GADBY'S HYMNS

A SELECTION OF HYMNS

FOR

PUBLIC WORSHIP

WILLIAM GADSBY

"Sing ye praises with understanding"
Psalm 47:7

SOLID GROUND CHRISTIAN BOOKS
BIRMINGHAM, ALABAMA USA

Solid Ground Christian Books
PO Box 660132
Vestavia Hills AL 35266
205-443-0311
sgcb@charter.net
solid-ground-books.com

Gadsby's Hymns
by William Gadsby (1773 – 1844)

First Solid Ground Edition May 2009

Taken from the 2003 edition published by
Grace and Truth Books, Sand Springs OK

Cover image by Borgo Design, Tuscaloosa, AL

ISBN: 978-159925-205-6

TABLE OF CONTENTS

PREFACE

TO WILLIAM GADSBY'S LAST EDITION.

———

To be employed with solemn pleasure in singing the praises of God with the spirit and with the understanding also, is a blessing peculiar to God's elect; nor can even they be thus engaged, only as the blessed Spirit influences the mind, and favours them with the unction of his grace. It is one thing to have the ear charmed, and another to have the heart engaged in this most delightful part of God's worship in his church below. "Blessed are the people that know the joyful sound."

It may be thought by many a great piece of folly for such an obscure mortal as I to publish a selection of hymns for the public worship of the eternal Three-One God; nor shall I attempt to make many apologies for having done so. Suffice it to say, that the church and people over which the Holy Ghost has made me overseer, had been in the constant habit, ever since I came among them, of using Dr. Watts's Psalms and Hymns, Rippon's Selection, and Hart's Composition. But though some of these hymns are big with the important truths of God, there are others, especially among Dr. Watts's and Rippon's, which give as legal a sound as if they had been forged at a certain foundry. This was one reason which induced me to publish a selection. Another was, we had three editions of Hart's Hymns amongst us, either differently arranged or differently paged; so that when any of those hymns were given out, one part of the congregation was unable to find them. These circumstances, together with a desire in my own breast and the express wish of others to have a selection of hymns in one book free from Arminianism, and sound in the faith, that the church might be edified and God glorified, were what induced me to attempt this work.

The last one hundred and fifty-seven hymns are of my own composing. In the former editions, many of these were too long for public worship, consequently comparatively useless, extending the size of the book without a proportionate benefit. In the present edition I have curtailed them; but as I have been careful to leave entire, or nearly so, the first verse of each, and as I have not materially altered the language of the remaining verses which still appear, I think but little inconvenience will be experienced, particularly if the hymns be given out from *this* edition, as in that case no verses can be read which are not in *all* the books. It will be seen that I have sometimes taken a line from another author, but for this, not professing perfection, I shall offer no apology.

My reason for putting those of my own composing together was, that I might publish a few copies of them separately from the selection, for the benefit of those who might wish to have them without being obliged to purchase the whole work; so that they may be had as they appeared originally, at full length, together with 112 more, since added, under the title of the " Nazarene's Songs."

The pages gained by the curtailment of my own Hymns, as above named, are occupied with a Supplement, consisting of 120 hymns, which have principally been selected from Hart and Berridge, these two men being, I believe, the sweetest and greatest experimental writers that have left any hymns on record.

If the dear Redeemer will be gracious to make this selection of hymns a blessing to his people, I hope the same grace which will accomplish this end will influence me to feel amply rewarded for my labour, and cheerfully give him all the glory.

WILLIAM GADSBY.

Manchester, November, 1838.

** If any of the Hymns be thought too long to sing at one time, the verses included in brackets, thus [ ], may be left out, without destroying the sense.

PREFACE

TO THE SECOND SUPPLEMENT.

———

IN a Collection of Hymns for the worship of God, three things seem desirable, if not essentially necessary—*savour*, *variety*, and *number*. Without the first, the sacrifice lacks salt (Lev. ii. 13); without the second, the various experiences of the Lord's people are not met; without the third, constant repetition of the choicest hymns has a tendency to deaden their effect.

When, then, in consequence of the destruction of the stereotype plates by the fire in Bouverie Street, it became necessary to publish a new edition of the late Mr. GADSBY'S Selection, it seemed desirable to increase the number of hymns; and as the proprietor and publisher liberally consented to enlarge the Hymn Book (already much increased in size and value by the addition of the remaining hymns of Hart), without a corresponding enlargement of price, I felt induced to select the Second Supplement.

In this difficult task, in the execution of which I have read many hundred hymns, I have been chiefly guided by two things: first, the savour which I have felt in the hymn itself; secondly, in its meeting the average experience of God's living family. As in music a tune may be pitched in too high a key for the average of voices, so a hymn may be written in too high a strain of assurance for the average of experiences; and as one would not choose a tune in which only a few voices could join, so one would not select a hymn which would require many to be mute.

I sensibly feel that the following Supplement is inferior to the first; but this has much arisen from the circumstance that the best hymns have already been inserted. Mine has been the gleaning of the grapes when the vintage is done. But such as it is, I hope it may please the Lord to make it a blessing to the souls of his people.

J. C. PHILPOT.

NOTE TO PRESENT EDITION.

THE Trustees wish to point out that some deviations appearing in previous editions, revert to the author's original in this edition. In two cases the original wording is deviated from. In each instance clear expression of the truth has been the first consideration.

It is hoped that the addition of eighteen *Occasional Hymns* will meet the need of such occasions as they arise.

INDEX OF AUTHORS

INDEX OF SUBJECTS

FOR EACH HYMN.

God's Care of her 269, 276, 277, 635, 1096, 1113
God her Defence 364, 1141
Good Men 538
Happy People 68, 137, 364, 526, 735, 966.
Heirs of God 531, 766
Her Springs in Christ 176
Holy People 16, 210, 601
Jewels 62, 832
Joint-Heirs with Christ 62, 766
Kings and Priests 102, 372
Leaning on her Beloved 92, 334, 994
Led by the Spirit 16
Lord's (The) Family 69, 79, 80, 531, 624, 1013
Mariners (See "Christ, Pilot")
Members of Christ 911
Peculiar People 598
Pilgrims 286, 289, 292, 308, 337, 347, 350, 417, 462, 747, 945
Poor and afflicted 91, 992, 993
Poor in Spirit 257, 918
Prayer for an increase in the Church 512, 683
— for the Minister 373, 450, 456, 508, 694, 864, 1130
Praying People 397, 725
Prisoners of Hope 998
Purchased 348, 351, 353
Ransomed 59, 532
Remnant 690
Righteous ones 350, 412
Safe in Christ 137, 214, 347, 348, 354, 568, 583, 625, 626, 629, 632, 667, 685, 772, 804, 921, 980, 993, 1000
Servants of God 955
Shulamites 612, 617, 678, 728
Settlement of a Church 365
Sheep 76, 345, 348, 349, 354, 768, 804, 944, 965, 1071
Sons and Daughters 1013
Spake often one to another 371, 911
They are not ashamed of Christ 427, 971, 1042
Tried People (See "Tribulation")
Unknown to the World 79, 243, 1013
Watched by the World 955

Witnesses 477
Zion 360-366, 369-372, 532, 540, 541, 569, 1021, 1027
See also "Prayer," "Love," "Worship," "Union")

COVENANT, THE.

All one in Christ 816, 921
Attributes of God displayed in the Covenant 17
Confirmed by Oath 83, 86
Covenant Favours 86, 912
Covenant Union 921, 766
Everlasting Covenant 87, 921
Gives Life Eternal 407
God keeping Covenant 85, 912
Hope in the Covenant 83
In all Things ordered well 411
Stability of the Covenant 82, 87, 757, 921
Made with Christ 86, 87, 411
Love, Peace, Mercy 87
Praise for the Covenant 84, 411
Rejoicing in the Covenant 68, 69
Restoring Grace in the Covenant 87
Sealed with Blood 86
Shalls and Wills 87
Stored with Promises 86
Support therein 84, 921
The Rainbow a Sign of the Covenant 791

DEATH.

462-472, 664, 665, 842-844 1155

DECREES OF GOD.

All things decreed 63
All things that respect the Church decreed 10, 61, 62, 64, 66
Rejoicing of Christ 71
Sonship decreed 61, 73
Source of Satisfaction 69, 70
Sovereignty of God 61, 69, 71
Unalterable 530
See also "Election," "Predestination"

DOXOLOGIES.

(Or giving Glory to God)
502-506, 867-870

ELECTION, Etc.

All of Grace 60, 68, 198, 201, 204, 211, 530, 1040
All settled 582, 680
Chosen in Christ 10, 60, 62, 65, 66, 530, 569, 572
Consolation of 69
Effectual Calling 74, 76
Elect ransomed 67, 80
Excludes Boasting 74
Ground of Perseverance 68, 72, 77, 205, 596, 795
No Condemnation 72, 96, 568, 921, 998, 1000
Sons through 69
Sovereign and Free 61, 66, 73, 75, 205
See also "Predestination," "Decrees," "Grace," "Salvation"

ENCOURAGEMENT.

Afflictions light 282, 286, 292, 307, 319, 337, 707
A Kingdom yours 257, 267
All for the best 88, 232, 298, 322, 412, 758
All in God's hands 64, 70
Blessed are the Poor 257, 740, 918, 978, 1112
— they that hunger 979
Captives released 892, 900, 989, 1006, 1034
Chastenings from Love 183, 275, 623
Crosses at God's Control 70, 335, 1113
David's God is yours 338
Deliverance sure 120, 782
Encouragement deriv. from ancient Israel 318
— from former Mercies 981
— from God incarnate 1095
— from the Covenant 87, 1097
Door of Hope 146, 585
Fear not 267, 273, 291, 328, 329, 396, 622, 909, 956, 957, 993, 1056
Folly of Doubts 323, 773
For Sinners afflicted 274, 328, 548, 705, 967, 976, 992, 1033, 1038, 1055
— backsliders to return 392, 858, 806 pt. 2, 1032, 1056, 1060
— black 145, 221, 669, 710, 775

Hope in Danger 290, 1096
— in Darkness 401, 727
— in God 917, 1010, 1062
Hope in Jesus' Blood 96, 214, 585, 1038, 1106
Hope in Trouble 927, 953
Hope of Mercy, &c., 997, 1108
Hope on the Ground of Adoption 70, 223, 243
Hope placed above the Skies 482
Hope through the Covenant 83, 1106
I will look again 1056
Jesus, God of Hope 244
Pierces thro' Clouds 244
Shall never fail 245
Shall be Crowned 997
Waiting 264, 893, 915, 1056, 1108, 1113
Who can tell 947

HUMILITY.

Approaching a Holy God 671, 1008
A View of God humbles 475, 555
Be still 275
Christ's Example 258
Desiring to do the Lord's Will 1003, 1064
Exhortation to 810
Humility under Chastisements 282, 871-873
It is the Lord 261
Keep close to me 708, 999
Praying for (See Prayer)
Resignation 259-262, 277, 307, 319, 682, 1079, 1083, 1086, 1110
Sit still 991
The Humble blessed 257, 263, 740, 918, 978, 1112
The Soul melted 158, 162, 1099
Though I be nothing 172, 708
Thy will be done 156, 307, 682, 1086
Walking with God 958 (See "Union")
Why me 69, 191, 680
Will ye also go away 999

JOY.

Doubts scattered 266, 323
Foretaste of Heaven 423, 484, 979
Happy Moments 735
Joy in Prospect of Heaven (See "Heaven")

Joy in Christ 581, 951
Joy in Free Grace 595
Joy and Shame 710, 918, 1062
Joy over a repenting Sinner 219, 422, 590
Joy unspeakable 933
Rejoicing in Hope 267
— in the Lord 265, 268, 269, 606, 607
— in Pardon 681, 933
Rejoice evermore 606, 607
Return of Joy 266, 323

JUSTIFICATION.

Justified by Christ 97, 110, 116, 344, 537, 544
Justified by Grace 80, 544
The Just shall live by Faith 605
Through Faith 111, 545, 565, 581

LAST JUDGMENT, THE.

493-497, 666, 847, 938

LAW, THE.

44-50, 101, 111, 146, 164, 188, 520, 522, 561, 565, 581, 809, 989

LORD'S SUPPER, THE.

435-449, 659-663, 734, 818-831, 1120-1123

LOVE.

A River 582, 914, 996
Brotherly Love 248, 258, 512, 609, 810, 1014, 1082
Christ's Love 88, 90, 92, 133, 149, 154, 157, 170, 208, 249, 339, 418, 529, 533, 535, 568, 569, 579-582, 584, 633, 688, 719, 720, 766, 914, 1012, 1053, 1059, 1117, 1118
Desiring to love God 25, 28-30, 247, 249, 283, 693, 905, 990, 1008, 1041, 1050, 1075
Desiring to love the Brethren 248, 258, 512, 609, 1014
Doing all things in Love 250
Effects of Love 250, 251
Love and Fear 252
Love and Shame 710
Love Divine 1053
Love flows from Forgiveness 158

Love I much 158
Love never fails 792
Lovest thou me 968, 1066
Love to Christ 246, 251, 268, 423, 798, 940, 1034, 1066
The Wine of Love 890

MAN'S MERIT.

44, 45, 52, 57, 111, 112, 143, 220, 221, 530, 544, 585, 668, 799, 800, 1042

MERCY.

A Debtor to Mercy 340
By Jesus' Blood 534 (See Redemption ")
Crying for (See Prayer)
From Calvary 93 (See also Sufferings, &c. of Christ.
Guards our Life 94
Holds us up 1016
Leads to Jesus 134, 146
Manifested 197, 565, 588
Mercy and Judgment 833
Mercy and Truth met 600
Mercy reigns 17
Mercy Seat 382, 388, 394, 395, 942
Praise for (See "Praise")
Recalls Backsliders 392, 806 pt. 2, 858
Singing of Mercy 11-13
Streams of Mercy 199, 932
Sure Mercy 13, 96
Surprising Mercy 95
Welcome News 218

OCCASIONAL.

Christian Marriage 375, 1153
Funeral 463, 466, 470, 665, 842-844, 1155 (See Death and "Last Judgment")
National trouble 808, 1142, 1143, 1145
Parting 500, 501, 1138
See "Times and Seasons"

PARDON.

A high Privilege 107, 681
A joyful Sound 755
Desiring an Earnest of Pardon 24, 1085
Freely given 218, 221
Hope of Pardon 44
Manifested 101, 151, 179, 233, 351, 908, 1025

For Fellowship with Christ (See Sufferings of Christ)

For Forgiveness (See " For Pardon ")

For Fruitfulness 400, 874

For godly Fear 335, 1060

For heavenly Intercourse (See " Union ")

For Help, &c. 393, 743, 1072, 1074

For Humility 258, 275, 277, 287, 390, 686, 695, 706, 874, 905, 991, 1024, 1051, 1058, 1060, 1076

For Liberty 288, 989, 1034

For Light, Life, &c. 193, 962, 1057, 1073

For living Bread 643, 1129

For Love, &c. 25, 28-30, 248, 249, 398, 609, 610, 906, 910, 970

For Mercy, Salvation, &c. 238, 262, 272, 384, 385, 393, 743, 895, 1009, 1030, 1056, 1060, 1068, 1069, 1098

For Nearness to God 610, 697, 704, 739, 945

For Pardon 164, 196, 390-392, 668, 682, 731, 753, 761, 860, 941, 948, 1019. 1060, 1067, 1084, 1098

For Preservation from Sin 199, 210, 214, 601, 693, 937, 1072

For quickening Grace 402, 515, 983, 1008

For Refuge 140, 143, 303. 739, 924, 926, 938, 944, 965, 1052, 1104

For Resignation 259-262, 275, 277, 682, 873, 1083, 1086, 1110

For Rest (See " Rest ")

For Restoration 390 - 392, 1041, 1056

For Shelter 143, 303, 944. 965, 1052

For Simplicity 686, 745, 1058

For single Sight 253

For Spring 400

For Steadfastness 296

For the Minister 373, 450, 456, 508, 694, 864, 1130 (See " Worship ")

For the Nation 808, 1142, 1143, 1145

PREDESTINATION.

PROMISES.

REDEMPTION.

GADSBY'S SELECTION.

PART I.

1   C.M.   WATTS.
The Infinity of God.—Ps. cxlvii. 5; Heb. iv. 13.

GREAT God! how infinite art thou!
  What worthless worms are we!
Let the whole race of creatures bow,
  And pay their praise to thee!

2 Thy throne eternal ages stood,
    Ere seas or stars were made;
  Thou art the ever-living God,
    Were all the nations dead.

3 [Nature and time quite naked lie
    To thy immense survey,
  From the formation of the sky,
    To the great burning day.]

4 Eternity, with all its years,
    Stands present in thy view;
  To thee there's nothing old appears—
    Great God! there's nothing new!

5 Our lives through various scenes are drawn,
    And vexed with trifling cares,
  While thy eternal thought moves on
    Thy undisturbed affairs.

6 Great God! how infinite art thou!
    What worthless worms are we!
  Let the whole race of creatures bow,
    And pay their praise to thee!

2   C.M.   WATTS.
The Eternity of God.—Ps. xc. 2; Lam. v. 19; Hab. i. 12.

LORD, raise my soul above the ground,
  And draw my thoughts to thee;
Teach me, with sweet and solemn sound,
  To praise the eternal Three.

2 Long ere the lofty skies were spread,
    Jehovah filled his throne;
  Or Adam formed, or angels made,
    The Maker lived alone.

3 His boundless years can ne'er decrease,
    But still maintain their prime;
  Eternity's his dwelling-place,
    And ever is his time.

4 While like a tide our minutes flow,
    The present and the past,
  He fills his own immortal NOW,
    And sees our ages waste.

5 The sea and sky must perish too,
    And vast destruction come!
  The creatures! look how old they grow,
    And wait their fiery doom.

6 Well; let the sea shrink all away,
    And flame melt down the skies,
  My God shall live an endless day
    When the old creation dies.

3   L.M.   BURNHAM.
The Power of God.—Exod. xv. 6; Ps. lxii. 11.

GOD is my everlasting King;
God is my Strength, and I will sing;
His power upholds my feeble frame,
And I'm victorious through his name.

2 Devils retreat when he appears;
  Then I arise above my fears,
  And every fiery dart repel,
  And vanquish all the force of hell.

3 Through the Redeemer's precious blood,
  I feel the mighty power of God;
  Through the rich aid divinely given,
  I rise from earth, and soar to heaven.

4 [Dear Lord, thy weaker saints inspire,
  And fill them with celestial fire;
  On thy kind arm may they rely,
  And all their foes shall surely fly.]

5 Now, Lord, thy wondrous power exert,
  And every ransomed soul support;
  Give us fresh strength to wing our way
  To regions of eternal day.

6 [There may we praise the great I AM,
  And shout the victories of the Lamb;
  Raise every chorus to his blood,
  And triumph in the power of God.] WATTS.

4   C.M.   Rom. ix. 15-18.
The Sovereignty of God.—Job xxiii. 13;

KEEP silence all created things,
  And wait your Maker's nod;
My soul stands trembling while she sings
  The honours of her God.

2 Life, death, and hell, and worlds unknown,
    Hang on his firm decree;
  He sits on no precarious throne,
    Nor borrows leave TO BE.

3 Chained to his throne a volume lies,
    With all the fates of men,
  With every angel's form and size,
    Drawn by the eternal pen.

4 His providence unfolds the book,
    And makes his counsels shine;

Each opening leaf, and every stroke,
  Fulfils some deep design.

5 Here he exalts neglected worms
  To sceptres and a crown ;
And there the following page he turns,
  And treads the monarch down.

6 [Not Gabriel asks the reason why,
  Nor God the reason gives ;
Nor dares the favourite angel pry
  Between the folded leaves.]

7 My God, I would not long to see
  My fate with curious eyes ;
What gloomy lines are writ for me,
  Or what bright scenes may rise.

8 In thy fair book of life and grace,
  O may I find my name
Recorded in some humble place,
  Beneath my Lord the Lamb.

5   C.M.   WATTS.
The Wisdom of God.—1 Cor. i. 24; Eph. iii. 9-11.

THE Lord, descending from above,
  Invites his children near,
While power, and truth, and boundless love
  Display their glories here.

2 Here, in thy gospel's wondrous frame,
  Fresh wisdom we pursue ;
A thousand angels learn thy name,
  Beyond whate'er they knew.

3 Thy name is writ in fairest lines ;
  Thy wonders here we trace ;
Wisdom through all the mystery shines,
  And shines in Jesus' face.

4 The law its best obedience owes
  To our incarnate God ;
And thy revenging justice shows
  Its honours in his blood.

5 But still the lustre of thy grace
  Our warmer thoughts employs ;
Gilds the whole scene with brighter rays,
  And more exalts our joys.

6   L.M.   BEDDOME.
The Wisdom and Knowledge of God.—Ps. cxxxix.

GOD'S ways are just, his counsels wise ;
No darkness can prevent his eyes ;
No thought can fly, nor thing can move,
Unknown to him that sits above.

2 He in the thickest darkness dwells ;
Performs his works, the cause conceals ;
But though his methods are unknown,
Judgment and truth support his throne.

3 In heaven, and earth, and air, and seas,

He executes his firm decrees ;
And by his saints it stands confessed,
That what he does is ever best.

4 Wait, then, my soul, submissive wait,
Prostrate before his awful seat ;
And, 'midst the terrors of his rod,
Trust in a wise and gracious God.

7   C.M.   MEDLEY.
The Wisdom and Goodness of God.—Exod. xxxiv. 6.

GOD shall alone the refuge be,
  And comfort of my mind ;
Too wise to be mistaken, He,
  Too good to be unkind.

2 In all his holy, sovereign will,
  He is, I daily find,
Too wise to be mistaken, still
  Too good to be unkind.

3 [When I the tempter's rage endure,
  'Tis God supports my mind ;
Too wise to be mistaken, sure,
  Too good to be unkind.]

4 [When sore afflictions on me lie,
  He is (though I am blind)
Too wise to be mistaken, yea,
  Too good to be unkind.]

5 What though I can't his goings see,
  Nor all his footsteps find ?
Too wise to be mistaken, He,
  Too good to be unkind.

6 Hereafter he will make me know,
  And I shall surely find,
He was too wise to err, and O,
  Too good to be unkind.

8   L.M.   BEDDOME.
The Justice and Goodness of God.—Deut. xxxii. 4.

GREAT God ! my Maker and my King,
Of thee I'll speak, of thee I'll sing ;
All thou hast done, and all thou dost,
Declare thee good, proclaim thee just.

2 Thy ancient thoughts and firm decrees ;
Thy threatenings and thy promises ;
The joys of heaven, the pains of hell,—
What angels taste, what devils feel ;

3 Thy terrors and thy acts of grace ;
Thy threatening rod, and smiling face ;
Thy wounding and thy healing word ;
A world undone, a world restored ;

4 While these excite my fear and joy,
While these my tuneful lips employ,
Accept, O Lord, the humble song,
The tribute of a trembling tongue.

9 L.M. MEDLEY.

The Loving-Kindness of God.—Ps. xxxvi. 7.

AWAKE, my soul, in joyful lays,
And sing thy great Redeemer's praise ;
He justly claims a song from me ;
His loving-kindness, O how free !

2 He saw me ruined in the fall,
Yet loved me notwithstanding all ;
He saved me from my lost estate ;
His loving-kindness, O how great !

3 [Though numerous hosts of mighty foes,
Though earth and hell my way oppose,
He safely leads my soul along ;
His loving-kindness, O how strong !]

4 [When trouble, like a gloomy cloud,
Has gathered thick and thundered loud,
He near my soul has always stood ;
His loving-kindness, O how good !]

5 Often I feel my sinful heart
Prone from my Saviour to depart ;
But though I have him oft forgot,
His loving-kindness changes not !

6 Soon shall I pass the gloomy vale ;
Soon all my mortal powers must fail ;
O may my last expiring breath
His loving-kindness sing in death !

7 Then let me mount and soar away
To the bright world of endless day,
And sing with rapture and surprise,
His loving-kindness in the skies.

10 L.M. KENT.

The Everlasting Love of God.—Jer. xxxi. 3; Eph. ii. 4, 5

'TWAS with an everlasting love
That God his own elect embraced ;

Before he made the worlds above,
Or earth on her huge columns placed.

2 Long ere the sun's refulgent ray
Primeval shades of darkness drove,
They on his sacred bosom lay,
Loved with an everlasting love.

3 Then in the glass of his decrees,
Christ and his bride appeared as one ;
Her sin, by imputation, his,
Whilst she in spotless splendour shone.

4 O love, how high thy glories swell !
How great, immutable, and free !
Ten thousand sins, as black as hell,
Are swallowed up, O love, in thee !

5 [Loved, when a wretch defiled with sin,
At war with heaven, in league with hell,
A slave to every lust obscene ;

Who, living, lived but to rebel.]

6 Believer, here thy comfort stands,—
From first to last salvation's free,
And everlasting love demands
An everlasting song from thee.

11 11s. STOCKER.

Singing of Mercy.—Ps. lxxxix. 1; ci. 1; Rom. xv. 9.

THY mercy, my God, is the theme of my song,
The joy of my heart, and the boast of my tongue ;
Thy free grace alone, from the first to the last,
Has won my affections, and bound my soul fast.

2
Thy mercy, in Jesus, exempts me from hell ;
Its glories I'll sing, and its wonders I'll tell ;
'Twas Jesus, my Friend, when he hung on the
Who opened the channel of mercy for me. [tree,

3
[Without thy sweet mercy I could not live here ;
Sin soon would reduce me to utter despair ;
But, thro' thy free goodness, my spirits revive,
And he that first made me still keeps me alive.]

4
[Thy mercy is more than a match for my heart,
Which wonders to feel its own hardness depart ;
Dissolved by thy goodness, I fall to the ground,
And weep to the praise of the mercy I found.]

5
The door of thy mercy stands open all day,
To the poor and the needy, who knock by the way.
No sinner shall ever be empty sent back,
Who comes seeking mercy for Jesus's sake.

6
Great Father of mercies, thy goodness I own,
And the covenant love of thy crucified Son ;
All praise to the Spirit, whose whisper divine
Seals mercy, & pardon, & righteousness mine.

12 8s. BURNHAM.

The All-Sufficient Mercy of God.—Ps. lxxxix. 28.

ALL glory to mercy we bring,
The mercy that reigns evermore,
The infinite mercy we sing,
The mercy eternal adore.

2 The mercy converting we prize ;
In mercy forgiving delight ;
For conquering mercy we rise,
We rise and triumphantly fight.

3 [And when we are wounded by sin,
And scarcely a prayer can repeat,
The mercy that heals us again,
Is mercy transportingly sweet.]

4 What though in the furnace we fall,
Free mercy the Saviour proclaims ;

Free mercy in Jesus we call,
And glorify God in the flames.

5 For mercy upholding we pray;
For mercy confirming aspire;
And mercy will bear us away
To God and the glorified choir.

13 C.M. HART.
The Everlasting Mercy of God.—Ps. cxxxvi.; c. 5.

GOD's mercy is for ever sure;
Eternal is his name;
As long as life and speech endure,
My tongue this truth proclaim.

2 I basely sinned against his love,
And yet my God was good;
His favour nothing could remove,
For I was bought with blood.

3 [That precious blood atones all sin,
And fully clears from guilt;
It makes the foulest sinner clean,
For 'twas for sinners spilt.]

4 He raised me from the lowest state,
When hell was my desert;
I broke his law, and, worse than that,
Alas! I broke his heart!

5 My soul, thou hast, let what will ail,
A never-changing Friend;
When brethren, friends, and helpers fail,
On him alone depend.

14 C.M. WATTS. 1-8.
Faithfulness of God.—Numb. xxiii. 19; Ps. lxxxix.

BEGIN, my tongue, some heavenly theme,
And speak some boundless thing;
The mighty works, or mightier name,
Of our eternal King.

2 Tell of his wondrous faithfulness,
And sound his power abroad;
Sing the sweet promise of his grace,
And the performing God.

3 Proclaim, " Salvation from the Lord,
For wretched dying men ";
His hand has writ the sacred word
With an immortal pen.

4 [Engraved as in eternal brass,
The mighty promise shines;
Nor can the powers of darkness rase
Those everlasting lines.]

5 He that can dash whole worlds to death,
And make them when he please,
He speaks, and that almighty breath
Fulfils his great decrees.

6 His every word of grace is strong

As that which built the skies;
The voice that rolls the stars along
Speaks all the promises.

15 C.M. WATTS & NEEDHAM.
The Holiness of God.—Ps. cxi. 9; cxlv. 17.

How shall I praise the eternal God,
That infinite Unknown?
Who can ascend his high abode,
Or venture near his throne?

2 Heaven's brightest lamps, with him compared
How mean they look, and dim!
The holy angels have no spots,
Yet can't compare with him.

3 Holy is he in all his works,
And truth is his delight;
But sinners, and their wicked ways,
Shall perish from his sight.

4 None but his favourites may draw near,
Who stand in Christ complete;
Those holy ones shall all appear
And worship at his feet.

5 In Jesus' image shining bright
With rapture they adore
The holy, holy, holy Lord,
In glory evermore.

16 C.M. BURNHAM.
Holiness.—Lev. xix. 2; 1 Sam. ii. 2; Heb. xii. 14.

THE Father is a holy God;
His holy Son he gave;
Who freely shed atoning blood,
A guilty world to save.

2 The Spirit brings the chosen race,
A holy Christ to view;
And while by faith they see his face,
Their souls grow holy too.

3 In holiness the saints delight,
While here on earth they dwell;
By faith they wrestle day and night,
More holiness to feel.

4 The Holy Spirit leads them on,
His holy truth to know;
Inscribes his laws in every son,
And works obedience too.

5 He makes them feel the cleansing grace,
That flows through Jesus' blood;
Unites in love the holy race—
The new-born sons of God.

17 L.M. TUCKER.
Harmony of the Perfections of God.—Rom. iii. 26.

O LOVE, beyond conception great,
That formed the vast stupendous plan,

Where all divine perfections meet,
To reconcile rebellious man.

2 There wisdom shines in fullest blaze
And justice all her rights maintains ;
Astonished angels stoop to gaze,
While mercy o'er the guilty reigns.

3 Yes, mercy reigns, and justice too ;
In Christ they both harmonious meet ;
He paid to justice all its due,
And now he fills the mercy-seat.

4 Such are the wonders of our God,
And the amazing depths of grace,
To save from wrath's vindictive rod,
The chosen sons of Adam's race.

18 L.M. WATTS.
2 Cor. iv. 6.
Glory and Grace in the Person of Christ.--
Now to the Lord a noble song !
Awake, my soul ; awake, my tongue !
Hosanna to the eternal Name,
And all his boundless love proclaim !

2 See where it shines in Jesus' face,
The brightest image of his grace !
God, in the person of his Son,
Has all his mightiest works outdone.

3 The spacious earth and spreading flood
Proclaim the wise, the powerful God ;
And thy rich glories from afar
Sparkle in every rolling star.

4 But in his looks a glory stands,
The noblest labour of thy hands ;
The pleasing lustre of his eyes
Outshines the wonders of the skies.

5 [Grace ! 'tis a sweet, a charming theme !
My thoughts rejoice at Jesus' name !
Ye angels, dwell upon the sound !
Ye heavens, reflect it to the ground !]

6 O may I live to reach the place
Where he unveils his lovely face,
Where all his beauties you behold,
And sing his name to harps of gold !

19 C.M. WATTS.
A New Song to the Lamb that was Slain.--Rev. v. 6-12.
BEHOLD the glories of the Lamb,
Amidst his Father's throne ;
Prepare new honours for his name,
And songs before unknown.

2 Let elders worship at his feet ;
The church adore around ;
With vials full of odours sweet,
And harps of sweeter sound.

3 Those are the prayers of the saints,

And these the hymns they raise,--
Jesus is kind to our complaints,
He loves to hear our praise.

4 [Eternal Father, who shall look
Into thy secret will ?
Who but the Son shall take that book,
And open every seal ?

5 He shall fulfil thy great decrees ;
The Son deserves it well ;
Lo ! in his hands the sovereign keys
Of heaven, and death, and hell.]

6 Now to the Lamb that once was slain,
Be endless blessings paid ;
Salvation, glory, joy remain
For ever on thy head.

7 Thou hast redeemed our souls with blood,
Hast set the prisoners free,
Hast made us kings and priests to God,
And we shall reign with thee.

8 The worlds of nature and of grace
Are put beneath thy power ;
Then shorten these delaying days,
And bring the promised hour.

20 L.M. WATTS.
Col.i. 16 ; 1 Tim. iii. 16
Deity and Humanity of Christ.--
ERE the blue heavens were stretched abroad,
From everlasting was the Word ;
With God he was ; the Word was God ;
And must divinely be adored.

2 By his own power were all things made ;
By him supported all things stand ;
He is the whole creation's Head,
And angels fly at his command.

3 [Ere sin was born, or Satan fell,
He led the host of morning stars ;
(Thy generation who can tell,
Or count the number of thy years ?)]

4 But lo ! he leaves those heavenly forms ;
The Word descends and dwells in clay,
That he may hold converse with worms,
Dressed in such feeble flesh as they.

5 Mortals with joy behold his face,
The eternal Father's only Son ;
How full of truth ! how full of grace !
When through his eyes the Godhead shone.

6 Bless'd angels leave their high abode,
To learn new mysteries here, and tell
The loves of our descending God,
The glories of Immanuel.

21 L.M. WATTS.
Sol. Song v. 9-16
A Description of Christ, the Beloved.--
THE wondering world inquires to know
Why I should love my Jesus so ;

"What are his charms," say they, "above
The objects of a mortal love?"

2 Yes, my Beloved to my sight
Shows a sweet mixture, red and white :
All human beauties, all divine,
In my Beloved meet and shine.

3 White is his soul, from blemish free ;
Red with the blood he shed for me ;
The fairest of ten thousand fairs ;
A sun amongst ten thousand stars.

4 [His head the finest gold excels ;
There wisdom in perfection dwells ;
And glory, like a crown, adorns
Those temples once beset with thorns.

5 Compassions in his heart are found,
Hard by the signals of his wound ;
His sacred side no more shall bear
The cruel scourge, the piercing spear.]

6 [His hands are fairer to behold
Than diamonds, set in rings of gold ;
Those heavenly hands that on the tree
Were nailed, and torn, and bled for me.]

7 [Though once he bowed his feeble knees,
Loaded with sins and agonies,
Now on the throne of his command,
His legs like marble pillars stand.]

8 [His eyes are majesty and love,
The eagle tempered with the dove ;
No more shall trickling sorrows roll
Through those dear windows of his soul.]

9 [His mouth, that poured out long complaints,
Now smiles, and cheers his fainting saints ;
His countenance more graceful is
Than Lebanon, with all its trees.]

10 All over glorious is my Lord ;
Must be beloved, and yet adored ;
His worth if all the nations knew,
Sure the whole world would love him too !

22   L.M.   WATTS.
Christ dwells in Heaven, but visits on Earth.-Song vi. 1
WHEN mourners stand and hear me tell
What beauties in my Saviour dwell,
Where he is gone they fain would know,
That they may seek and love him too.

2 My best Beloved keeps his throne
On hills of light, in worlds unknown ;
But he descends and shows his face
In the young gardens of his grace.

3 [In vineyards, planted by his hand,
Where fruitful trees in order stand,
He feeds among the spicy beds,

Where lilies show their spotless heads.]

4 He has engrossed my warmest love ;
No earthly charms my soul can move ;
I have a mansion in his heart,
Nor death nor hell shall make us part.

5 [He takes my soul, ere I'm aware,
And shows me where his glories are ;
No chariots of Amminadib
The heavenly rapture can describe.]

6 O may my spirit daily rise
On wings of faith above the skies ;
Till death shall make my last remove,
To dwell for ever with my Love.

23   C.M.   HART.
Christ very God and Man.—John i. 29 ; Isa. ix. 6.
A MAN there is, a real Man,
With wounds still gaping wide,
From which rich streams of blood once ran,
In hands, and feet, and side.

2 ['Tis no wild fancy of our brains,
No metaphor we speak ;
The same dear Man in heaven now reigns
That suffered for our sake.]

3 This wondrous Man of whom we tell,
Is true Almighty God ;
He bought our souls from death and hell ;
The price, his own heart's blood.

4 That human heart he still retains,
Though throned in highest bliss ;
And feels each tempted member's pains ;
For our affliction's his.

5 Come, then, repenting sinner, come ;
Approach with humble faith ;
Owe what thou wilt the total sum
Is cancelled by his death.

6 His blood can cleanse the blackest soul,
And wash our guilt away ;
He will present us sound and whole,
In that tremendous day.

24   C.M.   Rom. viii. 14, 16.   WATTS.
The Witnessing and Sealing Spirit.—
WHY should the children of a King
Go mourning all their days ?
Great Comforter ! descend and bring
Some tokens of thy grace.

2 Dost thou not dwell in all the saints,
And seal them heirs of heaven ?
When wilt thou banish my complaints,
And show my sins forgiven ?

3 Assure my conscience ot her part
In the Redeemer's blood ;

And bear thy witness with my heart,
   That I am born of God.

4 Thou art the earnest of his love,
   The pledge of joys to come ;
   And thy soft wings, celestial Dove,
   Will safe convey me home.

25   C.M.   WATTS.
Breathing after the Holy Spirit.—Ps. xliv. 25.
COME, Holy Spirit, heavenly Dove,
   With thy all-quickening powers ;
Kindle a flame of sacred love
   In these cold hearts of ours.

2 Look how we grovel here below,
   Fond of these trifling toys ;
   Our souls can neither fly nor go,
   To reach eternal joys.

3 In vain we tune our formal songs,
   In vain we strive to rise ;
   Hosannas languish on our tongues,
   And our devotion dies.

4 Dear Lord, and shall we ever live
   At this poor dying rate ?
   Our love so faint, so cold to thee,
   And thine to us so great ?

5 Come, Holy Spirit, heavenly Dove,
   With thy all-quickening powers ;
   Come shed abroad a Saviour's love,
   And that shall kindle ours.

26   L.M.   WATTS.
The Operations of the Holy Spirit.—Zech. iv. 6.
ETERNAL Spirit, we confess
And sing the wonders of thy grace ;
Thy power conveys our blessings down
From God the Father and the Son.

2 Enlightened by thy heavenly ray,
Our shades and darkness turn to day ;
Thy inward teachings make us know
Our danger and our refuge too.

3 Thy power and glory work within,
And break the chains of reigning sin ;
Do our imperious lusts subdue,
And guide our roving feet anew.

4 The troubled conscience knows thy voice ;
Thy cheering words awake our joys ;
Thy words allay the stormy wind,
And calm the surges of the mind.

27   S.M.   HART.
To the Holy Ghost.—Luke xi. 13: John xiv. 26; xv. 26.
   COME, Holy Spirit, come ;
   Let thy bright beams arise ;
Dispel the darkness from our minds,

And open all our eyes.

2 [Cheer our desponding hearts,
   Thou heavenly Paraclete ;*
Give us to lie, with humble hope,
   At our Redeemer's feet.]

3 Revive our drooping faith ;
   Our doubts and fears remove ;
And kindle in our breasts the flames
   Of never-dying love.

4 Convince us of our sin,   * Comforter.
   Then lead to Jesus' blood ;
And to our wondering view reveal
   The secret love of God.

5 [Show us that loving Man
   That rules the courts of bliss,
The Lord of Hosts, the Mighty God,
   The eternal Prince of Peace.]

6 ['Tis thine to cleanse the heart,
   To sanctify the soul,
To pour fresh life on every part,
   And new-create the whole.]

7 If thou, celestial Dove,
   Thy influence withdraw,
What easy victims soon we fall
   To conscience, wrath, and law !

8 [No longer burns our love ;
   Our faith and patience fail ;
Our sin revives, and death and hell
   Our feeble souls assail.]

9 Dwell, therefore, in our hearts ;
   Our minds from bondage free ;
Then shall we know, and praise, and love
   The Father, Son, and Thee.

28   C.M.   John vi. 63; xiv. 16   HART.
" It is the Spirit that quickeneth."—
BLEST Spirit of truth, eternal God,
   Thou meek and lowly Dove,
Who fill'st the soul through Jesus' blood,
   With faith, and hope, and love ;

2 Who comfortest the heavy heart,
   By sin and sorrow pressed ;
Who to the dead canst life impart,
   And to the weary rest ;

3 [Thy sweet communion charms the soul,
   And gives true peace and joy,
Which Satan's power can not control,
   Nor all his wiles destroy ;]

4 Come from the blissful realms above ;
   Our longing breasts inspire
With thy soft flames of heavenly love,
   And fan the sacred fire.

5 [Let no false comfort lift us up
   To confidence that's vain ;
Nor let their faith and courage droop,
   For whom the Lamb was slain.]

6 Breathe comfort where distress abounds,
   Make the whole conscience clean,
And heal, with balm from Jesus' wounds,
   The festering sores of sin.

7 Vanquish our lust, our pride remove,
   Take out the heart of stone ;
Show us the Father's boundless love,
   And merits of the Son.

8 The Father sent the Son to die ;
   The willing Son obeyed ;
The witness Thou, to ratify
   The purchase Christ has made.

29 8.8.6. HART.
Ezek. xxxvii. 5, 9; John xvi. 14.
Led by the Spirit.—

DESCEND from heaven, celestial Dove,
With flames of pure seraphic love
   Our ravished breasts inspire ;
Fountain of joy, blest Paraclete,
Warm our cold hearts with heavenly heat,
   And set our souls on fire.

2 Breathe on these bones, so dry and dead ;
Thy sweetest, softest influence shed
   In all our hearts abroad ;
Point out the place where grace abounds ;
Direct us to the bleeding wounds
   Of our incarnate God.

3 Conduct, blest Guide, thy sinner-train
To Calvary, where the Lamb was slain,
   And with us there abide ;
Let us our loved Redeemer meet,
Weep o'er his pierced hands and feet,
   And view his wounded side.

4 [From which pure fountain if thou draw
Water to quench the fiery law,
   And blood to purge our sin ;
We'll tell the Father in that day,
(And thou shalt witness what we say),
   "We're clean, just God, we're clean."]

5 Teach us for what to pray, and how ;
And since, kind God, 'tis only thou
   The Throne of Grace canst move,
Pray thou for us, that we, through faith,
May feel the effects of Jesus' death,
   Through faith, that works by love.

6 [Thou, with the Father and the Son,
Art that mysterious Three-in-One,

God blest for evermore !
Whom though we cannot comprehend,
Feeling thou art the sinner's Friend,
   We love thee and adore.]

30 C.M. HART.
The Fruit of the Spirit.—Acts ii. 3; Gal. v. 22; Eph. v.

THE soul that with sincere desires
   Seeks after Jesus' love,
That soul the Holy Ghost inspires
   With breathings from above.

2 [Not every one in like degree
   The Spirit of God receives ;
The Christian often cannot see
   His faith, and yet believes.

3 So gentle sometimes is the flame,
   That, if we take not heed,
We may unkindly quench the same,
   We may, my friends, indeed.]

4 Blest God ! that once in fiery tongues
   Cam'st down in open view,
Come, visit every heart that longs
   To entertain thee too.

5 [And though not like a mighty wind,
   Nor with a rushing noise,
May we thy calmer comforts find,
   And hear thy still small voice.]

6 Not for the gift of tongues we pray,
   Nor power the sick to heal ;
Give wisdom to direct our way,
   And strength to do thy will.

7 We pray to be renewed within,
   And reconciled to God ;
To have our conscience washed from sin
   In the Redeemer's blood.

8 We pray to have our faith increased,
   And O, celestial Dove !
We pray to be completely blessed
   With that rich blessing, love.

31 C.M. HART.
"The kingdom of God is in power."—1 Cor. iv. 28.

A FORM of words, though e'er so sound,
   Can never save a soul ;
The Holy Ghost must give the wound,
   And make the wounded whole.

2 Though God's election is a truth,
   Small comfort there I see,
Till I am told by God's own mouth,
   That he has chosen me.

3 [Sinners, I read, are justified,
   By faith in Jesus' blood ;
But when to me that blood's applied,
   'Tis then it does me good.]

4 [To perseverance I agree ;
   The thing to me is clear ;
Because the Lord has promised me
   That I shall persevere.]

5 [Imputed righteousness I own
   A doctrine most divine ;
For Jesus to my heart makes known
   That all his merit's mine.]

6 That Christ is God I can avouch,
   And for his people cares,
Since I have prayed to him as such,
   And he has heard my prayers.

7 That sinners black as hell, by Christ
   Are saved, I know full well ;
For I his mercy have not missed,
   And I am black as hell.

8 Thus, Christians glorify the Lord,
   His Spirit joins with ours
In bearing witness to his word,
   With all its saving powers.

32   C.M.   HART.
" He shall not speak of himself."—John xvi. 13; xv. 26.

WHATEVER prompts the soul to pride,
   Or gives us room to boast,
Except in Jesus crucified,
   Is not the Holy Ghost.

2 That blessed Spirit omits to speak
   Of what himself has done,
And bids the enlightened sinner seek
   Salvation in the Son.

3 He never moves a man to say,
   " Thank God, I'm made so good,"
But turns his eye another way,
   To Jesus and his blood.

4 Great are the graces he confers,
   But all in Jesus' name ;
He gladly dictates, gladly hears,
   " Salvation to the Lamb."

33   L.M.   WATTS.
Praise to the ever-blessed Trinity.-Col. ii. 2; Rev. xi. 17.

BLEST be the Father and his love,
   To whose celestial source we owe
Rivers of endless joy above,
   And rills of comfort here below.

2 Glory to thee, great Son of God,
   From whose dear wounded body rolls
A precious stream of vital blood,
   Pardon and life for dying souls.

3 We give thee, sacred Spirit, praise,
   Who in our hearts of sin and woe
Makes living springs of grace arise,
   And into boundless glory flow.

4 Thus God the Father, God the Son,
   And God the Spirit we adore ;
That sea of life and love unknown,
   Without a bottom or a shore.

34   L.M.   HART.
                              Tit. iii. 4.
Love of, and praise to, the blessed Trinity.—

To comprehend the great THREE-ONE,
   Is more than highest angels can ;
Or what the Trinity has done
   From death and hell to ransom man.

2 But all true Christians this may boast,
   (A truth from nature never learned),
That Father, Son, and Holy Ghost,
   To save our souls are all concerned.

3 [The Father's love in this we find,
   He made his Son our sacrifice ;
The Son in love his life resigned ;
   The Spirit of love his blood applies.]

4 Thus we the Trinity can praise
   In Unity through Christ our King ;
Our grateful hearts and voices raise
   In faith and love, while thus we sing :

5 Glory to God the Father be,
   Because he sent his Son to die ;
Glory to God the Son, that he
   Did with such willingness comply ;

6 Glory to God the Holy Ghost,
   Who to our hearts this love reveals ;
Thus God Three-One, to sinners lost
   Salvation sends, procures, and seals.

35   6.4. Ps. ix. 11; xxvii. 6.   C. W.
Praise to Father, Son, and Spirit.—

COME, thou almighty King,
   Help us thy name to sing ;
      Help us to praise :
   Father all glorious,
   O'er all victorious,
   Come and reign over us,
      Ancient of Days !

2 Jesus, our Lord, arise,
   Scatter our enemies,
      And make them fall !
   Let thy almighty aid
   Our sure defence be made,
   Our souls on thee be stayed ;
      Lord, hear our call !

3 Come, thou Incarnate Word,
   Gird on thy mighty sword ;
      Our prayers attend ;
   Come, and thy people bless,
   And give thy word success ;

Spirit of holiness,
On us descend!

4 Come, holy Comforter,
Thy sacred witness bear
In this glad hour!
Thou, who almighty art,
Now rule in every heart,
And ne'er from us depart,
Spirit of power!

5 To the great One-in-Three
Eternal praises be
Hence evermore!
His sovereign majesty
May we in glory see,
And to eternity
Love and adore!

36   7s.   C. W.
Christ's Nativity.—Luke ii. 13-15; 2 Cor. v. 19.

HARK! the herald-angels sing,
Glory to the new-born King;
Peace on earth and mercy mild,
God and sinners reconciled!

2 Sons of Zion, too, arise,
Join the triumph of the skies;
And with angels loud proclaim,
"Christ was born in Bethlehem!"

3 Veiled in flesh the Godhead see!
Hail the incarnate Deity!
Mild he lays his glory by,
Born that we no more may die!

4 Glory to the new-born King,
Let us now the anthem sing;
Peace on earth, and mercy mild,
God and sinners reconciled!

37   148th.   C. W.
The Incarnate God.—Isa. vii. 14; Matt. i. 23.

LET earth and heaven combine,
Angels and men agree,
To praise, in songs divine,
The incarnate Deity;
Our God contracted to a span,
Incomprehensibly made man.

2 He laid his glory by,
And wrapped him in our clay;
Unmarked by human eye,
The latent Godhead lay;
Infant of Days he here became,
And bore the loved Immanuel's name.

3 Unsearchable the love
That has the Saviour brought;
The grace is far above

Or man's or angel's thought;
Suffice for us, that God we know,
Our God, was manifest below!

38   S.M.   WATTS.
"Jesus."—Luke i. 31-33; ii. 10-14.

BEHOLD! the grace appears,
The promise is fulfilled!
Mary, the wondrous virgin, bears,
And Jesus is the child.

2 [The Lord, the highest God,
Calls him his only Son;
He bids him rule the lands abroad,
And gives him David's throne.]

3 [O'er Jacob shall he reign
With a peculiar sway;
The nations shall his grace obtain,
His kingdom ne'er decay.]

4 To bring the glorious news
A heavenly form appears;
He tells the shepherds of their joys,
And banishes their fears.

5 "Go, humble swains," said he,
"To David's city fly,
The promised Infant born to-day
Does in a manger lie.

6 "With looks and hearts serene,
Go visit Christ, your King";
And straight a flaming troop was seen;
The shepherds heard them sing:

7 "Glory to God on high,
And heavenly peace on earth;
Good will to men, to angels joy,
At the Redeemer's birth!"

8 [In worship so divine
Let saints employ their tongues;
With the celestial host we join,
And loud repeat their songs:

9 "Glory to God on high,
And heavenly peace on earth;
Good will to men, to angels joy,
At the Redeemer's birth!"]

39   C.M.   HART.
"Bethlehem."—Matt. ii. 1, 5, 6; Luke ii. 4-16.

COME, ye redeemed of the Lord,
Your grateful tribute bring;
And celebrate, with one accord,
The birthday of our King.

2 Let us with humble hearts repair
(Faith will point out the road)
To little Bethlehem, and there
Adore our infant God.

3 [In swaddling bands the Saviour view !
  Let none his weakness scorn ;
  The feeblest heart shall hell subdue,
    Where Jesus Christ is born.]

4 No pomp adorns, no sweets perfume
    The place where Christ is laid ;
  A stable serves him for his room,
    A manger is his bed.

5 The crowded inn, like sinners' hearts,
    (O ignorance extreme !)
  For other guests, of various sorts,
    Had room ; but none for him.

6 But see what different thoughts arise
    In our and angels' breasts ;
  To hail his birth *they* left the skies,
    We lodged him with the beasts !

7 Yet let believers cease their fears,
    Nor envy heavenly powers ;
  If sinless innocence be theirs,
    Redemption all is ours.

40   11s.   HART.
" And the Word was made flesh."—John i. 14.

How blest is the season at which we appear !
Bow down, sense & reason, faith only reign here.
'Tis heard by mere nature with coldness & scorn,
That God, our Creator, an infant was born.

2
Lost souls to recover, and form them afresh,
Our wonderful Lover took flesh of our flesh ;
From sin to release us—that yoke so long worn,
The holy child Jesus of Mary was born.

3
Poor sinners dejected, of comfort debarred,
Whose hearts are afflicted because they're so
    hard ;
Despairing of favour—cold, lifeless, forlorn,
Remember, the Saviour in winter was [?] born.

4
And ye that sincerely confide in the Lamb,
(He loves you most dearly) rejoice in his name;
No more the believer from God shall be torn ;—
To hold him for ever an Infant was born.

41   11s.   ALLEN AND BATTY.
Rejoicing in the Incarnation, &c. of Christ.-Matt. ii. 10

My God, my Creator, the heavens did bow,
To ransom offenders, and stooped very low ;
The body prepared by the Father assumes,
And on the kind errand most joyfully comes.

2
O wonder of wonders ! astonished I gaze,
To see in the manger the Ancient of Days ;
And angels proclaiming the stranger forlorn,

And telling the shepherds that Jesus is born.

3
For thousands of sinners the Lord bow'd his head ;
For thousands of sinners he groan'd and he bled.
My spirit rejoices—the work it is done !
My soul is redeeméd—salvation is won !

4
[Dear Jesus, my Saviour, thy truth I embrace—
Thy name and thy natures, thy Spirit and grace ;
And trace the pure footsteps of Jesus, my Lord,
And glory in Him whom proud sinners abhorred.]

5
My God is returnéd to glory on high ;
When death makes a passage, then to him I'll fly,
To join in the song of all praise thro' his blood,
To the Three who are One inconceivable God.

42   C.M.   S. STENNETT.   Luke xxiv. 32.
Excellency of the Scriptures.-Ps. xix. 10;

Let avarice, from shore to shore
  Her favourite god pursue ;
Thy word, O Lord, we value more
  Than India or Peru.

2 When God the Holy Ghost reveals
  The riches it contains,
And in the conscience safely seals
  The grandeur of its lines ;

3 Then mines of knowledge, love, and joy
  Are opened to our sight ;
The purest gold without alloy
  And gems divinely bright.

4 The counsels of redeeming grace
  Those sacred leaves unfold ;
And here the Saviour's lovely face
  Our raptured eyes behold.

5 Here light, descending from above,
  Directs our doubtful feet ;
Here promises of heavenly love
  Our ardent wishes meet.

6 Our numerous griefs are here redressed,
  And all our wants supplied ;
Nought we can ask to make us bless'd
  Is in this book denied.

43   8.7.4.   NEWTON.
The Word of God.—Ps. cxix. 50, 103; Jer. xv. 16.

Precious Bible ! what a treasure
  Does the word of God afford !
All I want for life or pleasure,
  Food and medicine, shield and sword,
    Is revealed
  In Jehovah's sacred word.

2 Food, to which the world's a stranger,
   Here my hungry soul enjoys ;
Of excess there is no danger ;
   Though it fills, it never cloys,
      While the Spirit
To my heart its truth applies.

3 When my faith is faint and sickly,
   Or when Satan wounds my mind,
Cordials to revive me quickly,
   Healing medicines, here I find,
      When my Jesus
Shines therein into my mind.

4 In the hour of dark temptation,
   Satan cannot make me yield ;
For the word of consolation
   Is to me a mighty shield,
      While Jehovah
Gives me faith the truth to wield.

5 [Vain his threats to overcome me,
   When in faith I take the sword ;
Then with ease I drive him from me ;
   Satan trembles at the word,
      When my Helper
Makes me strong in Christ my Lord.]

6 [Shall I envy, then, the miser,
   Doting on his golden store ?
Sure I am, or should be, wiser ;
   I am rich, 'tis he is poor :
      Having Jesus,
I have an immortal store.]

44   L.M.   MAXWELL.
Lawful Use of the Law.—Rom. iii. 19, 20; Eph. ii. 3-9

HERE, Lord, my soul convicted stands
Of breaking all thy ten commands ;
And on me justly mightst thou pour
Thy wrath in one eternal shower.

2 But, thanks to God, its loud alarms
Have warned me of approaching harms ;
And now, O Lord, my wants I see ;
Lost and undone, I come to thee.

3 I see my fig-leaf righteousness
Can ne'er thy broken law redress ;
Yet in thy gospel plan I see,
There's hope of pardon e'en for me.

4 Here I behold thy wonders, Lord,
How Christ has to thy law restored
Those honours, on the atoning day,
Which guilty sinners took away.

5 Amazing wisdom, power, and love,
Displayed to rebels from above !
Do thou, O Lord, my faith increase,
To love and trust thy plan of grace.

45   C.M.   HART.
Salvation by Christ alone.—Rom. xi. 6; Gal. iii. 10.

How can ye hope, deluded souls,
   To see what none e'er saw,
Salvation by the works obtained
   Of Sinai's fiery law ?

2 [There ye may toil, and weep, and fast,
   And vex your heart with pain ;
And, when you've ended, find at last
   That all your toil was vain.]

3 That law but makes your guilt abound ;
   Sad help ! and (what is worst)
All souls that under that are found,
   By God himself are curs'd.

4 [This curse pertains to those who break
   One precept, e'er so small ;
And where's the man, in thought or deed,
   That has not broken all ?]

5 Fly, then, awakened sinners, fly ;
   Your case admits no stay ;
The fountain's opened now for sin ;
   Come, wash your guilt away.

6 See how from Jesus' wounded side
   The water flows and blood !
If you but touch that purple tide,
   You then have peace with God.

7 Only by faith in Jesus' wounds
   The sinner finds release ;
No other sacrifice for sin
   Will God accept but this.

46   C.M.   WATTS.
Conviction of Sin by the Law.—Rom. v. 20.

LORD, how secure my conscience was,
   And felt no inward dread !
I was alive without thy law,
   And thought my sins were dead.

2 My hopes of heaven were firm and bright,
   But since the precept came
With a convincing power and light,
   I find how vile I am.

3 [My guilt appeared but small before,
   Till terribly I saw
How perfect, holy, just, and pure
   Was thy eternal law !

4 Then felt my soul the heavy load ;
   My sins revived again ;
I had provoked a dreadful God,
   And all my hopes were slain.]

5 Thy gracious throne I bow beneath ;
   Lord, thou alone canst save ;

O break the yoke of sin and death,
And thus redeem the slave.

47   L.M.   WATTS.

The Law and Gospel.—Luke xxiii. 34; 1 Cor. i. 18.

[CURS'D be the man, for ever curs'd,
That does one wilful sin commit;
Death and damnation for the first,
Without relief and infinite.

2 Thus *Sinai* roars, and round the earth
Thunder, and fire, and vengeance flings;
But Jesus, thy dear gasping breath
And *Calvary*, say gentler things:

3 " Pardon and grace, and boundless love,
Streaming along a Saviour's blood;
And life, and joy, and crowns above,
Obtained by a dear bleeding God."

4 Hark! how he prays, (the charming sound
Dwells on his dying lips,) " Forgive!"
And every groan and gaping wound
Cries, " Father, let the rebels live!"]

5 Go, ye that rest upon the law,
And toil and seek salvation there,
Look to the flame that Moses saw,
And shrink, and tremble, and despair.

6 But I'll retire beneath the cross;
Saviour, at thy dear feet I'll lie!
And the keen sword that justice draws,
Flaming and red, shall pass me by.

48   L.M.   WATTS.

The Law and Gospel.— Rom. viii. 3; Gal. iii. 10, 11.

WHAT curses does the law denounce
Against the man who fails but once!
But in the gospel Christ appears
Pardoning the guilt of numerous years.

2 My soul, no more attempt to draw
Thy life and comfort from the law;
Fly to the hope the gospel gives;
The man that trusts the promise lives.

49   L.M.   BERRIDGE.

The Law and Gospel.—Rom. viii. 3, 4; x. 5-15.

THE law demands a weighty debt,
And not a single mite will bate;
But gospel sings of Jesus' blood,
And says it made the payment good.

2 The law provokes men oft to ill,
And churlish hearts makes harder still
But gospel acts a kinder part,
And melts a most obdurate heart.

3 " Run, run, and work," the law commands,
Yet finds me neither feet nor hands;

But sweeter news the gospel brings;
It bids me fly, and lends me wings.

4 [Such needful wings, O Lord, impart,
To brace my feet and brace my heart;
Good wings of faith and wings of love
Will make a cripple sprightly move.]

5 With these a lumpish soul may fly,
And soar aloft, and reach the sky;
Nor faint nor falter in the race,
But cheerly work, and sing of grace.

50   S.M.   WATTS.

Moses and Christ.—John i. 17; Heb. iii. 1-6.

THE law by Moses came,
But peace, and truth, and love
Were brought by Christ (a nobler name)
Descending from above.

2 Amidst the house of God
Their different works were done;
Moses a faithful servant stood,
But Christ a faithful Son.

3 Then to his new commands
Be strict obedience paid;
O'er all his Father's house he stands
The Sovereign and the Head.

51   C.M.   S. STENNETT.

The Glorious Gospel.—Heb. ix. 24-28; 1 Tim. i. 11.

WHAT wisdom, majesty, and grace
Through all the gospel shine!
'Tis God that speaks, and we confess
The doctrine most divine.

2 Down from his shining throne on high
The Almighty Saviour comes,
Lays his bright robes of glory by,
And feeble flesh assumes.

3 The mighty debt his chosen owed
Upon the cross he pays;
Then through the clouds ascends to God,
Midst shouts of loftiest praise.

4 There he, our great High Priest, appears
Before his Father's throne;
There on his breast our names he wears,
And counts our cause his own.

52   11s.   TOPLADY (?).

The Gospel.—Mark ii. 17; 1 Tim. i. 15; Rev. xxii. 17.

THE gospel brings tidings to each wounded soul,
That Jesus the Saviour can make it quite whole;
And what makes this gospel most precious to me,
It holds forth salvation so perfectly free!

2

The gospel declares that God, sending his Son
To die for poor sinners, gave all things in one;
This, too, makes the gospel most precious to me;
Because 'tis a gospel as full as 'tis free!

3

Since Jesus has saved me, and that freely too,
I fain would in all things my gratitude show ;
But as to man's merit, 'tis hateful to me !
The gospel—I love it ; 'tis perfectly free !

53   L.M.   WATTS.
The Gospel.—Ezek. xi. 19; xxxvii. 9, 10.

THIS is the word of truth and love,
Sent to the nations from above ;
Jehovah here resolves to show
What his almighty grace can do.

2 Lo ! at its sound the dead revive,
Quickened by grace are made alive ;
Dry bones are raised and clothed afresh,
And hearts of stone are turned to flesh.

3 [Lions and beasts of savage name
Put on the nature of the lamb ;
While the vile world esteem it strange,
Gaze and admire, and hate the change.]

4 May but this grace my soul renew,
Let sinners gaze and hate me too ;
The word that saves me does engage
A sure defence from all their rage.

54   C.M.   WATTS.
Not ashamed of the Gospel.—Rom. i. 16; 2 Tim. i. 12.

I'M not ashamed to own my Lord,
Or to defend his cause,
Maintain the honour of his word,
The glory of his cross.

2 Jesus, my God, I know his name,
His name is all my trust ;
Nor will he put my soul to shame,
Nor let my hope be lost.

3 Firm as his throne his promise stands,
And he can well secure
What I've committed to his hands,
Till the decisive hour.

4 Then will he own my worthless name
Before his Father's face,
And in the new Jerusalem
Appoint my soul a place.

55   C.M.   HUMPHREYS.
Gracious Invitation.—Matt. xi. 28; John vi. 37.

COME, guilty souls, and flee away
To Christ, and heal your wounds ;
This is the welcome gospel-day
Wherein free grace abounds.

2 God loved the church, and gave his Son
To drink the cup of wrath ;
And Jesus says he'll cast out none
That come to him by faith.

56   C.M.   WATTS.
Gospel Invitation.—Song v. 1; Isa. lv. 1-3.

[LET every open ear attend,
And broken heart rejoice ;
The trumpet of the gospel sounds
With an inviting voice.]

2 Ho ! all ye hungry, starving souls,
That feed upon the wind,
And vainly strive with earthly toys
To fill an empty mind ;

3 Eternal Wisdom has prepared
A soul-reviving feast ;
And bids your longing appetites
The rich provision taste.

4 Ho ! ye that pant for living streams,
And pine away and die ;
Here you may quench your raging thirst,
With springs that never dry.

5 Rivers of love and mercy here
In a rich ocean join ;
Salvation in abundance flows,
Like floods of milk and wine.

6 [Ye perishing and naked poor,
Who work with mighty pain
To weave a garment of your own
That will not hide your sin ;

7 Come naked, and adorn your souls
In robes prepared by God,
Wrought by the labours of his Son,
And dyed in his own blood.]

8 Dear God ! the treasures of thy love
Are everlasting mines ;
Deep as our helpless miseries are,
And boundless as our sins !

9 The happy gates of gospel grace
Stand open night and day ;
Lord, we are come to seek supplies,
And drive our wants away.

57   L.M.   WATTS.
The Gospel the Power of God to Salvation.—Rom. i. 16.

WHAT shall the dying sinner do,
That seeks relief for all his woe ?
Where shall the guilty conscience find
Ease for the torment of the mind ?

2 How shall we get our crimes forgiven,
Or form our natures fit for heaven ?
Can souls, all o'er defiled with sin,
Make their own powers and passions clean ?

3 In vain we search, in vain we try,
Till Jesus brings his gospel nigh ;
'Tis there that power and glory dwell,
That save rebellious souls from hell.

4 This is the pillar of our hope,
    That bears our fainting spirits up ;
    We read the grace, we trust the word,
    And find salvation in the Lord.

5 [Let men or angels dig the mines
    Where nature's golden treasure shines ;
    Brought near the doctrine of the cross,
    All nature's gold appears but dross.]

6 Should vile blasphemers, with disdain,
    Pronounce the truths of Jesus vain,
    We'll meet the scandal and the shame,
    And sing and triumph in his name.

58   C.M.   WATTS
A Joyful Gospel.—Ps. lxxxix. 15-18; iii. 8.

BLESS'D are the souls that hear and know
    The gospel's joyful sound ;
    Peace shall attend the path they go,
    And light their steps surround.

2 Their joy shall bear their spirits up,
    Through their Redeemer's name ;
    His righteousness exalts their hope,
    Nor Satan dares condemn.

3 The Lord, our glory and defence,
    Strength and salvation gives :
    Israel, thy King for ever reigns .
    Thy God for ever lives.

59   148th.   C.W., *altered by Toplady.*
The Jubilee.—Lev. xxv. 8-18; Isa. xxxv. 10; lxi. 1-3.

BLOW ye the trumpet, blow
    The gladly solemn sound !
    Let poor insolvents know
    To earth's remotest bound :
The year of jubilee is come ;
Return, ye ransomed sinners, home.

2 Exalt the Lamb of God,
    The sin-atoning Lamb ;
    Redemption by his blood,
    To burdened souls proclaim : [The year, &c.

3 Ye slaves in Sinai's cell,
    Your liberty receive ;
    And safe in Jesus dwell,
    And blest in Jesus live :   [The year, &c.

4 The gospel-trumpet hear,
    The news of pardoning grace ;
    Ye happy souls, draw near,
    Behold your Saviour's face : [The year, &c.

5 Jesus, our great High Priest,
    Has full atonement made ;
    Ye weary spirits, rest ;
    Ye mournful souls, be glad ! [The year, &c

60   148th.   BURNHAM.
Chosen to Salvation.—Rom. xi. 5; 2 Thess. ii. 18.

ALL the elected train
    Were chosen in their Head,
    To all eternal good,
    Before the worlds were made ;
Chosen to know the Prince of Peace,
And taste the riches of his grace.

2 Chosen to faith and hope,
    To purity and love,
    To all the life of God,
    To all the things above ;
Chosen to prove salvation sure ;
Chosen to reign for evermore.

3 Nothing but grace appears
    In this eternal choice ;
    It charms the humble saint,
    And makes the soul rejoice ;
Its endless glories shine so bright,
It makes obedience all delight.

4 Now, Lord, to us reveal
    The all-confirming grace ;
    And may we all pursue
    The shining paths of peace ;
Run in the way to joys above,
And ever sing electing love.

61   L.M.   BURNHAM.
Predestination.—Acts xiii. 48; Rom. viii. 30.

'TWAS fixed in God's eternal mind
When his dear sons should mercy find ;
From everlasting he decreed
When every good should be conveyed.

2 Determined was the manner how
Eternal favours he'd bestow ;
Yea, he decreed the very place
Where he would show triumphant grace.

3 Also the means were fixed upon
Thro' which his sovereign love should run.
So time and place, yea, means and mode,
Were all determined by our God.

4 Vast were the settlements of grace
On millions of the human race ;
And every favour, richly given,
Flows from the high decree of heaven.

5 [In every mercy, full and free,
A sovereign God I wish to see ;
To see how grace, free grace has reigned,
In every blessing he ordained.

6 Yes, dearest Lord, 'tis my desire
Thy wise appointments to admire ;
And trace the footsteps of my God,
Through every path in Zion's road.]

62   L.M.   W. A. CLARKE.

God's Sovereignty displayed in Christ.—1 Cor. vi. 11.

SPACE and duration God does fill,
And orders all things by his will,
Respecting all the holy seed,
Chosen in Christ their blesséd Head.

2 God's jewels of election-love
Were sanctified in Christ above ;
In oneness with his nature pure,
Joint-heirs with him for evermore.

63   C.M.   WATTS.

All things decreed.--Matt. x. 29-31; Isa. xlv. 7; Dan. ii.

THERE's not a sparrow nor a worm
    But's found in God's decrees ;
He raises monarchs to their thrones,
    And sinks them if he please.

2 If light attend the course I run,
    'Tis he provides those rays ;
And 'tis his hand that hides my sun,
    If darkness cloud my days.

3 When he reveals the Book of Life,
    O may I read my name
Among the chosen of his love,
    The followers of the Lamb !

64   7s.   RYLAND.

God's Decrees.--Eccles. iii. 1-8, 17; Ps. xxxi. 14, 15.

SOVEREIGN Ruler of the skies.
Ever gracious, ever wise ;
All my times are in thy hand,
All events at thy command.

2 His decree who formed the earth
Fixed my first and second birth ;
Parents, native place, and time,
All appointed were by him.

3 He that formed me in the womb,
He shall guide me to the tomb :
All my times shall ever be
Ordered by his wise decree.

4 [Times of sickness ; times of health ;
Times of penury and wealth ;
Times of trial and of grief ;
Times of triumph and relief ;

5 Times the tempter's power to prove ;
Times to taste the Saviour's love ;
All must come, and last, and end,
As shall please my heavenly Friend.]

6 Plagues and deaths around me fly ;
Till he bids, I cannot die ;
Not a single shaft can hit,
Till the God of love sees fit.

65   L.M.   TUCKER.

Election in Christ.—Eph. i. 5, 11 ; 2 Tim. i. 9.

EXPAND, my soul, arise and sing
The matchless grace of Zion's King ;
His love, as ancient as his name,
Let all thy powers aloud proclaim.

2 Chosen of old, of old approved,
In Christ eternally beloved ;
Adopted too, and children made,
Ere sin its baleful poison spread.

3 Though sin and guilt infest them here,
In Christ they all complete appear ;
The whole that justice e'er demands
Received full payment from his hands.

4 In him the Father never saw
The least transgression of his law ;
Perfection, then, in him we view ;
His saints in him are perfect too.

5 Then let our souls in him rejoice,
As favoured objects of his choice ;
Redeemed, and saved by grace, we sing
Eternal praise to Christ our King.

66   L.M.   TUCKER.

Free Election.—John xvii. 23, 24; Rom. viii. 29.

DEEP in the everlasting mind
The great mysterious purpose lay,
Of choosing some from lost mankind,
Whose sins the Lamb should bear away.

2 Them, loved with an eternal love,
To grace and glory he ordained ;
Gave them a throne which cannot move,
And chose them both to means and end.

3 In these he was resolved to make
The riches of his goodness known ;
These he accepts for Jesus' sake,
And views them righteous in his Son.

4 No goodness God foresaw in his,
But what his grace decreed to give ;
No comeliness in them there is
Which they did not from him receive.

5 Faith and repentance he bestows
On such as he designs to save ;
From him their soul's obedience flows,
And he shall all the glory have.

67   8,8,6.   ADAMS.

The Elect Ransomed.—Isa. liii. 6, 7; 2 Cor. v. 21.

OUR Jesus loves his dear elect ;
With glory they shall all be decked
    Before his Father's face.
Not one of them for whom he bled,
But shall with joy behold their Head,
    In heaven their dwelling-place.

2 [They are the travail of his soul ;
His sweetest thoughts on them did roll
From all eternity.
And, as the jewels of his crown,
He'll give them honour, peace, renown,
And full felicity.]

3 Their sins upon him all were laid,
And he the dreadful debt has paid,
(A debt no more to pay ;)
Their Surety in their law-place stood,
Appeased stern Justice with his blood,
And bore their sins away.

68　　　11s.　　　TOPLADY.
Election.—Luke x. 20; John xiii. 1; Eph. i. 5, 6.

How happy are we our election who see,
And venture, O Lord, for salvation on thee !
In Jesus approved, eternally loved,
Upheld by his power, we cannot be moved.
2
['Tis sweet to recline on the bosom divine,
And experience the comforts peculiar to thine ;
While, born from above, & upheld by thy love,
With singing and triumph to Zion we move !]
3
Our seeking thy face was all of thy grace ;
Thy mercy demands and shall have all the praise.
No sinner can be beforehand with thee ;
Thy grace is eternal, almighty, and free !
4
Our Saviour and Friend, his love shall extend ;
It knew no beginning, and never shall end !
Whom once he receives, his Spirit ne'er leaves,
Nor ever repents of the grace that he gives.
5
[This proof we would give that thee we receive,
Thou art *precious* alone to the souls that *believe* ;
Be precious to us ;　all beside is as dross,
Compared with thy love & the blood of thy cross.]
6
[Through mercy we taste the invisible feast,
The bread of the kingdom, the wine of the blest !
Who grants us to know his drawings below
Will endless salvation and glory bestow.]

69　　　8.7.4.　　GOSPEL MAG., 1777.
The Consolation of Election.—Eph. i. 3-7; Deut. vii. 7.

SONS we are, through God's election,
Who in Jesus Christ believe ;
By eternal destination,
Saving grace we here receive ;
Our Redeemer
Does both grace and glory give.

2 Every soul of man, by sinning,
Merits everlasting pain ;

But thy love, without beginning,
Formed and fixed salvation's plan.
Countless millions
Shall in life through Jesus reign.

3 [Pause, my soul ! adore and wonder !
Ask, " O why such love to me ? "
Grace has put me in the number
Of the Saviour's family ;
Hallelujah !
Thanks, Eternal Love, to thee !]

4 These are springs of consolation,
To converted sons of grace ;
Finished, free, and full salvation
Shining in the Saviour's face !
Free grace only
Suits the wretched sinner's case.

5 When in that blest habitation,
Which my God for me ordained ;
When in glory's full possession,
I with saints and angels stand ;
Free grace only
Shall resound through Canaan's land !

70　　　S.M.　　TOPLADY, C. W., &c.
Divine Providence.—Deut. xxxiii. 27; Ps. lxxiii. 24.

THRICE comfortable hope
That calms my stormy breast ;
My Father's hand prepares the cup,
And what he wills is best.

2 My fearful heart he reads ;
Secures my soul from harms ;
While underneath his mercy spreads
Its everlasting arms.

3 His skill infallible,
His providential grace,
His power and truth, that never fail,
Shall order all my ways.

4 [The fictious power of *chance*
And *fortune* I defy ;
My life's minutest circumstance
Is subject to his eye.]

5 O might I doubt no more,
But in his pleasure rest ;
Whose wisdom, love, and truth, and power,
Engage to make me blest !

71　　　C.M.　　WATTS.
Free Grace in Revealing Christ.—Matt. xi. 25, 26.

JESUS, the Man of constant grief,
A mourner all his days ;
His spirit once rejoiced aloud,
And turned his joy to praise ;

2 " Father, I thank thy wondrous love,
That has revealed thy Son

To men unlearned ; and to babes
Has made the gospel known.

3 " The mysteries of redeeming grace
Are hidden from the wise ;
While pride and carnal reasonings join
To swell and blind their eyes."

4 Thus does the Lord of heaven and earth
His great decrees fulfil,
And order all his works of grace
By his own sovereign will.

72 L.M. WATTS.
The Triumph of Faith.—Rom. viii. 1, 33—39.

WHO shall the Lord's elect condemn ?
'Tis God that justifies their souls ;
And mercy, like a mighty stream,
O'er all their sins divinely rolls.

2 Who shall adjudge the saints to hell ?
'Tis Christ that suffered in their stead ;
And the salvation to fulfil,
Behold him rising from the dead !

3 He lives ! he lives ! and sits above,
For ever interceding there ;
Who shall divide us from his love,
Or what shall tempt us to despair ?

4 Shall persecution, or distress,
Famine, or sword, or nakedness ?
He that has loved us bears us through,
And makes us more than conquerors, too.

5 Faith has an overcoming power ;
It triumphs in the dying hour.
Christ is our life, our joy, our hope,
Nor can we sink with such a prop.

6 Not all that men on earth can do,
Nor powers on high, nor powers below,
Shall cause his mercy to remove,
Or wean our hearts from Christ our love.

73 L.M. WATTS.
Electing Grace.—Eph. i. 3-13; Jno. xx. 17.

JESUS, we bless thy Father's name ;
Thy God and ours are both the same,
What heavenly blessings from his throne
Flow down to sinners through his Son !

2 " Christ be my first elect," he said ;
Then chose our souls in Christ, our Head,
Before he gave the mountains birth,
Or laid foundations for the earth.

3 Thus did eternal love begin
To raise us up from death and sin ;
Our characters were then decreed,
Blameless in love, a holy seed.

4 Predestinated to be sons,
Born by degrees, but chose at once ;
A new regenerated race,
To praise the glory of his grace.

5 With Christ, our Lord, we share our part
In the affections of his heart ;
Nor shall our souls be thence removed,
Till he forgets his first Beloved.

74 C.M. WATTS.
Election excludes Boasting.—1 Cor. i. 26-31.

BUT few among the carnal wise,
But few of noble race,
Obtain the favour of thy eyes,
Almighty King of grace !

2 He takes the men of meanest name
For sons and heirs of God ;
And thus he pours abundant shame
On honourable blood.

3 He calls the fool and makes him know
The mysteries of his grace,
To bring aspiring wisdom low,
And all its pride abase.

4 Nature has all its glories lost,
When brought before his throne ;
No flesh shall in his presence boast,
But in the Lord alone.

75 L.M. WATTS.
Election Sovereign and Free.—Rom. ix. 20-23.

BEHOLD the potter and the clay ;
He forms his vessels as he please ;
Such is our God, and such are we,
The subjects of his high decrees.

2 [Does not the workman's power extend
O'er all the mass, which part to choose,
And mould it for a nobler end,
And which to leave for viler use ?]

3 May not the sovereign Lord on high
Dispense his favours as he will ?
Choose some to life, while others die,
And yet be just and gracious still ?

4 [What if, to make his terror known,
He let his patience long endure,
Suffering vile rebels to go on,
And seal their own destruction sure ?]

5 [What if he mean to show his grace,
And his electing love employs,
To mark out some of mortal race,
And form them fit for heavenly joys ?]

6 Shall man reply against his Lord,
And call his Maker's ways unjust,
The thunder of whose dreadful word
Can crush a thousand worlds to dust ?

7 But O, my soul, if truths so bright
Should dazzle and confound thy sight,
Yet still his written will obey,
And wait the great decisive day.

8 Then shall he make his justice known,
And the whole world before his throne,
With joy or terror shall confess
The glory of his righteousness.

76   L.M.   KENT.

Effectual Calling.—Ps. cii. 13; cx. 3; Ezek. xxxiv. 11-16

THERE is a period known to God
When all his sheep, redeemed by blood,
Shall leave the hateful ways of sin,
Turn to the fold, and enter in.

2 At peace with hell, with God at war,
In sin's dark maze they wander far,
Indulge their lust, and still go on
As far from God as sheep can run.

3 But see how heaven's indulgent care
Attends their wanderings here and there;
Still hard at heel where'er they stray,
With pricking thorns to hedge their way.

4 [When wisdom calls, they stop their ear,
And headlong urge the mad career;
Judgments nor mercies ne'er can sway
Their roving feet to wisdom's way.]

5 Glory to God, they ne'er shall rove
Beyond the limits of his love;
Fenced with Jehovah's *shalls* and *wills*,
Firm as the everlasting hills.

6 The appointed time rolls on apace,
Not to *propose* but *call* by grace;
To change the heart, renew the will,
And turn the feet to Zion's hill.

77   7.5.   HART.

Election.—Mark xiii. 20; John x. 28; xv. 16.

BRETHREN, would you know your stay,
What it is supports you still?
Why, though tempted every day,
Yet you stand, and stand you will?
    Long before our birth,
Nay, before Jehovah laid
The foundations of the earth,
We were chosen in our Head.

2 God's election is the ground
Of our hope to persevere;
On this rock your building found,
And preserve your title clear.
    Infidels may laugh;
Pharisees gainsay or rail;
Here's your tenure (keep it safe)—
God's elect can never fail!

78   L.M.   TUCKER.

Predestination.—Luke xvi. 26; Eph. i. 5-12.

FIXED was the eternal state of man,
Ere time its rapid course began;
Appointed, by God's firm decree,
To endless joy or misery.

2 Fixed was the vast eternal deep
Between the goats and chosen sheep;
Nor can a union e'er take place
'Twixt heirs of wrath and heirs of grace.

3 [Yet erring men make much ado,
And strive to force a passage through;
But, ah! what vain attempt is this,
To strive to ford that deep abyss!]

4 All glory to the great I AM,
Who chose me in the blessed Lamb;
Whilst millions of the human race
Will never know or taste his grace;

5 And blessings on atoning blood,
By which I'm reconciled to God;
And praise be to the Spirit given,
Who frees from sin and leads to heaven.

79   S.M.   WATTS. Rom. viii. 15.

The Glories of Adoption.—1 John iii. 1-3;

BEHOLD what wondrous grace
    The Father has bestowed
On sinners of a mortal race,
    To call them sons of God.

2 'Tis no surprising thing
    That we should be unknown;
The Jewish world knew not their King,
    God's everlasting Son.

3 Nor does it yet appear
    How great we must be made;
But when we see our Saviour there,
    We shall be like our Head.

4 A hope so much divine
    May trials well endure,
For we, as sons in Christ, are made
    As pure as he is pure.

5 If in my Father's love
    I share a filial part,
Send down thy Spirit, like a dove,
    To rest upon my heart.

6 We would no longer lie
    Like slaves before thy throne;
Our faith shall *Abba*, Father, cry,
    And thou the kindred own.

80   7s.   HUMPHREYS.

Privileges of Adoption.—Rom. iii. 24.

BLESSED are the sons of God,
They are bought with Jesus' blood;

They are ransomed from the grave
Life eternal they shall have.

2 God did love them in his Son
Long before the world began ;
They the seal of this receive,
When in Jesus they believe.

3 They are justified by grace ;
They enjoy a solid peace ;
All their sins are washed away ;
They shall stand in God's great day !

4 [They produce the fruits of grace,
Clothed in Jesus' righteousness ;
Born of God, they hate all sin ;
God's pure seed remains within !]

5 They have fellowship with God,
Through the Mediator's blood ;
One with God, through Jesus one,
Glory is in them begun !

6 Though they suffer much on earth,
Strangers to the worldling's mirth,
Yet they have an inward joy,
Pleasures which can never cloy.

81 S.M. BERRIDGE
Spirit of Adoption.—Rom. viii. 15.

WELL, canst thou read thy heart,
And feel the plague of sin ?
Does Sinai's thunder make thee start,
And conscience roar within ?

2 Expect to find no balm
On nature's barren ground ;
All human medicines will do harm ;
They only skin the wound.

3 To Jesus Christ repair,
And knock at mercy's gate ;
His blood *alone* can wash thee fair,
And make thy conscience sweet.

4 In season due he seals
A pardon on the breast ;
The wounds of sin his Spirit heals,
And brings the gospel-rest.

5 [So comes the peace of God,
Which cheers the conscience well ;
And love shed in the heart abroad,
More sweet than we can tell.]

6 Adopted sons perceive
Their kindred to the sky ;
The Father's pardoning love receive,
And " Abba, Father," cry.

82 L.M. WALLIN.
Stability of Covenant.—Ps. lxxxix. 28 ; Isa. liv. 9, 10.

REJOICE, ye saints, in every state,

Divine decrees remain unmoved ;
No turns of Providence abate
God's care for those he once has loved.

2 Firmer than heaven his covenant stands,
Though earth should shake and skies depart,
You're safe in your Redeemer's hands,
Who bears your names upon his heart.

3 Our Surety knows for whom he stood
And gave himself a sacrifice :
The souls once sprinkled with his blood,
Possess a life that never dies.

4 Though darkness spread around our tent,
Though fear prevail and joy decline,
God will not of his oath repent :
Dear Lord, thy people still are thine !

WATTS.

83 L.M. Isa. liv. 8.
Hope in the Covenant.—Heb. vi. 17-19 ;

How oft have sin and Satan strove
To rend my soul from thee, my God !
But everlasting is thy love,
And Jesus seals it with his blood.

2 The oath and promise of the Lord
Join to confirm the wondrous grace,
Eternal power performs the word,
And fills all heaven with endless praise.

3 Amidst temptations sharp and long,
My soul to this dear refuge flies ;
Hope is my anchor, firm and strong,
While tempests blow and billows rise.

4 The gospel bears my spirit up ;
A faithful and unchanging God
Lays the foundation of my hope
In oaths, and promises, and blood.

84 C.M. DODDRIDGE.
Support in the Covenant.—2 Sam. xxiii. 5 ; Ps. xxv. 14.

'TIS mine, the covenant of his grace,
And every promise mine ;
All flowing from eternal love,
And sealed by blood divine.

2 On my unworthy, favoured head,
Its blessings all unite ;
Blessings more numerous than the stars,
More lasting and more bright.

3 That covenant the last accent claims
Of this poor faltering tongue ;
And that shall the first notes employ
Of my celestial song.

85 C.M. WATTS.
God keeping Covenant.—Ps. lxxxix. 19-34.

OUR God, how firm his promise stands,
E'en when he hides his face !
He trusts in our Redeemer's hands
His glory and his grace.

2 Then why, my soul, these sad complaints,
　　Since Christ and thou are one ?
　Thy God is faithful to his saints,
　　Is faithful to his Son.

3 Beneath his smiles my heart has lived,
　　And part of heaven possessed.
　I'll praise his name for grace received,
　　And trust him for the rest.

86　　　S.M.　GOSPEL MAG , 1778.
Covenant Favours.—Deut. iv. 31 ; 2 Cor. i. 20; Heb. viii.
　THE covenant of free grace,
　　As made with Christ our Head,
　Is stored with precious promises,
　　By which our souls are fed.

2　The solemn oath of God
　　Confirms each promise true ;
　And Jesus, with his precious blood,
　　Has sealed the covenant, too !

3　Hence all our comforts flow,
　　And balm for every fear ;
　May we by sweet experience know
　　How choice, how rich they are.

87　　　148th.　　　KENT.
Everlasting Love.—Jer. xxxi 31-34; xxxiii. 20, 21.
　WITH David's Lord and ours,
　　A covenant once was made,
　Whose bonds are firm and sure,
　　Whose glories ne'er shall fade !
　Signed by the sacred Three-in-One,
　In mutual love, ere time began.

2　Firm as the lasting hills,
　　This covenant shall endure,
　Whose potent shalls and wills
　　Make every blessing sure :
　When ruin shakes all nature's frame,
　Its jots and tittles stand the same.

3　[Here the vast seas of grace,
　　Love, peace, and mercy flow,
　That all the blood-bought race
　　Of men, or angels know :
　O sacred deep, without a shore,
　Who shall thy limits e'er explore ?]

4　Here when thy feet shall fall,
　　Believer, thou shalt see
　Grace to restore thy soul,
　　And pardon, full and free ;
　Thee with delight shall God behold,
　A chosen sheep in Zion's fold.

5　And when through Jordan's flood
　　Thy God shall bid thee go,
　His arm shall thee defend,
　　And vanquish every foe ;

And in this covenant thou shalt view
Sufficient strength to bear thee through.

SECOND PART.　　　L.M.
Eph. ii.; Mal. iii. 6.
O THE mysterious depths of grace !
Who shall thy wandering mazes trace ?
Surpassing human thought to know
Where this abyss of love shall flow.

2 'Twas hid in God's eternal breast,
For all his sons in Jesus blest,
Whose mystic members, from of old,
Were in the book of life enrolled.

3 [Shall one, as now in thy embrace,
Before to-morrow fall from grace ;
Be doomed to Tophet's endless flame,
Where hope or mercy never came ?

4 No ! glory to his name we say,
He'll love to-morrow as to-day.
No wrath shall e'er his bosom move
Towards an object of his love.]

5 No heights of guilt, nor depths of sin,
Where his redeemed have ever been,
But sovereign grace was underneath,
And love eternal, strong as death.

6 Come, then, ye saints, in strains divine,
Rehearse the same in every line ;
Nor fear to sing the charming lay ;
You'll sing the same another day.

7 No other song will be the employ
Of saints, in worlds of endless joy,
But loud hosannas round the throne,
To the great sacred Three-in-One.

88　　　L.M.　　　HART.
The Wonders of Redeeming Love.—Ps. cxxx. 7.
How wondrous are the works of God,
Displayed through all the world abroad !
Immensely great ! immensely small !
Yet one strange work exceeds them all !

2 [He formed the sun, fair fount of light ;
The moon and stars, to rule the night ;
But night and stars, and moon and sun,
Are little works compared with one.]

3 [He rolled the seas and spread the skies,
Made valleys sink and mountains rise ;
The meadows clothed with native green,
And bade the rivers glide between.

4 But what are seas, or skies, or hills,
Or verdant vales, or gliding rills,
To wonders man was born to prove—
The wonders of redeeming love ?]

5 'Tis far beyond what words express,
What saints can feel or angels guess ;
Angels, that hymn the great I AM,
Fall down and veil before the Lamb.

6 The highest heavens are short of this ;
'Tis deeper than the vast abyss ;
'Tis more than thought can e'er conceive,
Or hope expect, or faith believe.

7 Almighty God sighed human breath !
The Lord of life experienced death !
How it was done we can't discuss,
But this we know, 'twas done for us.

8 Blest with this faith, then let us raise
Our hearts in love, our voice in praise ;
All things to us must work for good,
For whom the Lamb has shed his blood.

9 [Trials may press of every sort ;
They may be sore, they must be short ;
We now believe, but soon shall view,
The greatest glories God can show.]

89   112th.   HART.
Christ the Saviour.—1 Tim. i. 15 ; Rom. v. 12.

WHEN Adam by transgression fell,
And conscious, fled his Maker's face,
Linked in clandestine league with hell,
He ruined all his future race :
The seeds of evil once brought in,
Increased and filled the world with sin.

2 But lo ! the Second Adam came,
The serpent's subtle head to bruise ;
He cancels his malicious claim,
And disappoints his devilish views ;
Ransoms poor prisoners with his blood,
And brings the sinner back to God.

3 [To understand these things aright,
This grand distinction should be known :
Though all are sinners in God's sight,
There are but few so in their own.
To such as these our Lord was sent ;
They're only sinners who repent.]

4 [What comfort can a Saviour bring
To those who never felt their woe ?
A sinner is a sacred thing ;
The Holy Ghost has made him so.*
New life from him we must receive,
Before for sin we rightly grieve.]

5 This faithful saying let us own,
Well worthy 'tis to be believed,
That Christ into the world came down,
That sinners might by him be saved.
Sinners are high in his esteem,
And sinners highly value him.

90   7s.   LANGFORD.
Redeeming Love.-Gal. iii. 13 ; 1 John iii. 16 ; Isa. lxiii. 9.

Now begin the heavenly theme ;
Sing aloud in Jesus' name ;
Ye who his salvation prove,
Triumph in redeeming love.

2 Ye who see the Father's grace
Beaming in the Saviour's face,
As to Canaan on you move,
Praise and bless redeeming love.

3 Mourning souls, dry up your tears ;
Banish all your guilty fears ;
See your guilt and curse remove,
Cancelled by redeeming love.

4 [Welcome all by sin oppressed,
Welcome to his sacred rest ;

* That is, the Holy Ghost teaches and convinces
him what a sinner he is.—W. G.

Nothing brought him from above,
Nothing but redeeming love.]

5 When his Spirit leads us home,
When we to his glory come,
We shall all the fulness prove
Of our Lord's redeeming love.

6 [He subdued the infernal powers,
Those tremendous foes of ours
From their cursed empire drove,
Mighty in redeeming love.]

7 Hither, then, your music bring ;
Strike aloud each cheerful string ;
Join, ye saints, the hosts above ;
Join to praise redeeming love.

91   L.M.   NEWTON.
Christ a Redeemer and Friend.—Mat. xi. 19 ; Lu. vii. 34

POOR, weak, and worthless though I am,
I have a rich, almighty Friend ;
Jesus, the Saviour, is his name ;
He freely loves, and without end.

2 He ransomed me from hell with blood,
And by his power my foes controlled ;
He found me wandering far from God,
And brought me to his chosen fold.

3 He cheers my heart, my needs supplies,
And says that I shall shortly be
Enthroned with him above the skies ;
O what a Friend is Christ to me !

92   L.M.   WATTS.
The Strength of Christ's Redeeming Love.- Song viii. 5

WHO is this fair one in distress,
That travels from this wilderness ;
And, pressed with sorrows and with sins,
On her beloved Lord she leans ?

2 This is the spouse of Christ our God,
  Bought with the treasures of his blood ;
  And her request and her complaint
  Is but the voice of every saint :

3 " O let my name engraven stand
  Both on thy heart and on thy hand ;
  Seal me upon thy arm, and wear
  That pledge of love for ever there.

4 " Stronger than death thy love is known,
  Which floods of wrath can never drown ;
  And hell and earth in vain combine,
  To quench a fire so much divine.

5 " But I am jealous of my heart,
  Lest it should once from thee depart ;
  Then let thy name be well impressed,
  As a fair signet, on my breast.

6 " Till thou hast brought me to thy home,
  Where fears and doubts can never come,
  Thy countenance let me often see,
  And often thou shalt hear from me."

93   8.7.4.   EVANS, 1797.
" It is finished."—John xix. 30.

HARK ! the voice of love and mercy
  Sounds aloud from Calvary !
See ! it rends the rocks asunder,
  Shakes the earth and veils the sky !
    " It is finished ! "
  Hear the dying Saviour cry !

2 " It is finished ! "—O what pleasure
  Do these charming words afford !
Heavenly blessings, without measure,
  Flow to us from Christ the Lord.
    " It is finished ! "
  Saints, the dying words record.

3 [Finished, all the types and shadows
  Of the ceremonial law ;
Finished all that God had promised ;
  Death and hell no more shall awe.
    " It is finished ! "
  Saints, from hence your comfort draw.]

4 Tune your harps anew, ye seraphs ;
  Join to sing the pleasing theme ;
Saints on earth, and all in heaven,
  Join to praise Immanuel's name.
    Hallelujah !
  Glory to the bleeding Lamb !

94   C.M.   WATTS.
Redemption and Protection.— Ps. xl. 2, 3 ; cxvi. 8.

ARISE, my soul, my joyful powers,
  And triumph in thy God ;
Awake, my voice, and loud proclaim
  His glorious grace abroad.

2 He raised me from the depths of sin,
  The gates of gaping hell ;
And fixed my standing more secure
  Than 'twas before I fell.

3 The arms of everlasting love
  Beneath my soul he placed,
And on the Rock of Ages set
  My slippery footsteps fast.

4 The city of my blessed abode
  Is walled around with grace ;
Salvation for a bulwark stands,
  To shield the sacred place.

5 Satan may vent his sharpest spite,
  And all his legions roar ;
Almighty mercy guards my life,
  And bounds his raging power.

6 [Arise, my soul ! awake my voice,
  And tunes of pleasure sing ;
Loud hallelujahs shall address
  My Saviour and my King.]

95   C.M.   STEELE.
The Wonders of Redemption.—Phil. ii. 8 ; Heb. x. 10.

AND did the Holy and the Just,
  The Sovereign of the skies,
Stoop down to wretchedness and dust,
  That guilty worms might rise ?

2 Yes, the Redeemer left his throne,
  His radiant throne on high,
(Surprising mercy ! love unknown !)
  To suffer, bleed, and die !

3 He took the dying traitor's place,
  And suffered in his stead ;
For man (O miracle of grace !)
  For man the Saviour bled.

4 Dear Lord, what heavenly wonders dwell
  In thy atoning blood !
By this are sinners snatched from hell,
  And rebels brought to God.

5 What glad return can I impart
  For favours so divine ?
O take my all, this worthless heart,
  And make it wholly thine.

96   112th.   C.W. (ROTHE.)
Redemption Found.—2 Cor. v. 1 ; 1 Pet. i. 18-20.

Now I have found the ground wherein
My anchor, hope, shall firm remain,
The wounds of Jesus, for my sin
Before the world's foundation slain ;
Whose mercy shall unshaken stay,
When heaven and earth are fled away.

2 [O grace, thou bottomless abyss,
My sins are swallowed up in thee !
Covered is my unrighteousness ;
From condemnation I am free.
For Jesus' blood, through earth and skies,
Mercy, eternal mercy, cries.]

3 Jesus, I know, has died for me ;
Here is my hope, my joy, my rest ;
Hither, when hell assails, I flee ;
I look into my Saviour's breast.
Away, sad doubt and anxious fear ;
Mercy and love are written there.

4 Though waves and storms go o'er my head,
Tho' strength, and health, and friends be gone,
Though joys be withered all and dead,
And every comfort be withdrawn,
Steadfast on this my soul relies,
Redeeming mercy never dies.

5 Fixed on this ground will I remain,
Though my heart fail and flesh decay ;
This anchor shall my soul sustain,
When earth's foundations melt away.
Mercy's full power I then shall prove,
Loved with an everlasting love.

97   L.M.   C.W.
Finished Redemption.—John xix. 30. Isa. liii. 10, 11.
'Tis finished ! the Messiah dies !
Cut off for sins, but not his own ;
Accomplished is the sacrifice ;
The great redeeming work is done.

2 Finished our vile transgression is,
And purged the guilt of all our sin ;
And everlasting righteousness
Is brought, for all his people, in.

3 'Tis finished, all my guilt and pain,
I want no sacrifice beside.
For me, for me the Lamb was slain,
And I'm for ever justified.

4 Sin, death, and hell are now subdued ;
All grace is now to sinners given ;
And lo ! I plead the atoning blood,
For pardon, holiness, and heaven.

98   7.6.8.   C.W.
Redeeming Blood.—1 John i. 7; Isa. lxiv. 6.
LET the world their virtue boast,
And works of righteousness.
I, a wretch undone and lost,
Am freely saved by grace.
Take me, Saviour, as I am,
And let me lose my sins in thee.
Friend of sinners, spotless Lamb,
Thy blood was shed for me.

2 Full of truth and grace thou art,
And here is all my hope ;
False and foul as hell, my heart
To thee I offer up.
Thou wast given to redeem
My soul from all iniquity.   [Friend, &c.

3 Nothing have I, Lord, to pay,
Nor can thy grace procure,
Empty send me not away,
For I, thou know'st, am poor.
Dust and ashes is my name,
My all is sin and misery.   [Friend, &c.

99   7s.   ADAMS.
Salvation by Christ.--Ps. lxii. 6, 7; Isa. xii. 5.
BLESSED Jesus ! thee we sing ;
Thou of life the eternal spring ;
Thou art worthy, thou alone ;
Thou the Rock and Corner-Stone.

2 'Tis from thee salvation flows ;
This the ransomed sinner knows.
Thou, O Christ, art all his plea,
When he sees his poverty.

3 None shall glory in thy sight
Of their labours e'er so bright ;
All who are taught by thee shall know,
Living faith from God must flow.

4 Grace shall be our lovely theme ;
Free redemption, glorious scheme !
This will be the song above :
Praise to Jesus' bleeding love.

100   C.M.   WATTS.
Redemption by Price & Power.—John i. 29; Heb. ii. 14.
JESUS, with all thy saints above,
My tongue would bear her part ;
Would sound aloud thy saving love,
And sing thy bleeding heart.

2 Bless'd be the Lamb, my dearest Lord,
Who bought me with his blood,
And quenched his Father's flaming sword
In his own vital flood ;

3 The Lamb that freed my captive soul
From Satan's heavy chains,
And sent the lion down to howl
Where hell and horror reigns.

4 All glory to the dying Lamb,
And never-ceasing praise,
While angels live to know his name,
Or saints to feel his grace.

101   C.M.   BERRIDGE.
Freedom from the Law by the Redemption of Christ.
DOES conscience lay a guilty charge,
And Moses much condemn,

And bring in bills exceeding large ?
Let Jesus answer them.

2 He paid thy ransom with his hand,
And every score did quit ;
And Moses never can demand
Two payments of one debt.

3 Now justice smiles on mercy sweet,
And looks well reconciled ;
Joined hand in hand, they go to meet
And kiss a weeping child.

4 But ask the Lord for his receipt,
To show the payment good,
Delivered from the mercy-seat,
And sprinkled with his blood.

5 The law thy feet will not enlarge,
Nor give thy conscience rest,
Till thou canst find a full discharge
Locked up within thy breast.

6 [The sight of this will melt thy heart,
And make thy eyes run o'er.
A happy, pardoned child thou art,
And heaven is at thy door.]

102 148th. HART.
" Set your affection," &c.—Col. iii. 2 ; 1 Cor. vi. 20.
COME, raise your thankful voice,
Ye souls redeemed with blood ;
Leave earth and all its toys,
And mix no more with mud.
Dearly we're bought, highly esteemed ;
Redeemed, with Jesus' blood redeemed.

2 Christians are priests and kings,
All born of heavenly birth ;
Then think on nobler things,
And grovel not on earth. [Dearly, &c.

3 With heart, and soul, and mind,
Exalt redeeming love ;
Leave worldly cares behind,
And set your minds above. [Dearly, &c.

4 Lift up your ravished eyes,
And view the glory given ;
All lower things despise,
Ye citizens of heaven. [Dearly, &c.

5 Be to this world as dead,
Alive to that to come ;
Our life in Christ is hid, [Dearly, &c.
Who soon shall call us home.

103 L.M. C.W. (COUNT ZINZENDORF.)
The Imputed Righteousness of Christ.—Isa. lxi. 10.
JESUS, thy blood and righteousness
My beauty are, my glorious dress ;

Midst flaming worlds, in these arrayed,
With joy shall I lift up my head.

2 When from the dust of death I rise,
To take my mansion in the skies,
E'en then shall this be all my plea :
" Jesus has lived and died for me."

3 Bold shall I stand in that great day,
For who aught to my charge shall lay,
While through thy blood absolved I am,
From sin's tremendous curse and shame ?

4 [Thus Abraham, the friend of God,
Thus all the armies bought with blood,
Saviour of sinners, thee proclaim—
Sinners, of whom the chief I am.]

5 This spotless robe the same appears,
When ruined nature sinks in years ;
No age can change its glorious hue ;
The robe of Christ is ever new.

6 O let the dead now hear thy voice ;
Bid, Lord, thy banished ones rejoice ;
Their beauty this, their glorious dress,
Jesus, the Lord our righteousness.

104 8.3. HART.
The same.—Rom. iii. 22, 25 ; iv. 24 ; 2 Cor. v. 19.
RIGHTEOUSNESS to the believer,
Freely given, comes from heaven,
God himself the giver.

2 Christ has wrought this mighty wonder ;
God and man by him can
Meet, and never sunder.

3 All the law in human nature
He fulfilled ; reconciled
Creature and Creator.

4 Every one, without exemption,
That believes, now receives
Absolute redemption.

5 [Robes of righteousness imputed,
White and whole, clothe the soul,
Each exactly suited.]

6 'Tis a way of God's own finding ;
'Tis his act, and the pact
Cannot but be binding.

7 Here is no prevarication ;
Justice stands, and demands
Full and free salvation.

105 C.M. HART.
" Made him to be sin for us."—2 Cor. v. 21 ; Lu. xxii. 44.
WHEN I by faith my Maker see
In weakness and distress,
Brought down to that sad state for me
Which angels can't express ;

2 When that great God to whom I go
   For help, amazed I view,
By sin and sorrow sunk as low
   As I, and lower too ;

3 [For all our sins we his may call,
   As he sustained their weight ;
How huge the heavy load of all,
   When only mine's so great !]

4 Then, ravished with the rich belief
   Of such a love as this,
I'm lost in wonder, melt with grief,
   And faint beneath the bliss.

5 [Prostrate I fall, ashamed of doubt,
   And worship love divine ;
Thus may I always be devout ;
   Be this religion mine.]

6 In this alone I can confide ;
   Here's righteousness enough.
What's all the boast of nature's pride ?
   What unsubstantial stuff !

7 [Rounds of dead service, forms, and ways,
   Which some so much esteem,
Compared with this stupendous grace,
   What trivial trash they seem !]

8 Lord, help a worthless worm, so weak
   He can do nothing good ;
May all I act, or think, or speak,
   Be sprinkled with thy blood !

106   L.M.   HART.
" Is not this a brand plucked out of the fire ?"-Zech. iii.
   THUS saith the Lord to those that stand
   And wait to hear his great command,
   " I have a sinner to renew,
   And, lo ! this charge I give to you.

2 " Pull his polluted garments off ;
   Here, soul, here's raiment rich enough ;
Clothe thee with righteousness divine ;
   Not creature's righteousness, but mine.

3 " Satan, avaunt ; stand off, ye foes ;
   In vain ye rail, in vain oppose ;
Your cancelled claim no more obtrude ;
   He's mine ; I bought him with my blood.

4 " Sinner, thou stand'st in me complete ;
   Though they accuse thee, I acquit ;
I bore for thee the avenging ire,
   And plucked thee burning from the fire."

107   C.M.   HART.
"Thy sins be forgiven thee."—Mat. ix. 2; Ps. xxxii. 1, 2.
   How high a privilege 'tis to know
   Our sins are all forgiven ;
To bear about this pledge below,
   This special grant of heaven !

2 To look on this when sunk in fears,
   While each repeated sight,
Like some reviving cordial, cheers,
   And makes temptations light !

3 O what is honour, wealth, or mirth,
   To this well-grounded peace ?
How poor are all the goods of earth,
   To such a gift as this !

4 This is a treasure rich indeed,
   Which none but Christ can give ;
Of this the best of men have need ;
   This I, the worst, receive.

108   C.M.   HART.
"The Lord our righteousness."—Jer. xxiii. 6; Ex. xv. 2.
   JEHOVAH is my righteousness ;
   In him alone I'll boast ;

   My tongue his mercy shall confess
   Who seeks and saves the lost.

2 When sunk in fears, with anguish pressed,
   Bowed down with weighty woe,
My weary soul in him finds rest ;
   From him my comforts flow.

3 I'll lay me down, and sweetly sleep,
   For I have peace with God ;
And when I wake he shall me keep,
   Through faith in Jesus' blood.

4 Ten thousand and ten thousand foes
   Shall not my soul destroy ;
My God their counsels overthrows,
   And turns my grief to joy.

109   C.M.   WATTS.
The Robe of Righteousness, &c.—Isa. lxi. 3-10.
   AWAKE, my heart, arise, my tongue ;
   Prepare a tuneful voice ;
In God, the life of all my joys,
   Aloud will I rejoice.

2 'Tis he adorned my naked soul,
   And made salvation mine ;
Upon a poor, polluted worm
   He makes his graces shine.

3 And, lest the shadow of a spot
   Should on my soul be found,
He took the robe the Saviour wrought,
   And cast it all around.

4 [How far the heavenly robe exceeds
   What earthly princes wear !
These ornaments, how bright they shine !
   How white the garments are !]

5 [The Spirit wrought my faith, and love,
   And hope, and every grace ;

But Jesus spent his life to work
The robe of righteousness.]

6 Strangely, my soul, art thou arrayed
By the great sacred Three ;
In sweetest harmony of praise
Let all thy powers agree.

110 S.M. WATTS.
Salvation, Righteousness & Strength in Christ.-Isa. xlv

THE Lord on high proclaims
His Godhead from his throne :
" Mercy and Justice are the names
By which I will be known.

2 " Ye dying souls, that sit
In darkness and distress,
Look from the borders of the pit
To my recovering grace."

3 Sinners shall hear the sound ;
Their thankful tongues shall own,
" Our righteousness and strength are found
In thee, the Lord, alone."

4 In thee shall Israel trust,
And see their guilt forgiven ;
God will pronounce the sinners just,
And take the saints to heaven.

111 C.M. WATTS.
Justification not by Works.--Rom. iii. 19-23, 28.

VAIN are the hopes the sons of men
On their own works have built ;
Their hearts by nature all unclean,
And all their actions guilt.

2 Let Jew and Gentile stop their mouths,
Without a murmuring word ;
And the whole race of Adam stand
Guilty before the Lord.

3 In vain we ask God's righteous law
To justify us now,
Since to convince and to condemn
Is all the law can do.

4 Jesus, how glorious is thy grace !
When in thy name we trust,
Our faith receives a righteousness
That makes the sinner just.

112 L.M. WATTS.
The Value of Christ's Righteousness.—Rom. iii. 27

No more, my God, I boast no more
Of all the duties I have done ;
I quit the hopes I held before,
To trust the merits of thy Son.

2 Now, for the love I bear his name,
What was my gain I count my loss ;
My former pride I call my shame,
And nail my glory to his cross.

3 Yes, and I must and will esteem
All things but loss for Jesus' sake ;
O may my soul be found in him,
And of his righteousness partake !

4 The best obedience of my hands
Dares not appear before thy throne ;
But faith can answer thy demands,
By pleading what my Lord has done.

113 L.M. KENT.
" The Whole need not a Physician."—Matt. ix. 12.

WHO but the soul that's led to know
How just and holy is the law,
Will to the cross of Christ repair,
And seek salvation only there ?

2 [Jesus, my soul's compelled to flee
From all its wrath and curse to thee ;
Though oft, thro' pride, my stubborn will
To Sinai feels a cleaving still.]

3 Sinner, if thou art taught to see
How great thy guilt and misery,
In every thought and act impure,
The blood of Christ thy soul can cure.

4 Daily to feel thyself undone,
Will make thee haste to kiss the Son,
And on thy knees for pardon sue,
And praise, and bless, and love him too.

5 [To feel thy shame and nakedness,
Will make thee love that glorious dress
That sets from condemnation free,
And from the curse delivers thee.

6 Without a seam this garment's wove,
Bequeathed in everlasting love ;
Ere time began, designed to be
A royal robe to cover thee.]

7 We seek no other blood or name,
To cleanse our guilt and hide our shame,
But that wrought out by Christ the Son,
Which God imputes, and faith puts on.

114 S.M. BERRIDGE.
Glorying in Christ.--Jer. ix. 23, 24; 1 Cor. i. 31.

THE sons of earth delight
To spread their fame abroad,
To glory in their worth and might ;
But such are not of God.

2 The heavenly word declares,
And faithful is the word,
That Israel's seed, the royal heirs,
Shall glory in the Lord.

3 In Jesus they shall trust ;
From first to last each one,

Through Jesus, shall be counted just,
And boast in him alone.

4 Amen! the word is good;
My trust is in his name;
I have redemption through his blood,
And I will shout his fame.

5 [He hears my sad complaints,
And heals old wounds and new;
Hosanna to the King of saints;
His ways are just and true!

6 His worth I love to tell,
And wish the world to know;
And where the Son is honoured well,
The Father's honoured too.]

115 L.M. BERRIDGE.
The Carnal Mind & Christ's Righteousness.-1 Cor. ii. 14

[IMPUTED righteousness is strange,
Nor will with human fancies range;
We guess the lurking motive well,
And Paul the hateful truth shall tell.]

2 The lofty heart can not submit
To cast itself at Jesus' feet;
It scorns in borrowed robes to shine,
Though weaved with righteousness divine.

3 Proud nature cries, with loathing eyes,
"This imputation I despise",
And from it she will pertly start,
Till grace has broken down her heart.

4 O give me, Lord, thy righteousness,
To be my peace and wedding dress!
My sores it heals, my rags it hides,
And makes me dutiful besides.

116 7s. BRADFORD.
A Just God and a Saviour.—Isa. xlv. 21; Rom. vi. 22.

O THE power of love divine!
Who its heights and depths can tell—
Tell Jehovah's grand design,
To redeem our souls from hell?

2 Mystery of redemption this:
All my sins on Christ were laid;
My offence was reckoned his;
He the great atonement made!

3 Fully I am justified;
Free from sin, and more than free;
Guiltless, since for me he died;
Righteous, since he lived for me.

4 Jesus, now to thee I bow;
Let thy praise my tongue employ.
Saved unto the utmost now,
Who can speak my heartfelt joy?

117 C.M. TOPLADY.
Intercession.—John xvii. 24; Heb. v. 7; 1 John ii. 1.

AWAKE, sweet gratitude, and sing
The ascended Saviour's love;

Sing how he lives to carry on
His people's cause above.

2 With cries and tears he offered up
His humble suit below;
But with authority he asks,
Enthroned in glory now.

3 For all that come to God by him,
Salvation he demands;
Points to their names upon his breast,
And spreads his wounded hands.

4 His sweet atoning sacrifice
Gives sanction to his claim:
"Father, I will that all my saints
Be with me where I am."

5 Eternal life, at his request,
To every saint is given;

Safety on earth, and, after death,
The plenitude of heaven.

6 Founded on right, thy prayer avails;
The Father smiles on thee;
And now thou in thy kingdom art,
Dear Lord, remember me.

118 C.M. CENNICK.
Melchisedec a type of Christ.—Ps. cx. 4; Heb. v. 10.

THOU dear Redeemer, dying Lamb,
We love to hear of thee;
No music's like thy charming name
Nor half so sweet can be.

2 O let us ever hear thy voice;
In mercy to us speak;
And in our Priest we will rejoice,
Thou great Melchisedec.

3 Our Jesus shall be still our theme,
While in this world we stay;
We'll sing our Jesus' lovely name,
When all things else decay.

4 When we appear in yonder cloud
With all thy favoured throng,
Then will we sing more sweet, more loud,
And Christ shall be our song.

119 C.M. NEWTON.
Access to God in Christ.—Eph. ii. 18; iii. 12; Heb. x. 19.

GREAT God! from thee there's nought con-
Thou seest my inward frame; [cealed,
To thee I always stand revealed
Exactly as I am!

2 Since I can hardly, therefore, bear
What in myself I see;
How vile and black must I appear,
Most holy God, to thee!

3 But since my Saviour stands between,
    In garments-dyed in blood,
    'Tis he, instead of me, is seen,
    When I approach to God.

4 Thus, though a sinner, I am safe ;
    He pleads, before the throne,
    His life and death in my behalf,
    And calls my sins his own.

5 What wondrous love, what mysteries,
    In this appointment shine !
    My breaches of the law are his,
    And his obedience mine.

120   C.M.   WATTS.
Christ's Compassion.--Heb. iv. 15; v. 7; Matt. xii. 20.

    WITH joy we meditate the grace
    Of our High Priest above ;
    His heart is made of tenderness ;
    His bowels melt with love.

2 Touched with a sympathy within,
    He knows our feeble frame ;
    He knows what sore temptations mean,
    For he has felt the same.

3 But spotless, innocent, and pure,
    The great Redeemer stood,
    While Satan's fiery darts he bore,
    And did resist to blood

4 He, in the days of feeble flesh,
    Poured out his cries and tears ;
    And, in his measure, feels afresh
    What every member hears.

5 [He'll never quench the smoking flax,
    But raise it to a flame ;
    The bruised reed he never breaks,
    Nor scorns the meanest name.]

6 Then let our humble faith address
    His mercy and his power ;
    We shall obtain delivering grace,
    In the distressing hour.

121   C.M.   WATTS.
Christ and Aaron.—Exod. xxx. 10; Lev. ix. 7.

JESUS, in thee our eyes behold
    A thousand glories more
Than the rich gems and polished gold
    The sons of Aaron wore.

2 They first their own burnt offerings brought
    To purge themselves from sin ;
    Thy life was pure without a spot,
    And all thy nature clean.

3 [Fresh blood, as constant as the day,
    Was on their altar spilt ;
    But thy one offering takes away
    For ever all our guilt.

4 Their priesthood ran through several hands,
    For mortal was their race ;
    Thy never-changing office stands
    Eternal as thy days.]

5 [Once in the circuit of a year,
    With blood (but not his own),
    Aaron within the veil appears,
    Before the golden throne.

6 But Christ, by his own powerful blood,
    Ascends above the skies,
    And, in the presence of our God,
    Shows his own sacrifice.]

7 Jesus, the King of Glory, reigns
    On Zion's heavenly hill ;
    Looks like a lamb that has been slain,
    And wears his priesthood still.

8 He ever lives to intercede
    Before his Father's face ;
    Give him, my soul, thy cause to plead,
    Nor doubt the Father's grace.

122   148th.   WATTS.
The Offices of Christ glorious.—Phil. ii. 9; Col. iii. 11.

    JOIN all the glorious names
    Of wisdom, love, and power,
    That ever mortals knew,
    That angels ever bore ;
All are too mean to speak his worth,
Too mean to set my Saviour forth.

2   But O what gentle terms,
    What condescending ways,
    Does our Redeemer use
    To teach his heavenly grace !
My eyes with joy and wonder see
What forms of love he bears for me.

3   [Arrayed in mortal flesh,
    He like an angel stands,
    And holds the promises
    And pardons in his hands ;
Commissioned from his Father's throne,
To make his grace to mortals known.]

4   [Great Prophet of my God,
    My tongue would bless thy name ;
    By thee the joyful news
    Of our salvation came ;
The joyful news of sins forgiven,
Of hell subdued, and peace with heaven.]

5   [Be thou my Counsellor,
    My Pattern, and my Guide ;
    And through this desert land,
    Still keep me near thy side ;

O let my feet ne'er run astray,
Nor rove, nor seek the crooked way!]

6 [I love my Shepherd's voice;
His watchful eyes shall keep
My wandering soul among
The thousands of his sheep;
He feeds his flock, he calls their names;
His bosom bears the tender lambs.]

7 [To this dear Surety's hand
Will I commit my cause;
He answers and fulfils
His Father's broken laws.
Behold my soul at freedom set;
My Surety paid the dreadful debt.]

8 [Jesus, my great High Priest,
Offered his blood and died;
My guilty conscience seeks
No sacrifice beside.
His powerful blood did once atone,
And now it pleads before the throne.]

9 [My Advocate appears
For my defence on high;
The Father bows his ears,
And lays his thunder by.
Not all that hell or sin can say,
Shall turn his heart, his love away.]

10 [My dear, almighty Lord,
My Conqueror and my King,
Thy sceptre and thy sword,
Thy reigning grace I sing;
Thine is the power; behold, I sit,
In willing bonds, beneath thy feet.]

11 [Now let my soul arise,
And tread the tempter down!
My Captain leads me forth
To conquest and a crown.
A feeble saint shall win the day,
Though death and hell obstruct the way.]

12 Should all the hosts of death,
And powers of hell unknown,
Put their most dreadful forms
Of rage and mischief on,
I shall be safe, for Christ displays
Superior power and guardian grace.

123 L.M. WATTS.
Priesthood of Christ.—Heb. ix. 24-26; xii. 24.

BLOOD has a voice to pierce the skies:
"Revenge!" the blood of Abel cries;
But the dear stream, when Christ was slain,
Speaks peace as loud from every vein:

2 Pardon and peace from God on high;
Behold, he lays his vengeance by;

And rebels that deserve his sword,
Become the favourites of the Lord.

3 To Jesus let our praises rise,
Who gave his life a sacrifice;
Now he appears before our God,
And for our pardon pleads his blood.

124 C.M. WATTS.
Offices of Christ.—Luke vii. 16; Heb. iii. 1; vii. 1-3.

WE bless the Prophet of the Lord,
That comes with truth and grace;
Jesus, thy Spirit and thy word
Shall lead us in thy ways.

2 We reverence our High Priest above,
Who offered up his blood,
And lives to carry on his love,
By pleading with our God.

3 We honour our exalted King;
How sweet are his commands!
He guards our souls from hell and sin
By his almighty hands.

4 Hosanna to his glorious name,
Who saves by different ways!
His mercies lay a sovereign claim
To our immortal praise.

125 S.M. WATTS.
Faith in Christ our Sacrifice.—Rom. v. 11; Heb. ix. 12.

NOT all the blood of beasts
On Jewish altars slain,
Could give the guilty conscience peace,
Or wash away the stain.

2 But Christ, the heavenly Lamb,
Takes all our sins away;
A sacrifice of nobler name
And richer blood than they.

3 My faith would lay her hand
On that dear head of thine;
While like a penitent I stand,
And there confess my sin.

4 My soul looks back to see
The burdens thou didst bear,
When hanging on the accursed tree,
And hopes her guilt was there.

5 Believing, we rejoice
To see the curse remove;
We bless the Lamb with cheerful voice,
And sing his bleeding Love.

126 C.M. WATTS.
The Personal Glories & Government of Christ.—Ps. xlv.

I'LL speak the honours of my King.
His form divinely fair;

None of the sons of mortal race
  May with the Lord compare.

Sweet is thy speech, and heavenly grace
  Upon thy lips is shed ;
Thy God with blessings infinite
  Has crowned thy sacred head.

Gird on thy sword, victorious Prince,
  Ride with majestic sway ;
Thy terror shall strike through thy foes
  And make the world obey.

Thy throne, O God, for ever stands ;
  Thy word of grace shall prove
A peaceful sceptre in thy hands,
  To rule thy saints by love.

Justice and truth attend thee still,
  But mercy is thy choice ;
And God, thy God, thy soul shall fill
  With most peculiar joys.

127   148th.   C.W.
The Kingdom of Christ.—John i. 49 ; Phil. iv. 4.

REJOICE, the Lord is King ;
  Your God and King adore ;
Mortals, give thanks and sing,
  And triumph evermore.
Lift up the heart, lift up the voice ;
Rejoice aloud, ye saints, rejoice.

2 Rejoice, the Saviour reigns,
  The God of truth and love ;
When he had purged our stains,
  He took his seat above ; [Lift up, &c.

3 His kingdom cannot fail ;
  He rules o'er earth and heaven ;
The keys of death and hell
  Are to our Jesus given ; [Lift up, &c.

4 [He all his foes shall quell ;
  Shall all our sins destroy ;
And every bosom swell
  With pure seraphic joy ;][Lift up, &c.

5 Rejoice in glorious hope,
  Jesus, the Judge, shall come,
And take his servants up
  To their eternal home ;
We soon shall hear the Archangel's voice ;
The trump of God shall sound, Rejoice !

128   C.M.   NEWTON.
Priesthood and Perfections of Christ.—Exod. xxviii.29

CHRIST bears the name of all his saints,
  Deep on his heart engraved ;
Attentive to the state and wants
  Of all his love has saved.

2 In him a holiness complete,
  Light, and perfection shine ;

And wisdom, grace, and glory meet ;
  A Saviour all divine.

3 The blood, which, as a priest, he bears
  For sinners, is his own ;
The incense of his prayers and tears
  Perfumes the holy throne.

4 In him my weary soul has rest,
  Though I am weak and vile ;
I read my name upon his breast,
  And see the Father smile.

129   104th.   HART.
" Thine is the kingdom."—Matt. vi. 13 ; John xvii. 2.

YE souls that are weak, and helpless, and poor,
Who know not to speak, much less to do more,
Lo ! here's a foundation for comfort and peace—
In Christ is salvation ; the kingdom is his.

2 With power he rules, and wonders performs ;
  Gives conduct to fools, and courage to worms
Beset by sore evils without and within,
By legions of devils and mountains of sin.

3 Then be not afraid ; all power is given
  To Jesus, our Head, in earth and in heaven ;
Thro' him we shall conquer the mightiest foes ;
Our Captain is stronger than all that oppose.

4 [His power from above he'll kindly impart,
  So free is his love, so tender his heart ;
Redeemed with his merit, we're washed in his
    blood ;
Renewed by his Spirit, we've power with God.]

5 Thy grace we adore, Director divine ;
  The kingdom, and power, and glory are thine.
Preserve us from running on rocks or on shelves,
From foes strong and cunning, and most from
    ourselves.

6 Reign o'er us as King, accomplish thy will,
  And powerfully bring us forth from all ill ;
Till, falling before thee, we laud thy loved name,
Ascribing the glory to God and the Lamb.

130   S.M.   HART.
Character and Offices of Christ.—Col. iii. 11.

CHRIST is the eternal Rock,
  On which his church is built ;
The Shepherd of his little flock ;
  The Lamb that took our guilt ;
Our Counsellor, our Guide,
  Our Brother, and our Friend ;
The Bridegroom of his chosen bride,
  Who loves her to the end.

2 [He is the Son to free ;
  The Bishop he to bless ;

The full Propitiation he ;
The Lord our Righteousness ;
His body's glorious Head ;
Our Advocate that pleads ;
Our Priest that prayed, atoned, and bled,
And ever intercedes.]

3 Let all obedient souls
Their grateful tribute bring,
Submit to Jesus' righteous rules,
And bow before the King.
Our Prophet, Christ, expounds
His and our Father's will ;
This good Physician cures our wounds
With tenderness and skill.

4 [When sin had sadly made,
'Twixt wrath and mercy, strife,
Our dear Redeemer dearly paid
Our ransom with his life.
Faith gives the full release ;
Our Surety for us stood ;
The Mediator made the peace,
And signed it with his blood.]

5 [Soldiers, your Captain own ;
Domestics, serve your Lord ;
Sinners, the Saviour's love make known ;
Saints, hymn the incarnate Word ;
The Witness sure and true
Of God's good will to men,
The Alpha and the Omega too,
The First and Last. Amen.]

6 Poor pilgrims shall not stray,
Who frighted flee from wrath ;
A bleeding Jesus is the Way,
And blood tracks all the path.
Christians in Christ obtain
The Truth that can't deceive ;
And never shall they die again,
Who in the Life believe.

131　　7.7.4.　　　　C.W.
Christ the Head of the Church.—Eph. iv. 15, 16 ; v. 23
HEAD of the Church triumphant,
We joyfully adore thee ;
Till thou appear, thy members here
Shall thirst for greater glory.

2 We lift our hearts and voices,
With blest anticipation ;
And cry aloud, and give to God
The praise of our salvation.

3 While in affliction's furnace,
And passing through the fire,
Thy love we praise, which tries our ways,
And ever brings us higher.

4 We lift our hands, exulting
In thy almighty favour ;
The love divine which made us thine
Shall keep us thine for ever.

5 Thou dost conduct thy people
Through torrents of temptation ;
Nor will we fear, while thou art near,
The fire of tribulation.

6 [The world, with sin and Satan,
In vain our march opposes,
By thee we shall break through them all,
And sing the song of Moses.]

7 By faith we see the glory
To which thou shalt restore us,
The world despise for that high prize
Which thou hast set before us.

8 And if thou count us worthy,
We each, as dying Stephen,
Shall see thee stand at God's right hand,
To take us up to heaven.

132　　　　C.M.　　　SWAIN.
Christ a True Friend.—Prov. xvii. 17 ; xviii. 24.
A FRIEND there is, your voices join,
Ye saints, to praise his name,
Whose truth and kindness are divine,
Whose love's a constant flame.

2 When most we need his helping hand,
This Friend is always near ;
With heaven and earth at his command,
He waits to answer prayer.

3 His love no end or measure knows ;
No change can turn its course ;
Immutably the same, it flows
From one eternal source !

4 When frowns appear to veil his face,
And clouds surround his throne,
He hides the purpose of his grace,
To make it better known.

5 And if our dearest comforts fall
Before his sovereign will,
He never takes away our all—
Himself he gives us still.

6 [Our sorrows in the scale he weighs,
And measures out our pains ;
The wildest storm his word obeys ;
His word its rage restrains.]

133　　8.7.7.　　　NEWTON.
Christ a Friend.—Rom. v. 7 ; Prov. xviii. 24 ; Song v. 16.
ONE there is, above all others,
Well deserves the name of Friend ;
His is love beyond a brother's,—
Costly, free, and knows no end ;
They who once his kindness prove,
Find it everlasting love.

2 Which of all our friends, to save us,
　　Could or would have shed his blood ;
　But our Jesus died to have us
　　Reconciled in him to God.
　　This was boundless love indeed !
　　Jesus is a Friend in need !

3 O for grace our hearts to soften !
　　Teach us, Lord, at length to love ;
　We, alas ! forget too often
　　What a Friend we have above.
　　But when home our souls are brought,
　　We will praise thee as we ought.

134　　L.M.　　Brewer.
Christ the Sinner's Hiding-place.—Ps. xxxii. 7.

HAIL, sovereign love, that first began
The scheme to rescue fallen man !
Hail, matchless, free, eternal grace,
That gave my soul a hiding-place !

2 [Against the God who rules the sky
I fought with hand uplifted high ;
Despised the mention of his grace,
Too proud to seek a hiding-place.

3 But thus the eternal counsel ran :
" Almighty love, arrest that man ! "
I felt the arrows of distress,
And found I had no hiding-place.

4 Indignant Justice stood in view ;
To Sinai's fiery mount I flew ;
But Justice cried, with frowning face,
" This mountain is no hiding-place ! "

5 Ere long a heavenly voice I heard,
And Mercy's angel-form appeared ;
She led me on, with placid pace,
To Jesus, as my Hiding-place.]

6 Should storms of seven-fold thunder roll,
And shake the globe from pole to pole,
No flaming bolt could daunt my face,
For Jesus is my Hiding-place.

7 On him almighty vengeance fell,
That must have sunk a world to hell ;
He bore it for a chosen race,
And thus became their Hiding-place.

8 A few more rolling suns, at most,
Will land me on fair Canaan's coast,
Where I shall sing the song of grace,
And see my glorious Hiding-place.

135　　C.M.　　Newton.
The Name of Jesus.—Song i. 3 ; Mal. i. 11 ; Col. i. 19.

How sweet the name of Jesus sounds
　In a believer's ear !
It soothes his sorrows, heals his wounds,
　And drives away his fear.

2 It makes the wounded spirit whole,
　And calms the troubled breast ;
'Tis manna to the hungry soul,
　And to the weary rest.

3 Dear name ! the rock on which I build ;
　My shield and hiding-place ;
My never-failing treasury, filled
　With boundless stores of grace.

136　　C.M.　　Steele.
God our Refuge.—Deut. xxxiii. 27 ; Ps. ix. 9 ; xlvi. 1.

DEAR Refuge of my weary soul,
　On thee, when sorrows rise,
On thee, when waves of trouble roll,
　My fainting hope relies.

2 [To thee I tell each rising grief,
　For thou alone canst heal] ;
Thy word can bring a sweet relief
　For every pain I feel.]

3 But O ! when gloomy doubts prevail,
　I fear to call thee mine ;
The springs of comfort seem to fail,
　And all my hopes decline.

4 Yet, gracious God, where shall I flee ?
　Thou art my only trust ;
And still my soul would cleave to thee,
　Though prostrate in the dust.

5 [Hast thou not bid me seek thy face,
　And shall I seek in vain ?
And can the ear of sovereign grace
　Be deaf when I complain !

6 No ; still the ear of sovereign grace
　Attends the mourner's prayer ;
O may I ever find access
　To breathe my sorrows there !]

7 Thy mercy-seat is open still ;
　Here let my soul retreat ;
With humble hope attend thy will,
　And wait beneath thy feet.

137　　8.8.6.　　C.W.. &c.
Christ the Church's Safety.—Luke xii. 32 ; xviii. 7.

How happy is the little flock,
Who, safe beneath their guardian Rock,
　In all commotions rest !
When war and tumult's waves run high,
Unmoved above the storm they lie ;
　They lodge in Jesus' breast.

2 Whatever ills the world befall,
A pledge of endless love we call,
　A sign of Jesus near !

His chariot will not long delay ;
We hear the rumbling wheels, and pray,
   Triumphant Lord, appear !

3 Appear, and thy own flock protect,
  Avenge thy own despised elect,
   And make thy glory known.
  Gird on thy sword, thou King of kings,
  And smite through all inferior things
   That dare usurp thy throne.

138   DODDRIDGE.
C.M.   Ps. xlv. 17.
Jesus precious.— 1 Pet. ii. 4, 7 ; Phil. iii. 8 ;

JESUS, 1 love thy charming name ;
  'Tis music in my ear ;
Fain would I sound it out so loud,
  That earth and heaven might hear.

2 Yes, thou art precious to my soul,
  My transport and my trust ;
Jewels to thee are gaudy toys,
  And gold is sordid dust.

3 O may thy name upon my heart
  Shed a rich fragrance there ;
The noblest balm of all my wounds,
  The cordial of my care.

4 I'll speak the honours of thy name
  With my last labouring breath ;
And, dying, clasp thee in my arms,
  The Antidote of death !

139   WATTS.
C.M.   Psa. xxiii.
Christ a Shepherd.—John x. 11, 14,

MY Shepherd will supply my need ;
  Jehovah is his name.
In pastures fresh he makes me feed,
  Beside the living stream.

2 He brings my wandering spirit back,
  When I forsake his ways ;
And leads me, for his mercy's sake,
  In paths of truth and grace.

3 When I walk through the shades of death,
  Thy presence is my stay ;
A word of thy supporting breath
  Drives all my fears away.

4 Thy hand, in sight of all my foes,
  Does still my table spread ;
My cup with blessings overflows ;
  Thy oil anoints my head.

5 The sure provisions of my God
  Attend me all my days.
O may thy house be my abode,
  And all my work be praise !

6 [There would I find a settled rest,
  (While others go and come)
No more a stranger or a guest,
  But like a child at home.]

140   S.M.   WATTS.
Safety in God.—Ps. xlvi. 1 ; lxi. 1-6 ; Prov. xviii. 10.

WHEN, overwhelmed with grief,
  My heart within me dies,
Helpless and far from all relief,
  To heaven I lift my eyes.

2 O lead me to the Rock
  That's high above my head.
And make the covert of thy wings
  My shelter and my shade !

3 Within thy presence, Lord,
  For ever I'd abide ;
Thou art the Tower of my defence,
  The Refuge where I hide.

4 Thou givest me the lot
  Of those that fear thy name ;
If endless life be their reward,
  I shall possess the same.

141   C.M.   WATTS.
Christ the Foundation of the Church.-- Ps. cxviii. 22, 23

BEHOLD the sure foundation stone
  Which God in Zion lays,
To build our heavenly hopes upon,
  And his eternal praise.

2 Chosen of God, to sinners dear,
  And saints adore the name ;
They trust their whole salvation here,
  Nor shall they suffer shame.

3 The foolish builders, scribe and priest,
  Reject it with disdain ;
Yet on this rock the church shall rest,
  And envy rage in vain.

4 What though the gates of hell withstood ?
  Yet must this building rise ;
'Tis thy own work almighty God,
  And wondrous in our eyes.

142   L.M.   WATTS.
Characters of Christ.-Ps. xlv. 2 ; Song v. 10 ; Phil. ii. 10.

Go worship at Immanuel's feet ;
See in his face what wonders meet,
Earth is too narrow to express
His worth, his glory, or his grace.

2 [The whole creation can afford
But some faint shadows of my Lord ;
Nature, to make his beauties known,
Must mingle colours not her own.]

3 [Is he compared to Wine or Bread ?
Dear Lord, our souls would thus be fed.

That flesh, that dying blood of thine,
Is bread of life, is heavenly wine.]

4 [Is he a Tree ? the world receives
Salvation from his healing leaves ;
That righteous branch, that fruitful bough,
Is David's root and offspring too.]

5 [Is he a Rose ? not Sharon yields
Such fragrancy in all her fields ;
Or if the Lily he assume,
The valleys bless the rich perfume.]

6 [Is he a Vine ? his heavenly root
Supplies the boughs with life and fruit ;
O let a lasting union join
My soul to Christ, the living Vine !]

7 [Is he a Head ? each member lives,
And owns the vital power he gives—
The saints below and saints above,
Joined by his Spirit and his love.]

8 [Is he a Fountain ? there I bathe,
And heal the plague of sin and death ;
These waters all my soul renew,
And cleanse my spotted garments too.]

9 [Is he a Fire ? he'll purge my dross ;
But the true gold sustains no loss ;
Like a refiner shall he sit,
And tread the refuse with his feet.]

10 [Is he a Rock ? how firm he proves !
The Rock of Ages never moves ;
Yet the sweet streams that from him flow,
Attend us all the desert through.]

11 [Is he a Way ? he leads to God ;
The path is drawn in lines of blood ;
There would I walk with hope and zeal,
Till I arrive at Zion's hill.

12 Is he a Door ? I'll enter in ;
Behold the pastures large and green ;
A paradise divinely fair ;
None but the sheep have freedom there.]

13 [Is he designed the Corner-stone,
For men to build their heaven upon ?
I'll make him my foundation too,
Nor fear the plots of hell below.]

14 [Is he a Temple ? I adore
The indwelling majesty and power ;
And still to his most holy place,
Whene'er I pray, I'll turn my face.]

15 [Is he a Star ? he breaks the night,
Piercing the shades with dawning light ;
I know his glories from afar,
I know the bright, the Morning Star.]

16 [Is he a Sun ? his beams are grace,
His course is joy and righteousness ;
Nations rejoice when he appears
To chase their clouds and dry their tears.]

17 O let me climb those higher skies,
Where storms and darkness never rise !
There he displays his powers abroad,
And shines and reigns the incarnate God.

18 Nor earth, nor seas, nor sun, nor stars,
Nor heaven his full resemblance bears ;
His beauties we can never trace,
Till we behold him face to face.

143   7s.   TOPLADY.
Rock Smitten; or the Rock of Ages.–1 Cor. x. 4 ; Ps. li. 2

Rock of Ages, cleft for me ;
Let me hide myself in thee ;
Let the water and the blood,
From thy riven side which flowed,
Be of sin the double cure,
Cleanse me from its guilt and power.

2 [Not the labour of my hands,
Can fulfil thy law's demands ;
Could my zeal no respite know,
Could my tears for ever flow,
All for sin could not atone ;
Thou must save, and thou alone.]

3 [Nothing in my hand I bring ;
Simply to thy cross I cling ;
Naked, come to thee for dress ;
Helpless, look to thee for grace ;
Foul, I to the fountain fly ;
Wash me, Saviour, or I die.]

4 While I draw this fleeting breath,
When my eye-strings break in death,
When I soar through tracts unknown,
See thee on thy judgment throne,
Rock of Ages, cleft for me, &c.

144   L.M.   CENNICK.
Christ the Way.—John xiv. 6 ; Isa. xxxv. 8.

JESUS, my All, to heaven is gone,
He whom I fix my hopes upon ;
His track I see, and I'll pursue
The narrow way, till him I view.

2 [The way the holy prophets went,
The road that leads from banishment,
The King's highway of holiness
I'll go, for all his paths are peace.]

3 This is the way I long have sought,
And mourned because I found it not ;
My grief, my burden long has been,
Because I could not cease from sin.

4 The more I strove against its power,
I sinned and stumbled but the more :

Till late I heard my Saviour say,
"Come hither, soul, I AM THE WAY."

5 Lo! glad I come; and thou, blest Lamb,
Shalt take me to thee as I am;
Nothing but sin I thee can give;
Nothing but love shall I receive.

6 Then will I tell to sinners round,
What a dear Saviour I have found;
I'll point to thy redeeming blood,
And say, "Behold the way to God."

145   7s.   KENT.
Peace made by the Blood of the Cross.—Isa. lxiii. 2, 3.

CHRIST exalted is our song,
Hymned by all the blood-bought throng;
To his throne our shouts shall rise,
God with us by sacred ties.

2 Shout, believer, to thy God!
He has once the wine-press trod;
Peace procured by blood divine;
Cancelled all thy sins and mine.

3 Here thy bleeding wounds are healed;
Sin condemned and pardon sealed;
Grace her empire still maintains;
Christ without a rival reigns.

4 [Through corruption, felt within,
Darkness, deadness, guilt, and sin,
Still to Jesus turn thy eyes—
Israel's hope and sacrifice.]

5 In thy Surety thou art free;
His dear hands were pierced for thee;
With his spotless vesture on,
Holy as the Holy One.

6 O the heights, the depths of grace,
Shining with meridian blaze!

Here the sacred records show
Sinners black but comely too.

7 Saints dejected, cease to mourn;
Faith shall soon to vision turn;
Ye the kingdom shall obtain,
And with Christ exalted reign.

146   148th.   BERRIDGE.
Christ the Sinner's Hiding-place.—Rom. vi. 23; x. 4.

WHERE must a sinner fly,
Who feels his guilty load,
And stands condemned to die,
Out of the mouth of God?
Can any door of hope be found?
Not any sure, on nature's ground.

2 What if he mend his life,
And pour out floods of tears,
And pray with fervent strife?
These pay no past arrears.

The law, with unrelenting breath,
Declares the wage of sin is death.

3 [Who then shall reconcile
Such jarring things as these?
Say, how can Justice smile
At Mercy on her knees?
Or how can Mercy lift her head,
If all the legal debt is paid?]

4 Jesus, thy helping hand
Has made the contest cease,
Paid off each law demand,
And bought the blest release;
Stern Justice, satisfied by thee,
Bids Mercy bring the news to me.

5 O tidings sweet of grace,
To sinners lost and poor,
Who humbly seek thy face,
And knock at Mercy's door;
Who taste the peace thy blood imparts,
And feel the Saviour in their hearts.

6 All hail! we bless thee now,
Who bought us with thy blood!
Our gracious Shepherd thou,
To bring us home to God.
On earth we sing thy bleeding love,
And long to see thy face above.

147   7s.   BERRIDGE.
Christ a Protector of the Wretched.—1 Sam. xxii. 2.

ALL in debt or in distress,
Discontented more or less,
All who would protection have,
Post away to David's cave.

2 All who find their sinful debt
Deep and deeper growing yet;
All who have been Satan's tool—
Much his madman or his fool;

3 All who discontented are,
Full of guilt and full of fear;
Every soul who would not die,
Unto Jesus' cave must fly.

4 [Jesus all your debts will pay;
Chase your legal duns away;
Every foe he will subdue—
World, and flesh, and devil too.]

5 Haste, and seek the Saviour's face;
Rise, and bless him for his grace;
To his scorned cave repair;
He will wash and feast you there.

148   8.8.6.   BERRIDGE.
Christ his People's Surety.—Prov. xi. 15; Matt. xxvii. 29.

FOR wretched strangers such as I,
The Saviour left his native sky,
And surety would become;

He undertakes for sinners lost,
And, having paid the utmost cost,
   Returns triumphant home.
2 A judgment bond against me lay,
Law charges, too, which he must pay,
   But found a smarting debt.
The garden scene begins his woes,
And fetches agonising throes,
   And draws a bloody sweat.
3 His back with hardy stripes is hewed,
Till flakes of gore, and streams of blood,
   Besmear the frighted ground !
A scornful and a smarting crown
His holy head is thrust upon,
   And thorns begird it round.
4 He smarts with nails that pierce his feet,
And smarts with hanging all his weight
   Upon the accursed tree !
He smarts beneath a Father's rod,
And roars aloud, " Why, O my God,
   Hast thou forsaken me ? "
5 [May all my Saviour's love and smart,
Be sweetly graven on my heart,
   And with me fast abide ;
And let me sing thy praises well,
And love thee more than I can tell,
   And trust in none beside.]

149   8.8.6.   BERRIDGE.
A Friend closer than a brother.—Prov. xviii. 24.
   THERE is a Friend, who sticketh fast,
   And keeps his love from first to last,
      And Jesus is his name ;
   An earthly brother drops his hold,
   Is sometimes hot and sometimes cold,
      But Jesus is the same.
2 He loves his people, great and small,
And, grasping hard, embraces all,
   Nor with a soul will part ;
No tribulations which they feel,
No foes on earth, or fiends of hell,
   Shall tear them from his heart.
3 His love before all time began,
And through all time it will remain,
   And evermore endure ;
Tho' rods and frowns are sometimes brought,
And man may change, he changes not ;
   His love abideth sure.
4 [A method strange this Friend has shown,
Of making love divinely known
   To rebels doomed to die ;
Unasked, he takes our humblest form,
And condescends to be a worm,
   To lift us up on high.]

5 [The law demanded blood for blood,
And out he lets his vital flood
   To pay the mortal debt ;
He toils thro' life, and pants thro' death,
And cries, with his expiring breath,
   " 'Tis finish'd," and complete !]

6 [Let all the ransomed of the Lord
Exalt his love with one accord,
   And hallelujah sing ;
Adore the dying Friend of man,
And bless him highly as you can ;
   He is your God and King.]

150   104th.   BERRIDGE.
The Lamb of God.—Isa. liii. 7; John i. 29; Acts viii. 32.
THE sweet Lamb of God comes forth to be slain,
And offers his blood to purge off our stain ;
With bitterest anguish and groans on the tree,
The Saviour did languish for sinners like me.
2 Look on him, my soul, and gaze on his smart ;
   His cries may control the lusts of thy heart ;
His blood has set often the worst broken bones ;
His love too can soften hearts harder than stones.
3 [Right worthy indeed he is of high fame,
   And saints have all need to trust in his name ;
Not feed on their graces, nor strut with a frame,
But fall on their faces, and worship the Lamb.]
4 Lo ! here is a feast of delicate food,
For prodigals dressed, yet costly and good.
Our Father provided this Lamb for a treat ;
And if you are minded, you freely may eat.
5 None other repast my spirit would have ;
   Thy flesh let me taste, sweet Lamb, & yet crave ;
Thy blood ever flowing my pleasant cup be ;
Thy fleece on earth growing make clothing for me.
6 Thus covered and fed at thy proper cost,
   That path I would tread which pleases my host.
Thy patience inherit, thy lowliness prove,
Catch all thy sweet Spirit, and burn with thy love.

151   C.M.   HART.
Christ the Believer's Surety.—Mark ii. 5; John x. 15.
   WHAT slavish fears molest my mind,
   And vex my sickly soul !
   How is it, Lord, that thou art kind,
   And yet I am not whole ?
2 [Ah ! why should unbelief and pride,
   With all their hellish train,
   Still in my ransomed soul abide,
   And give me all this pain ?
3 Thy word is past, thy promise made ;
   With power it came from heaven ;

"Cheer up, desponding soul," it said,
  " Thy sins are all forgiven.
4 " Behold, I make thy cause my own ;
  I bought thee with my blood ;
Thy wicked works on me be thrown,
  And I will work thy good.
5 " I am thy God, thy Guide till death,
  Thy everlasting Friend ;
On me for love, for works, for faith,
  On me for all depend."]
6 Thy blood, dear Lord, has bought my peace,
  And paid the heavy debt ;
Has given a fair and full release,
  But I'm in prison yet.
7 Unjustly now these foes of mine
  Their devilish hate pursue ;
They made my Surety pay the fine,
  Yet plague the prisoner too.
8 What right can my tormentors plead,
  That I should not be free ?
Here's an amazing change indeed !
  Justice is now for me.
9 Lord, break these bars that thus confine,
  These chains that gall me so ;
Say to that ugly gaoler, Sin,
  " Loose him, and let him go."

152   S.M.   HART.
"I am the Way, the Truth, and the Life."—John xiv. 6.

  " I AM," says Christ, " the Way " ;
  Now, if we credit him,
All other paths must lead astray,
  How fair soe'er they seem.
2   " I am," says Christ, " the Truth " ;
  Then all that lacks this test,
Proceed it from an angel's mouth,
  Is but a lie at best.
3   " I am," says Christ, " the Life " ;
  Let this be seen by faith,
It follows, without further strife,
  That all besides is death.
4   If what those words aver,
  The Holy Ghost apply,
The simplest Christian shall not err,
  Nor be deceived, nor die.

153   L.M.   HART.
Christ's Passion.—Matt. xxvi. 36-46; Mark xiv. 32-41
COME, all ye chosen saints of God,
That long to feel the cleansing blood,
In pensive pleasure join with me,
To sing of sad Gethsemane.
2 [Gethsemane, *the olive press !*
(And why so called, let Christians guess ;)
Fit name ! fit place ! where vengeance strove,

And griped and grappled hard with love.]
3 'Twas here the Lord of life appeared,
And sighed, & groaned, & prayed, & feared ;
Bore all incarnate God could bear,
With strength enough, and none to spare.
4 The powers of hell united pressed,
And squeezed his heart & bruised his breast ;
What dreadful conflicts raged within,
When sweat and blood forced thro' the skin!
5 [Dispatched from heaven an angel stood,
Amazed to find him bathed in blood ;
Adored by angels, and obeyed,
But lower now than angels made.
6 He stood to strengthen, not to fight ;
Justice exacts its utmost mite,
This Victim vengeance will pursue ;
He undertook, and must go through.]
7 [Three favoured servants, left not far,
Were bid to wait and watch the war ;
But Christ withdrawn, what watch we keep !
To shun the sight, they sank in sleep.]
8 Backwards and forwards thrice he ran,
As if he sought some help from man ;
Or wished, at least, they would condole
('Twas all they could) his tortured soul.
9 [Whate'er he sought for, there was none ;
Our Captain fought the field alone ;
Soon as the Chief to battle led,
That moment every soldier fled.]
10 Mysterious conflict ! dark disguise !
Hid from all creatures' peering eyes ;
Angels, astonished, viewed the scene ;
And wonder yet what all could mean.
11 O Mount of Olives, sacred grove !
O Garden, scene of tragic love !
What bitter herbs thy beds produce !
How rank their scent, how harsh their juice!
12 [Rare virtues now these herbs contain ;
The Saviour sucked out all their bane ;
My mouth with these if conscience cram,
I'll eat them with the paschal Lamb.]
13 O Kedron, gloomy brook, how foul
Thy black, polluted waters roll !
No tongue can tell, but some can taste,
The filth that into thee was cast.

14 In Eden's garden there was food
Of every kind for man while good ;
But banished thence we fly to thee,
O garden of Gethsemane.

SECOND PART.

Matt. xxvii.; Mark xv.; John xv. 13; Eph. ii. 4, 5.

AND why, dear Saviour, tell me why,
Thou thus wouldst suffer, bleed, and die ;
What mighty motive could thee move ?
The motive's plain ; 'twas all for love.

2 For love of whom ? Of sinners base,
A hardened herd, a rebel race ;
That mocked and trampled on thy blood,
And wantoned with the wounds of God.

3 [When rocks and mountains rent with dread ;
And gaping graves gave up their dead ;
When the fair sun withdrew his light,
And hid his head, to shun the sight ;

4 Then stood the wretch of human race,
And raised his head and showed his face,
Gazed unconcerned when nature failed,
And scoffed, & sneered, & cursed, & railed.]

5 Harder than rocks and mountains are,
More dull than dirt and earth by far,
Man viewed unmoved thy blood's rich stream,
Nor ever dreamed it flowed for him.

6 [Such was the race of sinful men,
That gained that great salvation then ;
Such, and such only, still we see ;
Such they were all ; and such are we.

7 The Jews with thorns his temples crowned,
And lashed him when his hands were bound ;
But thorns, and knotted whips, and bands
By us were furnished to their hands.

8 They nailed him to the accursed tree ;
(They did, my brethren ; so did we) ;
The soldier pierced his side, 'tis true,
But we have pierced him thro' and thro'.]

9 O love of unexampled kind !
That leaves all thought so far behind ;
Where length, & breadth, & depth, & height
Are lost to my astonished sight.

10 For love of me, the Son of God
Drained every drop of vital blood.
Long time I after idols ran ;
But now my God's a martyred Man.

154   7s.   HART.

"Behold, & see, if there be any sorrow."—Lam. i. 12.

MUCH we talk of Jesus' blood ;
But how little's understood !
Of his sufferings so intense,
Angels have no perfect sense.
Who can rightly comprehend
Their beginning or their end ?
'Tis to God, and God alone,
That their weight is fully known.

2 [O thou hideous monster, Sin,
What a curse hast thou brought in !
All creation groans through thee,
Pregnant cause of misery.
Thou hast ruined wretched man,
Ever since the world began ;
Thou hast God afflicted too ;
Nothing less than that would do.

3 Would we then rejoice indeed ?
Be it that from thee we're freed ;
And our justest cause to grieve
Is that thou wilt to us cleave.
Faith relieves us from thy guilt,
But we think whose blood was spilt ;
All we hear, or feel, or see,
Serves to raise our hate to thee.]

4 Dearly we are bought, for God
Bought us with his own heart's blood ;
Boundless depths of love divine !
Jesus, what a love was thine !
Though the wonders thou hast done
Are as yet so little known,
Here we fix and comfort take—
Jesus died for sinners' sake.

155   104th.   HART.

Christ the Fountain for sin & uncleanness.-Zech. xiii. 1

THE fountain of Christ, assist me to sing,
The blood of our Priest, our crucified King ;
Which perfectly cleanses from sin and from filth,
And richly dispenses salvation and health.

2 This fountain so dear, he'll freely impart ;
Unlocked by the spear, it gushed from his heart,
With blood and with water ; the first to atone,
To cleanse us the latter ; the fountain's but one.

3 [This fountain is such (as thousands can tell),
The moment we touch its streams we are well.
All waters beside them are full of the curse ;
For all who have tried them, swell, rot, and grow worse.]

4 [This fountain, sick soul, recovers thee quite ;
Bathe here and be whole, wash here and be white ;
Whatever diseases or dangers befall,
The fountain of Jesus will rid thee of all.]

5 This fountain from guilt not only makes pure,
And gives soon as felt infallible cure ;
But if guilt removéd return and remain,
Its power may be provéd again and again.

6 This fountain unsealed stands open for all
That long to be healed, the great & the small.
Here's strength for the weakly that hither are led ;
Here's health for the sickly, here's life for the dead.

7 This fountain, though rich, from charge is
  quite clear ;
The poorer the wretch, the welcomer here ;
Come needy, come guilty, come loathsome & bare ;
You can't come too filthy ; come just as you are.
8 This fountain in vain has never been tried ;
  It takes out all stain whenever applied ;
The water flows sweetly with virtue divine,
To cleanse souls completely, tho' leprous as mine.

156   C.M.   HART.
The Wish.—Gen. xviii. 27; Zech. xii. 10; Heb. ii. 9.
  IF dust and ashes might presume,
    Great God, to talk to thee ;
  If in thy presence can be room
    For crawling worms like me ;
  I humbly would my *wish* present,
    For *wishes* I have none ;
  All my desires are now content
    To be comprised in one.

2 The single boon I would entreat
    Is, to be led by thee
  To gaze upon thy bloody sweat
    In sad Gethsemane.
  To view (as I could bear at least)
    Thy tender, broken heart,
  Like a rich olive, bruised and pressed
    With agonising smart.

3 [To see thee bowed beneath my guilt ;
    (Intolerable load !)
  To see thy blood for sinners spilt,
    My groaning, gasping God !
  With sympathising grief to mourn
    The sorrows of thy soul :
  The pangs and tortures by thee borne
    In some degree condole.]

4 There musing on thy mighty love,
    I always would remain ;
  Or but to Golgotha remove,
    And thence return again.
  In each dear place the same rich scene
    Should ever be renewed ;
  No object else should intervene,
    But all be love and blood.

5 For this one favour oft I've sought ;
    And if this one be given,
  I seek on earth no happier lot,
    And hope the like in heaven.
  Lord, pardon what I ask amiss,
    For knowledge I have none ;
  I do but humbly speak my wish ;
    And may thy will be done.

157   8.7.   BURNHAM.
Christ's Blood a cleansing Fountain.—John xix. 34.
  MOURNING souls, by sin distressed,
    Lost and ruined, void of good,
  You can never be released,
    But by faith in Jesus' blood.

2 Richly flowed the crimson river,
    Down Immanuel's lovely side ;
  And that blood will you deliver,
    Whensoever 'tis applied.

3 Christ is ready to receive you ;
    See his bloody cross appear.
  From your sins he will relieve you,
    And dissolve your every fear.

4 O behold the Lord expiring ;
    See the suffering Lamb of God !
  And that love be much admiring,
    Which appears in streams of blood.

158   8.7.   ALLEN & BATTY (altered).
Waiting at the Cross.—Jno. xix. 37; Heb. xii. 3.
  SWEET the moments, rich in blessing,
    Which before the cross I spend,
  Life, and health, and peace possessing
    From the sinner's dying Friend ;
  May I sit for ever viewing
  Mercy's streams in streams of blood ;
  Precious drops my soul bedewing,
    Plead and claim my peace with God !

2 Truly blessed is this station,
    Low before his cross to lie,
  While I see divine compassion
    Floating in his languid eye.
  Here it is I find my heaven,
    While upon the Lamb I gaze ;
  Love I much ? I've much forgiven ;
    I'm a miracle of grace.

3 Love and grief my heart dividing,
    With my tears his feet I'll bathe ;
  Constant still in faith abiding,
    Life deriving from his death.
  May I still enjoy this feeling,
    In all need to Jesus go ;
  Prove his wounds each day more healing,
    And himself more deeply know !

159   8s.   SWAIN.
The Sufferings and Death of Jesus.—Luke xxii. 44.
  How willing was Jesus to die,
    That we fellow-sinners might live !
  The life they could not take away,
    How ready was Jesus to give !
  They pierced his hands and his feet ;
    His hands and his feet he resigned ;

The pangs of his body were great,
  But greater the pangs of his mind.

2 That wrath would have kindled a hell
  Of never-abating despair,
In millions of creatures, which fell
  On Jesus, and spent itself there.
'Twas justice that burst in a blaze
  Of vengeance on Jesus, our Head;
Divinity's indwelling rays
  Sustained him till nature was dead.

3 Divinity back to his frame
  The life he had yielded restored,
And Jesus entombed was the same
  With Jesus in glory adored.
No nearer we venture than this,
  To gaze on a deep so profound,
But tread, whilst we taste of the bliss,
  With reverence the hallowed ground.

160   C.M.   COWPER.
The Fountain opened.—Zech. xiii. 1; 1 John i. 7.

THERE is a fountain filled with blood,
  Drawn from Immanuel's veins,
And sinners plunged beneath that flood,
  Lose all their guilty stains.

2 [The dying thief rejoiced to see
  That fountain in his day;
And there have I, as vile as he,
  Washed all my sins away.]

3 [Dear dying Lamb! thy precious blood
  Shall never lose its power,
Till all the ransomed church of God
  Be saved, to sin no more.]

4 E'er since, by faith, I saw the stream
  Thy flowing wounds supply,
Redeeming love has been my theme,
  And shall be till I die.

5 But when this lisping, stammering tongue
  Lies silent in the grave,
Then, in a nobler, sweeter song,
  I'll sing thy power to save.

161   11s.   C.W.
Christ our Sacrifice.—Isa. liii. 6, 12; John x. 15; xv. 13.

THE Lord, in the day of his anger, did lay
Our sins on the Lamb, and he bore them away.
He died to atone for our sins, not his own;
The Father has punished for us his dear Son.

2
[With joy we approve the design of his love;
'Tis a wonder below and a wonder above.
Our Ransom, our Peace, and our Surety he is;
Come, see if there ever were sorrow like his.]

3
[He came from above, the law's curse to remove;
He loved, he has loved us, because he would love;
And, when time is no more, we still shall adore
That ocean of love, without bottom or shore.]

4
Love moved him to die, and on this we rely,
Our Jesus has loved us, we cannot tell why;
But this we can tell, that he loved us so well,
As to lay down his life to redeem us from hell.

162   8s.   SWAIN.
The Soul melted.—Song v. 10; Luke vii. 38; 1 Pet. i. 11.

WHEN on my Beloved I gaze,
  So dazzling his beauties appear,
His charms so transcendently blaze,
  The sight is too melting to bear.

When from my own vileness I turn
  To Jesus exposed on the tree,
With shame and with wonder I burn,
  To think what he suffered for me.

2 [My sins, O how black they appear,
  When in that dear bosom they meet!
Those sins were the nails and the spear
  That wounded his hands and his feet.
'Twas justice that wreathed for his head
  The thorns that encircled it round;
Thy temples, Immanuel, bled,
  That mine might with glory be crowned.]

3 The wonderful love of his heart,
  Where he has recorded my name,
On earth can be known but in part;
  Heaven only can bear the full flame.
In rivers of sorrow it flowed,
  And flowed in those rivers for me,
My sins are all drowned in his blood;
  My soul is both happy and free.

163   8.8.6.   CENNICK.
Looking to Christ.—Job xxxiii. 24; Ps. cxxx. 3.

GREAT God! if thou shouldst bring me near,
To answer at thy awful bar,
  And my own self defend;
If Jesus did himself withdraw,
I know thy holy, fiery law
  My soul to hell would send.

2 A sinner self-condemned I come,
Worthy that thou shouldst me consume,
  But, O! one thing I plead:
The every mite to thee I owed,
Christ Jesus, with his own heart's blood,
  In pity for me paid.

3 Now shouldst thou me to judgment call,
Though Moses faced me there, and all
  My dreadful sins appeared,
I should not fear, but boldly stand ;
Through Jesus' piercéd heart and hand,
  I know I should be spared.

4 My full receipt should there be showed,
Written with iron pens in blood,
  On Jesus' hands and side.
"I'm safe ! " I'll shout, " O law and sin,
Ye cannot bring me guilty in,
  For Christ was crucified ! "

164 L.M. WATTS.
Christ's Passion and Sinners' Salvation.—1 Pet. i. 11

DEEP in our hearts let us record
The deeper sorrows of our Lord,
Behold the rising billows roll,
To overwhelm his holy soul.

2 In loud complaints he spends his breath,
While hosts of hell and powers of death,
And all the sons of malice join
To execute their cursed design.

3 Yet, gracious God ! thy power and love
Have made the curse a blessing prove ;
Those dreadful sufferings of thy Son
Atoned for sins which we had done.

4 The pangs of our expiring Lord,
The honours of thy law restored ;
His sorrows made thy justice known,
And paid for follies not his own.

5 O for his sake our guilt forgive,
And let the mourning sinner live.
The Lord will hear us in his name,
Nor shall our hope be turned to shame.

165 C.M. WATTS.
Christ and his Cross.—1 Cor. i. 18-24, iii. 6, 7.

CHRIST and his cross is all our theme ;
  The mysteries that we speak
Are scandal in the Jew's esteem,
  And folly to the Greek.

2 But souls enlightened from above
  With joy receive the word ;
They see what wisdom, power, and love
  Shine in their dying Lord.

3 The vital savour of his name
  Restores their fainting breath ;
Believing, they rejoice in him,
  The Antidote of death.

4 [Till God diffuse his graces down,
  Like showers of heavenly rain,
In vain Apollos sows the ground,
  And Paul may plant in vain.]

166 L.M. WATTS.
Salvation in the Cross.—Isa. xii. 2, 3 ; 1 Cor. ii. 2.

HERE at thy cross, my dying God,
I lay my soul beneath thy love,
Beneath the droppings of thy blood,
Jesus, nor shall it e'er remove.

2 Not all that tyrants think or say,
With rage and lightning in their eyes,
Nor hell shall fright my heart away,
Should hell with all its legions rise.

3 Should worlds conspire to drive me thence,
Moveless and firm this heart shall lie ;
Resolved (for that's my last defence),
If I must perish, there to die.

4 But speak, my Lord, and calm my fear ;
Am I not safe beneath thy shade ?
Thy vengeance will not strike me here,
Nor Satan dares my soul invade.

5 Yes, I'm secure beneath thy blood,
And all my foes shall lose their aim ;
Hosannah to my dying God,
And my best honours to his name !

167 S.M. WATTS.
The Passion and Exaltation of Christ.—Rom. vi. 9, 10.

COME, all harmonious tongues,
  Your noblest music bring,
'Tis Christ the everlasting God,
  And Christ the Man, we sing.

2 Tell how he took our flesh,
  To take away our guilt ;
Sing the dear drops of sacred blood,
  That hellish monsters spilt.

3 [Alas ! the cruel spear
  Went deep into his side ;
And the rich flood of purple gore
  Their murderous weapons dyed.]

4 [The waves of swelling grief
  Did o'er his bosom roll,
And mountains of almighty wrath,
  Lay heavy on his soul.]

5 Down to the shades of death
  He bowed his awful head ;
Yet he arose to live and reign,
  When death itself is dead.

6 No more the bloody spear ;
  The cross and nails no more ;
For hell itself shakes at his name,
  And all the heavens adore.

7 There the Redeemer sits,
  High on his Father's throne ;

The Father lays his vengeance by,
And smiles upon his Son.

8   [There his full glories shine,
     With uncreated rays ;
  And bless his saints' and angels' eyes,
     To everlasting days.]

168   C.M.   WATTS.
Christ's Victory, Death, and Dominion.—John xix. 30.

I SING my Saviour's wondrous death ;
  He conquered when he fell.
" 'Tis finished ! " said his dying breath,
  And shook the gates of hell.

2 " 'Tis finished ! " our Immanuel cries ;
  The dreadful work is done.
Hence shall his sovereign throne arise ;
  His kingdom is begun.

3 His cross a sure foundation laid
  For glory and renown,
When through the regions of the dead
  He passed to reach the crown.

4 Exalted at his Father's side,
  Sits our victorious Lord ;
To heaven and hell his hands divide
  The vengeance or reward.

5 The saints from his propitious eye
  Await their several crowns ;
And all the sons of darkness fly
  The terror of his frowns.

169   C.M.   BERRIDGE.
A saving knowledge of Christ crucified desirable.

SOME wise men of opinions boast,
  And sleep on doctrines sound ;
But, Lord, let not my soul be lost
  On such enchanted ground.

2 [Good doctrines can do me no good,
  While floating in the brain ;
Unless they yield my heart some food.
  They bring no real gain.]

3 O may my single aim be now
  To live on him that died ;
And nought on earth desire to know,
  But Jesus crucified !

4 [Disputings only gender strife,
  And gall a tender mind ;
But godliness, in all its life,
  At Jesus' cross we find.]

5 Lord, let thy wondrous cross employ
  My musings all day long,
Till, in the realms of purest joy,
  I make it all my song.

170   7s.   BERRIDGE.
Fellowship with Christ's Sufferings.—Luke xxiv. 26, 46

WHAT a doleful voice I hear !
What a garden-scene is there !
What a frightful, ghastly flood !
Jesus weltering in his blood !

2 Groaning on the ground he lies ;
Seems a slaughtered sacrifice !
Tells me, with a feeble breath,
" Sorrowful, yea, unto death ! "

3 [How his eyes astonished are !
Sure they witness conflict near !
On his face what sadness dwells !
Sure he feels a thousand hells !]

4 O my Jesus, let me know
What has brought this heavy woe ;
Swords are piercing through thy heart ;
Whence arose the torturing smart ?

5 " Sinner, thou hast done the deed ;
Thou hast made the Saviour bleed !
Justice drew its sword on me !
Pierced my heart to pass by thee !

6 " Now I take the deadly cup ;
All its dregs am drinking up ;
Read my anguish in my gore ;
Look, and pierce my heart no more "

7 O thou bleeding love divine,
What are other loves to thine ?
Theirs a drop, and thine a sea,
Ever full, and ever free !

8 If I loved my Lord before,
I would love him ten times more ;
Drop into his sea outright,
Lose myself in Jesus quite.

171   L.M.   MEDLEY.
" Him hath God exalted."—Acts v. 31 ; Phil. ii. 9.

JOIN, all who love the Saviour's name,
To sing his everlasting fame ;
Great God ! prepare each heart and voice
In Him for ever to rejoice.

2 Of Him what wondrous things are told !
In Him what glories I behold !
For Him I gladly all things leave ;
To Him, my soul, for ever cleave.

3 In Him my treasure's all contained ;
By Him my feeble soul's sustained ;
From Him I all things now receive ;
Through Him my soul shall ever live.

4 With Him I daily love to walk ;
Of Him my soul delights to talk ;
On Him I cast my every care ;
Like Him one day I shall appear.

5 Bless Him, my soul, from day to day ,
Trust Him to bring thee on thy way ;
Give Him thy poor, weak, sinful heart ;
With Him, O never, never part.

6 Take Him for strength and righteousness ;
Make Him thy refuge in distress ;
Love Him above all earthly joy,
And Him in everything employ.

7 Praise Him in cheerful, grateful songs ;
To Him your highest praise belongs ;
'Tis He who does your heaven prepare,
And Him you'll sing for ever there.

172 L.M. MEDLEY.
"Though I be nothing."—2 Cor. xii. 9, 11 ; vi. 10.

JEHOVAH'S awful name revere,
In humble praise, with holy fear ;
In glory throned, divinely bright,
All worlds are nothing in his sight.

2 [The numerous proud, self-righteous host,
Who fondly of their something boast,
Will find their something nothing more
Than what will prove them blind and poor.

3 O may my soul such folly shun,
Nor ever boast what I have done ;
But at God's footstool humbly fall,
And Jesus be my All in All.]

4 Though of myself I nothing am,
I'm dear to God and to the Lamb ;
Though I have nothing, I confess,
All things in Jesus I possess.

5 I can do nothing, Lord, 'tis true,
Yet in thy strength can all things do ;
Nothing I merit, Lord, I own,
Yet shall possess a heavenly throne.

6 [Thus something, Saviour, may I be,
Nothing in self, but all in thee ;
And when in glory I appear,
Be something, and yet nothing, there.]

173 L.M. MEDLEY.
Christ a Sanctuary.—Ps. lxiii. 2 ; xcvi. 6 ; Isa. viii. 14.

JESUS, before thy face I fall,
My Lord, my Life, my Hope, my All ;
For I have nowhere else to flee,
No sanctuary, Lord, but thee.

2 [In thee I every glory view,
Of safety, strength, and beauty too ;
Beloved Saviour, ever be
A Sanctuary unto me.]

3 [Whatever woes and fears betide,
In thy dear bosom let me hide ;

And, while I pour my soul to thee,
Do thou my Sanctuary be.]

4 Through life and all its changing scenes,
And all the grief that intervenes,
'Tis this supports my fainting heart,
That thou my Sanctuary art.

5 Apace the solemn hour draws nigh,
When I must bow my head and die ;
But O what joy this witness gives,
Jesus, my Sanctuary, lives !

6 He from the grave my dust will raise ;
I in the heavens will sing his praise ;
And when in glory I appear,
He'll be my Sanctuary there.

174 L.M. MEDLEY.
Christ is Precious.—1 Pet. ii. 4, 7 ; Ps. lxxiii. 25.

JESUS is precious, says the word ;
What comfort does this truth afford !
And those who in his name believe,
With joy this precious truth receive.

2 To them he is more precious far
Than life and all its comforts are ;
More precious than their daily food ;
More precious than their vital blood.

3 [Not health, nor wealth, nor sounding fame,
Nor earth's deceitful, empty name,
With all its pomp and all its glare,
Can with a precious Christ compare.]

4 He's precious in his precious blood,
That pardoning and soul-cleansing flood ;
He's precious in his righteousness,
That everlasting, heavenly dress.

5 [In every office he sustains,
In every victory he gains,
In every counsel of his will,
He's precious to his people still.]

6 As they draw near their journey's end,
How precious is their heavenly Friend !
And when in death they bow their head,
He's precious on a dying bed.

7 In glory, Lord, may I be found,
And, with thy precious mercy crowned,
Join the glad song, and there adore
A precious Christ for evermore.

175 L.M. ADAMS.
Christ All in All.—Col. iii. 11 ; Ps. xviii. 2 ; xxiii. 2.

CHRIST is my All, my sure Defence,
Nor shall my soul depart from thence ;
He is my Rock, my Refuge too,
In spite of all my foes can do.

2 Christ is my All, and he will lead
My soul in pastures green to feed ;

'Tis he supplies my every want,
And will all needful blessings grant.
3 Christ is my All! where should I go?
Without him I can nothing do.
Helpless and weak, a sinner great,
Yet in his righteousness complete.

176   C.M.   MEDLEY.
" All my springs are in thee.—Ps. lxxxvii. 7.
Now, dearest Lord, to praise thy name,
  Let all our powers agree;
Worthy art thou of endless fame;
  Our springs are all in thee.
2 Here in thy love will we rejoice,
  All sovereign, rich, and free;
Singing, we hope with heart and voice,
  Our springs are all in thee.
3 To whom, dear Jesus, O to whom
  Shall needy sinners flee
But to thyself, who bidst us come?
  Our springs are all in thee.
4 Some tempted, weak, and trembling saint
  Before thee now may be;
Let not his hopes or wishes faint;
  His springs are all in thee.
5 The poor supply, the wounded heal,
  Let sinners such as we,
Salvation's blessings taste and feel;
  Our springs are all in thee.
6 When we arrive at Zion's hill,
  And all thy glory see,
Our joyful songs shall echo still,
  Our springs are all in thee.

177   7s.   BERRIDGE.
Christ altogether lovely.—Ps. xlv. 2; Song v. 16.
Soon as faith the Lord can see,
Bleeding on the cross for me,

Quick my idols all depart,
Jesus gets and fills my heart.

2 [None among the sons of men,
None among the heavenly train,
Can with Jesus then compare;
None so sweet and none so fair.]

3 Then my tongue would fain express
All his love and loveliness;
But I lisp and falter forth
Broken words, not half his worth.

4 Vexed, I try and try again;
Still my efforts all are vain;
Living tongues are dumb at best;
We must die to speak of Christ.

5 [Blessed is the upper saint,
Who can praise and never faint,

Gazing on thee evermore,
And with flaming heart adore.]

6 [Let the Lord a smile bestow
On his lisping babes below,
That will keep their infant tongue
Prattling of him all day long.]

178   8.8.6.   BERRIDGE.
No Gathering to Profit but with Christ.—Mat. xii. 30.
Abundance of good folk, I find,
Are gathering goodness for the wind
  To scatter it about;
They seek, with human care and skill,
Their vessels with good wine to fill,
  But all the wine leaks out.

2 [A fretful soul his fault may spy,
And struggle much, and often try
  Some patience to obtain;
Yet after many toilsome years,
And many sighs and many tears,
  He has not got a grain.]

3 He that with Jesus gathers not,
May plough and sow, and weed his plot,
  But scatters all his corn;
No real goodness long can stand,
Which planted is by human hand;
  It dies as soon as born.

4 [They reap and scatter all the while;
They reap and gather nought but toil;
  'Tis labour lost, I see.
O Lord, do thou instruct my heart
With my own reaping-hook to part,
  And gather all with thee.]

5 In Christ my treasure gathered is;
My wisdom, wealth, and might are his,
  My peace at his command;
With him is free and plenteous store,
And faith may have enough and more,
  When gathered from his hand.

179   7s.   HART.
Jesus our All.—John x, 17: 1 Cor.ii. 2; Phil. iii. 7, 8.
Jesus is the chiefest good;
He has saved us by his blood;
Let us value nought but him;
Nothing else deserves esteem.

2 [Jesus, when stern Justice said,
" Man his life has forfeited,
Vengeance follows by decree,"
Cried, " Inflict it all on me."]

3 Jesus gives us life and peace,
Faith, and love, and holiness;
Every blessing, great or small,
Jesus freely gives us all.

4 Jesus, therefore, let us own :
Jesus we'll exalt alone ;
Jesus has our sins forgiven,
And will take us safe to heaven.

180   8.7.   HART.
Christ the believer's all.-Acts v. 31; Gal.vi. 14; Eph. i.

LAMB of God, we fall before thee,
Humbly trusting in thy cross ;
That alone be all our glory ;
  All things else are dung and dross ;
Thee we own a perfect Saviour,
  Only Source of all that's good :
Every grace and every favour
  Comes to us through Jesus' blood.

2 [Jesus gives us true repentance,
  By his Spirit sent from heaven ;
Jesus whispers this sweet sentence,
  " Son, thy sins are all forgiven."
Faith he gives us to believe it ;
  Grateful hearts his love to prize ;
Want we wisdom ?   He must give it ;
  Hearing ears, and seeing eyes.]

3 [Jesus gives us pure affections,
  Wills to do what he requires ;
Makes us follow his directions,
  And what he commands inspires.
All our prayers and all our praises,
  Rightly offered in his name,
He that dictates them is Jesus ;
  He that answers is the same.]

4 When we live on Jesus' merit,
  Then we worship God aright,
Father, Son, and Holy Spirit,
  Then we savingly unite.

Hear the whole conclusion of it ;
  Great or good, whate'er we call,
God, or King, or Priest, or Prophet,
  Jesus Christ is All in All.

181   C.M.   HART.
'Who of God is made   . wisdom."--1 Cor. i. 24, 30.

BELIEVERS own they are but blind ;
  They know themselves unwise ;
But wisdom in the Lord they find,
  Who opens all their eyes.

2 Unrighteous are they all, when tried ;
  But God himself declares
In Jesus they are justified ;
  His righteousness is theirs.

3 [That we're unholy needs no proof ;
  We sorely feel the fall ;
But Christ has holiness enough
  To sanctify us all.]

4 Exposed by sin to God's just wrath,
  We look to Christ and view
Redemption in his blood by faith,
  And full redemption too.

5 [Some this, some that good virtue teach,
  To rectify the soul ;
But we first after Jesus reach,
  And richly grasp the whole.]

6 To Jesus joined, we all that's good
  From Him, our Head, derive.
We eat his flesh and drink his blood,
  And by and in him live.

182   112th.   HART.
Dependence on Christ alone.—John xiii. 1; 1 Pet. i. 5

IF ever it could come to pass,
That sheep of Christ might fall away,
My fickle, feeble soul, alas !
Would fall a thousand times a day ;
Were not thy love as firm as free,
Thou soon wouldst take it, Lord, from me.

2 I on thy promises depend ;
At least I to depend desire ;
That thou wilt love me to the end,
Be with me in temptation's fire ;
Wilt for me work, and in me too,
And guide me right and bring me through.

3 No other stay have I beside ;
If these can alter, I must fall ;
I look to thee to be supplied
With life, with will, with power, with all.
Rich souls may glory in their store,
But Jesus will relieve the poor.

183   8s.   KENT.
" Look unto me."—Isa. xlv. 22; John x. 11-15.

" BY covenant transaction and blood,"
  Says Jesus, " my people are mine ;
Their sin-bearing Victim I stood ;
  Yea, for them my life did resign.
The curse of the law I sustained,
  Did them from all cursings set free,
That when by stern Justice arraigned,
  The sinner should look unto me.

2 " When darkness envelopes the mind,
  And troubles rush in as a flood,
Protection in me they shall find,
  And peace in my peace-speaking blood.
For wisdom their course to direct,
  As well as their danger to see,
My sheep, by my Father elect,
  I'll teach them to look unto me.

3 " When thirsty, or faint in the way,
　Or groping 'twixt hope and despair,
To faith I'll my fulness display,
　And bid the poor sinner look there.
When lost in themselves and undone,
　Like doves to my wounds they shall flee ;
For all that the gospel makes known,
　The sinner shall look unto me.

4 " By crosses I'll scourge them for sin,
　Not flowing from wrath, but in love ;
Yet, while they the furnace are in,
　The strength of my grace they shall prove.
And when at my footstool at last,
　They come with the suppliant knee,
Their sorrowful eyes they shall cast,
　And look for salvation in me."

184　　104th.　　FAWCETT.
The fulness of Christ.—John i. 16; Eph. i. 23; Col. i. 19.

A FULNESS resides in Jesus our Head,
And ever abides to answer our need ;
The Father's good pleasure has laid up in store
A plentiful treasure, to give to the poor.

2 Whate'er be our wants, we need not to fear ;
　Our numerous complaints his mercy will hear ;
His fulness shall yield us abundant supplies ;
His power shall shield us when dangers arise.

3 The fountain o'erflows, our woes to redress,
　Still more he bestows, and grace upon grace.
His gifts in abundance we daily receive ;
He has a redundance for all that believe.

4 Whatever distress awaits us below,
　Such plentiful grace will Jesus bestow
As still shall support us and silence our fear,
For nothing can hurt us while Jesus is near.

5 When troubles attend, or danger, or strife,
　His love will defend and guard us thro' life ;
And when we are fainting and ready to die,
Whatever is wanting, his grace will supply.

185　　S.M.　　WATTS.
God all in all.—Ps. xvi. 11; lxxiii. 25.

My God, my Life, my Love,
　To thee, to thee I call,
I cannot live if thou remove,
　For thou art all in all.

2　[Thy shining grace can cheer
　　This dungeon where I dwell ;
'Tis paradise when thou art here ;
　　If thou depart, 'tis hell.]

3　[The smilings of thy face,
　　How amiable they are !
'Tis heaven to rest in thy embrace,
　　And nowhere else but there.]

4　[To thee, and thee alone,
　　The angels owe their bliss ;
They sit around thy gracious throne,
　　And dwell where Jesus is.]

5　[Not all the harps above
　　Can make a heavenly place,
If God his residence remove,
　　Or but conceal his face.]

6　Nor earth, nor all the sky,
　　Can one delight afford ;
No, not a drop of real joy,
　　Without thy presence, Lord.

7　[Thou art the sea of love,
　　Where all my pleasures roll ;
The circle where my passions move,
　　And centre of my soul.]

8　[To thee my spirits fly,
　　With infinite desire ;
And yet how far from thee I lie ;
　　Dear Jesus, raise me higher.]

186　　C.M.　　WATTS.
God my only happiness.—Ps. lxxiii. 25; cxliv. 15.

My God, my Portion, and my Love,
　My everlasting All,
I've none but thee in heaven above,
　Or on this earthly ball.

2 [What empty things are all the skies,
　　And this inferior clod !
There's nothing here deserves my joys ;
　　There's nothing like my God.]

3 [In vain the bright, the burning sun
　　Scatters his feeble light ;
'Tis thy sweet beams create my noon ;
　　If thou withdraw, 'tis night.]

4 [And whilst upon my restless bed,
　　Amongst the shades I roll,
If my Redeemer shows his head,
　　'Tis morning with my soul.]

5 To thee we owe our wealth, and friends,
　　And health, and safe abode ;
Thanks to thy name for meaner things,
　　But they are not my God.

6 [How vain a toy is glittering wealth,
　　If once compared to thee !
Or what's my safety or my health,
　　Or all my friends to me ?]

7 [Were I possessor of the earth,
　　And called the stars my own,
Without thy graces and thyself,
　　I were a wretch undone !]

8 Let others stretch their arms like seas,
 And grasp in all the shore ;
 Grant me the visits of thy face,
 And I desire no more.

187   7s.   BURNHAM.
Jesus draws by effectual grace.—Jno. xii. 32; Song i. 4

JESUS draws the chosen race
 By his sweet resistless grace ;
 Causing them to hear his call,
 And before his power to fall.

2 From the blissful realms above,
 Swift as lightning flies his love ;
 Draws them to his tender breast ;
 There they find the gospel rest.

3 Then how eagerly they move
 In the happy paths of love !
 How they glory in the Lord,
 Pleased with Jesus' sacred word !

4 When the Lord appears in view,
 Old things cease, and all is new ;
 Love divine o'erflows the soul ;
 Love does every sin control.

188   C.M.   COWPER.
Evangelical Obedience.—Rom. vii. 9; Phil. ii. 13.

No strength of nature can suffice
 To serve the Lord aright ;
 And what she has she misapplies,
 For want of clearer light.

2 How long beneath the law I lay,
 In bondage and distress !
 I toiled the precept to obey,
 But toiled without success.

3 [Then to abstain from outward sin
 Was more than I could do ;
 Now, if I feel its power within,
 I feel I hate it too.]

4 [Then, all my servile works were done
 A righteousness to raise ;
 Now, freely chosen in the Son,
 I freely choose his ways.]

5 What shall I do, was then the word,
 That I may worthier grow ?
 What shall I render to the Lord ?
 Is my inquiry now.

6 To see the law by Christ fulfilled,
 And hear his pardoning voice,
 Changes a slave into a child,
 And duty into choice.

189   C.M.   ROZZELL.
Regeneration.—Ps. xl. 3; John iii. 3; 1 Pet. i. 23.

O LET my voice proclaim the joys
 My heart has known and felt ;

And let my tongue declare the woes
 My soul has known by guilt.

2 Long in the paths of sin I trod,
 And, in her foulest way,
 Provoked a kind and gracious God,
 And grieved him day by day.

3 I tried his patience with my crimes,
 By days and years of sin ;
 Resolved to mend in aftertimes,
 And wash the leper clean.

4 [I tried, resolved, and toiled, and tugged,
 But filthier still I grew ;
 My darling sins in secret hugged,
 Nor how to leave them knew.]

5 But when the Lord his arm made bare,
 And took my heart in hand,
 Effectual cleansing work was there,
 Which I could not withstand.

6 He doomed me in the dust to lie,
 In sorrows sharp and long ;
 Then changed my sadness into joy,
 My mourning to a song.

190   C.M.   WATTS.
New Birth.—John i. 13; iii. 3; Jas. i. 18; 1 Pet. i. 23.

NOT all the outward forms on earth,
 Nor rites that God has given,
 Nor will of man, nor blood, nor birth,
 Can raise a soul to heaven.

2 The sovereign will of God alone
 Creates us heirs of grace ;
 Born in the image of his Son,
 A new peculiar race.

3 Our quickened souls awake and rise
 From the long sleep of death ;
 On heavenly things we fix our eyes,
 And praise employs our breath.

191   C.M.   BURNHAM.
Grace Sovereign in Conversion.—Deut. vii. 8; Jno. xv. 16

O WHY did Jesus show to me
 The beauties of his face ?
 Why to my soul did he convey
 The blessings of his grace ?

2 O how could he so sweetly smile
 On such a wretch as I ;
 I who his name did once revile,
 And his dear truth deny ?

3 But 'twas because he loved my soul,
 Because he died for me,
 Because that nothing could control
 His great, his firm decree.

4 Lord, for thy manifested grace
    I'll raise a cheerful song,
Till I shall see thy brighter face
    'Midst the celestial throng.

192   C.M.   WATTS.
Reigning Grace.—Eph. ii. 10; Tit. ii. 11, 12; iii. 8, 14.

As new-born babes desire the breast,
    To feed, and grow, and thrive ;
So saints with joy the gospel taste,
    And by the gospel live.

2 [With inward gust their heart approves
    All that the Word relates.
They love the men the Father loves,
    And hate the works he hates.]

3 [Not all the chains that tyrants use
    Shall bind their souls to vice ;
Faith, like a conqueror, can produce
    A thousand victories.]

4 [Grace, like an uncorrupted seed,
    Abides and reigns within ;
Immortal principles forbid
    The sons of God to sin.]

5 Not by the terrors of a slave,
    Do they perform his will ;
But with the noblest powers they have,
    His sweet commands fulfil.

6 Lord, I address thy heavenly throne ;
    Call me a child of thine.
Send down the Spirit of thy Son
    To form my heart divine.

7 There shed thy choicest loves abroad,
    And make my comforts strong ;
Then shall I say, " My Father, God,"
    With an unwavering tongue.

193   C.M.   NEWTON.
" I am the Resurrection and the Life."—John xi. 25.

" I AM," says Christ, "your glorious Head,"
    (May we attention give,)
" The Resurrection of the dead,
    The Life of all that live.

2 " By faith in me the soul receives
    New life, though dead before ;
And he that in my name believes,
    Shall live to die no more.

3 " The sinner sleeping in his grave
    Shall at my voice awake,
And when I once begin to save,
    My work I'll ne'er forsake."

4 Fulfil thy promise, gracious Lord,
    On us assembled here ;
Put forth thy Spirit with the word,
    And cause the dead to hear.

5 [Preserve the power of faith alive
    In those who love thy name ;
For sin and Satan daily strive
    To quench the sacred flame.

6 Thy power and mercy first prevailed
    From death to set us free ;
And often since our life had failed,
    Had it not been in thee.]

7 To thee we look, to thee we bow,
    To thee for help we call ;
Our Life and Resurrection thou,
    Our Hope, our Joy, our All.

194   C.M.   WALLIN & TOPLADY.
Grace Invincible.—Ps. xlv.; cx. 2; Rev. vi. 2.

HAIL, mighty Jesus ! how divine
    Is thy victorious sword !
The stoutest rebel must resign
    At thy commanding word.

2 Deep are the wounds thy arrows give ;
    They pierce the hardest heart ;
Thy smiles of grace the slain revive,
    And joy succeeds to smart.

3 Still gird thy sword upon thy thigh,
    Ride with majestic sway ;
Go forth, sweet Prince, triumphantly,
    And make thy foes obey.

4 And when thy victories are complete,
    When all the chosen race
Shall round the throne of glory meet,
    To sing thy conquering grace ;

5 O may my blood-washed soul be found
    Among that favoured band !
And I, with them, thy praise will sound
    Throughout Immanuel's land.

195   L.M.   MEDLEY.
Grace exalted in the New Birth.—Jno. i. 13; Jas. i. 18.

ASSIST my soul, my heavenly King,
Thy everlasting love to sing ;
And joyful spread thy praise abroad,
As one, through grace, that's born of God.

2 [No, it was not the will of man
My soul's new heavenly birth began ;
Nor will nor power of flesh and blood
That turned my heart from sin to God.]

3 Herein let self be all abased,
And sovereign love alone confessed ;
This be my song through all the road,
That born I am, and born of God.

4 O may this love my soul constrain
To make returns of love again ;

That I, while earth is my abode,
May live like one that's born of God.

5 [May I thy praises daily show,
Who hast created all things new,
And washed me in a Saviour's blood
To prove that I'm a son of God.]

6 And when the appointed hour shall come,
That thou wilt call me to my home,
Joyful I'll pass the chilling flood,
And die as one that's born of God.

7 Then shall my soul triumphant rise
To its blest mansion in the skies ;
And in that glorious, bright abode,
Sing then as one that's born of God.

196   S.M.   NEWTON.
The Lamentation of a New-born Soul.—Job xl. 4.

O LORD, how vile am I,
Unholy and unclean !
How can I dare to venture nigh
With such a load of sin ?

2 Is this polluted heart
A dwelling fit for thee ?
Swarming, alas ! in every part,
What evils do I see !

3 [If I attempt to pray,
And lisp thy holy name ;
My thoughts are hurried soon away,
I know not where I am.]

4 [If in thy word I look,
Such darkness fills my mind;
I only read a sealed book,
And no relief can find.]

5 [Thy gospel oft I hear,
But hear it still in vain ;
Without desire, or love, or fear,
I like a stone remain.]

6 Myself can hardly bear
This wretched heart of mine !
How hateful, then, must it appear
To those pure eyes of thine !

7 And must I, then, indeed,
Sink in despair and die ?
Fain would I hope that thou didst bleed
For such a wretch as I.

8 That blood which thou hast spilt,
That grace which is thy own,
Can cleanse the vilest sinner's guilt,
And soften hearts of stone.

9 Low at thy feet I bow ;
O pity and forgive !
Here will I lie, and wait till thou
Shalt bid me rise and live.

197   104th.   TOPLADY.
Invincible Grace.—Ps. cx. 3 ; Titus iii. 5.

How mighty thou art, O Lord, to convert ;
Thou only couldst conquer so stubborn a heart,
For thy love to lost man alone could constrain
So stiff-necked a rebel to love thee again.

2 Thro' thee I embrace the ransoming grace,
Of him who has suffered and died in my place,
Tho' I strove to withstand the force of thy hand,
Thy Spirit would conquer, and I was constrained.

3 In vain I withstood, and fled from my God,
For mercy would save me thro' Jesus's blood.
I felt it applied, and I joyfully cried,
Me, me thou hast loved, and for me thou hast died.

4 For sinners like me thy mercy is free,
Who hunger and thirst for redemption by thee.
Lord, gather in more ; make this the glad hour ;
Compel them to yield in the day of thy power.

198   C.M.   NEWTON.
Faith's View.—Eph. ii. 4-8 ; 1 Chron. xvii. 16, 17.

AMAZING grace ! (how sweet the sound !)
That saved a wretch like me ;
I once was lost, but now am found ;
Was blind, but now I see.

2 'Twas grace that taught my heart to fear,
And grace my fears relieved ;
How precious did that grace appear
The hour I first believed !

3 Through many dangers, toils, and snares,
I have already come ;
'Tis grace has brought me safe thus far,
And grace will lead me home.

4 Yes, when this flesh and heart shall fail,
And mortal life shall cease,
I shall possess, within the vail,
A life of joy and peace.

5 The earth shall soon dissolve like snow,
The sun forbear to shine :
But God, who called me here below,
Will be for ever mine.

199   8.7.   LADY HUNTINGDON.
Free Grace.—1 Sam. vii. 12 ; Luke xv. 4-7 ; Eph. i. 6.

COME, thou Fount of every blessing,
Tune my heart to sing thy grace !
Streams of mercy, never ceasing,
Call for songs of loudest praise.
Teach me some melodious sonnet,
Sung by flaming tongues above ;
Praise the mount ! O fix me on it !
Mount of God's unchanging love.

2 Here I raise my Ebenezer ;
  Hither by thy help I'm come ;
And I hope, by thy good pleasure
  Safely to arrive at home.
Jesus sought me when a stranger,
  Wandering from the fold of God ;
He, to save my soul from danger,
  Interposed his precious blood.

3 O to grace how great a debtor
  Daily I'm constrained to be !
Let that grace, Lord, like a fetter,
  Bind my wandering heart to thee.
Prone to wander, Lord, I feel it ;
  Prone to leave the God I love ;
Here's my heart, Lord, take and seal it ;
  Seal it from thy courts above !

200   L.M.   PAICE, 1798.
Amazing Grace.—1 Cor. xv. 10; Eph. ii. 1-8; Zech.iii. 2.

AH ! but for free and sovereign grace,
I still had lived estranged from God,
Till hell had proved the destined place
Of my deserved but dread abode.

2 But O, amazed, I see the hand
That stopped me in my wild career ;
A miracle of grace I stand ;
The Lord has taught my heart to fear.

3 To fear his name, to trust his grace,
To learn his will be my employ ;
Till I shall see him face to face,
Himself my heaven, himself my joy.

201   S.M.   DODDRIDGE
Grace.—Rom. iii. 24; Eph. ii. 5-8; 2 Tim. i. 9.

GRACE ! 'tis a charming sound,
  Harmonious to the ear ;
Heaven with the echo shall resound,
  And all the earth shall hear.

2 Grace first contrived a way
  To save rebellious man,
And all the steps that grace display
  Which drew the wondrous plan.

3 Grace first inscribed my name
  In God's eternal book ;
'Twas grace that gave me to the Lamb,
  Who all my sorrows took.

4 Grace taught my soul to pray,
  And pardoning love to know ;
'Twas grace that kept me to this day,
  And will not let me go.

5 Grace all the work shall crown,
  Through everlasting days ;
It lays in heaven the topmost stone,
  And well deserves the praise.

202   C.M.   NEWTON.
Reigning Grace.—Rom. v. 21; viii. 37-39.

Now may the Lord reveal his face,
  And teach our stammering tongues
To make his sovereign, reigning grace
  The subject of our songs.

2 No sweeter subject can invite
  A sinner's heart to sing,
Or more display the glorious right
  Of our exalted King.

3 Grace reigns to pardon crimson sins,
  To melt the hardest hearts ;
And from the work it once begins
  It never once departs.

4 [The world and Satan strive in vain
  Against the chosen few ;
Secured by grace's conquering reign,
  They all shall conquer too.]

5 'Twas grace that called our souls at first ;
  By grace thus far we're come ;
And grace will help us through the worst,
  And lead us safely home.

203   S.M.   BURNHAM.
The Influence of Grace.—Rom. iii. 24.

FREE grace ! melodious sound !
  How it delights my ear !
It cheers my soul, revives my hope,
  And drowns my every fear.

2 Through grace I conquer hell,
  And break infernal chains ;
Through grace my soul aspires to heaven,
  Where the Redeemer reigns.

3 From his abounding grace
  I daily draw supplies ;
Grace is the never-ceasing spring
  Of all my swelling joys.

4 And when we meet our Lord,
  In yon celestial throng,
Grace shall inspire our souls to sing,
  And grace be all our song.

204   L.M.   RADFORD (?)
Free Grace.—Rom. iii. 24; 1 Cor. xv. 10; 1 Tim. i. 14.

SELF-RIGHTEOUS souls on works rely,
And boast their moral dignity ;
But if I lisp a song of praise,
Each note shall echo, Grace, free grace !

2 'Twas grace that quickened me when dead ;
'Twas grace my soul to Jesus led ;
Grace brings a sense of pardoned sin,
And grace subdues my lusts within.

3 Grace reconciles to every loss,
　And sweetens every painful cross ;
　Defends my soul when danger's near ;
　By grace alone I persevere.

4 When from this world my soul removes
　To mansions of delight and love,
　I'll cast my crown before his throne,
　And shout, Free grace, free grace alone !

205　8.7.4.　ADAMS.
Free Salvation.—Ps. lxviii. 20 ; Isa. xlv. 17 ; Acts iv. 12.

JESUS is our great salvation,
　Worthy of our best esteem ;
He has saved his favourite nation ;
　Join to sing aloud of him.
　　He has saved us !
　Christ alone could us redeem.

2 When involved in sin and ruin,
　And no helper there was found,
Jesus our distress was viewing ;
　Grace did more than sin abound
　　He has called us,
　With salvation in the sound.

3 [Let us never, Lord, forget thee ;
　Make us walk as children here.
We will give thee all the glory
　Of that love that brought us near.
　　Bid us praise thee,
　And rejoice with holy fear.]

4 Free election, known by calling,
　Is a privilege divine ;
Saints are kept from final falling ;
　All the glory, Lord, be thine !
　　All the glory,
　All the glory, Lord, is thine !

206　C.M.　GOSPEL MAG., 1777.
Salvation is of Grace.—Eph. ii. 8 ; 1 John iv. 10.

How sovereign is the love of God
　To Israel's favoured race !
Paid is the mighty debt they owed ;
　Salvation is of grace.

2 His love, without beginning, knew
　Each chosen sinner's case ;
And sent his equal Son to show
　Salvation is of grace.

3 Immanuel had not bled and died,
　Nor suffered in our place,
But for this truth (O sound it wide !),
　Salvation is of grace.

4 We had not known and loved the Son,
　Nor sung his worthy praise,
But that himself the work begun ;
　Salvation is of grace.

207　C.M.　WATTS.
Glorious Salvation.—Ps. xix. 1, 2 ; 1 Thess. v. 9, 10.

FATHER, how wide thy glory shines !
　How high thy wonders rise !
Known through the earth by thousand signs,
　By thousands through the skies !

2 Those mighty orbs proclaim thy power ;
　Their motion speaks thy skill ;
And on the wings of every hour,
　We read thy patience still.

3 But when we view thy strange design
　To save rebellious worms,
Where vengeance and compassion join,
　In their divinest forms :

4 Here the whole Deity is known,
　Nor dares a creature guess

Which of the glories brightest shone—
　The justice or the grace.

5 When sinners broke the Father's laws,
　The dying Son atones ;
O the dear mysteries of his cross,
　The triumph of his groans !

6 Now the full glories of the Lamb
　Adorn the heavenly plains ;
Sweet cherubs learn Immanuel's name,
　And try their choicest strains.

7 O may I bear some glorious part
　In that immortal song !
Wonder and joy shall tune my heart,
　And love command my tongue.

208　8.7.4.　ADAMS.
Salvation.—Acts iv. 12 ; Eph. iii. 17-19 ; Deut. xxxiii. 3.

JESUS, Lover of thy nation ;
　Saviour of thy people free !
Visit us with thy salvation ;
　Let us, Lord, thy glory see ;
　　O revive us,
　That we may rejoice in thee.

2 Let us find thy love surrounding
　Us, thy fickle children, here ;
And thy mighty grace abounding,
　Leading us in holy fear.
　　Guide us, Jesus ;
　To our souls be ever near.

3 May we never more forget thee ;
　(Base ingratitude indeed !)
Keep us with thy arm almighty,
　Us in verdant pastures lead.
　　Be our Guardian,
　Till from this vain world we're freed.

4 Then, O sweetest, lovely Jesus!
    When in heaven we see thy face,
Who from all our bondage freed us,
    We will give thee all the praise.
        All the glory
    Shall redound to thy free grace!

209   C.M.   T. GREENE.
Trust in God's Grace.—2 Cor. xii. 9; Psa. xxxviii. 9.

GRACE, like a fountain, ever flows,
    Fresh succours to renew;
The Lord my wants and weakness knows,
    My sins and sorrows too.

2 He sees me often overcome,
    And pities my distress;
And bids affliction drive me home,
    To anchor on his grace.

3 'Tis he directs my doubtful ways,
    When dangers line the road,
Here I my Ebenezer raise,
    And trust the gracious God.

210   S.M.   WATTS.
Dead to Sin by the Cross of Christ.—Rom. vi. 1, 2, 6.

SHALL we go on to sin,
    Because thy grace abounds?
Or crucify the Lord again,
    And open all his wounds?

2 Forbid it, mighty God!
    Nor let it e'er be said
That we, whose sins are crucified,
    Should raise them from the dead.

3 We will be slaves no more,
    Since Christ has made us free;
Has nailed our tyrants to his cross,
    And brought us liberty.

211   L.M.   WATTS.
Salvation by Grace in Christ.—2 Tim. i. 9, 10.

Now to the power of God supreme
Be everlasting honour given;
He saves from hell (we bless his name),
He calls our wandering feet to heaven.

2 [Not for our duties or deserts,
But of his own abounding grace,
He works salvation in our hearts,
And forms a people for his praise.]

3 'Twas his own purpose that began
To rescue rebels doomed to die;
He gave us grace in Christ his Son,
Before he spread the starry sky.

4 Jesus the Lord appears at last,
And makes his Father's counsels known;

Declares the great transactions past,
And brings immortal blessings down.

5 [He dies! and in that dreadful night
Did all the powers of hell destroy.
Rising, he brought our heaven to light,
And took possession of the joy.]

212   C.M.   WATTS.
Sufficiency of Pardon.—Isa. i. 18; 1 John i. 7.

WHY does your face, ye humble souls,
    Those mournful colours wear?
What doubts are these that try your faith,
    And nourish your despair?

2 [What though your numerous sins exceed
    The stars that fill the skies,
And, aiming at the eternal throne,
    Like pointed mountains rise?]

3 [What though your mighty guilt beyond
    The wide creation swell,
And has its cursed foundations laid
    Low as the deeps of hell?]

4 See, here an endless ocean flows
    Of never-failing grace;
Behold, a dying Saviour's veins
    The sacred flood increase!

5 It rises high, and drowns the hills;
    Has neither shore nor bound;
Now if we search to find our sins,
    Our sins can ne'er be found.

6 Awake, our hearts, adore the grace
    That buries all our faults;
And pardoning blood that swells above
    Our follies and our thoughts.

213   C.M.   WATTS.
Salvation.—Ps. xxxv. 9; Isa. lii. 10; Jonah ii. 9.

SALVATION! O the joyful sound!
    'Tis pleasure to our ears,
A sovereign balm for every wound,
    A cordial for our fears.

2 Buried in sorrow and in sin,
    At hell's dark door we lay;
But we arise by grace divine,
    To see a heavenly day.

3 Salvation! let the echo fly
    The spacious earth around;
While all the armies of the sky
    Conspire to raise the sound.

214   148th.   STEVENS (?).
"Lord, remember me."—Luke xxiii. 42; Ps. xxv. 7.

DEAR Lord, remember me,
    A sinner weak and vile,
    Full of impiety,
And fraught with sin and guile,

I cannot hope but in thy blood ;
Remember me, O Lord, for good.

2   [Unable to depend
    On nature-strength and power,
    Jesus, my soul befriend ;
    Teach me to trust thee more ;
    Save me from sin and all its smart ;
    O save me from my treacherous heart !]

3   Upon thy oath I rest ;
    My feeble soul secure ;
    By sin I am oppressed,
    But thy salvation's sure ;
    Though like a bottle in the smoke,
    I know thy vessels can't be broke.

4   ['Tis true, dear Lord, I am
    A sinner vile indeed !
    Yet hoping in the Lamb,
    Who deigned for such to bleed ;
    And while the Spirit seals my heart,
    My soul believes we ne'er shall part.]

5   Christ ever will defend
    The people of his choice ;
    He loves them without end,
    And in them does rejoice ;
    For them he shed his precious blood,
    And will present them all to God.

215   C.M.   DRACUP.
Free Grace.—Zech. iv. 7 ; Titus iii. 7.

FREE grace to every heaven-born soul
  Will be their constant theme ;
Long as eternal ages roll,
  They'll still adore the Lamb.

2 Free grace alone can wipe the tears
  From our lamenting eyes ;
Can raise our souls from guilty fears
  To joy that never dies.

3 [Free grace can death itself outbrave,
  And take its sting away ;
Can souls unto the utmost save,
  And them to heaven convey.

4 Our Saviour, by free grace alone,
  His building shall complete ;
With shouting bring forth the head stone,
  Crying, Grace, grace to it.

5 May I be found a living stone,
  In Salem's streets above ;
And help to sing before the throne,
  Free grace and dying love.

216   8.8.6.   STEVENS (altered).
Exulting in Salvation by Grace.—Ps. xxxiv. 1-6, 22.

LORD, come in thy appointed ways,
And teach me now to sing thy praise,

For thou art dear to me ;
And all the openings of thy love,
In coming from thy courts above,
  Prove I was dear to thee.

2 [Dear in primeval glory, when
Neither were angels made nor men,
  Nor aught exist but God.
E'en then thy heart was fixed on me ;
And now, through grace, I fix on thee,
  By faith in Jesus' blood.]

3 In this I make my greatest boast,
Though once to human reason lost,
  That I am saved by grace ;
With this bright hope I walk below—
That I thy purest love shall know,
  And see thee face to face.

4 [Dear Lord, more drops of honey send,
From Christ, thy Son, the sinner's Friend,
  And larger make my share ;
More grapes from Eshcol may I bring,
And of the heavenly Canaan sing,
  Whilst I am stationed here.

5 And thus with many foretastes blest
Of yonder everlasting rest,
  Held for me in thy hand,
May I thy house below resort,
And give my friends a good report
  Of Canaan's heavenly land.

6 And in these galleries of thy grace,
Show us, dear Lord, thy smiling face,
  And bring thy presence near ;
Nor from these earthly courts remove,
But send more showers of heavenly love,
  Upon thy garden here.]

217   8.8.6.   KENT.
A Song of Redemption.—Rom. iii. 24 ; Titus iii. 5-7.

LET Zion, in her songs, record
The honours of her dying Lord
  Triumphant over sin ;
How sweet the song, there's none can say
But he whose sins are washed away,
  Who feels the same within.

2 We claim no merit of our own,
But, self-condemned before thy throne,
  Our hopes on Jesus place ;
In heart, in lip, in life depraved,
Our theme shall be, a sinner saved,
  And praise redeeming grace.

3 We'll sing the same while life shall last,
And when, at the archangel's blast
  Our sleeping dust shall rise,

Then in a song for ever new
The glorious theme we'll still pursue,
Throughout the azure skies.

4 [Prepared of old, at God's right hand,
Bright, everlasting mansions stand,
For all the blood-bought race ;
And till we reach those seats of bliss,
We'll sing no other song but this :
A sinner saved by grace.]

218   C.M.   HART.

"He frankly forgave them both."—Luke vii. 41, 42.

MERCY is welcome news indeed
To those that guilty stand ;
Wretches that feel what help they need
Will bless the helping hand.

2 Who rightly would his alms dispose
Must give them to the poor.
None but the wounded patient knows
The comforts of his cure.

3 We all have sinned against our God ;
Exception none can boast ;
But he that feels the heaviest load
Will prize forgiveness most.

4 No reckoning can we rightly keep,
For who the sum can know ?
Some souls are fifty pieces deep,
And some five hundred owe.

5 But let our debts be what they may,
However great or small,
As soon as we have nought to pay,
Our Lord forgives us all.

6 'Tis perfect poverty alone
That sets the soul at large ;
While we can call one mite our own,
We have no full discharge.

219   S.M.   HART.

The Prodigal.—Luke xv. 11-32.

Now for a wondrous song,
(Keep distance, ye profane ;
Be silent, each unhallowed tongue,
Nor turn the truth to bane,)

2 The prodigal's returned—
The rebel bold and base,
That all his Father's counsel spurned,
And long abused his grace.

3 What treatment since he came ?
Love, tenderly expressed.
What robe is brought to hide his shame ?
The best, the very best.

4 Rich food the servants bring ;
Sweet music charms his ears ;
See what a beauteous, costly ring
The beggar's finger wears !

5 [Ye elder sons, be still ;
Give no bad passion vent ;
My brethren, 'tis our Father's will,
And you must be content.

6 All that he has is yours !
Rejoice, then, not repine ;
That love which all your state secures,
That love has altered mine.]

7 Dear Lord ! are these thy ways ?
If rebels thus are freed,
And favoured with peculiar grace,
Grace must be free indeed !

220   8s.   HART.

"If there arise among you a prophet."—Deut. xiii. 1.

No prophet, or dreamer of dreams,
No master of plausible speech,

To live like an angel who seems,
Or like an apostle to preach ;
No tempter, without or within,
No spirit, though ever so bright,
That comes crying out against sin,
And looks like an angel of light ;

2 Though reason, though fitness he urge,
Or plead with the words of a friend,
Or wonders of argument forge,
Or deep revelations pretend ;
Should meet with a moment's regard,
But rather be boldly withstood,
If anything, easy or hard,
He teach, save the Lamb and his blood.

3 [Remember, O Christian, with heed,
When sunk under sentence of death,
How first thou from bondage wast freed—
Say, was it by works, or by faith ?
On Christ thy affections then fixed,
What conjugal truth didst thou vow ?
With him was there anything mixed ?
Then what wouldst thou mix with him now ?

4 If close to thy Lord thou wouldst cleave,
Depend on his promise alone ;
His righteousness wouldst thou receive ?
Then learn to renounce all thy own.
The faith of a Christian, indeed,
Is more than mere notion or whim ;
United to Jesus, his Head,
He draws life and virtue from him.]

5 [Deceived by the father of lies,
Blind guides cry, Lo, here ! and, Lo, there !
By these our Redeemer us tries,
And warns us of such to beware.

Poor comfort to mourners they give
  Who set us to labour in vain ;
And strive, with a " Do this and live,'
  To drive us to Egypt again.]

6 But what says our Shepherd divine ?
  (For his blessed word we should keep)
" This flock has my Father made mine ;
  I lay down my life for my sheep ;
'Tis life everlasting I give ;
  My blood was the price my sheep cost ;
Not one that on me shall believe
  Shall ever be finally lost."

7 This God is the God we adore ;
  Our faithful, unchangeable Friend ;
Whose love is as large as his power,
  And neither knows measure nor end.
'Tis Jesus, the First and the Last,
  Whose Spirit shall guide us safe home :
We'll praise him for all that is past,
  And trust him for all that's to come.

221   104th.   HART.
Free Grace.—Rom. iii. 24; iv. 16; xi. 6; Titus iii. 7.

YE children of God, by faith in his Son,
Redeem'd by his blood, & with him made one ;
This union with wonder and rapture been seen,
Which nothing shall sunder, without or within.

2 This pardon, this peace, which none can
      destroy,
This treasure of grace, this heavenly joy,
The worthless may crave it; it always comes free;
The vilest may have it, 'twas given to *me*.

3 'Tis not for good deeds, good tempers, nor
    frames ;
From grace it proceeds, and all is the Lamb's ;
No goodness, no fitness, expects he from us ;
This I can well witness, for none could be worse.

4 Sick sinner, expect no balm but Christ's blood;
Thy own works reject, the bad and the good ;
None ever miscarry that on him rely,
Though filthy as Mary,* Manasseh, or I.

222   C.M.   HART.
"Because thou sayest, I am rich."—Rev. iii. 17.

WHAT makes mistaken men afraid
  Of sovereign grace to preach !
The reason is, if truth be said,
  Because they are so rich.

2 [Why so offensive in their eyes
  Does God's election seem ?
Because they think themselves so wise
  That they have chosen him.]

3 [Of perseverance why so loath
  Are some to speak or hear ?

Because, as masters over sloth,
  They vow to persevere.]

4 [Whence is imputed righteousness
  A point so little known ?
Because men think they all possess
  Some righteousness their own.]

5 Not so the needy, helpless soul,
  Prefers his humble prayer ;
He looks to him that works the whole,
  And seeks his treasure there.

6 His language is, " Let me, my God,
  On sovereign grace rely ;
And own 'tis free, because bestowed
  On one so vile as I.

7 " Election ! 'tis a word divine ;
  For, Lord, I plainly see,
      * Mary (Mark xvi. 9).
Had not thy choice prevented mine,
  I ne'er had chosen thee.

8 [" For perseverance strength I've none,
  But would on this depend—
That Jesus, having loved his own,
  Will love them to the end.]

9 " Empty and bare, I come to thee
  For righteousness divine ;
O may thy matchless merits be,
  By imputation, mine."

10 [Thus differ these ; yet hoping each
  To make salvation sure.
Now most men will approve the rich,
  But Christ has blessed the poor.]

223   8.8.6.   HART.
The Outcasts of Israel.—Isa. lxiii. 16; 1 Cor. iv. 11-13.

LORD, pity outcasts, vile and base,
The poor dependants on thy grace,
  Whom men disturbers call ;
By sinners and by saints withstood ;
For these too bad, for those too good ;
  Condemned or shunned by all.

2 Though faithful Abraham us reject,
And though his ransomed race elect
  Agree to give us up,
Thou art our Father, and thy name
From everlasting is the same ;
  On that we build our hope.

224   L.M.   STEVENS.
Perseverance the effect of grace.-Rom. iv. 16; Phil. i. 6.

GRACE is Jehovah's sovereign will,
In an eternal covenant sure ;
Which for his seed he will fulfil,
Longer than sun and moon endure.

2 Grace is a firm but friendly hand,
  Put forth by God to save his own ;
  And by that grace, through faith, we stand,
  Adoring at our Father's throne.

3 There grace its peaceful sceptre wields,
  Inviting souls to venture near ;
  There Christ his saving Spirit yields
  To those whose sins he deigned to bear.

4 Lord, help us on thy grace to stand,
  And every trial firm endure ;
  Preserved by thy sovereign hand,
  And by thy oath and covenant sure.

5 Thy willingness to save thy seed,
  Is as they stand in Christ their Head ;
  No act thy grace can supersede,
  For thine must live, though they were dead.

6 Thanks, everlasting thanks be given
  To God, to Christ, to matchless grace ;
  And to that Dove who seals for heaven
  All who shall sing Jehovah's praise !

225   S.M.   BEDDOME.
Faith.—Eph. ii. 8 ; 2 Pet. i. 1.

FAITH ! 'tis a precious grace,
  Where'er it is bestowed ;
It boasts of a celestial birth,
  And is the gift of God.

2   Jesus it owns a King,
    An all-atoning Priest ;
  It claims no merits of its own,
    But looks for all in Christ.

3   To him it leads the soul,
    When filled with deep distress ;
  Flies to the fountain of his blood,
    And trusts his righteousness.

4   Since 'tis thy work alone,
    And that divinely free,
  Come, Holy Spirit, and make known
    The power of faith in me.

226   C.M.   WATTS.
Faith the Evidence of Things unseen.—Heb. xi. 1, 3, 8.

FAITH is the brightest evidence
  Of things beyond our sight ;
Breaks through the clouds of flesh and sense,
  And dwells in heavenly light.

2 It sets time past in present view,
  Brings distant prospects home,
Of things a thousand years ago,
  Or thousand years to come.

3 By faith we know the worlds were made
  By God's almighty word ;

Abram, to unknown countries led,
  By faith obeyed the Lord.

4 He sought a city fair and high,
  Built by the eternal hands ;
  And faith assures us, though we die,
  That heavenly building stands.

227   8.8.6.   TOPLADY.
Faith takes Comfort in Christ's Atonement.-Isa. liii. 5.

FROM whence this fear and unbelief ?
Hast thou, O Father, put to grief
  Thy spotless Son for me ?
And will the righteous Judge of men
Condemn me for that debt of sin
  Which, Lord, was charged on thee ?

2 Complete atonement thou hast made,
And to the utmost farthing paid
  Whate'er thy people owed ;
How then can wrath on me take place,
If sheltered in thy righteousness,
  And sprinkled with thy blood ?

3 [If thou hast my discharge procured,
And freely in my room endured
  The whole of wrath divine,
Payment God cannot twice demand,
First at my bleeding Surety's hand,
  And then again at mine.]

4 Turn, then, my soul, unto thy rest ;
The merits of thy great High Priest
  Speak peace and liberty ;
Trust in his efficacious blood,
Nor fear thy banishment from God,
  Since Jesus died for thee.

228   C.M.   STEVENS.
Origin and Acts of Faith.—Heb. xii. 2 ; 1 Pet. i. 9.

FAITH owes its birth to sovereign grace,
  And lives beneath the throne,
Where grace maintains her dwelling-place,
  And reigns supreme alone.

2 [Faith yields to grace the glory due,
  Nor dares assume her place ;
But owns all doctrines must be true
  That spring from sovereign grace.]

3 The precious cleansing blood of Christ
  Is a delightful theme ;
When faith is lifted up the high'st,
  She sings of none but him.

4 Faith owns the sceptre through the cross,
  And yields obedience true ;
Counts all things else but earth and dross,
  To keep the Lamb in view.

5 To live upon his precious death
  Is faith's divine repast ;

The language of his dying breath,
  See how she holds it fast !
6 Faith views him dead upon the tree ;
  Then buried in the grave ;
And waits around the tomb to see
  Him rise with power to save.

7 Then to the Mount of Olives go ;
  There faith, with eager eye,
Beholds her Lord leave all below,
  To dwell and reign on high.

8 With tears of joy, faith now believes
  The day will surely come,
When he who Jesus' cross receives
  Shall see him crowned at home.

229   104th.
The Fight of Faith.—Ps. lxi. 2-4; Rom. viii. 37.

OMNIPOTENT Lord, my Saviour and King,
Thy succour afford, thy righteousness bring.
Thy promises bind thee compassion to have ;
Now, now let me find thee almighty to save.

2 Lord, thou art my hope; o'erwhelmed with grief,
  To thee I look up for certain relief ;
I dread no denial, no danger I fear,
Nor start from the trial if Jesus be here.

3 Yes ! God is above men, devils, and sin ;
  My Jesus's love the battle shall win ;
So terribly glorious his coming shall be,
His love all victorious shall conquer for me.

230   C.M.   T. GREENE.
2 Pet. i. 4.
Trust in God's Faithfulness.—2 Tim. ii. 13;

WHY should my fears so far prevail,
  When they my hopes accost ?
My faith, though weak, can never fail,
  Nor shall my hopes be lost.

2 A thousand promises are wrote
  In characters of blood ;
And those emphatic lines denote
  The ever-faithful God.

3 Through those dear promises I range ;
  And, blessed be his name,
Though I, a feeble mortal, change,
  His love is still the same.

231   L.M.   WATTS.
iv. 17, 18
" We walk by faith, not by sight."-2 Cor. v. 7;

'TIS by the faith of joys to come
We walk through deserts dark as night ;
Till we arrive at heaven our home,
Faith is our guide, and faith our light.

2 The want of sight she well supplies ;
She makes the pearly gates appear ;
Far into distant worlds she pries,
And brings eternal glories near.

3 Cheerful we tread the desert through,
  While faith inspires a heavenly ray,
Though lions roar, and tempests blow,
  And rocks and dangers fill the way.

4 So Abram, by divine command,
  Left his own house to walk with God ;
His faith beheld the promised land,
  And fired his zeal along the road.

232   104th.   NEWTON.
" I will trust and not be afraid."—Isa. xii. 2.

BEGONE, unbelief, my Saviour is near,
And for my relief will surely appear ;
By prayer let me wrestle, and he will perform ;
With Christ in the vessel, I smile at the storm.

2 Tho' dark be my way, since he is my Guide,
'Tis mine to obey, 'tis his to provide ;
Tho' cisterns be broken, and creatures all fail,
The word he has spoken shall surely prevail.

3 His love in time past forbids me to think
  He'll leave me at last in trouble to sink ;
Each sweet Ebenezer I have in review
Confirms his good pleasure to help me quite thro'.

4 Determined to save, he watched o'er my path,
  When, Satan's blind slave, I sported with death.
And can he have taught me to trust in his name,
And thus far have brought me to put me to shame ?

5 [Why should I complain of want or distress,
  Temptation or pain ? He told me no less ;
The heirs of salvation, I know from his word,
Thro' much tribulation must follow their Lord.
6 How bitter that cup, no heart can conceive,
  Which he drank quite up that sinners might live !
His way was much rougher & darker than mine ;
Did Christ, my Lord, suffer, and shall I repine ?]
7 Since all that I meet shall work for my good,
  The bitter is sweet, the medicine is food ;
Tho' painful at present, 'twill cease before long,
And then O how pleasant the conqueror's song !

233   8s.   HART.
Saving Faith.—Mark xvi. 16; Acts x. 43; xvi. 31.

THE sinner that truly believes,
  And trusts in his crucified God,
His justification receives,
  Redemption in full through his blood ;
Though thousands and thousands of foes
  Against him in malice unite,
Their rage he through Christ can oppose,
  Led forth by the Spirit to fight.

2 Not all the delusions of sin
  Shall ever seduce him to death ;

He now has the witness within,
  Rejoicing in Jesus by faith.
This faith shall eternally fail
  When Jesus shall fall from his throne ;
For hell against both must prevail,
  Since Jesus and he are but one.

3 The faith that lays hold on the Lamb,
  And brings such salvation as this,
Is more than mere notion or name ;
  The work of God's Spirit it is ;
A principle active and young,
  That lives under pressure and load ;
That makes out of weakness more strong,
  And draws the soul upwards to God.

4 [It treads on the world and on hell ;
  It vanquishes death and despair ;
And, what is still stranger to tell,
  It overcomes heaven by prayer ;
Permits a vile worm of the dust
  With God to commune as a friend ;
To hope his forgiveness is just,
  And look for his love to the end.]

5 [It says to the mountains, " Depart,"
  That stand betwixt God and the soul ;
It binds up the broken in heart,
  And makes their sore consciences whole ;
Bids sins of a crimson-like dye
  Be spotless as snow, and as white ;
And makes such a sinner as I
  As pure as an angel of light.]

234   8.6.8.   HART.
Difference and Degrees of Faith.—Gal. iii. 25-27.

HE that *believeth* Christ the Lord,
  Who shed for man his blood,
By giving credence to his word,
  Exalts the truth of God ;
So far he's right, but let him know,
Farther than this he yet must go.

2 He that believes *on* Jesus Christ,
  Has a much better faith.
His Prophet now becomes his Priest,
  And saves him by his death ;
By Christ he finds his sins forgiven,
And Christ has made him heir of heaven.

3 But he that *into* Christ believes,
  What a rich faith has he !
In Christ he moves, and acts, and lives
  From self and bondage free ;
He has the Father and the Son,
For Christ and he are now but one.

4 Till we attain to this rich faith,
  Though safe, we are not sound ;

Though we are saved from guilt and wrath,
  Perfection is not found.
Lord, make our union closer yet,
And let the marriage be complete.

235   7.7.4.   HART.
" Whom resist, steadfast in the faith."—1 Pet. v. 9.

IN all our worst afflictions,
  When furious foes surround us ;
When troubles vex, and fears perplex,
  And Satan would confound us ;
When foes to God and goodness,
  We find ourselves, by feeling,
To do what's right unable quite,
  And almost as unwilling ;

When, like the restless ocean,
  Our hearts cast up uncleanness,

Flood after flood, with mire and mud,
  And all is foul within us ;
When love is cold and languid,
  And different passions shake us ;
When hope decays, and God delays,
  And seems to quite forsake us ;

3   Then to maintain the battle
    With soldier-like behaviour ;
To keep the field, and never yield,
  But firmly eye the Saviour ;
To trust his gracious promise,
  Thus hard beset with evil,
This, this is faith will conquer death,
  And overcome the devil.

236   S.M.   HART.
True and False Faith.—Acts xv. 9 ; Rom. v. 1, 2.

FAITH'S a convincing proof,
  A substance sound and sure,
That keeps the soul secured enough,
  But makes it not secure.

2   [Notion's the harlot's test,
    By which the truth's reviled ;
The child of fancy, finely dressed,
  But not the living child.]

3   Faith is by knowledge fed,
    And with obedience mixed,
Notion is empty, cold, and dead,
  And fancy's never fixed.

4   True faith's the life of God ;
    Deep in the heart it lies ;
It lives and labours under load ;
  Though damped, it never dies.

5   Opinions in the head,
    True faith as far excels

As body differs from a shade,
Or kernels from the shells.

6 [To see good bread and wine,
Is not to eat and drink ;
So some who hear the word divine,
Do not believe, but think.]

7 True faith refines the heart,
And purifies with blood ;
Takes the whole gospel, not a part,
And holds the fear of God.

237 8.7. HART.
Faith and Repentance.—Rom. iv. 18 ; vii. 18-25.

LET us ask the important question,
(Brethren, be not too secure),
What it is to be a Christian,
How we may our hearts assure.
Vain is all our best devotion,
If on false foundations built ;
True religion's more than notion ;
Something must be known and felt.

2 ['Tis to trust our Well-Belovéd
In his blood has washed us clean ;
'Tis to hope our guilt's removéd,
Though we feel it rise within ;
To believe that all is finished,
Though so much remains to endure ;
Find the dangers undiminished,
Yet to hold deliverance sure.]

3 ['Tis to credit contradictions ;
Talk with him one never sees ;
Cry and groan beneath afflictions,
Yet to dread the thoughts of ease.
'Tis to feel the fight against us,
Yet the victory hope to gain ;
To believe that Christ has cleansed us,
Though the leprosy remain.]

4 ['Tis to hear the Holy Spirit
Prompting us to secret prayer ;
To rejoice in Jesus' merit,
Yet continual sorrow bear ;
To receive a full remission
Of our sins for evermore,
Yet to sigh with sore contrition,
Begging mercy every hour.]

5 To be steadfast in believing,
Yet to tremble, fear, and quake ;
Every moment be receiving
Strength, and yet be always weak ;
To be fighting, fleeing, turning ;
Ever sinking, yet to swim ;
To converse with Jesus, mourning
For ourselves or else for him.

SECOND PART.
Matt. xxvi. 36-46 ; 2 Cor. vii. 10.

GREAT High Priest, we view thee stooping
With our names upon thy breast ;
In the garden groaning, drooping
To the ground, with horrors pressed ;
Wondering angels stood confounded
To behold their Maker thus ;
And can we remain unwounded,
When we know 'twas all for us ?

2 On the cross thy body broken
Cancels every penal tie ;
Tempted souls produce this token,
All demands to satisfy.
All is finished ; do not doubt it ;
But believe your dying Lord,

Never reason more about it,
Only take him at his word.

3 Lord, we fain would trust thee solely ;
'Twas for us thy blood was spilt ;
Bruiséd Bridegroom, take us wholly,
Take and make us what thou wilt.
Thou hast borne the bitter sentence
Passed on man's devoted race ;
True belief and true repentance
Are thy gifts, thou God of grace.

238 L.M. FAWCETT.
Repentance.—Ps. xxv. 11 ; Acts xvi. 30 ; 2 Cor. vii. 10.

WITH melting heart and weeping eyes,
My guilty soul for mercy cries ;
What shall I do, or whither flee,
To escape the vengeance due to me ?

2 Till late, I saw no danger nigh ;
I lived at ease, nor feared to die ;
Wrapped up in self-conceit and pride,
" I shall have peace at last," I cried.

3 But when, great God, thy light divine
Had shone on this dark soul of mine,
Then I beheld, with trembling awe,
The terrors of thy holy law.

4 How dreadful now my guilt appears,
In childhood, youth, and growing years ;
Before thy pure discerning eye,
Lord, what a filthy wretch am I !

5 Should vengeance still my soul pursue,
Death and destruction are my due ;
Yet mercy can my guilt forgive,
And bid a dying sinner live.

6 Does not thy sacred word proclaim
Salvation free in Jesus' name ?

To him I look, and humbly cry,
"O save a wretch condemned to die!"

239   11s.   STEVENS.
Repentance the gift of God.—Acts v. 31.

THE Lamb is exalted repentance to give,
That sin may be hated, while sinners believe;
Contrition is granted, and God justified,
The sinner is humbled, and self is denied.

2
Repentance flows freely thro' Calvary's blood,
Produced by the Spirit and goodness of God.
The living possess it, thro' faith, hope, and love,
And own it a blessing sent down from above.

3
All born of the Spirit are brought to repent;
Free grace can make adamant hearts to relent.
Repentance is granted, God's justice to prove;
Remission is given, and both from his love.

4
The vilest of sinners forgiveness have found,
For Jesus was humbled that grace might abound;
Whoever repents of his sin against God,
Shall surely be pardoned thro' Calvary's blood.

240   C.M.   HART.
Repentance and Faith.—Matt. ix. 13; Luke xiii. 3.

[WHAT various ways do men invent,
To give the conscience ease!
Some say, Believe; and some, Repent;
And some say, Strive to please.

2 But, brethren, Christ, and Christ alone,
Can rightly do the thing;
Nor ever can the way be known,
Till he salvation bring.

3 What mean the men that say, Believe.
And let repentance go?
What comfort can the soul receive
That never felt its woe?]

4 Christ says, "That I might sinners call
To penitence, I'm sent;"
And, "Likewise ye shall perish all,
Except ye do repent."

5 Those who are called by grace divine
Believe, but not alone;
Repentance to their faith they join,
And so go safely on.

6 But should repentance, or should faith,
Should both deficient seem,
Jesus gives both, the Scripture saith;
Then ask them both of him.

241   C.M.   HART.
"Godly sorrow worketh repentance."—2 Cor. vii. 10.

REPENTANCE is a gift bestowed
To save a soul from death;

Gospel repentance towards God
Is always joined to faith.

2 Not for an hour, or day, or week,
Do saints repentance own;
But all the time the Lord they seek,
At sin they grieve and groan.

3 [Nor is it such a dismal thing
As 'tis by some men named;
A sinner may repent and sing,
Rejoice and be ashamed.]

4 'Tis not the fear of hell alone,
For that may prove extreme;
Repenting saints the Saviour own
And grieve for grieving him.

5 If penitence be quite left out,
Religion is but halt;
And hope, though e'er so clear of doubt,
Like offerings without salt.

242   8.8.6.   STEVENS.
Good hope, through grace.-2 Thes. ii. 16; Rom. xii. 12.

GOOD hope, thro' grace, the saints possess,
The fruit of Jesus' righteousness,
And by his Spirit given;
Faith eyes the promise firm and sure,
And hope expects for evermore
To dwell with Christ in heaven.

2 Good hope is born of sovereign grace,
And lives in Jesus' righteousness,
With faith, and peace, and love;
What faith believes good hope desires,
And after perfect bliss aspires,
In the bright world above.

3 [All through the wilderness below,
Good hope expects more good to know;
And thus is kept alive
The soul, that many a trial bears,
And conflicts hard with doubts and fears,
Till joy and peace arrive.]

4 [When sore temptations haunt the soul,
Good hope shall all their power control,
And save from sad despair;
While faith looks up to Jesus' blood,
Good hope rides safely o'er the flood;
Nor dreads destruction there.]

5 When gloomy death, in dread array,
Appears to call the saint away,
Faith looks beyond the flood,
And when the soul to march prepares,
Good hope sends out her fervent prayers,
And dies in peace with God.

243 11s. STEVENS (altered).
Hoping on the ground of Eternal Adoption.—Gal. iv. 5.

GREAT Father of glory, how rich is thy grace !
What wonderful love is displayed in thy face !
In Jesus thy image with brightness we view,
And hope to be formed to that likeness anew.

2

By favour adopted, thy sons we appear,
And led by thy Spirit, we boldly draw near ;
In Jesus beloved, and washed in his blood,
With hope we adore at the footstool of God.

3

The man who is blessed with hope in the cross,
Is freed from the bondage of guilt and the curse ;
The blood of his Surety by faith he reviews,
While hope in that fountain his spirit renews.

4

The world knows us not ; but in this we rejoice,
To God we're no strangers, but objects of choice.
His love from eternity gave us a home,
Where now we are hoping in safety to come.

5

Arrayed in obedience, all wrought by the Lamb,
By Christ our Jehovah, the ancient I AM ; [on,
With boldness we journey, while Christ leads us
And hope soon in glory to praise the Three-One.

244 C.M. BURNHAM.
Hope.—Ps. lxxi. 5; Lam. iii. 24-26; Rom. v. 2; xv. 13.

OUR Jesus is the God of hope ;
He works it by his power ;
It holds the weak believer up,
In the distressing hour.

2 The darkest cloud hope pierces through,
And waits upon the Lord,
Expects to prove that all is true
Throughout the sacred word.

3 True hope looks out for blessings great ;
And, though they're long delayed,
Yet hope's determined still to wait,
Until they are conveyed.

4 Hope long will wait, and wait again,
And ne'er can give it up,
Till the bless'd Lamb, who once was slain,
Appears the God of hope.

245 L.M. GOSPEL MAG., 1799.
"An anchor of the soul."—Heb. vi. 18, 19; Titus i. 2.

WE travel through a barren land,
With dangers thick on every hand ;
But Jesus guides us through the vale ;
The Christian's hope can never fail.

2 Huge sorrows meet us as we go,
And devils aim our overthrow ;
But vile infernals can't prevail ;
The Christian's hope shall never fail.

3 Sometimes we're tempted to despair,
But Jesus makes us then his care ;
Though numerous foes our souls assail,
The Christian's hope shall never fail.

4 We trust upon the sacred word—
The oath and promise of our Lord ;
And safely through each tempest sail ;
The Christian's hope shall never fail.

246 8s. B. FRANCIS.
On Love to Christ as a Redeemer, &c.—John xiv. 21.

MY gracious Redeemer I love ;
His praises aloud I'll proclaim,
And join with the armies above,
To shout his adorable name.
To gaze on his glories divine
Shall be my eternal employ ;

And feel them incessantly shine,
My boundless, ineffable joy.

2 He freely redeemed with his blood
My soul from the confines of hell,
To live on the smiles of my God,
And in his sweet presence to dwell ;
To shine with the angels of light,
With saints and with seraphs to sing ;
To view with eternal delight
My Jesus, my Saviour, my King.

3 In Meshech, as yet, I reside,
A darksome and restless abode ;
Molested with foes on each side,
And longing to dwell with my God.
O when shall my spirit exchange
This cell of corruptible clay
For mansions celestial, and range
Through realms of ineffable day ?

PAUSE.

4 My glorious Redeemer ! I long
To see thee descend on the cloud,
Amidst the bright numberless throng,
And mix with the triumphing crowd.
O when wilt thou bid me ascend,
To join in thy praises above,
To gaze on thee, world without end,
And feast on thy ravishing love ?

5 No sorrow, nor sickness, nor pain,
Nor sin, nor temptation, nor fear,
Shall ever molest me again ;
Perfection of glory reigns there.
This soul and this body shall shine
In robes of salvation and praise,
And banquet on pleasures divine,
Where God his full beauty displays.

6 Ye palaces, sceptres, and crowns,
    Your pride with disdain I survey ;
Your pomps are but shadows and sounds,
    And pass in a moment away.
The crown that my Saviour bestows,
    Yon permanent sun shall outshine ;
My joy everlastingly flows ;
    My God, my Redeemer, is mine !

247   C.M.   RYLAND.
Desiring to Love and Delight in God.—Ps.xxxvii. 4, 5.

    O LORD, I would delight in thee,
        And on thy care depend ;
    To thee in every trouble flee,
        My best, my only Friend.

2 [When all created streams are dried,
    Thy fulness is the same :
May I with this be satisfied,
    And glory in thy name.]

3 [Why should the soul a drop bemoan,
    Who has a fountain near—
A fountain which will ever run
    With waters sweet and clear ?]

4 No good in creatures can be found,
    But may be found in thee ;
I must have all things, and abound,
    While God is God to me.

5 O that I had a stronger faith,
    To look within the veil ;
To credit what my Saviour saith,
    Whose words can never fail.

6 He that has made my heaven secure
    Will here all good provide ;
While Christ is rich, I can't be poor ;
    What can I want beside ?
7 O Lord, I cast my care on thee ;
    I triumph and adore ;
Henceforth my great concern shall be
    To love and praise thee more.

248   7s.   C.W.
Brotherly love.-Ps. cxxxiii. 1; Jno. xv. 12, 17; Eph. v. 2.

    JESUS, Lord, we look to thee ;
    Let us in thy name agree ;
    Show thyself the Prince of Peace ;
    Bid all jars for ever cease.

2 By thy reconciling love,
    Every stumbling-block remove ;
    Each to each unite, endear ;
    Come and spread thy banner here.

3 Make us of one heart and mind,
    Courteous, pitiful, and kind ;
    Lowly, meek, in thought and word,
    Altogether like our Lord.

4 Let us each for other care ;
    Each another's burdens bear ;
    To thy church the pattern give ;
    Show how true believers live.

5 Let us then with joy remove
    To thy family above ;
    On the wings of angels fly ;
    Show how true believers die.

249   8.8.6.   C.W.
Love of God earnestly desired.—Song viii. 6; 1 Jno. iv. 9.

    O LOVE divine, how sweet thou art !
    When shall I find my willing heart
        All taken up by thee ?
    I thirst, and faint, and die to prove
    The greatness of redeeming love,
        The love of Christ to me.

2 Stronger his love than death or hell,
    Its riches are unsearchable ;
        The first-born sons of light
    Desire in vain its depth to see ;
    They cannot reach the mystery,
        The length, and breadth, and height.

3 God only knows the love of God ;
    O that it now were shed abroad
        In this poor stony heart !
    For this I sigh, for this I pine ;
    This only portion, Lord, be mine ;
        Be mine this better part.

250   8s.   TOPLADY (?).
All things in Love (or Charity).—Eph. iv. 2, 15.

    THOUGH justly of wrongs we complain,
    Or faithfully sinners reprove,
    Yet still we do all things in vain,
    Unless we do all things in love.
    'Tis love makes us humble and meek !
    The wounds of ill usage it cures ;
    It pities the falls of the weak,
    The pride of the lofty endures.

2 Has God a command to fulfil,
    Which nature untoward would shun ?
    Love brings to compliance the will,
    And causes the deed to be done.
    From Jesus the blessing must flow,
    To creatures beneath and above ;
    May he his good Spirit bestow,
    And we shall do all things in love.

251   C.M.   HART.
"And the Lord went his way," &c.—Gen. xviii. 33.

    WHEN Jesus, with his mighty love,
        Visits my troubled breast,

My doubts subside, my fears remove,
And I'm completely blest ;
2 [I love the Lord with mind and heart,
His people and his ways ;
Envy, and pride, and lust depart,
And all his works I praise ;]
3 Nothing but Jesus I esteem ;
My soul is then sincere ;
And everything that's dear to him,
To me is also dear.
4 But ah ! when these short visits end,
Though not quite left alone,
I miss the presence of my Friend,
Like one whose comfort's gone.
5 [I to my own sad place return,
My wretched state to feel ;
I tire, and faint, and mope, and mourn,
And am but barren still.]
6 More frequent let thy visits be,
Or let them longer last ;
I can do nothing without thee ;
Make haste, O God, make haste.

252 C.M. NEEDHAM.
Fear and Love.—Deut. x. 12, 13; Prov. xxiii. 17.
FEAR is a grace which ever dwells
With its fair partner, love ;
Blending their beauties, both proclaim
Their source is from above.
2 Let terrors fright the unwilling slave,
The child with joy appears ;
Cheerful he does his Father's will,
And loves as much as fears.
3 Let fear and love, most holy God,
Possess this soul of mine ;
Then shall I worship thee aright,
And taste thy joys divine.

253 S.M. BREEID
Singleness of Eye.—Prov. iv. 25; Matt. vi. 21-23.
To Canaan art thou bound ?
Walk on in Jesus' might ;
But mark, the way is holy ground,
And needs a heart upright.
2 Make Jesus all thy peace,
And make him all thy arm ;
Rely alone upon his grace,
To guard from every harm.
3 [To Jesus some will pray,
Yet not with single eye ;
They turn their eyes another way,
Some creature-help to spy.
4 In darkness such are held ;
And bound in legal fear ;

A double eye is in the child,
The heart is not sincere.
5 Such find no gospel rest,
But into bondage fall ,
The Lord will not uphold thy breast,
Till he is all in all.]
6 Lord, give me single sight,
And make it strong and clear,
So will my soul be full of light,
And feel the Saviour near.

254 104th. HART.
" The fear of the Lord."—Ps. cxi. 10; Prov. x. 27, &c.
THE fear of the Lord our days will prolong,
In trouble afford a confidence strong,
Will keep us from sinning, will prosper our ways,
And is the beginning of wisdom and grace.
2 The fear of the Lord preserves us from death,
Enforces his word, enlivens our faith,
It regulates passion, and helps us to quell
The dread of damnation and terrors of hell.
3 The fear of the Lord is soundness and health ;
A treasure well stored with heavenly wealth ;
A fence against evil, by which we resist
World, flesh, and the devil, and imitate Christ.
4 [The fear of the Lord is clean and approved ;
Makes Satan abhorred and Jesus beloved ;
It conquers in weakness ; is proof against strife ;
A cordial in sickness ; a fountain of life.]
5 [The fear of the Lord is lowly and meek ;
The happy reward of all that him seek ;
They only that fear him the truth can discern,
For, living so near him, his secrets they learn.]
6 [The fear of the Lord his mercy makes dear,
His judgments adored, his righteousness clear,
Without its fresh flavour, in knowledge there's fault ;
In doctrines no savour ; in duties no salt.]
7 [The fear of the Lord confirms a good hope ;
By this are restored the senses that droop ;
The deeper it reaches, the more the soul thrives ;
It gives what it teaches, & guards what it gives.]
8 The fear of the Lord forbids us to yield ;
It sharpens our sword & strengthens our shield.
Then cry we to heaven, with one loud accord,
That to us be given the fear of the Lord.

255 L.M. HART.
The same.—Ps. cxi. 10; Prov. xxviii. 14.
HAPPY the men that fear the Lord ;
They from the paths of sin depart ;

Rejoice and tremble at his word,
And hide it deep within their heart.
2 They in his mercy hope, through grace ;
Revere his judgments, not contemn ;
In pleasing him their pleasure's placed,
And his delight is placed in them.
3 This fear, a rich and endless store,
Preserves the soul from poisonous pride ;
The heart that wants this fear is poor,
Whatever it possess beside.
4 This treasure was by Christ possessed ;
In this his understanding stood ;
And every one that's with it blessed
Has free redemption in his blood.

256   L.M.   HART.
" The fear of the Lord is to hate evil."—Prov. viii. 13.
IN vain men talk of living faith,
When all their works exhibit death ;
When they indulge some sinful view,
In all they say and all they do.
2 The true believer fears the Lord ;
Obeys his precepts, keeps his word ;
Commits his works to God alone,
And seeks his will before his own.
3 A barren tree that bears no fruit,
Brings no great glory to its root ;
When on the boughs rich fruit we see,
'Tis then we cry, " A goodly tree."
4 Never did men, by faith divine,
To selfishness and sloth incline ;
The Christian works with all his power,
And grieves that he can work no more.

257   L.M.   STEELE.
" Blessed are the poor in spirit."—Mat. v. 3 ; Jas. ii. 5.
YE humble souls, complain no more ;
Let faith survey your future store.

How happy, how divinely blest,
The sacred words of truth attest.

2 In vain the sons of wealth and pride
Despise your lot, your hope deride ;
In vain they boast their little stores ;
Trifles are theirs, a kingdom yours.

3 [A kingdom of immense delight,
Where health, and peace, and joy unite ;
Where undeclining pleasures rise,
And every wish has full supplies.]

4 [A kingdom which can ne'er decay,
While time sweeps earthly thrones away ;
The state which power and truth sustain,
Unmoved for ever must remain.]

5 There shall your eyes with rapture view
The glorious Friend that died for you,
That died to ransom, died to raise
To crowns of joy and songs of praise.

6 Jesus ! to thee I breathe my prayer ;
Reveal, confirm my interest there ;
Whate'er my humble lot below,
This, this my soul desires to know.

258   8.7.   BURNHAM.
Christ's Example.—Phil. ii. 3-5 ; Ps. cxxxiii. 1.
JESUS, Source of our salvation,
May we now thy nature know ;
Then more bowels of compassion
We to thy dear saints shall show.
May the grace thou hast imparted,
In relieving our complaints,
Make us kind and tender-hearted
To the feeblest of thy saints.

2 When they are severely tempted,
We their sorrows would assuage,

Knowing we are not exempted
From the tempter's furious rage.
If by sin they're overtaken,
We'd their faults to them declare ;
But in strains of much compassion,
Lest we drive them to despair.

3 Keep us from a proud appearance,
In whate'er we do or say ;
Fill us with divine forbearance ;
Then how happy we shall be !
Hand in hand we would be walking,
Eyeing Jesus' new command ;
Of his love we'd e'er be talking,
Till we reach fair Canaan's land.

259   C.M.   COWPER.
Resignation.—Job v. 19 ; Ps. x. 17 ; Luke xxii. 35.
O LORD, my best desire fulfil,
And help me to resign
Life, health, and comfort to thy will,
And make thy pleasure mine.

2 Why should I shrink at thy command,
Whose love forbids my fears ?
Or tremble at the gracious hand
That wipes away my tears ?

3 No ; let me rather freely yield
What most I prize to thee,
Who never hast a good withheld,
Or wilt withhold from me.

4 Thy favour all my journey through,
Thou art engaged to grant ;
What else I want, or think I do,
'Tis better still to want.

5 Wisdom and mercy guide my way ;
Shall I resist them both—

A poor blind creature of a day,
And crushed before the moth ?

6 But ah ! my inmost spirit cries,
Still bind me to thy sway,
Else the next cloud that veils my skies
Drives all these thoughts away.

260 C.M. STEELE.
Filial Resignation.—Isa. lxiv. 8; Heb. xii. 7.
AND can my heart aspire so high
To say, " My Father, God ? "
Lord, at thy feet I fain would lie
And learn to kiss the rod.

2 I would submit to all thy will,
For thou art good and wise ;
Let every anxious thought be still,
Nor one faint murmur rise.

3 Thy love can cheer the darksome gloom,
And bid me wait serene ;
Till hopes and joys immortal bloom,
And brighten all the scene.

261 C.M. T. GREENE.
" It is the Lord," &c.—1 Sam. iii. 18; 2 Sam. xv. 26.
IT is the Lord, enthroned in light,
Whose claims are all divine,
Who has an undisputed right
To govern me and mine.

2 [It is the Lord ; should I distrust
Or contradict his will—
Who cannot do but what is just,
And must be righteous still ?

3 It is the Lord, who can sustain
Beneath the heaviest load ; .
From whom assistance I obtain
To tread the thorny road.]

4 [It is the Lord, whose matchless skill
Can from afflictions raise
Matter eternity to fill
With ever-growing praise.]

5 It is the Lord, my covenant God,
(Thrice blessed be his name !)
Whose gracious promise, sealed with blood,
Must ever be the same.

6 His covenant will my soul defend,
Should nature's self expire,
And the great Judge of all descend
In awful flames of fire.

7 [How can my soul, with hopes like these,
Be sullen, or repine ?
My gracious God, take what thou please,
But teach me to resign.]

262 104th. TOPLADY.
" The Lord is good unto them that wait for him."
THOU Fountain of bliss, thy smile I entreat ;
O'erwhelm'd with distress I mourn at thy feet;
The joy of salvation, when shall it be mine ?
The high consolation of friendship divine !

2 Awakened to see the depth of my fall,
For mercy on thee I earnestly call ;
'Tis thine the lost sinner to save and renew ;
Faith's mighty Beginner and Finisher too.

3 Thy Spirit alone repentance implants,
And gives me to groan at feeling my wants ;
'Midst all my dejection, dear Lord, I can trace
Some marks of election, some tokens of grace.

4 Thou wilt not despise a sinner distressed ;
All-kind and all-wise, thy season is best.
To thy sovereign pleasure resigned I would be,
And tarry thy leisure, and hope still in thee.

263 L.M. MEDLEY.
" Blessed are they that mourn."—Mat. v. 4; Isa. lxi. 3.
JESUS, the glorious Head of grace,
Knows every saint's peculiar case ;
What sorrows by their souls are borne,
And how for sin they daily mourn.

2 He knows how deep their groanings are,
And what their secret sighs declare ;
And, for their comfort, has expressed
That all such mourning souls are blessed.

3 They're blessed on earth, for 'tis by grace
They see and know their mournful case ;
Blessed mourners ! they shall shortly rise
To endless comfort in the skies.

4 There all their mourning days shall cease,
And they be filled with joy and peace ;
Comforts eternal they shall prove,
And dwell for ever in his love.

5 [Dear Lord, may I a mourner be,
Over my sins and after thee ;
And when my mourning days are o'er,
Enjoy thy comforts evermore.]

264 L.M. WATTS.
' I have waited for thy salvation, O Lord.'-Gen. xlix. 18.
FAR from my thoughts, vain world, begone ;
Let my religious hours alone ;
Fain would my eyes my Saviour see ;
I wait a visit, Lord, from thee.

2 My heart grows warm with holy fire,
And kindles with a pure desire ;
Come, my dear Jesus, from above,
And feed my soul with heavenly love.

3 [The trees of life immortal stand,
In fragrant rows at thy right hand ;

And in sweet murmurs by thy side,
Rivers of bliss perpetual glide.

4 Haste, then, but with a smiling face,
And spread the table of thy grace;
Bring down a taste of truth divine,
And cheer my heart with sacred wine.]

5 Bless'd Jesus! what delicious fare!
How sweet thy entertainments are!
Never did angels taste above,
Redeeming grace and dying love.

6 Hail, great Immanuel, all divine!
In thee thy Father's glories shine;
Thou brightest, sweetest, fairest One,
That eyes have seen or angels known.

265　　　　L.M.　　　　WATTS.
"My heart rejoiceth in the Lord."—1 Sam. ii. 1.
LORD, what a heaven of saving grace
Shines through the beauties of thy face,
And lights our passions to a flame!
Lord, how we love thy charming name!

2 When I can say, "My God is mine,"
When I can feel thy glories shine,
I tread the world beneath my feet,
And all that earth calls good or great.

3 While such a scene of sacred joys
Our raptured eyes and soul employs,
Here we could sit and gaze away,
A long, an everlasting day.

4 Well, we shall quickly pass the night
To the fair coasts of perfect light;
Then shall our joyful senses rove
O'er the dear Object of our love.

5 [There shall we drink full draughts of bliss,
And pluck new life from heavenly trees;

Yet now and then, dear Lord, bestow
A drop of heaven on worms below.]

6 [Send comforts down from thy right hand,
While we pass through this barren land,
And in thy temple let us see
A glimpse of love, a glimpse of thee.]

266　　　　C.M.　　　　WATTS.
Doubts scattered; or, spiritual joys restored.—Ps. xl. 3.
HENCE from my soul, sad thoughts, begone,
And leave me to my joys;
My tongue shall triumph in my God,
And make a joyful noise.

2 Darkness and doubts had veiled my mind,
And drowned my head in tears,
Till sovereign grace, with shining rays,
Dispelled my gloomy fears.

3 O what immortal joys I felt,
And raptures all divine,

When Jesus told me I was his,
And my Beloved mine!

4 In vain the tempter frights my soul,
And breaks my peace in vain;
One glimpse, dear Saviour, of thy face,
Revives my joys again.

267　　　　7s.　　　　CENNICK.
Rejoicing in Hope.—Rom. v. 2; Ps. cxxxviii. 5.
CHILDREN of the heavenly King,
As ye journey, sweetly sing;
Sing your Saviour's worthy praise,
Glorious in his works and ways.

2 Ye are travelling home to God
In the way the fathers trod;
They are happy now, and ye
Soon their happiness shall see.

3 [O ye banished seed, be glad;
Christ your Advocate is made;
You to save, your flesh assumes;
Brother to your souls becomes.]

4 Shout, ye little flock, and blest;
You on Jesus' throne shall rest;
There your seat is now prepared,
There your kingdom and reward.

5 Fear not, brethren, joyful stand
On the borders of your land;
Jesus Christ, your Father's Son,
Bids you undismayed go on.

6 Lord, submissive make us go,
Gladly leaving all below;
Only thou our Leader be,
And we still will follow thee.

268　　　　S.M.　　　　BERRIDGE.
The Drawings of Christ's Love followed.—Song ii. 10.
IF Jesus kindly say,
And with a whispering word,
"Arise, my love, and come away,"
I run to meet my Lord.

2 My soul is in my ears;
My heart is all on flame;
My eyes are sweetly drowned in tears,
And melted is my frame.

3 My raptured soul will rise,
And give a cheerful spring,
And dart through all the lofty skies,
To visit Zion's King.

4 He meets me with a kiss,
And with a smiling face;
I taste the dear, enchanting bliss,
And wonder at his grace.

5 The world now drops its charms ;
   My idols all depart ;
  Soon as I reach my Saviour's arms,
   I give him all my heart.
6 A soft and tender sigh
   Now heaves my hallowed breast ;
  I long to lay me down and die,
   And find eternal rest.

269   C.M.   WATTS.
God's tender Care of his Church.—Isa. xlix. 15-16.
  Now shall my inward joys arise,
   And burst into a song ;
  Almighty love inspires my heart,
   And pleasure tunes my tongue.
2 God on his thirsty Zion-hill
   Some mercy-drops has thrown,
  And solemn oaths have bound his love
   To shower salvation down.
3 Why do we, then, indulge our fears,
   Suspicions, and complaints ?
  Is he a God, and shall his grace
   Grow weary of his saints ?
4 Can a kind woman e'er forget
   The infant of her womb ?
  And 'mongst a thousand tender thoughts,
   Her suckling have no room ?
5 Yet, says the Lord, should nature change,
   And mothers monsters prove,
  Zion still dwells upon the heart
   Of everlasting love.

270   8.7.   HART.
"Put on the whole armour of God."—Eph.vi. 11-13.
  GIRD thy loins up, Christian soldier ;
   Lo ! thy Captain calls thee out ;
  Let the danger make thee bolder ;
   War in weakness, dare in doubt.
  Buckle on thy heavenly armour ;
   Patch up no inglorious peace ;
  Let thy courage wax the warmer,
   As thy foes and fears increase.

2 Bind thy golden girdle round thee,
   Truth to keep thee firm and tight ;
  Never shall the foe confound thee,
   While the truth maintains thy fight.
  Righteousness within thee rooted
   May appear to take thy part ;
  But let righteousness imputed
   Be the breastplate of thy heart.

3 Shod with gospel-preparation,
   In the paths of promise tread ;
  Let the hope of free salvation,
   As a helmet, guard thy head.

When beset with various evils,
   Wield the Spirit's two-edged sword,
  Cut thy way through hosts of devils,
   While they fall before the Word.
4 But when dangers closer threaten,
   And thy soul draws near to death ;
  When assaulted sore by Satan,
   Then object the shield of faith ;
  Fiery darts of fierce temptations,
   Intercepted by thy God,
  There shall lose their force in patience,
   Sheathed in love, and quenched in blood.
5 Though to speak thou be not able,
   Always pray and never rest ;
  Prayer's a weapon for the feeble ;
   Weakest souls can wield it best.
  Ever on thy Captain calling,
   Make thy worst condition known ;
  He shall hold thee up when falling,
   Or shall lift thee up when down.

271   L.M.   S. STENNETT.
Captain of Salvation.—Eph. vi. 11-18 ; Ps. xxvii. 1.
  MY Captain sounds the alarm of war—
  Awake ! the powers of hell are near !
  " To arms, to arms ! " I hear him cry ;
  " 'Tis yours to conquer, or to die ! "
2 Roused by the animating sound,
  I cast my eager eyes around ;
  Make haste to gird my armour on,
  And bid each trembling fear begone.
3 Hope is my helmet ; Christ my shield ;
  Thy Word, my God, the sword I wield ;
  With sacred truth my loins are girt,
  And holy zeal inspires my heart.
4 Thus armed, I venture on the fight,
  Resolved to put my foes to flight ;
  While Jesus kindly deigns to spread
  His conquering banner o'er my head.
5 In Him I hope ; in Him I trust ;
  His bleeding cross is all my boast ;
  Through troops of foes he'll lead me on,
  To victory and a victor's crown.

272   8.7.   NEWTON.
"Behold the blood of the Covenant."—Exod. xxiv. 8.
  DEAREST Saviour ! we adore thee,
   For thy precious life and death ;
  Melt each stubborn heart before thee ;
   Give us all the eye of faith.
  From the law's condemning sentence,
   To thy mercy we appeal ;
  Thou alone canst give repentance ;
   Thou alone our souls canst heal.

273   7s.   NEWTON.

To the Afflicted.—Isa. xli. 10, 14; liv. 4-11.

PENSIVE, doubting, fearful heart,
Hear what Christ the Saviour says ;
Every word should joy impart,
Change thy mourning into praise.
Yes, he speaks, and speaks to thee,
May he help thee to believe ;
Then thou presently wilt see
Thou hast little cause to grieve :

2 " Fear thou not, nor be ashamed ;
All thy sorrows soon shall end,
I, who heaven and earth have framed,
Am thy Husband and thy Friend ;
I, the High and Holy One,
Israel's God, by all adored,
As thy Saviour will be known,
Thy Redeemer and thy Lord.

3 " For a moment I withdrew,
And thy heart was filled with pain ;
But my mercies I'll renew ;
Thou shalt soon rejoice again ;
Though I seem to hide my face,
Very soon my wrath shall cease ;
'Tis but for a moment's space,
Ending in eternal peace.

4 " Though afflicted, tempest-tossed,
Comfortless awhile thou art,
Do not think thou canst be lost,
Thou art graven on my heart ;
All thy wastes I will repair ;
Thou shalt be rebuilt anew ;
And in thee it shall appear
What the God of love can do."

274   S.M.   ADAMS.

The afflicted secure in Christ.—Job v. 19; Ps. xxix. 10.

THE Lord in Zion reigns,
And will his people keep ;
'Tis he the universe sustains,
And well secures his sheep.

2 Though with afflictions sore
He may them exercise ;
Yet still his hand they shall adore,
And still his love shall prize.

3 Should poverty, and loss
Of every kind of good,
Conspire to make our weighty cross,
Our helper still is God.

4 May we for ever trust
And glory in his name ;
Jesus, the faithful, true, and just,
For ever is the same !

275   L.M.   MEDLEY.

" Be still, and know that I am God."—Ps. xlvi. 10.

LET me, thou sovereign Lord of all,
Low at thy footstool humbly fall ;
And while I feel affliction's rod,
Be still and know that thou art God.

2 Let me not murmur nor repine,
Under these trying strokes of thine ;
But while I walk the mournful road
Be still and know that thou art God.

3 When and wherever thou shalt smite,
Teach me to own thy sovereign right ;
And underneath the heaviest load,
Be still and know that thou art God.

4 Still let this truth support my mind,
Thou canst not err nor be unkind ;
And thus approve thy chastening rod,
And know thou art my Father, God !

5 When this afflicted soul shall rise
To ceaseless joys above the skies,
I shall, as ransomed by thy blood,
For ever sing, " Thou art my God ! "

276   8s.   NEWTON.

The Care God takes of his People.—1 Kings xvii. 6.

ELIJAH'S example declares,
Whatever distress may betide,
The saints may commit all their cares
To Him who will surely provide ;
When rain long withheld from the earth
Occasioned a famine of bread,
The prophet, secured from the dearth,
By ravens was constantly fed.

2 More likely to rob than to feed,
Were ravens, which live upon prey ;
But when the Lord's people have need,
His goodness will find out a way.
This instance to those may be strange
Who know not how faith can prevail ;
But sooner all nature shall change,
Than one of God's promises fail.

3 How safe and how happy are they
Who on the good Shepherd rely ;
He gives them out strength for their day,
Their wants he will surely supply.
He ravens and lions can tame !
All creatures obey his commands !
Then let us rejoice in his name,
And leave all our cares in his hands.

277   7s.   NEWTON.

" He careth for you."—1 Pet. v. 7; Ps. lv. 22.

Now I see, whate'er betide,
All is well if Christ be mine ;

He has promised to provide ;
May he teach me to resign.

2 When a sense of sin and thrall
Forced me to the sinner's Friend,
He engaged to manage all,
By the way and to the end.

3 "Cast," he said, "on me thy care ;
'Tis enough that I am nigh ;
I will all thy burdens bear ;
I will all thy needs supply."

4 Lord, I would indeed submit ;
Gladly yield my all to thee ;
What thy wisdom sees most fit,
Must be surely best for me.

5 Only when the way is rough,
And the coward flesh would start,
Let thy promise and thy love
Cheer and animate my heart.

278   S.M.   NEWTON.
Conflict.—Rom. vii. 15-24 ; Gal. v. 17.

I KNOW the Lord is nigh,
And would but cannot pray,
For Satan meets me when I try,
And frights my soul away.

2 I would, but can't repent,
Though I endeavour oft ;
This stony heart can ne'er relent
Till Jesus makes it soft.

3 I would, but cannot love,
Though wooed by love divine ;
No arguments have power to move
A soul so base as mine.

4 I would, but cannot rest
In God's most holy will ;
I know what he appoints is best,
Yet murmur at it still.

5 O could I but believe,
Then all would easy be ;
I *would*, but *cannot;* Lord, relieve !
My help must come from thee.

6 [By nature prone to ill,
Till thy appointed hour,
I was as destitute of will
As now I am of power.]

7 [Wilt thou not crown at length
The work thou hast begun ?
And with the will afford me strength
In all thy ways to run ?]

279   L.M.   HAMMOND.
Conflict.—Rom. vii. 15-24 ; Gal. v. 17.

How shall I pour out my complaint,
Or tell the Lord my sore distress ?

Yet he espies my every want,
My weakness, sin, and foolishness.

2 Stupid, secure, and hard, and blind,
Withered and dead, and rooted up ;
To endless death I seem consigned ;
So destitute of cheering hope.

3 Uneasy when I feel my load ;
Uneasy when I feel it not ;
Dissatisfied for want of God,
Though oft of him I've not a thought.

4 I cannot frame a good desire,
If all the world to me was given ;
I cannot to a wish aspire,
If one good wish would purchase heaven.

5 Sometimes I follow after God ;
Sometimes I carelessly retreat ;
For mercy now I cry aloud,
And now in stubborn silence sit.

6 O Prince of life, with power descend ;
Thy blood apply, my conscience clear ;
Then shall this legal conflict end,
And perfect love cast out sad fear.

280   7s.   HAMMOND.
Conflict.—Matt. xiv. 31.

WILL my doubting ne'er be o'er ?
Will the Lord return no more ?
When shall I the Saviour see,
And be sure he died for me ?

2 How I waver to and fro,
Rising high and sinking low !
Now to heaven I aspire,
Now to shades of death retire.

3 When a glimpse of hope appears,
Soon 'tis lost in doubts and fears.
O ! I fear 'tis all a cheat !
Keep me, Lord, from self-deceit.

4 Lord, thy light, thy love display ;
All my darkness chase away ;
Everlasting peace restore ;
Bid me disbelieve no more.

5 Put thy Spirit in my heart ;
Bid my doubts and fears depart ;
When thy face shall on me shine,
I shall know and feel thee mine.

281   C.M.   COWPER.
"Contrite heart."—Isa. lvii. 15 ; Ps. li. 17.

THE Lord will happiness divine
On contrite hearts bestow ;
Then tell me, gracious God, is mine
A contrite heart, or no ?

2 I hear, but seem to hear in vain ;
   Insensible as steel ;
If aught is felt, 'tis only pain,
   To find I cannot feel.

3 I sometimes think myself inclined
   To love thee, if I could ;
But often find another mind,
   Averse to all that's good.

4 My best desires are faint and few ;
   I fain would strive for more ;
But when I cry, " My strength renew,"
   Seem weaker than before.

5 Thy saints are comforted, I know,
   And love thy house of prayer ;
I sometimes go where others go,
   But find no comfort there.

6 O make this heart rejoice or ache,
   Decide this doubt for me ;
And if it be not broken, break,
   And heal it if it be.

282
7s.   COWPER.
Welcome Cross.—Rom. v. 3; Heb. xii. 5-11 ; 1Pet. i. 6.
   'TIS my happiness below,
   Not to live without the cross,
   But the Saviour's power to know,
   Sanctifying every loss.

2   Trials must and will befall ;
   But with humble faith to see
   Love inscribed upon them all,
   This is happiness to me.

3   Trials make the promise sweet ;
   Trials give new life to prayer ;
   Trials bring me to his feet,
   Lay me low and keep me there.

4   Did I meet no trials here,
   No chastisement by the way,
   Might I not with reason fear
   I should be a castaway ?

5   Bastards may escape the rod,
   Sunk in earthly, vain delight ;
   But the true-born child of God
   Must not, would not if he might

283
7s.   NEWTON.
Breathing after Love to Christ.—Matt. xxii. 37.
   'TIS a point I long to know,
   (Oft it causes anxious thought),
   Do I love the Lord, or no ?
   Am I his, or am I not ?

2   If I love, why am I thus ?
   Why this dull and lifeless frame ?
   Hardly, sure, can they be worse
   Who have never heard his name.

3 Could my heart so hard remain,
   Prayer a task and burden prove,
   Every trifle give me pain,
   If I knew a Saviour's love ?

4 [When I turn my eyes within,
   All is dark, and vain, and wild ;
   Filled with unbelief and sin,
   Can I deem myself a child ?

5 If I pray, or hear, or read,
   Sin is mixed with all I do ;
   You that love the Lord indeed,
   Tell me, is it thus with you ?

6 Yet I mourn my stubborn will
   Find my sin a grief and thrall ;
   Should I grieve for what I feel,
   If I did not love at all ?]

7 Could I joy his saints to meet,
   Choose the ways I once abhorred,
   Find at times the promise sweet,
   If I did not love the Lord ?

8 Lord, decide the doubtful case ;
   Thou who art thy people's Sun,
   Shine upon thy work of grace,
   If it be indeed begun.

9 Let me love thee more and more,
   If I love at all, I pray ;
   If I have not loved before,
   Help me to begin to-day.

284
7s.   LANGLEY.
The Mourner's sorrow and comfort.—Ps. vi. 6; xlii. 1-3.
   WHEN shall all my sorrows end ?
   When my days of mourning cease ?
   When shall I to Christ ascend,
   Only place of happiness ?

2   Thirsting, panting after home,
   Longing for that happy day,
   Still I cry, " My Saviour, come !
   Come, Lord Jesus, come away."

3   See what tribulations rise ;
   Earth and sin beset me round ;
   Sorrows, trickling from my eyes,
   Moisten all the weary ground.

4   Lord, thy pardoning love reveal ;
   Let my cry ascend thy ears.
   Sin, alas ! I deeply feel ;
   Sin, but ah ! thy blood appears !

5   Blood, that answers every claim,
   Tells me, Jesus died for me.
   Then, in his delightful name,
   Sin's subdued, and I am free.

GADSBY'S SELECTION.

285   L.M.   W. W. HORNE.
Complaint.—Ps. lxi. 2; Lam. i. 16.

O FOR a heart to seek my God,
Encouraged by his gracious word,
To view my Saviour all complete,
And lie submissive at his feet!

2 To thee, almighty God, to thee,
My Rock and Refuge, would I flee;
Now tides of sorrow, rolling high,
Appear to mingle earth and sky.

3 To see thy saints in mourning clad,
And foes by their distress made glad,
O'erwhelms my soul with poignant grief;
Lord, send thy servants sweet relief.

4 [Though safe in Christ thy saints abide,
Nor can their life be e'er destroyed;
While thy dear cause is thus suppressed,
My burdened soul can take no rest.]

5 Arise, O God, thy cause defend;
Deliverance unto Zion send.
Arise, arise, O God of might,
And put thy threatening foes to flight.

6 Pity thy poor, dejected few;
Our souls revive, our strength renew;
Collect thy scattered flock once more,
And open wide the gospel-door.

286   L.M.   SWAIN.
The Pilgrim's Consolation.—Ps. xxxiv. 19; Heb. xi. 13.

PILGRIMS we are, to Canaan bound;
Our journey lies along this road;
This wilderness we travel round,
To reach the city of our God.

2 And here as travellers we meet,
Before we reach the fields above,
To sit around our Master's feet,
And tell the wonders of his love.

3 Oft have we seen the tempest rise;
The world and Satan, hell and sin,
Like mountains, seemed to reach the skies,
With scarce a gleam of hope between.

4 But still, as oft as troubles come,
Our Jesus sends some cheering ray;
And that strong arm shall guide us home
Which thus protects us by the way.

5 A few more days, or months, or years,
In this dark desert to complain;
A few more sighs, a few more tears,
And we shall bid adieu to pain.

287   S.M.   HART.
"Pride."—Prov. viii. 13; xi. 2; xxix. 23.

INNUMERABLE foes
Attack the child of God;
He feels within the weight of sin,
A grievous, galling load.

2 [Temptations, too, without,
Of various kinds, assault;
Sly snares beset his travelling feet,
And make him often halt.

3 From sinner and from saint
He meets with many a blow;
His own bad heart creates him smart,
Which only God can know.]

4 But though the host of hell
Be neither weak nor small,
One mighty foe deals wondrous woe,
And hurts beyond them all.

5 'Tis pride, accursed pride,
The spirit by God abhorred;
Do what we will, it haunts us still,
And keeps us from the Lord.

6 [It blows its poisonous breath,
And bloats the soul with air;
The heart uplifts with God's own gifts,
And makes e'en grace a snare.]

7 [Awake, nay, while we sleep,
In all we think or speak,
It puffs us glad, torments us sad;
Its hold we cannot break.

8 In other ills we find
The hand of heaven not slack;
Pride only knows to interpose,
And keep our comforts back.]

9 ['Tis hurtful when perceived;
When not perceived, 'tis worse;
Unseen or seen, it dwells within,
And works by fraud or force.]

10 [Against its influence pray,
It mingles with the prayer;
Against it preach, it prompts the speech;
Be silent, still 'tis there.]

11 [In every outward act,
In every thought within,
The heart it draws to seek applause,
And mixes all with sin.]

12 Thou meek and lowly Lamb,
This haughty tyrant kill,
That wounded thee, though thou wast free,
And grieves thy Spirit still.

13 Our condescending God,
(To whom else shall we go?)
Remove our pride, whate'er betide,
And lay and keep us low.

14 [Thy garden is the place
Where pride cannot intrude ;
For should it dare to enter there,
'Twould soon be drowned in blood.]

288　　C.M.　　NEWTON.
The Prisoner.—Ps. vi. 4; cxlii. 7.

WHEN the poor prisoner, through a grate,
Sees others walk at large,
How does he mourn his lonely state,
And long for a discharge !

2 Thus I, confined in unbelief,
My loss of freedom mourn ;
And spend my hours in fruitless grief,
Until my Lord return.

3 The beam of day which pierces through
The gloom in which I dwell,
Only discloses to my view
The horrors of my cell.

4 [Ah ! how my pensive spirit faints,
To think of former days,
When I could triumph with the saints,
And join their songs of praise !]

5 Dear Saviour, for thy mercy's sake,
My strong, my only plea,
These gates and bars in pieces break,
And set the prisoner free.

289　　L.M.　　FAWCETT.
" And he led them forth by the right way."—Ps. cvii. 7.

THUS far my God has led me on,
And made his truth and mercy known ;
My hopes and fears alternate rise,
And comforts mingle with my sighs.

2 [Through this wide wilderness I roam,
Far distant from my blissful home ;

Lord, let thy presence be my stay,
And guard me in this dangerous way.]

3 [Temptations everywhere annoy,
And sins and snares oft make me sigh ;
My earthly joys are from me torn,
And oft an absent God I mourn.]

4 My soul, with various tempests tossed,
Her hopes o'erturned, her projects crossed,
Sees every day new straits attend,
And wonders where the scene will end.

5 Is this, dear Lord, that thorny road
Which leads us to the mount of God ?
Are these the toils thy people know,
While in this wilderness below ?

6 'Tis even so ; thy faithful love
Does all thy children's graces prove ;
'Tis thus our pride and self must fall
That Jesus may be all in all.

290　　L.M.　　COWPER.
Hope in Danger.—John xvi. 33.

DANGERS of every shape and name
Attend the followers of the Lamb,
Who leave the world's deceitful shore,
And leave it to return no more.

2 O Lord, the pilot's part perform,
And guide and guard me through the storm ;
Defend me from each threatening ill ;
Control the waves ; say, " Peace ! be still ! "

3 Amidst the roaring of the sea,
My soul still hangs her hopes on thee ;
Thy constant love, thy faithful care,
Is all that saves me from despair.

291　　C.M.　　ROZZELL.
" Be strong; fear not."—Isa. xxxv. 3, 4; Rom. viii. 31.

How prone the mind to search for ill,
To fancy mighty woes !

Shortly the cup of life will fill,
And rob it of repose.

2 [How sharp and numerous are the pangs
Imagination gives !
So sharp, that life itself oft hangs
In doubt, nor dies nor lives.]

3 [Could we our woes with truth divide,
The sterling and ideal,
What crowds would stand on fancy's side !
How few upon the real !]

4 Creatures of fear, we drag along,
And fear where no fear is ;
Our griefs we labour to prolong !
Our joys in haste dismiss.

5 Spirit of power, thy strength impart ;
This fearful spirit chase
Far off, and make my feeble heart
Thy constant dwelling-place.

6 O if to me thy strength be given,
If thou be on my side,
Then hell as soon shall conquer heaven
As I can be destroyed.

292　　7.6.　　ROZZELL.
The Pilgrim.—Heb. xi. 13-16; Psa. xxxix. 12.

AMIDST ten thousand dangers,
Which everywhere abound,
The pilgrims and the strangers
Alone secure are found ;
For on their Lord they're waiting,
They seek him night and day ;
His aid they're supplicating
In his appointed way.

2 [How signal are the blessings
My Saviour has bestowed !

He taught me wisdom's lessons,
  When I had lost the road.
From death he has me raised,
  By his almighty power ;
Let his great name be praised,
  Both now and evermore.]

3 Through Christ, the Mediator,
  To God access we find ;
The Spirit's own dictator,
  Who knows the Father's mind.
Thus through this world of trouble
  His saints in safety go ;
They count the world a bubble,
  All vanity below.

293   8s.   TOPLADY.
Longing for God's presence in soul-trouble.—Ps. lxi. 2.

ENCOMPASSED with clouds of distress,
  And tempted all hope to resign,
I pant for the light of thy face,
  That I in thy beauty may shine.
Disheartened with waiting so long,
  I sink at thy feet with my load ;
All plaintive I pour out my song,
  And stretch forth my hands unto God.

2 [Shine, Lord, and my terror shall cease ;
  The blood of atonement apply ;
And lead me to Jesus for peace,
  The Rock that is higher than I.
Speak, Saviour, for sweet is thy voice ;
  Thy presence is fair to behold ;
I thirst for thy Spirit, with cries
  And groanings that cannot be told.]

3 If sometimes I strive, as I mourn,
  My hold of thy promise to keep,
The billows more fiercely return,
  And plunge me again in the deep.
While harassed and cast from thy sight,
  The tempter suggests with a roar,
" The Lord has forsaken thee quite ;
  Thy God will be gracious no more."

4 Yet, Lord, if thy love has designed
  No covenant blessing for me,
Ah ! tell me, how is it I find
  Some sweetness in waiting for thee ?
Almighty to rescue thou art,
  Thy grace is immortal and free ;
Lord, succour and comfort my heart,
  And make me live wholly to thee.

294   148th.   DE COURCY.
The Christian's Spiritual Voyage.—Ps. cvii. 23-28.

JESUS, at thy command

I launch into the deep ;
  And leave my native land,
Where sin lulls all asleep ;
For thee I would the world resign,
And sail to heaven with thee and thine.

2 Thou art my Pilot wise ;
  My compass is thy word ;
My soul each storm defies,
  While I have such a Lord ;
I trust thy faithfulness and power,
To save me in the trying hour.

3 Though rocks and quicksands deep
  Through all my passage lie ;
Yet Christ will safely keep,
  And guide me with his eye ;
My anchor, hope, shall firm abide,
And I each boisterous storm outride.

4 By faith I see the land—
  The port of endless rest ;
My soul, thy sails expand,
  And fly to Jesus' breast !
O may I reach the heavenly shore
Where winds and waves distress no more.

5 [Whene'er becalmed I lie,
  And storms forbear to toss ;
Be thou, dear Lord, still nigh,
  Lest I should suffer loss ;
For more the treacherous calm I dread,
Than tempests bursting o'er my head.]

6 Come, Holy Ghost, and blow
  A prosperous gale of grace ;
Waft me from all below
  To heaven, my destined place,
Then, in full sail, my port I'll find,
And leave the world and sin behind.

295   L.M.   NEWTON.
Prayer answered by Crosses.—Ps. lxv. 5 ; Acts xiv. 22

I ASKED the Lord that I might grow
In faith, and love, and every grace ;
Might more of his salvation know,
And seek more earnestly his face.

2 ['Twas he who taught me thus to pray,
And he, I trust, has answered prayer ;
But it has been in such a way
As almost drove me to despair.]

3 I hoped that in some favoured hour,
At once he'd answer my request ;
And, by his love's constraining power,
Subdue my sins, and give me rest.

4 Instead of this, he made me feel
The hidden evils of my heart,

And let the angry powers of hell
Assault my soul in every part.

5 Yea, more, with his own hand he seemed
Intent to aggravate my woe ;
Crossed all the fair designs I schemed,
Blasted my gourds, and laid me low.

6 " Lord, why is this ? " I trembling cried ;
" Wilt thou pursue thy worm to death ?
" 'Tis in this way," the Lord replied,
" I answer prayer for grace and faith.

7 " These inward trials I employ,
From self and pride to set thee free ;
And break thy schemes of earthly joy,
That thou mayst seek thy all in me."

296 L.M. BEDDOME.

Inconstancy.—Ps. cix. 23: Hos. vi. 4.

THE wandering star and fleeting wind
Both represent the unstable mind ;
The morning cloud and early dew
Bring our inconstancy to view.

2 But cloud, and wind, and dew, and star,
Faint and imperfect emblems are ;
Nor can there aught in nature be
So fickle and so false as we.

3 [Our outward walk and inward frame,
Scarce through a single hour the same.
We vow, and straight our vows forget,
And then those very vows repeat.

4 We sin forsake, to sin return ;
Are hot, are cold ; now freeze, now burn ;
In deep distress, then raptures feel ;
We soar to heaven, then sink to hell.]

5 With flowing tears, Lord, we'd confess
Our folly and unsteadfastness ;

When shall these hearts more fixéd be—
Fixed by thy grace, and fixed on thee ?

297 104th. KENT.

The Trial of Faith.—Ps. xi. 5: Mal. iii. 3.

JEHOVAH has said, 'tis left on record,
" The righteous are one with Jesus the Lord ;"
At all times he loves them ; 'twas for them he died ;
Yet ofttimes he proves them, for grace must be
tried.

2 When faint in the way, or lifeless and cold,
Or sunk in dismay, and none to uphold ;
Yet firm to his promise thy God shall abide ;
But grace, tho' the smallest, shall surely be tried.

3 [Temptations and sins in legions shall rise,
As spears in thy side or thorns in thy eyes ;
And oft, to thy sorrow, his face he shall hide,
For God has determined his grace shall be tried.]

4 With him on the mount to-day thou shalt be,
Indulged by thy Lord his glory to see ;
There he may caress thee, & call thee his bride,
Yet grace, tho' he bless thee, shall surely be tried.

5 [The tempest shall blow, the billows shall swell,
Thy soul, full of woe, shall pass as thro' hell ;
And all this to prove thee, to stain thy curs'd pride ;
Yet still he will love thee ; but grace must be tried.]

6 He'll ne'er thee forsake, but surely perform
His word, tho' he take his way in the storm ;
Yea, oft in the clouds of dejection he'll ride,
For he has determined his grace shall be tried.

7 He'll cause thee to bring thy griefs to his throne,
But answers of peace to thee shall send none ;
Then sorrow and sadness thy heart shall divide,
Because he's determined his grace shall be tried.

8 As gold from the flame, he'll bring thee at last,
To praise him for all thro' which thou hast past ;
Then love everlasting thy griefs shall repay,
And God from thy eyes wipe all sorrows away.

298 8s. KENT.

" The Canaanites . . . in that land."—Jos. xvii. 12.

THE Canaanites still in the land,
To harass, perplex, and dismay,
Brought Israel of old at a stand,
For Anak was stronger than they.
What God had designed they possessed,
Supported and kept by his hand ;
Yet, lest on their lees they should rest,
The Canaanites dwelt in the land.

2 'Tis thus with the Israel on earth,
Who groan with a body of sin,
Partake of a spiritual birth,
The work of God's Spirit within ;
To-day, with a taste of his love,
Jehovah their souls will expand,
To-morrow he'll give them to prove
The Canaanites still in the land.

3 [Corruptions like vapours shall rise ;
Light, love, and delight shall be gone ;
The sun shall be dark in the skies,
And hell, with its legions, come on ;
Yet all things shall work for their good,
Afflictions, temptations, or pain ;
And still, through the Lamb and his blood
Their cause they shall ever maintain.]

4 [Like Gad, by a troop overcome,
They fall, through the workings of sin ;
Yet glory they not in their shame,
But mourn their defilement within.
On Zion's bright summit above,
Victorious at last they shall stand,

Though now for a season they prove
  The Canaanites still in the land.]

5 [A thorn in the flesh they shall have,
  Their roving affections to win,
To teach them how Jesus can save,
  And show them the depth of their sin ;
Yea, down to the Jordan of death,
  His foes shall the Christian withstand,
And feel, when resigning his breath,
  The Canaanites still in the land.]

6 [To them he his oath shall fulfil,
  A poor, little, faint-hearted band ;
For 'tis of their Father's good will
  The Canaanites dwell in the land.
Their place of repose is on high,
  No Canaanite enters therein,
To drink of the rivers of joy,
  Remote from the regions of sin.]

299   C.M.   BERRIDGE.
"Thou didst hide thy face, I was troubled."—Ps. xxx.

If but a single moment's space,
  My Lord himself withdraws,
Dark clouds and storms come on apace,
  And debts, and broken laws.

2 My heart reveals its dross and dung,
  And loathsome is my breath ;
My harp is on the willows hung,
  And Esau vows my death.

3 My eyes refuse to lend a tear ;
  My throat is hoarse and dry ;
I lisp and falter in my prayer,
  And sick and faint am I.

4 If Jesus loves the gospel-poor,
  That broken-hearted be,

A mourner waiteth at thy door,
  Who wants a sight of thee.

5 Look from the windows of thy grace,
  And cheer a drooping heart ;
A single smile from thy sweet face
  Will bid my griefs depart.

6 Thou art the life of all my joys ;
  Thy presence makes my heaven ;
Whatever else my Lord denies,
  Thy presence, Lord, be given.

300   C.M.   BERRIDGE.
"Tribulation worketh patience."—Rom. v. 3.

How simple are thy children, Lord,
  Unskilled in what they pray ;
Full oft they lift a hearty word,
  Yet know not what they say.

2 For patience when I raised a cry,
  Fresh burdens made me roar ;
My foolish heart would then reply,
  For patience pray no more.

3 So much my Master seemed to blame,
  I thought to leave his school ;
But now I learn to blush for shame,
  And see myself a fool.

4 [I fancied patience would be brought
  Before my troubles rose ;
And by such granted help I thought
  To triumph o'er my woes.

5 But Christ has cleared my misty sight,
  And, taught by him, I find
That tribulations, working right,
  Produce a patient mind.]

6 When our dear Master would bestow
  Much patience on his friends,
He loads their shoulders well with woe,
  And thus obtains his ends.

7 I must expect a daily cross ;
  Lord, sanctify the pain ;
Bid every furnace purge my dross
  And yield some patient gain.

301   7s.   BERRIDGE.
Inconstancy.—Ps. xxxix. 5-7, 11 ; Job xxv. 6.

WELL, at length I plainly see,
Every man is vanity ;
In his best and brightest form,
But a shadow or a worm.

2 Such a shade I am in view,
Empty, dark, and fleeting too ;
Such a worm of nothing worth,
Crawling out and in the earth.

3 [Very foolish, very base,
Notwithstanding Jesus' grace.
Murmuring oft for gospel-bread,
Growing wanton when full fed.]

4 [Brisk and dull in half an hour,
Hot and cold, and sweet and sour ;
Sometimes grave at Jesus' school,
Sometimes light, and play the fool.]

5 What a motley wretch am I !
Full of inconsistency !
Sure the plague is in my heart,
Else I could not act this part.

6 Let me come unto my Lord,
Self-condemned and abhorred ;
Take the sinner's safe retreat,
Lie and blush at Jesus' feet.

7 [If my heart is broken well,
God will surely with me dwell ;

Yet amazed I would be,
How the Lord should dwell with me.]

302   8.8.6.   BERRIDGE.
Pressing to Jesus through the crowd.—Phil. iii. 12-14.

IF unto Jesus thou art bound,
A crowd about him will be found;
  Attending day and night ;
A worldly crowd to din thy ears,
And crowds of unbelieving fears,
  To hide him from thy sight.

2 Yet all the vain and noisy crowd
Is but a thin and lowering cloud,
  A mist before thy eyes ;
If thou press on, the crowds will fly,
Or if thou faint, to Jesus cry,
  And he will send supplies.

3 This only way can pilgrims go,
And all complain, as thou wilt do,
  Of crowds that daily come ;
Yet though beset by crafty foes,
And passing through a thousand woes,
  They get securely home.

4 [But such as seem to run the race,
And meet no crowd to check their pace,
  Are only rambling still ;
Not fairly entered on the list,
The gate and narrow way they missed,
  Which lead to Zion's hill.]

5 O Lord, a cheering look bestow,
Or lend a hand to help me through,
  And draw me up to thee ;
And when, through fear, I only creep,
Or dare not move a single step,
  Yet thou canst come to me.

303   7s.   C.W.
Tempted ; but flying to Christ the Refuge.—Ps. lvii. 1.

JESUS, Lover of my soul,
Let me to thy bosom fly,
While the raging billows roll,
While the tempest still is high.
Hide me, O my Saviour, hide,
Till the storm of life is past ;
Safe into the haven guide ;
O receive my soul at last !

2 [Other refuge have I none,
Hangs my helpless soul on thee ;
Leave, ah ! leave me not alone ;
Still support and comfort me.
All my trust on thee is stayed ;
All my help from thee I bring ;
Cover my defenceless head
With the shadow of thy wing.]

3 Thou, O Christ, art all I want ;
All in all in thee I find ;
Raise the fallen, cheer the faint,
Heal the sick, and lead the blind.
Just and holy is thy name ;
I am all unrighteousness ;
Vile and full of sin I am ;
Thou art full of truth and grace.

4 Plenteous grace with thee is found ;
Grace to pardon all my sin ;
Let the healing streams abound ;
Make and keep me pure within.
Thou of life the Fountain art ;
Freely let me take of thee ;
Spring thou up within my heart,
Rise to all eternity.

304   L.M.   HART.
Unsettledness.—Job vii. 3 ; Ps. lv. 1.

LORD, what a riddle is my soul !
Alive when wounded, dead when whole !
Fondly I flee from pain, yet ease
Cannot content, nor pleasure please.

2 Thou hid'st thy face, my sins abound ;
World, flesh, and Satan all surround ;
Fain would I find my God, but fear
The means, perhaps, may prove severe.

3 [If thou the least displeasure show,
And bring my vileness to my view,
Timorous and weak, I shrink and say,
" Lord, keep thy chastening hand away."

4 If reconciled I see thy face,
Thy matchless mercy, boundless grace,
O'ercome with bliss, I cry, " Remove
That killing sight, I die with love."]

5 My dear Redeemer, purge this dross ;
Teach me to hug and love the cross ;
Teach me thy chastening to sustain,
Discern the love, and bear the pain.

6 Nor spare to make me clearly see
The sorrows thou hast felt for me ;
If death must follow, I comply ;
Let me be sick with love, and die.

305   C.M.   HART.
Tribulation.—2 Tim. iii. 12.

THE souls that would to Jesus press,
Must fix this firm and sure,
That tribulation, more or less,
They must and shall endure.

2 From this there can be none exempt ;
'Tis God's own wise decree ;
Satan the weakest saint will tempt,
Nor is the strongest free.

3 [The world opposes from without,
    And unbelief within ;
We fear, we faint, we grieve, we doubt,
    And feel the load of sin.]

4 [Glad frames too often lift us up,
    And then how proud we grow !
Till sad desertion makes us droop,
    And down we sink as low.]

5 [Ten thousand baits the foe prepares
    To catch the wandering heart ;
And seldom do we see the snares
    Before we feel the smart.]

6 But let not all this terrify ;
    Pursue the narrow path ; ·
Look to the Lord with steadfast eye,
    And fight with hell by faith.

7 Though we are feeble, Christ is strong ;
    His promises are true ;
We shall be conquerors all ere long,
    And more than conquerors too.

306   7.6.   HART.
"Lord, . . thou canst make me clean."—Mat. viii. 2.

O THE pangs by Christians felt,
    When their eyes are open ;
When they see the gulfs of guilt
    They must wade and grope in ;
When the hell appears within,
    Causing bitter anguish,
And the loathsome stench of sin
    Makes the spirit languish.

2 Now the heart disclosed, betrays
    All its hid disorders,
Enmity to God's right ways,
    Blasphemies and murders ;

Malice, envy, lust, and pride,
    Thoughts obscene and filthy ;
Sores corrupt and putrefied,
    No part sound or healthy.

3 [All things to promote our fall
    Show a mighty fitness ;
Satan will accuse withal,
    And the conscience witness ;
Foes within, and foes without,
    Wrath, and law, and terrors,
Rash presumption, timid doubt,
    Coldness, deadness, errors.]

4 Brethren, in a state so sad,
    When temptations seize us,
When our hearts we feel thus bad,
    Let us look to Jesus.
He that hung ·· ﹁ the cross,

For his people bleeding,
Now in heaven sits, for us
    Always interceding.

5 Vengeance, when the Saviour died,
    Quitted the believer ;
Justice cried, " I'm satisfied,
    Now, henceforth, for ever."
" It is finished," said the Lord,
    In his dying minute ;
Holy Ghost, repeat the word,
    Full salvation's in it.

6 [Leprous soul, press through the crowd
    In thy foul condition ;
Struggle hard, and call aloud
    On the great Physician.
Wait till thy disease he cleanse,
    Begging, trusting, cleaving ;

When, and *where*, and *by what means*,
    To his wisdom leaving.]

307   148th.   HART.
" Blessed is the man that endureth temptation."

AND must it, Lord, be so ?
    And must thy children bear
Such various kinds of woe,
    Such soul-perplexing fear ?
Are these the blessings we expect ?
Is this the lot of God's elect ?

2 [Boast not, ye sons of earth,
    Nor look with scornful eyes ;
Above your highest mirth,
    Our saddest hours we prize ;
For though our cup seems filled with gall,
There's something secret sweetens all.]

3 How harsh soe'er the way,
    Dear Saviour, still lead on,
Nor leave us till we say
    " Father, thy will be done."
At most we do but taste the cup,
For thou alone hast drunk it up.

4 Shall guilty man complain ?
    Shall sinful dust repine ?
    And what is all our pain ?
    How light compared with thine !
Finish, dear Lord, what is begun ;
Choose thou the way, but still lead on.

308   S.M.   HART.
The Narrow Way.--Matt. vii. 13, 14; Luke xiii. 24.

WIDE is the gate of death ;
    The way is large and broad ;
And many enter in thereat,
    And walk that beaten road.

2 Because the gate of life
   Is narrow, low, and small ;
The path so pressed, so close, so strait,
   There seems no path at all.

3 [This way, that's found by few,
   Ten thousand snares beset,
To turn the seeker's steps aside,
   And trap the traveller's feet.]

4. [Before we've journeyed far,
   Two dangerous gulfs are fixed,
Dead sloth and pharisaic pride,
   Scarce a hair's breadth betwixt.]

5 [False lights delude the eyes,
   And lead the steps astray ;
That traveller treads the surest here
   That seldom sees his way.]

6 [Guides cry, " Lo here ! " " Lo there ! "
   " On this, on that side keep ; "
Some overdrive, some frighten back,
   And others lull to sleep.]

7 [On the left hand and right,
   Close, cragged rocks are seen,
Distrust and self-wrought confidence ;
   'Tis hard to squeeze between.]

8 [Sometimes we seem to gain
   Great lengths of ground by day ;
But find, alas ! when night comes on,
   We quite mistook the way.]

9 [Sometimes we have no strength ;
   Sometimes we want the will ;
And sometimes, lest we might go wrong,
   We choose to stand quite still.]

10 [Again, through heedless haste,
   We catch some dangerous fall ;
Then, fearing we may move too fast,
   We hardly move at all.]

11 [Deep quagmires choke the way ;
   Corruptions foul and thick ;
Whose stench infects the air, and makes
   The strongest traveller sick.]

12 [Through these we long must wade,
   And oft stick fast in mire ;
Now heat consumes, now frost benumbs,
   As dangerous as the fire.]

13 [Spectres, of various forms,
   Allure, enchant, affright ;
Presumption tempts us every day ;
   Despair assaults by night.]

14 [Companions if we find,
   Alas ! how soon they're gone !
For 'tis decreed that most must pass
   The darkest paths alone.]

15 Distressed on every side
   With evils, felt or feared ;
We pray, we cry, but cannot find
   That prayers or cries are heard.

16 Thickets of briers and thorns
   Our feeble feet enclose ;
And every step we take betrays
   New dangers and new foes.

17 When all these foes are quelled,
   And every danger past,
That ghastly phantom, Death, remains
   To combat with at last.

SECOND PART.

   If this be, Lord, thy way,
      Then who can hope to gain

That prize such numbers never seek,
   Such numbers seek in vain ?

2 'Tis thy almighty grace
   That can suffice alone ;
Thou giv'st us strength to run the race,
   And then bestow'st a crown.

3 Cheer up, ye travelling souls ;
   On Jesus' aid rely ;
He sees us when we see not him,
   And always hears our cry.

4 [Without cessation pray ;
   Your prayers will not prove vain ;
Our Joseph turns aside to weep,
   But cannot long refrain.]

5 [Sudden he stands confessed ;
   We look, and all is light ;
The foe, confounded, swift as thought,
   Sneaks off, and skulks from sight.]

6 [His presence cheers the soul,
   And smooths the rugged way ;
He often makes the crooked straight,
   And turns the night to day.]

7 [We then move cheerful on ;
   The ground feels firm and good ;
And, lest we should mistake the way,
   He lines it out with blood.]

8 [Again, we cannot see
   His helping hand, but feel ;
And though we neither feel nor see,
   His hand sustains us still.]

9 He gently leads us on ;
   Protects from fatal harms ;
And when we faint and cannot walk,
   He bears us in his arms.

10 [He guides, and moves our steps,
　For though *we* seem to move,
His Spirit all the motion gives,
　By springs of fear and love.]

11 The meek with love he draws ;
　Restrains the rash by fear ;
Searches and finds the wandering out,
　And brings the distant near.

12 When for a time we stop,
　Perplexed and at a loss,
He, like a beacon on a hill,
　Erects his bloody cross.

13 Forward again we press,
　And, while that mark's in view,
Though hosts of foes beset the way,
　We boldly venture through.

14 When all these foes are quelled,
　And every danger past,
Though Death remains, he but remains
　To be subdued at last.

309　　11.9.　　HART.
The Christian's Life a Paradox.—2 Cor. iv. 8-11.

How strange is the course that a Christian
　must steer !
　How perplexed is the path he must tread !
The hope of his happiness rises from fear,
　And his life he receives from the dead.

2 His fairest pretensions must wholly be waived,
　And his best resolutions be crossed ;
Nor can he expect to be perfectly saved,
　Till he finds himself utterly lost.

3 When all this is done, and his heart is assured
　Of the total remission of sins,　[procured,
When his pardon is signed and his peace is
　From that moment his conflict begins.

310　　C.M.　　HART.
" Create in me a clean heart."—Ps. li. 10 ; Mark vii. 21.

LORD, when thy Spirit descends to show
　The badness of our hearts,
Astonished at the amazing view,
　The soul with horror starts.

2 [The dungeon, opening foul as hell,
　Its loathsome stench emits ;
And, brooding in each secret cell,
　Some hideous monster sits.]

3 [Swarms of ill thoughts their bane diffuse,
　Proud, envious, false, unclean ;
And every ransacked corner shows
　Some unsuspected sin.]

4 Our staggering faith gives way to doubt ;
　Our courage yields to fear ;
Shocked at the sight, we straight cry out,
　" Can ever God dwell here ? "

5 None less than God's Almighty Son
　Can move such loads of sin ;
The water from his side must run,
　To wash this dungeon clean.

6 O come, thou much-expected Guest !
　Lord Jesus, quickly come !
Enter the chamber of my breast ;
　Thyself prepare the room.

7 For shouldst thou stay till thou canst meet
　Reception worthy thee,
With sinners thou wouldst never sit—
　At least I'm sure with me.

8 When, when will that blest time arrive,
　When thou wilt kindly deign
With me to sit, to lodge, to live ;
　And never part again ?

311　　S.M.　　HART.
Faith is the Victory.—Acts xiii. 38. 39 ; 1 John v. 4,

WHOE'ER believes aright
　In Christ's atoning blood,
Of all his guilt's acquitted quite,
　And may draw near to God.

2 But sin will still remain ;
　Corruptions rise up thick ;
And Satan says the medicine's vain
　Because we yet are sick.

3 But all this will not do ;
　Our hope's on Jesus cast ;
Let all be liars and him be true,
　We shall be well at last.

312　　S.M.　　HART.
Temptation.—Mat. iv. 3-10 ; 1 Cor. x. 13 ; Heb. iv. 15.

YE tempted souls, reflect
　Whose name 'tis you profess ;
Your Master's lot you must expect,—
　Temptations more or less.

2 Dream not of faith so clear
　As shuts all doubtings out ;
Remember how the devil dared
　To tempt e'en Christ to doubt.

3 [" If thou'rt the Son of God,"
　(O what an IF was there !)
" These stones here, speak them into food,
　And make that Sonship clear."]

4 [View that amazing scene !
　Say, could the tempter try
To shake a tree so sound, so green ?
　Good God, defend the dry !]

5 Think not he now will fail
　To make us shrink and droop ;

Our faith he daily will assail,
And dash our every hope.

6 [That impious IF he thus
At God incarnate threw,
No wonder if he cast at us,
And make us feel it too.]

7 To cause despair's the scope
Of Satan and his powers ;
Against hope to believe in hope,
My brethren, must be ours.

8 *Buts, ifs,* and *hows* are hurled
To sink us with the gloom
Of all that's dismal in this world,
Or in the world to come.

9 But here's our point of rest :
Though hard the battle seem,
Our Captain stood the fiery test,
And we shall stand through him.

313   148th.   HART.
" The spirit . . . lusteth to envy.—James iv. 5.
WHAT tongue can fully tell
That Christian's grievous load,
Who would do all things well,
And walk the ways of God,
But feels within foul envy lurk,
And lust, and work, engendering sin ?

2 [Poor, wretched, worthless worm !
In what sad plight I stand !
When good I would perform,
Then evil is at hand.
My leprous soul is all unclean,
My heart obscene, my nature foul.]

3 To trust to Christ alone,
By thousand dangers scared,
And righteousness have none,
Is something very hard.
Whate'er men say, the needy know
It must be so, it is the way.

4 Thou all-sufficient Lamb,
God blest for evermore,
We glory in thy name,
For thine is all the power.
Stretch forth thy hand, and hold us fast,
Our First and Last, in thee we stand.

314   S.M.   HART.
" O wretched man that I am," &c.—Rom. vii. 13-24.
How sore a plague is sin,
To those by whom 'tis felt !
The Christian cries, "*Unclean, unclean !* '
E'en though released from guilt.

2 O wretched, wretched man !

What horrid scenes I view !
I find, alas ! do all I can,
That I can nothing do.

3 When good I would perform,
Through fear or shame I stop,
Corruption rises like a storm,
And blasts the promised crop.

4 [Of peace if I'm in quest,
Or love my thoughts engage,
Envy and anger in my breast
That moment rise and rage.]

5 [When for a humble mind
To God I pour my prayer,
I look into my heart, and find
That pride will still be there.]

6 How long, dear Lord, how long
Deliverance must I seek ;
And fight with foes so very strong,
Myself so very weak ?

7 I'll bear the unequal strife,
And wage the war within ;
Since death, that puts an end to life,
Shall put an end to sin.

315   7.6.   HART.
" But thou shalt know hereafter."—John xiii. 7.
RIGHTEOUS are the works of God ;
All his ways are holy ;
Just his judgments, fit his rod
To correct our folly.

2 All his dealings wise and good,
Uniform, though various ;
Though they seem, by reason viewed,
Cross, or quite contrarious.

3 These are truths, and happy he
Who can well receive them ;
Brethren, though we cannot see,
Still we should believe them.

4 Why through darksome paths we go,
We may know no reason ;
Yet we shall hereafter know,
Each in his due season.

5 Could we see how all is right,
Where were room for credence ?
But by faith, and not by sight,
Christians yield obedience.

6 Let all fruitless searches go,
Which perplex and teaze us ;
We determine nought to know,
But a bleeding Jesus.

316   L.M.   HART.
Stony Heart.—Isa. lxiv. 1 ; Ezek. xi. 19 ; xxxvi. 26.
O FOR a glance of heavenly day,
To take this stubborn stone away :

And thaw, with beams of love divine,
This heart, this frozen heart of mine !

2 [The rocks can rend, the earth can quake,
The seas can roar, the mountains shake ;
Of feeling all things show some sign,
But this unfeeling heart of mine.]

3 To hear the sorrows thou hast felt,
Dear Lord, an adamant would melt ;
But I can read each moving line,
And nothing move this heart of mine.

4 Thy judgments, too, unmoved I hear,
(Amazing thought !) which devils fear ;
Goodness and wrath in vain combine
To stir this stupid heart of mine.

5 But something yet can do the deed,
And that dear something much I need ;
Thy Spirit can from dross refine,
And move and melt this heart of mine.

317   L.M.   WATTS.
Distinguishing Love.—Rom. ix. 15; 2 Pet. ii. 4-9.

FROM heaven the sinning angels fell,
And wrath and darkness chained them down;
But man, vile man, forsook his bliss,
And mercy lifts him to a crown.

2 Amazing work of sovereign grace,
That could distinguish rebels so !
Our guilty treasons called aloud
For everlasting fetters too.

3 To thee, to thee, Almighty Love,
Our souls, ourselves, our all we pay ;
Millions of tongues shall sound thy praise
On the bright hills of heavenly day.

318   S.M.   WATTS.
God's unchangeable Love.—Ps. cvi. 7-48;
Lev. xxvi. 40.

GOD of eternal love,
How fickle are our ways !
And yet how oft did Israel prove
Thy constancy and grace !

2 [They saw thy wonders wrought,
And then thy praise they sung ;
But soon thy works of power forgot,
And murmured with their tongue.]

3 Now they believe his word,
While rocks with rivers flow ;
Now with their lusts provoke the Lord,
And he reduced them low.

4 Yet, when they mourned their faults,
He hearkened to their groans,
Brought his own covenant to his thoughts,
And called them still his sons.

5 [Their names were in his book ;
He saved them from their foes ;
Oft he chastised, but ne'er forsook

The people that he chose.]

6 Let Israel bless the Lord,
Who loved their ancient race ;
And Christians join the solemn word,
Amen, to all the praise.

319   8s.   SWAIN.
Comfort under Affliction.—Zech. iii. 2; 2 Cor. i. 4.

How light, while supported by grace,
Are all the afflictions I see,
To those the dear Lord of my peace,
My Jesus, has suffered for me !
To him every comfort I owe,
Above what the fiends have in hell ;
And shall I not sing as I go,
That Jesus does everything well ?

2 [*That* Jesus who stooped from his throne,
To pluck such a brand from the fire.
A wretch that had nought of his own,
Not even a holy desire.
My only inheritance sin,
A slave to rebellion and lust ;
Polluted without and within,
A child of corruption and dust.

3 Such was I when Jesus looked down,
When none but himself could relieve ;
What could I expect but a frown ?
Yet kindly he smiled, and said, " Live ! "
And shall I impatiently fret
And murmur beneath his kind rod ?
His love and his mercy forget,
And fly in the face of my God ?]

4 Dear Jesus, preserve me in love,
And teach me on thee to rely ;
Give wisdom and strength from above,
Nor let me against thee reply ;
Then I thy great name will adore,
And cheerfully bear up the cross,
Nor wish thee to lessen the power
Which purges my conscience from dross.

320   C.M.   COWPER.
Light shining out of darkness.—Ps. lxxvii. 19.

GOD moves in a mysterious way
His wonders to perform ;
He plants his footsteps in the sea,
And rides upon the storm.

2 Deep in unfathomable mines
Of never-failing skill,
He treasures up his bright designs,
And works his sovereign will.

3 Ye fearful saints, fresh courage take ;
The clouds ye so much dread

Are big with mercy, and shall break
   In blessings on your head.

4 Judge not the Lord by feeble sense,
   But trust him for his grace ;
   Behind a frowning providence
   He hides a smiling face.

5 His purposes will ripen fast,
   Unfolding every hour ;
   The bud may have a bitter taste,
   But sweet will be the flower.

6 Blind unbelief is sure to err,
   And scan his work in vain ;
   God is his own interpreter,
   And he will make it plain.

321   104th.   MEDLEY.
" The Lord will appear."—Lev. ix. 4; Is. lxvi. 5.

MY soul, Lord, inflame with zeal from above,
Thy praise to proclaim and sing of thy love;
To lift up my voice in thanksgiving sincere.
This truth to rejoice in, The Lord will appear.

2 How joyful this sound, while daily I find
Afflictions abound in body and mind !
It oft has afforded relief from my fear,
To find it recorded, The Lord will appear.

3 [I have, as I seem, when left in the dark,
Of light not a beam, of love not a spark ;
And though thus in pain for an evidence clear,
I can't wait in vain, for The Lord will appear.]

4 [A warfare I find without and within,
With legions combined, world, Satan, & sin.
Tho' sore they annoy me, I'll be of good cheer,
They cannot destroy me, The Lord will appear.]

5 My fears sometimes say I never shall find,
In death's awful day true peace in my mind ;
But tho' thus surrounded, yet, when I come there,
I can't be confounded, The Lord will appear.

6 My dust he will raise, and glory he'll give ;
And I to his praise in heaven shall live ;
There he will deliver my soul from all fear,
And to me, for ever, The Lord will appear.

322   104th.   MEDLEY.
'Tis all for the best.—Rom. viii. 28.

MY soul, now arise, my passions, take wing ;
Look up to the skies, and cheerfully sing ;
Let God be the Object in praises addressed,
And this be my subject, 'Tis all for the best.

Search all the world thro', examine and see,
And what canst thou view more suited to the
than this declaration, in Scripture expressed,
That God, thy Salvation. does all for the best ?

Tho' here, day by day, his love shall see good

Upon thee to lay his fatherly rod ;
Yet be not dejected, however oppressed,
Though sorely afflicted, 'tis all for the best.

4 The beams of his grace are passing all worth,
The smiles of his face are heaven on earth ;
When to me he shows them, what joy fills my
   breast !   [best.
And when he withdraws them, 'tis all for the

5 But O, the blest day, and soon 'twill arise,
When, freed from my clay, I mount to the
   skies ;
Then gladly I'll enter my heavenly rest,
And there sing for ever, 'Tis all for the best.

323   L.M.   COWPER.
Return of Joy.—Isa. liv. 7-10; Job xxxiv. 29.

WHEN darkness long has veiled my mind,
And smiling day once more appears,
Then, my Redeemer, then I find
The folly of my doubts and fears.

2 I chide my unbelieving heart,
And blush that I should ever be
Thus prone to act so base a part,
Or harbour one hard thought of thee.

3 O let me then at length be taught
(What I am still so slow to learn)
That God is love, and changes not,
Nor knows the shadow of a turn.

4 Sweet truth, and easy to repeat !
But when my faith is sharply tried,
I find myself a learner yet,
Unskilful, weak, and apt to slide.

5 But, O my Lord, one look from thee
Subdues the disobedient will ;
Drives doubt and discontent away,
And thy rebellious worm is still.

6 Thou art as ready to forgive
As I am ready to repine ;
Thou, therefore, all the praise receive ;
Be shame and self-abhorrence mine.

324   104th.   NEWTON.
" The Lord will provide."—Gen. xxii. 14; Matt. vi.26.

THOUGH troubles assail and dangers affright ;
Tho' friends should all fail, and foes all unite,
Yet one thing secures us, whatever betide,
The Scripture assures us, The Lord will provide.

2 When Satan appears to stop up our path,
And fills us with fears, we triumph by faith ;
He cannot take from us, tho' oft he has tried,
This heart-cheering promise, The Lord will
   provide.

3 He tells us we're weak, our hope is in vain,
The good that we seek we ne'er shall obtain ;
But when such suggestions our spirits have
plied,   [vide.
This answers all questions, The Lord will pro-
4 No strength of our own, or goodness we claim ;
Yet since we have known the Saviour's great
name,
In this our strong tower for safety we hide,
The Lord is our power, The Lord will provide.
5 When life sinks apace, and death is in view,
This word of his grace shall comfort us thro' ;
No fearing or doubting with Christ on our side ;
We hope to die shouting, The Lord will pro-
vide.

325   C.M.   WATTS.
Assistance and victory in spiritual warfare.—Ps. lv. 18.
FOR ever blesséd be the Lord,
    My Saviour and my shield ;
He sends his Spirit with his word,
    To arm me for the field.

2 When sin and hell their force unite,
    He makes my soul his care ;
Instructs me to the heavenly fight,
    And guards me through the war.

3 A Friend and Helper so divine,
    Does my weak courage raise ;
He makes the glorious victory mine,
    And his shall be the praise.

326   L.M.   WATTS.
Our Weakness, and Christ our Strength.—2 Cor. xii. 9.
LET me but hear my Saviour say,
" Strength shall be equal to thy day ; "
Then I rejoice in deep distress,
Leaning on all-sufficient grace.

2 I glory in infirmity,
That Christ's own power may rest on me ;
When I am weak, then am I strong ;
Grace is my shield, and Christ my song.

3 I can do all things, or can bear
All sufferings, if my Lord be there ;
Sweet pleasures mingle with the pains
While his left hand my head sustains.

4 But if the Lord be once withdrawn,
And we attempt the work alone,
When new temptations spring and rise,
We find how great our weakness is.

327   C.M.   WATTS.
Jehovah the Strength of his People.—Isa. xl. 29.
WHENCE do our mournful thoughts arise ?
    And where's our courage fled ?
Has restless sin and raging hell

Struck all our comforts dead ?

2 Have we forgot the almighty Name
    That formed the earth and sea ?
And can an all-creating arm
    Grow weary, or decay ?

3 Treasures of everlasting might
    In our Jehovah dwell ;
He gives the conquest to the weak,
    And treads their foes to hell.

4 Mere mortal power shall fade and die,
    And youthful vigour cease ;
But we that wait upon the Lord
    Shall feel our strength increase.

5 The saints shall mount on eagles' wings,
    And taste the promised bliss,
Till their unwearied feet arrive
    Where perfect pleasure is.

328   L.M   FAWCETT.
As thy days, so shall thy strength be.—Deut. xxxiii. 2
AFFLICTED saint, to Christ draw near,
Thy Saviour's gracious promise hear ;
His faithful word declares to thee,
That as thy days, thy strength shall be.

2 Let not thy heart despond, and say,
" How shall I stand the trying day ? "
He has engaged, by firm decree,
That as thy days, thy strength shall be.

3 Thy faith is weak, thy foes are strong ;
And if the conflict should be long,
Thy Lord will make the tempter flee ;
For as thy days, thy strength shall be.

4 Should persecution rage and flame,
Still trust in thy Redeemer's name ;
In fiery trials thou shalt see,
That as thy days, thy strength shall be.

5 When called to bear the weighty cross,
Or sore affliction, pain, or loss,
Or deep distress, or poverty,
Still, as thy days, thy strength shall be.

6 When ghastly death appears in view,
Christ's presence shall thy fears subdue ;
He comes to set thy spirit free,
And as thy days, thy strength shall be.

329   11s.   KIRKHAM (?).
Exceeding great and precious Promises.—2 Pet. i. 4.
How firm a foundation, ye saints of the Lord,
Is laid for your faith in his excellent word !
What more can he say than to you he has said
You who unto Jesus for refuge have fled ?
                        2
In every condition—in sickness, in health,
In poverty's vale, or abounding in wealth ;

At home, or abroad, on the land, on the sea,
" As thy days may demand, shall thy strength
    ever be.   3

" Fear not, I am with thee ; O be not dismayed ;
, I am thy God, and will still give thee aid ;
'll strengthen thee, help thee, and cause thee
    to stand,
Upheld by my righteous, omnipotent hand.

    4

" When through the deep waters I call thee to go,
The rivers of woe shall not thee overflow ;
For I will be with thee, thy troubles to bless,
And sanctify to thee thy deepest distress.

    5

" When thro' fiery trials thy pathway shall lie,
My grace all-sufficient shall be thy supply ;
The flame shall not hurt thee ; I only design
Thy dross to consume, and thy gold to refine.

    6

" E'en down to old age, all my people shall prove
My sovereign, eternal, unchangeable love ;
And when hoary hairs shall their temples adorn,
Like lambs they shall still in my bosom be borne.

    7

" The soul that on Jesus has leaned for repose,
I will not, I will not desert to his foes ;
That soul, tho' all hell should endeavour to shake,
I'll never, no never, no never forsake."

330   S.M.   TOPLADY.
Weak Believers encouraged.—Ps. xxvii. 14 ; Isa. xlix. 23
    YOUR harps, ye trembling saints,
      Down from the willows take ;
  Loud to the praise of Christ our Lord,
      Bid every string awake.
2   Though in a foreign land,
      We are not far from home ;
  And nearer to our house above,
      We every moment come.
3   His grace shall to the end,
      Stronger and brighter shine ;
  Nor present things, nor things to come,
      Shall quench the spark divine.
4   The time of love will come,
      When we shall clearly see,
  Not only that he shed his blood,
      But each shall say, " *For me.*"
5   Tarry his leisure, then ;
      Wait till the appointed hour ;
  Wait till the Bridegroom of your souls
      Reveal his love with power.
6   [Blest is the man, O God,
      Whose mind is stayed on thee ;

    Who waits for thy salvation, Lord,
      Shall thy salvation see.]

331   L.M.   DODDRIDGE.
Choosing the Better Part.—Luke x. 42 ; Ps. xlvi. 1-3.
  BESET with snares on every hand,
  In life's uncertain path I stand ;
  Saviour divine, diffuse thy light,
  To guide my doubtful footsteps right.
2 Engage this roving, treacherous heart
  To fix on Christ, my better part ;
  To scorn the trifles of a day,
  For joys that none can take away.
3 Then let the wildest storms arise ;
  Let tempests mingle earth and skies ;
  No fatal shipwreck shall I fear,
  But all my treasures with me bear.
4 If thou, my Jesus, still be nigh,
  Cheerful I live, and joyful die ;
  Secure, when mortal comforts flee,
  To find ten thousand worlds in thee.

332   L.M.   DODDRIDGE.
  " God is faithful," &c.—1 Cor. x. 13.
  Now let the feeble all be strong,
  And make Jehovah's arm their song ;
  His shield is spread o'er every saint,
  And thus supported, who shall faint ?
2 What though the hosts of hell engage
  With mingled cruelty and rage ?
  A faithful God restrains their hands,
  And chains them down in iron bands.
3 Bound by his word, he will display
  A strength proportioned to our day ;
  And when united trials meet,
  Will show a path of safe retreat.
4 Thus far we prove that promise good,
  Which Jesus ratified with blood ;
  Still is he gracious, wise, and just,
  And still in him let Israel trust.

333   8.7.4.   FAWCETT.
Cast down, yet hoping in God.—Ps. xlii. 5-11 ; xliii. 5.
  O MY soul, what means this sadness ?
    Wherefore art thou thus cast down ?
  Let thy griefs be turned to gladness ;
    Bid thy restless fears be gone ;
      Look to Jesus,
    And rejoice in his dear name.
2 What though Satan's strong temptations
    Vex and teaze thee day by day,
  And thy sinful inclinations
    Often fill thee with dismay ?

Thou shalt conquer,
Through the Lamb's redeeming blood.

3 Though ten thousand ills beset thee,
From without and from within,
Jesus says he'll ne'er forget thee,
But will save from hell and sin ;
He is faithful,
To perform his gracious word.

4 Though distresses now attend thee,
And thou tread'st the thorny road,
His right hand shall still defend thee ;
Soon he'll bring thee home to God ;
Therefore praise him ;
Praise the great Redeemer's name.

5 O that I could now adore him
Like the heavenly host above,
Who for ever bow before him,
And unceasing sing his love !
Happy songsters !
When shall I your chorus join ?

334   8s.   KENT.
The Church coming from the Wilderness.—Song viii. 5

BEHOLD, from the desert of sin,
The world, and the curse of the law,
A fair one, whose garments are clean,
Does with her Beloved withdraw ;
Retiring from thence, she appears
Dejected, and often complains,
Surrounded with sorrows and fears,
Yet on her Beloved she leans.

2 Thus up from the desert she goes,
Sustained both in fire and in flood ;
Victorious, to vanquish her foes,
And all through the Lamb and his blood.
By faith she's enabled to view
Fair Canaan's delectable plains,
And faint, yet her course shall pursue,
When on her Beloved she leans.

3 [When darkness envelops her mind,
By faith she shall hold on her way ;
And, in the sweet promise, shall find
Her strength shall suffice for the day ;
No fiery afflictions shall burn
Beyond what his wisdom ordains,
But times of refreshing return,
When on her Beloved she leans.]

4 Her woes are permitted of God,
Her faith and her patience to prove ;
The kiss, or a stroke of his rod,
Is all from immutable love.
By crosses and losses, at last
From self her affections he weans,

That on him her hopes may stand fast,
While on her Beloved she leans.

5 When foiled by the tempter, she goes
And makes the atonement her plea,
There pardon eternally flows,
And love wipes her sorrows away ;
And when with her pardon she's blessed,
Communion with Jesus she gains,
No longer a sinner distressed,
For on her Beloved she leans.

335   S.M.   BERRIDGE.
Crosses at the Control of Christ.—Heb. xii. 5 ; Job v. 17.

POOR angry bosom, hush,
Nor discontented grow ;
But at thy own sad folly blush,
Which breedeth all the woe.

2 If sick, or lame, or poor,
Or by the world abhorred,
Whatever cross lies at thy door,
It cometh from the Lord.

3 The lions will not tear,
The billows cannot heave,
The furnace shall not singe thy hair,
Till Jesus give them leave.

4 The Lord is just and true,
And upright in his way ;
He loves, but will correct us too,
Whene'er we run astray.

5 [With caution we should tread,
For as we sow we reap,
And oft bring mischief on our head,
By some unwary step.]

6 Lord, plant a godly fear
Before my roving eyes,
Lest some hid snake or wily snare
My heedless feet surprise.

7 Or should I start aside,
And meet a scourging God,
Let not my heart grow stiff with pride,
But weep and kiss the rod.

336   C.M.   BERRIDGE.
God's presence makes glad.—Ps. xxx. 5-12 ; Jer. xxxi. 4

WHEN I can sit at Jesus' feet,
And he anoints my head,
Such peace ensues, so calm and sweet,
I think my foes all dead.

2 My simple heart then fondly dreams,
It will see war no more ;
Too firm to shrink my mountain seems,
And every storm blows o'er.

3 [While thus a queen in state I sit,
Self hunts about for praise ;
Talks much of frames and victories great,
That you may hear and gaze.]

4 Then Jesus sends a trying hour,
    This lurking pride to quell ;
My dead foes rise with dreadful power,
    And drag me down to hell.
5 Now faints my heart within me quite,
    My mountain disappears ;
All grace is vanished from my sight,
    And faith seems lost in fears.
6 At length my Lord, with sweet surprise,
    Returns to loose my bands,
Brings kind compassion in his eyes,
    And pardon in his hands.
7 I drop my vile head in the dust,
    And at my Lord's feet fall ;
His grace is now my song and boast,
    And Christ my All in All.

337   S.M.   NEWTON.
The Pilgrim's Song.—Heb. xi. 13, 27.
    FROM Egypt lately freed,
    By the Redeemer's grace,
A rough and thorny path we tread,
    In hopes to see his face.
2   The flesh dislikes the way,
    But faith approves it well ;
This only leads to endless day
    All others lead to hell.
3   The promised land of peace,
    Faith keeps in constant view ;
How different from the wilderness
    We now are passing through !
4   Here often from our eyes
    Clouds hide the light divine ;
There we shall have unclouded skies,
    Our Sun will always shine.
5   Here griefs, and cares, and pains,
    And fears distress us sore ;
But there eternal pleasure reigns,
    And we shall weep no more.
6   Lord, pardon our complaints ;
    We follow at thy call ;
The joy prepared for suffering saints,
    Will make amends for all.

338   148th.   COWPER.
The Lord my Banner.—Exod.xvii. 15.
[BY whom was David taught
To aim the dreadful blow,
When he Goliath fought,
And laid the Gittite low ?
No sword nor spear the stripling took,
But chose a pebble from the brook.
2   'Twas Israel's God and King,
    Who sent him to the fight,
    Who gave him strength to sling
    And skill to aim aright ;

Ye feeble saints, your strength endures,
Because young David's God is yours.]
3   [Who ordered Gideon forth,
    To storm the invader's camp,
    With arms of little worth—
    A pitcher and a lamp ?
The trumpets made his coming known,
And all the host was overthrown.]
4   O ! I have seen the day,
    When, with a single word,
    God helping me to say,
    " My trust is in the Lord,"
My soul has quelled a thousand foes,
Fearless of all that could oppose.
5   But unbelief, self-will,
    Self-righteousness, and pride,
    How often do they steal
    My weapon from my side !

Yet David's Lord and Gideon's Friend,
Will help his servant to the end.

339   148th.   HAMMOND.
Immutability of God's Will.—Phil. i. 6; Heb. x. 35.
    O MY distrustful heart,
    How small thy faith appears !
    But greater, Lord, thou art,
    Than all my doubts and fears.
Did Jesus once upon me shine ?
Then Jesus is for ever mine.

2   Unchangeable his will ;
    Whatever be my frame,
    His loving heart is still
    Eternally the same.
My soul through many changes goes ;
His love no variation knows.

3   Thou, Lord, wilt carry on,
    And perfectly perform,
    The work thou hast begun
    In me, a sinful worm ;
'Midst all my fear, and sin, and woe,
Thy Spirit will not let me go.

4   The bowels of thy grace
    At first did freely move ;
    I still shall see thy face,
    And feel that God is love.
My soul into thy arms I cast ;
I trust I shall be saved at last.

340   8s.   TOPLADY.
Saints' final perseverance.-Rom. viii. 33-39; Is. xlix. 15.
    A DEBTOR to mercy alone,
    Of covenant mercy I sing ;
Nor fear, with thy righteousness on,
    My person and offerings to bring.

The terrors of law and of God
  With me can have nothing to do ;
My Saviour's obedience and blood
  Hide all my transgressions from view.

2 The work which his goodness began,
  The arm of his strength will complete ;
His promise is *Yea* and *Amen*,
  And never was forfeited yet.
Things future, nor things that are now,
Not all things below nor above,
Can make him his purpose forego,
  Or sever my soul from his love.

3 My name from the palms of his hands
  Eternity will not erase,
Impressed on his heart it remains,
  In marks of indelible grace ;
Yes, I to the end shall endure,
  As sure as the earnest is given ;
More happy, but not more secure,
  The glorified spirits in heaven.

341   C.M.   FAWCETT.
Perseverance desired.—Ps. cxix. 117; lxxiii. 24.

LORD, hast thou made me know thy ways ?
  Conduct me in thy fear ;
And grant me such supplies of grace,
  That I may persevere.

2 Let but thy own almighty arm
  Sustain a feeble worm,
I shall escape, secure from harm
  Amid the dreadful storm.

3 Be thou my all-sufficient Friend,
  Till all my toils shall cease ;
Guard me through life, and let my end
  Be everlasting peace.

342   7s.   HAMMOND.
"My beloved is mine, and I am his."—Song ii. 16.

CHRIST is mine, and I am his ;
Centre, source, and sum of bliss ;
Earth and hell in vain combine
Me and Jesus to disjoin.

2 Thou my fortress art and tower ;
Having thee, I want no more.
Strong in thy full strength I stand ;
None can pluck me from thy hand.

3 Nothing in myself I am ;
All I have is in the Lamb.
While his face on me does shine,
All in heaven and earth is mine.

4 In my Jesus' arms secure,
To the end I shall endure ;
Join with me, ye angels, join !
Praise his name in hymns divine.

343   104th.   HAMMOND.
" The mountains shall depart," &c.—Isa. liv. 10.

IF Jesus is ours, we have a true-Friend,
  Whose goodness endures the same to the end ;
Our comforts may vary, our frames may decline,
We cannot miscarry ; our aid is divine.

2 Though God may delay to show us his light,
  And heaviness may endure for a night,
Yet joy in the morning shall surely abound ;
No shadow of turning in Jesus is found.

3 The hills may depart, and mountains remove,
  But faithful thou art, O Fountain of Love.
The Father has graven our names on thy hands,
Our building in heaven eternally stands.

4 A moment he hid the light of his face,
  Yet firmly decreed to save us by grace ;
And tho' he reproved us, and still may reprove,
For ever he loved us, and ever will love.

344   C.M.   HAMMOND.
Perseverance.—Ps. lxxxix. 28-34; Isa. xlix. 16.

FOR us the dear Redeemer died ;
  Why are we then ashamed ?
We stand for ever justified,
  And cannot be condemned.

2 Though we believe not, he is true ;
  The work is in his hand ;
His gracious purpose he will do,
  And all his word shall stand.

3 If once the love of Christ we feel
  Upon our hearts impressed,
The mark of that celestial seal
  Can never be erased.

4 The Lord will scourge us if we stray,
  And wound us with distress ;
But he will never take away
  His covenant of peace.

5 The peace which Jesus' blood secures,
  And fixes in our hearts,
To all eternity endures,
  Nor finally departs.

345   S.M.   DODDRIDGE.
Christ knows and keeps his Sheep.—John x. 27-30.

MY soul, with joy attend,
  While Jesus silence breaks ;
No angel's harp such music yields
  As what my Shepherd speaks.

2 " I know my sheep," he cries ;
  " My soul approves them well ;
Vain is the treacherous world's disguise,
  And vain the rage of hell.

3   " I freely feed them now
      With tokens of my love.
    But richer pastures I prepare,
      And sweeter streams above.

4.   " Unnumbered years of bliss
      I to my sheep will give ;
    And while my throne unshaken stands,
      Shall all my chosen live.

5   This tried almighty hand
      Is raised for their defence ;
    Where is the power can reach them there,
      Or what can force them thence ? "

6   Enough, my gracious Lord,
      Let faith triumphant cry ;
    My heart can on this promise live ;
      Can on this promise die.

346   8s.   TOPLADY.
Divine Protection.—Ps. iii. 3-6; cxxi. 4; 1 Sam. vii. 12.

    A SOVEREIGN Protector I have,
      Unseen, yet for ever at hand ;
    Unchangeably faithful to save,
      Almighty to rule and command ;
    He smiles, and my comforts abound ;
      His grace as the dew shall descend ;
    And walls of salvation surround
      The souls he delights to defend.

2   Kind Author and ground of my hope,
      Thee, thee for my God I avow ;
    My glad Ebenezer set up,
      And own thou hast helped me till now.
    I muse on the years that are past,
      Wherein my defence thou hast proved ;
    Nor wilt thou relinquish at last
      A sinner so signally loved.

347   7s.   ADAMS.
Safety in Christ.—Ps. iii. 1-3; Prov. xxi. 31.

    LORD, how many are my foes !
    Many they that me oppose ;
    Thou my strong Protector be ;
    All my safety is in thee.

2   Satan and my wicked heart
    Often use their treacherous art ;
    Fain would make my soul to flee ;
    But my safety is in thee.

3   Thou hast said and thou art true,
    " As I live, ye shall live too ; "
    Thou my Rock wilt ever be ;
    All my safety is in thee.

4   I'm a pilgrim here below ;
    Guide me all the desert through ;
    Let me, as I journey, see
    All my safety is in thee.

5   Then, when landed on that shore,
    Where my mind was fixed before,
    In sweet raptures I shall see
    All my safety was in thee.

348   C.M.   TOPLADY.
Safety in Christ.—John xiv. 19.

    THY purchased people, gracious Lamb,
      Thou never canst forget ;
    The piercing nails have wrote their name
      Upon thy hands and feet.

2   Satan, in vain, with rage assails
      Thy dear peculiar ones ;
    For them thy righteousness avails ;
      For them thy blood atones.

3   Vainly against the sheep he strives,
      And wars with the Most High ;
    Their glorious Head for ever lives,
      Nor can his members die.

4   Jesus shall his elect avenge,
      Nor from his own remove ;
    Nor cancel his decree, nor change
      His everlasting love.

349   8.7.4.   ADAMS.
Seeking Christ.—John x. 11, 28; v. 24; Isa. xl. 11.

    JESUS, Shepherd of thy people,
      Lead us through this desert land ;
    We are weak, and poor, and feeble,
      Yet we trust thy mighty hand ;
        Great Protector !
      By thy power alone we stand.

2   All thy sheep shall come to Zion ;
      With them thou wilt never part ;
    Beasts of prey, nor roaring lion,
      None shall pluck them from thy heart ;
        All thy chosen
      Cost thee wounds, and blood, and smart.

3   In thy bosom safely lodgéd,
      Thine shall rest from danger free ;
    They shall never more be judgéd,
      Nor shall condemnation see ;
        Blessed Jesus,
      Let us thus rejoice in thee.

350   11.8.   H. FOWLER.
" The righteous shall hold on his way."—Job xvii. 9.

    YE pilgrims of Zion, and chosen of God,
      Whose spirits are filled with dismay,
    Since ye have eternal redemption thro' blood,
      Ye cannot but hold on your way.

2   As Jesus, in covenant love, did engage
      A fulness of grace to display,

The powers of darkness in malice may rage,
The righteous shall hold on his way.

3 This truth, like its Author, eternal shall stand,
Though all things in nature decay,
Upheld by Jehovah's omnipotent hand,
The righteous shall hold on his way.

4 They may on the main of temptation be tossed ;
Their sorrows may swell as the sea ;
But none of the ransomed shall ever be lost ;
The righteous shall hold on his way.

5 Surrounded with sorrows, temptations, & cares,
This truth with delight we survey,
And sing, as we pass thro' this valley of tears,
The righteous shall hold on his way.

351　　C.M.　　HART.
" Having loved, he loved them to the end."—John xiii.

THE sinner that, by precious faith,
Has felt his sins forgiven,
Is manifestly passed from death,
And sealed an heir of heaven.

2 [Though thousand snares enclose his feet,
Not one shall hold him fast ;
Whatever dangers he may meet,
He shall get safe at last.]

3 Not as the world the Saviour gives ;
He is no fickle friend ;
Whom once he loves he never leaves,
But loves him to the end.

4 [The spirit that would this truth withstand,
Would pull God's temple down,
Wrest Jesus' sceptre from his hands,
And spoil him of his crown.

5 Satan might then full victory boast ;
The church might wholly fall ;
If one believer may be lost,
It follows, so may all.

6 But Christ in every age has proved
His purchase firm and true ;
If this foundation be removed,
What shall the righteous do ?]

7 Brethren, by this, your claim, abide—
This title to your bliss ;
Whatever loss you bear beside,
O never give up this.

352　　L.M.　　HART.
" Heaven and earth shall pass away."—Mat. xxiv. 35.

THE moon and stars shall lose their light,
The sun shall sink in endless night ;
Both heaven and earth shall pass away ;
The works of nature all decay.

2 But they that in the Lord confide,
And shelter in his wounded side,
Shall see the danger overpast,
Stand every storm, and live at last.

3 What Christ has said must be fulfilled ;
On this firm rock, believers build ;
His word shall stand, his truth prevail,
And not one jot or tittle fail.

4 His word is this (poor sinners, hear) ;
" Believe on me, and banish fear ;
Cease from your own works, bad or good,
And wash your garments in my blood."
HART.

353　　148th.　　Ex. xv. 13.
" Thou hast guided them in thy strength."—

MISTAKEN men may brawl
Against the grace of God,
And threat with final fall
The purchase of his blood ;
But, though they own the Saviour's name,
From him such gospel never came.

2　Shall babes in Christ, bereft
Of God's rich gift of faith,
Be to their own will left,
And sin the sin to death ?
Shall any child of God be lost,
And Satan cheat the Holy Ghost ?

3　Dark unbelief and pride,
With Pharisaic zeal,
We lay you all aside,
And trust a surer seal ;
We rest our souls on Jesus' word,
And give the glory to the Lord.

4　Led forth by God's free grace,
And guided by his power,
We reach his holy place,
And live for evermore ;
'Twas this place Moses had in view ;
Of this he sang, and we sing too.

354　　C.M.　　WATTS.
Saints in the Hand of Christ.—John vi. 39 ; x. 27-29.

FIRM as the earth thy gospel stands,
My Lord, my Hope, my Trust ;
If I am found in Jesus' hands,
My soul can ne'er be lost.

2 His honour is engaged to save
The meanest of his sheep ;
All that his heavenly Father gave
His hands securely keep.

3 Nor death, nor hell, shall e'er remove
His favourites from his breast ;
In the dear bosom of his love
They must for ever rest.

355   C.M.   HART.

"Let God be true and every man a liar."—Rom. iii. 4.

THE God I trust is true and just ;
  His mercy has no end ;
Himself has said my ransom's paid,
  And I on him depend.

2 Then why so sad, my soul ? though bad,
  Thou hast a Friend that's good ;
He bought thee dear (abandon fear) ;
  He bought thee with his blood.

3 So rich a cost can ne'er be lost,
  Though faith be tried by fire ;
Keep Christ in view ; let God be true ;
  And every man a liar.

356   7s.   NEWTON.

Rest for Weary Souls.—Matt. xi. 28; Gen. viii. 9.

DOES the gospel-word proclaim
Rest for those who weary be ?
Then, my soul, put in thy claim ;
Sure that promise speaks to thee.
Marks of grace I cannot show ;
All polluted is my breast ;
Yet I weary am, I know,
And the weary long for rest.

2 Burdened with a load of sin ;
Harassed with tormenting doubt ;
Hourly conflicts from within ;
Hourly crosses from without ;
All my little strength is gone ;
Sink I must without supply ;
Sure upon the earth there's none
Can more weary be than I.

3 In the ark the weary dove
Found a welcome resting-place ;
Thus my spirit longs to prove
Rest in Christ, the Ark of grace.
Tempest-tossed I long have been,
And the flood increases fast ;
Open, Lord, and take me in,
Till the storm be overpast.

357   S.M.   WATTS.

The Lord's Day.—Ps. lxxxiv. 1-10; Matt. xviii. 20.

WELCOME, sweet day of rest,
  That saw the Lord arise ;
Welcome to this reviving breast,
  And these rejoicing eyes.

2 The King himself comes near,
  And feasts his saints to-day ;
Here we may sit and see him here,
  And love, and praise, and pray.

3 One day amidst the place
  Where my dear God has been,

Is sweeter than ten thousand days
  Of pleasurable sin.

4 My willing soul would stay
  In such a frame as this,
And sit and sing herself away
  To everlasting bliss.

358   8.8.6.   HART.

The Sabbath.—Deut. v. 14, 15; Exod. xx. 8-11.

GOD thus commanded Jacob's seed,
When, from Egyptian-bondage freed,
  He led them by the way :
" Remember, with a mighty hand
I brought thee forth from Pharaoh's land ;
  Then keep my Sabbath Day."

2 [In six days God made heaven and earth
Gave all the various creatures birth,
  And from his working ceased ;
These days to labour he applied ;
The seventh he blessed and sanctified.
  And called the day of rest.]

3 To all God's people now remains
A Sabbatism, a rest from pains,
  And works of slavish kind ;
When tired with toil, and faint thro' fear,
The child of God can enter here,
  And sweet refreshment find.

4 To this, by faith, he oft retreats ;
Bondage and labour quite forgets,
  And bids his cares adieu ;
Slides softly into promised rest,
Reclines his head on Jesus' breast,
  And proves the Sabbath true.

5 [This, and this only, is the way
To rightly keep the Sabbath Day,
  Which God has holy made.
All keepers that come short of this,
The substance of the Sabbath miss,
  And grasp an empty shade.]

359   S.M.   S. STENNETT.

Worship.—Ps. lxxxiv. 1, 2.

How charming is the place,
  Where my Redeemer, God,
Unveils the beauties of his face,
  And sheds his love abroad !

2 Not the fair palaces
  To which the great resort,
Are once to be compared to this,
  Where Jesus holds his court.

3 Here, on the mercy-seat,
  With radiant glory crowned,
Our joyful eyes behold him sit,
  And smile on all around.

4 [To him their prayers and cries
Each humble soul presents ;
He listens to their broken sighs,
And grants them all their wants.

5 To them his sovereign will
He graciously imparts ;
And in return accepts with smiles,
The tribute of their hearts.]

6 Give me, O Lord, a place
Within thy blest abode,
Among the children of thy grace,
The servants of my God.

360 L.M. WATTS.
The Church the birth-place of the saints.—Ps. lxxxvii.

GOD in his earthly temples lays
Foundations for his heavenly praise ;
He likes the tents of Jacob well,
But still in Zion loves to dwell.

2 His mercy visits every house,
That pay their night and morning vows ;
But makes a more delightful stay
Where churches meet to praise and pray.

3 What glories were described of old !
What wonders are of Zion told !
Thou city of our God below,
Thy fame shall Tyre and Egypt know.

4 Egypt and Tyre, and Greek and Jew,
Shall there begin their lives anew ;
Angels and men shall join to sing
The hill where living waters spring.

5 When God makes up his last account
Of natives in his holy mount,
'Twill be an honour to appear
As one new-born or nourished there.

361 C.M. WATTS.
The Church.—Ps.c. 4 ; cxxii.

How did' my heart rejoice to hear
My friends devoutly say,
" In Zion let us all appear,
And keep the solemn day " !

2 I love her gates ; I love the road ;
The church, adorned with grace,
Stands like a palace built for God
To show his milder face.

3 Up to her courts, with joys unknown,
The holy tribes repair ;
The Son of David holds his throne,
And sits in judgment there.

4 He hears our praises and complaints,
And, while his awful voice

Divides the sinners from the saints,
We tremble and rejoice.

5 Peace be within this sacred place,
And joy a constant guest ;
With holy gifts and heavenly grace,
Be her attendants blest.

6 My soul shall pray for Zion still,
While life or breath remains ;
There my best friends, my kindred dwell ;
There God my Saviour reigns.

362 122nd. WATTS.
The Church.—Psalm cxxii. 1-7 ; Zech. viii. 21.

How pleased and blest was I,
To hear the people cry,
" Come, let us seek our God to-day ! "
Yes, with a cheerful zeal,
We haste to Zion's hill,
And there our vows and honours pay.

2 Zion, thrice happy place !
Adorned with wondrous grace,
And walls of strength embrace thee round ;
In thee our tribes appear,
To pray, and praise, and hear
The sacred gospel's joyful sound.

3 There David's greater Son
Has fixed his royal throne ;
He sits for grace and judgment there.
He bids the saints be glad ;
He makes the sinner sad,
And humble souls rejoice with fear.

4 May peace attend thy gate,
And joy within thee wait,
To bless the soul of every guest ;
The man that seeks thy peace,
And wishes thy increase,
A thousand blessings on him rest.

5 My tongue repeats her vows,
" Peace to this sacred house,"
For there my friends and kindred dwell ;
And since my glorious God
Makes thee his blest abode,
My soul shall ever love thee well.

363 L.M. WATTS.
The Church the garden of Christ.—Song iv. 12-15 ; v. 1.

WE are a garden walled around,
Chosen and made peculiar ground ;
A little spot enclosed by grace, .
Out of the world's wide wilderness.

2 Like trees of myrrh and spice we stand,
Planted by God the Father's hand ;
And all his springs in Zion flow
To make the young plantation grow.

3 Awake, O heavenly wind, and come,
  Blow on this garden of perfume ;
  Spirit divine, descend and breathe
  A gracious gale on plants beneath.

4 Make our best spices flow abroad,
  To entertain our Saviour, God ;
  And faith, and love, and joy appear,
  And every grace be active here.

5 [Let my Beloved come and taste
  His pleasant fruits at his own feast.
  " I come, my spouse, I come," he cries,
  With love and pleasure in his eyes.]

6 [Our Lord into his garden comes,
  Well pleased to smell our poor perfumes ;
  And calls us to a feast divine,
  Sweeter than honey, milk, or wine :

7 " Eat of the tree of life, my friends ;
  The blessings that my Father sends ;
  Your taste shall all my dainties prove,
  And drink abundance of my love."]

8 [Jesus, we will frequent thy board,
  And sing the bounties of our Lord ;
  But the rich food on which we live
  Demands more praise than tongue can give.]

364   L.M.   WATTS.
God the Glory and Defence of Zion.—Isa. lx. 18-21.
HAPPY the church, thou sacred place ;
  The seat of thy Creator's grace ;
  Thy holy courts are his abode,
  Thou earthly palace of our God.

2 Thy walls are strength, and at thy gates
  A guard of heavenly warriors waits ;
  Nor shall thy deep foundations move,
  Fixed on his counsels and his love.

3 Thy foes in vain designs engage ;
  Against his throne in vain they rage :
  Like rising waves with angry roar,
  That dash and die upon the shore.

4 Then let our souls in Zion dwell,
  Nor fear the wrath of men or hell ;
  His arms embrace this happy ground,
  Like brazen bulwarks built around.

5 God is our Shield, and God our Sun ;
  Swift as the fleeting moments run ;
  On us he sheds new beams of grace,
  And we reflect his brightest praise.

365   L.M.   WATTS.
At the Settlement of a Church.—Ps. cxxxii. 5, 13-18.
WHERE shall we go to seek and find
  A habitation for our God ;

A dwelling for the Eternal Mind,
  Amongst the sons of flesh and blood ?

2 The God of Jacob chose the hill
  Of Zion, for his ancient rest ;
  And Zion is his dwelling still ;
  His church is with his presence blessed.

3 " Here will I fix my gracious throne,
  And reign for ever," says the Lord ;
  " Here shall my power and love be known,
  And blessings shall attend my word.

4 " Here I will meet the hungry poor,
  And fill their souls with living bread ;
  Sinners that wait before my door,
  With sweet provisions shall be fed.

5 " Girded with truth, and full of grace,
  My priests, my ministers shall shine ;
  Not Aaron, in his costly dress,
  Made an appearance so divine.

6 " The saints, unable to contain
  Their inward joys, shall shout and sing,
  The Son of David here shall reign,
  And Zion triumph in her King."

366   C.M.   WATTS.
The Church the Dwelling of God.—Ps. cxxxii. 5-15.
[THE Lord in Zion placed his name ;
  His ark was settled there ;
  To Zion the whole nation came
  To worship thrice a year.

2 But we have no such lengths to go,
  Nor wander far abroad ;
  Where'er thy saints assemble now,
  There is a house for God.]

3 Arise, O King of grace, arise,
  And enter to thy rest ;
  Lo ! thy church waits with longing eyes,
  Thus to be owned and blessed.

4 Enter with all thy glorious train,
  Thy Spirit and thy Word ;
  All that the ark did once contain,
  Could no such grace afford.

5 Here, mighty God ! accept our songs ;
  Here let thy praise be spread ;
  Bless the provisions of thy house,
  And fill thy poor with bread.

6 Here let the Son of David reign ;
  Let God's anointed shine ;
  Justice and truth his court maintain,
  With love and power divine.

7 Here let him hold a lasting throne,
  And as his kingdom grows,
  Fresh honours shall adorn his crown,
  And shame confound his foes.

367　　C.M.　　MEDLEY.
On opening a new Place of Worship.—Zech. viii. 7-9.

GREAT God ! thy glory and thy love
　Our humble songs employ ;
Propitious from thy throne above,
　Look down, and aid our joy.

2 Thy presence and thy glories, Lord,
　Fill all the realms of space ;
O let thy presence, by thy word,
　Divinely fill this place.

3 Sacred to thy eternal name,
　Behold, these walls we raise ;
Long may they stand to show thy fame,
　And echo to thy praise.

4 This day begins the solemn sound
　Of sacred worship here ;
May every saint with joy abound,
　And reverential fear.

5 Dear Jesus ! Zion's holy King,
　Enter with all thy train,
And here thy choicest blessings bring,
　And long may they remain.

6 Eternal Spirit ! heavenly Dove !
　Enter and fill this place ;
Reveal Immanuel's matchless love
　And open all his grace.

368　　L.M.　　DODDRIDGE.
The same.—Ps. xxxvi. 8.

O LORD, descend and fill this place
With choicest tokens of thy grace !
These walls we to thy honour raise ;
Long may they echo with thy praise.

2 Here let the great Redeemer reign,
With all the graces of his train ;
While power divine his word attends,
To conquer foes and cheer his friends.

369　　L.M.　　WATTS.
The Pleasure of Public Worship.—Ps. lxxxiv. 1-10.

How pleasant, how divinely fair,
O Lord of Hosts, thy dwellings are !
With long desire my spirit faints,
To meet the assemblies of thy saints.

2 Blest are the saints who sit on high,
Around the throne of majesty ;
Thy brightest glories shine above,
And all their work is praise and love.

3 Blest are the souls that find a place
Within the temple of thy grace ;
There they behold thy gentler rays,
And seek thy face, and learn thy praise.

4 Blest are the men whose hearts are set

To find the way to Zion's gate ;
God is their strength, and through the road
They lean upon their helper, God.

370　　L.M.　　WATTS.
Grace and Glory.—Ps. lxxxiv. 1, 8-12 ; Jer. xvii. 7.

GREAT God ! attend, while Zion sings
The joy that from thy presence springs ;
To spend one day with thee on earth,
Exceeds a thousand days of mirth.

2 God is our Sun, he makes our day ;
God is our Shield, he guards our way
From all the assaults of hell and sin,
From foes without, and foes within.

3 All needful grace will God bestow,
And crown that grace with glory too ;
He gives us all things, and withholds
No real good from upright souls.

4 O God, our King, whose sovereign sway
The glorious hosts in heaven obey ;
And devils at thy presence flee ;
Blest is the man who trusts in thee.

371　　122nd.　　SWAIN.
Social Worship.—Ps. ix. 11 ; lxvi. 16.

How pleasant is the gate
　Where willing converts wait
For fellowship with Zion here ;
　Where they with wonder tell
　How they escaped from hell,
And hope in glory to appear.

2　With wonder we attend,
　While they the Sinner's Friend,
With tears of holy joy, extol ;
　Each heart, once hard as steel,
　Now made for sin to feel,
Bears tokens of a ransomed soul.

3　No more of self they boast,
　But humbly own the cost
Of their salvation freely paid ;
　The sins which make them groan,
　And must have sunk them down,
They now behold on Jesus laid.

372　　8.7.　　NEWTON.
Zion.—Ps. lxxxvii. 3 ; Isa. xxxiii. 20, 21 ; xxvi. 1.

GLORIOUS things of thee are spoken,
　Zion, city of our God !
He whose word can not be broken,
　Formed thee for his own abode ;
On the Rock of Ages founded,
　What can shake thy sure repose ?
With salvation's walls surrounded,
　Thou may'st smile at all thy foes.

2 See ! the streams of living waters,
　　Springing from eternal love,
Well supply thy sons and daughters,
　　And all fear of want remove.
Who can faint while such a river
　　Ever flows their thirst to assuage ?
Grace, which, like the Lord, the giver,
　　Never fails from age to age.

3 Round each habitation hovering,
　　See the cloud and fire appear,
For a glory and a covering,
　　Showing that the Lord is near.
Thus deriving from their banner,
　　Light by night and shade by day,
Safe they feed upon the manna
　　Which he gives them when they pray.

4 Bless'd inhabitants of Zion,
　　Washed in the Redeemer's blood !
Jesus, whom their souls rely on,
　　Makes them kings and priests to God
'Tis his love his people raises
　　Over self to reign as kings ;
And as priests, his solemn praises
　　Each for a thank-offering brings.

373　　L.M.　　SEAGRAVE ( ).
Prayer for a Minister.—2 Thess. iii. 1, 2; Heb. xiii. 13

WITH heavenly power, O Lord, defend
Him whom we now to thee commend ;
His person bless, his soul secure ;
And make him to the end endure.

2 Gird him with all-sufficient grace ;
Direct his feet in paths of peace ;
Thy truth and faithfulness fulfil,
And help him to obey thy will.

3 Before him thy protection send ;
O love him, save him to the end !
Nor let him as thy pilgrim rove
Without the convoy of thy love.

4 Enlarge, inflame, and fill his heart ;
In him thy mighty power exert ;
That thousands, yet unborn, may praise
The wonders of redeeming grace.

374　　148th.　　BERRIDGE.
Prayer for increase of faithful Ministers.—Mat. ix. 38.

SEND help, O Lord, we pray,
　　And thy own gospel bless ;
For godly men decay,
　　And faithful pastors cease ;
The righteous are removéd home,
And scorners rise up in their room.

2 While Satan's troops are bold,
　　And thrive in number too,
The flocks in Jesus' fold,
　　Are growing lank and few ;
Old sheep are moving off each year,
And few lambs in the fold appear.

3 Old shepherds, too, retire,
　　Who gathered flocks below,
And young ones catch no fire,
　　Or worldly-prudent grow ;
Few run with trumpets in their hand,
To sound alarms by sea and land.

4 O Lord, stir up thy power,
　　To make the gospel spread ;
And thrust out preachers more,
　　With voice to raise the dead ;
With feet to run where thou dost call ;
With faith to fight and conquer all.

5 [The flocks that long have dwelt
　　Around fair Zion's hill,
And thy sweet grace have felt,
　　Uphold and feed them still ;
But fresh folds build up everywhere,
And plenteously thy truth declare.]

6 As one Elijah dies,
　　True prophet of the Lord,
Let some Elisha rise
　　To blaze the gospel-word ;
And fast as sheep to Jesus go,
May lambs recruit his fold below.

This hymn was occasioned by the death of Whitefield.

375　　C.M.　　BERRIDGE.
On a Christian Marriage.—John ii. 1, 2; Heb. xiii. 4.

OUR Jesus freely did appear
　　To grace a marriage feast ;
And, Lord, we ask thy presence here
　　To make a wedding-guest.

2 Upon the bridal pair look down ;
　　Who now have plighted hands ;
Their union with thy favour crown,
　　And bless the nuptial bands.

3 With gifts of grace their hearts endow ;
　　(Of all rich dowries best !)
Their substance bless, and peace bestow,
　　To sweeten all the rest.

4 In purest love their souls unite,
　　And linked in kindly care,
To render family burdens light,
　　By taking mutual share.

5 True helpers may they prove indeed,
　　In prayer, and faith, and hope ;
And see with joy a godly seed,
　　To build thy household up.

6 As Isaac and Rebecca give
　　A pattern chaste and kind ;
　So may this new-met couple live,
　　In faithful friendship joined.

376　　　7s.　　　NEWTON.
" I will not let thee go, except thou bless me."
　LORD, I cannot let thee go,
　Till a blessing thou bestow ;
　Do not turn away thy face ;
　Mine's an urgent, pressing case.

2 [Dost thou ask me who I am ?
　Ah, my Lord, thou know'st my name ;
　Yet the question gives a plea,
　To support my suit with thee.]

3 Thou didst once a wretch behold,
　In rebellion blindly bold ;
　Scorn thy grace ; thy power defy ;
　That poor rebel, Lord, was I.

4 Once a sinner near despair
　Sought thy mercy-seat by prayer ;
　Mercy heard and set him free ;
　Lord, that mercy came to me.

5 Many days have passed since then ;
　Many changes I have seen ;
　Yet have been upheld till now ;
　Who could hold me up but thou ?

6 Thou hast helped in every need ;
　This emboldens me to plead ;
　After so much mercy past,
　Canst thou let me sink at last ?

7 No ; I must maintain my hold ;
　'Tis thy goodness makes me bold ;
　I can no denial take,
　When I plead for Jesus' sake.

377　　　L.M.　　　MEDLEY.
Encouragement to pray.—Isa. xlv. 19-25 ; Ps. ix. 10.
　MY soul, take courage from the Lord ;
　Believe and plead his holy word ;
　To him alone do thou complain,
　Nor shalt thou seek his face in vain.

2 Upon him call in humble prayer,
　Thou still art his peculiar care ;
　He'll surely turn and smile again,
　Nor shalt thou seek his face in vain.

3 However sinful, weak, and poor,
　Still wait and pray at mercy's door ;
　Faithful Jehovah must remain,
　Nor shalt thou seek his face in vain.

4 [Though the vile tempter's hellish rage
　Will, with his darts, thy soul engage,

God through the fight shall thee sustain,
Nor shalt thou seek his face in vain.]

5 [Though the corruptions of thy heart
　Daily new cause of grief impart,
　Pray that thy lusts may all be slain,
　Nor shalt thou seek his face in vain.]

6 [Though sharp afflictions still abound,
　And clouds and darkness thee surround,
　Still pray, for God will all explain,
　Nor shalt thou seek his face in vain.]

7 In him, and him alone, confide ;
　Still at the throne of grace abide ;
　Eternal victory thou shalt gain,
　Nor shalt thou seek his face in vain.

378　　　C.M.　　　MEDLEY.
The Beggar's Prayer.—Matt. viii. 2 ; Mark i. 40.
　A BEGGAR poor, at mercy's door,
　　Lies such a wretch as I ;

　Thou know'st my need is great indeed ,
　　Lord, hear me when I cry.

2 With guilt beset, and deep in debt,
　　For pardon, Lord, I pray ;
　O let thy love sufficient prove
　　To take my sins away.

3 A wicked heart is no small part
　　Of my distress and shame ;
　Let sovereign grace its crimes efface,
　　Through Jesus' blessed name.

4 [My darkened mind, I daily find,
　　Is prone to go astray ;
　Lord, on it shine, with light divine,
　　And guide it in thy way.]

5 [My stubborn will opposes still
　　Thy wise and holy hand ;
　Thy Spirit send to make it bend
　　To thy supreme command.]

6 Affections wild, by sin defiled,
　　Oft hurry me away ;
　Lord, bring them home, nor let them roam
　　From Christ, the Living Way.

7 [A conscience hard does oft retard
　　My walk in holy peace ;
　Let it by thee made tender be,
　　And all its hardness cease.]

8 [My memory bad, but what is sad,
　　Can folly still retain ;
　O fill it, Lord, with thy sweet word,
　　And let it there remain.]

9 Before thy face I've told my case ;
　　Lord, help, and mercy send ;
　Pity my soul, and make me whole,
　　And love me to the end.

379   7s.   NEWTON.
" Ask what I shall give thee."—1 Kings iii. 5.

COME, my soul, thy suit prepare,
Jesus loves to answer prayer ;
He himself has bid thee pray,
Therefore will not say thee, Nay.

2 [Thou art coming to a King ;
Large petitions with thee bring ;
For his grace and power are such,
None can ever ask too much.

3 With my burden I begin ;
Lord, remove this load of sin ;
Let thy blood, for sinners spilt,
Set my conscience free from guilt.]

4 Lord, I come to thee for rest ;
Take possession of my breast ;
There thy blood-bought right maintain,
And without a rival reign.

5 As the image in the glass
Answers the beholder's face,
Thus unto my heart appear ;
Print thy own resemblance there.

6 While I am a pilgrim here,
Let thy love my spirit cheer ;
As my Guide, my Guard, my Friend,
Lead me to my journey's end.

7 Show me what I have to do ;
Every hour my strength renew ;
Let me live a life of faith ;
Let me die thy people's death.

380   8s.   BURNHAM.
Praying for Confidence.—Mark ix. 23, 24.

O JESUS, thou fountain of grace,
Enlighten, enliven my heart,
And show the sweet smiles of thy face
And from me bid evil depart ;

Pronounce, O pronounce I am thine ;
A sinner once purchased by blood ;
And may I for ever recline
On the bosom of Jesus, my Lord.

2 Thou great and compassionate King,
Drive all my sad doubtings away ;
And let me with confidence sing,
" The Saviour expired for me."
The witness that I am thy child,
O Jesus, to me now impart ;
The pleasing sensation will yield
Unspeakable joy to my heart.

3 Bestow this rich blessing on me,
And heaven below I shall prove ;
I'll then go exulting in thee,
And tell of thy wonderful love.
Lord, teach me thy cause to maintain ;

For constant support to thee fly ;
And fight till the conquest I gain.
Resolved for thy glory to die.

381   L.M.   COWPER.
The House of Prayer.—Mark xi. 17 ; 1 Cor. iii. 16, 17.

THY mansion is the Christian's heart,
O Lord, thy dwelling-place secure !
Bid the unruly throng depart,
And leave the consecrated door.

2 Devoted as it is to thee,
A thievish swarm frequents the place ;
They steal away my joys from me,
And rob my Saviour of his praise.

3 There, too, a sharp designing trade,
Sin, Satan, and the world maintain ;
Nor cease to press me, and persuade
To part with ease and purchase pain.

4 I know them, and I hate their din ;
Am weary of the bustling crowd ;
But while their voice is heard within,
I cannot serve thee as I would.

5 O for the joy thy presence gives ;
What peace shall reign when thou art here ;
Thy presence makes this den of thieves
A calm, delightful house of prayer.

6 And if thou make thy temple shine,
Yet, self-abased, will I adore ;
The gold and silver are not mine ;
I give thee what was thine before.

382   C.M.   MEDLEY.
The Throne of Grace.—Heb. iv. 16 ; x. 19-22.

DEAR Lord ! to us assembled here
Reveal thy smiling face,
While we, by faith, with love and fear,
Approach the throne of grace.

2 Thy house is called the house of prayer,
A solemn sacred place ;
O let us now thy presence share,
While at the throne of grace.

3 With holy boldness may we come,
Though of a sinful race,
Thankful to find there yet is room
Before the throne of grace.

4 Our earnest, fervent cry attend,
And all our faith increase,
While we address our heavenly Friend
Upon the throne of grace.

5 [His tender pity and his love
Our every fear will chase ;
And all our help, we then shall prove,
Comes from the throne of grace.]

6 Dear Lord, our many wants supply ;
　Attend to every case ;
　While humbled in the dust we lie,
　Low at the throne of grace.

7 We bless thee for thy word and laws ;
　We bless thee for thy peace ;
　And we do bless thee, Lord, because
　There is a throne of grace.

383   C.M.   MEDLEY.
The Ground and Foundation of Prayer.—Heb. vii. 25.

WHEREWITH shall we approach the Lord,
　And bow before his throne ?
By trusting in his faithful word,
　And pleading Christ alone.

2 The blood, the righteousness, and love
　Of Jesus, will we plead ;
　He lives within the vail above,
　For us to intercede.

3 Sure ground, and sure foundation too,
　We find in Jesus' name ;
　Herein we every blessing view,
　And every favour claim.

4 Then let his name for ever be
　To us supremely dear ;
　Our only, all-prevailing plea,
　For all our hope is there.

5 This is the name the Father loves
　To hear his children plead ;
　And all such pleading he approves,
　And blesses them indeed.

384   L.M.   MEDLEY.
"O save me for thy mercies' sake."—Ps. vi. 2-4.

REGARD, great God ! my mournful prayer ;
Make my poor trembling soul thy care ;
For me in pity undertake,
And save me for thy mercies' sake.

2 [My soul's cast down within me, Lord,
And only thou canst help afford ;
Let not my heart with sorrow break,
But save me for thy mercies' sake.]

3 Such dismal storms are raised within,
By Satan and indwelling sin,
Which all my soul with horror shake ;
O save me for thy mercies' sake.

4 [I've foes and fears of every shape,
Nor from them can my soul escape ;
Upon me, Lord, some pity take,
And save me for thy mercies' sake.]

5 [I've scarce a glimmering ray of light ;
With me 'tis little else but night ;
O for my help do thou awake,

And save me for thy mercies' sake.]

6 To me, dear Saviour, turn once more ;
To my poor soul thy joys restore ;
Let me again thy smiles partake.
Lord, save me for thy mercies' sake.

385   L.M.   MEDLEY.
"God be merciful to me a sinner."—Luke xviii. 13.

HEAR, gracious God, a sinner's cry,
For I have nowhere else to fly ;
My hope, my only hope's in thee ;
O God, be merciful to me !

2 [To thee I come, a sinner poor,
And wait for mercy at thy door ;
Indeed, I've nowhere else to flee ;
O God, be merciful to me !]

3 [To thee I come, a sinner weak,
And scarce know how to pray or speak ;

From fear and weakness set me free ;
O God, be merciful to me !]

4 [To thee I come, a sinner vile ;
Upon me, Lord, vouchsafe to smile ;
Mercy, through blood, I make my plea ;
O God, be merciful to me !]

5 [To thee I come, a sinner great,
And well thou knowest all my state ;
Yet full forgiveness is with thee ;
O God, be merciful to me !]

6 To thee I come, a sinner lost,
Nor have I aught wherein to trust ;
But where thou art, Lord, I would be ;
O God, be merciful to me !

7 To glory bring me, Lord, at last,
And there, when all my fears are past,
With all thy saints I'll then agree,
God has been merciful to me !

386   C.M.   MEDLEY.
Desiring Rest and Peace.—Job iii. 17.

WEARY of earth, myself, and sin,
　Dear Jesus, set me free,
And to thy glory take me in,
　For there I long to be.

2 Burdened, dejected, and oppressed,
　Ah ! whither shall I flee
But to thy arms, for peace and rest ?
　For there I long to be.

3 Empty, polluted, dark, and vain,
　Is all this world to me ;
May I the better world obtain ;
　For there I long to be.

4 Lord, let a tempest-tossed soul
　That peaceful harbour see,

Where waves and billows never roll ;
　For there I long to be.

5 Let a poor labourer here below,
　When from his toil set free,
To rest and peace eternal go ;
　For there I long to be.

387　　L.M.　　SWAIN.

Sweetness of waiting at throne of grace.—Ps. cxix. 103.

How sweet to wait upon the Lord,
While he fulfils his gracious word ;
To seek his face, and not in vain,
To be beloved, and love again !

2 To see, while prostrate at his feet,
Jehovah on the mercy-seat ;
And Jesus, at the Lord's right hand,
With his divine atonement stand !

3 " Father," he cries, " I will that these
Before thee on their bended knees,
For whom my life I once laid down,
Be with me soon on this my throne."

4 Amen ! our hearts with rapture cry,
May we with reverence look so high ;
Ascended Saviour, fix our eyes,
By faith upon this glorious prize !

5 With this delightful prospect fired,
We'll run, nor in thy ways be tired ;
And all the trials here we see,
Will make us long to reign with thee.

388　　C.M.　　NEWTON.

An approach to the Mercy-Seat.—Ps. xxxii. 5-7.

APPROACH, my soul, the mercy-seat,
Where Jesus answers prayer ;
There humbly fall before his feet,
For none can perish there.

2 Thy promise is my only plea ;
With this I venture nigh ;
Thou callest burdened souls to thee,
And such, O Lord, am I.

3 Bowed down beneath a load of sin ;
By Satan sorely pressed ;
By wars without, and fears within,
I come to thee for rest.

4 Be thou my shield and hiding-place,
That, sheltered near thy side,
I may my fierce accuser face,
And tell him thou hast died.

5 [O wondrous love ! to bleed and die ;
To bear the cross and shame ;
That guilty sinners such as I,
Might plead thy gracious name.]

6 [" Poor tempest-tossed soul, be still ;
My promised grace receive ;

I'll work in thee both power and will ;
Thou shalt in me believe."]

389　　7s.　　ADAMS.

Drawn by Divine Love.—Song i. 4 ; John vi. 44.

DRAW my soul to thee, my Lord ;
Make me love thy precious word !
Bid me seek thy smiling face ;
Willing to be saved by grace.

2 Dearest Jesus, bid me come ;
Let me find thyself my home ;
Thou the Refuge of my soul,
Where I may my troubles roll.

3 Lord, thy powerful work begun,
Thou wilt never leave undone ;
Teach me to confide in thee ;
Thy salvation's wholly free.

390　　7.6.8.　　C.W.
　　　　　　　　Isa. liii. 6.

Praying for Restoration.—Luke xxii. 61, 62:

JESUS, let thy pitying eye
　Call back a wandering sheep ;
False to thee, like Peter, I
　Would fain like Peter, weep ;
Let me be by grace restored ;
On me be all its freeness shown ;
　Turn, and look upon me, Lord,
　And break my heart of stone.

2 Saviour, Prince, enthroned above,
　Repentance to impart,
Give me, through thy dying love,
　The humble, contrite heart.
Give, what I have long implored,
A portion of thy love unknown,
　Turn, and look upon me, Lord,
　And break my heart of stone.

3 Look as when thy pitying eye
　Was closed, that we might live ;
" Father," (at the point to die,
　My Saviour gasped), " forgive ! "
Surely, with that dying word,
He turns, and looks, and cries, " 'Tis done."
　O my loving, bleeding Lord,
　This breaks the heart of stone.

391　　7.6.8.　　C.W.

The same.—Hos. xiv. 4 ; Jer. xiv. 7.

JESUS, Friend of sinners, hear
　A feeble creature pray ;
From my debt of sin set clear,
　For I have nought to pay.
Speak, O speak my kind release ,
A poor backsliding soul restore ;
　Love me freely, seal my peace,
　And let me rove no more.

2 [Though my sins as mountains rise,
    And swell, and reach to heaven,
  Mercy is above the skies,
    And I shall stand forgiven.
  Mighty is my guilt's increase,
  But greater is thy mercy's store !
    Love me freely, &c.]

3 From the oppressive weight of sin,
    My struggling spirit free ;
  Blood and righteousness divine
    Can rescue even me.
  Holy Spirit, shed thy grace,
  And let me feel the softening shower ;
    Love me freely, &c.

392 C.M. STEELE.
Confession.—Jer. iii. 12 : Ps. cxix. 176 ; Hos. vi. 1.

  How oft, alas, this wretched heart
    Has wandered from the Lord,
  How oft my roving thoughts depart,
    Forgetful of his word !

2 Yet sovereign mercy calls, " Return ! "
    Dear Lord, and may I come ?
  My vile ingratitude I mourn ;
    O take the wanderer home.

3 And canst thou, wilt thou yet forgive,
    And bid my crimes remove ?
  And shall a pardoned rebel live,
    To speak thy wondrous love ?

4 Almighty grace, thy healing power
    How glorious, how divine !
  That can to life and bliss restore
    So vile a heart as mine !

5 Thy pardoning love, so free, so sweet,
    Dear Saviour, I adore ;
  O keep me at thy sacred feet,
    And let me rove no more.

393 C.M. FAWCETT.
Craving a Crumb of Mercy.—Mat. xv. 27 ; Lu. xviii. 39

  A CRUMB of mercy, Lord, I crave,
    Unworthy to be fed
  With dainties such as angels have,
    Or with the children's bread.

2 Have pity on my needy soul ;
    Thy peace and pardon give ;
  Thy love can make the wounded whole,
    And bid the dying live.

3 Behold me prostrate at thy gate ;
    Do not my suit deny ;
  With longing eyes for thee I wait ;
    O help me, or I die.

4 When thou dost give a heart to pray,
    Thou wilt incline thy ear ;
  From me turn not thy face away,
    But my petition hear.

5 So shall my joyful soul adore
    The riches of thy grace ;
  No sinner needed mercy more,
    That ever sought thy face.

394 L.M. COWPER.
Exhortation to Prayer.—1 Thess. v. 17.

  WHAT various hindrances we meet,
  In coming to the mercy-seat !
  Yet who that knows the worth of prayer,
  But wishes to be often there ?

2 Prayer makes the darkened cloud withdraw,
  Prayer climbs the ladder Jacob saw ;
  Gives exercise to faith and love ;
  Brings every blessing from above.

3 Restraining prayer, we cease to fight ;
  Prayer makes the Christian's armour bright ;
  And Satan trembles when he sees
  The weakest saint upon his knees.

4 [While Moses stood with arms spread wide,
  Success was found on Israel's side ;
  But when, through weariness, they failed,
  That moment Amalek prevailed.]

5 [Have you no words ? ah ! think again ;
  Words flow apace when you complain,
  And fill your fellow-creatures' ear
  With the sad tale of all your care.

6 Were half the breath thus vainly spent,
  To heaven in supplication sent,
  Your cheerful song would oftener be,
  " Hear what the Lord has done for me."]

395 S.M. NEWTON.
The Throne of Grace.—Heb. iv. 16 ; John xiv. 13, 14.

  BEHOLD the Throne of grace !
    The promise calls me near ;
  There Jesus shows his smiling face ;
    And waits to answer prayer.

2 That rich atoning blood
    Which, sprinkled round, I see,
  Provides for those who come to God
    An all-prevailing plea.

3 My soul, ask what thou wilt,
    Thou canst not be too bold ;
  Since his own blood for thee he spilt,
    What else can he withhold ?

4 Beyond thy utmost wants
    His love and power can bless.
  To praying souls he always grants
    More than they can express.

396   8.7.   NEWTON.
The Prayer of Necessity.—Ps. xci. 15, 16; Heb. iv. 16.

COULD the creatures help or ease us,
  Seldom should we think of prayer;
Few, if any, come to Jesus,
  Till reduced to self-despair.
Long we either slight or doubt him,
  But, when all the means we try
Prove we cannot do without him,
  Then at last to him we cry.

2 Fear thou not, distressed believer;
  Venture on his mighty name;
He is able to deliver,
  And his love is still the same.
Can his pity or his power
  Suffer thee to pray in vain?
Wait but his appointed hour,
  And thy suit thou shalt obtain.

397   7s.   NEWTON.
The Power of Prayer.—Ps. l. 15; Jas. v. 16-18.

IN themselves as weak as worms,
How can poor believers stand,
When temptations, foes, and storms,
Press them close on every hand?

2 Weak, indeed, they feel they are,
But they know the Throne of Grace;
And the God who answers prayer,
Helps them when they seek his face.

3 Though the Lord awhile delay,
Succour they at length obtain;
He who taught their hearts to pray,
Will not let them cry in vain.

4 Wrestling prayer can wonders do;
Bring relief in deepest straits!

Prayer can force a passage through
Iron bars and brazen gates.

5 For the wonders he has wrought,
Let us now our praises give;
And, by sweet experience taught,
Call upon him while we live.

398   C.M.   NEWTON.
Worship.—Ps. lxxx. 1, 2.

DEAR Shepherd of thy people, here
Thy presence now display;
As thou hast given a place for prayer,
So give us hearts to pray.

2 Show us some token of thy love,
Our fainting hope to raise;
And pour thy blessings from above,
That we may render praise.

3 Within these walls let holy peace,
  And love, and concord dwell;
Here give the troubled conscience ease;
  The wounded spirit heal.

4 May we in faith receive thy word,
  In faith present our prayers,
And, in the presence of our Lord,
  Unbosom all our cares.

5 And may the gospel's joyful sound,
  Enforced by mighty grace,
Awaken many sinners round,
  To come and fill the place.

399   L.M.   TUCKER.
Praying for Christ to be revealed.—2 Cor. iv. 6.

AMIDST ten thousand anxious cares,
The world and Satan's deep-laid snares,
This my incessant cry shall be,
Jesus, reveal thyself to me.

2 When Sinai's awful thunder rolled,
And struck with terror all my soul,
No gleam of comfort could I see,
Till Jesus was revealed to me.

3 When by temptations sore oppressed,
Distressful anguish fills my breast!
All, all is grief and misery,
Till Jesus is revealed to me.

4 When various lusts imperious rise,
And my unguarded soul surprise;
I'm captive led, nor can get free,
Till Christ reveals himself to me.

5 When darkness, thick as beamless night,
Hides the loved Saviour from my sight,
Nothing but this my ardent plea,
Jesus, reveal thyself to me.

6 'Tis he dispels the dismal gloom;
Gives light and gladness in its room;
Then have I joy and liberty
As Christ reveals himself to me.

400   7s.   NEWTON.
Prayer for Spring.—Song ii. 10-13; iv. 16.

LORD, afford a spring to me;
Let me feel like what I see;
Ah! my winter has been long!
Chilled my hopes and stopped my song.
Winter threatens to destroy
Faith, and love, and every joy;
If thy life was in the root,
Still I could not yield thee fruit.

2 Speak, and by thy gracious voice
Make my drooping soul rejoice;
O, beloved Saviour, haste,
Tell me all the storms are past!

On thy garden deign to smile ;
Raise the plants, enrich the soil ;
Soon thy presence will restore
Life to what seemed dead before.

401   L.M.   WATTS.
Hope in Darkness.—Ps. xiii.; Job xiii. 24.

How long, O Lord, shall I complain
Like one that seeks his God in vain ?
Canst thou thy face for ever hide,
And I still pray and be denied ?

2 Shall I for ever be forgot,
As one whom thou regardest not ?
Still shall my soul thy absence mourn,
And still despair of thy return ?

3 How long shall my poor troubled breast
Be with these anxious thoughts oppressed ?
And Satan, my malicious foe,
Rejoice to see me sunk so low ?

4 How would the powers of darkness boast
Should but one praying soul be lost !
But I have trusted in thy grace,
And shall again behold thy face.

5 Whate'er my fears or foes suggest,
Thou art my hope, my joy, my rest ;
My heart shall feel thy love, and raise
My cheerful voice to songs of praise.

402   C.M.   WATTS.
Praying for Quickening Grace.—Ps. cxix. 20, 25, 37, 40.

My soul lies cleaving to the dust ;
Lord, give me life divine ;
From vain desires and every lust,
Turn off these eyes of mine.

2 I need the influence of thy grace
To speed me in my way,

Lest I should loiter in my race,
Or turn my feet astray.

3 When sore afflictions press me down,
I need thy quickening powers ;
Thy word that I have rested on,
Shall help my heaviest hours.

4 Are not thy mercies sovereign still,
And thou a faithful God ?
Wilt thou not grant me warmer zeal
To run the heavenly road ?

5 Does not my heart thy precepts love,
And long to see thy face ?
And yet how slow my spirits move
Without enlivening grace !

6 Then shall I love thy gospel more,
And ne'er forget thy word,

When I have felt its quickening power,
To draw me near the Lord.

403   148th.   S. STENNETT.
A Song of Praise to Christ.—Phil. ii. 6-11 ; Rev. v. 9-13.

Come, every gracious heart,
That loves the Saviour's name,
Your noblest powers exert,
To celebrate his fame ;
Tell all who fear the Lord below,
The debt of love to him you owe.

2   He left his starry crown,
And laid his robes aside,
On wings of love came down,
And wept, and bled, and died ;
What he endured no tongue can tell,
To save our souls from death and hell.

3   From the dark grave he rose,
The mansion of the dead ;
And thence his mighty foes
In glorious triumph led ;
Up through the sky the Conqueror rode,
And reigns on high, the Saviour, God.

4   From thence he'll quickly come ;
His chariots will not stay ;
And bear our spirits home,
To realms of endless day.
There shall we see his lovely face,
And ever dwell in his embrace.

404   104th.—Ps. lxxi. 22, 23 ; ciii. 4.   CENNICK.
Praise to the Prince of Peace.—Ps. lxxi. 22, 23 ; ciii. 4.

Our Saviour alone, the Lord, let us bless,
Who reigns on his throne, the Prince of our
peace ;
Who evermore saves us by shedding his blood ;
All hail, holy Jesus ! our Lord and our God.

2 We thankfully sing thy glory and praise,
Thou merciful Spring of pity and grace ;
Thy kindness for ever to men we will tell,
And say, our dear Saviour redeemed us from hell.

3 Preserve us in love, while here we abide ;
O never remove thy presence, nor hide
Thy glorious salvation, till each of us see,
With joy, the bless'd vision completed in thee.

405   L.M.   KENT.
Exulting in eternal union with Jesus.—Jno. xvii. 21-23.

'Twixt Jesus and the chosen race,
Subsists a bond of sovereign grace,
That hell, with its infernal train,
Shall ne'er dissolve nor rend in twain !

2 This sacred bond shall never break,
Though earth should to her centre shake ;
Rest, doubting saint, assured of this,
For God has pledged his holiness.

3 [He swore but once ; the deed was done ;
'Twas settled by the great Three-One ;
Christ was appointed to redeem
All that his Father loved in him.]

4 Hail, sacred union, firm and strong !
How great the grace ! how sweet the song !
That worms of earth should ever be
One with incarnate Deity !

5 [One in the tomb ; one when he rose ;
One when he triumphed o'er his foes ;
One when in heaven he took his seat,
While seraphs sang all hell's defeat.]

6 This sacred tie forbids their fears,
For all he is or has is theirs ;
With him, their Head, they stand or fall—
Their Life, their Surety, and their All.

7 [The sinner's Peace, the Daysman he,
Whose blood should set his people free ;
On them his fond affections ran,
Before creation-work began.]

8 Blessed be the wisdom and the grace,
The eternal love and faithfulness,
That's in the gospel-scheme revealed,
And is by God the Spirit sealed.

406 8.8.6. KENT. Rev. v. 9.

Praise for Reigning Grace.—Rom. v. 20, 21 ;

HARK ! how the blood-bought hosts above
Conspire to praise redeeming love,
    In sweet harmonious strains ;
And while they strike the golden lyres,
This glorious theme each bosom fires,
    That grace triumphant reigns.

2 Join thou, my soul, for thou canst tell
How grace divine broke up thy cell,
    And loosed thy native chains ;

And still, from that auspicious day,
How oft art thou constrained to say,
    That grace triumphant reigns.

3 [Grace, till the tribes redeemed by blood,
Are brought to know themselves and God,
    Her empire shall maintain ;
To call when he appoints the day,
And from the mighty take the prey,
    Shall grace triumphant reign.]

4 When called to meet the King of dread,
Should love compose my dying bed,
    And grace my soul sustain,
Then, ere I quit this mortal clay,
I'll raise my fainting voice, and say,
    Let grace triumphant reign.

407 L.M.

Praise to the Redeemer.—Ps. cvii. 1, 2 ; 1 John i. 7, 9.

DEAR Lord ! my panting soul inflame,
To spread abroad thy matchless fame,
And with a solemn pleasure tell,
The grace which saves from death and hell.

2 Here's pardon full for sin that's past ;
It matters not how black their cast ;
And O my soul, with wonder view,
For sins to come here's pardon too.

3 The nation, thus redeemed from sin,
Was chosen, loved, and blessed in him ;
They ne'er shall die while Jesus lives ;
His covenant life eternal gives.

4 Let saints prepare to crown his brow
With bright immortal trophies now ;
And let their songs record his name,
His honours, and his deathless fame.

408 104th. C.W.

Thanksgiving.—Ps. lxxxix. 14-17 ; cl. 2 : Isa. xlv. 25.

O WHAT shall I do my Saviour to praise,
So faithful and true, so plenteous in grace ;
So strong to deliver, so good to redeem,
The weakest believer that hangs upon him ?

2 How happy the man whose heart is set free,
The people that can be joyful in thee !
Their joy is to walk in the light of thy face,
And still they are talking of Jesus's grace.

3 Their daily delight shall be in thy name ;
They shall, as their right, thy righteousness
    claim.   [thy blood,
Thy righteousness wearing, and cleansed by
Bold shall they appear in the presence of God.

4 For thou art their boast, their glory, & power ;
    And I also trust to see the glad hour ;
My soul's new creation, alive from the dead ;
The day of salvation that lifts up my head.

5 Yes, Lord, I shall see the bliss of thy own ;
    Thy secret to me shall soon be made known ;
For sorrow and sadness I joy shall receive,
And share in the gladness of all that believe.

409 148th. WATTS.

A Song of Praise to the Eternal Three.—Eph. i. 3, 4.

To Him that chose us first,
    Before the world began ;
To Him that bore the curse,
    To save rebellious man ;
To Him that formed our hearts anew,
Is endless praise and glory due.

2 The Father's love shall run
    Through our immortal songs ;
We bring to God the Son,
    Hosannas on our tongues ;

Our lips address the Spirit's name,
With equal praise and zeal the same.

3   Let every saint above,
    And angel round the throne,
    For ever bless and love
    The sacred Three-in-One ;
Thus heaven shall raise his honours high,
When earth and time grow old and die.

410   L.M.   MEDLEY.
" He hath done all things well."—Mark vii. 37.
O FOR a heart prepared to sing,
To God, my Saviour and my King ;
While with his saints I join to tell,
My Jesus has done all things well.

2 [All worlds his glorious power confess ;
His wisdom all his works express ;
But O his love what tongue can tell ?
My Jesus has done all things well.]

3 How sovereign, wonderful, and free,
Is all his love to sinful me !
He plucked me as a brand from hell ;
My Jesus has done all things well.

4 And since my soul has known his love,
What mercies has he made me prove :
Mercies which all my praise excel ;
My Jesus has done all things well.

5 [Whene'er my Saviour and my God
Has on me laid his gentle rod,
I know, in all that has befel,
My Jesus has done all things well.]

6 [Sometimes he's pleased his face to hide,
To make me pray, or stain my pride ;
Yet am I helped on this to dwell,
My Jesus has done all things well.]

7 Soon shall I pass the vale of death,
And in his arms shall lose my breath ;
Yet then my happy soul shall tell,
My Jesus has done all things well.

8 And when to that bright world I rise,
And join the anthems in the skies,
Among the rest this note shall swell,
My Jesus has done all things well.

411   C.M.   KENT.
" An everlasting covenant."—2 Sam. xxiii. 5.
COME, saints, and sing in sweet accord,
    With solemn pleasure tell,
The covenant made with David's Lord ;
    In all things ordered well.

2 This covenant stood ere time began,
    That God with man might dwell ;

Eternal wisdom drew the plan ;
    In all things ordered well.

3 This covenant, O believer, stands,
    Thy rising fears to quell ;
Sealed by thy Surety's bleeding hands ;
    In all things ordered well.

4 'Twas made with Jesus, for his bride,
    Before the sinner fell ;
'Twas signed, and sealed, and ratified ;
    In all things ordered well.

5 When rolling worlds depart on fire,
    And thousands sink to hell,
This covenant shall the saints admire ;
    In all things ordered well.

6 In glory, soon, with Christ their King,
    His saints shall surely dwell ;
And this blest covenant ever sing ;
    In all things ordered well.

412   S.M.   KENT.
" It shall be well with the righteous."—Isa. iii. 10.
WHAT cheering words are these ;
    Their sweetness who can tell ?
In time and to eternal days,
    " 'Tis with the righteous well."

2   In every state secure,
    Kept as Jehovah's eye,
'Tis well with them while life endure,
    And well when called to die.

3   [Well when they see his face,
    Or sink amidst the flood ;
Well in affliction's thorny maze,
    Or on the mount of God.]

4   [Well when the gospel yields
    Pure honey, milk, and wine ;
Well when thy soul her leanness feels,
    And all her joys decline.]

5   ['Tis well when joys arise ;
    'Tis well when sorrows flow ;
'Tis well when darkness veils the skies,
    And strong temptations blow.]

6   'Tis well when at his throne
    They wrestle, weep, and pray ;
'Tis well when at his feet they groan,
    Yet bring their wants away.

7   'Tis well when they can sing
    As sinners bought with blood ;
And when they touch the mournful string,
    And mourn an absent God.

8   'Tis well when on the mount
    They feast on dying love ;
And 'tis as well, in God's account,
    When they the furnace prove.

9   'Tis well when Jesus calls,
    " From earth and sin arise,
    Join with the host of virgin souls,
    Made to salvation wise."

KENT.

413   C.M.   Jer. xxxii. 40.
" He hateth putting away."—Mal. ii. 16:

LET Zion songs of triumph sing ;
    Let gladness crown the day ;
Jehovah is her God and King,
    He hates to put away.

2 'Graved on his hands divinely fair,
    Who did their ransom pay,
The golden letters still appear ;
    He hates to put away.

3 Think not that he'll thy suit reject,
    Or spurn thy humble plea ;
He hears the groans of his elect,
    And hates to put away.

4 [When loathsome in thy sins and blood,
    He did thy state survey,
And for a stranger Surety stood ;
    He hates to put away.]

5 Salvation's of the Lord alone ;
    Grace is a shoreless sea ;
In heaven there's ne'er a vacant throne ;
    He hates to put away.

414   11s.   WATTS
Praise to the Saviour.—Matt. xxi. 9; Ps. xl. 7, 8.

I LONG for a concert of heavenly praise,
To Jesus, my God, the omnipotent Son !
My soul should awake in harmonious lays,
Could it tell half the wonders that Jesus has
        done.   2

I'd sing how he left his own mansions of light ,
The robes made of glory that dressed him above,
Yet pleased with his journey & swift in his flight ;
He came on the pinions of covenant love !

3

Quick down to the place of our distant abode,
He came, we adore him, to raise us on high ;
He came to atone the dread justice of God,
And took up a life to be able to die !

4

All hell and its lions stood roaring around ;
His flesh and his spirit with malice they tore,
While oceans of sorrow lay pressing him down,
As vast as the burden of guilt which he bore.

5

Fast bound in the chains of imperious death,
The Infinite Captive a prisoner lay ;
The Infinite Captain arose from the earth,
And leaped to the hills of ethereal day !

6

Then mention no more of the vengeance of God,
The lions of hell, and their roaring no more ;
We lift up our eyes to his shining abode ;
Our loudest hosannas his name shall adore !

7

His conquest is crowned with the honours he won ;
Hosanna through all the ethereal groves ;
The God and the Man, how he fills up his throne !
How he shines ! how he smiles ! how he looks !
    how he loves !

415   6.4.   ALLEN & BATTY.
" Worthy the Lamb."—Rev. v. 12, 13 ; Ps. cxlviii. 13.

GLORY to God on high !
    Let earth and skies reply,
        Praise ye his name !

His love and grace adore,
Who all our sorrow bore ;
Sing aloud evermore,
    Worthy the Lamb !

2 Jesus, our Lord and God,
Bore sin's tremendous load !
    Praise ye his name !
Tell what his arm has done,
What spoils from death he won ;
Sing his great name alone ;
    Worthy the Lamb !

3 While they around the throne
Cheerfully join in one,
    Praising his name,
Ye who have felt his blood
Sealing your peace with God,
Sound his dear fame abroad ;
    Worthy the Lamb !

NEWTON.
416   8.7.7.   Rev. i. 5.
Praise for Atoning Blood.—1 Cor. vi. 11, 20;

LET us love, and sing, and wonder ;
    Let us praise the Saviour's name ;
He has hushed the law's loud thunder ;
    He has quenched Mount Sinai's flame ;
    He has washed us in his blood ;
    He has brought us home to God !

2 Let us love the Lord who bought us ;
    Pitied us when enemies ;
Called us by his grace, and taught us ;
    Gave us ears, and gave us eyes ;
    He has washed us, &c.

3 Let us sing though fierce temptation
    Threatens hard to bear us down ;

Jesus is our strong salvation ;
    He will surely give the crown ;
    He has washed us, &c.

4 [Let us wonder ! grace and justice
    Join and point to mercy's store ;
    When, through grace, in Christ our trust is,
    Justice smiles, and asks no more ;
    He has washed us, &c.]

5 Let us praise, and join the chorus
    Of the saints enthroned on high ;
    Here they trusted him before us,
    Now their praises fill the sky ;
    He has washed us, &c.

6 Yes, we praise thee, gracious Saviour ;
    Wonder, love, and bless thy name ;
    Pardon, Lord, our poor endeavour ;
    Pity, for thou know'st our frame ;
    Wash our souls and songs with blood,
    For by thee we come to God.

417   104th.   SWAIN.
The Pilgrim's Joy.—Isa. xxxv. 10; xxv. 8; Rev. vii. 17.

To Zion we go, the seat of our King,
And yet while below we cannot but sing ;
Though few here esteem us, the God we adore
Has died to redeem us ! what could he do more !

2 What Jesus has done to save us from hell ;
What conquests he won, when he himself fell ;
The depths of his sorrow ; the heights of his love ;
Can never be known till we sing them above.

418   C.M.   STEELE.
Praise to the Redeemer.—Phil. ii. 7-9; Eph. iii. 19.

To our Redeemer's glorious name,
    Awake the sacred song ;
O may his love (immortal flame !)
    Tune every heart and tongue.

2 His love, what mortal thought can reach,
    What mortal tongue display ?
Imagination's utmost stretch
    In wonder dies away !

3 He left his radiant throne on high !
    Left the bright realms of bliss !
And came to earth to bleed and die !
    Was ever love like this ?

4 Dear Lord, while we adoring pay
    Our humble thanks to thee,
May every heart with rapture say,
    "The Saviour died for me."

419   L.M.   WATTS.
Rejoicing in God.—Ps. xviii. 30-35, 46.

JUST are thy ways and true thy word,
Great Rock of my secure abode ;
Who is a God beside the Lord ?
Or where's a refuge like our God ?

2 'Tis he that girds me with his might ;
Gives me his holy sword to wield ;
And while with sin and hell I fight,
Spreads his salvation for my shield.

3 He lives (and blessed be my Rock),
The God of my Salvation lives ;
The dark designs of hell are broke ;
Sweet is the peace my Father gives.

4 Before the scoffers of the age
I will exalt my Father's name ;
Nor tremble at their mighty rage,
But meet reproach and bear the shame.

5 To David and his royal seed
Thy grace for ever shall extend ;
Thy love to saints, in Christ their Head,
Knows not a limit nor an end.

420   S.M.   WATTS.
Praise for spiritual and temporal mercies.—Ps. ciii. 1.

O BLESS the Lord, my soul !
    Let all within me join,
And aid my tongue to bless his name,
    Whose favours are divine.

2   O bless the Lord, my soul !
    Nor let his mercies lie
Forgotten in unthankfulness,
    And without praises die.

3   'Tis he forgives thy sins ;
    'Tis he relieves thy pain ;
'Tis he that heals thy sicknesses,
    And makes thee young again.

4   He crowns thy life with love,
    When ransomed from the grave ;
He that redeemed my soul from hell
    Has sovereign power to save.

5   He fills the poor with good ;
    He gives the sufferers rest ;
The Lord has judgments for the proud,
    And justice for the oppressed.

6   His wondrous works and ways
    He made by Moses known ;
But sent the world his truth and grace,
    By his beloved Son.

421   S.M.   WATTS.
Praise for Preserving Grace.—Jude 24, 25; Rom. xvi. 25

To God the only wise,
    Our Saviour and our King,
Let all the saints below the skies
    Their humble praises bring.

2   'Tis his almighty love,
    His counsel and his care,

Preserves us safe from sin and death,
And every hurtful snare.

3   He will present our souls
Unblemished and complete
Before the glory of his face,
With joys divinely great.

4   Then all the chosen seed
Shall meet around the throne ;
Shall bless the conduct of his grace,
And make his wonders known.

5   To our Redeemer, God,
Wisdom and power belongs ;
Immortal crowns of majesty,
And everlasting songs.

422   L.M.   WATTS.
Joy in heaven over a repenting sinner.-Mat. xviii. 12-14
WHO can describe the joys that rise
Through all the courts of Paradise,
To see a prodigal return,
To see an heir of glory born ?

2 With joy the Father does approve
The fruit of his eternal love ;
The Son with joy looks down and sees
The purchase of his agonies.

3 The Spirit takes delight to view
The holy soul he formed anew ;
And saints and angels join to sing,
The growing empire of their King.

423   S.M.   WATTS.
" Whom having not seen, ye love."—1 Pet. i. 8.
NOT with our mortal eyes
Have we beheld the Lord ;
Yet we rejoice to hear his name,
And love him in his word.

2   On earth we want the sight
Of our Redeemer's face ;
Yet, Lord, our inmost thoughts delight
To dwell upon thy grace.

3   And when we taste thy love,
Our joys divinely grow
Unspeakable, like those above,
And heaven begins below

424   C.M.   WATTS.
Christ's Victory.—Hos. xiii. 14; Eph. iv. 8; Col. ii. 15.
HOSANNA to our conquering King !
The prince of darkness flies ;
His troops rush headlong down to hell,
Like lightning from the skies.

2 There, bound in chains, the lions roar,
And fright the rescued sheep ;
But heavy bars confine their power
And malice to the deep.

3 Hosanna to our conquering King !
All hail, incarnate Love !
Ten thousand songs and glories wait
To crown thy head above.

4 Thy victories and thy deathless fame
Through the wide world shall run,
And everlasting ages sing
The triumphs thou hast won.

425   S.M.   STEVENS.
Following Christ.—Matt. xvi. 24; iii. 13; Mark i. 9.
WITH pleasure we behold
Immanuel's offspring come ;
As sheep are gathered to the fold,
And left no more to roam.

2   The way the Shepherd trod
They freely choose to go ;

Moved by the powerful love of God,
They leave this world below.

3   This watery path they own ;
Their Saviour's cross they view ;
And resting on his blood alone,
By faith they journey through.

4   Among the flock they rest,
In pastures fresh and green ;
With peace and safety ever blest,
And pleasures all serene.

426   C.M.   STEVENS.
" We see Jesus."---Heb. ii. 9; Matt. xxviii. 6.
How great and solemn is the thing,
For which we here are come ;
To view the death of Zion's King,
And gaze upon his tomb ;

2 To see him, under death's arrest,
Enter the dismal grave ;
Awhile in that dark cell to rest,
Our mortal flesh to save ;

3 To see him in his grave-clothes lie,
His life and glory gone ;
To ask ourselves the reason why
This wondrous deed was done ;

4 To view the wounds of which he died
And own our sins the cause ;
To honour Christ the crucified,
Adhering to his laws ;

5 To trace him rising from the tomb
In victory over all ;
The first-born Son of nature's womb,
That rose no more to fall.

6 Here, humble saints, your tribute pay ;
A risen Saviour sing ;
Come, be baptized without delay,
In honour of your King

427 L.M. GRIGG

Not ashamed of Christ.—Mark viii. 38; Luke ix. 26

JESUS, and shall it ever be,
A mortal man ashamed of thee ?
Ashamed of thee, whom angels praise ;
Whose glories shine to endless days ?

2 [Ashamed of Jesus ! sooner far
Let evening blush to own a star ;
He sheds his beams of light divine
O'er this benighted soul of mine.]

3 [Ashamed of Jesus ! just as soon
Let midnight be ashamed of noon ;
'Tis midnight with my soul till he,
Bright Morning Star, bids darkness flee.]

4 Ashamed of Jesus ! that dear Friend,
On whom my hopes of heaven depend !
No ; when I blush, be this my shame,
That I no more revere his name.

5 Ashamed of Jesus ! yes, I may,
When I've no guilt to wash away ;
No tear to wipe ; no good to crave ;
No fears to quell ; no soul to save.

6 Till then, nor is my boasting vain,
Till then I boast a Saviour slain ;
And O may this my glory be,
That Christ is not ashamed of me.

7 [His institutions would I prize ;
Take up my cross, the shame despise ;
Dare to defend his noble cause,
And yield obedience to his laws.]

428 8.7. FAWCETT.

Baptism.—Acts ii. 38; xxii. 16; Mark xvi. 16.

HUMBLE souls, who seek salvation
  Through the Lamb's redeeming blood,

Hear the voice of revelation ;
  Tread the path that Jesus trod.
Flee to him, your only Saviour ;
  In his mighty name confide ;
In the whole of your behaviour,
  Own him for your Sovereign Guide.

2 Hear the blessed Redeemer call you ;
  Listen to his gracious voice ;
Dread no ills that can befall you,
  While you make his ways your choice.
Jesus says, " Let each believer
  Be baptized in my name."
He himself, in Jordan's river,
  Was immersed beneath the stream.

3 Plainly here his footsteps tracing,
  Follow him without delay ;
Gladly his command embracing ;
  Lo ! your Captain leads the way.

View the rite with understanding ;
  Jesus' grave before you lies ;
Be interred at his commanding ;
  After his example rise.

429 C.M. FELLOWS.

Baptism.—Matt. iii. 13-17; x. 38; Mark i. 9.

DEAR Lord ! and will thy pardoning love
  Embrace a wretch so vile ?
Wilt thou my load of guilt remove,
  And bless me with thy smile ?

2 Hast thou the cross for me endured,
  And all its shame despised ?
And shall I be ashamed, O Lord,
  With thee to be baptized ?

3 Didst thou the great example lead
  In Jordan's swelling flood ?

And shall my pride disdain the deed
  That's worthy of my God ?

4 Dear Lord, the ardour of thy love
  Reproves my cold delays ;
And now my willing footsteps move
  In thy delightful ways.

430 8.8.6. NORMAN (?).

" Thus it becometh us," &c.—Matt. iii. 15.

'TIS not as led by custom's voice,
We make these ways our favoured choice,
  And thus with zeal pursue ;
No ; Zion's great and gracious Lord
Has, in the precepts of his word,
  Enjoined us thus to do.

2 Thou everlasting, gracious King,
Assist us now thy grace to sing,
  And still direct our way
To those bright realms of peace and rest,
Where all the exulting tribes are blessed
  With one great choral day.

431 L.M. BEDDOME.

" Can any man man forbid water? "&c.—Acts x. 47.

COME, ye beloved of the Lord,
Behold the Lamb, the incarnate Word ;
He died and rose again for you ;
What more could your Redeemer do ?

2 We to this place are come to show
What we to boundless mercy owe ;
The Saviour's footsteps to explore,
And tread the path he trod before.

432 L.M. WATTS.

Buried with Christ in Baptism.—Rom. vi. 3-11.

Do we not know that solemn word,
That we are buried with the Lord ;

Baptized into his death, and then
Put off the body of our sin ?

2 Our souls receive diviner breath,
Raised from corruption, guilt, and death ;
So from the grave did Christ arise,
And lives to God above the skies.

3 No more let sin or Satan reign
Over our mortal flesh again ;
The various lusts we served before,
Shall have dominion now no more.

433   8.7.   FELLOWS.
" Therefore we are buried with him," &c.—Rom. vi. 4.
JESUS, mighty King in Zion !
   Thou alone our Guide shalt be,
Thy commission we rely on ;
   We would follow none but thee.

2 As an emblem of thy passion,
   And thy victory o'er the grave,
We, who know thy great salvation,
   Are baptized beneath the wave.

3 Fearless of the world's despising,
   We the ancient path pursue ;
Buried with our Lord, and rising
   To a life divinely new.

434   C.M.   BEDDOME.
   " I will run the way," &c.—Ps. cxix. 32.
How great, how solemn is the work
   Which we attend to-day !
Now for a holy, solemn frame,
   O God, to thee we pray.

2 [O may we feel as once we felt,
   When pained and grieved at heart,
Thy kind, forgiving, melting look
   Relieved our every smart.

3 Let graces, then in exercise,
   Be exercised again ;
And nurtured by celestial power,
   In exercise remain.]

4 Awake our love, our fear, our hope ;
   Wake, fortitude and joy ;
Vain world, begone ; let things above
   Our happy thoughts employ.

5 Whilst thee, our Saviour and our God,
   To all around we own,
Drive each rebellious, rival lust,
   Each traitor from thy throne.

6 Instruct our minds ; our wills subdue ;
   To heaven our passions raise ;
That hence our lives, our all may be
   Devoted to thy praise.

435   L.M.   WATTS.
Remember Jesus!—Luke xxii. 19; 1 Cor. xi. 24.
THE Lord of life this table spread,
With his own flesh and dying blood ;
We on the rich provision feed,
And taste the wine, and bless our God.

2 May sinful sweets be all forgot,
And earth grow less in our esteem ;
Christ and his love fill every thought,
And faith and hope be fixed on him.

436   S.M.   BERRIDGE.
For the Lord's Presence.—John xiv. 21; xv. 9.
THE table now is spread ;
   We meet around the board ;
Dear Jesus, bless the wine and bread,
   And heavenly life afford.

2 O may the Lord appear,
   With looks divinely mild,
And whisper in each humble ear,
   " I love thee well, my child."

437   S.M.   (altered) WATTS.
Communion with Christ & with saints.-1 Cor. x. 16, 17.
JESUS invites his saints
   To meet around his board ;
Here pardoned rebels sit, and hold
   Communion with their Lord.

2 [For food he gives his flesh ;
   He bids us drink his blood ;
Amazing favour, matchless grace
   Of our descending God !]

3 By faith, the bread and wine
   Maintain our fainting breath,
By union with our living Lord,
   And interest in his death.

4 Our heavenly Father calls
   Christ and his members one ;
We the young children of his love,
   And he the first-born Son.

5 We are but several parts
   Of the same broken bread ;
One body has its several limbs,
   But Jesus is the Head.

6 Let all our powers be joined
   His gracious name to raise ;
Pleasure and love fill every mind,
   And every voice be praise.

438   C.M.   WATTS.
Christ's dying Love.—Isa. lxiii. 9; John xv. 13.
THIS was compassion like a God,
   That when the Saviour knew
The price of pardon was his blood,
   He pity ne'er withdrew.

2 Now though he reigns exalted high,
   His love is still as great ;
Well he remembers Calvary,
   Nor let his saints forget.

3 [Here we behold his bowels roll,
   As kind as when he died ;
And see the sorrows of his soul
   Bleed through his wounded side.]

439   L.M.   WATTS.
Crucifixion to the World by the Cross.— Gal. vi. 14.

WHEN I survey the wondrous cross
On which the Prince of Glory died,
My richest gain I count but loss,
And pour contempt on all my pride.

2 Forbid it, Lord, that I should boast,
Save in the death of Christ, my God ;
All the vain things that charm me most,
I sacrifice them to his blood.

3 See ! from his head, his hands, his feet,
Sorrow and love flow mingled down ;
Did e'er such love and sorrow meet,
Or thorns compose so rich a crown ?

440   C.M.   WATTS.
Divine Love making a Feast.—Luke xiv. 17, 22, 23.

How sweet and awful is the place,
   With Christ within the doors,
While everlasting love displays
   The choicest of her stores.

2 Here every bowel of our God
   With soft compassion rolls ;
Here peace and pardon, love and blood,
   Is food for dying souls.

3 [While all our hearts and all our songs
   Join to admire the feast,

Each of us cry, with thankful tongues,
   " Lord, why was I a guest ?

4 " Why was I made to hear thy voice,
   And enter while there's room ;
When thousands make a wretched choice,
   And rather starve than come ? "]

5 'Twas the same love that spread the feast
   That sweetly forced us in ;
Else we had still refused to taste,
   And perished in our sin.

441   L.M.   BEDDOME.
" Jesus wept."—John xi. 35 ; Luke xix. 41 ; Heb. v. 7.

So fair a face bedewed with tears ;
What beauty e'en in grief appears !
He wept, he bled, he died for you ;
What more, ye saints, could Jesus do ?

2 Enthroned above, with equal glow
His warm affections downward flow ;

In our distress he bears a part,
And feels a sympathetic smart.

3 Still his compassions are the same ;
He knows the frailty of our frame ;
Our heaviest burdens he sustains ;
Shares in our sorrows and our pains

442   7s.   BERRIDGE.
" Peace I leave with you."—John xiv. 27.

ERE we leave thy table, Lord,
Drop us down a pledge of peace ;
Give us all a parting word,
Sealed with a parting kiss.

443   104th.   BERRIDGE.
Praise for the heavenly feast.-Song v. 1 ; Prov. ix. 1-5.

THE Lord of the feast we solemnly bless,
And pray that each guest may grow in his grace ;
Thanks for his preparing his banquet of love ;
O may we all share in the banquet above.

444   S.M.   BERRIDGE.
The Leper's Prayer.—Matt. viii. 2 ; Mark i. 40.

DEFILED I am indeed ;
   Defiled throughout by sin ;
Thy purple fountain, Lord, I need,
   To wash a leper clean.

2   The fountain open stands,
   Yet on its brink I dwell ;
O put me in with thy own hands,
   And that will make me well.

445   148th.   HART.
The Love of Christ.—John xv. 13 ; Rom. v. 7, 8.

JOIN, every tongue, to sing
   The mercies of the Lord ;
The love of Christ, our King,
   Let every heart record.
He saved us from the wrath of God,
And paid our ransom with his blood.

2   What wondrous grace was this !
   We sinned, and Jesus died ;
He wrought the righteousness,
   And we were justified.
We ran the score to lengths extreme,
And all the debt was charged on him.

3   Hell was our just desert,
   And he *that* hell endured ;
Guilt broke his guiltless heart
   With wrath that we incurred ;
We bruised his body, spilt his blood,
And both became our heavenly food.

446   S.M.   HART.
The Bread of Heaven.—John vi. 33-58.

WHEN through the desert vast
   The chosen tribes were led,

They could not plough, nor till, nor sow,
Yet never wanted bread.

2 Around their wandering camp,
The copious manna fell ;
Strewed on the ground, a food they found,
But *what* they could not tell.

3 But better bread by far
Is now to Christians given ;
Poor sinners eat immortal meat,
The Living Bread from heaven.

4 We eat the flesh of Christ,
Who is the Bread of God ;
Their food was coarse compared with ours,
Though theirs was angels' food.

447   L.M.   HART.
Sighing for the Substance.—Luke xiv. 22 ; John vi. 53.

PITY a helpless sinner, Lord,
Who would believe thy gracious word,
But own my heart, with shame and grief,
A sink of sin and unbelief.

2 Lord, in thy house I read there's room,
And, venturing hard, behold I come ;
But can there, tell me, can there be
Amongst thy children room for me ?

3 I eat the bread, and drink the wine ;
But oh ! my soul wants more than sign !
I faint unless I feed on thee,
And drink the blood as shed for me.

4 For sinners, Lord, thou cam'st to bleed ;
And I'm a sinner vile indeed ;
Lord, I believe, thy grace is free,
O magnify that grace in me.

448   148th.   HART.
Tokens of Christ's Love.—John xv. 9 ; Matt. xi. 30.

WHEN Jesus undertook
To rescue ruined man,
The realms of bliss forsook,
And to relieve us ran ;
He spared no pains, declined no load,
Resolved to buy us with his blood.

2 No harsh commands he gave,
No hard conditions brought ;
He came to seek and save,
And pardon every fault.
Poor trembling sinners hear his call ;
They come, and he forgives them all.

3 When thus we're reconciled,
He sets no rigorous tasks ;
His yoke is soft and mild,
For love is all he asks.

E'en *that* from him we first receive,
And well he knows we've none to give.

4 This pure and heavenly gift,
Within our hearts to move,
The dying Saviour left
These tokens of his love ;
Which seem to say, " While this you do.
Remember Him that died for you."

449   104th.   HART.
The Banqueting Song.—2 Thess ii. 13, 14 ; Eph. i. 3.

WHAT creatures beside are favoured like us ?
Forgiven, supplied, and banqueted thus
By God, our good Father, who gave us his Son,
And sent him to gather his children in one.

2 Salvation's of God, the effect of free grace,
Upon us bestowed before the world was ;
God *from* everlasting be blest, and, again,
Blest *to* everlasting. Amen, and amen.

450   L.M.   BURNHAM.
" A burning and a shining light."—John v. 35.

O BLESS thy servant, dearest Lord,
While he shall preach thy gospel word ;
May he declare delightful things,
Touching the glorious King of kings.

2 O grant him bright celestial views,
While he proclaims the gospel news ;
With fiery zeal his soul inflame,
While he exalts the bleeding Lamb.

3 Give him clear light, and burning love ;
Shower down thy blessings from above ;
O may we hear the Saviour's voice,
And in his precious name rejoice.

451   L.M.   NEWTON.
Before Sermon.—John v. 25 ; Col. ii. 13 ; Isa. lxi. 1-3.

MAY this be a much-favoured hour
To souls in Satan's bondage led !
Lord, clothe thy word with sovereign power
To break the rocks, and raise the dead.

2 To mourners speak a cheering word ;
On seeking souls vouchsafe to shine ;
Let poor backsliders be restored,
And all thy saints in praises join.

452   148th.   NEWTON.
After Sermon.—1 Cor. iii. 6 ; Isa. lv. 11.

ON what has now been sown,
Thy blessing, Lord, bestow ;
The power is thine alone
To make it spring and grow.
Do thou the gracious harvest raise,
And thou alone shalt have the praise.

453 L.M. S. STENNETT.
Between Prayer and Sermon.—Matt. xviii. 20.

[" WHERE two or three, with sweet accord,
Obedient to their sovereign Lord,
Meet to recount his acts of grace,
And offer solemn prayer and praise ;

2 " There," says the Saviour, " will I be,
Amid this little company ;
To them unveil my smiling face,
And shed my glories round the place."]

3 We meet at thy command, dear Lord ;
Relying on thy faithful word ;
Now send thy Spirit from above ;
Now fill our hearts with heavenly love.

454 112th. FAWCETT.
Before Sermon.—Isa. lv. 11 ; 2 Thess. iii. 1.

THY presence, gracious God, afford ;
Prepare us to receive thy word ;
Now let thy voice engage our ear,
And faith be mixed with what we hear ;
Thus, Lord, thy waiting servants bless,
And crown thy gospel with success.

2 [Distracting thoughts and cares remove,
And fix our hearts and hopes above ;
With food divine may we be fed,
And satisfied with living bread.
Thus, Lord, thy waiting servants, &c.]

3 To us the sacred word apply,
With sovereign power and energy ;
And may we, in thy faith and fear,
Reduce to practice what we hear.
Thus, Lord, thy waiting servants, &c.

4 Father, in us thy Son reveal ;
Teach us to know and do thy will ;
Thy saving power and love display,
And guide us to the realms of day.
Thus, Lord, thy waiting servants, &c.

455 C.M. HART.
The same.—Song iv. 16 ; Gen. xlix. 18 ; Isa. xxxiii. 2.

ONCE more we come before our God ;
Once more his blessing ask ;
O may not duty seem a load,
Nor worship prove a task.

2 Father, thy quickening Spirit send
From heaven, in Jesus' name,
To make our waiting minds attend,
And put our souls in frame.

3 May we receive the word we hear,
Each in an honest heart ;
Hoard up the precious treasure there,
And never with it part.

4 To seek thee all our hearts dispose ;
To each thy blessings suit ;

And let the seed thy servant sows
Produce a copious fruit.

5 Bid the refreshing north wind wake ;
Say to the south wind, Blow ;
Let every plant the power partake,
And all the garden grow.

6 Revive the parched with heavenly showers ;
The cold with warmth divine ;
And as the benefit is ours,
Be all the glory thine.

456 104th. HART.
The same.—Isa. lxiv. 2.

THE good hand of God has brought us again
(A favour bestowed, we hope not in vain)
To hear from our Saviour the word of his grace ;
Then be our behaviour becoming the place.

2 Remember the ends for which we are met ;
Alas ! my dear friends, we're apt to forget ;
The motives that brought us, the Lord only sees ;
But if he has taught us, our ends should be these :

3 To worship the Lord with praise & with prayer ;
To practise his word, as well as to hear,
To own with contrition the deeds we have done,
And take the remission God gives in his Son.

4 Blest Spirit of Christ, descend on us thus ;
Thy servant assist ; teach him to teach us ;
O send us thy unction, to teach us all good ;
And touch with compunction, and sprinkle with
blood.

457 L.M. HART.
Dismission.—Ps. lxxxv. 7 ; xxix. 11 ; Isa. liv. 13.

DISMISS us with thy blessing, Lord ,
Help us to feed upon thy word ;
All that has been amiss forgive,
And let thy truth within us live.

2 Though we are guilty, thou art good ;
Wash all our works in Jesus' blood ;
Give every fettered soul release,
And bid us all depart in peace.

458 S.M. HART.
The same.—Luke ii. 19, 51 ; Hos. vi. 3 ; Ps. lxxxix. 1.

ONCE more before we part,
We'll bless the Saviour's name :
Record his mercies, every heart ;
Sing, every tongue, the same.

2 Hoard up his sacred word,
And feed thereon and grow ;
Go on to seek to know the Lord,
And practise what you know.

459 C.M. HART.
The same.—Jer. xxxi. 14; Isa. lv. 11.
LORD, help us on thy word to feed ;
In peace dismiss us hence ;
Be thou, in every time of need,
Our refuge and defence.
2 We now desire to bless thy name,
And in our hearts record,
And with our thankful tongues proclaim,
The goodness of the Lord.

460 8s. BURNHAM.
After Sermon.—1 Thess. i. 5; Eph. ii. 17; Acts x. 36.
THE gospel's a message of peace,
We oft by experience have felt ;
'Tis filled with Immanuel's grace,
And sweeps away mountains of guilt.
O sweet revelation divine !
Delighted, we've heard its contents ;
All through it our Jesus does shine.
A lover of all his dear saints.
2 Through various scenes of distress,
Perplexed with sin, guilt, and fear ;
This glorious message of grace
Has frequently yielded good cheer.
Dear Lord, may we prize the rich peace,
The peace so abundantly given ;
It flows through the word of thy grace,
And makes us anticipate heaven.

461 8.7.4. TOPLADY.
Dismission.—Heb. xiii. 20, 21 ; Ps. lxxxix. 15-17.
LORD, dismiss us with thy blessing ;
Fill our hearts with joy and peace ;
Let us each, thy love possessing,
Triumph in redeeming grace.
O refresh us !
Travelling through this wilderness.

2 Thanks we give and adoration,
For thy gospel's joyful sound ;
May the fruits of thy salvation
In our hearts and lives be found ;
May thy presence
With us evermore abound.
3 So, whene'er the signal's given,
Us from earth to call away,
Borne on angels' wings to heaven,
Glad to leave our cumbrous clay,
May we ready,
Rise and reign in endless day.

462 8.7.4. W. WILLIAMS.
Christ a Guide through Death to Glory.—Ps. lxxiii. 24.
GUIDE me, O thou great Jehovah !
Pilgrim through this barren land ;
I am weak, but thou art mighty ;

Hold me with thy powerful hand ;
Bread of heaven,
Feed me now and evermore.
2 Open thou the crystal fountain,
Whence the healing streams do flow ;
Let the fiery, cloudy pillar
Lead me all my journey through ;
Strong Deliverer,
Be thou still my strength and shield.
3 When I tread the verge of Jordan,
Bid my anxious fears subside ;
Death of deaths, and hell's Destruction,
Land me safe on Canaan's side ;
Songs of praises,
I will ever give to thee.

463 8.7. HART.
The Burial of a Saint.—1 Cor. xv. 42-44; 1 John iii. 2.
SONS of God, by blest adoption,
View the dead with steady eyes ;
What is sown thus in corruption,
Shall in incorruption rise ;
What is sown in death's dishonour,
Shall revive to glory's light ;
What is sown in this weak manner,
Shall be raised in matchless might.

2 Earthly cavern, to thy keeping
We commit our [brother's] dust ;
Keep it safely, softly sleeping,
Till our Lord demand thy trust.
Sweetly sleep, dear saint, in Jesus ;
Thou with us shalt wake from death ;
Hold he cannot, though he seize us ;
We his power defy by faith.

3 Jesus, thy rich consolations
To thy mourning people send ;
May we all, with faith and patience,
Wait for our approaching end.
Keep from courage, vain or vaunted,
For our change our hearts prepare ;
Give us confidence undaunted,
Cheerful hope and godly fear.

464 C.M. WATTS.
Victory over Death.--Hos. xiii. 14; 1 Cor. xv. 55-57.
O FOR an overcoming faith,
To cheer my dying hours,
To triumph o'er the monster, Death,
And all his frightful powers.
2 Joyful with all the strength I have
My quivering lips should sing,
" Where is thy boasted victory, Grave ?
And where's the monster's sting ? "
3 If sin be pardoned, I'm secure ;
Death has no sting beside ;

The law gives sin its damning power,
  But Christ, my ransom, died.
4 Now to the God of victory
    Immortal thanks be paid,
  Who makes us conquerors, though we die,
  Through Christ our living Head.

465   C.M.   WATTS.
Afflictions and Death under Providence.—Job v. 6-8.

NOT from the dust affliction grows,
  Nor troubles rise by chance ;
  Yet we are born to cares and woes—
  A sad inheritance !

2 As sparks break out from burning coals,
    And still are upwards borne,
  So grief is rooted in our souls,
    And man grows up to mourn.

3 Yet with my God I leave my cause
    And trust his promised grace ;
  He rules me by his well-known laws
    Of love and righteousness.

4 Not all the pains that e'er I bore
    Shall spoil my future peace ;
  For death and hell can do no more
    Than what my Father please.

466   C.M.   WATTS.
The Death and Burial of a Saint.—1 Thess. iv. 13, 14.

WHY do we mourn departed friends,
  Or shake at death's alarms ?
  'Tis but the voice that Jesus sends,
  To call them to his arms.

2 Are we not tending upward too,
    As fast as time can move ?
  Nor should we wish the hours more slow,
  To keep us from our love.

3 Why should we tremble to convey
    Their bodies to the tomb ?
  There the dear flesh of Jesus lay,
  And left a long perfume.

4 [The graves of all his saints he blessed,
    And softened every bed ;
  Where should the dying members rest,
    But with their dying Head ?]

5 Thence he arose, ascending high,
    And showed our feet the way ;
  Up to the Lord our flesh shall fly,
    At the great rising day.

6 Then let the last loud trumpet sound,
    And bid our kindred rise ;
  Awake, ye nations under ground ;
    Ye saints, ascend the skies.

467   C.M.   SWAIN.
Looking to Jesus in Death.—Tit. ii. 13, 14; Ps. xxiii. 4.

WHY should we shrink at Jordan's flood,
  Or dread the unknown way ?
  See, yonder rolls a stream of blood,
  That bears the curse away.

2 Death lost his sting when Jesus bled ;
    When Jesus left the ground,
  Disarmed, the King of terrors fled,
    And felt a mortal wound.

3 And now his office is to wait
    Between the saints and sin ;
  A *porter* at the heavenly gate,
    To let the pilgrims in.

4 And though his pale and ghastly face
    May seem to frown the while ;
  We soon shall see the King of grace,
    And he'll for ever smile.

468   C.M.   W. W. HORNE.
" To die is gain."—Phil. i. 21; Rev. xiv. 13.

DEATH is no more a frightful foe ;
  Since I with Christ shall reign,
  With joy I leave this world of woe.;
  For me to die is gain.

2 To darkness, doubts, and fears, adieu ;
    Adieu, thou world so vain ;
  Then shall I know no more of you ;
  For me to die is gain.

3 No more shall Satan tempt my soul,
    Corruption shall be slain ;
  And tides of pleasure o'er me roll ;
  For me to die is gain.

4 Nor shall I know a Father's frown,
    But ever with him reign,
  And wear an everlasting crown,
  For me to die is gain.

5 Sorrow for joy I shall exchange,
    For ever freed from pain ;
  And o'er the plains of Canaan range ;
  For me to die is gain.

6 Fain would my raptured soul depart,
    Nor longer here remain,
  But dwell, dear Jesus, where thou art ;
  For me to die is gain.

469   C.M.   NEWTON.
Hope beyond the Grave.—1 Peter i. 3—5; John xiv. 2.

MY soul, this curious house of clay,
  Thy present frail abode,
  Must quickly fall to worms a prey,
  And thou return to God.

2 Canst thou, by faith, survey with joy,
    The change before it come,

And say, " Let Death this house destroy,
I have a heavenly home ?

3 " The Saviour, whom I then shall see,
With new admiring eyes,
Already has prepared for me
A mansion in the skies.

4 " I feel this mud-walled cottage shake,
And long to see it fall ;
That I my willing flight may take
To Him who is my All.

5 " Burdened and groaning then no more,
My rescued soul shall sing,
As up the shining path I soar,
' Death, thou hast lost thy sting.' "

6 Dear Saviour, help us now to seek,
And grant thy Spirit's power ;
That we may all this language speak,
Before the dying hour.

470   L.M.   MEDLEY.
Death viewed in Jesus.—Job iii. 17; Heb. ii. 9-15.

DEATH and the grave are doleful themes,
For sinful mortal worms to sing ;
Except a Saviour's brighter beams
Dispel the gloom, and touch the string.

2 Death ! awful sound ! the fruit of sin,
And terror of the human race ;
Who, except Jesus smiles within,
Can look the monster in the face ?

3 Yet, dearest Lord, when viewed in thee,
The monster loses all his dread ;
There all his frightful horrors flee,
And joy surrounds a dying bed.

4 Jesus, the mighty Saviour, lives,
And he has conquered death and hell :
This truth substantial comfort gives,
And dying saints can sing, " 'Tis well."

471   S.M.   ELLIOTT & TOPLADY.
Preparation for Death.—Ps. x. 17; 1 Chron. xxix. 18.

PREPARE me, gracious God,
To stand before thy face ;
Thy Spirit must the work perform,
For it is all of grace.

2 In Christ's obedience clothe,
And wash me in his blood ;
So shall I lift my head with joy
Among the sons of God.

3 Do thou my sins subdue ;
Thy sovereign love make known,
The spirit of my mind renew,
And save me in thy Son.

4 Let me attest thy power ;
Let me thy goodness prove,

Till my full soul can hold no more
Of everlasting love.

472   C.M.   TOPLADY.
The Sweetness of Spiritual Things.—Ps. civ. 34.

WHEN languor and disease invade
This trembling house of clay,
'Tis sweet to look beyond our cage,
And long to fly away.

2 [Sweet to look inward, and attend
The whispers of his love ;
Sweet to look upward to the place
Where Jesus pleads above.]

3 Sweet to look back, and see my name
In life's fair book set down ;
Sweet to look forward, and behold
Eternal joys my own.

4 Sweet to reflect how grace divine
My sins on Jesus laid ;
Sweet to remember that his blood
My debt of suffering paid.

5 Sweet in his righteousness to stand,
Which saves from second death ;
Sweet to experience, day by day,
His Spirit's quickening breath.

6 [Sweet in his faithfulness to rest,
Whose love can never end ;
Sweet on his covenant of grace
For all things to depend.]

7 Sweet in the confidence of faith
To trust his firm decrees ;
Sweet to lie passive in his hands,
And know no will but his.

8 If such the sweetness of the streams,
What must the fountain be ?
Where saints and angels draw their bliss
Immediately from thee !

473   L.M.   WATTS.
The Sinner's Portion, and Saint's Hope.—Ps. xvii. 9-15.

LORD, I am thine, but thou wilt prove
My faith, my patience, and my love ;
When men of spite against me join,
They are the sword, the hand is thine.

2 Their hope and portion lie below ;
'Tis all the happiness they know ;
'Tis all they seek ; they take their shares
And leave the rest among their heirs.

3 What sinners value I resign ;
Lord, 'tis enough that thou art mine.
I shall behold thy blissful face,
And stand complete in righteousness.

4 This life's a dream, an empty show,
  But the bright world to which I go,
  Has joys substantial and sincere ;
  When shall I wake and find me there ?

5 O glorious hour ! O blest abode !
  I shall be near, and like my God !
  And flesh and sin no more control
  The sacred pleasures of my soul.

6 My flesh shall slumber in the ground,
  Till the last trumpet's joyful sound ;
  Then burst the chains with sweet surprise,
  And in my Saviour's image rise.

474   C.M.   WATTS.

Support under Trials on Earth.—Rev. xxi. 4; vii. 17.

WHEN I can read my title clear,
  To mansions in the skies,
I bid farewell to every fear,
  And wipe my weeping eyes.

2 Should earth against my soul engage,
  And hellish darts be hurled,
Then I can smile at Satan's rage,
  And face a frowning world.

3 Let cares like a wild deluge come,
  And storms of sorrow fall ;
May I but safely reach my home,
  My God, my Heaven, my All.

4 There shall I bathe my weary soul
  In seas of heavenly rest,
And not a wave of trouble roll
  Across my peaceful breast.

475   C.M.   WATTS.

Desiring to Depart.—Phil. i. 23; 2 Cor. v. 8; Isa. vi. 3.

FATHER, I long, I faint to see
  The place of thy abode ;
I'd leave thy earthly courts and flee
  Up to thy seat, my God !

2 Here I behold thy distant face,
  And 'tis a pleasing sight ;
But to abide in thy embrace
  Is infinite delight.

3 I'd part with all the joys of sense
  To gaze upon thy throne ;
Pleasure springs fresh for ever thence,
  Unspeakable, unknown.

4 [There all the heavenly hosts are seen ;
  In shining ranks they move,
And drink immortal vigour in,
  With wonder and with love.]

5 [There at thy feet, with awful fear,
  The adoring armies fall ;
With joy they shrink to *nothing* there,
  Before the eternal All.]

6 [There would I vie with all the host,
  In duty and in bliss,
While *less than nothing* I could boast,
  And *vanity* confess.]

7 The more thy glories strike my eyes
  The humbler I shall lie ;
Thus, while I sink, my joys shall rise
  Unmeasurably high.

476   C.M.   WATTS.

The Glory of Christ.—Phil. ii. 10; Ps. xlv. 1-7.

O THE delights, the heavenly joys,
  The glories of the place,
Where Jesus sheds the brightest beams
  Of his o'erflowing grace.

2 Sweet majesty and awful love
  Sit smiling on his brow,
And all the glorious ranks above
  At humble distance bow.

3 [Princes to his imperial name
  Bend their bright sceptres down ;
Dominions, thrones, and powers rejoice
  To see him wear the crown.]

4 Bless'd angels sound his lofty praise
  Through every heavenly street,
And lay their highest honours down,
  Submissive at his feet.

5 [Those soft, those blessed feet of his,
  That once rude iron tore,
High on a throne of light they stand,
  And all the saints adore.]

6 [His head, the dear majestic head,
  That cruel thorns did wound,
See what immortal glories shine,
  And circle it around.]

7 This is the Man, the exalted Man,
  Whom we, unseen, adore ;
But when our eyes behold his face,
  Our hearts shall love him more.

8 [Lord, how our souls are all on fire
  To see thy bless'd abode !
Our tongues rejoice in tunes of praise
  To our incarnate God.

9 And while our faith enjoys this sight,
  We long to leave our clay ;
And wish thy fiery chariots, Lord,
  To fetch our souls away.]

477   C.M.   WATTS.

The Example of Christ and his Saints.—Heb. xii. 1, 2.

GIVE me the wings of faith to rise
  Within the veil, and see

The saints above, how great their joys,
　How bright their glories be.
2 Once they were mourning here below,
　And wet their couch with tears ;
　They wrestled hard, as we do now,
　With sins, and doubts, and fears.
3 I ask them whence their victory came,
　They with united breath,
　Ascribe their conquest to the Lamb,
　Their triumph to his death.
4 They marked the footsteps that he trod,
　(His zeal inspired their breast) ;
　And following their incarnate God,
　Possess the promised rest.
5 Our glorious Leader claims our praise
　For his own pattern given ;
　While the long cloud of witnesses
　Shows the same path to heaven.

478   C.M.   WATTS.
Sight through a glass, and face to face.—1 Cor. xiii. 12.
　I LOVE the windows of thy grace,
　　Through which my Lord is seen,
　And long to meet my Saviour's face,
　　Without a glass between.
2 O that the happy hour were come,
　　To change my faith to sight !
　I shall behold my Lord at home,
　　In a diviner light.
3 Haste, my Beloved, and remove
　　These interposing days ;
　Then shall my passions all be love,
　　And all my powers be praise.

479   C.M.   WATTS.
The Meditation of Heaven.—2 Cor. iv. 17, 18.
　MY thoughts surmount these lower skies,
　　And look within the veil,
　There springs of endless pleasure rise,
　　The waters never fail.
2 There I behold, with sweet delight,
　　The blessed Three-in-One ;
　And strong affections fix my sight
　　On God's incarnate Son.
3 His promise stands for ever firm ;
　　His grace shall ne'er depart ;
　He binds my name upon his arm,
　　And seals it on his heart.
4 Light are the pains that nature brings ;
　　How short our sorrows are,
　When with eternal, future things,
　　The present we compare !
5 I would not be a stranger still
　　To that celestial place,
　Where I for ever hope to dwell,
　　Near my Redeemer's face.

480   L.M.   WATTS.
A sight of God mortifies to the world.—Ps. lxxiii. 25.
　UP to the fields where angels lie,
　And living waters gently roll,
　Fain would my thoughts leap out and fly,
　But sin hangs heavy on my soul.
2 Thy wondrous blood, dear dying Christ,
　Can make this world of guilt remove ;
　And thou canst bear me where thou fliest,
　On thy kind wings, celestial Dove.
3 [O might I once mount up and see
　The glories of the eternal skies,
　What little things these worlds would be ;
　How despicable to my eyes.]
4 Had I a glance of thee, my God,
　Kingdoms and men would vanish soon ;
　Vanish as though I saw them not,
　As a dim candle dies at noon.
5 Then they might fight, and rage, and rave,
　I should perceive the noise no more
　Than we can hear a shaking leaf,
　While rattling thunders round us roar.
6 Great All in All, eternal King !
　Let me but view thy lovely face,
　And all my powers shall bow and sing
　Thy endless grandeur and thy grace.

481   L.M.   WATTS.
The Sight of God and Christ in Heaven.—Col. iii. 4.
　DESCEND from heaven, immortal Dove,
　Stoop down and take us on thy wings,
　And mount and bear us far above
　The reach of these inferior things ;
2 Beyond, beyond this lower sky,
　Up where eternal ages roll,
　Where solid pleasures never die,
　And fruits immortal feast the soul.
3 O for a sight, a pleasing sight,
　Of our almighty Father's throne ;
　There sits our Saviour crowned with light,
　Clothed in a body like our own.
4 [Adoring saints around him stand,
　And thrones and powers before him fall ;
　The God shines gracious through the Man,
　And sheds sweet glories on them all.
5 O what amazing joys they feel,
　While to their golden harps they sing
　And sit on every heavenly hill,
　And spread the triumphs of their King !]
6 When shall the day, dear Lord, appear,
　That I shall mount to dwell above,

And stand and bow amongst them there
And view thy face, and sing thy love ?

482   L.M.   GOSPEL MAG., 1796.
The Believer's Treasure.—Col. i. 5,6; Matt. vi. 20, 21.

IN heaven my choicest treasure lies,
My hopes are placed above the skies ;
'Tis Christ, the bright and Morning Star,
Draws my affections from afar.

2 O that my anxious mind were free
From this vile tenement of clay,
That I might view the immortal Word,
And live and reign with Christ my Lord.

3 Then should I see, and feel, and know,
What 'tis to rest from sin and woe ;
And all my soul be tuned to sing
The praises due to Christ my King.

4 [Hail, blessed time ! Lord, bid me come,
And enter my celestial home,
And drown the sorrows of my breast,
In seas of unmolested rest.]

483   7.6.   GOSPEL MAG., 1804.
The Christian's Prospect of Heaven.—John xiv. 3.

YES, I shall soon be landed
On yonder shores of bliss.
There, with my powers expanded,
Shall dwell where Jesus is.

2 Yes, I shall soon be seated,
With Jesus on his throne,
My foes be all defeated,
And sacred peace made known.

3 With Father, Son, and Spirit,
I shall for ever reign,
Sweet joy and peace inherit,
And every good obtain.

4 I soon shall reach the harbour,
To which I speed my way,
Shall cease from all my labour,
And there for ever stay.

5 Sweet Spirit, guide me over
This life's tempestuous sea ;
Keep me, O holy Lover,
For I confide in thee.

6 O that in Jordan's swelling
I may be helped to sing,
And pass the river, telling
The triumphs of my King.

484   8.3.   HART.
The Saint's Inheritance.—2 Cor. vii. 1 ; 1 Pet. i. 4.

PERFECT holiness of spirit,
Saints above, full of love,
With the Lamb inherit.

2 This inheritance, believer,
Faith alone makes thy own,
Safe and sure for ever.

3 True, 'twas thine from everlasting,
But the bliss of it is
Known to thee by tasting.

4 Though thou here receive but little ;
Scarce enough for the proof
Of thy proper title ;

5 Urge thy claim through all unfitness ;
Sue it out, spurning doubt ;
The Holy Ghost's thy witness.

6 Cite the will of his own sealing ;
Title good, signed with blood,
Valid and unfailing.

7 When thy title thou discernest,
Humbly then sue again
For continual earnest.

485   7s.   C.W.
The Resurrection.—1 Cor. xv. 20, 55; Matt. xxviii. 2–7.

CHRIST, the Lord, is risen to-day,
Sons of men and angels say,
Raise your joys and triumphs high ;
Sing, ye heavens, and earth reply.

2 Love's redeeming work is done ;
Fought the fight, the battle won.
Lo ! the sun's eclipse is o'er ;
Lo ! he sets in blood no more !

3 Vain the stone, the watch, the seal ;
Christ has burst the gates of hell ;
Death in vain forbids his rise ;
Christ has opened paradise.

4 Lives again our glorious King ;
Where, O Death, is now thy sting ?
Once he died our souls to save ;
Where's thy victory, boasting Grave ?

5 [Soar we now where Christ has led,
Following our exalted Head ;
Made like him, like him we rise ;
Ours the cross, the grave, the skies !]

6 Hail ! the Lord of earth and heaven !
Praise to thee by both be given !
Thee we greet, triumphant now !
Hail ! the *Resurrection* thou !

486   C.M.   HART.
Christ's Resurrection.—Matt. xx. 19; Luke xxiv. 2–7

SEE from the dungeon of the dead,
Our great Deliverer rise ;

While conquests wreathe his heavenly head,
And glory glads his eyes.

2 The struggling Hero, strong to save,
Did all our miseries bear
Down to the chambers of the grave,
And left the burden there.

3 [See, how the well-pleased angel rolls
The stone, and opes the prison !
Lift up your heads, ye sin-sick souls,
And sing, The Lord is risen.]

4 No more indictments justice draws ;
It sets the soul at large ;
Our Surety undertook the cause,
And faith's a full discharge.

5 To save us, our Redeemer died ;
To justify us, rose ;
Where's the condemning power beside
Has right to interpose ?

6 The Lord is risen ! thou trembling soul,
Let fears no more confound !
Let heaven and earth, from pole to pole,
The Lord is risen resound !

487   S.M.   HART.
The same.—Luke xxiv. 34; Ps. xvi. 10; Acts xiii. 34.
CHRISTIANS, dismiss your fear ;
Let hope and joy succeed ;
The great good news with gladness hear,
The Lord is risen indeed.

2   The shades of death withdrawn,
His eyes their beams display ;
So wakes the sun, when rosy dawn
Unbars the gates of day.

3   The promise is fulfilled ;
Salvation's work is done ;
Justice with mercy's reconciled,
And God has raised his Son.

4   He quits the dark abode,
From all corruption free ;
The holy, harmless Child of God
Could no corruption see.

5   [Angels, with saints above,
The rising Victor sing ;
And all the blissful seats of love
With loud hosannas ring.

6   Ye pilgrims, too, below,
Your hearts and voices raise ;
Let every breast with gladness glow,
And every mouth sing praise.]

7   My soul, thy Saviour laud,
Who all thy sorrows bore ;
Who died for sin, but lives to God,
And lives to die no more.

8   His death procured thy peace,
His resurrection's thine ;
Believe ; receive the full release ;
Tis signed with blood divine.

488   L.M.   HART.
The same.—Luke xxiv. 4–7; 1 Pet. i. 3; Isa. xlii. 21.
UPRISING from the darksome tomb,
See the victorious Jesus come ;
The Almighty Prisoner quits the prison,
And angels tell, The Lord is risen.

2 Ye guilty souls, that groan and grieve,
Hear the glad tidings, hear and live !
God's righteous law is satisfied,
And justice now is on your side.

3 Your Surety, thus released by God,
Pleads the rich ransom of his blood ;
No new demand, no bar remains,
But mercy now triumphant reigns.

4 Believers, hail your rising Head,
The first-begotten from the dead ;
Your resurrection's sure, through his,
To endless life and boundless bliss !

489   C.M.   HART.
Christ's Ascension.—Luke xxiv. 51-53; Ps. lxviii. 18.
Now for a theme of thankful praise
To tune the stammerer's tongue ;
Christians, your hearts and voices raise,
And join the joyful song.

2 The Lord's ascended up on high,
Decked with resplendent wounds ;
While shouts of victory rend the sky,
And heaven with joy resounds.

3 See, from the regions of the dead,
Through all the ethereal plains,
The powers of darkness captive led,
The dragon dragged in chains.

4 Ye eternal gates, your leaves unfold !
Receive the conquering King ;
Ye angels, strike your harps of gold ;
And saints, triumphant sing.

5 Sinners, rejoice ! he died for you ;
For you prepares a place ;
Sends down his Spirit to guide you through
With every gift of grace.

6 His blood, which did your sins atone,
For your salvation pleads ;
And, seated on his Father's throne,
He reigns and intercedes.

490   7s.   HART.
Christ's Resurrection and Ascension.—Acts i. 9.
JESUS, our triumphant Head,
Risen victorious from the dead,

To the realms of glory gone,
To ascend his rightful throne.

2 Cherubs on the Conqueror gaze ;
Seraphs glow with brighter blaze ;
Each bright order of the sky
Hails him as he passes by.

3 [Saints the glorious triumph meet,
See their enemies at his feet !
By his scars his toils are viewed,
And his garments rolled in blood.]

4 [Heaven its King congratulates ;
Opens wide her golden gates ;
Angels songs of victory sing ;
All the blissful regions ring.]

5 Sinners, join the heavenly powers,
For redemption all is ours ;
None but burdened sinners prove
Blood-bought pardon, dying love.

6 Hail, thou dear, thou worthy Lord ;
Holy Lamb, incarnate Word !
Hail, thou suffering Son of God !
Take the trophies of thy blood.

491   8.7.   HART.
The same.—Rev. i. 8-18; Isa. xxv. 8; Matt. xxv. 31-41.
PLEASED we read in sacred story,
How our Lord resumed his breath ;
Where's, O Grave, thy conquering glory ?
Where's thy sting, thou phantom Death ?
Soon thy jaws, restrained from chewing,
Must disgorge their ransomed prey ;
Man first gave thee power to ruin ;
Man, too, takes that power away.

2 I am Alpha, says the Saviour,
I Omega likewise am !
I was dead and live for ever,
God Almighty and the Lamb.
In the Lord is our perfection,
And in him our boast we'll make ;
We shall share his resurrection,
If we of his death partake.

3 Ye that die without repentance,
Ye must rise when Christ appears ;
Rise to hear your dreadful sentence,
While the saints rejoice in theirs :
You to dwell with fiends infernal,
They with Jesus Christ to reign ;
They go into life eternal,
You to everlasting pain.

492   L.M.   HART.
The same.—Heb. ii. 14; Eph. iv. 8; 1 Cor. xv. 54.
YE Christians, hear the joyful news,
Death has received a deadly bruise ;

Our Lord has made his empire fall,
And conquered him that conquered all.

2 Though doomed are all men once to die,
Yet we by faith death's power defy ;
We soon shall feel his bands unbound,
Awakened by the Archangel's sound.

3 The trump of God shall rend the rocks,
And open adamantine locks ;
Come forth the dead from death's dark dome,
And Jesus call his ransomed home.

493   8.7.4.   CENNICK, C. W.
AND MADAN.
The Second Coming of Christ.—Rev. i. 7.
Lo ! he comes, with clouds descending,
Once for favoured sinners slain,
Thousand, thousand saints attending,
Swell the triumph of his train,
And with pleasure,
Magnify his awful name !

2 Every eye shall now behold him,
Robed in dreadful majesty ;
Those who set at naught and sold him,
Pierced and nailed him to the tree,
Deeply wailing,
Shall the true Messiah see.

3 Every island, sea, and mountain—
Heaven and earth, shall flee away ;
All who hate him must, confounded,
Hear the trump proclaim the day ;
Come to judgment !
Come to judgment ! come away !

4 Now redemption, long expected,
See in solemn pomp appear !
All his saints, by man rejected,
Now shall meet him in the air !
Hallelujah !
See the day of God appear !

494   148th.   BURNHAM.
"Shall see the Son of Man coming."—Matt. xxv. 30.
ON yonder glorious height,
King Jesus does appear,
Upon the judgment-seat,
With millions at his bar ;
Behold the awful Judge is come,
To fix their everlasting doom.

2 Sinners must now come forth
And stand before the Lord,
Whose word they scorned on earth,
Whose children they abhorred ;
Then speaks the Judge, " Ye sinners, go
From my blessed face to endless woe."

3 But now, my soul, behold
   That host at his right hand ;
   O see the blood-washed world
   Boldly before him stand ;
How pleased they look, how bright they shine,
While Jesus cries, " These, these are mine ! "

4 " These are my holy race ;
   These did resound my fame ;
   These prized redeeming grace ;
   These loved and feared my name ;
And these shall now ascend with me
To mansions of eternal day."

495   8.7.4.   SWAIN.

Coming of Christ to Judgment.—Matt. xxv. 31—46.

Lo ! he comes, arrayed in vengeance,
   Riding down the heavenly road ;
Floods of fury roll before him :
   Who can meet an angry God ?
     Tremble, sinners ;
   Who can stand before his rod ?

2 Lo ! he comes in glory shining ;
   Saints, arise and meet your King !
" Glorious Captain of salvation,
   Welcome, welcome," hear them sing !
     Shouts of triumph
   Make the heavens with echoes ring.

3 Now, despisers, look and wonder !
   Hear the dreadful sound, " Depart ! "
Rattling like a peal of thunder,
   Through each guilty rebel's heart !
     Lost for ever !
   Hope and sinners here must part.

4 [Still they hear the dreadful sentence ;
   Hell resounds the dreadful roar ;
While their heart-strings rend with anguish,
   Trembling on the burning shore ;
     Justice seals it ;
   Down they sink to rise no more.

5 How they shrink with horror, viewing
   Hell's deep caverns opening wide ;
Guilty thoughts, like ghosts, pursuing,
   Plunge them down the rolling tide !
     Now consider,
   Ye who scorn the Lamb that died.]

6 Hark ! ten thousand harps resounding !
   Formed in bright and grand array ;
See the glorious armies rising,
   While their Captain leads the way ;
     Heaven before them,
   Opens an eternal day.

496   8.7.4.   NEWTON.

Day of Judgment.—Matt. xii. 36 ; xxv. 31—46.

DAY of judgment, day of wonders !
   Hark ! the trumpet's awful sound,
Louder than a thousand thunders,
   Shakes the vast creation round !
     How the summons
   Will the sinner's heart confound !

2 See the Judge our nature wearing,
   Clothed in Majesty divine
You who long for his appearing,
   Then shall say, " This God is mine ! "
     Gracious Saviour,
   Own me in that day for thine.

3 [At his call the dead awaken,
   Rise to life from earth and sea !
All the powers of nature, shaken
   By his looks, prepare to flee !
     Careless sinner,
   What will then become of thee ?

4 Horrors, past imagination,
   Will surprise your trembling heart,
When you hear your condemnation,
   " Hence ! accursèd wretch, depart !
     Thou with Satan
   And his angels have thy part."

5 But to those who have confessèd,
   Loved, and served the Lord below,
He will say, " Come near, ye blessèd,
   See the kingdom I bestow ;
     You for ever
   Shall my love and glory know."]

6 Under sorrows and reproaches
   May this thought our courage raise ;
Swiftly God's great day approaches ;
   Sighs shall then be changed to praise !
     We shall triumph
   When the world is in a blaze.

497   50th   WATTS.

The Last Judgment.—1 Thess. iv. 16, 17 ; Ps. i. 5.

THE God of glory sends his summons forth,
Calls the south nations and awakes the north;
From east to west his sovereign orders spread,
Thro' distant worlds, and regions of the dead
The trumpet sounds ; hell trembles, heaven rejoices ;
Lift up your heads, ye saints, with cheerful voices.

2 No more shall Atheists mock his long delay ;
His vengeance sleeps no more, behold the day !

Behold, the Judge descends ; his guards are nigh ;
Tempests and fire attend him down the sky !
When God appears, all nature shall adore him ;
While sinners tremble, saints rejoice before him.

3 " Heaven, earth, and hell, draw near : let all things come
To hear my justice, and the sinner's doom ;
But gather first my saints," the Judge commands ; [lands."
" Bring them, ye angels, from their distant
When Christ returns, wake ev'ry cheerful passion;
And shout, ye saints, he comes for your salvation.

4 " Behold ! my covenant stands for ever good,
Sealed by the eternal sacrifice in blood,
And signed with all their names, the Greek, the Jew,
That paid the ancient worship, or the new."
There's no distinction here ; join all your voices
And raise your heads, ye saints, for heaven rejoices.

5 " Here," says the Lord, " ye angels, spread their thrones ;
And near me seat my favourites, and my sons ;
Come, my redeemed, possess the joys prepared
Ere time began---'tis your divine reward ; "
When Christ returns, wake ev'ry cheerful passion ;
And shout, ye saints, he comes for your salvation.

498 C.M. WATTS.
Shortness of Life, and Goodness of God.—Ps. lxv. 11

TIME ! what an empty vapour 'tis !
And days how swift they are !
Swift as an Indian arrow flies,
Or like a shooting star.

2 [The present moments just appear,
Then slide away in haste,
That we can never say, " They're here,"
But only say, " They're past."]

3 [Our life is ever on the wing,
And death is ever nigh ;
The moment when our lives begin,
We all begin to die.]

4 Yet, mighty God ! our fleeting days
Thy lasting favours share ;
Yet with the bounties of thy grace,
Thou load'st the rolling year.

5 'Tis sovereign mercy finds us food,
And we are clothed with love ;
While grace stands pointing out the road
That leads our souls above.

6 His goodness runs an endless round ;
All glory to the Lord !
His mercy never knows a bound ;
And be his name adored.

7 Thus we begin the lasting song,
And, when we close our eyes,
Let the next age thy praise prolong
Till time and nature dies.

499 S.M. MEDLEY.
New Year.—Ps. lii. 1 ; lxv. 11.

GREAT God ! before thy throne
We joyfully appear,
In songs to make thy glories known,
And thus begin the year.

2 [What favours all divine ;
What mercies shall we share ;
What blessings all around us shine
To open this new year !]

3 Indulgent goodness spares
And still preserves us here,
And bounty all divine prepares
Supplies for this new year.

4 Our follies past forgive ;
Our souls divinely cheer :
And help us more to thee to live,
Dear Lord, in this new year.

5 Prepare us for thy will,
Whatever may appear ;
And let thy loving-kindness still
Preserve us through the year.

6 Confirm our souls in thee,
In faith and holy fear ;
And let a precious Jesus be
Our song through all the year.

500 8.7. NEWTON.
The favour of the Trinity desired.—2 Cor. xiii. 14.

MAY the grace of Christ, our Saviour,
And the Father's boundless love,
With the Holy Spirit's favour,
Rest upon us from above.
Thus may we abide in union
With each other and the Lord ;
And possess, in sweet communion,
Joys which earth cannot afford.

501 7s. NEWTON.
At Parting.—Acts xviii. 21 ; 1 Cor. iv. 19.

FOR a season called to part,
Let us now ourselves commend
To the gracious eye and heart
Of our ever-present Friend.

2 Jesus, hear our humble prayer,
Tender Shepherd of thy sheep ;

Let thy mercy and thy care
All our souls in safety keep.
3 In thy strength may we be strong ;
Sweeten every cross and pain ;
Give us, if we live, ere long,
Here to meet in peace again.
4 Then, if thou thy help afford,
Ebenezers shall be reared ;
All our souls shall praise the Lord,
Who our poor petitions heard.

502   S.M.   HART.
1 John v. 7; Ps. ciii. 20-22.
WITH all the heavenly host,
Let Christians join to laud
The Father, Son, and Holy Ghost,—
Our Saviour and our God.

503   7s.   HART.
1 John v. 7.
GLORY to the Eternal be,
Three-in-One, and One-in-Three ;
God that pitied sinners lost,—
Father, Son, and Holy Ghost.

504   8.8.6.   HART.
1 Chron. xvi. 28.
YE saints on earth, your voices raise,
And sing the eternal Father's praise,
And glorify the Son ;
Give glory to the Holy Ghost,
And join with all the angelic host
To bless the great Three-One.

505   C.M.   WATTS.
1 Cor. x. 31 ; 1 Pet. ii. 9.
GLORY to God the Father's name,
Who, from our sinful race,
Chose out his favourites to proclaim
The honours of his grace.
2 Glory to God the Son be paid
Who dwelt in humble clay,
And, to redeem us from the dead,
Gave his own life away.
3 Glory to God the Spirit give,
From whose almighty power
Our souls their heavenly birth derive,
And bless the happy hour.
4 Glory to God that reigns above,
The eternal Three-in-One,
Who, by the wonders of his love,
Has made his nature known.

506   148th.   WATTS.
John v. 23.
To God the Father's throne
Perpetual honours raise ;

Glory to God the Son ;
To God the Spirit praise ;
And while our lips their tribute bring,
Our faith adores the name we sing.

506ᴬ   L.M.   BISHOP KEN.
Ps. cxvii. ; cl. 6 ; cxlviii. 2-4.
PRAISE God, from whom all blessings flow ;
Praise him all creatures here below ;
Praise him above, ye heavenly host ;
Praise Father, Son, and Holy Ghost.

507   C.M.   D. HERBERT.
" Turn thou me, and I shall be turned."—Jer. xxxi. 18.
How oft I grumble and repine,
With blessings in my hand ;
There's nothing here can satisfy,
Nor gold, nor house, nor land.

2 Sometimes the Lord bestows on me,
His fretful child, a toy,
On which I raise my prospects high,
And look for certain joy.

3 But soon there's something intervenes ;
I've something else in view ;
The former mercy is forgot,
And I want something new.

4 [Oh ! this unstable heart of mine
Is like the troubled sea ;
The more I have, the more I want ;
When shall I settled be ?]

5 I know this wretched world can't fill
This anxious soul of mine ;
O could I to my Father's will
My soul, my all resign !

6 [Sometimes, alas ! I think I can ;
I'll trust the world no more ;
But when I meet some little cross,
I'm fretful as before.

7 Why am I captivated thus,
By such poor trifling toys ?
Alas ! how oft this wretched world
Annoys my better joys !]

8 I want to trust, but cannot trust,
A God of providence ;
Although he bless from day to day,
I'm full of diffidence.

9 [When troubles roll in thick and fast,
Ah ! then my faith gives way ;
Sometimes I think I cannot stand,
No, not another day.]

10 Sometimes, like Ephraim, I rebel,
I cannot bear the yoke ;

I kick and murmur at the rod,
  And shrink at every stroke ;

11 But when my Father smiles again,
  Then what a fool am I !
'Tis then, like Ephraim, I repent,
  And smite upon my thigh.

12 Like him I mourn, like him I cry,
  " Lord, hold me with thy hand ;
And draw me by thy special grace ;
  Hold up, and I shall stand."

508   C.M.   D. HERBERT.
Before Sermon.—Isa. lv. 11; Deut. xxxii. 2, 3.
LORD, fill thy servant's soul to-day
  With pure seraphic fire,
And set his tongue at liberty,
  And grant his soul's desire.

2 O may he preach the word of God
  With energy and power ;
May gospel-blessings spread around,
  Like a refreshing shower.

3 May God's eternal love and grace
  Be sweetly felt within ;
While he is preaching Christ the Lord,
  Who bore our curse and sin.

4 May burdened sinners lose their load,
  And downcast souls rejoice ;
May doubting souls believe to-day
  They are Jehovah's choice.

5 May Christ be first, and Christ be last,
  And Christ be all in all,
Who died to make salvation sure,
  And raise us from the fall.

6 O may thy servant now to-day
  Proclaim salvation free,

  As finished by the Son of God,
    For such poor souls as we.

509   C.M.   D. HERBERT.
" He shall call upon me, I will answer."—Ps. xci. 15.
COME, come, my soul, with boldness come,
  Unto the throne of grace ;
There Jesus sits to answer prayer,
  And shows a smiling face.

2 Our Surety stands before the throne,
  And personates our case ;
And sends the blessed Spirit down
  With tokens of his grace.

3 There's not a groan, nor wish, nor sigh,
  But penetrates his ears ;
He knows our sins perplex and tease,
  And cause our doubts and fears.

4 But he upholds us with his arm,
  And will not let us fall ;
When Satan roars, and sin prevails,
  He hears our mournful call.

5 He knows we have no strength at all ;
  He knows our foes are strong ;
But though ten thousand foes engage,
  The weakest sha'n't go wrong.

6 Then let us all unite and sing
  The praises of free grace ;
Those souls who long to see him now,
  Shall surely see his face.

510   C.M.   D. HERBERT.
" O Lord, rebuke me not in thine anger."—Ps. vi. 1, 4.
O LORD, rebuke me not in wrath ;
  Thy anger who can bear ?
'Tis heaven to live beneath thy smiles ;
  Thy frowns create despair.

2 I'm but a mass of filthiness ;
  I own my wretched case ;
O heal my loathsome, stinking wounds,
  And magnify thy grace.

3 [Ah ! must I die with this sad plague ?
  What ! is thy pity gone ?
Lord, look, and heal my broken bones ;
  O look on God the Son !]

4 On thee I'll wait ; in thee I'll trust ;
  For thou art still my God ;
Crush not my soul beneath thy hand,
  O take away thy rod.

5 Lord, let not guilt thus plague my soul ;
  I would be rid of sin.
From head to foot I'm nought but wounds,
  But, ah ! I'm worse within.

6 [Within, O what a hellish crew !
  Who knows what dwells within ?
How oft some darling lust creeps out,
  Some unsuspected sin !]

7 Lord Jesus, heal this malady,
  And set my broken bones ;
Let my petitions reach thy ears,
  Though only sighs and groans.

8 Base as I am, yet, blessed Lord,
  I dare to make this plea :
As Jesus died to save the lost,
  Perhaps he died for me.

511   C.M.   FRANKLIN.
Jesus, the soul's help in times of trouble.—Ps. xxxi. 7.
IN all my troubles and distress,
  The Lord my soul does own ;
Jehovah does my griefs redress,
  And make his mercy known.

2 He helps me on him to rely ;
   He is my strength and tower ;
   'Tis he that hears me when I cry,
   And manifests his power.

3 In every storm, in every sea,
   My Jesus makes a way ;
   His light shall make the darkness flee,
   And turn the shade to day.

4 'Tis he in trouble bears me up,
   And leads me safely through ;
   My Jesus does maintain my cup,
   And daily strength renew.

512   C.M.   FRANKLIN.
Prayer for increase and union in the Church.—Acts ii.

THY church, O Lord, that's planted here,
   O make it to increase
With numbers, blessed with filial fear,
   Enjoying heavenly peace.

2 O may we all, dear Lord, as one,
   United ever be,
Rejoicing in what Christ has done,
   Who groaned upon the tree.

3 May all each other's burdens bear ;
   Be simple, meek, and kind ;
And keep us safe from every snare,
   And all of humble mind.

513   L.M.   FRANKLIN.
" Jehovah-Jireh."—Gen. xxii. 14.

IN mounts of danger and of straits,
My soul for his salvation waits ;
Jehovah-Jireh will appear,
And save me from my gloomy fear.

2 He, in the most distressing hour,
Displays the greatness of his power ;

In darkest nights he makes a way,
And turns the gloomy shade to day.

3 Jehovah-Jireh is his name ;
From age to age he proves the same ;
He sees when I am sunk in grief,
And quickly flies to my relief.

4 The Lord Jehovah is my guide ;
He does and will for me provide ;
And in the mount it shall be seen,
How kind and gracious he has been.

PART II.

HYMNS BY W. GADSBY.

514   8.7.4.
"The glory of the Lord shall be revealed."—Isa. xi. 5.

O WHAT matchless condescension
  The eternal God displays ;
Claiming our supreme attention,
  To his boundless works and ways.
    His own glory
  He reveals in gospel days.

2 In the person of the Saviour,
  . All his majesty is seen !
Love and justice shine for ever ;
  And, without a veil between,
    Worms approach him,
  And rejoice in his dear name.

3 Would we view his brightest glory,
  Here it shines in Jesus' face ;
Sing and tell the pleasing story,
  O ye sinners saved by grace ;
    And with pleasure,
  Bid the guilty him embrace.

4 In his highest work, redemption,
  See his glory in a blaze ;
Nor can angels ever mention
  Aught that more of God displays ;
    Grace and justice
  Here unite to endless days.

5 True, 'tis sweet and solemn pleasure,
  God to view in Christ the Lord ;
Here he smiles and smiles for ever ;
  May my soul his name record ;
    Praise and bless him,
And his wonders spread abroad.

515   7s.
Person and power of the Spirit.—John vi. 63 ; xvi. 13.

HOLY GHOST, we look to thee ;
Raise the dead ; the captive free ;
From the mighty take the prey,
Teach the weak to watch and pray.

2 Now, dear Lord, the heavens rend ;
Make some haughty rebel bend ;
Life, and light, and truth impart,
To some careless sinner's heart.

3 If it be thy holy will,
Now thy gracious word fulfil ;
Quicken souls, and make them cry,
"Jesus, save me, or I die."

4 [Nor thy mourning saints forget ;
Thy sweet unction still repeat ;

Daily lead us unto Christ,
As our Prophet, King, and Priest.]

5 Thine it is the church to bless,
And to comfort in distress ;
Trembling, helpless souls to guide,
Safe to Jesus' wounded side.

6 Out of self to Jesus lead !
For and in us intercede ;
Guide us down to death, and there
Banish all our guilt and fear.

7 There and then support the mind ;
May we be to death resigned ;

And with an immortal song,
Haste to join the heavenly throng.

516   8s.
Jehovah united in Salvation.—1 Sam. xii. 22.

THE Triune Jehovah we praise,
  In essence eternally one,
Who has, by the word of his grace,
  His counsels eternal made known ;
The Father, the Spirit, and Word,
  As three in one God, and no more,
In Zion's salvation accord ;
  Then let us this one God adore.

2 No change can take place in his mind :
  His counsels are settled of old ;
To Zion he'll ever be kind,
  And to her his glory unfold.
Though men, sin, and devils unite
  To drive the believer to hell,
Jehovah will put them to flight,
  And Zion shall surely prevail.

3 In Jesus, and Jesus alone,
  The church stands for ever complete ;
And whilst he remains on his throne,
  He will not the weakest forget ;
They're his and shall ever be his,
  And with him in glory shall reign,
The triune Jehovah to bless,
  For ever and ever. Amen.

517   6.4.
The Trinity.—1 John v. 7 ; 1 Cor. xii. 4-6 ; Eph. iv. 4.

WE bless the triune God—
  The Father and the Word,
    And Holy Ghost ;

God, who must ever be
The mighty One-in-Three ;
To all eternity
   The Lord of Hosts.

2 Holy, immortal Three,
One God eternally,
   Teach us to praise ;
Mysterious Three-in-One,
To us thy grace make known,
And lead us safely on
   In thy own ways.

3 While we in Meshech dwell,
May we thy wonders tell,
   Nor yield to fear.
Though men and devils rage,
And all their powers engage,
Zion, from age to age,
   Is thy own care.

4 We bless the Father's name,
Whose love is still the same ;
   We also praise
The Spirit and the Word ;
Be this one God adored,
In solemn, sweet accord,
   To endless days.

518   7s.
"Glory to God in the highest."—Luke ii. 14.
At the birth of Christ our King,
Angels made the heavens ring,
Singing, with a solemn joy,
"Glory to the Lord on high."

2 Glory in the highest height,
Blazing with majestic light,
Shines in David's root and rod,
The incarnate Son of God.

3 Sinners here by faith may view,
What Omnipotence can do ;
And in measure sweetly trace
The rich treasures of his grace.

4 Come, ye mourning souls, rejoice ;
Look, and, with a cheerful voice,
Sing the honours of your Lord,
Blazing in the incarnate Word.

5 Soon the whole elect shall view
All the glory God can shew !
And in bliss immortal sing,
Hallelujah to their King.

519   S.M.
"Let fall some handfuls."—Ruth ii. 16.
[When Ruth a-gleaning went,
Jehovah was her guide ;

To Boaz' field he led her straight,
And she became his bride.]

2 Jesus my Boaz is ;
My strength and portion too ;
His word of grace the precious field,
Where I a-gleaning go.

3 O what a heavenly field !
What handfuls it contains !
What strength and comfort gleaners get,
To recompense their pains !

4 Rejoice, ye mourning souls ;
Ye broken hearts, be strong ;
The field is ripe for harvest now,
And ye shall glean ere long.

5 Ye gleaners, one and all,
Let Christ be all your song ;
He is your strength and portion too,
And you to him belong.

6 [All blessings he contains ;
He cannot let you starve :
The meanest gleaner in his field,
At length shall walk at large.]

520   104th.
"The law is good if a man use it lawfully."—1 Tim. i. 8
The law of the Lord is perfect and good,
But cannot afford nor comfort nor food,
To sinners distressed, o'erwhelmed with fear,
But Jesus the blessed can yield them good cheer.

2 The sinner may toil with care and with pain,
Some comfort to bring from Sinai's flame,
Spend long nights in sorrow, and days in distress,
Yet find on the morrow the law does him curse.

3 Where then can he flee for help or relief ?
A sinner is he, a rebel in chief ;
He feels himself guilty, and what can he do ?
He's unsound and filthy, and no good can show.

4 Thanks be to the Lamb, the great King of kings,
Who comes just in time, & glad tidings brings,
Applies peace & pardon, with power from above,
The poor soul to gladden, and calls him his love.

5 [These tidings Christ brings, and they reach
   the heart ;
The Spirit he sends his truth to impart ;
The sweet Spirit seals him a son and an heir,
And comforts and cheers him, & banishes fear.]

6 Then ravished with joy, and o'ercome with
   love,   [my God,
"Abba, Father," he'll cry, "my Lord and
My Friend & my Portion, my Head & my All ;
Thou art my Salvation from guilt, sin, & thrall."

521 104th.
"Dead to the law," —Gal. ii. 19-21; Rom. vii. 4, 6.

THANKS be to my Head, the great King of kings,
My life from the dead, the death of my sins ;
Who took all my woes, and was made sin for me ;
Who died, and who rose, and from sin set me free.

2 His Spirit he sent, to soften my heart ;
The old veil to rend, and life to impart ;
To bring me from darkness to light in the Lord,
And kill me to Moses, to sin, and the world.

3 Thus I, through the law, dead to the law am,
Yet married am I to Jesus the Lamb !
This union is sealed, all heaven's agreed ;
From sin and from Moses I henceforth am freed.

4 My soul, then, rejoice ; let Christ be thy song ;
With heart and with voice, with lip and with
tongue,
Before men or angels, sing, Worthy's the Lamb
Of unceasing praises, for ever. Amen.

522 122nd.
Saints freed from Hagar.-Gen. xxi. 9-12; Gal. iv. 21-31.

WHAT ! must the Christian draw
His comforts from the law,
That can do nothing but condemn ?
If this be Zion's rule,
Then unto Hagar's school,
Must Sarah send her free-born son.

2 But the bond-woman's son
With such shall not be one,
Isaac alone is lawful heir ;
So Abra'm must obey,
And Ishmael send away,
Nor Hagar must continue there.

3 Jehovah has decreed,
None but the chosen seed
Shall ever be accounted free ;
Not one shall e'er possess
The promised land of bliss,
But Abra'm's lawful family.

4 And these shall all be freed
From bondage, guilt, and dread,
And bliss, immortal bliss enjoy ;
Beyond, beyond the grave,
The land of promise have,
And live with God eternally.

523 8s.
The Law of Liberty.—James i. 25; John xiii. 17.

THE gospel's the law of the Lamb ;
My soul of its glories shall sing ;

With pleasure my tongue shall proclaim
The law of my Saviour and King ;
A sweet law of liberty this ;
A yoke that is easy and mild ;
Of love it the precious law is,
Unknown unto all but a child.

2 [The law of the Spirit of life,
That takes the old yoke from our neck,
Proves Zion to be the Lamb's wife,
And Zion with beauty does deck ;
Provides her a clothing divine,
And makes her all-glorious within ;
Nor angels are clothed more fine,
Nor can it be sullied with sin.]

3 Its beauties all centre in Christ,
For Christ is the substance of it ;
It makes broken hearts to rejoice,
And insolvent debtors will fit.

'Tis wisdom, 'tis strength, and 'tis love,
'Tis all that a sinner can need ;
And all that are born from above,
By Jesus from Moses are freed.

4 This law is the poor pilgrim's rule ;
With boldness this truth I'll maintain ;
Thrice happy's the man, though a fool,
That in it can look and remain ;
This man shall be blest in his deed,
For Jesus and he are but one ;
He'll therefore supply all his need,
For ever and ever. Amen.

524 11s.
Glad Tidings.—Isa. lxi. 1-3; Matt. xi. 5, 28.

THE gospel brings tidings, glad tidings indeed,
To mourners in Zion, who want to be freed
From sin, & from Satan, & Mount Sinai's flame,
Good news of salvation, through Jesus the Lamb.

2

What sweet invitations the gospel contains,
To men heavy laden with bondage and chains ;
It welcomes the weary to come and be blessed
With ease from their burdens, in Jesus to rest.

3

For every poor mourner, who thirsts for the Lord,
A fountain is opened in Jesus the Word ;
Their poor parched conscience to cool & to wash
From guilt & pollution, from dead works & dross.

4

A robe is provided, their shame now to hide,
In which none are clothed but Jesus's bride ;
And though it be costly, yet is the robe free,
And all Zion's mourners shall decked with it be.

5

[A ring that denotes his unchangeable love,
Is put on the finger, God's kindness to prove,
(This love no beginning can know, nor an end,)
And Zion shall wear it in praise of her Friend.]

525 L.M.

Good News.—Eph. i. 3; Numb. xxiii. 21.

WHAT joyful news the gospel is,
To guilty sinners in distress !
It speaks of mercy, rich and free,
For such polluted worms as we.

2 Jesus, my Shepherd, lived and died,
Rose, and now lives to intercede ;
He bears my name upon his heart,
Nor will he ever with me part.

3 For me he bore the wrath of God ;
For me he in the wine-press trod ;
He magnified the law for me,
And I for ever am set free.

4 [He loved me ere the world began ;
Nor did my Saviour love alone ;
The Spirit and the Father joined,
As one Jehovah, in one mind.]

5 In endless love, the Holy Three
All blessings have secured for me ;
All good that's worthy of a God,
For me in Jesus Christ is stored.

6 What glory, yea, what matchless grace,
Appears in my Redeemer's face !
All Deity can there agree
To smile upon a worm like me.

526 148th.

"The joyful sound."—Ps. lxxxix. 15; Matt. xviii. 11.

THRICE happy are the men,
Who know the joyful sound ;

They glory in the Lamb ;
Their hopes upon him found ;
They see how justice, truth, and grace,
Agree and shine in Jesus' face.

2 A joyful sound indeed,
To sinners in distress,
Who have no works to plead
But what are vile and base ;
Who feel their hearts a dreadful den
Of every murderous, hateful sin.

3 For such to hear and know
Salvation is of God,
That Jesus will bestow
The riches of his love
On sinners who have nought to bring,
Will make their very souls to sing.

4 He pardons all their sins,
And makes them white as wool,
And the sweet Spirit sends,
To fill their vessels full
Of faith, and love, and joy, and peace,
And seal them sons and heirs of grace.

527 C.M.

The Gospel.—Rom. x. 15; Isa. lii. 7; Rom. i. 16.

WHAT a divine harmonious sound
The gospel-trumpet gives ;
No music can with it compare ;
The soul that knows it lives.

2 Ten thousand blessings it contains,
Divinely rich and free,
For helpless, wretched, ruined man,
Though vile and base as we.

3 It speaks of pardon, full and free,
Through Christ, the Lamb once slain ;

Whose blood can cleanse the foulest soul,
And take away all stain.

4 The vilest sinner out of hell,
Who lives to feel his need,
Is welcome to a Throne of Grace,
The Saviour's blood to plead.

5 The Lord delights to hear them cry,
And knock at mercy's door ;
'Tis grace that makes them feel their need,
And pray to him for more.

6 Nor will he send them empty back,
Nor fright them from the door ;
The Father has in Jesus stored
All blessings for the poor.

528 C.M.

The Gospel.—Rom. x. 15; Isa. lxi. 1-3; Nahum i. 15.

THE gospel is good news indeed,
To sinners deep in debt ;
The man who has no works to plead,
Will thankful be for it.

2 To know that when he's nought to pay,
His debts are all discharged,
Will make him blooming look as May,
And set his soul at large.

3 No news can be compared with this,
To men oppressed with sin ;
Who know what legal bondage is,
And labour but in vain.

4 Freedom from sin and Satan's chains,
And legal toil as well,
The gospel sweetly now proclaims ;
Which tidings suit them well.

5 How gladly does the prisoner hear
    What gospel has to tell!
  'Tis perfect love that casts out fear,
    And brings him from his cell.

6 The man that feels his guilt abound,
    And knows himself unclean,
  Will find the gospel's joyful sound
    Is welcome news to him.

529   8s.
The Law of the Wise.—Prov. xiii. 14; xiv. 27.

SWEET Jesus! how great is thy love;
  Thy mercy and truth know no end;
And all that are born from above,
  Shall find thee a permanent Friend;
Dear Saviour, enlighten my eyes,
  That I may the wonders behold
Contained in the law of the wise,
  Too grand and too great to be told.

2 O what a rich field of delight!
  How sweet and how fragrant the smell!
Its beauties astonish me quite,
  Nor am I yet able to tell
The half of the glory I see
  In that divine treasure of grace;
Sweet wonders are shown unto me,
  When I behold Jesus's face.

3 Dear Jesus! thy glories unfold,
  Nor let me be wanting of sight;
O may I with pleasure behold
  Thy statutes, and in them delight.
I want to know nothing beside;
  Here's room for my soul to expand;
Nor can I be better employed,
  In Meshech's discouraging land.

530   C.M.
Election.—Eph. i. 4-9; ii. 9; Deut. vii. 8; Matt. xi. 26.

ELECTION is a truth divine,
  As absolute as free;
Works ne'er can make the blessing mine;
  'Tis God's own wise decree.

2 Before Jehovah built the skies,
  Or earth, or seas, or sun,
He chose a people for his praise,
  And gave them to his Son.

3 Eternal was the choice of God,
  A sovereign act indeed;
And Jesus, the incarnate Word,
  Secures the chosen seed.

4 He loved and chose because he would;
  Nor did his choice depend
On sinners' work, or bad or good,
  But on his sovereign mind

5 Nor law, nor death, nor hell, nor sin,
  Can alter his decree;
The elect eternal life shall win,
  And all God's glory see.

6 His counsel stands for ever sure,
  Immortal and divine;
And justice, mercy, truth, and power,
  Unite to make it mine.

531   L.M.
" Now are we the sons of God."—1 John iii. 1; Gal. iv. 7

BELOVED of the Lord most high,
Let praises be your sweet employ;
Ye sons of God, rejoice, and sing
The honours of your Lord and King.

2 Your heavenly Father ever lives,
And all his choicest treasure gives

To you, the favourites of his heart,
Nor will he ever with you part.

3 [Whatever be your lot below,
Though you through gloomy paths may go,
Your heavenly Father is your Light,
And he will guide your footsteps right.]

4 In every changing scene below,
'Tis yours by faith this grace to know:
Now are we sons and heirs of God,
Fast hastening to our blest abode.

5 In every trying, deep distress,
In poverty and wretchedness,
This truth sweet comfort should afford:
E'en now we are the sons of God.

6 Let worldlings know we scorn the toys
Which they so highly love and prize;
We must possess all real good,
Since we are sons and heirs of God.

7 Dear Father, bless us with this grace,
While travelling through this wilderness;
Our sonship still to keep in view,
And honour thee in all we do.

532   148th.
" The ransomed shall return unto Zion."—Isa. xxxv. 10.

THE ransomed of the Lord
  Shall unto Zion come;
A faithful, loving God
  Will surely bring them home;
He gave his life a ransom-price
And Zion shall in him rejoice.

2 The promise of the Lord
  Shall stand for ever good,
And Zion shall record
  The wonders of his love.

Redemption's glorious work is done ;
The ransomed shall to Zion come.

3 [The Holy, Wise, and Just,
His Well-Beloved gave ;
And shall the man be cursed
That Jesus came to save ?
Shall sin and Satan Jesus cheat,
Or prove the ransom incomplete ?]

4 [O vanity extreme !
And base that heart must be
Whose tongue can dare proclaim
The ransomed damned shall be.
The debt is paid ; the victory won ;
The ransomed shall to Zion come.]

5 They shall rejoice in him,
And in him they shall boast ;
He saves from wrath and sin,
From guilt, law, and the curse.
To Zion they shall all be led,
And joy shall rest upon their head.]

6 'Tis no uncertain sound
The gospel-trumpet gives ;
The church in Christ is found,
And by and in him lives ;
While Jesus lives to bring them home,
The ransomed shall to Zion come.

533 C.M.
The Love of Christ.—1 John iii. 16 ; Eph. v. 25.
How condescending and how wise
Is the eternal God !
On wings of love, from heaven he flies,
The church to buy with blood.

2 He saw her rolling in her filth,
More beastly far than swine ;

Her only clothing sin and guilt ;
Exposed to wrath divine.

3 He came to save her soul from hell,
And bring her home to God ;
Her debts and guilt upon him fell ;
He made the payment good.

4 His life he gave a ransom-price,
Resolved to set her free ;
And make her in his name rejoice,
To all eternity.

534 7s.
The Blood of Sprinkling.—Heb. xii. 24 ; Isa. liii. 6.
MERCY speaks by Jesus' blood ;
Hear and sing, ye sons of God ;
Justice satisfied indeed ;
Christ has full atonement made.

2 Jesus' blood speaks loud and sweet ;
Here all Deity can meet,
And, without a jarring voice,
Welcome Zion to rejoice.

3 Should the law against her roar,
Jesus' blood still speaks with power,
" All her debts were cast on me,
And she must and shall go free."

4 Peace of conscience, peace with God,
We obtain through Jesus' blood ;
Jesus' blood speaks solid rest ;
We believe, and we are blest.

535 8.7.4.
Redeeming Love.—Jer. xxxi. 3 ; Heb. ix. 12.
O THE love of Christ to sinners !
Who can make its wonders known ?
Sin-born slaves, through grace, are winners
Of a bright celestial crown ;
Jesus gives us
Endless glory and renown.

2 We, by nature, are disgraceful ;
Nothing but the filth of hell ;
All our righteousnesses hateful ;
Who can half our baseness tell ?
Satan's captives,
And we loved his service well.

3 Jesus saw us sunk in ruin,
And, determined us to save,
Shed his blood, and brought us to him ;
For our life his own he gave ;
He redeemed us
From sin, Satan, and the grave.

4 Endless love he fixed upon us,
In eternity that's past ;
Nor will ever take it from us ;
Endless love shall ever last ;
Love redeemed us,
And will ever hold us fast.

536 L.M.
" He hath made him to be sin for us."—2 Cor. v. 14, 21.
BEHOLD a scene of matchless grace,
'Tis Jesus in the sinner's place ;
Heaven's brightest Glory sunk in shame,
That rebels might adore his name.

2 Tremendous clouds of wrath and dread,
In vengeance burst upon his head ;
Ten thousand horrors seize his soul,
And vengeful mountains on him roll.

3 He sighed ; he groaned ; he sweat ; he cried ;
Through awful floods he passed and died ;
All penal wrath to Zion due,
Infinite justice on him threw.

4 He rose in triumph from the dead ;
Justice declared the debt was paid ;
Then Christ with kingly grandeur flew,
And took his throne in glory too.

5 Come, saints, with solemn pleasure trace
The boundless treasures of his grace ;
He bore almighty wrath for you,
That you might all his glory view.

537 148th.

Work and Righteousness of Christ.—Rom. iii. 24-26.

THE work of Christ I sing,
And glory in his name ;
Immortal life to bring,
The Lord of Glory came ;
He gave himself for wretched me,
And sets my soul at liberty.

2 He magnified the law
And made an end of sin ;
Without a single flaw,
A righteousness brought in.
Come, mourning souls, in Jesus trust ;
His righteousness makes sinners just.

538 L.M.

The Good Man.—Acts xi. 24 ; Rom. iv. 8-11.

BY nature, none of Adam's race
Can boast of goodness in God's sight ;
Sin plunged them all in sad disgrace ;
Now nothing merely human's right.

2 Good men there are ; but, be it known,
Their goodness dwells in Christ their Head !
United to God's only Son,
Their holiness can never fade.

3 In him they stand complete and just ;
His righteousness he gives to them ;
Of this they sing, of this they boast,
Nor law nor Satan can condemn.

4 The One-in-Three, and Three-in-One,
Sets up his kingdom in their breasts ;
And there, to make his wonders known,
He ever lives, and reigns, and rests.

5 Life, light, and holiness divine,
From Jesus they by faith receive ;
The Spirit makes his graces shine,
And gives them power in Christ to live.

539 148th.

" Rejoice in the Lord."—Joel ii. 23, 26 ; Ps. xxxii. 11.

CHRISTIANS, rejoice, and sing
Your Maker's lovely praise ;
He is your God and King,
Ancient of endless days ;

He lives, he reigns, and sits above,
The King of kings, and God of love.

2 No place can him contain ;
Immensity he fills ;
He measures, with a span,
The world with all its hills ;
In heaven he reigns your God and King,
And will you to his glory bring.

3 He saves you by his grace ;
O matchless grace indeed,
That such a rebel race
From sin and Satan's freed !
His mercy, truth, and justice join,
To make you in full glory shine.

4 The time will shortly come,
When you, with sweet surprise,
Will find yourself at home
With Christ, above the skies ;
With him to live, with him to reign,
And never, never part again.

540 S.M.

Jesus, King of Zion.—Ps. cxlix. 2 ; John i. 49.

JESUS, the Lord, is King,
And be his name adored ;
Let Zion with sweet pleasure sing
The honours of her God.

2 His laws are just and mild,
All pregnant with delight ;
The church at large, and every child,
Shall prove his burden light.

3 Let Christians all attend
To his commanding voice ;
His mercies never have an end ;
Then be his ways our choice.

4 On Zion's hill he reigns,
And still displays his love ;
Bids saints remember all his pains,
And lift their hearts above.

541 S.M.

Jesus, King in Zion.— Jer. viii. 19 ; Ps. ii. 6 ; Zech. ix. 9.

THE Lord is Zion's King ;
Let Zion in him trust ;
'Midst friends and foes his goodness sing,
And of his mercy boast.

2 He rules on Zion's hill,
With laws of peace and grace,
Laws that bespeak his kindness still,
And human pride abase.

3 Let saints his sceptre own ;
His righteous laws obey ;
Acknowledge him the Lord alone,
And walk the heavenly way.

542 7s.

Christ, our High Priest.—Heb. iii. 1; vii. 26; ii. 17.

JESUS is my great High Priest;
Bears my name upon his breast;
And that we may never part,
I am sealed upon his heart.

2 All my sins were on him thrown:
He for them did once atone;
He did all my debts discharge,
And has set my soul at large.

3 By his own atoning blood,
He my wounded spirit cured;
Washed and made me white as snow;
Cleansed me well from top to toe.

4 [He the vail has rent in twain;
Through his flesh I enter in;
And with him for ever rest,
In the Lord's most holy place.]

5 He has bought me with his blood;
Reconciled my soul to God;
Made me meet for glory too,
And will bring me safely through.

543 7s.

"I am the Way."—John xiv. 6.

JESUS is the way to God;
Jesus is the way to bliss;
In this way the church has trod,
Down from Adam's day to this.

2 [Jesus is the living way;
All beside to ruin lead;
They are safe, and only they,
Who are one in Christ their Head.]

3 [Jesus is a holy way;
Leads to endless joys above;
Holy men, and only they,
Walk in this blest way of love.]

4 [Jesus is the narrow way;
Hagarenes have here no room;
Sons, and only sons are they,
Who can travel this way home.]

5 [Jesus is a humble way;
Pride and self must be brought down;
Nothing like a beast of prey
Ever can in this way run.]

6 [Jesus is the way of strength;
Yet the strong this way can't come;
And the Lord will prove at length,
Weaklings have the victory won.]

7 [Jesus is the way of peace,
Paved from end to end with love;
Yes, this way abounds with grace,
And the needy it approve.]

8 All a helpless soul can need,
All a faithful God can give,
In this way is to be had;
Here the hungry eat and live.

544 8s.

The Path of the Just.—Isa. xxvi. 7, 8.

BY nature can no man be just,
Since all are conceived in sin;
No room is now left us to boast,
For works cannot God's favour win;
But such who in Jesus believe,
Are justified freely by grace;
United to Jesus their Head,
He's made unto them righteousness.]

2 The Lord is the path of the just,
And brighter and brighter shall shine,
To Adam revealed at first;
To Abra'm made known in due time.
The saints saw the path in those days,
But still the path brighter did shine
When God gave to Moses his ways,
In shadows and types so sublime.

3 Now Jesus, the true Light, is come,
The path is far brighter than day;
Nor can that fair body, the sun,
Shine equal to Jesus, the Way;
The light that in Moses appeared,
Though great, was but dim at the best,
When with that divine Light compared,
With which the true church is now blest.

545 7s.

Christ All in All.—Col. iii. 11.

TRULY that poor soul is just,
Who, by faith, in Christ can trust;
In him live, upon him rest,
As the Lord his Righteousness.

2 Sins as foul as hell he'll find
Rising up against his mind;
Nor will Satan spare to say,
He has quite mistook the way.

3 Yet, through all the scenes of time,
Jesus as his Way shall shine,
Brighter than the blaze of day,
Suited to him as his Way.

4 When he feels his dreadful woes,
And the craft of Satan knows,
Faith shall trace in Christ, his Head,
All his helpless soul can need.

5 So his path shall brighter shine,
   Faith increase, and fears decline ;
   He from faith to faith shall go,
   Till he nought but Christ shall know.
6 And when he resigns his breath,
   To the icy hand of death,
   In the Lord, his Living Way,
   He shall fly to endless day.

546 S.M.
Christ a Sun.—Mal. iv. 2; Ps. lxxxiv. 11; 2 Pet. i. 9.
   JEHOVAH is my Sun ;
   He shines into my heart ;
Though clouds do often interpose,
   My Sun shall not depart.
2 This Sun has warmed my soul,
   When chilled by sin and death ;
Its beams have shone with strength and heat,
   And made me strong in faith.
3 Whatever be my frame,
   My Sun no change can know ;
Though I am dark, he still remains
   My light and glory too.
4 Nor death, nor sin, nor hell,
   Shall make him cease to shine ;
And, though I cannot always feel
   His beams, he's ever mine.
5 'Tis no precarious light
   That shines on Zion's hill ;
'Tis God, essential light itself,
   And therefore cannot fail.

547 C.M.
Christ the Believer's Shield.—Gen. xv. 1; Ps. iii. 2, 8.
   WHEN foes within, and foes without,
      Against my soul unite,

By faith, I wield my Shield about,
      And put them all to flight.
2 Should hell against my soul conspire,
   And send their darts like hail,
My Shield's a match for all their power,
   Nor shall they e'er prevail.
3 No fiery darts from Satan's den
   Can sons of God destroy ;
Their Shield is Christ ; by faith in him
   They can them all defy.
4 Then let the weaklings all be strong ;
   Take up their Shield, nor fear ;
They shall be conquerors all ere long,
   And crowns of victory wear.
5 Nor shall it e'er be said at last,
   Here's one among the damned
That, by a precious faith in Christ,
   Behind this Shield did stand.

548 11s.
Christ a Physician.—Matt. ix. 12, 13; Mark ii. 17.
A PHYSICIAN, I learn, abides in this place,
Profound in his wisdom, abounding in grace ;
His skill in all cases infallible is ;
Effectual his medicines, nor ever did miss.

2
Poor sinners tormented with sickness or sore
Are heartily welcome to knock at his door ;
He will not deceive them, nor spurn them away,
But freely will heal them by night or by day.

3
All plagues and distempers, all sickness and pain,
He cures without money ; nor will he disdain
The vilest of sinners, that unto him go,
But surely will heal them, and perfectly too.

4
[The strong and the healthy, in vain 'tis to ask
To try this Physician ; they'd think it a task ;
They feel no disorder, no danger they see,
But boast of a heart that from sickness is free.]

5
[Nor will the afflicted to Jesus apply,
Till quacks give them up, and they think they
      must die ;   [past,
When pockets are emptied, and carnal hopes
To Christ they will come, and he'll cure them
      at last.]

549 104th.
David in the Cave.—1 Sam. xxii. 1, 2; xviii. 6, 7.
   [WHEN Jesse's young son was honoured of
   The stripling began to publish abroad [God,
The love of Jehovah ; his strength and his might ;
Which brought down Goliath in Israel's sight.
2 What joy in the land at once did appear !
   Hosanna was sung to David, we hear ;
But soon he was forced into Adullam's cave,
And thousands pursued him his life to bereave.
3 To Adullam's cave the wretched all run ;
   Which David must have, their captain become ;
And thus he is furnished with men, to be sure,
But, O be astonished! they're helpless and poor.]
4 In David I see a greater by far ;
   'Tis Jesus, 'tis he who saves from despair ;
No sinner dejected that flees to the Lamb,
Shall e'er be neglected, for David's his name.

550 148th.
Christ the Nail in a sure place.—Isa. xxii. 23.
   MY soul, rejoice and sing
   Thy Father's glorious praise ;

And let his precious love
Employ thee all thy days;
Proclaim, with honour to his name,
That God is love, and still the same.

2   To save my soul from hell
Was his eternal will;
And, bless his precious name,
His purpose to fulfil,
He took the Lord, the great I AM,
And as a nail he fastened him.

3   [When deep calls unto deep,
And sins like mountains rise,
And the old prince of hell
Says, All the Bible's lies,
This Nail is fastened in my heart,
Nor will it e'er from me depart.

4   My wicked heart has said,
Again, yea, and again,
That Christ my soul will leave
To perish in my sin;
But though I feel as cold as clay,
He will not, cannot go away.]

5   He's fastened there as God,
As Shepherd, Priest, and King,
My Lord, my Life, my Head,
From whom all blessings spring;
As all I need, as all I have,
While here, and when beyond the grave.

551   7s.   Song ii. 14.
Christ the Rock.—Isa. xxxii. 2; 1 Cor. x. 4;

JESUS Christ, the sinner's Friend,
Loves his people to the end;
And that they may safe abide,
He's the Rock in which they hide.

2   As a rock, he guards them well
From the rage of sin and hell.
Such a rock is Christ to me,
I am safe, though thousands flee!

3   Sheltered in his wounded side,
Now no ill can me betide;
From the tempest covered o'er;
One with Him for evermore.

552   C.M.
'The Lord is my Helper.''—Heb. xiii. 6; Ps. xxx. 8-10.

THE Lord's my Helper and Support,
My Saviour and my Friend;
He bears my sinking spirits up,
And will my soul defend.

2   Though earth, and hell, and sin agree,
My comfort to destroy,
The Lord of glory fights for me,
Nor will he let me die.

553   C.M.
The Breaker.—Micah ii. 13; Jer. xxiii. 29.

THE Breaker is gone forth in love,
With power and skill divine;
Descending from the realms above,
To quell his foes and mine.

2   In love to Zion, he has broke
The powers of death and hell;
And her from Sinai's dreadful yoke
Has broken off as well.

3   Though death, and law, and sin agree
This Breaker to arrest,
He breaks their bonds, himself sets free,
With Zion on his breast.

4   He breaks his children's hearts in twain,
And brings proud nature down;

The hearts he breaks he heals again,
And on them puts a crown.

5   [He breaks through every darksome cloud,
And shows his lovely face;
Which makes the sinner sing aloud,
"Salvation is of grace."]

6   [He breaks the traps and gins that lie
To catch poor pilgrims' feet;
And, when they stumble, makes them fly
To him, their safe retreat.]

7   He'll break the strings of nature soon,
And bid the prisoner fly
Beyond the reach of sin and gloom,
His glory to enjoy.

554   C.M.
"I will make all my goodness pass before thee."

THOUGH we walk through this wilderness
God's promise is our stay;
His goodness he will make to pass
Before us in the way.

2   Goodness, immortal and divine,
The bliss of endless day,
The Lord our God will make to pass
Before us in the way.

3   The boundless treasures of his grace,
He surely will display,
And all his goodness make to pass
Before us in the way.

4   [Though hosts of enemies rise up,
To fill us with dismay,
The Lord will make his goodness pass
Before us in the way.

5   To keep our eyes on Jesus fixed,
And there our hope to stay,

The Lord will make his goodness pass
  Before us in the way.]

6 To make his saints his glory view,
  And sing their cares away,
The Lord will make his goodness pass
  Before them in the way.

555   S.M.
" And I will proclaim my name."—Exod. xxxiii. 19.
WHEN God proclaims his name,
  Then Zion hears with joy;
His grace, from age to age the same,
  Shall all her needs supply.

2   When he descends to show
    The wonders of his heart,
His presence lays proud nature low,
  And guilty fears depart.

3   Rich mercy he proclaims
    To sinners in distress ;
And, by the most endearing names,
  Reveals to them his grace.

556   S.M.
The Name of the Lord.—Exod. xxxiii. 19; xxxiv. 6.
THE Lord proclaims his name ;
  And sinners hear his voice ;
His mercy ever stands the same,
  And we'll in him rejoice.

2   His name is gracious still,
    And freely he bestows
The bounty of his sovereign will,
  On all who feel their woes.

3   His patience long endures,
    And saved sinners know,
A God, long-suffering, still restores
  Their joy and peace below.

4   The thousands whom he loves
    He pardons and forgives,
Their persons he in Christ approves,
  And will while Jesus lives.

5   Lord, help us to believe,
    And make thy name our choice ;
Thy mercy freely to us give,
  And we'll in thee rejoice.

557   8.8.6.
" In his name shall the Gentiles trust."—Matt. xii. 21.
How sweet and precious is the name
Of Jesus Christ, the Lord, the Lamb,
  To sinners in distress !
A name just suited to their case ;
Pregnant with mercy, truth, and grace,
  With strength and righteousness.

2 [His name, as Jesus, suits them well ;
He saves from sin, wrath, law, and hell,
  From guilt and slavish fears.
His name is Wonderful indeed ;
An able Counsellor, to plead,
  Just suits a case like theirs.]

3 [Immanuel ! thrice-blessèd name !
The God we trust is still the same !
  An endless Father, He ;
A most illustrious Prince of Peace ;
A Tower, a precious Hiding-place,
  Is Jesus Christ to me.]

4 [Yes, if his name be Lord of Hosts,
Of his almighty power I'll boast ;
  He all my foes shall quell ;
He's all the helpless soul can need ;
No ointment put on Aaron's head,
  Could give so sweet a smell.]

5 In him the Gentile church shall trust ;
Of him shall sing ; of him shall boast ;
  On him cast all their care ;
He is their God, and they shall know
What his almighty power can do,
  Nor death, nor danger fear.

558   7s.
The Name of Christ.—Col. i. 19; ii. 9, 10; Matt. i. 21.
SWEET the name of Christ must be,
  From and to eternity ;
For it pleased the Father well,
  Fulness all in Christ should dwell.

2   Jesus is his name, and Christ ;
  He my Surety is, and Priest ;
He has saved my soul from sin,
  And I stand complete in him.

3   [Unctuous is his heavenly love ;
  He anoints me from above ;
When his heavenly odours flow,
  I have joy and peace below.]

4   Head o'er all is Christ to me,
  And I shall his glory see ;
Therefore in his name I'll trust,
  And of him will make my boast.

5   All a hungry soul can want,
  Jesus' name will richly grant ;
Not a blessing God can give,
  But with Christ the church shall have.

6   May I ever here confide,
  Let whatever ills betide ;
And if sufferings must ensue,
  Gladly bear those sufferings too.

7   May this name be all my choice ;
  If reproached, let me rejoice ;

And with pleasure keep in view,
What the Lord for me went through.

559   148th.
"Great is the Lord."—1 Chron. xvi. 25.
THE works of God proclaim
The greatness of his power ;
Jehovah is his name ;
The saints his name adore ;
All creatures are at his control ;
He rules and reigns from pole to pole.

2 Such his omnipotence,
And such his justice too,
A world he drowns at once,
Except a very few ;
He sends his millions down to hell,
And yet is just and holy still.

3 But, O my soul ! admire ;
He looks with smiling face ;
Though awful is his ire,
Yet boundless is his grace ;
Mercy and justice here agree,
To save a guilty wretch like me.

4 That Zion might be free,
The angry powers of hell
As settled by decree,
Upon the Saviour fell ;
'Twas in this way the Lord did show
What his almighty love could do.

5 [Justice unsheathed its sword,
"Awake," the Father cries,
"And smite the Son of God,
My Fellow, from the skies ;
Fall on him with thy wrathful power
Nor spare him in the trying hour."

6 Justice obeyed the word ;
The Lord a victim fell ;
Shed all his vital blood ;
Then spoiled the powers of hell ;
He rose and triumphed o'er the grave,
And ever lives the church to save.]

7 Here I with wonder see
The Lord is great indeed ;
Great is his love to me,
And all his chosen seed ;
He's great, and Zion shall record
The greatness of the mighty Lord.

560   8.7.4.
"Awake, O sword, against my Shepherd."—Zec. xiii.7.
O THOU mighty God and Saviour
Give us faith thy works to trace ;
Heavenly Warrior, may we never

From thee turn away our face ;
May we view thee,
Standing in our wretched place.

2 Armed with wrath and righteous vengeance,
Justice once unsheathed its sword ;
Death and hell were its attendants,
And Jehovah gave the word :
"Smite the Shepherd ;
Let my wrath on him be poured."

3 All obeyed with fixed attention,
And in dreadful troops drew near ;
Horrors we can never mention
Seized our Lord and Saviour there ;
Armed with vengeance,
Free from either dread or fear.

4 Gaze, ye Christians, gaze and wonder ;
See the mighty Hero fight ;
He has burst their bands asunder,
And completely spoiled their might,
Yes, this Warrior,
Put the hosts of hell to flight.

5 Now the battle's fought and gainéd ;
Jesus, our victorious Lord,
Rushed into the hosts, and stainéd
All his garments in their blood ;
But he conquered,
And redeemed the church to God.

561   C.M.
"Every battle . . is with confused noise."—Isa. ix. 5.
JESUS our heavenly Warrior is,
He fights our battles well ;
His wisdom, love, and power displays,
And conquers death and hell.

2 When this almighty Warrior stood
The church's woes to bear,
Sin, Satan, and the curse of God,
In blazing wrath drew near.

3 He bore their every poisonous dart,
Nor from God's vengeance fled ;
Hell seized his agonised heart,
And, lo ! he bowed his head.

4 He stained his garments in their blood,
And, O victorious King !
In triumph rose the conquering God,
Sweet victory to sing.

5 He satisfied the claims of law,
In that tremendous day ;
Let saints from hence their comfort draw,
And sing their cares away.

6 O for a living faith to view
The victories of the Lamb ;

And sweetly lean upon him too,
Nor fear to trust his name.

562 7s.
Fellowship with Christ's Suffering.—Phil. iii. 10.

JESUS is the King of kings,
And in him are all my springs ;
Jesus lived and died for me,
And from bondage sets me free.

2 That I might be saved from hell,
Vengeance on my Saviour fell ;
Bathed in blood was Christ for me :
Loved me from eternity.

3 All the sorrows he endured,
Were by his own spouse procured ;
Yet his tender, loving heart
Never will from her depart.

563 8.7.4.
"Called unto the fellowship of Christ."—1 Cor. i. 9.

COME, thou now exalted Saviour,
Bless us with a solemn frame ;
Teach us now, henceforth, for ever,
To adore thy precious name ;
Lovely Jesus,
Never let us stray again.

2 Lead us forth by thy sweet Spirit,
Now to feed on heavenly food ;
And by faith may we inherit
The true riches of our God ;
And with pleasure,
Trace the wonders of thy blood.

3 Into thy heart-breaking sorrows,
May our souls be sweetly led ;
May we gaze upon the furrows
That within thy back were made ;
And, believing,
Fellowship with Jesus have.

4 May we never rest, or glory
In a form, without the power ;
Jesus, make us wise and holy,
Thee to love and to adore ;
And, in living,
Live in thee for evermore.

5 [While in Meshech we must wander,
Lead us out of self to thee ;
And, with a transporting wonder,
May we oft thy glory see ;
And, when dying,
Sing of deathless victory.]

564 C.M.
Glorying in the Cross of Christ.—Gal. vi. 14.

DEAR Lord, forbid that we should boast,
Save in the cross of Christ,

Here may we confidently trust,
And solemnly rejoice.

2 A triune God is here displayed
In all his glorious hue ;
Here sinners may approach and live,
Behold and love him too.

3 Here we have power to plead with God,
And call the Lord our own ;
With pleasure view our Father sit
Upon a smiling throne.

4 Lose sight of Jesus and his cross,
And soon we fall a prey ;
Our lust and pride, by power or craft,
Will carry us away.

5 But when, by faith, the cross we view,
Such is its mighty power,
Though earth and hell unite with sin,
We conquer and adore.

565 8s.
Deliverance from Guilt by Christ.—1 Thess. i. 10.

REJOICE, and let Christ be thy song,
For he is thy All and in All ;
He leads my soul safely along,
In spite of the world, sin, or thrall ;
Though poor in myself, yet in him
I've riches immense and divine ;
Nor can I be brought guilty in,
For Jesus, my Lord, paid the fine.

2 Once I was enveloped in debt,
My poor mind was burdened with sin,
And strove hard to make matters straight,
That I the Lord's favour might win !
But ah ! my soul laboured in vain,
And only the debt did increase,
Which greatly increased my pain,
And filled me with shame and disgrace.

3 I looked to the law for some help,
And hoped it some mercy would show ;
But O, my soul trembled, and felt
The law could but doom me to woe ,
I saw it too just to forgive ;
Too holy at sin to connive ;
Then speechless I stood, as if dead,
Nor did I expect a reprieve.

4 But while I stood trembling with fear,
The Saviour of sinners came in,
Who smiled, and said, " Be of good cheer,
I surely will save thee from sin ;

I'm Jesus, the First and the Last ;
  Thy debts have been chargéd on me—
The future, the present, the past—
  And thou shalt for ever go free."

566   8s.
Christ All and in All.—Col. iii. 11 ; i. 19 : ii. 9.

Ye famishing, naked, and poor,
  Distressed, tormented, forlorn,
In Christ is a suitable store,
  For all that unto him will come ;
He's Bread, and the Bread of Life too ;
  Well suited the hungry to fill ;
Nor one that unto him shall go,
  But what will approve the Bread well.

2 Yes, he is the true paschal Lamb,
  Of which all his Israel must eat ;
Not sodden, but roast in the flame
  Of Sinai's most horrible heat.
This, this is the true fatted calf
  The Father gave orders to kill,
That prodigals might have enough
  When feasting on fair Zion's hill.

3 [The Wine of the Kingdom is Christ,
  Provided for beggars distressed !
Which makes broken hearts to rejoice,
  When with it the soul is refreshed.
He's Water to cleanse and to heal ;
  The thirsty are welcome to drink ;
A River that never can fail ;
  A Fountain that never can sink.

4 It always is full to the brim,
  Of water of life and of peace ;
From which blessings flow like a stream,
  As free as the sun runs its race.

He's marrow and fatness as well,
  A fulness of every good ;
Nor Gabriel is able to tell,
  The blessings that in him are stored.]

567   C.M.
"Christ the Hope of Glory."—Col. i. 27.

Jesus, the Lord, my Saviour is,
  My Shepherd, and my God ;
My light, my strength, my joy, my bliss ;
  And I his grace record.

2 Whate'er I need in Jesus dwells,
  And there it dwells for me ;
'Tis Christ my earthen vessel fills
  With treasures rich and free.

3 Mercy and truth and righteousness,
  And peace, most richly meet

In Jesus Christ, the King of grace,
  In whom I stand complete.

4 As through the wilderness I roam,
  His mercies I'll proclaim ;
And when I safely reach my home,
  I'll still adore his name.

5 "Worthy the Lamb," shall be my song,
  "For he for me was slain ; "
And with me all the heavenly throng
  Shall join, and say, "Amen."

568   104th.
Christ the Believer's Song.—Rev. v. 12 ; xiv. 3.

Ye saints of the Lord, rejoice in your King ;
His mercy record ; his faithfulness sing ;
His infinite power and wisdom proclaim ;
His free grace adore, and sing, "Worthy's the
  Lamb ! "

2 Complete and all pure in Jesus you are ;
Your baseness he bore, and makes you all fair ;
Nor Gabriel can boast of a robe more divine,
Than on you is cast, and in which you shall shine.

3 'Midst worlds in a blaze, and wrath streaming
  forth,
While millions shall gaze divested of hope,
In dread consternation, distracted with fear
Of just condemnation and utter despair,

4 True Christians shall stand, without fear or
  shame,
At Jesus' right hand, in glory to reign,
The dread conflagration their joy can't decrease,
Complete's their salvation, and all is of grace.

5 Hallelujah, amen ; salvation's of God !
Repeat it again, and publish abroad
The love of your Saviour ; what theme's so
  complete ?   [great.
He'll leave you ? No, never ! his love is too

569   8s.
Christ and his Church.—Eph. v. 25-27 ; Jer. xxxi. 3.

The Father, in eternal love,
  His heart upon Zion did set ;
Her name he enrolled above ;
  Nor will he fair Zion forget,
He chose her in Jesus his Son,
  And gave her to him for a wife ;
Who freely accepted the same,
  Though knowing she'd cost him his life.

2 He saw her polluted with sin,
  Enveloped in debt and distress ;
Determined her heart he would win,
  Engaged to save her by grace,

He took all her debts and her woes,
   And for her was surely made sin ;
He fought and he conquered her foes,
   And with him she shall live and reign.

570   C.M.
Christ & his blessings a gift.—Eph. i. 22; John iii. 16.

THE Lord on high his love proclaims,
   And makes his goodness known ;
To men deserving endless pains
   He gave his only Son.

2 He gave his Son their life to be,
   To save them from despair ;
From death and hell to set them free,
   In glory to appear.

3 All real good in Jesus dwells,
   And freely is bestowed
On such as cannot help themselves,
   And cry for help to God.

4 Then, mourning souls, dry up your tears;
   Though wretched be your case,
His love shall banish all your fears ;
   He'll save you by his grace.

571   148th.
"Behold my Servant whom I uphold."-Is. xlii. 1; lxv. 1

BEHOLD, with wondering eyes,
   The Servant of the Lord ;
On wings of love he flies,
   His counsels to unfold !
He comes, he comes with truth and grace !
And Zion shall behold his face.

2 Behold him as your Head ;
   Your Husband, and your Friend ;
Your Saviour, and your God,
   Your Way, your Life, your End.
Behold him as your Shepherd dear,
And on him rest when danger's near.

3 Behold him as your King,
   Whose laws are peace and love ;
Mercy and judgment sing,
   And set your minds above.
Behold him as your great High Priest,
With Zion's name upon his breast.

4 Your Counsellor to plead,
   Your Prophet he to teach ;
A Daysman he is made,
   To make up every breach.
On him depend ; before him fall ;
Behold him as your All in All.

572   8.8.6.
"Mine Elect, in whom my soul delighteth."-Is. xlii. 1.

BEFORE the earth or seas were made,

Jesus was chosen as our Head,
   The Father's first Elect ;
In him the church was chosen too,
   And he engaged to bring them through ;
   Nor will he them neglect.

2 He undertook the care and charge,
   And promised they should walk at large,
   And all his glory view.
Anon the Father's set time came,
Nor did the Saviour then disdain
   The Father's will to do.

3 " Behold him now," the Father cries ;
   " Ye mourning souls, lift up your eyes
   And view your Saviour dear.
In him my soul delighteth well ;
My great commands he shall fulfil,
   And banish all your fear.

4 " Ye tried, ye tempted sinners, look
   To my Elect, who undertook
   To ransom you with blood.
In him I'm ever, ever pleased,
And you shall of your pain be eased,
   And see a smiling God.

5 " Whatever be your frame of mind,
   You never will perfection find,
   But in the Lord alone.
No spot nor wrinkle can I see
In them that unto Jesus flee ;
   For they and he are one."

573   8.7.4.
The One Thing Needful.—Luke x. 42; Acts iv. 12.

JESUS is the one thing needful ;
   I without him perish must.
Gracious Spirit, make me heedful ;
   Help me in his name to trust ;
     And with pleasure,
In him, as my portion, boast.

2 In the councils of Jehovah,
   He was needed much indeed ;
There to stand (a mighty Lover !)
   In the church's room and stead,
     As her Surety,
And her everlasting Head.

3 He is needful in all stations,
   While in Meshech I reside ;
All my springs and consolations
   In him, as my Head, abide ;
     And in glory,
I shall sing to him that died.

574   7.6.
The One Thing Needful.—Luke x. 42; Eph. i. 3.

WHAT a precious, needful thing,
   Is the Lord and Saviour !

Zion shall his mercy sing,
Now, henceforth, and ever.
In him a rich fulness dwells,
And is freely given;
Law and conscience Jesus quells;
Crooked things makes even.

2 Mercy from his bosom flows,
Free as any river;
He redresses all the woes
Of a weak believer.
Sinners in corruption's pit
Know they greatly need him;
He and he alone is fit
From it to relieve them.

3 He is needful as our All;
May we cleave unto him;
Every blessing, great and small,
Flows to Zion through him;
Happy is the man indeed,
Who has such a Saviour;
Every blessing he can need,
Dwells in him for ever.

575 7s.
"Called of God."--Heb. v. 4; 2 Tim. i. 9; 1 Pet. v. 10.

CALLED to see God's righteous law
Holy is without a flaw;
Called to feel its vengeful power,
And to tremble in that hour.

2 Called the cleansing blood to feel;
Called to know it me can heal;
Called to feel my guilt depart,
Through the Saviour's bleeding heart.

3 Called, and called by grace divine,
In full glory I shall shine.

Called while here, to sing and tell,
Jesus has done all things well.

4 Called to part with flesh and sin,
And eternal life to win;
And, when Jesus bids me fly,
Sing his praise beyond the sky.

576 7s.
Saved by Grace.—Eph. ii. 5, 8; Acts xv. 11.

SAVED, and saved alone by grace;
Saved to see my Saviour's face;
Saved from Satan's iron yoke,
And the law that I had broke.

2 Saved from sin, that hateful foe
That has millions plunged in woe,
Saved from all its reigning power;
Saved to serve my lusts no more.

3 Saved, nor can I be condemned;
Jesus Christ, the sinner's Friend,
Took my place and vengeance bore,
Me to save for evermore.

4 Death, nor hell, nor world, nor sin,
Foes without, nor foes within,
Ever can my soul destroy;
I am saved eternally.

577 11s.
Free Grace.—1 Pet. ii. 24.

Is Jesus my Saviour, my Husband, and Friend,
And my Elder Brother, who loves to the end?
Then of him, with pleasure, for ever I'll sing;
He is my rich treasure, my God, and my King.

2
His love he fixed on me before time began,
Nor will he take from me the love he had then;
Determined to save me, he bore all my guilt;
And rather than lose me his own blood he spilt.

578 8s.
Free Grace.—Rom. v. 6-9; iii. 24.

FREE grace is the theme of my song;
A subject divinely sublime;
Though weak in myself, yet I'm strong,
For Jehovah-Jesus is mine.
He's mine, and with pleasure I see,
We both are united in one;
And such is my Jesus to me,
I never can from him be torn.

579 C.M.
The love of God to his people.—Jer. xxxi. 3: Ps. iii. 8.

SALVATION! O my soul, rejoice;
Salvation is of God;
He speaks, and that almighty voice
Proclaims his grace abroad.

2 How wonderful, how grand the plan!
All Deity's engaged
To rescue rebel, ruined man
From Satan's power and rage.

3 The Father loved us ere we fell,
And will for ever love;
Nor shall the powers of earth or hell
His love from Zion move.

4 'Twas love that moved him to ordain
A Surety just and good;
And on his heart inscribe the name
Of all for whom he stood.

5 Nor is the Surety short of love;
He loves beyond degree;
No less than love divine could move
The Lord to die for me.

6 And O what love the Spirit shows!
 When Jesus he reveals
 To men oppressed with sin and woes,
 He all their sorrows heals.

7 The Three-in-One and One-in-Three,
 In love for ever rest;
 And Zion shall in glory be,
 And with his love be blessed.

580   8.8.6.
Sinners married to Christ.—Rom vii. 4; Jer. iii. 14.

 MY soul with holy wonder views
 The love the Lord the Saviour shows,
 To wretched, dying man;
 So strange, so boundless is his grace,
 He takes the vilest of our race
 With him to live and reign.

2 He'll charm them with a holy kiss,
 And make them know what union is;
 He'll draw them to his breast;
 A smiling eye upon them cast,
 Which brings them to his feet in haste,
 Each singing, "I am blest!

3 "I'm blest, I'm blest, for ever blest;
 My rags are gone, and I am dressed
 In garments white as snow;
 I'm married to the Lord the Lamb,
 Whose beauties I can ne'er explain,
 Nor half his glory show."

581   8s.
Christ's love to his spouse made known.—John xiv. 21.

 I'LL speak forth the love of my Lord,
 His praises my tongue shall employ;
 He bought me with his precious blood,
 Nor Gabriel is loved more than I;
 Though pure, he for me was made sin;
 Though rich, he for me became poor;
 Though free, yet a debtor brought in;
 For me he has paid the long score.

2 [These truths to my heart he proclaimed,
 When helpless I stood and distressed,
 When I at the bar was arraigned,
 With law, sin, and terrors oppressed.
 No hand to my help did appear;
 The witness against me was true;
 Which filled me with horror and fear,
 Till Jesus, my Lord, came in view.]

3 He saw me distressed, and he said,
 "Fear not, I procured thy discharge;
 I'm Jesus, who lives, and was dead,
 And now will I set thee at large."
 Not one in the court did object,

But all gave a smile when he spoke;
 He then took the yoke off my neck,
 And ravished my soul with his look.

4 What joy filled my soul, who can tell?
 But surely I ne'er shall forget;
 My Jesus has all things done well,
 And therefore his love I'll repeat.
 To him all the glory belongs;
 My soul shall speak well of his name;
 He now is the theme of my songs,
 And shall be for ever the same.

582   8.7.4.
Love of Christ immeasurable.—John iii. 16; Eph. iii. 19

 HIGH beyond imagination
 Is the love of God to man;
 Far too deep for human reason;
 Fathom that it never can;
 Love eternal
 Richly dwells in Christ the Lamb.

2 Love like Jesus' none can measure,
 Nor can its dimensions know;
 'Tis a boundless, endless river,
 And its waters freely flow.
 O ye thirsty,
 Come and taste its streams below.

3 Jesus loved, and loves for ever;
 Zion on his heart does dwell;
 He will never, never, never
 Leave his church a prey to hell.
 All is settled,
 And my soul approves it well.

583   8.7.4.
"I lay down my life for the sheep."—John x. 15.

 O MY soul, admire and wonder;
 Jesus lived and died for thee;
 He has broke the bands asunder,
 And from bondage set thee free.
 Sweet deliverance
 Jesus Christ has wrought for me.

2 [I a slave to sin and Satan
 Once did live, and liked it well;
 But the God of my salvation
 Died to save my soul from hell.
 Precious Saviour
 Let me ever with thee dwell.]

3 All the debts I had contracted,
 He, in mercy, called his own;
 And lest I should be neglected,
 Drew me near his gracious throne;
 Paid all charges,
 Then, and for the time to come.

4 Soon I hope to see his glory,
  And, with all the saints above,
Sing and tell the pleasing story,
  In the highest strains of love ;
    And for ever
Live and reign with him above.

584   7s.
"In his love he redeemed them," &c.—Isa. lxiii. 9.
JESUS lived, and loved, and died,
  Rose, and lives to intercede ;
And with Zion on his breast,
  He has said he'll ever rest.

2 Long before this world was made,
  Or that monster, Sin, appeared,
God was love, and loved the men
  He designed to redeem.

3 [Love constrained the Lamb to die,
  For a wretch so vile as I ;
Love, immensely great and free,
  Christ has shown to worthless me.]

4 Once I rolled in guilt and sin,
  Heeded not a heart unclean ;
But I now with wonder tell,
  Jesus saved my soul from hell.

585   148th.
No Help for Sinners but in Christ.—Acts iv. 12.
WHERE must a sinner fly,
  That feels himself undone ?
On what kind hand rely,
  Eternal wrath to shun ?
Can wit or reason help him out,
And bring a lasting peace about ?

2 Reason no help can give,
  But leaves him in distress ;
Nor can he be reprieved
  By works of righteousness ;
The law as loud as thunder cries,
"The soul that sins against me, dies."

3 [Should creatures all agree,
  To give him settled rest,
They cannot set him free,
  Nor cheer his troubled breast ;
No human arm his case can reach,
Nor men, nor angels heal the breach.]

4 Salvation is of God ;
  Jehovah is his name ;
The Saviour shed his blood ;
  The Lord of Life was slain ;
And by his own atoning blood,
He made a precious way to God.

5 Here sinners may draw near,

With all their sin and guilt ;
  Nor death nor danger fear,
Since Jesus' blood was spilt ;
A door of hope is opened wide,
In Jesus' bleeding hands and side.

586   148th.
Sinners welcome to Christ.—Dan. ix. 24 ; Mark xvi. 15.
YE servants of the Lord,
  Ye messengers of grace,
Go forth with one accord,
  Proclaim a full release ;
Jesus has made an end of sin,
And righteousness divine brought in.

2 With tidings great and grand ;
  Tidings immensely good ;
Proclaim, through all the land,
  Redemption through his blood.
Jesus has made, &c.

3 Ye sinners in distress,
  The tidings are for you ;
Salvation is of grace,
  And full salvation too ;
Jesus has made an end of sin,
And righteousness divine brought in.

587   S.M.
Gospel Invitation.—Rev. xxii. 17 ; Isa. lv. 1.
COME, whosoever will,
  Nor vainly strive to mend ;
Sinners are freely welcome still
  To Christ, the sinner's Friend.

2 The gospel-table's spread
  And richly furnished too,
With wine and milk, and living bread,
  And dainties not a few.

3 [The guilty, vile, and base,
  The wretched and forlorn,
Are welcome to the feast of grace,
  Though goodness they have none.]

4 No goodness he expects ;
  He came to save the poor ;
Poor helpless souls he ne'er neglects,
  Nor sends them from his door.

5 His tender, loving heart
  The vilest will embrace ;
And freely to them will impart
  The riches of his grace.

588   C.M.
The Beggar.—Mark x. 46, 47 ; Ps. xxxiv. 6 ; lxxii. 12.
A LIMPING beggar, clothed in rags ;
  Disgraceful and forlorn ;
In self a mass of hateful dregs,
  In Satan's image born ;

2 To Jesus comes, with all his woes,
   And loud for mercy cries;
And mercy, like a river, flows
   From Jesus' heart and eyes.

3 He takes the rebel to his breast,
   And, with a touch divine,
Heals him of all his wretchedness,
   And makes his face to shine.

4 Himself he binds by oath and blood,
   To take the wretch to bliss;
Then gives his soul a glimpse of God,
   And kills him with a kiss.

5 Salvation unto God belongs!
   Amen! we'll bless his name;
And when we have immortal tongues,
   We'll still repeat the same.

589   8.8.6.
The Beggar's Needs all in Christ.—1 Sam. ii. 8.

A BEGGAR, vile and base, I come,
Without a friend, without a home,
   And knock at mercy's door;
A friendless, helpless wretch indeed,
Nor have I one good work to plead,
   Yet crave a living store.

2 My wants are great and many too;
O Lamb of God, some pity show,
   Or I must surely die;
No other hand can help but thee;
I've tried the rest, and plainly see
   They cannot me supply.

3 But though my wants are very great,
In Jesus they most richly meet;
   With him I've all the rest;
And wilt thou give thyself to me?
From sin and Satan set me free?
   Then I'm completely blest.

4 Source of delight! Fountain of bliss!
In thee I all things do possess;
   My treasure is divine;
With holy wonder I adore
The God who thus does bless the poor,
   And make their faces shine.

590   148th.
The Prodigal.—Luke xv. 11-24.

Now for a song of praise,
   To our Redeemer God;
Whose glorious works and ways
   Proclaim his love abroad;
Ye prodigals, lift up your voice,
And let us all in him rejoice.

2 A sinner, saved by grace,
   And God calls him his son,
From Jesus turned his face,
   And from his Father ran;
Spent all he had with harlots base,
And brought himself into disgrace.

3 And now, in his distress,
   A servant he becomes;
Some legalising priest,
   Has hired him, it seems;
Then sends him forth to feed his swine,
And husks he now must eat, or pine.

4 So off the rebel sets,
   And to the herd he goes;
Then tries to eat his husks,
   But now he feels his woes;
With hunger pinched, he cried and said,
"My Father's house abounds with bread.

5 "Alas! what can I do?
   I starving am for want;
I'll to my Father go,
   And tell him my complaint;
I'll tell him, too, how base I am,
Not worthy to be called his son,"

6 He said, and off he goes
   Towards his Father's house,
With neither shoes nor hose,
   Nor any other dress,
Except his base and filthy rags,
Of sin and guilt the very dregs.

7 But O good news of grace!
   The Father saw him come,
And, with a smiling face,
   He ran to fetch him home;
He ran, and fell upon his neck,
And kissed him, for his mercy's sake.

8 "Father," the rebel cries,
   "I've sinned against thy love;"
The Father then replies,
   "Bring hither the best robe;
Yes, bring it forth, and put it on,
For this my son's alive again.

9 "Put shoes upon his feet,
   And on his hand a ring;
Bring forth the fatted calf,
   And let us eat and sing;"
And now the Father's house abounds
With joy, and sweet harmonious sounds.

591   11.8.
The man blessed who believes in Christ.—John xiv. 1-3.

How blest is the man who in Jesus believes
   And on him can cast all his cares;

A righteousness full and complete he receives,
    That hides all his guilt, sin, and fears.

2 [No creature on earth is more happy than he,
    Nor Gabriel himself is more blest;
He lives on the bounty of grace, rich and free—
    A glorious, immortal repast.]

3 Whate'er be his lot, while on earth he resides,
    His glory can never depart;
He's one in the Lord, and in him he abides,
    United together in heart.

4 The time is now fixed, and soon it will come,
    When Christ will his messenger send,
To fetch him from Meshech & carry him home;
    And then all his sorrows will end.

592   8.8.6.
"Mighty to save."—Isa. lxiii. 1; xix. 20; xliii. 11.
MIGHTY to save is Christ the Lamb;
Let all the saints adore his name,
    And make his goodness known;
With one accord proclaim abroad,
The wonders of their Saviour, God,
    Whose blood did once atone.

2 Mighty to save! nor all sin's power
Can hold the sinner in that hour
    When Jesus calls him home;
Nor Moses, with his iron rod,
Can keep the trembling soul from God,
    When the set time is come.

3 [Mighty to save! he saves from hell;
A mighty Saviour suits me well;
    A helpless wretch am I;
With sin oppressed, by law condemned,
With neither feet nor legs to stand,
    Nor wings from wrath to fly.]

4 [Mighty to save! he saves from death;
O may I, with my latest breath,
    His mighty power proclaim.
Ye sinners lost, and wretched too,
He came to save such worms as you,
    And mighty is his name.]

5 [Mighty to save! let Zion sing
The honours of her God and King,
    Whose love no change can know.
With cheerful hearts, and cheerful voice,
We'll in the mighty God rejoice,
    And sing his praise below.]

6 And when the icy hand of death
Shall steal away our mortal breath,
    Our joy shall still increase;
Yes, with a loud immortal tongue,
We'll sing, and Christ shall be our song,
    In realms of endless peace.

593   8.7.4.
A mighty Saviour.—Isa. xliii. 11; Heb. vii. 25.
JESUS is a mighty Saviour;
    Helpless souls have here a Friend;
He has borne their misbehaviour,
    And his mercy knows no end;
      O ye helpless,
Come, and on his grace depend.

2 He, to save your souls from ruin,
    Shed his blood upon the tree!
O ye needy, haste unto him;
    His salvation's full and free;
      Vilest sinners
Shall his great salvation see.

3 [Whatsoe'er your age or case be,
    None can save you but the Lamb;

If in prison, he can set free,
    And a full release proclaim;
      He is mighty,
And to save the lost he came.]

4 Yes, the very worst of sinners,
    Who upon his grace rely,
Shall of endless bliss be winners;
    And shall sing, beyond the sky,
      Songs of praises
To the Lamb that once did die.

594   7s.
"My peace I give unto you."—John xiv. 27; Eph. ii. 14.
O MY soul, with wonder tell,
Jesus has done all things well;
And, through his atoning blood,
I've a settled peace with God.

2 He bequeathed his peace to me,
As a gift divinely free;
And it is his righteous will,
That my soul in peace shall dwell.

3 [Love to such vile worms as I,
Brought the Saviour from the sky;
Every foe for them to quell,
Jesus conquered death and hell.]

4 [Gifts like this, so full and free,
Stand as firm as Deity;
God has sworn, nor can he lie,
It shall last eternally.]

5 Justice, mercy, truth, and love,
Every attribute of God,
Join to make this peace secure,
And it must and shall endure.

6 What a solid basis this!
Such a peace can never miss,

But produce a grateful mind,
To a God so vastly kind.

7 [Mourning souls who feel the smart
Of a guilty, treacherous heart,
And with mighty care and pain,
Struggle hard relief to gain;

8 Labour hard you may, and long,
But you'll find your foes too strong;
Solid peace can ne'er be had,
Only through a Saviour's blood.]

9 Jesus, mighty Prince of Peace,
Now proclaim a full release;
Set poor captive sinners free;
Give them solid peace in thee.

595 8s.

Free Grace.—Eph. i. 7; ii. 5-8; Rom. v. 20.

FREE grace is the joy of my heart;
Its glories, with wonder, I trace;
To me it does freely impart
Rich blessings, just suiting my case;
No monster more wretched could be,
Nor less of God's favour deserve;
Yet such is free grace unto me,
I never, no never can starve.

2 [Grace takes all my ruin and woe,
Nor murmurs my burdens to bear;
And grace in return makes me know
In Jesus I'm comely and fair.
In self I'm polluted and vile;
But grace sweetly speaks unto me,
It tells me, and that with a smile,
In Jesus I'm perfect and free.]

3 Its blessings, though rich and divine,
Are all without money and price;

A soul, though as wretched as mine,
May venture to hope and rejoice;
Its highest delight is to give
True riches to sinners undone;
Nor can it, nor will it deceive,
The soul that with Jesus is one.

596 C.M.

Saved by Grace.—Titus ii. 11-14; Eph. ii. 5, 8.

GOD is a Spirit, just and wise;
His footsteps who can trace?
His love, more ancient than the skies,
Breaks forth in boundless grace.

2 In vast eternity he chose
A people for his praise;
And saves them from their guilt and woes,
By his almighty grace.

3 Redeemed, with Jesus' blood redeemed,
His beauties called to trace,
No angel can be more esteemed
Than sinners saved by grace.

4 [Immortal love no change can know
Though clouds surround his face;
All Israel must to glory go,
As trophies of his grace.]

5 [Satan and sin may vex the mind,
And threaten with disgrace;
But, after all, the saint shall find
He's saved, and saved by grace.]

6 The work begun is carried on,
Nor hell can it deface;
The whole elect with Christ are one
And must be saved by grace.

7 Where Jesus is, there they must be,
And view his lovely face;

And sit to all eternity,
In chanting forth his grace.

597 8s.

"I will in no wise cast out."—John vi. 37.

JEHOVAH, the Saviour, appears,
A world to redeem from its woes;
From guilt, sin, wrath, bondage, and fears,
From Satan and all that oppose.
Adored be his name for his grace,
His faithfulness, justice, and truth;
He saves, and he smiles in the face,
Nor scorns neither aged nor youth.

598 148th.

"A peculiar people."—Titus ii. 14; 1 Pet. ii. 9.

PECULIAR are the saints,
And God does them esteem;
Though numerous are their wants,
They all things have in him;
He is their treasure and their joy,
Nor can they ever starve or die.

2 [Loved from eternity,
And chosen in the Lamb,
The eternal One-in-Three,
Jehovah, Great I AM,
Himself has bound, by holy ties,
To take them up beyond the skies.]

3 [Peculiar is the grace,
Which makes their bliss secure;
Its beauties none can trace,
Nor know its saving power;
None but this little favoured few
Can know what endless love can do.]

4 Bought with the blood of Christ,
(Peculiar price indeed!)

Their God becomes their Priest,
And they from sin are freed ;
Peculiar must the blessing be,
Which makes insolvent wretches free.

5 [Their birth is from above ;
Peculiar indeed ;
Begotten, not of blood,
But of immortal seed :
From Christ, their Head, their life proceeds,
And to him it most surely leads.]

6 They live, and live to God ;
A life that's known by few :
Their Father's staff and rod,
Support and comfort too ;
Christ is their Life, nor can they die,
For hell can ne'er their life destroy.

599　　148th.
" But ye are come to Mount Zion."—Heb. xii. 22.

YE sons of God, be wise,
And learn your Father's will ;
By faith lift up your eyes
To yonder shining hill ;
No smoke, no thunderbolts are there,
Nor wrath to sink you in despair.

2 [A pleasant mount indeed,
Where God unfolds his grace
To all the chosen seed,
And, with a smiling face,
Speaks peace to every troubled breast,
And bids the weary in him rest.

3 To worship on this ground,
Is not a legal task ;
A solid peace is found,
And faith has all it asks ;
There Jesus sits with smiling face,
And rules and reigns the God of grace.

600　　8.7.4.
" Mercy and truth are met together."—Ps. lxxxv. 10.

TRUTH and mercy meet together,
Righteousness and peace embrace ;
Each perfection of Jehovah
Meets and shines in Jesus' face ;
Here the Father
Can be just and save by grace.

2 What a field of consolation !
Here no jarring notes are found ;
Zion has a full salvation,
And shall all her foes confound ;
Each believer
Has for hope a solid ground.

3 Justice has no loss sustained ;
Truth remains in perfect light ;
Not an attribute is stained ;
All in one grand cause unite ;
Saved sinners
Must and shall in God delight.

4 Here's a cord which can't be broken ;
O my soul, with wonder tell ;
God himself the word has spoken.
Zion in her Lord shall dwell ;
And with Jesus
Live in spite of earth and hell.

5 [O ye much-esteemed sinners,
Who in Jesus Christ are found,
Rest assured you shall be winners,
Soon with glory shall be crowned ;
And for ever
Shall the praise to Christ redound.]

601　　S.M.
" Shall we sin because . . not under law ?"-Rom. vi. 15.

WHAT, then ! shall Christians sin,
Because freed from the law ?
Shall sinners, saved by grace divine,
From holiness withdraw ?

2 Shall grace seduce the mind,
And lead the soul astray ?
And souls who under grace are found,
Delight to disobey ?

3 Great God, forbid the thought !
Preserve thy saints in love,
While Pharisees set grace at nought,
Saints shall thy ways approve.

602　　148th.
" Jesus the Author and Finisher of our faith."-Heb. xii.

[JESUS the Author is
Of true and living faith ;
This blessed grace he gives,
And saves our souls from death ;
By faith in him we live, and view
The wonders God alone can do.]

2 [The principle of faith
From Jesus we receive ;
And all the power it hath,
The Lord the Saviour gave ;
'Tis Jesus gives us faith to view
The wonders God alone can do.]

3 'Tis Jesus gives us faith
To fight and overcome ;
To vanquish hell and death,
And trust in him alone ;
With sweet surprise to sit and view
The wonders God alone can do.

4   Nor death, nor sin, nor hell,
    Against this faith can stand;
    She eyes the Saviour well,
    And Jesus holds her hand;
    He gives her power to live and view
    The wonders God alone can do.

5   Through every trying scene,
    Down to the gates of death,
    Jehovah will maintain
    The life and power of faith;
    For death can never keep from view
    The wonders God alone can do.

603   S.M.
Precious and holy Faith.—2 Pet. i. 1; Jude 20.
    FAITH! 'tis a grace divine,
    A gift both rich and free;
    'Twas grace that made this blessing mine,
    From guilt to set me free.

2   The faith of God's elect
    Is precious, pure, and good;
    Such is its power, and its effect,
    True faith prevails with God.

3   To Jesus and his blood,
    It looks for life and peace;
    The oaths and promises of God,
    Its power and zeal increase.

4   [When saints in darkness roam
    With sin and guilt distressed,
    Faith in Christ's righteousness alone
    Can set the soul at rest.]

5   Faith lives in spite of hell;
    And, when the soul's oppressed
    With miseries more than tongue can tell,
    It leans on Jesus' breast.

6   Though death and dangers fly
    Like lightning from the skies;
    He that believes shall never die;
    Faith must obtain the prize.

604   C.M.
" We walk by faith, not by sight."—2 Cor. v. 7; iv. 18.
    WHY should a pilgrim grope within,
    And judge by what he feels?
    A loathsome stench of death and sin
    No consolation yields.

2 Corruptions, base and foul as hell,
    May vex and tease the soul;
    But Jesus' blood its rage can quell,
    And make the conscience whole.

3 I have no life, no light, no love,
    No truth or righteousness,
    That God, my Father, can approve,
    Or justice can caress,

4   But what I have in Christ, my Head,
    And grace on me bestows;
    My life with Christ in God is hid,
    And he'll redress my woes.

5 In this dear Christ I all things have;
    Why should I yield to fear?
    All that a living soul can crave,
    Is richly treasured here.

6 In him I stand completely just;
    His heart is my abode;
    Though in myself, at best, but dust,
    In him I've power with God.

605   S.M.
" The just shall live by faith."—Heb. x. 38; Rom. i. 17.
    THE just by faith shall live,
    Nor fear the powers of hell;
    All blessings that a God can give,
    In Christ most richly dwell.

2   By faith in Jesus' blood,
    The just shall live indeed;
    Shall have a settled peace with God,
    And from their sins be freed.

3   When sense and reason fail,
    And all things dark appear,
    By faith, the just shall say, 'Tis well,
    Jehovah will appear.

4   If providence should frown,
    And crosses still increase;
    By faith, the just shall live and own
    God their salvation is.

5   By faith in Christ, as God,
    As Prophet, Priest, and King,
    The just shall live, and live to prove,
    That death has lost its sting.

606   S.M.
" Rejoice in the Lord."—Hab. iii. 18; Joel ii. 23.
    LET saints lift up their hearts,
    And, with a cheerful voice,
    The wonders of their King proclaim,
    And in the Lord rejoice.

2   Whatever be thy frame,
    Though dark and cold as ice,
    No change has taken place in him;
    Then in the Lord rejoice.

3   Till God can change his mind,
    And swear he has no choice,
    The soul that in the Lord believes,
    Shall in the Lord rejoice.

4   As sure as God is God,
    And Abra'm heard his voice,

He'll love his saints unto the end,
Then let them all rejoice.

5 Nor sin, nor death, nor hell,
Can make him hate his choice ;
The cause of love is in himself ;
And in him we'll rejoice.

6 He made an end of sin,
And bought us with a price ;
Our life, our hope, our all's in him,
And we'll in him rejoice.

607   148th.
" Rejoice evermore."—1 Thess. v. 16 ; Luke x. 20.
REJOICE, ye saints, rejoice,
In Christ, your glorious Head ;
With heart, and soul, and voice,
His matchless honours spread ;
Exalt his love, proclaim his name,
And sweetly sing the Lamb once slain.

2 The blood and righteousness
Of the incarnate Word ;
The wisdom, truth, and grace,
Of your exalted Lord,
Unite, with one immortal voice,
To bid the saints of God rejoice.

3 God's promise and his oath,
And covenant of grace,
Abide secure enough,
To all the chosen race ;
And with a solemn, heavenly voice
Invite believers to rejoice.

4 The whole of Deity,
With all his grace contains,
In sweetest harmony
A solemn joy proclaims ;

The Father, Word, and Spirit's voice
Unite to bid the saints rejoice.

608   148th.
" Walk worthy of the Lord."—Col. i. 10 ; Eph. iv. 1.
YE souls, redeemed with blood,
And called by grace divine,
Walk worthy of your God,
And let your conduct shine ;
Keep Christ, your living Head, in view,
In all you say, in all you do.

2 Has Jesus made you free ?
Then you are free indeed ;
Ye sons of liberty,.
Ye chosen royal seed,
Walk worthy of your Lord, and view
Your glorious Head, in all you do.

3 Shall sons of heavenly birth
Their dignity debase ?
Unite with sons of earth,
And take a servant's place ?
The slaves to sin and Satan too ?
Forget to keep their Lord in view ?

4 Forbid it, mighty God !
Preserve us in thy fear ;
Uphold with staff and rod,
And guard from every snare ;
Teach us to walk with Christ in view,
And honour him in all we do.

5 Increase our faith and love,
And make us watch and pray ;
O fix our souls above,
Nor let us ever stray ;
Dear Lord, do thou our strength renew,
And lead us on with Christ in view.

609   7s.
" Walk in love."—Eph. v. 2 ; Rom. xii. 10, 15.
LORD, we fain would walk in love,
But, alas ! how slow we move ;
Pride, that haughty monster, pride,
Often makes us start aside.

2 Lamb of God, thy power make known ;
Sweetly draw, and we will run ;
Make our love to thee and thine
Like the sun at noon-day shine.

3 As the purchase of thy blood,
May we seek each other's good ;
And be it our great concern,
Thee to view, of thee to learn.

4 May we mourn with those that mourn ;
Make each other's cause our own ;
Ever keeping this in mind,
We are to each other joined.

5 Flesh of flesh, and bone of bone,
With the King of glory one ;
Of one body each a part,
Jesus, make us one in heart.

6 King of kings, enthroned above,
Come and shed abroad thy love ;
Fill us with that source of joy,
Which can never, never cloy.

610   8.7.4.
Panting for Christ, the Friend of sinners.—Ps. xlii. 1.
PRECIOUS Jesus ! Friend of sinners ;
We, as such, to thee draw near ;
Let thy spirit now dwell in us,
And with love our souls inspire ;
Fill, O fill us
With that love which casts out fear.

2 Matchless Saviour ! let us view thee
  As the Lord our Righteousness ;
  Cause each soul to cleave unto thee,
  Come, and with thy presence bless.
      Dear Immanuel,
  Feast us with thy sovereign grace.

3 Open now thy precious treasure :
  Let the blessings freely flow ;
  Give to each a gracious measure
  Of thy glory here below ;
      Loving Bridegroom,
  'Tis thyself we want to know.

4 [Come, and claim us as thy portion,
  And let us lay claim to thee ;
  Leave us not to empty notion,
  But from bondage set us free ;
      King of glory !
  We would live and reign with thee.]

611   7s.
Changeableness.—Gal. v. 17; John iii. 6.
  LORD, I freely would confess,
  I am all unrighteousness ;
  Base and vile, from head to feet ;
  Full of pride and self-conceit.

2 [When thy presence I enjoy,
  I can say, My God is nigh ;
  And with holy wonder tell,
  Thou, dear Lord, dost all things well.]

3 When deliverance thou hast wrought,
  I can of thy wonders talk,
  And too often proudly say,
  Nothing more shall me dismay.

4 [When, by faith, I view my Lord,
  Bathed in agonies and blood,
  I with joy his love repeat,
  Sink to nothing at his feet.]

5 But, alas ! how soon I stand
  At a distance, unconcerned ;
  And the trifles of a day
  Almost carry me away.

6 Lord, with shame and grief I own,
  I to evil still am prone ;
  Vile and base I am indeed ;
  When from sin shall I be freed ?

7 Make me strong and steadfast too ;
  Help me all thy will to do ;
  And with patience may I wait,
  Ever knocking at thy gate.

612   11s.
" What will ye see in the Shulamite ? "—Song vi. 13.

IN every believer two armies are seen,
The new man of grace, and the old man of sin ;

In Christ he is perfect, and free from all guilt,
Yet in himself evils are both seen and felt.

2
As one in the Lord, he's a true son of peace ;
In himself, he is nothing but sin and disgrace ;
His body's the temple of the Holy Ghost,
And Christ in him dwelleth as King of one host.

3
When Christ takes possession, and proves him-
    self King,   [bring ;
Then sin, world, and Satan, their forces will
Nor will they be wanting of gun-shot from hell ;
The old prince of darkness will furnish them well.

4
Yet such is the power and love of our King,
In spite of all hell we of victory sing ;

For though sin and devils against us unite,
'Tis Christ fights our battles, and puts them to
    flight.

5
The victory is thine ! then let hell do its worst ;
For Christ will still reign, and of Christ thou
    shalt boast ;   [wear,
And when the fight's ended, the crown thou shalt
And glory immortal with Christ thou shalt share.

613   148th.
Glorying in Infirmities.—2 Cor. xi. 30; xii. 5, 9, 10.
  A HELPLESS worm am I,
  Yet often start aside ;
  Infirmities annoy,
  And enemies deride ;
  Ten thousand evils me assault,
  And wound my soul, and make me halt.

2 I want to be set free
  From every hateful foe,
  From each infirmity,
  And only pleasure know ;
  But 'tis my heavenly Father's will,
  That I infirmities should feel.

3 [Infirmities, as means,
  Have taught my soul to see,
  That nought, how fair it seems,
  But Christ will do for me ;
  I must have Christ as All in all,
  Or sink in ruin, guilt, and thrall.]

4 I'll gladly glory, then,
  In my infirmity,
  That Jesus' power and name,
  May ever rest on me ;
  I'll bless his name ; he'll bring me through,
  And he'll have all the glory too.

614   S.M.
"The Lord trieth the righteous."—Ps. xi. 5.

THE Lord the righteous tries ;
Yet we'll adore his name ;
He never will their cause despise,
Nor put their hope to shame.

2 He brings them to the test,
And tries them by his law ;
Then leads them to the promised rest,
From whence they comfort draw.

3 Then he his face conceals,
And lets them grope within ;
And by his Spirit's power reveals
The dreadful plague of sin.

4 We straightway cry, "Unclean !
A monstrous mass of woe !
What can such hosts of evil mean ?
And whither can we go ? "

5 "Look here," the Lord replies ;
"Thy beauty's all in me ;
'Tis thine to flee from self, and prize
Salvation full and free.

6 "Whate'er my wisdom does,
Or lets the tempter do,
Thy guilt and ruin to disclose,
One thing I keep in view,—

7 "To teach thee how to live
By faith in Jesus' name ;
For guilt and sin to mourn and grieve,
And sing the Lamb once slain."

615   8.7.4.
"In the world ye shall have tribulation."—John xvi. 33

SINNERS, called by grace, and blessèd
With a living faith in Christ.
Must not think to be caressèd
By a world of sin and vice ;
Satan's agents
Cannot love the Saviour's choice.

2 Let this thought the Christian strengthen ;
Jesus' name is life and peace ;
Angels have not skill to mention
Half his wisdom, power, or grace.
Souls that trust him,
Soon shall see him face to face.

3 Though they suffer for a season,
For the name of Christ, their Lord ;
And at times may know no reason
Why such sorrows are endured ;
Soon he'll teach them,
That the whole has worked for good.

4 [Happy is the savèd sinner,
That endures for Jesus' sake ;
He of endless life's a winner ;
Of his glory shall partake ;
Jesus will not,
Cannot, such a soul forsake.]

5 O for love, for faith, and patience !
Jesus, fix our souls on thee !
Nor let Satan's dire vexations,
Make us start aside or flee ;
May we ever
Cling and twine, dear Lord, to thee.

616   7s.
Reproach of Christ esteemed by faith.—Heb. xi. 26.

PRECIOUS Jesus ! must it be,
Is it thy all-wise decree,
That afflictions must attend
Zion to her journey's end ?

2 [Must the heirs of endless bliss
Travel through a wilderness,
And, by savage beasts of prey,
Be tormented night and day ?]

3 Yes, affliction is their lot ;
Earth is a polluted spot,
Where a million evils dwell,
All in league with death and hell.

4 Pains and sorrows, sins and woes,
Will the Christian's way oppose ;
Every day brings something new,
Zion's troubles to renew.

5 Yet, when faith is strong and true,
They with cheerfulness go through,
Scorning all created good,
When opposed to Christ, their God.

6 Living faith will still esteem
The reproaches of the Lamb,
Greater riches than this earth
Can afford the sons of mirth.

7 O for faith this choice to make,
And endure, for Jesus' sake,
The reproaches of his cross,
Counting all things else but dross !

617   148th.
Flesh and Spirit.—Gal. v. 17; Rom. vii. 15-24.

THE new man and the old
By no means can agree ;
The one in sin is bold,
From sin the other's free.
The principles of grace and sin
A constant warfare must maintain.

2 [One loves to watch and pray,
And walk in Jesus' path ;

The other hates the way,
And loves the road to death ;
Christ is the new man's boast and joy ;
Flesh does the old man satisfy.]

3   Christ, and him crucified,
    The new man loves to view ;
    Lust, vanity and pride,
    The old man will pursue ;
    One pants with God to live and reign ;
    The other hates his sovereign name.

4   The principle of grace
    On Jesus puts the crown ;
    But sin, with shameless face,
    Would pull his glory down.
    Jesus shall reign, the new man cries ;
    His right to reign the flesh denies.

5   Well, let old nature toil ;
    The warfare can't be long ;
    And Christians, with a smile,
    Shall sing the conqueror's song ;
    Through Christ we shall victorious prove,
    And live and reign with him above.

618   148th
"I will lead them in paths that they have not known."

    THE path that Christians tread
    To reason's eye is strange ;
    Through regions of the dead,
    They frequently must range ;
    Ten thousand monstrous beasts of prey
    Beset the soul by night and day.

2   We must not learn God's truth
    As school-boys learn their task ;
    Such knowledge is not proof
    Against delusion's blast.

    An empty knowledge bloats with air,
    But dies when dreadful storms appear.

3   Christians oft pray for faith ;
    To trace God's beauties more ;
    To triumph over death ;
    And Jesus' name adore.
    God hears and answers their desire ;
    But 'tis through scenes of floods and fire.

4   [Sin, armed with all the spleen
    Of enmity to God,
    Oft rises up within,
    And scorns the Saviour's blood ;
    A world of filth, too base to name,
    Beset and plunge the soul in shame.

5   To pray, he thinks too bold ;
    While he in silence moans,

His bones keep waxing old,
By reason of his groans ;
And by such means, though strange to tell,
The Lord will teach him Jesus well.]

6   When self and nature die,
    And all our beauty's gone,
    The Saviour brings us nigh,
    To trust in him alone ;
    'Tis then we trust his righteousness,
    And rest alone on sovereign grace.

7   Thus Jesus wears the crown ;
    We gladly trace the power
    That brings all nature down,
    And leads us to adore
    Jesus, the Lord our Righteousness,
    Who saves in every deep distress.

619   7s.
"I shall be satisfied, . . . with thy likeness."

    CREATURES are but vain at best ;
    In them is no solid rest.
    All the world calls good or great
    Cannot perfect bliss create.

2   Souls renewed by grace divine,
    Carnal pleasures will resign ;
    Holiness, without a stain,
    They are thirsting to obtain.

3   Satisfied ! not they indeed,
    Till with Christ, their living Head,
    They in heavenly bliss appear,
    And his likeness fully bear.

4   [Heart and flesh may fail, 'tis true ;
    Sin and Satan plague them too !
    Hell and earth their powers unite,
    Christ to banish from their sight ;

5   For a season they may be
    Left at an uncertainty,
    Overwhelmed with fear and doubt,
    Scarcely know what they're about ;

6   Yet they feel a panting mind
    For a God supremely kind ;
    Satisfied they cannot be,
    But as they his beauty see.]

620   L.M.
The heart is deceitful above all things.—Jer. xvii. 9.

    SIN has a thousand pleasing charms,
    Which flatter to preserve from harms ;
    She richly gilds her pleasing baits,
    And calls her trash delicious sweets.

2   Young men and maidens, rich and poor,
    Are pleased with her deceptive ore ;

There's scarce an eye that views the light,
But she can charm by day or night.

3 Nor are the vessels of the Lord
Free from the chirpings of this bird ,
Her craft and spleen she'll make them feel,
And make them like a drunkard reel.

4 Her nature's serpentine indeed ;
Her strength could make a Samson yield ;
Nor David could against her stand,
When David's God withheld his hand.

5 Good God ! what can a mortal do,
With such a cursed, artful foe ?
Let grace divine my soul defend,
Nor let me to this monster bend.

6 [Work in me, Lord, to will and do,
My way to Zion to pursue ;
And while I tread the thorny road,
Teach me to lean upon my God.]

621 L.M.
The carnal mind is enmity against God.-- Rom. viii. 7.

THE carnal mind takes different ways,
And different objects she surveys ;
She's pleased with things that suit her taste,
But hates the God of truth and grace.

2 No beauty in the Lord she views,
Nor is she charmed with gospel-news ;
She sets at nought, with vain contempt,
The Man the Lord Jehovah sent.

3 She hates him as the mighty God,
The church's Wisdom, Life, and Head ;
His priestly office she disdains,
And wantons with his wounds and pains.

4 Whatever office Jesus bears,
Or in what glorious form appears,

She was, and is, and still will be
Against him dreadful enmity.

5 [Is this the case ? Yes, Lord, 'tis true ;
And I've a carnal nature too,
That fights, with all its hellish might,
Against the God of my delight.

6 Yet, bless the Lord, through grace I feel
I have a mind that loves him well ;
Nor shall the dreadful power of sin,
My better part from Jesus win.]

7 [May grace not only live and reign,
But may its powers be felt and seen ;
Dear God, my every foe subdue,
And make me more than conqueror too.]

622 L.M.
"Be not dismayed, for I am thy God."--Isa. xli. 10

POOR fearful saint, be not dismayed,

Nor dread the dangers of the night ;
Thy God will ever be thy aid,
And put the hosts of hell to flight.

2 Nor sin, nor Satan, can o'ercome
The arm that vindicates thy cause ;
God, thy own God, will lead thee home,
In spite of all that may oppose.

3 [Should hosts within, and hosts without,
At once unite to make thee yield,
Thy God shall put them all to rout,
And make thee master of the field.]

4 In every sore and deep distress,
"I am thy God " shall be thy stay ;
Thy God shall all thy woes redress,
And drive thy guilty fears away.

5 This soul-supporting truth contains
All blessings that a God can give ;

In sorrows, sicknesses, or pains,
Thy God will every need relieve.

623 7s.
" Whom the Lord loveth he chasteneth."—Heb. xii. 6.

WHOM the Lord Jehovah loves,
He in various ways reproves ;
'Tis his settled, wise decree,
That his sons chastised shall be.

2 Them to wean from self and sin,
Try the grace he works within ;
Strip them of each idol god ;
Make them prize the Saviour's blood ;

3 Teach them what and where they are ;
Draw forth patience, faith, and prayer ;
Make them closer cling to Christ,
And in him alone rejoice ;

4 These are ends he has in view,
And he'll them accomplish too ;
Nor shall our poor peevish heart
Make him from his purpose start.

5 [Yet his love and grace are such,
He will ne'er afflict too much ;
But, in every chastening, prove
His paternal care and love.]

6 Father, make us clearly view
What thy love designs to do ;
And in every trying case,
Trust thy faithfulness and grace.

624 S.M.
God, the Father of his People.—Ps. ciii. 13.

THE Lord Jehovah is
Our Father and our Friend ;
Immortal majesty is his,
Nor can his glory end.

2 He guards his children well,
    Nor shall they starve for want;
When they their needs unto him tell,
    He'll answer their complaint.

3 He bids his saints draw nigh,
    Nor fear to call him theirs;
And, though he reigns enthroned on high,
    He calls them sons and heirs.

4 His sympathising heart
    Feels for them in distress;
And love divine he will impart,
    With strength and righteousness.

5 [Though they in darkness walk,
    He is their Father still;
And when insulting Ishmaels mock
    He will his grace reveal.]

6 [His children he supplies
    With food and raiment too;
He with his wisdom makes them wise,
    And will their strength renew.]

7 Should men and devils try
    To make the saints a prey;
The Lord, their Father, still is nigh,
    To guard them in his way.

8 Through all the scenes of time,
    He'll make his goodness known;
His sons, in every age and clime,
    His sovereign grace shall own.

625   L.M.
God a Father.—Jer. xxxi. 9; 2 Thess. ii. 16.
God is a Father, just and wise,
And reigns enthroned above the skies;
Yet all his saints on earth shall know,
He condescends to dwell below.

2 He'll make his sons and daughters wise,
  And teach them all his ways to prize;
He'll lead them forth with love and power,
  And save them in a trying hour.

3 To them he will his secrets tell,
  And save them from the power of hell;
And when they leave this world of woe,
  He'll take them all to glory too.

626   7s.
" And ye are Christ's."—1 Cor. iii. 23; Rom. xiv. 8.
Sinners who on Jesus rest,
  Must eternally be blest;
All Jehovah's love can give,
  They from Jesus shall receive.

2 Loved of God, to Jesus given,
  In the purposes of heaven;

They are bought with blood divine,
  And they must in glory shine.

3 They are Jesus' flesh and bone,
  Nor from him shall e'er be torn;
Can a part be sent to hell,
  And the whole in Zion dwell?

4 No! we bless the Lord on high,
  Not a single joint can die;
Every member lives in him;
  He's the life of every limb.

5 They are Christ's by ties divine;
  Here his brightest glories shine;
All creation must give place
  To the subjects of his grace.

6 Matchless Jesus! may we be
  Wholly taken up with thee!
And, in every deep distress,
  Lean upon thy truth and grace.

627   8s.
Encouragement to flee to Christ.—Matt. xi. 28.
Poor sinner, dejected with fear,
  Unbosom thy mind to the Lamb;
No wrath on his brow he does wear,
  Nor will he poor mourners condemn;
His arm of omnipotent grace
  Is able and willing to save;
A sweet and a permanent peace
  He'll freely and faithfully give.

2 [Come just as thou art, with thy woe,
  Fall down at the feet of the Lamb;
He will not, he cannot say, Go,
  But surely will take out thy stain.
A fountain is opened for sin,
  And thousands its virtues have proved;
He'll take thee, and plunge thee therein,
  And wash thee from filth in his blood.]

3 The soul that on Jesus relies,
  He'll never, no never deceive;
He freely and faithfully gives
  More blessings than we can conceive;
Yea, down to old age he will keep,
  Nor will he forsake us at last;
He knows, and is known by, his sheep;
  They're his, and he will hold them fast.

628   8s.
The Fulfilment of God's promise sure.—Hab. ii. 3.
My soul shall with wonder proclaim
  The love of my Father and God,
Whose promises ever remain,
  And each in its course is made good;
They're great, and exceeding great too;
  More precious than rubies by far;

Like streams from the fountain they flow,
And Zion preserve from despair.

2 Like Abra'm and Sarah, have I
Endeavoured with reason and wit,
Some blessing to get and enjoy
Much sooner than God promised it ;
Like them too, I've proved in the end,
My labour brought bondage and pain ;
And yet (O how faithful's my Friend !)
In due time the true blessing came.

629 148th.
Christ, the Beggar's Friend.—Ps. cxxxii. 15.
The Lord will feed the poor,
Nor shall their fare be mean ;
Rich blessings are in store,
In grace's magazine ;
From which rich treasure Christ will feed
The hungry soul that feels his need.

2 Poor trembling sinner, come
And knock at mercy's door ;
Though ruined and undone,
The Lord relieves the poor ;
He knows and loves the beggar's knock,
Nor will he send them empty back.

3 He came to save the lost,
Nor will he change his mind ;
The souls that in him trust
He will not leave behind ;
With him they shall for ever reign,
And glorify the Lamb once slain.

630 148th.
"My soul, wait thou only upon God."—Ps. lxii. 5.
What foolish worms are we !
How prone to start aside,
And in our troubles flee
From Jesus' wounded side ;
To wait on self, or something base,
Instead of trusting sovereign grace !

2 O that our souls could wait
At all times on the Lord ;
And watch at wisdom's gate,
Whose mercy will afford
A constant flow of every good,
To souls that trust alone in God.

3 The Lord is rich indeed,
And richly will supply
The waiting sinner's need,
With blessings from on high ;
My expectation is from God ;
Then wait, my soul, upon the Lord.

4 If darkness him surround,
His mercy's still the same ;
He never will confound
The soul that waits on him ;
He is my All ; of him I'll boast ;
On him I'll wait, and in him trust.

631 C.M.
"The Lord be with you all."—2 Thess. iii. 16.
The Lord himself be with you all,
To teach you his own will ;
And guide you safe from every thrall,
To Zion's heavenly hill.

2 Be with you to unfold his grace,
And prove his truth divine ;
Unveil the glories of his face,
And make his counsels shine.

3 Whatever be your state or case,
The Lord himself be near ;
Support, protect, defend, embrace,
And make your passage clear.

4 Thus may you prove his promise true,
And glorify his name ;
And every day your songs renew,
While life and breath remain.

5 The Lord be with you to the end,
And land you safe above ;
A long eternity to spend,
In singing, "God is love."

632 8s.
The Believer in Christ, secure.—John iii. 15, 16.
Whoever in Jesus believes,
The blessing is sure to obtain ;
A full and free pardon Christ gives,
To all that confide in his name ;
Nor Moses, nor Satan, nor sin,
Can sentence believers to hell ;
No evil, without or within,
Shall ever against them prevail.

2 Till He who immensity fills,
Whose name is Jehovah, I AM,
Who governs the sun, moon, and stars,
And measures the earth with a span ;
Till this God can fall from his throne,
His promise and faithfulness fail,
Omnipotence weakness become,
And hell against heaven prevail,—

3 Till then the believer's secure,
Though devils against him unite ;
His faith stands in Jesus's power,
And Christ all his battles will fight ;
The feeble shall all be made strong ;
Then let them rejoice in their King ;

The warfare will cease before long,
And they a sweet victory sing.

633 L.M.
Having loved his own .. in the world.—John xiii. 1.
THE love of Christ is rich and free ;
Fixed on his own eternally ;
Nor earth, nor hell, can it remove ;
Long as he lives, his own he'll love.

2 His loving heart engaged to be
Their everlasting Surety ;
'Twas love that took their cause in hand,
And love maintains it to the end.

3 Love cannot from its post withdraw ;
Nor death, nor hell, nor sin, nor law,
Can turn the Surety's heart away ;
He'll love his own to endless day.

4 [Love has redeemed his sheep with blood ;
And love will bring them safe to God ;
Love calls them all from death to life ;
And love will finish all their strife.]

5 He loves through every changing scene,
Nor aught can him from Zion wean ;
Not all the wanderings of her heart
Can make his love from her depart.

6 At death, beyond the grave, he'll love ;
In endless bliss, his own shall prove
The blazing glory of that love
Which never could from them remove.

634 148th.
Saints safe in Christ.—John x. 28, 29 ; xiv. 19 ; Col. iii.
WHEN saints together meet
God's goodness to declare,
The season will be sweet,
If Jesus be but there ;
Of Christ they speak ; of Christ they boast ;
While Jesus lives, they can't be lost.

2 What though their house with God
Be not as they could wish,
And oft a Father's rod
Fills them with deep distress,
Yet in the Lord they firm abide,
United to him as his bride.

3 [What if their lust rebel,
And threaten to devour,
To plunge their souls to hell,
In some unguarded hour ?
Their standing fast is in the Lord,
And they his faithfulness record.]

4 The Lord will guard them well,
Nor shall they ever be

A prey to death and hell,
For Christ has made them free ;
He bought them with his own heart's blood,
And he will bring them home to God.

635 8s.
The Church the Body of Christ.—1 Cor. xii. 27.
THE body, the church, ever stood
In Christ their mysterious Head ;
To save them he shed his own blood,
And they from his fulness are fed.
A body united indeed ;
Cemented together by love ;
And richly supplied from its Head,
With blessings from heaven above.

2 [Each joint is the care of the Lord,
And he will preserve it from hell ;
His aid and his influence afford,
And so supply each member well.
When creatures to time bid adieu,
Each part shall appear in its place,
And live to eternity too,
Where Jesus unveileth his face.]

3 The arm, and the eye, and the breast,
Or members less comely to sight,
Shall ever be honoured and blest,
In glory's ineffable light.
No schism can ever take place ;
'Tis built and supported by God ;
A temple of infinite grace,
A mansion of immortal love.

636 8.8.6.
The Sabbath.—Heb. iv. 8-11 ; Exod. xxxi. 15.
THE Sabbath was a day of rest ;
The day the Lord Jehovah blest ;
A lively type of Christ ;
The labouring poor may venture here ;
The guilty banish all their fear,
And lean on Jesus' breast.

2 When foes without, and foes within,
Wrath, law, and Satan, guilt and sin,
The child of God molest ;
Fatigued with sin, distressed with fear,
He enters into Christ, and there
He finds a settled rest.

3 Jesus is Zion's only rest ;
Thrice happy is the man, and blest,
That into him believes ;
His six days' toil is finished then ;
His slavish fear for ever gone ;
By faith in Christ he lives.

4 [A precious resting-place indeed ;
Whatever weary pilgrims need
Is richly treasured here.

Here sinners may commune with God,
And drink full draughts of heavenly love,
Nor death nor danger fear.]

5 O may I ever rest in him,
And never, never stray again,
Nor after strangers roam ;
Dear Jesus, fix my roving heart,
Nor ever let me from thee start,
Till thou shalt take me home.

637 C.M. Isa. xi. 10; xxviii. 12.
Christ, the Believer's Rest.—

JESUS, thou art our only rest
From sin, and guilt, and fears ;
We love to lean upon thy breast,
And on thee cast our cares.

2 With anxious care and painful thought,
We toiled and toiled again ;
True holiness was what we sought,
But this we sought in vain.

3 Stripped naked, and exposed to shame,
We loud for mercy cried ;
The Lord gave faith to eye the Lamb,
And fasten in his side.

4 The works of nature, bad or good,
Availed nothing here ;
Faith viewed the Saviour's precious blood,
And banished guilt and fear.

5 [Here's life, and light, and holiness,
And righteousness divine ;
A boundless treasure, all of grace,
And faith says, All is mine.]

6 O what a rest is Christ to me !
How precious and how true !

From guilt and sin he sets me free,
And gives me glory too.

7 I have, I want no rest beside ;
Here's all a God can give ;
Here would I constantly abide,
And every moment live.

638 C.M.
No Rest but Christ.—Heb. iv. 3-11 ; Matt. xi. 28.

WITH sin and guilt poor Zion toils,
And labours hard for peace ;
But till the Lord the Saviour smiles,
Her conscience gets no ease.

2 [Her efforts all abortive prove ;
Her working makes her worse ;
Nought but the Saviour's flesh and blood
Can save her from the curse.]

3 The Lord the Saviour is her rest ;
On him she casts her cares ;

By faith she leans upon his breast,
And banishes her fears.

4 But till the Holy Ghost applies
The Saviour's precious blood,
Above her guilt she cannot rise,
Nor lean upon her God.

639 104th.
Return unto thy rest, O my soul."—Ps. cxvi. 7.

RETURN to thy rest, my soul, and rejoice ;
Let Christ be thy boast, for thou art his choice ;
And tho' sin and Satan, and their hellish guest,
Do vex and dishearten, Jehovah's thy rest.

2 A sweet resting-place is Jesus to thee ;
A fulness of grace, rich, sovereign, and free ;
From slavish works cease, then, and rest in the
Lamb, [sin.
For Christ is thy freedom from wrath, law, and

3 O yield not to fear, rest only in Christ ;
His promise is sure ; he's Jesus thy Priest ;
And by one atonement thy sin has condemned,
Then by himself sworn that he'll love to the end.

4 Return, then, my soul, to Jesus, thy Rest ;
By faith on him roll, and lean on his breast ;
He will not deceive thee ; his faithfulness prove ;
He never can leave thee, till God is not love.

640 7s.
" Lord, teach us to pray."—Luke xi. 1.

BLESSED Jesus, Lord of all,
Teach us on thy name to call ;
Help us to be much in prayer,
And upon thee cast our care.

2 Draw us, Lord, by thy sweet power,
In temptation's darkest hour ;
Make us cry to thee our Friend,
And upon thy grace depend.

3 At all times, in every case,
Lead us to thy Throne of Grace ;
Let our needs be what they may,
Teach us how and what to pray.

4 Jesus, deign to bless us thus,
And to glory in thy cross ;
Then, though men and devils roar,
We will ever thee adore.

641 8.7.4.
Desiring to be led by the Lord.—Ps. xxv. 5 : xxxi. 3.

JESUS, mighty God and Saviour,
Lead me forth by thy right hand ;
And be it my fixed endeavour,
To obey thy sweet command ;
Let me never
At a trifling distance stand.

2 Guide, O guide me by thy Spirit ;
    Leave me not to walk alone ;
    And by faith may I inherit
    The eternal Three-in-One ;
        And with boldness,
    Make thy matchless wonders known.

3 May my soul be sweetly filled,
    With the treasures of my God ;
    And my tongue be rightly skilled,
    To proclaim thy truth abroad ;
        And with pleasure,
    God's eternal love record.

642   148th.
Prayer for the Presence of Christ.—Ex. xxxiii. 15.

ONCE more, dear God of grace,
    Thy earthly courts we tread ;
    We come to see thy face,
    And banquet with our Head ;
We long, we faint, we pant for thee ;
And hope that with us thou wilt be.

2   Though base and vile we are,
    Nor goodness have to bring,
    We cannot well despair,
    While Jesus is our King ;
He welcomes all by sin oppressed,
Upon his grace to come and feast.

3   With Christ we would be fed ;
    By faith upon him live ;
    We wish no other bread,
    And thou hast this to give ;
Lord, fill us well with this rich food,
And let us drink thy precious blood.

643   8.8.6.
Praying for Living Bread.—Ps. xxviii. 9.

AGAIN, dear Lord, we would be fed ;
We come to seek for living bread,
    And feast on love divine ;
Dear Father, let thy presence be
Enjoyed by all thy family,
    And make each face to shine.

2 In thee all blessings richly meet ;
Come, then, and give our souls a treat,
    And let us feast indeed ;
O let us banquet with the King,
And love, and pray, and praise, and sing,
    As sons from bondage freed.

3 May faith be strong, and pierce the skies,
And we with pleasure realise

The glory now prepared ;
Commune with Jesus as our Friend ;
Upon him live ; his love commend ;
    And carnal things discard.

4 If this be granted, we'll adore
The hand that gives, yet keeps in store
    A boundless stock of grace ;
In every time of need we'll cry,
And thou shalt all our needs supply,
    And that with smiling face.

644   11s.
" Watch and be sober."—1 Thess. v. 6 ; 1 Pet. v. 8.

WATCH, watch, and be sober, ye children of God ;
Your wonderful Lover has bought you with
    blood ;   [life ;
Your Husband and Saviour for you gave his
Then be your behaviour becoming his wife.

2

O watch against trusting to your native strength ;
Behold Peter boasting, but o'ercome at length ;
Your strength will forsake you, & leave you to fall,
Unless the Lord make you to trust him for all.

3

Treat all as deceivers that lead not to Christ ;
As holy believers, rely on your Priest ;
Watch ye against sleeping, and stand to your post,
Lest you should go weeping, while Canaanites
    boast.   4

By awful temptations attacked and distressed,
Tho' thousand vexations each moment molest,
Yet watch against falling, & yield not to doubt,
On Christ your Lord calling, your foes you shall
    rout.

645   7s.
" Watch and pray."—Matt. xxvi. 41 ; Mark xiv. 38.

DANGEROUS is the path we go,
In this wilderness below,
Savage beasts, of every kind,
Aiming to distress the mind.

2 Scarce an hour but pilgrims see
They from danger are not free ;
In some unexpected way,
Something fills them with dismay.

3 Thus beset, they daily feel
They have neither strength nor skill
Rightly to oppose the foe,
Or to guard against the woe.

4 How, then, can they persevere ?
Must they of the prize despair ?
No ; 'tis theirs to watch and pray,
For the Lord will guard the way.

5 Christ the Master, Lord of all,
Bids his children watch and call;
May it be our blessed case,
Both to watch and seek his face.

6 When we watch, then may we pray,
And in prayer watch every day;
And with pleasure ever prove
All our strength is from above.

7 [Thus supported, we shall be
More than conquerors, Lord, through thee;
And when every danger's past,
Live and reign with thee at last.]

646 C.M.
Hymn for a Fast-Day.—Ps. xcix. 1; xciii. 1—4.
GREAT God! whose universal power
Through all the earth is known;
Who governs heaven and earth, nor sits
On a precarious throne;

2 No strange commotions on the earth,
No wars have taken place,
But what were ever in thy view,
Almighty God of grace.

3 Creatures of every sort and kind
Are all at thy control;
The God that fills immensity
Must reign from pole to pole.

4 Our wars and tumults all arise
As the effect of sin;
Sin is the cause of all the woes
The world has felt or seen.

5 Dear Lord, we fall before thy face;
Our guilt and folly own;
And pray thee, for thy mercy's sake,
To make thy goodness known.

6 In mercy put a stop to war;
In mercy send us peace;
Nor let thy vengeance on us fall,
Almighty King of grace.

7 Yet, Lord, whate'er thy will may be,
We pray to be resigned;
We know thou art too wise to err,
Too good to be unkind.

647 8.8.6.
A Song of Praise to the Holy Three.—Rev. xix. 5.
WHEN will the happy moment come
That I shall meet my Lord at home,
And all his glory view?
Where sin no more shall vex my soul,
Nor Satan any more control,
Nor guilt shall me pursue?

2 [Christ loved, and chose, and ransom'd me.
From sin and Satan set me free,
And washed me in his blood;
He clothed me well from top to toe,
Adorned me with his glory too,
And brought me home to God.]

3 When such a guilty wretch as I,
Deserving nought but misery,
Shall in full glory be,
With all the blood-bought throng above,
I'll sing the riches of thy love,
Through vast eternity.

4 I'll tell the Father and the Son,
And the bless'd Spirit, Three-in-One,
I'm saved by grace divine;
And, with a strong, immortal voice,
In this One God will I rejoice,
Nor ever more repine.

648 148th.
Baptism.—Matt. iii. 13-15; John xv. 14; Luke vi. 46.
WITH wonder and with love,
We at thy courts appear;
Thy ways our hearts approve,
And thy great name revere;
We own the Lamb, our Leader wise,
Nor would we dare his ways despise.

2 [What Jesus does command,
His children should obey;
He's King in Zion's land,
And does his sceptre sway;
Let Zion, then, with one accord,
Obey the precepts of her Lord.]

3 Can anything be mean,
That's worthy of our God?
The King himself was seen
In Jordan's swelling flood;
And shall the subject scorn to tread
The path the King himself has made?

4 Come, fill our souls with love,
With faith, and peace, and joy,
Nor let the price of blood
Against her God reply;
Dear Father, draw, and we will run,
In sweet obedience to thy Son.

649 7s.
The same.—Luke xii. 50; Rom. vi. 4; Col. ii. 12.
PRECIOUS Jesus! here we are,
Come to witness and declare
We are thine, redeemed with blood,
Called and proved the sons of God.

2 Jesus, ere he gave his blood,
Was immersed in Jordan's flood,

There, and in that way, to show
What he had to undergo.

3. In the watery grave we see,
Looking through it, Lord, to thee,
Jesus, overwhelmed in blood,
Sunk in wrath's tremendous flood.

4 And shall we for whom he died,
Rose, and lives to intercede,
Be too proud to be despised,
And with him to be baptized ?

5 No, dear Saviour, we will go
In the watery grave, to show
We are buried with our King,
And we rise his praise to sing.

6 Precious Spirit, make us see
Love immense, beyond degree ;
Now, and when beneath the flood,
Fill us with the love of God.

650 7s.
The same.—John xv. 14 ; Luke xii. 50.

Jesus, we thy name adore ;
Thine the kingdom is and power ;
Thou shalt reign on Zion's hill ;
We would gladly do thy will.

2 Thou hast bought our souls with blood,
And hast brought us home to God.
We would gladly thee obey,
In thy own appointed way.

3 [We through grace are dead indeed,
And from our old husband freed,
But are married to the Lord,
And would gladly do his word.]

4 Thou didst sink in floods of wrath,
Us to save from guilt and death ;
And with such a scene in view,
We would thy commandments do.

5 Thou hast claimed us as thy bride ;
Keep us near thy wounded side ;
Dead to every lord but thee,
We would fain obedient be.

651 8.7.4.
The same.—Rom. vi. 4 ; Luke xii. 50 ; Col. ii. 12.

Jesus, our exalted Saviour,
We adore thy matchless grace ;
Thou hast borne our misbehaviour,
Suffered in our wretched place ;
Wrath and terror
Sank thy soul in deep disgrace.

2 For us thou hast borne the horrors
Of a sin-avenging God :
Who can understand the sorrows
Of thy soul in wrath's deep flood ?
'Tis a mystery
Only fully known to God.

3 [Yet, through grace, we know in measure
What thy love has for us borne,
And we hope, through thy good pleasure,
To behold thee on thy throne,
And for ever
Sing the victories thou hast won.]

4 As an emblem of thy passion,
We with thee would be baptized ;
And to show thy great salvation,
From the liquid grave we rise ;
May we never,
Never dare thy ways despise.

652 S.M.
The same.—Rom. vi. 4, 8 ; Luke xii. 50 ; Col. ii. 12.

Jesus, our Lord and King,
Thou art our hope and trust ;
Thy boundless love and grace we sing,
And of thee we will boast.

2 As sinners saved by grace,
And made alive to God
Thy righteous laws we would embrace,
And tread the heavenly road.

3 Thy wisdom did ordain
This solemn rite, to show
How thou wast plunged in wrath and pain,
To save our souls from woe.

4 We come thy name to own,
And solemnly confess,
Thou art our Life, our Joy, our Crown,
Our Strength, and Righteousness.

653 S.M.
"One Lord, one faith, one baptism."—Eph. iv. 5.

Of one Lord will we sing,
And spread his fame abroad,
Jehovah Jesus is our King,
And be his name adored.

2 One living, vital faith,
Each Christian will approve ;
A faith that triumphs over death,
And sweetly works by love.

3 One baptism we own ;
A sacred, solemn sign
Of what the Saviour's undergone,
To wash away our sin.

4 [His overwhelming pain,
And burial we see ;

His rising from the grave again,
  To set his children free.]

5 Here we by faith may view,
    That every Christian's dead
To Satan, sin, and Moses too,
    Through Christ, our living Head.

6 In rising from the flood,
    Saints solemnly proclaim
Their life is hid with Christ in God,
    And they shall with him reign.

654   7s.

Baptism.—Matt. iii. 15; Luke iii. 21; Acts x. 47.

WE adore the Lord the Lamb,
And rejoice in his dear name ;
He has shed his precious blood,
To redeem our souls to God.

2 Once we lay immersed in sin ;
Every part and power unclean ;
Enemies to all that's good,
We despised the Saviour's blood.

3 But the Lord, by grace divine,
Brought us to abhor the crime ;
And, to make his wonders known,
Gave us faith in Christ, his Son.

4 Thus redeemed and saved by blood,
We esteem the ways of God,
And would gladly him obey,
In his own appointed way.

5 'Tis from love to Christ, our Head,
We his footsteps wish to tread ;
And when we his unction feel,
We with pleasure do his will.

655   L.M.

The same.—Phil. iii. 10; Acts viii. 38; Isa. lxiii. 9.

JESUS, the Lord, enthroned on high,
To thee we look, to thee we cry ;
We long to view thy lovely face,
And sweetly sing thy matchless grace.

2 Thou hast redeemed our souls from death,
And blessed us with a living faith ;
And thou wilt safely lead us home,
Where sins and sorrows never come.

3 As children loved and taught of God,
We now descend into the flood :
Nor will we fear, nor blush with shame,
To be baptized in thy name.

4 Dear condescending God, appear,
And bless us with a holy fear ;
Give solid joy and sacred love,
And every idle thought remove.

5 [Bless with true fellowship with thee,
When weltering in Gethsemane ;
Thy resurrection's power display,
While we thy sacred rite obey.]

6 Then shall we feel a solemn frame,
And magnify thy sovereign name ;
And with a holy, reverend awe,
Yield sweet obedience to thy law.

656   8.7.4.

The same.—Luke xii. 50; Acts x. 47; Heb. ii. 9.

PRECIOUS Jesus ! we adore thee ;
  Thou hast conquered death and hell ;
We in wonder fall before thee ;
  Thy salvation suits us well ;
    May we love thee,
And obey thy righteous will.

2 Here we raise our Ebenezer,
  Monuments of grace divine ;
Thou art all our joy and treasure,
  We are wholly, doubly thine ;
    Loved for ever,
And redeemed with blood divine.

3 [Give us faith to view thee sighing,
  Under our tremendous load ;
Agonising, groaning, dying,
  Overwhelmed in sweat and blood ;
    Floods of vengeance
Covering our incarnate God.]

4 By thy precious love constrained,
  We are come to own thy name ;
Thou for us all shame disdained ;
  We for thee would do the same.
    Saviour, bless us
With a holy, solemn frame.

5 Then, with a transporting pleasure,
  We with Christ will be baptized ;
Follow him, our glorious Leader,
  Let whoever will despise ;
    And for ever
Sing his praise beyond the skies.

657   7s.

The same.—Acts x. 47; John xv. 14; Luke xii. 50.

TUNED with love divine, we sing,
Glory to our God and King ;
Matchless in his grace and power ;
We behold, and we adore.

2 Once in floods of wrath, the Lamb
Sank, and called it baptism ;
Overwhelmed was he indeed,
That his chosen might be freed.

3 [But he conquered when he fell,
  And destroyed the powers of hell ;
  He in holy triumph broke
  Sin and death's tremendous yoke.]

4 [One with Christ, our living Head,
  We were each considered dead ;
  With him, too, we rose again,
  And with him must ever reign.]

5 Now with pleasure we attend
  To his wise and just command,
  And by faith therein we view
  What the Lord for us went through.

658   7s.
The same.—Rom. vi. 4, 8; Luke xii. 50; Acts x. 47.
  MIGHTY King, thy power display,
  Give us grace to watch and pray ;
  Strengthened by thy Spirit's might,
  May we in thy ways delight.

2 For us Jesus was baptized
  In tremendous agonies ;
  Mighty vengeance, like a flood,
  Overwhelmed the Lamb of God.

3 Come, ye saints, with wonder view
  What the Lord has done for you ;
  View the mighty waters roll,
  And break in upon his soul.

4 View the swelling floods of wrath
  Sink your Saviour low as death ;
  Grief him covered like a grave,
  When he died, your souls to save.

5 Sons of God, lift up your eyes ;
  See your slaughtered Saviour rise !
  He has conquered death and hell ;
  With him you shall ever dwell.

659   S.M.
The Church's Sins charged upon Christ.—2 Cor. v. 21.
  THE Lord my Saviour is ;
  For me he shed his blood ;
  And shall I scorn his name to own ?
  Forbid it, mighty God.

2 With me upon his heart,
  He stooped to bleed and die ;
  And when my guilt was to him charged,
  The charge did not deny.

3 The debt, though great, he paid,
  That I might be set free ;
  No charge against me can be brought,
  For Jesus died for me.

4 ['Midst all his vast concerns,
  He could not me forget ;
  Then let my heart, my soul, my tongue,
  His dying love repeat.]

660   C.M.
The Lord's Supper.—1 Cor. x. 16, 17; Acts ii. 42.
  WITH wondering eyes, Lord, we admire
  The feast prepared by grace ;
  Come, Lord, and set our souls on fire,
  And fill each heart with peace.

2 These emblems of thy precious love,
  By faith may we receive !
  And with a solemn pleasure prove,
  We in thy name believe.

3 [No goodness of our own we bring ;
  We're sinners vile and base ;
  Christ is our all ; of Christ we sing,
  And long to see his face.]

4 O may we each, with heart and tongue
  Sing, " Worthy is the Lamb " ;

  To him alone the praise belongs,
  And we'll adore his name.

661   C.M.
The Same.—1 Cor. v. 7, 8; xi. 23-28; Luke xxii. 19.
  ONCE more, like children, we are come,
  To banquet with our God ;
  May each one feel himself at home,
  And feast upon thy love.

2 While we receive the bread and wine,
  As emblems of thy death,
  Lord, raise each soul above the sign,
  To feast on Christ by faith.

3 [We would not come as strangers, Lord,
  Who only see the sign,
  But, as the objects of Christ's love,
  Would feel we're one in him.]

4 Like free-born sons, we would be free
  From every legal chain ;
  Praise him who brought our liberty,
  And ever with him reign.

662   7s.
" Do this in remembrance of me."—Luke xxii. 19.
  O THE matchless love of God !
  He has bought our souls with blood !
  Jesus, our exalted Head,
  For us sighed, and groaned, and bled.

2 He invites us to this feast ;
  Bids our souls his glories taste,
  And with pleasure keep in view,
  What he once for us went through.

3 Hear him speak, ye saved few,
  For this word is sent to you,
  You, the objects of his choice,
  Listen to his saving voice :

4 "This my body is, and blood ;
Take, receive it as your food !
But, as oft as this you do,
Keep your slaughtered Lord in view.

5 [" View him in your wretched place,
Overwhelmed in deep disgrace ;
Plunged in horror's dreadful flood,
The vindictive wrath of God.]

6 " View him, and with wonder tell,
He has vanquished death and hell ;
Cancelled all your sins with blood,
And will bring you home to God."

663   S.M.
Sympathy with Christ.--Luke xxiii. 46 ; Ps. xlii. 7.

BELOVED, we are come
With Christ to sympathise ;
For us he has the victory won,
And we shall share the prize.

2 But O remember him ;
View justice, armed with wrath ;
The vengeance due to Zion's sin,
Stung Zion's Lord to death.

3 In miseries great he sighed ;
He groaned ; he cried ; he bled ;
He sank in wrath's tremendous tide,
And dying, bowed his head..

4 Christians, repeat his love ;
With solemn pleasure sing
The bloody conflicts of your God ;
The victories of your King.

664   C.M.
" There the weary be at rest."—Job iii. 17.

WHAT solemn tidings reach our ears !
How awful and how grand !
A *brother* [*or sister*] landed safe from fears,
On Canaan's happy land.

2 No clouds shall now obstruct *his* sun,
But all be life and peace ;
With *him* 'tis ever, ever noon,
Nor can *his* joy decrease.

3 *He's* gone in endless bliss to dwell,
And I am left below,
To struggle with the powers of hell,
Till Jesus bids me go.

4 Though *he's* more happy, I'm secure ;
God's promise cannot fail ;
O may I patiently endure
My heavenly Father's will.

5 The counsel of the Lord shall stand,
And all his will be done ;
I'll therefore wait in Meshech's land,
Until he fetch me home.

665   S.M.
On the Death of Believers.—Prov. x. 7.

GRACE taught our friends to know
What rebels they had been ;
'Twas grace redeemed them from their woe,
And made their conscience clean.

2 Grace taught them to commune
With Christ the Lamb once slain ;
To hate the sins that made him mourn,
And put his soul to pain.

3 Grace taught their souls to sing
Salvation through his blood ;
Through grace they loved him as their King,
Their Saviour, and their God.

4 Grace must and will relieve
From such a waste as this,
All souls that in the Lord believe,
And take them to his bliss.

666   148th.
Last Judgment.—Matt. xxv. 31—46 ; 2 Tim. iv. 1.

WITH great and awful power,
Jesus, the Judge, shall come,
To bid his foes depart,
And take his children home ;
How will the wicked quake and fear,
When they before him must appear.

2 He comes, the world to judge,
Nor will he take a bribe ;
His wrath none can escape,
But his beloved bride ;
Millions will unto mountains call,
To hide them and upon them fall.

3 Poor soul, what is thy hope ?
On what dost thou depend ?
Art thou a stranger still
To Christ, the sinner's Friend ?
Soon thou must leave thy all below,
And then, O then, what wilt thou do ?

4 Christians, lift up your heads ;
Say, what has Jesus done ?
His matchless grace to you
The Saviour has made known ;
Yes, you shall all his glory see,
And from the second death be free.

667   10s.
Safety in Christ.—Heb. xiii. 6 ; Phil. iv. 19.

IMMORTAL honours rest on Jesus' head ;
My God, my Portion, and my Living Bread ;
In him I live, upon him cast my care ;
He saves from death, destruction, and despair.

2 He is my Refuge in each deep distress ;
The Lord my strength & glorious righteousness ;
Through floods and flames he leads me safely on,
And daily makes his sovereign goodness known.

3 My every need he richly will supply ;
Nor will his mercy ever let me die ;
In him there dwells a treasure all divine,
And matchless grace has made that treasure
    mine.

4 O that my soul could love and praise him more,
His beauties trace, his majesty adore ;
Live near his heart, upon his bosom lean ;
Obey his voice, and all his will esteem.

668   10s.
Panting for Pardon.—Ezra ix. 5, 6; Job xiii. 6.

JEHOVAH God ! eternal Lord most high !
Permit a worm to bow before thy throne ;
A worm deserving endless misery,
But pleads the blood that did for sin atone.

2 [I feel myself a rebel, base and vile ;
From head to feet, a mass of sin and guilt ;
Nor have I skill the malady to heal,
But plead the blood that once for sin was spilt.]

3 A base, ungrateful monster I have been,
And now with shame my guilt and folly own ;
I cannot, dare not, on my own works lean,
But plead the blood that did for sin atone.

4 Nor dare I promise future good to bring ;
I know my heart deceitful is indeed ;
Compelled I am on Christ alone to hang, [freed.
And plead that blood by which the church is

5 If thou, dear Lord, so base a wretch wilt save,
Then all the glory shall redound to thee ;
While here, and when I reach beyond the grave,
My soul shall sing salvation full and free.

669   10s.
Welcome to Jesus.—Isa. xliv. 22: Dan. ix. 9.

POOR sinners, sunk in sin's tremendous cell,
Tormented with the fiery darts of hell,
On Jesus call, though wretched be your case ;
He came the lost to seek and save by grace.

2 What tho' your sins like mountains on you fall,
And God's just law with terror fills your soul,
Jehovah Jesus is the sinner's Friend,
And he has answered all the law's demand.

3 'Tis true, in self you have no ground for joy,
Nor can you hope the law to satisfy ;
But Jesus' blood has full atonement made,
And faith therein will make the conscience glad.

4 Here sinners, black as hell, obtain relief ;
A filthy Mary, and a dying thief ;
And guilty I, though vile as they could be,
Have proved his mercy sovereign, rich, and free.

670   8s.
" Without me ye can do nothing."—John xv. 5.

UNITED to Jesus, the Vine,
We've life, strength, and righteousness
But this he will teach us in time,   too,
Without him we nothing can do.
Our hope of performing what's right,
And strictly obeying our God,
If not wholly built on his might,
Will leave us exposed to his rod.

2 Unless he uphold by his grace,
We sink under Satan and sin,
And plunge into shame and disgrace,
Nor can we deliverance obtain ;
We neither can hope nor believe,
Nor pray in a time of distress,
But as we from Jesus receive
The fruits of his own righteousness.

PART III.

FIRST SUPPLEMENT.

671   148th.   BERRIDGE.
Approaching a Holy God.—Ezra ix. 6; Ps. li. 2-10.

How shall I come to thee,
O God, who holy art,
And cannot evil see,
But with a loathing heart ?
I am defiled throughout by sin,
And by my very birth unclean.

2   Soon as my heart could beat,
It drank in various woe ;
Pride, lust, and self-deceit ;
Through all its channels flow ;
A captive born, a child of earth,
It knows and craves no higher birth.

3   From this polluted spring
All filthy waters rise ;
From this diseased thing
I date my maladies ;
My heart, a most degenerate root,
Produces only cankered fruit.

4   And what can wash me clean
But Jesus' precious blood ?
This *only* purgeth sin,
And bringeth nigh to God ;
Lord, wash my sores, and heal them too,
And all my leprosy subdue.

5   Thy heavenly image draw
Upon my panting heart,

And well engrave thy law
Upon the inward part ;
My soul in mercy upward raise,
And teach me how to love and praise.

672   148th.   BERRIDGE.
Spiritual Longing.—Ps. cxix. 174; lv. 6.

JESUS, I long for thee,
And sigh for Canaan's shore,
Thy lovely face to see,
And all my warfare o'er ;
Here billows break upon my breast
And brooding sorrows steal my rest.

2   [I mourn to see thy blood
So foully trampled on ;
And sinners, daring God,
To swift destruction run ;
With heedless heart and simpering face,
They dance the hell-ward road apace.]

3   I pant, I groan, I grieve
For my untoward heart ;

How full of doubts I live,
Though full of grace thou art !
What poor returns I make to thee
For all the mercy shown to me !

4   And must I ever smart,
A child of sorrows here ?
Yet, Lord, be near my heart,
To soothe each rising tear ;
Then at thy bleeding cross I'll stay,
And sweetly weep my life away.

673   148th.   BERRIDGE.
No Rest but Christ.—Isa. xi. 10; Matt. xi. 28, 29.

WHEN Jesus' gracious hand
Has touched our eyes and ears,

O what a dreary land
The wilderness appears !
No healing balm springs from its dust ;
No cooling stream to quench the thirst.

2   Yet long I vainly sought
A resting-place below ;
And that sweet land forgot
Where living waters flow ;
I hunger now for heavenly food,
And my poor heart cries out for God.

3   [Lord, enter in my breast,
And with me sup and stay ;
Nor prove a hasty guest,
Who tarries but a day ;
Upon my bosom fix thy throne,
And pull each fancy idol down.]

4   My sorrow thou canst see,
For thou dost read my heart ;
It pineth after thee,
And yet from thee will start ;
Reclaim thy roving child at last,
And fix my heart and bind it fast.

5   I would be near thy feet,
Or at thy bleeding side ;
Feel how thy heart does beat,
And see its purple tide ;
Trace all the wonders of thy death,
And sing thy love in every breath.

674   148th.   BERRIDGE.
The Power is of God.—Ps. lxii. 11; Phil. ii. 13.

How sinners vaunt of power
A ruined soul to save,
And count the fulsome store
Of worth they seem to have,

And by such visionary props
Build up and bolster sandy hopes !

2   But God must work the will,
And power to run the race ;
And both through mercy still,
A work of freest grace ;
His own good pleasure, not our worth,
Brings all the will and power forth.

3   Disciples who are taught
Their helplessness to feel,
Have no presumptuous thought,
But work with care and skill ;
Work with the means, and for this end,
That God the will and power may send.

4   [They feel a daily need
Of Jesus' gracious store,
And on his bounty feed,
And yet are always poor ;
No manna can they make or keep ;
The Lord finds pasture for his sheep.]

5   Renew, O Lord, my strength
And vigour every day,
Or I shall tire at length,
And faint upon the way ;
No stock will keep upon my ground ;
My all is in thy storehouse found.

675   C.M.   D. HERBERT.

Freedom of Access to a Throne of Grace.—Heb. iv. 16.

COME boldly to a throne of grace,
Ye wretched sinners, come ;
And lay your load at Jesus' feet,
And plead what he has done.

2 " How can I come ? " some soul may say,
" I'm lame, and cannot walk ;

My guilt and sin have stopped my mouth ;
I sigh, but dare not talk."

3 Come boldly to the throne of grace,
Though lost, and blind, and lame ;
Jehovah is the sinner's Friend,
And ever was the same.

4 He makes the dead to hear his voice ;
He makes the blind to see ;
The sinner lost he came to save,
And set the prisoner free.

5 Come boldly to the throne of grace,
For Jesus fills the throne ;
And those he kills he makes alive ;
He hears the sigh or groan.

6 Poor bankrupt souls, who feel and know
The hell of sin within,

Come boldly to the throne of grace ;
The Lord will take you in.

676   C.M.   D. HERBERT.

The Doubting Soul's Soliloquy.—Job xii. 14 ; Ps. lv. 6.

O COULD I lift this heart of mine
Above these creature things,
I'd fly, and leave this world below,
As though on eagle's wings.

2 [But ah ! I feel no love at all,
Can neither praise nor pray ;
O would the Lord but shine again,
And turn this night to day !]

3 But whither can I go to lodge
My sorrow and complaint ?
Unless the Lord is pleased to shine,
I mope, I grieve, I faint.

4 I find my striving all in vain,
Unless my Lord is near ;
My heart is hard ; I'm such a wretch—
Can neither love nor fear.

5 I ask my soul this question then,
For here I would begin :
O do I feel a want of Christ
To save me from my sin ?

6 The souls redeemed by precious blood
Are taught this lesson well ;
'Tis not of him that wills or runs,
But Christ who saves from hell.

677   C.M.   D. HERBERT.

Prayer Meeting.—Ps. xvii. 1 ; xxxii. 5, 6.

BEHOLD, dear Lord, we come again,
To supplicate thy grace ;
We feel our leanness and our wants ;
We want to see thy face.

2 Thou know'st, dear Lord, for what we're
Each heart is known to thee.   [come ;
Lord, give our burdened spirits rest,
And bid us all go free.

3 We've nothing of our own to plead,
We come just as we are ;
And who can tell but God may bless,
And drive away our fear ?

4 While one is pleading with our God,
May each one wrestle too ;
And may we feel the blessing come,
And cheer us ere we go.

5 Then shall we sing of sovereign grace
And feel its power within ;
And glory in our Surety, Christ,
Who bore our curse and sin.

6 For this we come, for this we plead,
    In spite of every foe ;
Until thou give this blessing, Lord,
    We would not let thee go.

678   C.M.   D. HERBERT.
The Warfare.—Acts iv. 12; Rom. vii. 21.
THERE'S not a man that's born of God,
    But readily will say,
" If ever my poor soul be saved,
    'Tis Christ must be the way."

2 There's not a man that's born of God,
    But feels the plague of sin :
And though his outside be kept clean,
    He feels the filth within.

3 The old man struggles hard to gain
    The conquest over grace ;
And oft he seems to gain the field,
    When Jesus hides his face.

4 God knows we can do nothing well,
    He knows we are but dust ;
He came to seek poor sinners out,
    And you and me the worst.

679   C.M.   D. HERBERT.
Prayer.—Matt. xviii. 20; Exod. xx. 24.
COME, thou Almighty Comforter,
    And bring upon thy wing
Sweet consolation to each soul,
    That we may praise and sing.

2 We want to feel, we want to see,
    We want to know thee more ;
We want sweet foretastes of thy love,
    As we have had before.

3 And shall we come in vain to God ?
    Dear Lord, that cannot be ;
Thy promise stands engaged to come,
    And bless e'en two or three.

4 Come, Lord, and grant each soul to feel
    Its interest in thy grace ;
And give us faith, and hope, and love,
    And strength to run the race.

5 [If thou shouldst leave us, we must fall ;
    Without thee, cannot rise ;
For when our Jesus hides his face,
    Our hope, our comfort, dies.]

6 Lord, give more faith, more solid faith,
    More confidence in thee ;
Break off our legal chains, O God,
    And let our souls go free.

680   C.M.   D. HERBERT.
Eternal Settlements.—Eph. i. 3-12; 2 Tim. i. 9; Tit. i. 2.
BEFORE all worlds, the glorious plan,
    The blessed eternal deed,

Was settled by the eternal Three,
    That Christ for man should bleed.

2 Astonished angels stand amazed,
    That Christ should die for man ;
This proves the eternal love of God,
    Who gloried in his plan.

3 But what can poor lost sinners say,
    When once they get a view ;
And hear the blessed Spirit say,
    " All this was done for you " ?

4 ". Why me, why me, O blessed God,
    Why such a wretch as me ?
Who must for ever lie in hell,
    Were not salvation free."

5 All those that God had foreordained,
    These shall and must believe ;

Not all the craft of earth or hell
    Shall one of these deceive.

681   L.M.   HART.
" Son, . . thy sins be forgiven thee."—Matt. ix. 2.
BLESSED are they whose guilt is gone,
Whose sins are washed away with blood,
Whose hope is fixed on Christ alone,
Whom Christ has reconciled to God.

2 Though, travelling through this vale of tears,
He many a sore temptation meet,
The Holy Ghost this witness bears,
He stands in Jesus still complete.

3 This pearl of price no works can claim ;
He that finds this is rich indeed ;
This pure white stone contains a name,
Which none but who receives can read.

4 This precious gift, this bond of love,
The Lord oft gives his people here ;
But what we all shall be above
Does not, my brethren, yet appear.

5 Yet this we safely may believe,
'Tis what no words will e'er express ;
What saints themselves cannot conceive,
And brightest angels can but guess.

682   S.M.   GADSBY.
" Thy will be done."—Matt. vi. 10; Luke xi. 2.
WHILE Jesus whispers peace,
    And unctuously displays
The matchless beauties of his grace,
    Our hearts approve his ways.

2 But when the Lord withdraws
    The unction of his love,
His will we wickedly oppose,
    His judgments disapprove.

3 So fickle, false, and blind,
Are these unstable hearts,
We only are to God resigned,
As he the grace imparts.

4 Father, thy will be done,
In words we oft express ;
When in our hearts we want our own,
And wish our sufferings less.

5 Dear God, our guilt forgive,
Thy pardoning love display ;
And may we to thy glory live,
Thy righteous will obey.

6 [Thy presence let us view,
And give our conscience rest ;
The visits of thy love renew,
Then do what thou think'st best.]

683　　　S.M.　　　GADSBY.
"Thy kingdom come."—Matt. vi. 10; Dan. ii. 44.
GREAT God ! thy kingdom come,
With reverence would we pray,
May the eternal Three-in-One
His sovereign sceptre sway.

2 May grace triumphant reign,
And Christ exalted be ;
Sinners, deserving endless pain,
Thy great salvation see.

3 May mercy, truth, and peace,
Fill each believer's soul,
And the sweet kingdom of thy grace,
Their raging lusts control.

4 [May love and harmony
Among thy saints abide,
Thy presence set each bosom free
From enmity and pride.]

5 Go on, thou mighty God,
Thy wonders to make known,
Till every sinner bought with blood,
Shall trust in thee alone.

6 Thus let thy kingdom come,
And free salvation reign,
Till all thy saints arrive at home,
And never part again.

684　　　C.M.　　　BERRIDGE.
Living Waters.—Jer. ii. 13; John iv. 10.
OF cistern waters art thou sick,
And loath'st the mire they bring ?
Then hither stretch thy thirsty neck,
And taste a living spring.

2 A spring that issues from a rock,
Where purest waters flow ;
And rocky hearts, by Moses struck,
May to these waters go.

3 No spring will quench a thirst like this ;
It makes a conscience whole,
Inspires the heart with heavenly bliss,
And purifies the soul.

4 Whoe'er can truly say, " I thirst,"
May come and take his fill ;
'Tis free for sinners, vile and lost ;
'Tis God who works the will.

5 [Its owner is a heavenly King ;
And by his winning ways,
He draws the thirsty to his spring,
Who drink and sing his praise.]

6 Lord, draw me by thy secret touch,
Or backward I shall start ;
For sure I want entreating much,
So fearful is my heart.

685　　　C.M.　　　HART.
"And the Lord shut him in."—Gen. vii. 16.
WHEN Noah, with his favoured few,
Was ordered to embark,
Eight human souls, a little crew,
Entered on board his ark

2 Though every part he might secure
With bar, or bolt, or pin,
To make the preservation sure,
Jehovah shut him in.

3 The waters then might swell their tides,
The billows rage and roar,
They could not stave the assaulted sides,
Nor burst the battered door.

4 So souls that into Christ believe,
Quickened by vital faith,
Eternal life at once receive,
And never shall see death.

5 In his own heart the Christian puts
No trust ; but builds his hopes
On him that opes, and no man shuts ;
And shuts, and no man opes.

6 In Christ, his Ark, he safely rides,
Not wrecked by death or sin.
How is it he so safe abides ?
The Lord has shut him in.

686　　　7s.　　　BERRIDGE.
Praying for Humility.—Luke xxii. 61, 62; Matt. v. 3.
JESUS, cast a look on me ;
Give me sweet simplicity ;
Make me poor, and keep me low,
Seeking only thee to know.

2 [Weaned from my lordly self,
Weaned from the miser's pelf,

Weaned from the scorner's ways,
Weaned from the lust of praise.]

3 All that feeds my busy pride,
Cast it evermore aside ;
Bid my will to thine submit ;
Lay me humbly at thy feet.

4 Make me like a little child,
Of my strength and wisdom spoiled,
Seeing only in thy light,
Walking only in thy might.

5 Leaning on thy loving breast,
Where a weary soul may rest ;
Feeling well the peace of God
Flowing from thy precious blood.

6 In this posture let me live,
And hosannas daily give ;
In this temper let me die,
And hosannas ever cry.

687   104th.   BERRIDGE.
" Wait on the Lord."—Ps. xxvii. 14 ; Isa. viii. 17.
YE broken hearts all, who cry out, " Unclean,"
And taste of the gall of in-dwelling sin ;
Lamenting it truly, and loathing it too,
And seeking help duly, as sinners must do ;

2 The Lord whom ye seek is nigh to your call,
Attends when you speak, nor lets a word fall ;
Your sorrow and sighing are felt in his breast ;
He pities your crying, and will give you rest.

3 [If often he hides his face from his friends,
And silent abides for merciful ends,
At length he uncovers himself from his cloud,
And sweetly discovers his face and his blood.]

4 All penitent cries his Spirit imparts,
And fetches out sighs from sin-feeling hearts ;
He puts you in mourning, the dress that you want,
A meek suit adorning both sinner and saint.

5 A time he has set to heal up your woes,
A season most fit his love to disclose ;
And till he is ready to show his good-will,
Be patient and steady, and wait on him still.

688   L.M.   C.W.
" Behold the Man."—John xix. 5 ; Lam. i. 12.
YE that pass by, behold the Man !
The Man of griefs condemned for you ;
The Lamb of God for sinners slain,
Weeping to Calvary pursue.

2 See there his temples crowned with thorns ;
His bleeding hands extended wide ;
His streaming feet transfixed and torn ;
The fountain gushing from his side.

3 O thou dear suffering Son of God,
How does thy heart to sinners move !

Sprinkle on me thy precious blood ;
Help me to taste thy dying love.

4 The rocks could feel thy powerful death,
And tremble, and asunder part ;
O rend with thy expiring breath,
The harder marble of my heart.

689   8.7.   SWAIN.
" He bare our sins .. on the tree."—1 Pet. ii. 24.

ON the wings of faith uprising,
Jesus crucified I see ;
While his love, my soul surprising,
Cries, I suffered all for thee.

2 Then beneath the cross adoring,
Sin does like itself appear ;
When, the wounds of Christ exploring,
I can read my pardon there.

3 Here I'd feast my soul for ever ;
While this balm of life I prove,
Every wound appears a river
Flowing with eternal love.

4 Who can think without admiring ?
Who can hear and nothing feel ?
See the Lord of life expiring,
Yet retain a heart of steel ?

5 [Angels here may gaze and wonder,
What the God of love could mean,
When he tore the heart asunder,
Never once defiled with sin.]

690   8.8.6.   BERRIDGE.
" A remnant shall be saved."—Rom. ix. 27 ; xi. 4. 5.
ON wings of love the Saviour flies,
And freely left his native skies,
To take a human birth ;
The wise and righteous men go near,
His wonders see, his sermons hear,
And think him nothing worth.

2 A remnant small of humble souls
His grace mysteriously controls
By sweet alluring call ;
They hear it, and his person view,
They learn to love and follow too,
And take him for their all.

3 One of this remnant I would be,
A soul devoted unto thee,
Allured by thy voice ;
No more on gaudy idols gaze,
No longer tinsel grandeur praise,
But fix on thee my choice.

4 Thou knowest well my secret smart,
And readest all my aching heart,
And hearest every sigh ;

Can any creature give me rest,
Or any blessing make me blest,
　Unless my Lord is nigh ?

5 While walking on the gospel-way,
　I would see Jesus every day,
　　And see in all his grace ;
　See him my Prophet, Priest, and King ;
　See him by faith, and praises sing ;
　　Then see him face to face.

691　　C.M.　　NEWTON.
　The Thaw.—Job xii. 14; John xv. 5.

ALL outward means, till God appears,
　Will ineffectual prove ;
Though much the sinner sees and hears,
　He cannot learn to love.

2 But let the stoutest sinner feel
　The softening warmth of grace,
Though hard as ice, or rocks, or steel,
　His heart dissolves apace.

3 Feeling the blood which Jesus spilt,
　To save his soul from woe,
His hatred, unbelief, and guilt,
　All melt away like snow.

4 Jesus, we in thy name entreat ;
　Reveal thy gracious arm ;
And grant thy Spirit's kindly heat,
　Our frozen hearts to warm.

692　　L.M.　　NEWTON.
　"Ask what I shall give thee."—1 Kings iii. 5.

IF Solomon for wisdom prayed,
The Lord before had made him wise ;
Else he another choice had made,
And asked for what the worldlings prize.

2 Thus he invites his people still,
　But first instructs them how to choose,
Then bids them ask whate'er they will,
　Assured that he will not refuse.

3 And dost thou say, " Ask what thou wilt " ?
Lord, I would seize the golden hour ;
I pray to be released from guilt,
And freed from sin and Satan's power.

4 More of thy presence, Lord, impart,
　More of thy image let me bear ;
Erect thy throne within my heart,
　And reign without a rival there.

5 Give me to read my pardon sealed,
　And from thy joy to draw my strength ;
To have thy matchless love revealed
　In all its height, and breadth, and length.

6 Grant these requests, I ask no more,
　But to thy care the rest resign ;

Sick or in health, or rich or poor,
All will be well if thou art mine.

693　　10s.　　GADSBY.
　Desiring love's sanctifying effects.—1 Jno. v. 3.

LORD, let me feel the unction of thy love,
To cheer my heart, and set my mind above ;
Give me a precious glimpse of thy sweet face,
And make me gladly all thy will embrace.

2 Draw me from all forbidden toil and care,
From lust, and pride, and every hurtful snare ;
Make Satan and his hellish powers to flee,
And let me have true intercourse with thee.

3 Subdue that monstrous host that dwells within,
That cursed train of unbelief and sin ;
Let faith be active in the Lamb once slain,
And all my soul adore, and love his name.

694　　8.7.　　GADSBY.
　The Church praying for themselves and their Minister.

LORD, direct thy own-sent servant ;
　Teach him how and what to speak ;
Make him humble, wise and fervent,
　　Skilled the bread of life to break ;
Let each child enjoy a portion,
　Feel their souls alive to God ;
Freed from pride and empty notion,
　Eat thy flesh and drink thy blood.

2 Father, Son, and Holy Spirit,
　Dwell thou sensibly in us ;
And may we thy love inherit,
　　Freed from guilt, law, and the curse.
Sweetly view and feel thy glory,
　Open all our hearts to thee ;
Sing and tell the pleasing story,
　Matchless grace has set us free.

695　　7s.　　GADSBY.
　Prayer to the blessed Spirit.—John xvi. 14; Gal. v. 5.

BLESSED Comforter, appear
To thy waiting children here ;
Bless us with a solemn frame ;
Magnify the Saviour's name.

2 Raise our souls from earth and sin ;
Let us feel thy power within,
Make the blessings of free grace
Unctuously suit every case.

3 Make us humble and sincere ;
Free us from each carking care ;
Jesus' love and blood impart,
Drive each rival from the heart.

4 Shower down blessings from above ;
Fill our souls with heavenly love ;

May we mutually agree,
With the Father, Son, and Thee.

696   148th.   GADSBY.
Public Meeting Place.—1 Kings viii. 28, 29, 43.

WITHIN these walls, dear Lord,
Display thy matchless grace ;
Thy constant aid afford,
And show thy smiling face ;
And may thy blessed family
Enjoy salvation full and free.

2 Here may the eternal Three
His glorious power make known,
Set captive sinners free,
Bring wandering sinners home ;
Display the wonders of his love,
And fix his children's hearts above.

3 May watchmen, taught of God,
Jehovah's love declare ;
Proclaim a Saviour's blood,
To vanquish guilty fear ;
And may the heavenly Paraclete,
Their message seal in Zion's heart.

697   8.7.   GADSBY.
Prayer for nearness to the Lord.—Ezek. xxxvi. 25.

O THOU lovely, loving Saviour,
Bless us with a solemn frame,
Teach us now, henceforth, and ever,
To adore thy matchless name.
Give us, blessed Jesus, give us,
A sweet glimpse of thy sweet face ;
From all carking care relieve us ;
Fill us with thy boundless grace.

2 [Let the unction of redemption
Supple every conscience well ;
Give us now a sweet exemption
From the rage of sin and hell.
Tell us, Lord, and make us feel it,
We are thine, for ever thine.
Take each wounded heart and heal it,
Let thy glory in us shine.]

3 Plunge us in that crimson ocean,
Thy atonement made for sin ;
Freed from trusting empty notion,
May we feel thy power within.
With thy presence, Lord, refresh us,
Aid and keep us by thy power ;
May we ever be ambitious
Thee to love, crown, and adore.

698   8.7.4.   GADSBY.
"The Lord is at hand."—Phil. iv. 5; Amos iv. 12.

PAUSE, my soul ! and ask the question,
Art thou ready to meet God ?
Am I made a real Christian,
Washed in the Redeemer's blood ?
Have I union
To the church's living Head ?

2 Am I quickened by his Spirit ;
Live a life of faith and prayer ?
Trusting wholly to his merit ;
Casting on him all my care ?
Daily panting,
In his likeness to appear ?

3 If my hope on Christ is stayed,
Let him come when he thinks best ;
O my soul ! be not dismayed,
Lean upon his loving breast ;
He will cheer thee
With the smilings of his face.

4 But, if still a total stranger
To his precious name and blood,
Thou art on the brink of danger ;
Canst thou face a holy God ?
Think and tremble,
Death is now upon the road.

699   10s.   GADSBY.
New Year.—Ps. lxv. 11; ciii. 4.

LORD, we adore thee, and would fain express
Thy matchless goodness and our worthlessness ;
Ashamed of self, we prostrate at thy door,
Confess our sin, and thy free grace implore.

2 Another year of our short life is gone,
And many are the wonders we have known ;
Our path's been strewed with blessings rich and
    rare,
Proceeding from thy special love and care.

3 Sometimes in solemn silence we have sat,
Then peevishly cried out, How hard's our lot !
Each trial we have viewed with fretful eye,
And every mercy passed in silence by.

4 We've swelled our woes to an immense degree,
And often said, None are so tried as we ;
God's righteous ways our carnal hearts despise,
And often say they're neither just nor wise.

5 Yet sovereign favours we have oft enjoyed ;
To us the Holy Ghost has them applied ;
Through God's free goodness, mercies, rich and
    rare,   [fear.
Have cheered our souls and vanquished every

6 Christ, and him crucified, has been our song ;
His unctuous love has tuned our hearts and
    tongue ;
We've been abashed, our vileness have confessed,
And felt that God in blessing has us blessed.

700 148th. GADSBY.
New Year.—Hab. iii. 2; Psa. lxv. 11.

GREAT God, to thee we come,
And solemnly confess,
Our hearts are prone to roam
From paths of righteousness;
We view the year already past,
And see great cause to be abashed.

2 Thy sovereign love and care
Thus far have brought us on,
'Midst sins, and woes, and fear,
Thy goodness is made known.
That grace must needs be rich and free,
Which saves such worthless worms as we.

3 We now begin the year,
Dependant on thy grace;
May we possess thy fear,
And often see thy face;
Lord, make us daily live by faith,
Triumphant over sin and death.

4 [Revive thy work within,
And make us watch and pray;
Subdue each hateful sin,
And guide us in thy way;
In Jesus may we live and rest,
And sweetly lean upon his breast.]

701 10s. GADSBY.
No solid comfort but in Christ.—Ps. xxx. 7.

WHEN my dear Jesus hides his smiling face,
Nor lets me feel the unction of his grace;
I feel my loss, nor can my spirit rest,
Till with his lovely presence I am blest.

2 I mourn like one bereft of home and friend,
And often wonder where the scene will end;

Tortured with anxious care, without repose,
I feel as one immersed in gloomy woes.

3 The means of grace afford no sweet relief,
But often tend to aggravate my grief;
I cannot rest without my resting-place,
Sweet Jesus, come, and let me thee embrace.

702 7s. BERRIDGE.
The Rock.—Ezek. xxxvi. 26; xi. 19; Ps. li. 10.

SELF-condemned and abhorred,
How shall I approach the Lord?
Hard my heart, and cold, and faint;
Full of every sad complaint.

2 What can soften hearts of stone?
Jesus' precious blood alone;
When the Spirit it imparts,
That will soften hardest hearts.

3 This would bruise my bosom well,
Make it with God's praises swell;

Squeeze my idols from my breast,
Bring the blessed gospel-rest.

4 O! the rock which Moses struck,
Soon would make my heart a brook;
Only this can make me feel;
Bring it with thy burial-seal.

5 With its oil my limbs anoint;
That will supple every joint.
Of its honey let me eat;
That will make my temper sweet.

703 10s. GADSBY.
The Nativity of Christ.—John i. 14; Lu. ii. 7—14.

YE souls redeemed with Jesus' precious blood,
Proclaim the grace of your incarnate God;
Sing that amazing, boundless, matchless love,
Which brought the Lord of glory from above.

2 The eternal Word, who built the earth and
skies,
Takes on him flesh, and in a manger lies;
In that dear Babe of Bethlehem I see
My God, contracted to a span for me.

3 Mary's first-born was God and man in one;
David's own God, and David's blessed Son.
Well might the angels wing their way to earth,
To celebrate so glorious a birth.

4 They sang, with new surprise and fresh de-
lights,
Glory to God, in all the angelic heights;
Surrounded with God's glory, in a blaze
To heaven they fly, the incarnate God to praise

5 Shall angels sing the honours of his name,
And sinners, saved by grace, silent remain?
Good God, forbid! inflame us with thy love,
And set our grovelling minds on things above.

6 This God-like mystery we will gladly sing,
And own the virgin's Babe our God and King
Jehovah Jesus, we will thee adore,
And crown thee Lord of all for evermore.

704 7s. HART.
Heb. iv. 11.
"Let us labour, . . to enter into that rest."—

LORD, we lie before thy feet;
Look on all our deep distress;
Thy rich mercy may we meet;
Clothe us with thy righteousness;
Stretch forth thy almighty hand;
Hold us up, and we shall stand.

2 O that closer we could cleave
To thy bleeding, dying breast!
Give us firmly to believe,
And to enter into rest;

Lord increase, increase our faith ;
Make us faithful unto death.

3 Make thy mighty wonders known ;
Let us see thy sufferings plain ;
Let us hear thee sigh and groan,
Till we sigh and groan again ;
Rend, O rend the vail between ;
Open wide the bloody scene.

4 Let us trust thee evermore ;
Every moment on thee call,
For new life, new will, new power ;
Let us trust thee, Lord, for all ;
May we nothing know beside
Jesus, and him crucified.

705   112th.   BERRIDGE.
He is touched, &c.—Isa. liv. 11 ; Heb. ii. 18.
THOU poor, afflicted, tempted soul,
With fears, and doubts, and tempests tossed,
What if the billows rise and roll,
And dash thy ship, it is not lost ;
The winds and waves, and fiends may roar,
But Christ will bring thee safe on shore.

2 What ails those eyes bedewed with tears ?
Those labouring sighs that heave thy breast ?
Those oft-repeated, broken prayers ?
Dost thou not long for Jesus' rest ?
And can the Lord pass heedless by,
And see a mourning sinner die ?

706   7s.   HART.
Christ the Christian's only Help.—Ps. xxvii. 9.
GRACIOUS God, thy children keep ;
Jesus, guide thy silly sheep ;
Fix, O fix our fickle souls ;
Lord, direct us ; we are fools.

2 Bid us in thy care confide ;
Keep us near thy wounded side ;
From thee let us never stir,
For thou know'st how soon we err.

3 Lay us low before thy feet,
Safe from pride and self-conceit ;
Be the language of our souls,
" Lord, protect us ; we are fools."

4 [O defend thy purchased flock ;
See, the insulting Ishmaels mock ;
Guard us from a world of sin ;
Foes without, and worse within.

5 Look upon the unequal war ;
Saviour, do not go too far ;
Crafty is the foe, and strong ;
Saviour, do not tarry long.]

6 By thy word we fain would steer,
Fain thy Spirit's dictates hear ;
Save us from the rocks and shelves,
Save us chiefly from ourselves.

7 Never, never may we dare,
What we're not to say we are ;
Make us well our vileness know ;
Keep us very, very low.

707   L.M.   HART.
" Our light affliction."—2 Cor. iv. 16, 17 ; Ps. xli. 3.
WHEN pining sickness wastes the frame,
Acute disease, or tiring pain ;
When life fast spends her feeble flame,
And all the help of man proves vain ;

2 Then, then to have recourse to God,
To pour a prayer in time of need,
And feel the balm of Jesus' blood,
This is to find a friend indeed.

3 And this, O Christian, is thy lot,
Who cleavest to the Lord by faith ;
He'll never leave thee (doubt it not)
In pain, in sickness, or in death.

4 Himself shall be thy helping Friend,
Thy good Physician and thy nurse ;
To make thy bed shall condescend,
And from the affliction take the curse.

5 Shouldst thou a moment's absence mourn ;
Should some short darkness intervene ;
He'll give thee power, till light return,
To trust him, with the cloud between.

708   C.M.   HART.
" It is good for me to draw near to God."—Ps. lxxiii. 28.
As when a child, secure of harms,
Hangs at the mother's breast,
Safe folded in her anxious arms,
Receiving food and rest :

2 And, while through many a painful path
The travelling parent speeds,
The fearless babe, with passive faith,
Lies still, and yet proceeds.

3 Should some short start his quiet break,
He fondly strives to fling
His little arms about her neck,
And seems to closer cling ;

4 Poor child, maternal love alone
Preserves thee, first and last ;
Thy parent's arms, and not thy own,
Are those that hold thee fast !

5 So souls that would to Jesus cleave,
And hear his secret call,
Must every fair pretension leave,
And let the Lord be all.

6 "Keep close to me, thou helpless sheep,"
   The Shepherd softly cries ;
  "Lord, tell me what 'tis close to keep,"
   The listening sheep replies.

7 "Thy whole dependence on me fix ;
   Nor entertain a thought
  Thy worthless schemes with mine to mix,
   But venture to be nought.

8 "Fond self-direction is a shelf ;
   Thy strength, thy wisdom flee ;
  When thou art nothing in thyself,
   Thou then art close to me."

709   C.M.   HART.
"Who hath despised the day of small things ?"

THE Lord that made both heaven and
   And was himself made man,   earth,
  Lay in the womb, before his birth,
   Contracted to a span.

2 Behold, from what beginnings small
   Our great salvation rose ;
  The strength of God is owned by all ;
   But who his weakness knows ?

3 Let not the strong the weak despise ;
   Their faith, though small, is true ;
  Though low they seem in others' eyes,
   Their Saviour seemed so too.

4 Nor meanly of the tempted think ;
   For O what tongue can tell
  How low the Lord of life must sink,
   Before he vanquished hell ?

5 As in the days of flesh he grew
   In wisdom, stature, grace,
  So in the soul that's born anew,
   He keeps a gradual pace.

6 No less almighty at his birth,
   Than on his throne supreme ;
  His shoulders held up heaven and earth,
   When Mary held up him.

710   104th.   BERRIDGE.
"The heart is deceitful."—Jer. xvii. 9 ; Song i. 5.

No wisdom of man can spy out his heart,
  The Lord only can show his hidden part,
Nor yet are men willing to have the truth told,
The sight is too killing for pride to behold.

2 A look from the Lord discovers our case,
  And bringeth his word attended with grace ;
The man is convicted and feeleth his hell,
And groweth afflicted more than he can tell.

3 If once the sun shines upon a soul clear,
  He reads the dark lines which sin has writ
Begins to discover his colour and make, [there ;
And cries, I'm all over as any fiend black.

4 But when the Lord shows his satisfied face ;
  And buries our woes in triumphant grace,
This blessed look stilleth the mourner's com-
   plaint,
And with a song filleth the mouth of the saint.

5. Sweet love and sweet shame now hallow his
   breast ;
Yet black is his name, tho' by his Lord blest ;
I am, he says, homely, deformed in each part ;
All black, and yet comely, through Jesus' desert.

6 A look of thy love is all that we want ;
  Ah ! look from above, and give us content.
Looks set us adoring thy person most sweet,
And lay us abhorring ourselves at thy feet.

711   L.M.   D. HERBERT.
The Hiding Place.—Isa. xxxii. 2 ; Ps. xxxii. 7.

AMIDST the sorrows of the way,
Lord Jesus, teach my soul to pray ;
And let me taste thy special grace,
And run to Christ, my Hiding-place.

2 Thou know'st the vileness of my heart,
So prone to act the rebel's part ;
And when thou veil'st thy lovely face,
Where can I find a hiding-place ?

3 Lord, guide my silly, wandering feet,
And draw me to thy mercy-seat.
I've nought to trust but sovereign grace ;
Thou only art my Hiding-place.

4 O how unstable is my heart !
Sometimes I take the tempter's part,
And slight the tokens of thy grace,
And seem to want no hiding-place.

5 But when thy Spirit shines within,
And makes me feel the plague of sin ;
Then how I long to see thy face !
'Tis then I want a hiding-place.

6 Lord Jesus, shine, and then I can
Feel sweetness in salvation's plan ;
And as a sinner, plead for grace,
Through Christ, the sinner's Hiding-place.

712   L.M.   HART.
Christ in the Garden.—Matt. xxvi. 36-46.

COME hither, ye that fain would know
The exceeding sinfulness of sin ;
Come see a scene of matchless woe,
And tell me what it all can mean.

2 Behold the darling Son of God
Bowed down with horror to the ground,

Wrung at the heart, and sweating blood,
His eyes in tears of sorrow drowned !

3 See how the Victim panting lies,
His soul with bitter anguish pressed ;
He sighs, he faints, he groans, he cries,
Dismayed, dejected, shocked, distressed.

4 What pangs are these that tear his heart ?
What burden's this that's on him laid ?
What means this agony of smart ?
What makes our Maker hang his head ?

5 'Tis Justice, with its iron rod,
Inflicting strokes of wrath divine ;
'Tis the avenging hand of God,
Incensed at all your sins and mine.

6 Deep in his breast our names were cut ;
He undertook our desperate debt ;
Such loads of guilt were on him put,
He could but just sustain the weight.

7 Then let us not ourselves deceive ;
For, while of sin we lightly deem,
Whatever notions we may have,
Indeed we are not much like him.

713   S.M.   GADSBY.
Faith.—1 John v. 4 ; Heb. iv. 3 ; Gal. iii. 22.
WHEN faith to Sinai looks,
It fills the heart with dread ;
And justifies the dreadful stroke
That strikes the sinner dead.

2 And when by faith we trace
Christ is the only way
From endless wrath to endless bliss,
We for the blessing pray.

3 But when faith views the Lamb,
As my atoning Priest,

It magnifies his precious name,
And sets the heart at rest.

4 How precious is the faith
That God to Zion gives !
It triumphs over sin and death,
And in Jehovah lives.

714   C.M.   BERRIDGE.
For a believer in darkness and distress.—Ps. xlii. 6-8.
WHY so cast down, dejected soul ?
A loving Christ is near ;
Thy broken bones he can make whole,
And drooping spirit cheer.

2 If guilty stings thy conscience feel,
And pierce thee through and through,
Yet past backslidings Christ can heal,
And love thee freely too.

3 If justice draw its flaming sword,
And seems intent to kill,
On Jesus call, and trust his word,
And thou shalt praise him still.

4 Thy soul with tempests may be tossed,
And Satan sorely thrust ;
Yet sure no soul shall e'er be lost
Who makes the Lord his trust.

5 Dear Jesus, show thy smiling face,
And Calvary's peace impart,
Display the power of saving grace,
And cheer a troubled heart.

6 Refresh his eye with sweeter light,
And whisper in his ear,
" Thy soul is precious in my sight,
No need thou hast to fear."

715   8.8.6.   HART.
The Day of Pentecost.—Acts ii. 1-12, 17.
WHEN the blessed day of Pentecost
Was fully come, the Holy Ghost
Descended from above,
Sent by the Father and the Son,
To bring immortal blessings down,
And shed abroad God's love.

2 Sudden a rushing wind they hear ;
And fiery cloven tongues appear ;
And sat on every one ;
Cloven, perhaps, to be a sign,
That God no longer would confine
His word to Jews alone.

3 And were these first disciples blessed
With heavenly gifts ? And shall the rest
Be passed unheeded by ?
What ! has the Holy Ghost forgot
To quicken souls that Christ has bought,
And lets them lifeless lie ?

4 No, thou Almighty Paraclete,
Thou shedd'st thy heavenly influence yet,
Thou visit'st sinners still ;
The breath of life, thy quickening flame,
Thy power, thy Godhead, still the same,
We own, because we feel.

716   L.M.   BERRIDGE.
The blood of sprinkling.—Heb. xii. 24 ; Ps. li. 7.
DEAR dying Friend, we look on thee,
And own our foul offences here ;
We built thy cross on Calvary,
And nailed and pierced thy body there.

2 Yet, let the blood our hands have spilt
Be sprinkled on each guilty heart,

To purge the conscience well from guilt,
And everlasting life impart.
3 So will we sing thy lovely name,
For grace so rich and freely given ;
And tell thy love, and tell our shame,
That one we murdered gives us heaven.

717   7.6.   HART.
" These are they which came out of great tribulation."
BRETHREN, those who come to bliss
  Come through sore temptations ;
May we all, remembering this,
  Pray for faith and patience.

2 See the suffering church of Christ,
  Gathered from all quarters ;
All contained in that red list
  Were not murdered martyrs.

3 Th' Holy Ghost will make the soul
  Feel its sad condition ;
For the sick, and not the whole,
  Need the good Physician.

4 Of that mighty multitude,
  Who of life were winners,
This we safely may conclude,
  All were wretched sinners.

5 All were loathsome in God's sight,
  Till the blood of Jesus
Washed their robes, and made them white;
  Now they sing his praises.

718   L.M.   HART.
Baptism.—Rom. vi. 3, 4 ; Col. ii. 12, 13.
BURIED in baptism with our Lord,
We rise with him, to life restored ;
Not the bare life in Adam lost,
But richer far, for more it cost.

2 Water can cleanse the flesh, we own ;
But Christ well knows, and Christ alone,
How dear to him our cleansing stood,
Baptized with fire, and bathed in blood.

3 Not but we taste his bitter cup ;
But only he could drink it up.
To burn for us was his desire ;
And he baptizes us with fire.

4 This fire will not consume, but melt !
How soft, compared with that he felt !
Thus cleansed from filth, & purged from dross,
Baptized Christian, bear the cross.

719   8.7.   HART.
Loved and Saved freely.—Rev. i. 5, 6 ; Matt. ix. 12.
COME, ye Christians, sing the praises
  Of your condescending God ;

Come and hymn the holy Jesus,
  Who has washed us in his blood.
We are poor, and weak, and silly,
  And to every evil prone ;
Yet our Jesus loves us freely,
  And receives us for his own.

2 Though we're mean in man's opinion,
  He has made us priests and kings ;
Power, and glory, and dominion,
  To the Lamb the sinner sings.
Leprous souls, unsound and filthy,
  Come before him as you are :
'Tis the sick man, not the healthy,
  Needs the good Physician's care.

3 O beware of fondly thinking
  God accepts thee for thy tears ;
Are the shipwrecked saved by sinking ?
  Can the ruined rise by fears ?

O beware of trust ill-grounded ;
  'Tis but fancied faith at most,
To be cured, and not be wounded ;
  To be saved before you're lost.

4 No big words of ready talkers,
  No dry doctrine will suffice ;
Broken hearts, and humble walkers,
  These are dear in Jesus' eyes.
Tinkling sounds of disputation,
  Naked knowledge, all are vain ;
Every soul that gains salvation
  Must and shall be born again.

720   7s.   GADSBY.
" Worthy is the Lamb to receive blessing."—Rev. v. 12.
ENDLESS blessings on the Lamb !
Broken hearts, repeat the same ;
His dear heart was broken too,
When he bore the curse for you.

2 Your dread crimes once pierced his heart !
Sank his soul in vengeful smart ;
But his sin-atoning blood
Now maintains your peace with God.

3 Endless blessings on him rest !
Broken hearts in him are blessed ;
And though they may trembling stand,
He upholds them with his hand.

4 In his heart they have a place,
'Stablished there through sovereign grace ;
And, in his set time and way,
He will change their night to day.

5 Trust in him, ye tempted saints ;
Tell him all your sad complaints ;
He a present help will be—
Give you strength and victory.

6 Blessed Jesus ! fill each heart
With thy love, and blood, and smart ;
Then thy wonders we'll proclaim,
And adore thy matchless name.

7 Endless blessings rest on thee !
Thou hast set the captive free ;
We would shout aloud and sing,
Glory to our God and King !

721   L.M.   SWAIN.

Praise for Complete Saviour.—Rev. v. 9-13; iv. 13.

To Him that loved us, ere we lay
Concealed within the passive clay ;
To Him that loved us though we fell,
And saved us from the pains of hell !

2 To him that found us dead in sin,
And planted holy life within ;
To Him that taught our feet the way
From endless night to endless day ;

3 To Him that wrought our righteousness,
And sanctified us by his grace ;
To Him that brought us back to God,
Through the red sea of his own blood :

4 To Him that sits upon the throne,
The great eternal Three-in-One ;
To Him let saints and angels raise
An everlasting song of praise.

722   7s.   GADSBY.

" At evening time it shall be light."—Zech. xiv. 7.

WHAT am I, and where am I ?
Strange myself and paths appear ;
Scarce can lift a thought on high,
Or drop one heart-feeling tear.

2 Yet I feel I'm not at home,
But know not which way to move :

Lest I farther yet should roam
From the Object of my love.

3 Some small glimmering light I have,
Yet too dark to see my way ;
Jesus' presence still I crave ;
When, O when will it be day ?

4 Is the evening time at hand ?
Will it then indeed be light ?
Will the sun its beams extend,—
Chase away the shades of night ?

5 Will the Lord indeed appear,
Give me light, and joy, and rest,
Drive away my gloomy fear,
Draw me to his lovely breast ?

6 Then his love is rich and free ;
Jesus, let me feel its power,
And my soul will cling to thee,
Love and praise thee and adore.

723   8.7.4.   HART (altered).

Come and welcome to Jesus Christ.—Isa. lv. 1.

COME, ye sinners, poor and wretched,
Weak and wounded, sick, and sore ;
Jesus ready stands to save you,
Full of pity, joined with power ;
He is able,
He is willing ; doubt no more.

2 Let not conscience make you linger,
Nor of fitness fondly dream ;
All the fitness he requireth,
Is to feel your need of him ;
This he gives you,
'Tis the Spirit's rising beam.

3 Come, ye weary, heavy laden,
Lost and ruined by the fall ;

If you tarry till you're better,
You will never come at all.
Not the righteous,
Sinners Jesus came to call.

724   8.8.6.   SWAIN.

Praise for redeeming Love.—Isa.liii. 3-7; Heb. ii. 14.

How vast the sufferings, who can tell,
When Jesus fought sin, death, and hell,
And was in battle slain ?
How great the triumph, who can sing,
When from the grave the immortal King
Triumphant rose again ?

2 Yet we'll attempt his name to bless,
While we pass through the wilderness
To Canaan's happy shore.
But when we reach the plains above,
And every breath we draw is love,
We'll sing his glories more.

725   S.M.   GADSBY.

Prayer.—Acts ix. 11; ii. 21; 2 Chron. xxxiii. 12, 13.

THE sinner born of God,
To God will pour his prayer,
In sighs, or groans, or words expressed,
Or in a falling tear.

2 The feelings of his heart
Ascend to the Most High ;
And though the Lord awhile forbear,
His needs he will supply

3 A form of words may please
A sinner dead in sin ;
But quickened sinners want to pray
As prompted from within.

4   The Holy Ghost indites
     All real vital prayer ;
     And prayer indited by the Lord,
     The Lord will surely hear.

726   7s.   C.W.
"I am the bright and morning star."—Rev. xxii. 16.

CHRIST, whose glory fills the skies,
Christ, the true, the only Light,
Sun of Righteousness, arise,
Triumph o'er the shades of night ;
Day-spring from on high, be near,
Day-star, in my heart appear.

2   Dark and cheerless is the morn,
     Unaccompanied by thee ;
     Joyless is the day's return,
     Till thy mercy's beams I see ;
     Till they inward light impart,
     Glad my eyes, and warm my heart.

3   Visit, then, this soul of mine ;
     Pierce the gloom of sin and grief
     Fill me, Radiancy Divine !
     Scatter all my unbelief ;
     More and more thyself display,
     Shining to the perfect day.

727   C.M.   WATTS.
"O that I knew where I might find him."—Job xxiii. 3.

O THAT I knew the secret place
   Where I might find my God !
I'd spread my wants before his face,
   And pour my woes abroad.

2   I'd tell him how my sins arise,
     What sorrows I sustain ;
   How grace recedes and comfort dies,
     And leaves my heart in pain.

3   He knows what arguments I'd take
     To wrestle with my God ;
   I'd plead for his own mercy's sake,
     And for my Saviour's blood.

4   But stay, my soul, to hope give place ;
     He'll banish every fear ;
   He calls thee to his throne of grace,
     To spread thy sorrows there.

728   112th.   NEWTON.
"The flesh lusteth against the spirit," &c.—Gal. v. 17.

STRANGE and mysterious is my life ;
What opposites I feel within !
A stable peace, a constant strife ;
The rule of grace, the power of sin ;
Too often I am captive led,
Yet often triumph in my Head.

2   I prize the privilege of prayer,
     But O what backwardness to pray !
   Though on the Lord I cast my care,
     I feel its burden every day ;
   I'd seek his will in all I do,
   Yet find my own is working too.

3   I call the promises my own,
     And prize them more than mines of gold ;
   Yet though their sweetness I have known,
     They leave me unimpressed and cold ;
   One hour upon the truth I feed,
   The next I know not what I read.

4   Thus different powers within me strive,
     And grace and sin by turns prevail ;
   I grieve, rejoice, decline, revive,
     And victory hangs in doubtful scale ;
   But Jesus has his promise passed
   That grace shall overcome at last.

729   S.M.   NEWTON.
"Waiting for the moving of the waters."—John v. 2-9.

BESIDE the gospel-pool
   Appointed for the poor,
From time to time my helpless soul
   Has waited for a cure.

2   But my complaints remain ;
     I feel, alas ! the same ;
   As full of guilt, and fear, and pain,
     As when at first I came.

3   O would the Lord appear
     My malady to heal !
   He knows how long I've languished here,
     And what distress I feel.

4   How often have I thought,
     Why should I longer lie ?
   Surely the mercy I have sought
     Is not for such as I.

5   No ; he is full of grace ;
     He never will permit
   A soul that fain would see his face,
     To perish at his feet.

730   C.M.   E. PERRONET (altered).
"Jesus Christ, Lord of All."—Rev. xix. 16 ; Acts x. 36.

ALL hail the power of Jesus' name,
   Let angels prostrate fall,
Bring forth the royal diadem,
   And crown him Lord of all.

2   Ye souls redeemed of Gentile race,
     Ye ransomed from the fall ;
   Hail him who saves you by his grace,
     And crown him Lord of all.

3   Let every kindred, every tribe,
     Throughout this earthly ball,

To him all majesty ascribe,
And crown him Lord of all.

4 We too, amid the sacred throng,
Low at his feet would fall,
Join in the everlasting song,
And crown him Lord of all.

731 C.M. COWPER.
"I am the Lord that healeth thee."—Exod. xv. 26.

HEAL us, Immanuel, here we are,
Waiting to feel thy touch;
Deep-wounded souls to thee repair,
And, Saviour, we are such.

2 Our faith is feeble, we confess;
We faintly trust thy word;
But wilt thou pity us the less?
Be that far from thee, Lord.

3 Remember him who once applied,
With trembling for relief;
"Lord, I believe," with tears he cried,
"O help my unbelief."

4 She, too, who touched thee in the press,
And healing virtue stole,
Was answered, "Daughter, go in peace;
Thy faith hath made thee whole."

5 Like her, with hopes and fears we come,
To touch thee, if we may;
O send us not despairing home;
Send none unhealed away.

732 148th. KENT.
"How precious are thy thoughts unto me, O God!"

INDULGENT God, how kind
Are all thy ways to me,
Whose dark benighted mind
Was enmity with thee;

Yet now, subdued by sovereign grace,
My spirit longs for thy embrace!

2 How precious are thy thoughts,
Which o'er my bosom roll!
They swell beyond my faults,
And captivate my soul;
How great their sum, how high they rise,
Can ne'er be known beneath the skies.

3 Preserved in Jesus when
My feet made haste to hell;
And there should I have gone,
But thou dost all things well;
Thy love was great, thy mercy free,
Which from the pit delivered me.

4 A monument of grace,
A sinner saved by blood;
The streams of love I trace

Up to the fountain, God;
And in his wondrous mercy see,
Eternal thoughts of love to me.

733 S.M. BEDDOME.
"Out of the heart proceed evil thoughts."—Matt. xv.

ASTONISHED and distressed,
I turn my eyes within;
My heart with loads of guilt oppressed,
The seat of every sin.

2 What crowds of evil thoughts,
What vile affections there!
Distrust, presumption, artful guile,
Pride, envy, slavish fear.

3 Almighty King of saints,
These tyrant-lusts subdue;
Expel the darkness of my mind,
And all my powers renew.

4 This done, my cheerful voice
Shall loud hosannas raise;
My soul shall glow with gratitude,
My lips proclaim thy praise.

734 C.M. HART.
The Lord's Supper.—Zech. xii. 10; Luke xxii. 19, 20

LORD, who can hear of all thy woe,
Thy groans and dying cries,
And not feel tears of sorrow flow,
And sighs of pity rise?

2 Much harder than the hardest stone
That man's hard heart must be;
Alas! dear Lord, with shame we own
That just such hearts have we.

3 The symbols of thy flesh and blood
Will (as they have been oft)
With unrelenting hearts be viewed,
Unless thou make them soft.

4 Dissolve these rocks; call forth the stream,
Make every eye a sluice;
Let none be slow to weep for him
Who wept so much for us.

5 And while we mourn, and sing, and pray,
And feed on bread and wine,
Lord, let thy quickening Spirit convey
The substance with the sign.

735 8.7.4. IRONS.
"Happy is that people in such a case."—Ps. cxliv. 15.

O THE happiness arising
From the life of grace within,
When the soul is realising
Conquests over hell and sin!
Happy moments!
Heavenly joys on earth begin.

2 On the Saviour's fulness living,
   All his saints obtain delight ;
With the strength which he is giving,
   They can wrestle, they can fight.
      Happy moments !
   When King Jesus is in sight.

3 Nearer, nearer, to him clinging,
   Let my helpless soul be found,
All my sorrows to him bringing,
   May his grace in me abound ;
      Happy moments !
With new covenant blessings crowned.

736   L.M.   C. COLE.
"Show me a token for good."—Ps. lxxxvi. 17.

SHOW me some token, Lord, for good,
Some token of thy special love ;
Show me that I am born of God,
And that my treasure is above.

2 My supplication, Lord, is this,
That all my sins may be subdued ;
That all thy precious promises
May be to me and for my good.

3 O seal my pardon to my soul,
And then proclaim my peace with thee ;
Thus make my wounded conscience whole,
And that will be for good to me.

4 Let thy good Spirit rule my heart,
And govern all my words and ways ;
Let grace abound in every part,
And teach my tongue to sing thy praise.

5 Thus may I see that I am thine,
And feel my heart to thee ascend ;
Then shall I know that thou art mine,
My God, my Father, and my Friend.

737   7s.   HAMMOND.
"He gave his only-begotten Son."—John iii. 16.

GRACIOUS Lord, incline thy ear ;
My requests vouchsafe to hear ;
Hear my never-ceasing cry ;
Give me Christ, or else I die.

2 Wealth and honour I disdain,
Earthly comforts, Lord, are vain ;
These can never satisfy ;
Give me Christ, or else I die.

3 Lord, deny me what thou wilt,
Only ease me of my guilt.
Suppliant at thy feet I lie ;
Give me Christ, or else I die.

4 All unholy and unclean,
I am nothing else but sin ;

On thy mercy I rely ;
Give me Christ, or else I die.

5 Thou dost freely save the lost ;
In thy grace alone I trust.
With my earnest suit comply ;
Give me Christ, or else I die.

6 Thou dost promise to forgive
All who in thy Son believe ;
Lord, I know thou canst not lie ;
Give me Christ, or else I die.

738   L.M.   SWAIN.
The House of Prayer.—Isa. lvi. 7; Eph. ii. 13.

JESUS, how heavenly is the place,
Where thy dear people wait for thee !
Where the rich fountain of thy grace
Stands ever open, full, and free.

2 Hungry, and poor, and lame, and blind,
Hither the blood-bought children fly ;
In thy deep wounds a balsam find,
And live while they behold thee die.

3 Here they forget their doubts and fears,
While thy sharp sorrows meet their eyes ;
And bless the hand that dries their tears,
And each returning want supplies.

4 O the vast mysteries of thy love !
How high, how deep, how wide it rolls !
Its fountain springs in heaven above,
Its streams revive our drooping souls.

739   S.M.   BERRIDGE.
The Soul flying to Christ .. Refuge.—Heb. vi. 18.

No help in self I find,
   And yet have sought it well ;
The native treasure of my mind
   Is sin, and death, and hell.

2 To Christ for help I fly,
   The Friend of sinners lost,
A refuge sweet, and sure, and nigh,
   And there is all my trust.

3 Lord, grant me free access
   Unto thy pierced side,
For there I seek my dwelling-place,
   And there my guilt would hide.

4 In every time of need,
   My helpless soul defend,
And save me from all evil deed,
   And save me to the end.

5 And when the hour is near
   That flesh and heart will fail,
Do thou in all thy grace appear,
   And bid my faith prevail.

740   L.M.   HART.
"Blessed be ye poor."—Luke vi. 20; Matt. v. 3.

LORD, when I hear thy children talk,
(And I believe 'tis often true),
How with delight thy ways they walk,
And gladly thy commandments do ;

2 In my own breast I look and read
Accounts so very different there,
That, had I not thy blood to plead,
Each sight would sink me to despair.

3 Needy, and naked, and unclean,
Empty of good, and full of ill,
A lifeless lump of loathsome sin,
Without the power to act or will.

4 I feel my fainting spirits droop ;
My wretched leanness I deplore ;
Till gladdened with a gleam of hope
From this, The Lord has blest the poor.

5 Then, while I make my secret moan,
Upwards I cast my eyes, and see,
Though I have nothing of my own,
My treasure is immense in thee.

6 My treasure is thy precious blood ;
Fix there my heart, and for the rest,
Under thy forming hands, my God,
Give me that frame which thou lik'st best.

741   8.7.   ALLEN AND BATTY & TOPLADY.
"Why weepest thou ?"—John xx. 11, 13, 15.

I NO more at Mary wonder
Dropping tears upon the grave,
Earnest asking all around her,
     "Where is he that died to save ? "

2 Dying love her heart attracted.
Soon she felt its rising power,
He who Mary thus affected,
     Bids his mourners weep no more.

742   7s.   BERRIDGE.
"He that trusteth in his own heart is a fool."

HE that trusts in his own heart,
Acts a raw and foolish part ;
Base it is, and full of guile,
Brooding mischief in a smile.

2 Does it boast of love within ?
So it may, and yet may sin ;
Peter loved his Master well,
Yet a loving Peter fell.

3 Does it feel a melting frame ?
David also felt the same ;
Yet he made a woeful trip,
And perceived his mountain slip.

4 Does it talk of faith, and boast ?
Abra'm had as much as most ;
Yet, beguiled by unbelief,
Twice he durst deny his wife.

5 Every prop will, first or last,
Sink or fail, but Jesus Christ ;
On this sure foundation stone
Let me build and rest alone.

743   C.M.   ERSKINE & BERRIDGE.
Waiting for Help.—Luke xvi. 20; Prov. viii. 34.

MY business lies at Jesus' gate,
     Where many a Lazar comes ;
And here I sue, and here I wait
     For mercy's falling crumbs.

2 My rags and wounds my wants proclaim,
     And help from him implore ;
The wounds do witness I am lame,
     The rags that I am poor.

3 The Lord, I hear, the hungry feeds,
     And cheereth souls distressed ;
He loves to bind up broken reeds,
     And heal a bleeding breast.

4 His name is Jesus, full of grace,
     Which draws me to his door ;
And will not Jesus show his face,
     And bring his gospel store ?

5 Supplies of every grace I want,
     And each day want supply ;
And if no grace the Lord will grant,
     I must lie down and die.

744   112th.   BERRIDGE.
"He shall convince of sin."—John xvi. 8.

No awful sense we find of sin,
The sinful life and sinful heart ;
No loathing of the plague within,
Until the Lord that feel impart ;
But when the Spirit of truth is come,
A sinner trembles at his doom.

2 Convinced and pierced through and through,
He thinks himself the sinner chief ;
And, conscious of his mighty woe,
Perceives at length his unbelief ;
Good creeds may stock his head around,
But in his heart no faith is found.

3 No power his nature can afford
To change his heart, or purge his guilt ;
No help is found but in the Lord,
No balm but in the blood he spilt ;
A ruined soul, condemned he stands,
And unto Jesus lifts his hands.

4 So lift I up my hands and eyes,
And all my help in Jesus seek.

Lord, bring thy purging sacrifice
To wash me white, and make me meek ;
And give me more enlarged faith,
To view the wonders of thy death.

745   8.8.6.   BERRIDGE.
Simple-Hearted.—Luke xiv. 13. 21 : Matt. xxii. 9, 10.

WHEN Jesus would his grace proclaim,
He calls the simple, blind, and lame
  To come and be his guest ;
Such simple folk the world despise ;
Yet simple folk have sharpest eyes,
  And learn to walk the best.

2 They view the want of Jesus' light,
Of Jesus' blood, and Jesus' might,
  Which others cannot view ;
They walk in Christ, the living Way,
And fight, and win the well-fought day,
  Which others cannot do.

3 They all declare, I nothing am,
My life is bound up in the Lamb,
  My wit and might are his ;
My worth is all in Jesus found,
He is my Rock, my anchor-ground,
  And all my hope of bliss.

4 Such simple soul I fain would be,
The scorn of man, the joy of thee,
  Thy parlour guest and friend ;
Do make me, Lord, a little child,
Right simple-hearted, meek and mild,
  And loving to the end.

746   8.7.   HART.
Faith and Repentance.—Acts v. 31 ; 2 Cor. vii. 10.

JESUS is our God and Saviour,
  Guide, and Counsellor, and Friend ;
Bearing all our misbehaviour,
  Kind and loving to the end.
Trust him, he will not deceive us,
  Though we hardly of him deem ;
He will never, never leave us ;
  Nor will let us quite leave him.

2 Nothing but thy blood, O Jesus !
  Can relieve us from our smart ;
Nothing else from guilt release us ;
  Nothing else can melt the heart.
Law and terrors do but harden,
  All the while they work alone ;
But a sense of blood-bought pardon
  Soon dissolves a heart of stone.

3 Teach us, by thy patient Spirit,
  How to mourn and not despair ;
Let us, leaning on thy merit,
  Wrestle hard with God in prayer.

Whatsoe'er afflictions seize us,
  They shall profit, if not please ;
But defend, defend us, Jesus,
  From security and ease.

4 Softly to thy garden lead us,
  To behold thy bloody sweat ;
Though thou from the curse hast freed us,
  Let us not the cost forget.
Be thy groans and cries rehearsed
  By the Spirit in our ears,
Till we, viewing whom we've pierced,
  Melt in sympathetic tears.

747   C.M.   HART.
God's various dealings with his children.—John xxi. 18

How hard and rugged is the way
  To some poor pilgrims' feet :
In all they do, or think, or say,
  They opposition meet.

2 Others, again, more smoothly go,
  Secured from hurts and harms ;
Their Saviour leads them gently through,
  Or bears them in his arms.

3 Faith and repentance all must find ;
  But yet we daily see
They differ in their time and kind,
  Duration and degree.

4 Some long repent and late believe,
  But when their sin's forgiven,
A clearer passport they receive,
  And walk with joy to heaven.

5 Their pardon some receive at first,
  And then, compelled to fight,
They feel their latter stages worst,
  And travel much by night.

6 But be our conflicts short or long,
  This commonly is true ;
That wheresoever faith is strong,
  Repentance is so too.

748   L.M.   BERRIDGE.
Light in God's Light.—Ps. xxxvi. 9 ; Isa. lx. 19.

IN darkness born, I went astray,
And wandered from the gospel way ;
And since the Saviour gave me sight,
I cannot see without his light.

2 So poor, and blind, and lame I am,
My all is bound up in the Lamb ;
And blessed am I when I see
My spirit's inmost poverty.

3 I cannot walk without his might,
I cannot see without his light ;

I can have no access to God,
But through the merits of his blood.

4 It makes me feel my ruined state,
It lays my soul at mercy's gate ;
And Jesus smiles at such a guest ;
And cheers him with a heavenly feast.

749   148th.   BERRIDGE.
When I cry .. he shutteth out my prayer.—Lam. iii. 8.

I HEAR a righteous man,
A prophet good and great,
In deep distress complain,
And thus his grief relate :
' I call on God, and cry and shout,
But all my prayer he shutteth out."

2 He cries, and cries again,
And yet no answers come ;
He shouts aloud through pain,
And still the Lord is dumb ;
Like some abandoned wretch he moans,
And Jesus seems to mock his groans.

3 Let every drooping saint
Keep waiting evermore ;
And though exceeding faint,
Knock on at mercy's door ;
Still cry and shout till night is past,
For daylight will spring up at last.

4 If Christ do not appear,
When his disciples cry,
He marketh every tear,
And counteth every sigh ;
In all their sorrows bears a part,
Beholds their grief, and feels their smart.

5 He lends an unseen hand,
And gives a secret prop,
Which keeps them waiting stand,
Till he complete their hope !
So let me wait upon this Friend,
And trust him till my troubles end.

750   C.M.   G. BURDER
" God is love."—1 John iv. 8, 16 ; Eph. ii. 4.

COME, ye that know and fear the Lord,
And lift your souls above ;
Let every heart and voice accord,
To sing that God is love !

2 This precious truth his word declares,
And all his mercies prove ;
Jesus, the Gift of gifts appears,
To show that God is love !

3. Behold his patience lengthened out,
To those who from him rove ;
And calls effectual reach their hearts,
To teach them God is love !

4 The work begun is carried on
By power from heaven above ;
And every step, from first to last,
Proclaims that God is love !

5 O may we all, while here below,
This best of blessings prove ;
Till warmer hearts in brighter worlds,
Shall shout that God is love !

751   L.M.   MEDLEY. (altered)
" Because I live, ye shall live also."—John xiv. 19.

THE Saviour lives no more to die !
He lives, the Lord enthroned on high !
He lives, triumphant o'er the grave !
He lives, eternally to save !

2 He lives, to still his people's fears !
He lives, to wipe away their tears !

He lives, to calm their troubled heart !
He lives, all blessings to impart !

3 He lives, all glory to his name !
He lives, unchangeably the same !
He lives, their mansions to prepare,
He lives, to bring them safely there !

752   L.M.   WATTS.
" The Wisdom of God in a mystery."—1 Cor. ii. 7.

NATURE with open volume stands,
To spread her Maker's praise abroad,
And every labour of his hands,
Shows something worthy of a God.

2 But in the grace that rescued man,
His brightest form of glory shines ;
Here on the cross 'tis fairest drawn,
In precious blood, and crimson lines.

3 O the sweet wonders of that cross,
Where God the Saviour loved and died !
Her noblest life my spirit draws
From his dear wounds and bleeding side.

4 I would for ever speak his name,
In sounds to mortal ears unknown ;
With angels join to praise the Lamb,
And worship at his Father's throne.

753   8.7.4.   KELLY.
Whoso trusteth in the Lord, happy is he.—Pro. xvi. 20.

LORD, we plead with thee for pardon ;
Who can need it more than we ?
Make us as a watered garden !
Fruitful let thy people be ;
'Tis thy pleasure
That thy people live to thee.

2 Keep us in a world of sorrow ;
When we call, O hear our prayer !

Let us trust thee for the morrow,
　Free from boasting, free from care ;
　　When we trust thee,
　Truly happy then we are.

754 7s. H. FOWLER.
" He will guide you into all truth."—John xvi. 13-15.
HOLY Comforter, descend,
Testify of Christ, the Lamb ;
From the foe our hearts defend,
And with zeal our hearts inflame.

2 Send a spark of heavenly fire,
Quick as lightning to the soul :
This shall melt and bring us nigher,
Raise us up and make us whole.

3 Teach us truly how to pray,
Carnal else will be our cries ;
Turn us, Lord, from self away,
And from Jesus send supplies.

4 Every burdened soul relieve,
Wipe away the mourner's tears ;
Help them fully to believe,
And on thee to cast their cares.

755 L.M. GIBBONS.
" There is forgiveness with thee."—Ps. cxxx. 4.
FORGIVENESS ! 'tis a joyful sound
To malefactors doomed to die ;
Lord, may this bliss in me be found ;
May I redeeming grace enjoy.

2 'Tis the rich gift of love divine ;
'Tis full, out-measuring every crime ;
Unclouded shall its glories shine,
And feel no change by changing time.

3 O'er sins unnumbered as the sand,
And like the mountains for their size,

The seas of sovereign grace expand,
The seas of sovereign grace arise.

4 For this stupendous love of heaven,
What grateful honours shall we show ?
Where much transgression is forgiven,
May love in equal ardour glow.

756 C.M. BERRIDGE.
" Unto you which believe he is precious."—1 Pet. ii. 7.
EXCEEDING precious is my Lord ;
His love divinely free !
And his dear name does health afford,
To sickly souls like me.

2 It cheers a debtor's gloomy face,
And breaks his prison door ;
It brings amazing stores of grace
To feed the gospel poor.

3 And if with lively faith we view
His dying toil and smart,
And hear him say, " It was for you ! "
This breaks the stony heart.

4 A heavenly joy his words convey ;
The bowels strangely move ;
We blush, and melt, and faint away,
O'erwhelmed with his love.

5 In such sweet posture let me lie,
And wet thy feet with tears,
Till, joined with saints above the sky,
I tune my harp with theirs.

757 C.M. KENT.
" God hath revealed them by his Spirit."—1 Cor. ii. 10.
GREAT God, how deep thy counsels lie :
Supreme in power art thou ;
All things to thy omniscient eye,
Are one eternal NOW.

2 Thy thoughts of peace to Israel's race,
From everlasting flowed ;
And when thou hid'st thy lovely face
Thou still art Israel's God.

3 In ties of blood, and nothing less,
We view thee as our own ;
And God the eternal Spirit bless,
Who makes the kindred known.

4 Long as the covenant shall endure,
Made by the great Three-One,
Salvation is for ever sure,
To every blood-bought son.

758 8.7.4. KENT.
Chosen in the furnace of affliction.—Isa. xlviii. 10.
SONS of God, in tribulation,
Let your eyes the Saviour view ;
He's the Rock of our salvation,
He was tried and tempted too ;
　All to succour
Every tempted, burdened son.

2 'Tis if need be, he reproves us,
Lest we settle on our lees ;
Yet he in the furnace loves us ;
'Tis expressed in words like these :
　" I am with thee,
Israel, passing through the fire."

3 To his church, his joy, and treasure,
Every trial works for good ;
They are dealt in weight and measure,
Yet how little understood !
　Not in anger,
But from his dear covenant love.

4 If to-day he deigns to bless us
With a sense of pardoned sin,

Perhaps to-morrow he'll distress us,
    Make us feel the plague within ;
        All to make us
    Sick of self and fond of him.

759   8.7.   KENT.
" He healeth the broken in heart."—Ps. cxlvii. 3.
JESUS heals the broken-hearted,
    O how sweet that sound to me !
Once beneath my sin he smarted,
    Groaned, and bled to set me free.

2 By his sufferings, death, and merits ;
    By his Godhead, blood, and pain ;
Broken hearts, or wounded spirits,
    Are at once made whole again.

3 Broken by the law's loud thunder,
    To the cross for refuge flee !
O'er his pungent sorrows ponder,
    'Tis his stripes that healeth thee.

4 Oil and wine to heal and cherish,
    Jesus still to Israel gives ;
Nor shall e'er a sinner perish,
    Who in his dear name believes.

5 In his righteousness confiding,
    Sheltered safe beneath his wing ;
Here they find a sure abiding,
    And of covenant mercy sing.

6 Seek, my soul, no other healing,
    But in Jesus' balmy blood ;
He, beneath the Spirit's sealing,
    Stands thy great High Priest with God.

760   8.7.4.   KENT.
" To the uttermost."—Heb. vii. 25.
ALL-SUFFICIENT is our Jesus,
    Though our sins are black as hell ;

From pollution he can raise us,
    Or from nature's deepest cell ;
        He on Calvary
    Cancelled all his people's sin.

2 Weeping saint, forget thy mourning ;
    Why cast down, or troubled so ?
To the cross thy eyes be turning ;
    See what healing virtues flow ;
        Christ exalted,
    Is the hope of Israel now.

761   L.M.   WATTS.
Pleading for Pardon.—Ps. li. 1-9.
SHOW pity, Lord ; O Lord, forgive ;
Let a repenting rebel live ;
Are not thy mercies large and free ?
May not a sinner trust in thee ?

2 My crimes are great, but don't surpass
The power and glory of thy grace ;
Great God ! thy nature has no bound,
So let thy pardoning love be found.

3 O wash my soul from every sin,
And make my guilty conscience clean ;
Here on my heart the burden lies,
And past offences pain my eyes.

4 My lips with shame my sins confess,
Against thy law, against thy grace ;
Lord, should thy judgments grow severe,
I am condemned, but thou art clear.

5 Should sudden vengeance seize my breath,
I must pronounce thee just in death ;
And if my soul were sent to hell,
Thy righteous law approves it well.

6 Yet save a trembling sinner, Lord,
Whose hope, still hovering round thy word,

Would light on some sweet promise there,
Some sure support against despair.

762   L.M.   S. STENNETT.
" A bruised reed shall he not break," &c.—Isa. xlii. 3.
    How soft the words my Saviour speaks,
    How kind the promises he makes !
    A bruised reed he never breaks,
    Nor will he quench the smoking flax.

2 The humble poor he'll not despise,
    Nor on the contrite sinner frown ;
    His ear is open to their cries,
    And quickly sends salvation down.

3 He sees the struggles that prevail
    Between the powers of grace and sin,
    He kindly listens while they tell
    The bitter pangs they feel within.

4 Though pressed with fears on every side,
    They know not how the strife may end ;
    Yet he will soon the cause decide,
    And judgment unto victory send.

763   C.M.   WATTS.
Godly sorrow arising from the sufferings of Christ.
    ALAS ! and did my Saviour bleed ?
    And did my Sovereign die ?
    Would he devote that sacred head
    For such a worm as I ?

2 Thy body slain, sweet Jesus, thine,
    And bathed in its own blood ;
    While all exposed to wrath divine
    The glorious Sufferer stood.

3 Was it for crimes that I had done
    He groaned upon the tree ?
    Amazing pity ! grace unknown !
    And love beyond degree.

4 Well might the sun in darkness hide,
 And shut his glories in,
When God, the mighty Maker, died
 For man, the creature's sin.

5 Thus might I hide my blushing face,
 While his dear cross appears ;
Dissolve my heart in thankfulness,
 And melt my eyes in tears.

764   C.M.   WATTS.
Faith in Christ for Pardon and Sanctification.

How sad our state by nature is ;
 Our sin how deep its stains ;
And Satan binds our captive minds
 Fast in his slavish chains.

2 But there's a voice of sovereign grace
 Sounds from the sacred word ;
" Ho ! ye despairing sinners come,
 And trust upon the Lord."

3 My soul obeys the almighty call,
 And runs to this relief ;
I would believe thy promise, Lord ;
 O help my unbelief.

4 To the dear fountain of thy blood,
 Incarnate God, I fly ;
Here let me wash my spotted soul
 From crimes of deepest dye.

5 Stretch out thy arm, victorious King,
 My reigning sins subdue ;
Drive the old dragon from his seat,
 With all his hellish crew.

6 A guilty, weak, and helpless worm,
 On thy kind arms I fall,
Be thou my strength and righteousness,
 My Jesus, and my all.

765   C.M.   BERRIDGE.
Out of . . . my grief have I spoken.—1 Sam. i. 16.

AND does thy heart for Jesus pine,
 And make its secret moan ?
He understands a sigh divine,
 And marks a secret groan.

2 These pinings prove that Christ is near,
 To testify his grace ;
Call on him with unceasing prayer
 For he will show his face.

3 Though much dismayed, take courage still,
 And knock at mercy's door ;
A loving Saviour surely will
 Relieve his praying poor,

4 He knows how weak and faint thou art,
 And must appear at length ;

A look from him will cheer thy heart,
 And bring renewed strength.

766   8.7.4.   KENT.
" The grace of our Lord . . abundant."—1 Tim. i. 14.

SOVEREIGN grace o'er sin abounding !
 Ransomed souls, the tidings swell ;
'Tis a deep that knows no sounding ;
 Who its breadth or length can tell ?
 On its glories,
Let my soul for ever dwell.

2 What from Christ that soul can sever,
 Bound by everlasting bands ?
Once in him, in him for ever ;
 Thus the eternal covenant stands.
 None shall pluck thee
From the Strength of Israel's hands.

3 Heirs of God, joint-heirs with Jesus,
 Long ere time its race begun ;
To his name eternal praises ;
 O what wonders love has done !
 One with Jesus,
By eternal union one.

4 On such love, my soul, still ponder,
 Love so great, so rich, so free ;
Say, whilst lost in holy wonder,
 Why, O Lord, such love to me ?
 Hallelujah !
Grace shall reign eternally.

767   7s.   STOCKER.
" Uphold me with thy free Spirit."—Ps. li. 12.

GRACIOUS Spirit, Dove divine,
Let thy light within me shine ;
All my guilty fears remove,
With atoning blood and love.

2 Speak thy pardoning grace to me ;
Set the burdened sinner free ;
Lead me to the Lamb of God ;
Wash me in his precious blood.

3 Life and peace to me impart ;
Seal salvation on my heart ;
Breathe thyself into my breast,
Earnest of immortal rest.

4 Guard me round on every side ;
Save me from self-righteous pride ;
Me with Jesus' mind inspire ;
Melt me with celestial fire.

5 Thou my dross and tin consume ;
Let thy inward kingdom come ;
All my prayer and praise suggest ;
Dwell and reign within my breast.

768   7s.   HAMMOND.
"I know my sheep, and am known of mine."—John x.
Jesus, Shepherd of the sheep,
Thou thy flock dost feed and keep ;
Sweetest pasture dost prepare,
Watchest them with tender care.

2 Thee the sheep profess and own,
Thee they love, and thee alone ;
Thee they follow in the way ;
Strangers will they not obey.

3 Thou dost call them by their names ;
In thy bosom bear'st the lambs ;
They protection seek, and rest,
In their Shepherd's loving breast.

4 Lord, thy wandering sheep behold ;
Bring them back into thy fold ;
On thy shoulders bear them home ;
Suffer them no more to roam.

5 Lead them into pastures green,
Where thy lovely face is seen ;
Make them to those fountains go,
Where the living waters flow.

769 8.7.4. H. FOWLER.
"He bringeth them unto their desired haven."
Jesus, o'er the billows steer me,
Be my Pilot in each storm ;
Hold me fast and keep me near thee,
For thou know'st I'm but a worm ;
 What concerns me,
By thy power and love perform.

2 Soon the tempest will be over,
To our destined port we sail ;
Jesus, our eternal Lover,
Says his word shall never fail.
 Storms shall never
Reach us more within the vail.

3 In the midst of tribulation,
Oft we cast a wishful eye
To our future habitation,
And by faith the shore espy ;
 Blest assurance !
We shall mount to dwell on high.

4 With what raptures he'll embrace us,
Wipe away each falling tear !
Near himself for ever place us,
And with love our bosoms cheer ;
 Hallelujah !
We shall with the Lamb appear !

770 S.M. WATTS.
Joy in the Prospect of Heaven.—Ps. xlviii. 14.
The God that rules on high,
And thunders when he please ;

That rides upon the stormy sky,
And manages the seas ;

2 This awful God is ours,
Our Father and our love ;
He shall send down his heavenly powers,
To carry us above.

3 There shall we see his face,
And never, never sin ;
There, from the rivers of his grace,
Drink endless pleasures in.

771 L.M. BURNHAM.
Knowledge of Christ.—Phil. iii. 7-10 ; John xvii. 3.
To know my Jesus crucified,
By far excels all things beside ;
All earthly good I count but loss,
And triumph in my Saviour's cross.

2 Knowledge of all terrestrial things
Ne'er to my soul true pleasure brings ;
No peace, but in the Son of God ;
No joy, but through his pardoning blood.

3 O could I know and love him more,
And all his wondrous grace explore,
Ne'er would I covet man's esteem,
But part with all, and follow him.

4 Lord, may I bear my every loss ;
Be patient under every cross ;
Never may I my Saviour blame,
Though I'm despised for his dear name.

5 Thus make me willing, glorious Lamb,
To suffer all things for thy name ;
At last be where my Jesus is,
And rise to everlasting bliss.

772 C.M. BURNHAM.
Christ the Keeper of his Saints.-Ps. cxxi. 5 ; Jno. vi. 39.
Christ is the Keeper of his saints,
He guards them by his power ;
Subdues their numerous complaints,
In every gloomy hour.

2 What though they fear each dread alarm,
Tried, and severely tossed ;
Held by the Saviour's mighty arm,
None, none can e'er be lost.

3 He'll lead them on fair Zion's road,
Though weary, weak, and faint ;
For O ! they ne'er shall lose their God,
Or God e'er lose a saint.

4 How sure his great salvation shines ;
How full the vast reward ;
How firm the promise e'er remains :
How faithful is the Lord !

PART IV.

HART'S HYMNS.

The following Hymns by Joseph Hart were added to the Selection after Mr. Gadsby's death. Several, though hardly suitable for public singing, will be found profitable for private meditation.

773   C.M.
The Doubting Christian.—Matt. xiv. 31; Mark xvi. 16.

Ir unbelief's that sin accursed,
  Abhorred by God above,
Because, of all opposers worst,
  It fights against his love,

2 How shall a heart that doubts like mine,
  Dismayed at every breath,
Pretend to live the life divine,
  Or fight the fight of faith?

3 Conscience accuses from within,
  And others from without;
I feel my soul the sink of sin,
  And this produces doubt.

4 [When thousand sins, of various dyes,
  Corruptions dark and foul,
Daily within my bosom rise,
  And blacken all my soul,

5 I groan, and grieve, and cry, and call
  On Jesus for relief;
But, that delayed, to doubting fall,
  Of all my sins the chief.

6 Such dire disorders vex my soul,
  That ill engenders ill;
And when my heart I feel so foul,
  I make it fouler still.]

7 In this distress, the course I take
  Is still to call and pray,
And wait the time when Christ shall speak,
  And drive my foes away.

8 For that blessed hour I sigh and pant,
  With wishes warm and strong;
But dearest Lord, lest these should faint,
  O do not tarry long.

774   C.M.
Sanctification.—Acts xv. 9; 1 Cor. i. 2; Heb. ix. 14.

THE Holy Ghost in Scripture saith
  Expressly, in one part,
Speaking by Peter's mouth, " By faith
  God purifies the heart."

2 Now, what in holy writ he says,
  In part or through the whole,
The self-same truths, by various ways,
  He teaches in the soul.

3 Experience likewise tells us this;
  Before the Saviour's blood
Has washed us clean, and made our peace,
  We can do nothing good.

4 [But here, my friends, the danger lies;
  Errors of different kind
Will still creep in, which devils devise
  To cheat the human mind.

5 " I want no work within," says one;
  " 'Tis all in Christ the Head; "
Thus, careless, he goes blindly on,
  And trusts a faith that's dead.

6 " 'Tis dangerous," another cries,
  " To trust to faith alone;
Christ's righteousness will not suffice
  Except I add my own."

7 Thus he, that he may something do,
  To shun the impending curse,
Upon the old will patch the new,
  And make the rent still worse.

8 Others affirm, " The Spirit of God
  To true believers given,
Makes all their thoughts and acts so good,
  They're always fit for heaven."

9 The babe of Christ, at hearing this,
  Is filled with anxious fear;
Conscience condemns, corruptions rise,
  And drive him near despair.

10 These trials weaklings suffer here;
  Censure and scorn without.
And from within, what's worse to bear,
  Despondency and doubt.

11 But, gracious Lord, who once didst feel
  What weakness is and fears,
Who gott'st thy victory over hell
  With groans, and cries, and tears;

12 Do thou direct our feeble hearts
  To trust thee for the whole;
The work of grace in all its parts
  Accomplish in the soul.

13 Thy Holy Spirit into us breathe;
  A perfect Saviour prove;
Lord, give us faith, and let that faith
  Work all thy will by love.]

775   S.M.

The Enlightened Sinner.—Eph. v. 8; 1 Tim. i. 13-15.

My God, when I reflect
How, all my life-time past,
I ran the roads of sin and death
With rash impetuous haste,

2   My foolishness I hate ;
My filthiness I loathe ;
And view, with sharp remorse and shame,
My filth and folly both.

3   [With some the tempter takes
Much pains to make them mad ;
But me he found, and always held,
The easiest fool he had.

4   His deep and dangerous lies
So grossly I believed,
He was not readier to deceive,
Than I to be deceived.

5   His light and airy dreams,
I took for solid good,
And thought his base, adulterate coin,
The riches of thy blood.]

6   And dost thou still regard,
And cast a gracious eye
On one so foul, so base, so blind,
So dead, so lost, as I ?

7   Then sinners black as hell
May hence for hope have ground ;
For who of mercy needs despair,
Since I have mercy found ?

776   8.7.

Christ's Nativity.—Luke ii. 7-14: Matt. i. 21; ii. 11.

LET us all, with grateful praises,
Celebrate the happy day,
When the lovely, loving Jesus
First partook of human clay ;
When the heavenly host, assembled,
Gazed with wonder from the sky ;
Angels joyed, and devils trembled,
Neither fully knowing why.

2 Long had Satan reigned imperious,
Till the woman's promised Seed,
Born a babe, by birth mysterious,
Came to bruise the serpent's head.
Crush, dear Babe, his power within us,
Break our chains, and set us free ;
Pull down all the bars between us,
Till we fly and cleave to thee.

3 [Shepherds on their flocks attending,
Shepherds, that in night-time watched,
Saw the messenger descending,
From the court of heaven dispatched.

Beams of glory decked his mission,
Bursting through the veil of night ;
Fear possessed them at the vision ;
Sinners tremble at the light.

4 Dove-like meekness graced his visage ;
Joy and love shone round his head ;
Soon he cheered them with his message ;
Comfort flowed from all he said :
" Fear not, favourites of the Almighty !
Joyful news to you I bring ;
You have now, in David's city,
Born a Saviour, Christ the King.

5 " Go and find the royal stranger
By these signs : A Babe you'll see,
Weak and lying in a manger,
Wrapped and swaddled ; that is he."

Straight a host of angels glorious
Round the heavenly herald throng,
Uttering in harmonious chorus,
Airs divine ; and this the song :

6 " Glory first to God be given
In the highest heights, and then
Peace on earth, proclaimed by heaven—
Peace and great goodwill to men ! "
Thus they sang with rapture, kindling
In the shepherds' hearts a flame,
Joy and wonder sweetly mingling ;
All believers feel the same.]

7 Lo, sweet Babe, we fall before thee ;
Jesus, thee we all adore ;
To thee, kingdom, power, and glory
Be ascribed for evermore.
Glory to our God be given
In the highest heights, and then
Peace on earth brought down from heaven—
Peace and great goodwill to men.

777   148th.

New Year's Day.—Eph. v. 16; Psa. lxv. 11.

ONCE more the constant sun,
Revolving round his sphere,
His steady course has run,
And brings another year.
He rises, sets, but goes not back,
Nor ever quits his destined track.

2   What now should be our task ?
Or rather, what our prayer ?
What good thing shall we ask,
To prosper this new year ?

PART IV.—HART'S HYMNS.

With one accord our hearts we'd lift,
And ask our Lord some new year's gift.

3 No trifling gift or small,
    Should friends of Christ desire.
  Rich Lord, bestow on all
    Pure gold, well tried by fire.
Faith that stands fast when devils roar,
And love that lasts for evermore.

778   104th.
"Hitherto hath the Lord helped us."—1 Sam. vii. 12.

THOUGH strait be the way, with dangers beset,
  And we on the way are no farther yet,
Our good Guide and Saviour has helped us
    thus far ;
And 'tis by his favour we are what we are.

2 [A favour so great we highly should prize ;
  Not murmur, nor fret, nor small things
    despise.   [called sum !
But what call we small things—sin's whole can-
'Tis greater than all things, except those to come.]

3 My brethren, reflect on what we have been,
  How God had respect to us under sin ;
When lower and lower we every day fell,
He stretched forth his power, and snatched us
    from hell.

4 Then let us rejoice, and cheerfully sing,
  With heart and with voice, to Jesus our King,
Who thus far has brought us from evil to good ;
The ransom that bought us, no less than his
    blood.

5 For blessings like these, so bounteously given,
  For prospects of peace & foretastes of heaven,
'Tis grateful, 'tis pleasant, to sing, and adore ;
Be thankful for present, and then ask for more.

779   7.6.8.
Cleaving to Christ, by Faith.—Heb. xi. 33-40; xii. 1.

FAITH, implanted from above,
  Will prove a fertile root,
Whence will spring a tree of love,
  Producing precious fruit.
Though bleak winds the boughs deface,
The rooted stock shall still remain ;
  Leaves may languish, fruit decrease,
  But more shall grow again.

2 Happy souls ! who cleave to Christ
    By pure and living faith,
  Finding him their King and Priest,
    Their God and guide till death.
God's own foe may plague his sons ;
Sin may distress, but not subdue ;
  Christ, who conquered for us once,
  Will in us conquer too.

780, 1   7.6.
Dialogue between a Believer and his Soul.—Ps. xliii. 5.

Bel. COME, my soul, and let us try,
    For a little season,
  Every burden to lay by ;
    Come, and let us reason.
What is this that casts thee down ?
  Who are those that grieve thee ?
Speak, and let the worst be known ;
  Speaking may relieve thee.

Soul. O I sink beneath the load
    Of my nature's evil !
Full of enmity to God ;
    Captived by the devil ;
Restless as the troubled seas ;
  Feeble, faint, and fearful ;
Plagued with every sore disease ;
  How can I be cheerful ?

Bel. Think on what thy Saviour bore
    In the gloomy garden,
Sweating blood at every pore,
    To procure thy pardon !
See him stretched upon the wood,
  Bleeding, grieving, crying,
Suffering all the wrath of God,
  Groaning, gasping, dying !

Soul. This by faith I sometimes view,
    And those views relieve me ;
But my sins return anew ;
    These are they that grieve me.
Oh ! I'm leprous, stinking, foul,
  Quite throughout infected ;
Have not I, if any soul,
  Cause to be dejected ?

Bel. Think how loud thy dying Lord
    Cried out, " It is finished ! "
Treasure up that sacred word,
  Whole and undiminished :
Doubt not he will carry on,
    To its full perfection,
That good work he has begun ;
  Why, then, this dejection ?

Soul. Faith when void of works is dead ;
    This the Scriptures witness ;
And what works have I to plead,
    Who am all unfitness ?
All my powers are depraved,
  Blind, perverse, and filthy ;
If from death I'm fully saved,
  Why am I not healthy ?

Bel. Pore not on thyself too long,
    Lest it sink thee lower ;

Look to Jesus, kind as strong—
  Mercy joined with power ;
Every work that thou must do,
  Will thy gracious Saviour
For thee work, and in thee too,
  Of his special favour.

Soul. Jesus' precious blood, once spilt,
  I depend on solely,
To release and clear my guilt ;
  But I would be holy.
Bel. He that bought thee on the cross
  Can control thy nature ;
Fully purge away thy dross ;
  Make thee a new creature.

Soul. That he can I nothing doubt,
  Be it but his pleasure.
Bel. Though it be not done throughout,
  May it not in measure ?
Soul. When that measure, far from great,
  Still shall seem decreasing ?
Bel. Faint not then, but pray and wait,
  Never, never ceasing.

Soul. What when prayer meets no regard ?
Bel. Still repeat it often.
Soul. But I feel myself so hard.
Bel.   Jesus will thee soften.
Soul. But my enemies make head.
Bel. Let them closer drive thee.
Soul. But I'm cold, I'm dark, I'm dead.
Bel. Jesus will revive thee.

782   C.M.
Deliverance Sure.—Deut. vii. 22 : 2 Cor. xii. 7-9.

THE Lord assured the chosen race,
  From Egypt's bondage brought,
They should obtain the promised place ;
  And find the rest they sought.

2 [Strong nations now possess the land,
  Yet yield not thou to doubt ;
With arm outstretched, and mighty hand,
  Thy God shall drive them out.

3 Not all at once, for fear thou find,
  The ravenous beasts of prey
Rising upon thee from behind,
  As dangerous foes as they.

4 By little and by little, he
  Will chase them from thy sight ;
Believers are not called, we see,
  To sleep or play, but fight.

5 Spiritual pride, that rampant beast,
  Would rear its haughty head ;
True faith would soon be dispossessed,
  And carelessness succeed.

6 Corruptions make the mourners shun
  Presumption's dangerous snare,
Force us to trust to Christ alone,
  And fly to God by prayer.

7 By them we feel how low we're lost,
  And learn, in some degree,
How dear that great salvation cost,
  Which comes to us so free.

8 If such a weight to every soul
  Of sin and sorrow fall,
What love was that which took the whole,
  And freely bore it all !]

9 O when will God our joy complete,
  And make an end of sin ?
When shall we walk the land, and meet
  No Canaanite therein ?

10 [Will this precede the day of death,
  Or must we wait till then ?
Ye struggling souls, be strong in faith,
  And quit yourselves like men.]

11 Our dear Deliverer's love is such,
  He cannot long delay ;
Meantime, that foe can't boast of much,
  Who makes us watch and pray.

783, 4   C.M.
" Stand still."—Exod. xiv. 13 ; Matt. vii. 14.

OH what a narrow, narrow path
  Is that which leads to life !
Some talk of works, and some of faith,
  With warmth, and zeal, and strife.

2 But after all that's said or done,
  Let men think what they will,
The strength of every tempted son
  Consists in standing still.

3 [" Stand still," says one, " that's easy sure ;
  'Tis what I always do."
Deluded soul, be not secure ;
  This is not meant to you.

4 Not driven by fear, nor drawn by love,
  Nor yet by duty led ;
Lie still you do, and never move ;
  For who can move that's dead ?

5 But for a living soul to stand,
  By thousand dangers scared,
And feel destruction close at hand,
  O this indeed is hard !

6 To shun this danger, others run
  To hide they know not where ;
Or though they fight, no victory's won ;
  They only beat the air.]

7 He that believes, the Scripture says,
   Shall not confusedly haste.
Thus danger threats both him that stays
   And him that runs too fast.

8 [Haste grasps at all, but nothing keeps ;
   Sloth is a dangerous state ;
And he that flees, and he that sleeps,
   Cannot be said to wait.]

9 Lord, let thy Spirit prompt us when
   To go, and when to stay ;
Attract us with the cords of men,
   And we shall not delay.

10 Give power and will, and then command,
   And we will follow thee ;
And when we're frightened, bid us stand
   And thy salvation see.

785   C.M.
The Crucifixion.—Ps. xxii. 11-17; lxix. 19-21.
OH ! what a sad and doleful night
   Preceded that day's morn,
When darkness seized the Lord of light,
   And sin by Christ was borne !

2 When our intolerable load
   Upon his soul was laid,
And the vindictive wrath of God
   Flamed furious on his head !

3 We in our Conqueror well may boast ;
   For none but God alone
Can know how dear the victory cost,
   How hardly it was won.

4 [Forth from the garden fully tried,
   Our bruised Champion came,
To suffer what remained beside
   Of pain, and grief, and shame.

5 Mocked, spit upon, and crowned with thorn,
   A spectacle he stood ;
His back with scourges lashed and torn :
   A victim bathed in blood.

6 Nailed to the cross through hands and feet,
   He hung in open view ;
To make his sorrows quite complete,
   By God deserted too !]

7 Through nature's works the woes he felt
   With soft infection ran ;
The hardest thing could break or melt,
   Except the heart of man.

8 This day before thee, Lord, we come ;
   O melt our hearts, or break ;
For, should we now continue dumb,
   The very stones would speak.

9 [True, thou hast paid the heavy debt,
   And made believers clean,
But he knows nothing of it yet,
   Who is not grieved at sin.

10 A faithful friend of grief partakes ;
   But union can be none
Betwixt a heart like melting wax
   And hearts as hard as stone ;

11 Betwixt a head diffusing blood
   And members sound and whole ;
Betwixt an agonising God
   And an unfeeling soul.]

12 Lord, my longed happiness is full,
   When I can go with thee
To Golgotha ; the place of skull
   Is heaven on earth to me.

786   8.8.6.
Another.—Gal. i. 17; Col. i. 27; 2 Cor. iv. 10.
THAT day when Christ was crucified,
The mighty God, Jehovah, died
   An ignominious death.
He that would keep this solemn day,
And true disciples safely may,
   Must keep it firm in faith.

2 For, though the mournful tragedy
May call up tears in every eye,
   Yet, brethren, rest not here.
Would you condole your dying Friend ?
Let each into his soul descend,
   And find his Saviour there.

3 This only can our hearts assure,
And make our outward worship pure
   In God's all-searching sight.
When all we do with love is mixed,
And steadfast faith on Jesus fixed,
   My brethren, then we're right.

787   7.6.8.
Another.—Heb. iv. 15; xii. 3; Zech. xiii. 1.
COME, poor sinners, come away ;
   In meditation sweet,
Let us go to Golgotha,
   And kiss our Saviour's feet.
Let us in his wounded side
Wash till we every whit are clean ;
   That's the fountain opened wide
   For filthiness and sin.

2 [Zion's mourners, cease your fear ;
   For lo ! the dying Lamb
Utterly forbids despair
   To all that love his name.

Him your fellow-sufferer see ;
He was in all things like to you.
Are you tempted ? So was he.
Deserted ? He was too.]

3 Jesus, our Redeemer, shed
 For us his vital blood,
 We, through our victorious Head
 Can now come near to God.
 Sin and sorrow may distress ;
 But neither shall us quite control ;
 Christ has perfect holiness
 For every sin-sick soul.

788   7s.

Following and praising the Lamb.— Rev. v. 9, 10.

 COME, ye humble sinner-train,
 Souls for whom the Lamb was slain,
 Cheerful let us raise our voice ;
 We have reason to rejoice.
 Let us sing, with saints in heaven,
 Life restored, and sin forgiven ;
 Glory and eternal laud
 Be to our incarnate God.

2 Now look up with faith and see
 Him that bled for you and me.
 Seated on his glorious throne,
 Interceding for his own.
 What can Christians have to fear,
 When they view the Saviour there ?
 Hell is vanquished, heaven appeased,
 God is satisfied and pleased.

3 Snares and dangers may beset,
 For we are but travellers yet.
 As the way, indeed, is hard,
 May we keep a constant guard.

 Neither lifted up with air,
 Nor dejected to despair ;
 Always keeping Christ in view ;
 He will bring us safely through.

789   7s.

No Pardon out of Christ.—Heb. ix. 22 ; Acts iv. 12.

 O YE sons of men, be wise ;
 Trust no longer dreams and lies.
 Out of Christ, almighty power
 Can do nothing but devour.

2 God, you say, is good. 'Tis true,
 But he's pure and holy too ;
 Just and jealous in his ire,
 Burning with vindictive fire.

3 [This of old himself declared ;
 Israel trembled when they heard.
 But the proof of proofs indeed

Is, he sent his Son to bleed.

4 When the blessed Jesus died,
 God was clearly justified.
 Sin to pardon without blood
 Never in his nature stood.]

5 Worship God, then, in his Son ;
 There he's love and there alone ;
 Think not that he will, or may,
 Pardon any other way.

6 [See the suffering Son of God
 Panting, groaning, sweating blood !
 Brethren, this had never been
 Had not God detested sin.]

7 Be his mercy, therefore, sought
 In the way himself has taught ;
 There his clemency is such,
 We can never trust too much.

8 He that better knows than we,
 Bids us now to Jesus flee ;
 Humbly take him at his word,
 And your souls shall bless the Lord.

790   112th.

Jabez's Prayer.—1 Chron. iv. 9, 10.

A SAINT there was in days of old
(Though we but little of him hear)
In honour high, of whom is told
A short, but an effectual prayer.
This prayer, my brethren, let us view,
And try if we can pray so too.

2 [He called on Israel's God, 'tis said ;
Let us take notice first of that ;
Had he to any other prayed,
To us it had not mattered what ;
For all true Israelites adore
One God, Jehovah, and no more.]

3 " O that thou wouldst me bless indeed,
And that thou wouldst enlarge my bound ;
And let thy hand in every need
A guide and help be with me found ;
That thou wouldst cause that evil be
No cause of pain and grief to me."

4 [What is it to be blest indeed,
But to have all our sins forgiven ;
To be from guilt and terror freed,
Redeemed from hell, and sealed for heaven ;
To worship an incarnate God,
And know he saved us by his blood ?

5 And next, to have our coast enlarged
Is, that our hearts extend their plan ;
From bondage and from fear discharged,
And filled with love to God and man ;

To cast off every narrow thought,
And use the freedom Christ has brought.

6 To use this liberty aright,
And not the grace of God abuse,
We always need his hand, his might,
Lest what he gives us we should lose ;
Spiritual pride would soon creep in,
And turn his very grace to sin.]

7 This prayer, so long ago preferred,
Is left on sacred record thus ;
And this good prayer by God was heard,
And kindly handed down to us.
Thus Jabez prayed, for that's his name.
May all believers pray the same.

791 L.M.
The Rainbow.—Gen. viii. 20-22 ; ix. 13, 14.
WHEN, deaf to every warning given,
Man braved the patient power of heaven,
Great in his anger, God arose,
Deluged the world, and drowned his foes.

2 Vengeance, that called for this just doom,
Retired to make sweet mercy room ;
God, of his wrath repenting, swore
A flood should drown the earth no more.

3 That future ages this might know,
He placed in heaven his radiant bow ;
The sign, till time itself shall fail,
That waters shall no more prevail.

4 [The beauties of this bow but shine
To vulgar eyes as something fine ;
Others investigate their cause
By mediums drawn from nature's laws.

5 But what great ends can men pursue
From schemes like these, suppose them true
Describe the form, the cause define,
The rainbow still remains a sign.

6 A sign in which by faith we read
The covenant God with Noah made ;
A noble end and truly great ;
But something greater lies there yet.]

7 This bow that beams with vivid light,
Presents a sign to Christian sight,
That God has sworn
                (who dares condemn ?)
He will no more be wroth with them.

8 [Thus the believer, when he views
The rainbow in its various hues,
May say, " Those lively colours shine
To show that heaven is surely mine.

9 " See in yon cloud what tinctures glow,
And gild the smiling vales below ;

So smiles my cheerful soul to see
My God is reconciled to me."]

792, 3 S.M.
" Charity never faileth."—1 Cor. xiii. 8, 13 ; xvi. 14.
FAITH in the bleeding Lamb,
O what a gift is this !
Hope of salvation in his name,
How comfortable 'tis !

2 [Knowledge of what is right,
How God is satisfied,
A foe received a favourite,
An alien made a child ;

3 Blessings, my friends, like these,
Are very, very great ;
But soon they every one must cease,
Nor are they now complete.

4 Faith will to bliss give place ;
In sight we hope shall lose ;
For who needs trust for things he has,
Or hope for what he views ?

5 The little too that's known,
Which, children-like, we boast,
Will fade, like glow-worms in the sun,
Or drops in ocean lost.]

6 But love shall still remain,
Its glories cannot cease,
No other change shall that sustain,
Save only to increase.

7 Of all that God bestows,
In earth or heaven above,
The best gift saint or angel knows,
Or e'er will know, is love.

8 [Love all defects supplies,
Makes great obstructions small ;
'Tis prayer, 'tis praise, 'tis sacrifice,
'Tis holiness, 'tis all !]

9 Descend, celestial Dove,
With Jesus' flock abide ;
Give us that best of blessings, love,
Whate'er we want beside.

794 L.M. xvi. 4]
The High Priest.—Ps. xlv. 7, 8 ; Heb. v. 6, 7. [cf. Lev.
[WHEN Aaron, in the holiest place,
Atonement made for Israel's race,
The names of all their tribes expressed,
He wore conspicuous on his breast.

2 Twelve lettered stones, with sculpture bold,
Deep seated in the wounded gold,
Glowed on the breastplate richly bright,
And beamed with characteristic light.

3 His hands a golden censer held,
With burning coals and incense filled,

Which clouded all the holy room
With odorous streams of rich perfume.

4 And, lest the priest the place defile,
A costly, consecrating oil,
With mingled gums and spices sweet,
Had for his office made him meet.

5 The liquid compound from his head
Its unctuous odours downward spread ;
Delicious drops, like balmy dews,
O'er all the man their sweets diffuse.

6 Arrayed in hallowed vests he stood,
Sprinkled with holy oil and blood ;
The tabernacle's sacred frame,
And all within it shared the same.

7 So, when our great Melchisedec
The true atonement came to make,
A holy oil anoints Him too,
Richer than Aaron ever knew.

8 His body, bathed in sweat and blood,
Showered on the ground a purple flood ;
The rich effusion copious ran,
To glad the heart of God and man.

9 Deep in his breast engraved he bore
Our names, with every penal score,
When pressed to earth he prostrate lay ;
Shocked at the sum, yet prompt to pay.

10 The fragrant incense of his prayer
To heaven went up through yielding air ;
Perfumed the throne of God on high,
And calmed offended Majesty.

795   7.6.
Election.—1 Pet. i. 2 ; 2 Tim. ii. 19 ; 1 Thess. v. 24.
MIGHTY enemies without,
Much mightier within,
Thoughts we cannot quell or rout,
Blasphemously obscene ;
Coldness, unbelief, and pride,
Hell and all its murderous train,
Threaten death on every side,
And have their thousands slain.

2 Thus pursued, and thus distressed,
Ah ! whither shall we fly ?
To obtain the promised rest,
On what sure hand rely ?
Shall the Christian trust his heart ?
That, alas ! of foes the worst,
Always takes the tempter's part ;
Nay, often tempts him first.

3 If to-day we be sincere,
And can both watch and pray,
Watchfulness, perhaps, and prayer,

To-morrow may decay.
If we now believe aright,
Faithfulness is God's alone,
We are feeble, fickle, light,
To changes ever prone.

4 But we build upon a base
That nothing can remove,
When we trust electing grace
And everlasting love.
Victory over all our foes
Christ has given with his blood,
Perseverance he bestows
On every child of God.

796   7.6.
All from above.—Jas. i. 17 ; Mark xiii. 31.
WHEN we pray, or when we sing,
Or read, or speak, or hear,
Or do any holy thing,
Be this our constant care :
With a fixed and constant faith
Jesus Christ to keep in view,
Trusting wholly in his death
In all we ask or do.

2 Holiness in all its parts,
Affections placed above,
Self-abhorrence, contrite hearts,
Humility, and love ;
Every virtue, every grace,
All that bears the name of good,
Perseverance in our race,
We draw from Jesus' blood.

3 Lamb of God, in thee we trust,
On thy fixed love depend ;
Thou art faithful, true, and just,
And lovest to the end.
Heaven and earth shall pass away,
But thy word shall firm abide ;
That's thy children's steadfast stay
When all things fail beside.

797   L.M.
The Crucifixion.—John xviii. ; xix. ; Isa. liii. 3.
Now, from the garden to the cross,
Let us attend the Lamb of God.
Be all things else accounted dross,
Compared with sin-atoning blood.

2 [See how the patient Jesus stands,
Insulted in his lowest case !
Sinners have bound the Almighty's hands !
And spit in their Creator's face !

3 With thorns his temples gored and gashed,
Send streams of blood from every part !

His back's with knotted scourges lashed,
But sharper scourges tear his heart !]

4 Nailed naked to the accursed wood,
Exposed to earth and heaven above,
A spectacle of wounds and blood,
A prodigy of injured love !

5 [Hark ! how his doleful cries affright
Affected angels, while they view !
His friends forsook him in the night,
And now his God forsakes him too !

6 O what a field of battle's here ;
Vengeance and love their powers oppose !
Never was such a mighty pair ;
Never were two such desperate foes.]

7 Behold that pale, that languid face,
That drooping head, those cold dead eyes !
Behold in sorrow and disgrace,
Our conquering Hero hangs and dies !

8 Ye that assume his sacred name,
Now tell me what can all this mean ?
What was it bruised God's harmless Lamb ?
What was it pierced his soul, but sin ?

9 Blush, Christian, blush ; let shame abound ;
If sin affects thee not with woe,
Whatever spirit be in thee found,
The Spirit of Christ thou dost not know.

798   7.6.8.
Faith, hope, love, righteousness, peace.—1 Thess. i. 3.

FAITH in Jesus can repel
The darts of sin and death ;
Faith gives victory over hell ;
But who can give us faith ?

Hope in Christ the soul revives,
Supports the spirits when they droop ;
Hope celestial comfort gives ;
But who can give us hope ?

2 Love to Jesus Christ and his,
Fixes the heart above ;
Love gives everlasting bliss ;
But who can give us love ?
To believe's the gift of God ;
Well-grounded hope he sends from heaven
Love's the earnest of his blood,
To all his children given.

3 Jesus, from thy boundless store,
Thy treasuries of grace,
On thy feeble followers pour
Thy righteousness and peace.
Of thy righteousness alone

Continual mention we will make ;
We have nothing of our own ;
But soul and all's at stake.

799   8.3.
Man's Righteousness.—Isa. lvii. 12; Zech. iii. 3.

MAN, bewail thy situation ;
Hell-born sin, once crept in,
Mars God's fair creation.

2 Vaunt thy native strength no longer ;
Vain's the boast ; all is lost ;
Sin and death are stronger.

3 Enemies to God and goodness,
Great and small, since the fall,
Sink in lust and lewdness.

4 If to this thou art a stranger,
While thou liest out of Christ,
Greater is thy danger.

5 [Trust not to thy smooth behaviour ;
All's deceit ; and the cheat
Keeps thee from the Saviour.]

6 Oft we're best when dangers fright us,
Jesus came to reclaim
Sinners, not the righteous.

7 Sick men feel their bad condition ;
But the soul that is whole
Slights the good Physician.

800   8.3.
The Linsey-Woolsey Garment.—Deut. xxii. 11.

DARK is he whose eye's not single ;
Foolish man never can
Hell with heaven mingle.

2 [Everything we do we sin in.
Chosen Jews must not use
Woollen mixed with linen.]

3 God is holy in his nature ;
And by that needs must hate
Sin in every creature.

4 Infinite in truth and justice,
He surveys all our ways ;
Knows in whom our trust is.

5 Partial service is his loathing ;
He requires pure desires ;
All the heart, or nothing.

6 [If we think of reconciling
Black with white, dark with light,
'Tis but self-beguiling.]

7 Righteousness to full perfection
Must be brought, lacking nought,
Fearless of rejection.

801   7.6.8.

"All my springs are in thee."—Ps. lxxxvii. 7.

BLESS the Lord, my soul, and raise
A glad and grateful song
To my dear Redeemer's praise,
For I to him belong.
He, my Goodness, Strength, and God,
In whom I live, and move, and am,
Paid my ransom with his blood ;
My portion is the Lamb.

2 [Though temptations seldom cease,
Though frequent griefs I feel,
Yet his Spirit whispers peace,
And he is with me still.
Weak of body, sick in soul,
Depressed at heart, and faint with fears,
His dear presence makes me whole,
And with sweet comfort cheers.]

3 O my Jesus, thou art mine,
With all thy grace and power ;
I am now, and shall be thine
When time shall be no more ;
Thou revivest me by thy death ;
Thy blood from guilt has set me free ;
My fresh springs of hope, and faith,
And love, are all in thee.

802   7s.

Gethsemane.—John xviii. 1, 2 ; Matt. xxvi. 36.

JESUS, while he dwelt below,
As divine historians say,
To a place would often go ;
Near to Kedron's brook it lay ;
In this place he loved to be,
And 'twas named Gethsemane.

2 ['Twas a garden, as we read,
At the foot of Olivet,
Low, and proper to be made
The Redeemer's lone retreat ;
When from noise he would be free,
Then he sought Gethsemane.

3 Thither, by their Master brought,
His disciples likewise came ;
There the heavenly truths he taught
Often set their hearts on flame ;
Therefore they, as well as he,
Visited Gethsemane.

4 Here they oft conversing sat,
Or might join with Christ in prayer ;
O what blest devotion's that,
When the Lord himself is there !

All things to them seemed to agree
To endear Gethsemane.

5 Here no strangers durst intrude ;
But the Prince of Peace could sit,
Cheered with sacred solitude,
Wrapt in contemplation sweet ;
Yet how little could they see
Why he chose Gethsemane !

6 Full of love to man's lost race,
On his conflict much he thought ;
This he knew the destined place,
And he loved the sacred spot ;
Therefore 'twas he liked to be
Often in Gethsemane.

7 They his followers, with the rest,
Had incurred the wrath divine ;
And their Lord, with pity prest,
Longed to bear their loads—and mine ;
Love to them, and love to me,
Made him love Gethsemane.

8 Many woes had he endured,
Many sore temptations met,
Patient, and to pains inured ;
But the sorest trial yet,
Was to be sustained in thee,
Gloomy, sad Gethsemane.

9 Came at length the dreadful night,
Vengeance, with its iron rod,
Stood, and with collected might
Bruised the harmless Lamb of God ;
See, my soul, thy Saviour see,
Grovelling in Gethsemane.

10 View him in that olive press,
Squeezed and wrung till 'whelmed in blood,
View thy Maker's deep distress !
Hear the sighs and groans of God !
Then reflect what sin must be,
Gazing on Gethsemane.

11 Poor disciples, tell me now,
Where's the love ye lately had,
Where's that faith ye all could vow ?
But this hour is too, too sad !
'Tis not now for such as ye
To support Gethsemane.

12 O what wonders love has done !
But how little understood !
God well knows, and God alone,
What produced that sweat of blood ;
Who can thy deep wonders see,
Wonderful Gethsemane ?

13 There my God bore all my guilt ;
This through grace can be believed ;

But the horrors which he felt,
Are too vast to be conceived.
None can penetrate through thee,
Doleful, dark Gethsemane.

14 Gloomy garden, on thy beds,
Washed by Kedron's waters foul,
Grow most rank and bitter weeds ;
Think on these, my sinful soul ;
Wouldst thou sin's dominion flee,
Call to mind Gethsemane.

15 Sinners vile like me, and lost,
If there's one so vile as I,
Leave more righteous souls to boast :
Leave them, and to refuge fly ;
We may well bless that decree
Which ordained Gethsemane.

16 We can hope no healing hand,
Leprous quite throughout with sin ;
Loathed incurables we stand,
Crying out, " Unclean, unclean ! "
Help there's none for such as we,
But in dear Gethsemane.

17 Eden, from each flowery bed,
Did for man short sweetness breathe ;
Soon, by Satan's counsel led,
Man wrought sin, and sin wrought death ;
But of life, the healing tree
Grows in rich Gethsemane.

18 Hither, Lord, thou didst resort,
Ofttimes with thy little train ;
Here wouldst keep thy private court ;
O confer that grace again ;
Lord, resort with worthless me
Ofttimes to Gethsemane.

19 True, I can't deserve to share
In a favour so divine ;
But, since sin first fixed thee there,
None have greater sins than mine ;
And to this my woeful plea,
Witness thou, Gethsemane.

20 Sins against a holy God ;
Sins against his righteous laws ;
Sins against his love, his blood ;
Sins against his name, and cause ;
Sins immense as is the sea—
Hide me, O Gethsemane !

21 Here's my claim, and here alone ;
None a Saviour more can need ;
Deeds of righteousness I've none ;
No, not one good work to plead ;
Not a glimpse of hope for me,
Only in Gethsemane.]

22 Saviour, all the stone remove
From my flinty, frozen heart ;
Thaw it with the beams of love,
Pierce it with the blood-dipt dart ;
Wound the heart that wounded thee ;
Melt it in Gethsemane.

23 Father, Son, and Holy Ghost,
One almighty God of love,
Hymned by all the heavenly host
In thy shining courts above ;
We poor sinners, gracious THREE,
Bless thee for Gethsemane.

803 C.M.

The Death and Excellency of Christ.—Isa. xiii. 12.

THE things on earth which men esteem,
And of their richness boast,
In value less or greater seem,
Proportioned to their cost.

2 [The diamond, that's for thousands sold,
Our admiration draws ;
For dust men seldom part with gold,
Or barter pearls for straws.]

3 Then what inestimable worth
Must in those crowns appear,
For which the Lord came down to earth,
And bought for us, so dear !

4 The Father dearly loves the Son,
And rates his merits high ;
For no mean cause he sent him down
To suffer, grieve, and die.

5 The blessings from his death that flow,
So little we esteem,
Only because we slightly know,
And meanly value him.

6 ['Twas our Creator for us bled,
The Lord of life and power ;
Whom angels worship, devils dread,—
God blest for evermore.]

7 O could we but with clearer eyes
His excellences trace,
Could we his person learn to prize,
We more should prize his grace.

SECOND PART.

1 Cor. ii. 9 ; Heb. xi. 16 ; 1 Pet. i. 18, 19.

AND did the darling Son of God
For sinners deign to bleed ?
The purchase of that precious blood
Must needs be rich indeed.

2 God's wisdom would not pay for toys
So great a price as this ;

'Tis God-like glory, boundless joys ;
'Tis unexampled bliss.

3 Saints, raise your expectations high ;
Hope all that heaven has good ;
The blood of Christ has brought you nigh—
Invaluable blood !

4 Eye has not seen, nor ear has heard,
Nor can the heart conceive,
What blessings are for them prepared
Who in the Lord believe.

5 By others, for their virtue fair,
Let rich rewards be sought ;
Give me, my God, to freely share
What thou hast freely bought.

804   104th.

The Lambs safe.—Ps. xxiii.; xxxiv. 10; 1 Thess. v. 14.

YE lambs of Christ's fold, ye weaklings in
faith,
Who long to lay hold on life by his death ;
Who fain would believe him, and in your best
room
Would gladly receive him, but fear to presume ;

2 Remember one thing, O may it sink deep ;
Our Shepherd and King cares much for his
sheep ;
To trust him endeavour ; the work is his own ;
He makes the believer, and gives him his crown.

3 Those feeble desires, those wishes so weak,·
'Tis Jesus inspires, and bids you still seek ;
His Spirit will cherish the life he first gave ;
You never shall perish if Jesus can save.

4 [Proud lions, that boast when lusty & young,
Soon find, to their cost, self-confidence wrong ;

Tormented with hunger, they feel their strength
vain ;
For famine is stronger, and gnaws them with
pain.

5 But lambs are preserved, though helpless in
kind ;   [find ;
When lions are starved, they nourishment
Their Shepherd upholds them, when faint, in
his arms ;   [them from harms.
And feeds them, and folds them, and guards

6 Though sometimes we see the case is not thus ;
Bad shepherds will flee, yet what's that to us ?
The Shepherd that chose us must surely be good,
Who rather than lose us would shed his heart's
blood.]

7 Blest soul that can say, " Christ only I seek."
Wait for him alway; be constant tho' weak ;

The Lord whom thou seekest will not tarry long ;
And to him the weakest is dear as the strong.

805   C.M.

The Robe of Righteousness.—Isa. lxi. 10; Luke xv. 22.

OF all the creatures God has made,
There is but man alone
That stands in need to be arrayed
In coverings not his own.

2 [By nature, bears, and bulls, and swine,
With fowls of every wing,
Are much more warm, more safe, more
fine,
Than man, their fallen king.]

3 Naked and weak, we want a screen ;
But when with clothes we're decked,
Not only lies our shame unseen,
But we command respect.

4 [Can sinful souls, then, stand unclad,
Before God's burning throne,
All bare, or, what is quite as bad,
In coverings of their own ?

5 Rich garments must be worn to grace
The marriage of the Lamb ;
Not nasty rags to foul the place,
Nor nakedness to shame.]

6 Robes of imputed righteousness
Will gain us God's esteem ;
No naked pride, no fig-leaf dress.
How fair soe'er it seem.

7 ['Tis call'd a robe, perhaps to mean
Man has by nature none ;
It grows not native, like our skin,
But is by faith put on.]

8 A sinner clothed in this rich vest,
And garments washed in blood,
Is rendered fit with Christ to feast,
And be the guest of God.

806   7.7.8.7.

Happy Mourners.—Matt. v. 4; John xvi. 22.

CHRIST is the Friend of sinners ;
Be that forgotten never ;
A wounded soul, and not a whole,
Becomes a true believer ;
To see sin smarts but slightly ;
To own, with lip confession,
Is easier still ; but O to feel
Cuts deep beyond expression.

2 [Trust not to joyous fancies,
Light hearts, or smooth behaviour ;
Sinners can say, and none but they,
" How precious is the Saviour ! "
Then hail, ye happy mourners ;
How blest your state to come is !

Ye soon will meet with comfort sweet ;
It is the Lord's own promise.]

3   The contrite heart and broken
    God will not give to ruin ;
This sacrifice he'll not despise,
    For 'tis his Spirit's doing.
Then hail, ye happy mourners,
    Who pass through tribulation ;
Sin's filth and guilt, perceived and felt,
    Make known God's great salvation.

4   [Dry doctrine cannot save us,
    Blind zeal, or false devotion ;
The feeblest prayer, if faith be there,
    Exceeds all empty notion.
Then hail, ye happy mourners,
    Ye will at last be winners ;
By Jesus' blood, the righteous God
    Now reconciles poor sinners.]

PART II.

8.6.8.8.
" Return, thou backsliding Israel."—Jer. iii.12, 14.

Come, ye backsliding sons of God,
    For many such there are,
Who long the paths of sin have trod,
    Come, cast away despair ;
Return to Jesus Christ, and see
There's mercy still for such as we.

2   'Tis true we can't pretend to much
    Of usefulness or fruit ;
But yet the love of Christ is such,
    We still retain the root ;
Returning prodigals shall find,
Though they are base, their Father's kind.

3   The indignation of the Lord
    Awhile we will endure,
For we have sinned against his word ;
    But still his grace is sure ;
'Tis all a gift ; let no man boast ;
For Jesus came to save the lost.

807   8.8.8.

" Love not the world."—1 John ii. 15—17;
Matt. vi. 24.

My brethren, why these anxious fears,
These warm pursuits and eager cares
For earth and all its gilded toys ?
If the whole world you could possess,
It might enchant ; it could not bless ;
False hopes, vain pleasures, and light joys.

2   [Remember, brethren, whose you are ;
Whose cause you own, whose name you bear ;
Is it not His who could not call
His own (though he had all things made)

A place whereon to lay his head—
A servant, though the Lord of all ?

3   If wealth or honour, power or fame,
Can bring you nearer to the Lamb,
    Then follow these with all your might ;
But if they only make you stray,
And draw your hearts from him away,
    Reflect in what you thus delight.]

4   Jesus has said (who surely knew
Much better what we ought to do
    Than we can e'er pretend to see),
" No thought e'en for the morrow take ;
And " He that will not for my sake
    Relinquish all, 's unworthy me."

5   [Let no vain words your souls deceive,
Nor Satan tempt you to believe
    The world and God can hold their parts ;

True Christians long for Christ alone.
The sacrifices God will own,
    Are broken, not divided, hearts.

6   Great things we are not here to crave ;
But if we food and raiment have,
    Should learn to be therewith content.
Into the world we nothing brought,
Nor can we from it carry aught ;
    Then walk the way your Master went.

808   C.M.

For Public Fast or Humiliation.—Joel i. 14 ; ii. 15—17.

Lord, look on all assembled here,
    Who in thy presence stand
To offer up united prayer
    For this our sinful land.

2   [Oft have we each in private prayed
    Our country might find grace ;
Now hear the same petitions made
    In this appointed place.

3   Or, if among us some be met,
    So careless of their sin,
They have not cried for mercy yet,
    Lord, make them now begin.]

4   Thou, by whose death poor sinners live,
    By whom their prayers succeed,
Thy Spirit of supplication give,
    And we shall pray indeed.

5   We will not slack, nor give thee rest,
    But importune thee so
That, till we shall by thee be blest,
    We will not let thee go.

6   Great God of Hosts, deliverance bring ;
    Guide those that hold the helm ;
Support the state, preserve the king,
    And spare the guilty realm.

7 Or, should the dread decree be past,
  And we must feel thy rod,
  May faith and patience hold us fast
  To our correcting God.

8 Whatever be our destined case,
  Accept us in thy Son ;
  Give us his gospel and his grace,
  And then, Thy will be done.

809   C.M.

The Law and Grace.—John i. 17 ; Rom. iii. 31.

Is, then, the law of God untrue,
  Which he by Moses gave ?
No ! but to take it in this view,
  That it has power to save.

2 [Legal obedience were complete,
  Could we the law fulfil ;
But no man ever did so yet,
  And no man ever will.]

3 The law was never meant to give
  New strength to man's lost race ;
We cannot act before we live,
  And life proceeds from grace.

4 But grace and truth by Christ are given ;
  To him must Moses bow ;
Grace fits the new-born soul for heaven,
  And truth informs us how.

5 By Christ we enter into rest,
  And triumph o'er the fall ;
Whoe'er would be completely blest
  Must trust to Christ for all.

810   L.M.

"Condescend to men of low estate."—Rom. xii. 16.

To you who stand in Christ so fast,
  Ye know your faith shall ever last ;

The Lord, on whom that faith depends,
  This kind, important message sends :

2 If light, exulting thoughts arise,
  Your weaker brethren to despise,
  Remember all to me are dear ;
  Who most is favoured most should bear.

3 If strong thyself, support the weak ;
  If well, be tender to the sick ;
  To babes I oft reveal my mind,
  And they who seek my face shall find.

4 If faith be strong as well as true,
  Then strive that love may be so too ;
  Boast not, but meek and lowly be ;
  The humblest soul is most like me.

5 [Should I, displeased, my face but turn,
  Ye sadly would your folly mourn ;
  Who now seemed best would soon be worst ;

I often make the last the first.]

6 Encourage souls that on me wait,
  And stoop to those of low estate.
  Contempt or slight I can't approve ;
  Be love your aim, for I am love.

811   S.M.

Flesh and Spirit.—Rom. vii. 14-25 ; Gal. v. 17-24.

Though void of all that's good,
  And very, very poor,
Through Christ I hope to be renewed,
  And live for evermore.

2 I view my own bad heart,
  And see such evils there,
The sight with horror makes me start,
  And tempts me to despair.

3 Then with a single eye
  I look to Christ alone ;

And on his righteousness rely,
  Though I myself have none.

4 By virtue of his blood,
  The Lord declares me clean.
Now serves my mind the law of God,
  My flesh the law of sin.

812, 13   C.M.

Jesus my Guide.—Ps. lxxiii. 24 ; 2 Cor. v. 7.

Whene'er I make some sudden stop—
  For many such I make—
And cannot see the cloud cleared up
  Nor know which path to take,

2 I to my Saviour speed my way,
  To tell my dubious state ;
Then listen what the Lord will say,
  And hope to follow that.

3 If Jesus seem to hide his face,
  What anxious fears I feel !
But if he deign to whisper peace,
  I'm happy ! all is well.

4 Confirmed by one soft, secret word,
  I seek no farther light ;
But walk, depending on my Lord,
  By faith, and not by sight.

5 Of friends and counsellors bereft,
  I often hear him say,
" Decline not to the right or left ;
  Go on ; lo ! here's the way."

6 Weak in myself, in him I'm strong ;
  His Spirit's voice I hear.
The way I walk cannot be wrong,
  If Jesus be but there.

7 [He is my Helper and my Guide ;
　　I trust in him alone ;
　No other helps have I beside ;
　　I venture all on One.]

814　　　　　P.M.
A General Admonition.—Heb. xiii. 22; Matt. vi. 19-21.

　BRETHREN, why toil ye thus for toys,
　　And reckon trash for treasure ?
　Call gay deceptions solid joys,
　　Intoxication pleasure ?

2 If more refined amusements please,
　　As knowledge, arts, or learning,
　A moment puts an end to these,
　　And sometimes short's the warning.

3 What balm could wretches ever find
　　In wit to heal affliction ?
　Or who can cure a troubled mind
　　With all the pomp of diction ?

4 Reflect what trifles ye pursue,
　　So anxious and so heedful ;
　For, after all, you'll find it true,
　　There is but one thing needful.

5 God in his Scriptures to reveal
　　His will has condescended ;
　What there is said he will fulfil,
　　Though man may be offended.

6 This written word with reverence treat ;
　　Join prayer with each inspection ;
　And be not wise in self-conceit ;
　　'Tis folly to perfection.

7 True wisdom, of celestial birth,
　　Can both instruct and cherish ;
　Other attainments are of earth,
　　And all that's earth must perish.

8 The chief concern of fall'n mankind
　　Should be to enjoy God's favour ;
　What safety can a sinner find
　　Before he finds a Saviour ?

9 This Saviour must be one that can
　　From sin and death release us,
　Make up the breach 'twixt God and man ;
　　Which none can do but Jesus.

10 Jesus is Judge of quick and dead ;
　　And there is none beside him,
　Whether his power we slight or dread,
　　Adore him or deride him.

11 Whate'er we judge ourselves, we must
　　Or stand or fall by *his* doom ;
　And they that in this Jesus trust,
　　Have found eternal wisdom.

12 Mercy and love, from Jesus felt,

Can heal a wounded spirit ;
Mercy that triumphs over guilt,
　And love that seeks no merit.

815　　　　　L.M.
An End of Sin.—Dan. ix. 24 ; John xix. 18-30.

JESUS, when on the bloody tree
He hung, through soul and body pierced,
That all things might accomplished be
Contained in Scripture, said, " I thirst."

2 Hyssop, the plant ordained by God,
　And held by Jews in high esteem,
　Which sprinkled them with paschal blood,
　Sharp vinegar conveyed to him.

3 This done, our dear, our dying Lord
　Exerts his short, expiring breath ;
　Utters this rich, important word,
　" 'Tis finished ! " and submits to death.

4 Henceforth an end is put to sin
　(The important word implies not less).
　Now for believers is brought in
　An everlasting righteousness.

5 The Son of God and man, has died,
　Sinners as black as hell to save ;
　And, that they might be justified,
　Is risen victorious from the grave.

6 In heaven he lives, our King, our Priest ;
　There for his people ever pleads :
　How sure is our salvation !　Christ
　Died, rose, ascended, intercedes.

816　　　　　C.M.
" And ye are complete in him."—Col. ii. 10; Gal. v. 6.

WHEN is it Christians all agree,
　And let distinctions fall ?
When, nothing in themselves, they see
　That Christ is all in all.

2 But strife and difference will subsist
　While men will something seem ;
　Let them but singly look to Christ
　And all are one in him.

3 The infant and the aged saint,
　The worker and the weak,
　They who are strong and seldom faint,
　And they who scarce can speak.

4 Eternal life's the gift of God ;
　It comes through Christ alone ;
　'Tis his, he bought it with his blood ;
　And therefore gives his own.

5 We have no life, no power, no faith,
　But what by Christ is given ;
　We all deserve eternal death,
　And thus we are all even.

817   148th.
The Author's Confession, &c.—Gen. xxvii. 20.
AND now the work is done,
Without much pains or cost ;
The author's merit's none,
And therefore none his boast ;
He only claims whate'er's amiss ;
Alas ! how large a share is his !

2   Some time it took to beat
And hunt for tinkling sound ;
But the rich savoury meat
Was very quickly found ;
For every truly Christian thought
Was by the God of Isaac brought.

3   May he that sings or reads
That precious blessing know
That comes by Jacob's kids,
And not from Esau's bow.
O bring no price ! God's grace is free
To Paul, to Magdalene, to me !

4   Glory to God alone
(Let man forbear to boast),
To Father, and to Son,
And to the Holy Ghost :
Eternal life's the gift of God ;
The Lamb procured it by his blood.

818, 19   C.M.
For the Lord's Supper.—Prov. ix. 1—5 ; Luke xxii. 19.
THE King of heaven a feast has made,
And to his much-loved friends,
The faint, the famished, and the sad,
This invitation sends :

2 " Beggars, approach my royal board,
Furnished with all that's good ;
Come, sit at table with your Lord,
And eat celestial food.

3 " My body and my blood receive,
It comes entirely free ;
I ask no price for all I give,
But O remember *Me !* "

4 Lo, at thy gracious bidding, Lord,
Though vile and base, we come ;
O speak the reconciling word,
And welcome wanderers home.

5 [Rich wine, and milk, and heavenly meat,
We come to buy and live ;
Since nothing is the price that's set,
And we have nought to give.]

6 Impart to all thy flock below
The blessings of thy death.
On every begging soul bestow
Thy love, thy hope, thy faith.

7 May each, with strength from heaven endued,
Say, " My Beloved's mine :
I eat his flesh, and drink his blood,
In signs of bread and wine."

820   S.M.
The broken body & blood-shedding of Christ.-Mark xiv.
GLORY to God on high !
Our peace is made with heaven ;
The Son of God came down to die,
That sin might be forgiven.

2   His precious blood was shed,
His body bruised for sin ;
Remember this in eating bread,
And that in drinking wine.

3   Approach his royal board,
In his rich garments clad ;
Join, every tongue, to praise the Lord,
And every heart be glad.

4   [The Father gives the Son ;
The Son his flesh and blood ;
The Spirit applies, and faith puts on,
The righteousness of God.]

5   Sinners the gift receive,
And each says, " I am chief ;
Thou know'st, O Lord, I would believe ;
O help my unbelief ! "

6   Lord, help us from above ;
The power is all thy own ;
Faith is thy gift, and hope, and love,
For of ourselves we've none.

821   C.M.
Wonderful Love.—Heb. x. 19, 20 ; John iii. 16 ; xvi. 27.
FATHER of heaven, almighty King,
How wondrous is thy love,
That worms of dust thy praise should sing,
And thou their songs approve !

2 [Since by a new and living Way
Access to thee is given,
Poor sinners may with boldness pray,
And earth converse with heaven.]

3 Give each some token, Lord, for good,
And send the Spirit down,
To feed us with celestial food,
The body of thy Son.

4 The feast thou hast been pleased to make
We would by faith receive,
That all that come their part may take,
And all that take may live.

5 Let every tongue the Father own,
Who, when we all were lost,

To seek and save us sent the Son,
 And gives the Holy Ghost.

822   C.M.
" Drink ye all of it."—Matt. xxvi. 27 ; John vi. 54, 56.

THE blest memorials of thy grief,
 Thy sufferings, and thy death,
We come, dear Saviour, to receive ;
 But would receive with faith.

2 The tokens sent us to relieve
 Our spirits when they droop,
We come, dear Saviour, to receive ;
 But would receive with hope.

3 The pledges thou wast pleased to leave,
 Our mournful minds to move,
We come, dear Saviour, to receive ;
 But would receive with love.

4 Here, in obedience to thy word,
 We take the bread and wine,
The utmost we can do, dear Lord,
 For all beyond is thine.

5 Increase our faith, and hope, and love ;
 Lord, give us all that's good ;
We would thy full salvation prove,
 And share thy flesh and blood.

823   7.6.8.
" In remembrance of Me."—1 Cor. xi. 23-25.

HAIL, thou Bridegroom, bruised to death,
 Who hast the wine-press trod
Of the Almighty's burning wrath !
 Hail, slaughtered Lamb of God ;
Melt our hearts with love like thine,
While we behold thee on the tree,
 Sweetly mourning o'er each sign,
  In memory of thee.

2 Hail, thou mighty Saviour, blest
 Before the world began
In the eternal Father's breast,
 Hail, Son of God and man !
Thee we hymn in humble strains ;
And to receive we now agree,
 These blest symbols of thy pains,
  In memory of thee.

3 Break, O break these hearts of stone.
 By some endearing word.
Jesus, come ! May every one
 Behold his suffering Lord.
The Holy Ghost into us breathe ;
Help us to take, from doubtings free,
 These dear tokens of thy death
  In memory of thee.

4 [Thou, our great Melchisedec,
 Bring'st forth thy bread and wine ;

Thou hast wrought out, for our sake,
 A righteousness divine.
Send thy blessing from above,
When worms partake, such worms as we,
 These rich pledges of thy love,
  In memory of thee.]

824   L.M.
" Reproach hath broken my heart."—Ps. lxix. 20.

O THAT our flinty hearts could melt,
While to remembrance, Lord, we call
Part of that weight which thou hast felt ;
For who can comprehend it all ?

2 Ye sinners, while these symbols dear
Present your suffering Lord to view,
Drop the soft tribute of a tear,
For he shed many a tear for you.

3 In the sad garden, on the wood,
His body bruised, from every part
Poured on the ground a purple flood,
Till sorrow broke his tender heart.

4 Lord, while we thus show forth thy death,
O send thy Spirit from above ;
Help us to feed on thee by faith,
And sigh, and sing, and mourn, and love.

825   S.M.
" Evermore give us this Bread."—John vi. 34, 51-58.

LORD, send thy Spirit down
 On babes that long to learn ;
Open our eyes, and make us wise,
 Thy body to discern.

2 'Tis by thy word we live,
 And not by bread alone ;
The word of truth from thy blest mouth,
 O make it clearly known.

3 With what we have received
 Impart thy quickening power ;
We would be fed with living bread,
 And live for evermore.

826   8.7.
" God's Goodness for the Poor."—Ps. lxviii. 10.

O HOW good our gracious God is !
 What rich feasts does he provide !
Bread and wine to feed our bodies ;
 But much more is signified :
All his sheep (amazing wonder !)
 Feeds he with his flesh and blood ;
Where's the power can ever sunder
 Souls united thus to God ?

2 When we take the sacred symbols
 Of his body, bread and wine :

While the heart relents and trembles,
　We rejoice with joy divine ;
Jesus makes the weakest able,
　Feeds us with his flesh and blood ;
Needy beggars at his table
　Are the welcome guests of God.

3 Cease thy fears, then, weak believer ;
　Jesus Christ is still the same,
Yesterday, to-day, for ever,
　Saviour is his unctuous name ;
Lowliness of heart, and meekness
　To the bleeding Lamb belong ;
Trust to him, and by thy weakness
　Thou shalt prove that Christ is strong.

827　　　　7.6.
"And shall mourn for him."—Zech. xii. 10.
SUFFERING Saviour, Lamb of God,
　How hast thou been used ?
With the Almighty's wrathful rod
　Soul and body bruised !

2 We, for whom thou once wast slain,
　We, whose sins did pierce thee,
Now commemorate thy pain,
　And implore thy mercy.

3 We would with thee sympathise
　In thy bitter passion ;
With soft hearts and weeping eyes
　See thy great salvation.

4 [Thine's an everlasting love ;
　We have dearly tried thee ;
Whom have we in heaven above,
　Whom on earth beside thee ?

5 What can helpless sinners do
　When temptations seize us ?
Nought have we to look unto
　But the blood of Jesus.]

6 Pardon all our baseness, Lord ;
　All our weakness pity ;
Guide us safely by thy word
　To the heavenly city.

7 O sustain us on the road
　Through this desert dreary ;
Feed us with thy flesh and blood
　When we're faint and weary.

8 Bid us call to mind thy cross,
　Our hard hearts to soften ;
Often, Saviour, feast us thus,
　For we need it often.

828　　　　C.M.
He that eateth this bread shall live for ever.—Jn. vi. 50.
THE tender mercies of the Lord
　On those that fear his name,

For every thankful tongue afford
　An everlasting theme.

2 [He pities all that feel his fear,
　When wounded, pained or weak ;
As tender mothers grieve to hear
　Their infants moan when sick.]

3 He to the needy and the faint
　His mighty aid makes known ;
And, when their languid life is spent,
　Supplies it with his own.

4 The body in his bounty shares,
　Sustained with corn and wine ;
But for the soul himself prepares
　A banquet more divine.

5 By faith received, his flesh and blood
　Shall life eternal give ;
For he that eats immortal food,
　Immortally must live.

829　　　　C.M.
"He gave himself for me."—Gal. ii. 20 ; Luke xxii. 19.
THAT doleful night before his death,
　The Lamb, for sinners slain,
Did almost with his latest breath
　This solemn feast ordain.

2 To keep thy feast, Lord, are we met,
　And to remember thee ;
Help each poor trembler to repeat,
　"For me he died, for me."

3 Thy sufferings, Lord, each sacred sign
　To our remembrance brings ;
We eat the bread and drink the wine,
　But think on nobler things.

4 O tune our tongues, and set in frame
　Each heart that pants to thee,
To sing, "Hosanna to the Lamb,
　The Lamb that died for me ! "

830　　　　7s.
"Show the Lord's death till he come."—1 Cor. xi. 26.
JESUS, once for sinners slain,
　From the dead was raised again,
And in heaven is now set down
　With his Father in his throne.

2 There he reigns a King supreme ;
　We shall also reign with him ;
Feeble souls, be not dismayed ;
　Trust in his almighty aid.

3 He has made an end of sin,
　And his blood has washed us clean ;
Fear not, he is ever near ;
　Now, e'en now, he's with us here.

4 Thus assembling, we, by faith,
Till he come, show forth his death ;
Of his body bread's the sign,
And we drink his blood in wine.

5 Bread, thus broken, aptly shows
How his body God did bruise ;
When the grape's rich blood we see,
Lord, we then remember thee.

6 [Saints on earth, with saints above,
Celebrate his dying love,
And let every ransomed soul
Sound his praise from pole to pole.]

831 S.M.
"The Free Feast."—Isa. lv. 1, 2 ; Luke i. 53.
THE God that first us chose,
The eternal Father, praise ;
What wondrous bounties he bestows ;
And by what wondrous ways !

2 His creatures all are filled
By him with proper food ;
But O ! he gives to every child
His Son's own flesh and blood.

3 Here hungry souls appear,
And eat celestial bread ;
The needy beggar banquets here,
With royal dainties fed.

4 Here thirsty souls approach,
And drink immortal wine :
The entertainment is for such,
Prepared by grace divine.

5 [God bids us bring no price ;
The feast is furnished free ;
His bounteous hand the poor supplies,
And who more poor than we ?

6 His Spirit from above
The Father sends us down,
And looks with everlasting love
On all that love the Son.]

832 S.M.
The Fear of the Lord.—Ecc. viii. 12 ; Ps. xxv. 14.
THE men that fear the Lord,
In every state are blest ;
The Lord will grant whate'er they want ;
Their souls shall dwell at rest.

2 [His secrets they shall share,
His covenant shall learn ;
Guided by grace, shall walk his ways,
And heavenly truths discern.]

3 [He pities all their griefs ;
When sinking, makes them swim ;

He dries their tears, relieves their fears,
And bids them trust in him.]

4 In his remembrance-book
The Saviour sets them down,
Accounting each a jewel rich,
And calls them all his own.

5 This fear's the spirit of faith,
A confidence that's strong ;
An unctuous light to all that's right,
A bar to all that's wrong.

6 It gives religion life
To warm, as well as light ;
Makes mercy sweet, salvation great,
And all God's judgments right.

833 S.M.
"I will sing of mercy and judgment."—Ps. ci. 1.
THY mercy, Lord, we praise ;
Of judgment too we sing ;

For all the riches of thy grace
Our grateful tribute bring.

2 Mercy may justly claim
A sinner's thankful voice ;
And judgment joining in the theme,
We tremble and rejoice.

3 Thy mercies bid us trust ;
Thy judgments strike with awe ;
We fear the last, we bless the first,
And love thy righteous law.

4 Who can thy acts express,
Or trace thy wondrous ways ?
How glorious is thy holiness ;
How terrible thy praise !

5 Thy goodness how immense
To those that fear thy name !
Thy love surpasses thought or sense,
And always is the same.

6 Thy judgments are too deep
For reason's line to sound.
Thy tender mercies to thy sheep
No bottom know, nor bound.

834 C.M.
Praise for Creation and Redemption.—Ps. ciii. 22.
WHILE heavenly hosts their anthems sing,
In realms above the sky,
Let worms of earth their tribute bring,
And laud the Lord most high.

2 In thankful notes your voices raise,
Ye ransomed of the Lord ;
And sing the eternal Father's praise,
The God by all adored.

3 All creatures to his bounty owe
　Their being and their breath ;
　But greatest gratitude should flow
　In men redeemed from death.

4 His only Son he deigned to give ;
　What love this gift declares !
　And all that in the Son believe,
　Eternal life is theirs.

835 112th.
Desertion.—Ps. xxv. 16, 17; lxix. 1. 2; cxliii. 4.

DEEP in a cold, a joyless cell,
A doleful gulf of gloomy care,
Where dismal doubts and darkness dwell,
The dangerous brink of black despair ;
Chilled by the icy damps of death,
I feel no firm support of faith.

2 [How can a burdened cripple rise ?
How can a fettered captive flee ?
Ah ! Lord, direct my wishful eyes,
And let me look, at least, to thee.
Alas ! my sinking spirits droop ;
I scarce perceive a glimpse of hope.]

3 Extend thy mercy, gracious God ;
Thy quickening Spirit vouchsafe to send ;
Apply the reconciling blood,
And kindly call thy foe thy friend ;
Or, if rich cordials thou deny,
Let patience comfort's place supply.

4 Let hope survive, though damped by doubt;
Do thou defend my battered shield ;
O let me never quite give out ;
Help me to keep the bloody field ;
Lord, look upon the unequal strife ;
Delay not, lest I lose my life.

836 L.M.
Christ's Resurrection.—Matt. xxviii. 6; Eph. i. 20-22.

BELIEVER, lift thy drooping head ;
Thy Saviour has the victory gained ;
See all thy foes in triumph led,
And everlasting life obtained.

2 God from the grave has raised his Son :
The powers of darkness are despoiled ;
Justice declares the work is done,
And God and man are reconciled.

3 Lo ! the Redeemer leaves the tomb ;
See the triumphant Hero rise !
His mighty arms their strength resume,
And conquest sparkles in his eyes.

4 Death his death's wound has now received ;
An end of sin's entirely made ;
Prisoners of hope are quite reprieved,
And all the dreadful debt is paid.

837 L.M.
" Repent ye, and believe the Gospel."—Mark i. 15.

REPENT, awakened souls, repent ;
Hear the good tidings God has sent,
Of sinners saved, and sins forgiven,
And beggars raised to reign in heaven.

2 God sent his Son to die for us,
Die to redeem us from the curse ;
He took our weakness, bore our load,
And dearly bought us with his blood.

3 In guilt's dark dungeon when we lay,
Mercy cried, " Spare ; " and Justice, " Slay."
But Jesus answered, " Set them free,
And pardon them and punish me."

4 Salvation is of God alone ;
Life everlasting in his Son ;
And he that gave his Son to bleed,
Will freely give us all we need.

5 Believe the gospel, and rejoice ;
Sing to the Lord with cheerful voice ;
His goodness praise, his wonders tell,
Who ransomed our poor souls from hell.

838, to 41 L.M.
Sickness.—Isa. xxxviii. 12; Job vii. 3-5; Ps. cii. 4-5.

LORD, hear a restless wretch's groans ;
To thee my soul in secret moans :
My body's weak, my heart's unclean ;
I pine with sickness and with sin.

2 My strength decays, my spirits droop ;
Bowed down with guilt, I can't look up ;
I lose my life, I lose my soul,
Except thy mercy make me whole.

3 Sin's rankling sores my soul corrode ;
O heal them with thy balmy blood !
And, if thou dost my health restore,
Lord, let me ne'er offend thee more.

4 Or, if I never more must rise,
But death's cold hand must close my eyes,
Pardon my sins, and take me home ;
O come, Lord Jesus, quickly come !

842 S.M.
" Sorrow not."—1 Thess. iv. 13, 14; 2 Sam. xii. 19-23.

THE spirits of the just,
　Confined in bodies, groan,
Till death consigns the corpse to dust,
　And then the conflict's done.

2 Jesus, who came to save,
　The Lamb for sinners slain,
Perfumed the chambers of the grave,
　And made e'en death our gain.

3   Why fear we, then, to trust
     The place where Jesus lay ?
  In quiet rests our *brother's* dust,
     And thus it seems to say :

4   " Forbear, my friends, to weep,
     Since death has lost its sting ;
  Those Christians that in Jesus sleep,
     Our God will with him bring."

5   This message, then, receive,
     And grief indulge no more ;
  Return to pray awhile ; believe,
     And wait the welcome hour.

843   7.6.8.
At the Interment of a Believer.—Job xix. 26

CHRISTIANS, view this solemn scene,
  And if your souls be sad,
Look beyond the cloud between,
  And let your hearts be glad.
Never from your memory lose
The resurrection of the just.
  Death's a blessing now to those
    Who in our Jesus trust.

2   Deep interred in earth's dark womb
    The mouldering body lies ;
  But the Christian from the tomb
    Shall soon triumphant rise.
  Jesus Christ, the righteous Judge,
  For all his people's sins was slain ;
  Give the Saviour, without grudge,
    The purchase of his pain.

3   Now, the grave's a downy bed,
    Embroidered round with blood ;
  Say not the believer's dead,
    He only rests in God.

  Lord, we long to be at home,
  Lay down our heads, and sleep in thee ;
  Come, Lord Jesus, quickly come,
    And set thy prisoners free.

844   L.M.
At the Interment of a Believer.—Hos. xiii. 14.

FOUNTAIN of life, who gavest us breath,
Eternal Sire, by all adored ;
Who makest us conquerors over death,
Through Jesus, our victorious Lord,

2 We give thee thanks, we sing thy praise,
For calling thus thy children home ;
And shortening tribulation days
To hide them in the peaceful tomb.

3 Jesus, confiding in thy name,
Thou King of saints, thy body's Head,
We give to earth the breathless frame,
Remembering thou thyself wast dead.

4 Thine was a bitter death indeed,
Thou harmless, suffering Lamb of God !
Thou hast from hell thy people freed,
And drowned destruction in thy blood.

845, 6   C.M.
The Resurrection.—1 Cor. xv. 36-44 ; Acts xxiv. 15.

THE praise of Christ, ye Christians, sound ;
  His mighty acts be told ;
Death has received a deadly wound ;
  He takes, but cannot hold.

2 [Clipt are the greedy vulture's claws ;
  No more we dread his power ;
He gapes with adamantine jaws,
  And grins, but can't devour.]

3 Believers in their darksome graves
  Shall start, to light restored ;

  Forsake their monumental caves,
    And mount to meet the Lord.

4 Not long in ground the dying grain
  Is hid, or lies forlorn ;
But soon revives, and springs again,
  And comes to standing corn.

5 So, waking from the womb of earth,
  Where Christ has lain before,
And bursting to a better birth,
  We rise to die no more.

6 The wicked, too, shall rise again,
  The difference will be this :
They rise to everlasting pain,
  And saints to endless bliss.

847, 8, 9   S.M.
The Day of Judgment.—2 Cor. v. 10 ; Mark xiii. 33.

BEHOLD ! with awful pomp
  The Judge prepares to come ;
The archangel sounds the dreadful trump,
  And wakes the general doom.

2   Nature, in wild amaze,
    Her dissolution mourns ;
Blushes of blood the moon deface ;
    The sun to darkness turns.

3   The living look with dread ;
    The frighted dead arise,
Start from the monumental bed,
    And lift their ghastly eyes.

4   Horrors all hearts appal ;
    They quake, they shriek, they cry ;
Bid rocks and mountains on them fall,
    But rocks and mountains fly.

5   Great God, in whom we live,
    Prepare us for that day ;

Help us in Jesus to believe,
To watch, and wait, and pray.

850   C.M.

Heaven.—Rev. vii. 15-17; 2 Cor. v. 1; Heb. vi. 20.

YE souls that trust in Christ, rejoice ;
Your sins are all forgiven ;
Let every Christian lift his voice,
And sing the joys of heaven.

2 Heaven is that holy, happy place,
Where sin no more defiles ;
Where God unveils his blissful face,
And looks, and loves, and smiles ;

3 [Where Jesus, Son of man and God,
Triumphant from his wars,
Walks in rich garments, dipped in blood,
And shows his glorious scars ;]

4 [Where ransomed sinners sound God's praise
The angelic host among ;
Sing the rich wonders of his grace,
And Jesus leads the song ;]

5 [Where saints are free from every load
Of passions, or of pains ;
God dwells in them, and they in God ;
And love for ever reigns.]

6 Lord, as thou show'st thy glory there,
Make known thy grace to us ;
And heaven will not be wanting here
While we can hymn thee thus :

7 Jesus, our dear Redeemer, died
That we might be forgiven ;
Rose that we might be justified,
And sends the Spirit from heaven.

851   C.M.

Good Works.—Jas. ii. 17; Gal. v. 6; 1 John iii. 7.

WHEN filthy passions or unjust
Professors' minds control ;
When men give up the reins to lust,
And interest sways the whole ;

2 Or when they seek themselves to please,
Decline each thorny road,
Indulge their sloth, consult their ease,
And slight the fear of God ;

3 The faith is vain such men profess ;
It comes not from above ;
The righteous man does righteousness,
And true faith works by love.

4 [Men's actions with their minds will suit :
By them the heart is viewed ;
A tree that bears corrupted fruit,
Cannot be called good.]

5 The Christian seeks his brother's good,
Sometimes beyond his own ;
Or, if self-interest will intrude,
It does not reign alone.

6 Help us, dear Lord, to honour thee ;
Let our good works abound ;
Thou art that green, that fruitful tree ;
From thee our fruit is found.

852   S.M.

"Faith without works is dead."—Jas. ii. 20-26.

VAIN man, to boast forbear,
The knowledge in thy head ;
The sacred Scriptures this declare :
"Faith without works is dead."

2 When Christ the Judge shall come
To render each his due,
He'll deal thy deeds their righteous doom,
And set thy works in view.

3 Food to the hungry give ;
Give to the thirsty drink ;
To follow Christ is to believe ;
Dead faith is but to think.

4 The man that loves the Lord
Will mind whate'er he bid ;
Will pay regard to all his word,
And do as Jesus did.

5 [The dead professor counts
Good works as legal ties ;
His faith to action seldom mounts ;
On doctrine he relies.

6 But words engender strife :
Behold the gospel plan :
Trust in the Lord alone for life,
And do what good you can.]

853   P.M.

"Believe only."—Luke viii. 50; John vi. 29.

ZEAL extinguished to a spark ;
Life is very, very low ;
All my evidences dark,
And good works I've none to show.
Prayer, too, seems a load ;
Ordinances tease or tire ;
I can feel no love to God ;
Hardly have a good desire.

2 Though thy fainting spirits droop,
Yet thy God is with thee still.
To believe in hope 'gainst hope,
And against thee all things feel ;
Only to believe,
'Midst thy coldness, doubts, and death,

Canst thou not, poor soul, perceive
This is now thy work of faith ?

854 7.6.8.
Christ is holy.—Ps. xxii. 3; Rev. iv. 8; Isa. vi. 3.

JESUS, Lord of life and peace,
  To thee we lift our voice ;
Teach us at thy holiness
  To tremble and rejoice.
Sweet and terrible's thy word ;
Thou and thy word are both the same.
Holy, holy, holy Lord,
  We love thy holy name.

2 Burning seraphs round thy throne,
    Beyond all brightness bright,
  Bow their bashful heads, and own
    Their own diminished light.
  Worthy thou to be adored,
  Lord God Almighty, great I AM !
  Holy, holy, holy Lord, &c.

3 Saints, in whom thy Spirit dwells,
    Pour out their souls to thee ;
  Each his tale in secret tells,
    And sighs to be set free.
  Christ admired, themselves abhorred,
  They cry with awe, delight, and shame,
  Holy, holy, holy Lord, &c.

4 [Men whose hearts admit not fear,
    At thy perfections awed,
  Use thy name, but not revere
    The holy child of God ;
  These thy kingdom own in word ;
  Save us from loyalty so lame.
  Holy, holy, holy Lord, &c.

5 Just and righteous is our King ;
    Glorious in holiness ;
  Though we tremble while we sing,
    We would not wish it less.
  Souls by whom the truth's explored
  Wonders of mercy best proclaim.
  Holy, holy, holy Lord, &c.]

855 C.M.
The holy Trinity.—Isa. lvii. 15; 1 Pet. i. 16.

GOD is a high and holy God,
  Eternally the same ;
Holiness is his blest abode,
  And holy is his name.

2 The holy Father, Holy Ghost,
  Men readily will own ;
But 'tis a blessing few can boast,
  To know the holy Son.

3 [With hearts of flint, and fronts of brass,
  Some talk of Christ their Head ;
And make the living Lord, alas !
  Companion with the dead.

4 Familiar freedom, luscious names,
  To Christ some fondly use ;
Visions of wonder, flashy frames,
  Are others' utmost views.

5 By things like these men often run
  To this or that extreme ;
But that man truly knows the Son
  Who loves to live like him.]

6 Lord, help us by thy mighty power
  To gain our constant view ;
Which is, that we may know thee more,
  And more resemble too.

856 C.M.
" Worthy is the Lamb that was slain."—Rev. v. 6-12.

WE sing thy praise, exalted Lamb,
  Who sitt'st upon thy throne ;
Ten thousand blessings on thy name,
  Who worthy art alone.

2 Thy bruised, broken body bore
  Our sins upon the tree ;
And now thou liv'st for evermore,
  And now we live through thee.

3 Poor sinners, sing the Lamb that died ;
  What theme can sound so sweet ?
His drooping head, his streaming side,
  His pierced hands and feet ;

4 With all that scene of suffering love
  Which faith presents to view :
For now he lives and reigns above,
  And lives and reigns for you.

5 [Was ever grace, Lord, rich as thine ?
  Can aught be with it named ?
What powerful beams of love divine
  Thy tender heart inflamed !]

6 Ye angels, hymn his glorious name,
  Who loved and conquered thus ;
And we will likewise laud the Lamb,
  For he was slain for us.

857 7s.
Praising Christ.—Rev. i. 5, 6; 1 Tim. vi. 16.

JESUS Christ, God's holy Lamb,
We will laud thy lovely name ;
We were saved by God's decree,
And our debt was paid by thee.

2 Thou hast washed us in thy blood,
  Made us kings and priests to God ;
  Take this tribute of the poor ;
  Less we can't, we can't give more.

3 Souls redeemed, your voices raise,
  Sing your dear Redeemer's praise ;
  Worthy thou of love and laud,
  King of saints, incarnate God.

4 Righteous are thy ways, and true ;
  Endless honours are thy due ;
  Grace and glory in thee shine ;
  Matchless mercy, love divine.

5 We for whom thou once wast slain,
  We thy ransomed sinner-train,
  In this one request agree,
  " Make us more resemble thee."

858, 9 L.M.
" Return, thou backsliding Israel."—Jer. iii. 12, 14, 22.

BACKSLIDING souls, return to God ;
  Your faithful God is gracious still ;
  Leave the false ways ye long have trod,
  For God will your backslidings heal.

2 Your first espousals call to mind ;
  'Tis time ye should be now reclaimed.
  What fruit could ever Christians find
  In things whereof they're now ashamed ?

3 The indignation of the Lord
  Awhile endure, for 'tis your due ;
  But firm and steadfast stands his word ;
  Though you are faithless, he is true.

4 The blood of Christ, a precious blood !
  Cleanses from all sin, doubt it not,
  And reconciles the soul to God,
  From every folly, every fault.

860 C.M.
" Pardon my iniquity, for it is great."—Ps. xxv. 11.

FROM poisonous errors, pleasing cheats,
  And gilded baits of sin,
  Which, swallowed as delicious meats,
  Infect and rot within ;

2 Lord, pardon a backslider base,
  Returning from the dead ;
  Ashamed to show his shameful face,
  Or lift his guilty head.

3 Ah ! what a fool have I been made !
  Or rather made myself ;
  That mariner's mad part I played,
  That sees, yet strikes the shelf.

4 How weak must be this wicked heart,
  Which, boasting much to know,
  Made light of all thy bitter smart
  And wantoned with thy woe !

5 Monstrous ingratitude I own,
  Well worthy wrath divine ;
  Can blood such horrid crimes atone ?
  Yes, blood so rich as thine.

6 Then, since thy mercy makes me melt,
  My baseness I deplore ;
  Regard the grief and shame I've felt,
  And daily make them more.

861 C.M.
Salvation to the Lamb.—Rev. vii. 10; Jer. iii. 23.

POOR sinner, come, cast off thy fear,
  And raise thy drooping head ;
  Come, sing with all poor sinners here,
  Jesus, who once was dead.

2 Salvation sing, no word more meet
  To join to Jesus' name ;
  Let every thankful tongue repeat,
  " Salvation to the Lamb."

3 Saints, from the garden to the cross,
  Your conquering Lord pursue,
  Who, dearly to redeem your loss,
  Groaned, bled, and died for you.

4 Now reigns victorious over death
  The glorious great I AM ;
  Let every soul repeat with faith,
  " Salvation to the Lamb."

5 When we incurred the wrath of God—
  Alas ! what could we worse ?
  He came, and, with his own heart's blood,
  Redeemed us from the curse.

6 This paschal Lamb, our heavenly meat,
  Was roasted in the flame ;
  Repeat, ye ransomed souls, repeat,
  " Salvation to the Lamb."

862 C.M.
Baptism.—Rom. vi. 3, 4 ; Acts x. 47.

FATHER of heaven, we thee address ;
  Obedience is our view ;
  Accept us in thy Son, and bless
  The work we have to do.

2 Jesus, as water well applied
  Will make the body clean,
  So in the fountain of thy side
  Wash thou the soul from sin.

3 Celestial Dove, descend from high,
  And on the water brood ;
  And with thy quickening power apply
  The water and the blood.

4 Great God, Three-One, again we call,
  And our requests renew ;

Accept in Christ, and bless withal
The work we've now to do.

863 S.M.
Baptism.—1 Pet. iii. 21; Gal. iii. 27.

BY what amazing ways
The Lord vouchsafes to explain
The wonders of his sovereign grace
Towards the sons of men !

2 He shows us first how foul
Our nature's made by sin ;
Then teaches the believing soul
The way to make it clean.

3 Our baptism first declares
What need we've all to cleanse ;
Then shows that Christ to all God's heirs
Can purity dispense.

4 Water the body laves ;
And, if 'tis done by faith,
The blood of Jesus surely saves
The sinful soul from death.

5 Water no man denies ;
But, brethren, rest not there ;
'Tis faith in Christ that justifies,
And makes the conscience clear.

6 Baptized into his death,
We rise to life divine ;
The Holy Spirit works the faith,
And water is the sign.

864 8.7.
At Recommending a Minister.—1 Cor. iii. 21-23.

HOLY Ghost, inspire our praises,
Touch our hearts, and tune our tongues ;
While we laud the name of Jesus,
Heaven will gladly share our songs.

Hosts of angels, bright and glorious,
While we hymn our common King,
Will be proud to join the chorus ;
And the Lord himself shall sing.

2 Raise we, then, our cheerful voices
To our God, who, full of grace,
In our happiness rejoices,
And delights to hear his praise.
Whoso lives upon his promise,
Eats his flesh and drinks his blood ;
All that's past, and all to come, is
For that soul's eternal good.

3 [Happy soul, that hears and follows
Jesus speaking in his word !
Paul, and Cephas, and Apollos,
All are his in Christ the Lord.
Every state, howe'er distressing,

Shall be profit in the end ;
Every ordinance a blessing,
Every providence a friend.]

4 [Christian, dost thou want a teacher,
Helper, counsellor, or guide ?
Wouldst thou find a proper preacher ?
Ask thy God, for he'll provide.
Build on no man's parts or merit,
But behold the gospel plan ;
Jesus sends his Holy Spirit,
And the Spirit sends the man.]

5 [Bless, dear Lord, each labouring servant ;
Bless the work they undertake ;
Make them able, faithful, fervent ;
Bless them, for thy church's sake.
All things for our good are given ;
Comforts, crosses, staffs, or rods ;

All is ours in earth and heaven ;
We are Christ's, and Christ is God's.]

865 7.6.
At Dismission.—Mark iv. 20; John iv. 36.

GUARDIAN of thy helpless sheep,
Jesus, almighty Lord,
Help our heedful hearts to keep
The treasure of thy word ;
Let not Satan steal what's sown ;
Bid it bring forth precious fruit ;
Thou canst soften hearts of stone,
And make thy word take root.

866 ?.6.8.
At Dismission.—1 Cor. iii. 6; 2 Thess. iii. 5.

FATHER, ere we hence depart,
Send thy good Spirit down,
To reside in every heart,
And bless the seed that's sown ;
Fountain of eternal love,
Thou freely gavest thy Son to die ;
Send thy Spirit from above,
To quicken and apply.

867 C.M.
Praise to the Trinity.—Isa. xlii. 10-12; Ps. cl. 6.

O PRAISE the Lord, ye heavenly hosts !
The same on earth be done ;
Praise Father, Son, and Holy Ghost,
The great, the good Three-One.

868 L.M.
Praise to the Trinity.—Ps. cxlviii. 7-11; cxvii. 1.

To the great Godhead, Father, Son,
And Holy Spirit, Three-in-One,
Be glory, praise, and honour given
By all on earth, and all in heaven.

869   104th.
Praise to the Trinity.—Psa. lxvii. 3, 5.

GIVE glory to God, ye children of men,
And publish abroad, again and again,
The Son's glorious merit, the Father's free grace,
The gifts of the Spirit, to Adam's lost race.

870   C.M.
Praise to the Trinity.—Rom. xv. 11.

WE laud thy name, almighty Lord,
  The Father of all grace ;
We laud thy name, incarnate Word,
  Who savedst a sinful race ;

2 We laud thy name, blest Spirit of truth,
  Who dost salvation seal ;
Incline the heart, unclose the mouth,
  And sanctify the will.

871   C.M.
Chastisement.—Heb. xii. 5-10; Ps. xciv 12.

HAPPY the man that bears the stroke
  Of his chastising God ;
Nor stubbornly rejects his yoke,
  Nor faints beneath his rod.

2 They who the Lord's correction share
  Have favour in his eyes ;
As kindest fathers will not spare
  Their children to chastise.

3 Thy Lord for nothing would not chide ;
  Thou highly shouldst esteem
The cross that's sent to purge thy pride,
  And make thee more like him.

4 For this correction render praise ;
  'Tis given thee for thy good.
The lash is steeped he on thee lays,
  And softened in his blood.

5 [Know, whom the Saviour favours much,
  Their faults he oft reproves ;
He takes peculiar care of such,
  And chastens whom he loves.]

6 Then kiss the rod ; thy sins confess ;
  It shall a blessing prove ;
And yield the fruits of righteousness—
  Humility and love.

872   S.M.
Chastisement.—Zech. xiii. 9; Mal. iii. 3; Prov. iii. 11.

GOLD in the furnace tried
  Ne'er loses aught but dross ;
So is the Christian purified
  And bettered by the cross.

2 Afflictions make us see,
  What else would 'scape our sight.

How very foul and dim are we,
  And God how pure and bright.

3 [The punished child repents ;
  The parent's bowels move ;
The offended father soon relents,
  And turns with double love.]

4 If God rebuke for pride,
  He'll humble thy proud heart ;
If for thy want of love he chide,
  That love he will impart.

5 He shall by means like these
  Thy stubborn temper break ;
Soften thy heart by due degrees,
  And make thy spirit meek.

6 His chastening, therefore, prize,
  The privilege of a saint ;
Their hearts are hard who that despise,
  And theirs too weak who faint.

873   L.M.
Chastisement.—Ps. vi. 1; xxx. 8-10; cxviii. 18.

To thee, my God, I make my plaint ;
To thee my trembling soul draws near ;
Let not thy chastening make me faint,
Nor guilt o'erwhelm me with despair.

2 What though thou frown to try my faith ?
What though thy heavy hand afflict ?
Thou wilt not give me up to death,
Nor enter into judgment strict.

3 I know thy judgments, Lord, are right ;
Thy rod commands me to repent ;
If with my sin compared, 'tis light,
And all in faithfulness is sent.

4 What would my blood avail, if spilt ?
Thou hast in richer blood been paid,
When all my dreadful debt of guilt
Was on my dying Saviour laid.

5 Then help me by thy grace to bear
Whate'er thou send to purge my dross ;
If in his crown I hope to share,
Why should I grudge to bear his cross ?

6 Though thou severely with me deal,
Still will I in thy mercy trust ;
Accomplish in me all thy will ;
Only remember I am dust.

874   7s.
Be clothed with humility.—1 Pet. v. 5; Isa. lxiv. 6.

LORD, if with thee part I bear ;
If I through thy word am clean ;
In thy mercy if I share ;
If thy blood has purged my sin ;
To my needy soul impart
Thy good Spirit from above,

To enrich my barren heart
With humility and love.

2 Lord, my heart, a desert vast,
Thy reviving hand requires ;
Sin has laid my vineyard waste,
Overgrown with weeds and briars.
Thou canst make this desert bloom ;
Breathe, O breathe, celestial Dove,
Till it blow with rich perfume
Of humility and love.

3 Vanquish in me lust and pride ;
All my stubbornness subdue ;
Smile me into fruit, or chide,
If no milder means will do.
Ah ! compassionate my case ;
Let the poor thy pity move ;
Give me of thy boundless grace,
Give humility and love.]

4 [Why should one that bears thy name,
Why should thy adopted child,
Be in rags, exposed to shame,
Like a savage, fierce and wild ?
With thy children I would sit,
And not like an alien rove ;
Clothe my soul and make it fit,
With humility and love.]

5 [Greatest sinners, greatly spared,
Love much, and themselves abase ;
Mine's a paradox too hard—
Rich of mercy, poor of grace ;
Me thou hast forgiven much ;
(This my sins too plainly prove).
Give me what thou givest such,—
Much humility and love.]

875   L.M.

"My leanness, my leanness ! "—Isa. xxiv. 16 ; xxxii. 15.
JESUS, to thee I make my moan ;
My doleful tale I tell to thee ;
For thou canst help, and thou alone,
A lifeless lump of sin like me.

2 Fain would I find increase of faith ;
Fain would I see fresh graces bloom ;
But ah ! my heart's a barren heath,
Blasted with cold, and black with gloom.

3 True, thou hast kindly given me light ;
I know what Christians ought to be ;
But did the blind receive their sight
Nothing but dismal things to see ?

4 Though winter waste the earth awhile,
Spring soon revives the verdant meads ;
The ripening fields in summer smile,
And autumn with rich crops succeeds ;

5 But I from month to month complain ;
I feel no warmth ; no fruits I see ;
I look for life, but dead remain :
'Tis winter all the year with me.

6 [Yet sin's rank weeds within me live ;
Barrenness is not all I bear ;
I do not so for *nothing* grieve :
Alas ! there's worse than *nothing* there.]

7 Still on thy promise I'll rely,
From whom alone my fruit is found,
Until the Spirit from on high
Enrich the dry and barren ground.

876, 7   8.8.7.
The Brazen Serpent.—Num. xxi. 9 ; John iii. 14.
WHEN the chosen tribes debated
'Gainst their God, as hardly treated,
And complained their hopes were spilt,

God, for murmuring to requite them,
Fiery serpents sent to bite them ;
Lively type of deadly guilt !

2 Stung by these, they soon repented ;
And their God as soon relented ;
Moses prayed ; he answer gave :
" Serpents are the beasts that strike them ;
Make of brass a serpent like them ;
That's the way I choose to save."

3 Vain was bandage, oil, or plaster ;
Rankling venom killed the faster ;
Till the serpent Moses took,
Reared it high, that all might view it ;
Bid the bitten look up to it ;
Life attended every look.

4 Jesus, thus for sinners smitten,
Wounded, bruised, serpent-bitten,
To his cross directs their faith.
Why should I, then, poison cherish ?
Why despair of cure, and perish ?
Look, my soul, though stung to death.

5 Thine's alas ! a lost condition ;
Works cannot work thee remission,
Nor thy goodness do thee good.
Death's within thee, all about thee ;
But the remedy's without thee ;
See it in thy Saviour's blood.

6 See the Lord of glory dying !
See him gasping ! Hear him crying !
See his burdened bosom heave !
Look, ye sinners, ye that hung him ;
Look how deep your sins have stung him ;
Dying sinners, look and live.

878, 9   S.M.
The Scriptures.—2 Tim. iii. 16; Prov. xiii. 13; viii. 8.

SAY, Christian, wouldst thou thrive
In knowledge of thy Lord ?
Against no Scripture ever strive,
   But tremble at his word.

2   Revere the sacred page ;
    To injure any part
Betrays, with blind and feeble rage,
   A hard and haughty heart.

3   If aught there dark appear,
    Bewail thy want of sight ;
No imperfection can be there,
   For all God's words are right.

4   The Scriptures and the Lord
    Bear one tremendous name ;
The written and the incarnate Word
   In all things are the same.

880, 1   S.M.
Treasure in Heaven.—1 Tim. vi. 17-19; Prov. xi. 24.

REMEMBER, man, thy birth ;
Set not on gold thy heart ;
Naked thou cam'st upon the earth,
   And naked must depart.

2   This world's vain wealth despise ;
    Happiness is not here ;
To Jesus lift thy longing eyes,
   And seek thy treasure there.

5   If profit be thy scope,
    Diffuse thy alms about ;
The worldling prospers laying up,
   The Christian laying out.

6   Returns will not be scant
    With honour in the high'st ;

For who relieves his brethren's want,
   Bestows his alms on Christ.

7   Give gladly to the poor,
    'Tis lending to the Lord ;
In secret so increase thy store,
   And hide in heaven the hoard.

8   There thou may'st fear no thief,
    No rankling rust or moth ;
Thy treasure and thy heart are safe ;
   Where one is, will be both.

882   L.M.
" Pray without ceasing."—1 Thess. v. 17; Eph. vi. 18.

PRAYER was appointed to convey
The blessings God designs to give.
Long as they live should Christians pray ;
For only while they pray they live.

2 The Christian's heart his prayer indites ;
He speaks as prompted from within ;
The Spirit his petition writes,
And Christ receives and gives it in.

3 'Tis prayer supports the soul that's weak,
Though thought be broken, language lame ;
Pray, if thou canst or canst not speak ;
But pray with faith in Jesus' name.

4 Depend on him, thou canst not fail ;
Make all thy wants and wishes known ;
Fear not, his merits must prevail ;
Ask what thou wilt, it shall be done.

PART V.

SECOND SUPPLEMENT.

883   148th.   BERRIDGE.
Draw me, we will run after thee.-Song i. 4; Lam. v. 21.

How backward is my heart
In search of endless life !
How loth with toys to part,
Which only bring me grief !
Small riddance in the race I make,
Yet pant for breath each step I take.

2 I cannot well abide
The cross's daily load,
It makes me start aside,
And leave the narrow road ;
Like some raw bullock not well broke,
My shoulder frets beneath the yoke.

3 Erewhile I sit and sigh,
And loathe my folly too ;
Then up I get and try
What human might can do ;
Lay to my arm, but all in vain ;
No arm of mine can break the chain.

4 Ah ! whither must I go,
Since flesh and reason fail ?
No help on earth, I know,
Can o'er my heart prevail ;
No arm can reach my desperate case
But His whose name is Truth and Grace.

5 To him I lift my eyes ;
Thou Son of David, hear,
And let my feeble cries
Bring thy salvation near ;
My froward heart is in thy hand,
And it will move at thy command.

884   148th.   BERRIDGE.
" My heart and my flesh crieth out."—Ps. lxxxiv. 2.

WITH solemn weekly state
The worldling treads thy court,
Content to see thy gate,
And such as there resort ;
But ah ! what is the house to me,
Unless the Master I can see ?

2 Nought will content my heart
But fellowship with him ;
And when from him I start,
My life is all a dream ;
I seem to eat and take my fill,
But wake and feel my hunger still.

3 In vain I seek for rest
In all created good ;
It leaves me yet unblest,
And makes me pant for God ;
And restless sure my heart must be

Till finding all its rest in thee.

4 For thee my soul would cry,
And send a labouring groan ;
For thee my heart would sigh,
And make a pensive moan ;
And each for thee would daily pine,
And would be always only thine.

885   148th.   BERRIDGE.
" What have I to do any more with idols ? "—Hos. xiv.

OUR fancy loves to range
In search of earthly good,
And freely would exchange
A pearl for rotten wood ;
Snaps at a shadow, thin and vain,
Is fooled and vexed, yet snaps again.

2 Fain would the heart unite
A Christ with idols base,
And link mid-day with night,
Or mammon foul with grace ;
And in one bosom, false as hell,
Would have the ark and Dagon dwell.

3 But Christ will not allow
A rival near his throne ;
A jealous God art thou,
And wilt be King alone !
Dagon shall fall before thy face,
Or thy sweet ark will leave the place.

4 Dear Jesus, thou art true,
Though false from thee I slide ;
And wilt thou not subdue
And link me to thy side ?
I would give all my ramblings o'er ;
Speak, Lord, and bid me stray no more.

886   148th.   BERRIDGE.
" Thou art my portion, O Lord."—Ps. cxix. 57.

I SEEK and hope to find
A portion for my soul,
To heal a feverish mind,
And make a bankrupt whole ;
A cup of blessing for the poor,
That's free, and full, and flowing o'er.

2 No satisfying rest
Earth's fluttering joys impart ;
The portion of a beast
Will not content my heart ;
The God of spirits only can
Fill up the vast desires of man.

3 Then, Jesus, wilt thou be
My portion and my all ?

For I would wait on thee,
And listen to thy call ;
My daily wants thou canst supply,
And find me food, and bring me joy.

4 Whate'er I wish or want
Can come from thee alone,
Thou canst my heart content ;
Then let thy grace be shown ;
I'd choose thee for my portion, Lord ;
Supply me well from mercy's board.

887 148th. BERRIDGE.
" Pull me out of the net."—Ps. xxxi. 4 ; Isa. xlii. 22.

A THOUSAND snares beset
A pilgrim in his walk,
To trap him by the feet,
Or catch him in his talk ;
The creature often proves a bait,
And Satan lays his wily net.

2 A stubborn guest is sin,
And makes a rueful rout ;
We may let idols in,
But cannot turn them out :
The Saviour's arm is wanted here,
To pluck the sinner from a snare.

3 What if the tyrant roar,
And of his conquest boast ?
The Lord will help the poor,
That in his mercy trust ;
And he has gained high renown
In bringing proud Goliaths down.

888 148th. BERRIDGE.
No man can come to me, except the Father draw him.

No wit or will of man,
Or learning he may boast,
No power of reason can
Draw sinners unto Christ ;
So fallen is nature, such her flaw,
None come except the Father draw.

2 His Spirit must disclose
The deadly plague within,
Uncover all our woes,
And show the man of sin ;
And feeling thus our ruined state,
We humbly fall at Jesus' feet.

3 [The Comforter must teach
The Saviour's toil and smart,
And with conviction preach
Atonement to the heart ;
Then sinners gaze with ravished eyes,
And feast upon the sacrifice.]

4 [The Spirit, too, must show
The power of Jesus' arm,
To vanquish every foe,
And guard the soul from harm ;

Believers then grow strong in faith,
And triumph over sin and death.]

5 So let my heart be drawn
To Jesus Christ the Lord,
And learn to feast upon
His person and his word,
Feel sweet redemption through his blood,
And give the glory all to God.

889 148th. BERRIDGE.
The Lord is nigh unto them that are of a broken heart.

SAY, is thy heart well broke,
And feels the plague of sin ?
And hateth Satan's yoke,
It sweetly once drew in ?
Give Christ the praise ; he broke thy heart,
And taught thee how to feel the smart.

2 [What if Mount Sinai's smoke
Should darken all the skies,
And thy weak stomach choke,
And bring on weeping eyes ?
It points the road to Zion's hill,
Where grace and peace for ever dwell.

3 Thick glooms lie in the way
To Jesus' heavenly light ;
Before a gospel day,
He sends a legal night ;
And while the legal nights abide,
No Christ is seen, although the Guide.]

4 The Lord is surely near
When drooping sinners pray,
And lends a gracious ear,
But steals himself away ;
Regards their moan with pitying eye,
And brings at length salvation nigh.

5 O let the Lord bestow
That broken heart on me,
Which feeleth well its woe,
And blushing, looks to thee ;
Amazed to see myself so vile,
And Jesus smiling all the while.

890 S.M. BERRIDGE.
Wine, which cheereth God and man.—Judges ix. 13.

A WONDROUS wine there is,
None can with it compare,
Creating most exalted bliss,
Which God and man will cheer.

2 It is the wine of Love,
That precious love divine
Which knits and cheers all hearts above,
And makes their faces shine.

3   Believers know its taste,
      And can its virtues tell ;
    Oft when their hearts are sinking fast,
      One sip has made them well.

4   It is the cordial true ;
      Lord, cheer me with it still ;
    Till at thy seat I drink it new,
      And take my hearty fill.

891   S.M.   BERRIDGE.
Turn thee yet again, and thou shalt see.—Ezk. viii. 6.
    THAT image-chamber foul
      Which met Ezekiel's eye,
    Points out the breast of every soul,
      Where lurking idols lie.

2   Yet ask for further light,
      And turn to see thy woe,
    And God will clear thy misty sight,
      And deeper visions show.

3   As we the light can bear
      To break upon our eyes,
    Still deeper idols shall appear,
      And more will after rise.

4   Thus pride is broken down,
      And humbled in the dust,
    We view our vileness, and must own
      The Lord is all our trust.

5   May Jesus Christ disclose
      The plagues within my heart ;
    And as my soul more humbled grows,
      A brighter faith impart.

892   C.M.   BERRIDGE.
"He shall let go my captives."—Isa. xlv. 13.
    ART thou by sin a captive led ?
      Is sin thy daily grief ?
    The Man who brake the serpent's head
      Can bring thee sweet relief.

2   His name is Jesus, for he saves,
      And setteth captives free ;
    His office is to purchase slaves,
      And give them liberty.

3   No money for thy ransom take,
      But mercy much entreat ;
    Go, with the chains about thy neck,
      And fall before his feet.

4   Tell how thy bosom tyrants lash,
      And rage without control ;
    Show where the fetters gall thy flesh,
      And bruise thy inmost soul.

5   The sight will melt his piteous heart,
      Soon touched with human woe ;
    And healing up thy guilty smart,

His freed-man thou shalt go.

893   C.M.   BERRIDGE.
"Though it tarry, wait for it."—Hab. ii. 3.
IF guilt pursue thee with its cry,
    And would to prison hale ;
To Jesus Christ, the Surety, fly,
    And he will give in bail.

2 If hope, that used thy soul to cheer,
    Now leaves thee dark as night,
  And neither sun nor stars appear,
    Yet wait for morning light.

3 Still look to Christ with longing eyes,
    Though both begin to fail ;
  Still follow with thy feeble cries,
    For mercy will prevail.

4 What if he drop no gracious smile,
    Or bid thee leave his door ?

    Yet still knock on, and wait awhile ;
    He must relieve the poor.

5 He tarries oft till men are faint,
    And comes at evening late ;
  He hears and will relieve complaint :
    'Tis ours to pray and wait.

894   C.M. BERRIDGE, ERSKINE, &c.
I kill, I make alive: I wound. I heal.—Deut. xxxii. 39.
    THE Saviour empties whom he fills,
      And quickens whom he slays,
    Our legal hope he kindly kills,
      To teach us gospel praise.

2 He wraps in frowns as well as smiles,
    Some tokens of his love;
  And if he wounds, or if he heals,
    In both his grace we prove.

3 No sooner we begin to mourn,
    And feel a broken heart,
  But Jesus cries, " Return, return,
    And let me heal thy smart."

4 My legal self may Jesus kill,
    And make my heart alive ;
  My guilty wounds may Jesus heal,
    And make my spirit thrive.

895   7s.   BERRIDGE.
"The wages of sin is death."—Rom. vi. 23; Gen. ii. 17.
    AWFUL is thy threatening, Lord ;
    Let me mark the solemn word ;
    What the righteous Ruler saith :
    " Wages due to sin is death."

2   Then I stand condemned to die
    By the mouth of God most high.
    Sins I have, a thousand too,
    And a thousand deaths are due.

3 Should I spend my life in prayers,
    Water all my couch with tears,
    Turn from every evil past,
    Still I am condemned and cast.

4 [Lord, I own the sentence just,
    Drop my head into the dust ;
    If my soul is cast to hell,
    Thou, O Lord, art righteous still.]

5 In myself I have no hope ;
    Justice every plea will stop ;
    Yet for mercy I may plead,
    Springing from the church's Head.

6 Knock I may at Jesus' door,
    Mercy for his sake implore,
    Mercy, such as thou wilt give ;
    Show it, Lord, and let me live.

896 L.M. CENNICK & BERRIDGE.
A Fountain opened for Sin.—Zech. xiii. 1 ; 1 Cor. vi. 11.
    A FOUNTAIN ! cries the man of God,
    A fountain with a purple flood ;
    A fountain opened for the poor,
    Where sickly souls may find a cure.

2 It softens well the heart of stone,
    And kindly knits a broken bone,
    Restoring hearing, speech, and sight,
    And puts all guilty fears to flight.

3 It heals the soul of feverish heat,
    And helps a pulse with grace to beat ;
    The fretful look, the wanton eye,
    And lordly self before it fly.

4 No spring like this makes lepers whole,
    Not that renowned Bethesda's pool,
    Nor Siloam's stream, nor Jordan's flood,
    Were altogether half so good.

5 Fast by this fountain let me stay,
    And drink, and wash my sores away ;
    If but a moment I depart,
    Sick is my head, and faint my heart.

897 L.M. BERRIDGE.
Believe that ye receive them, and ye shall have them.
    YE poor afflicted souls, give ear,
    Who seek the Lord, but fear his frown ;
    What things ye ask in fervent prayer,
    Believing, Christ will send them down.

2 If sin is loathsome to thy heart,
    And shows a most ill-favoured face ;
    If guilt affords thee fearful smart,
    It flows from Jesus' love and grac

3 A feast is now prepared for thee,
    In spite of all thy unbelief ;
    A feast of mercy, sweetly free
    For sinners and the sinners' chief.

4 Take courage, then ; ask and believe,
    Expecting mercy from the Lord ;
    The promise runs, " Ask and receive,"
    And Christ is faithful to his word.

5 O Lord, increase my feeble faith,
    And give my straitened bosom room
    To credit what thy promise saith,
    And wait till thy salvation come.

898 112th. BERRIDGE.
" A rod for the fool's back."—Prov. xxvi. 3 ; x. 13.
    I WONDER not if giddy men
    Run roving all the world about,
    Pursuing folly with much pain,
    And wearied oft, yet give not out ;
    The world must be their fluttering aim,
    Who see no charm in Jesus' name.

2 Yet none so foolish are and base,
    As those who've felt the legal lash,
    And having tasted gospel-grace,
    Good manna leave for earthly trash ;
    When such from wisdom's teaching start,
    A rod shall make their shoulders smart.

3 In vain they seek the world's relief ;
    The Lord will weary them with woe,
    And lash them well with grief on grief,
    With rods and stinging scorpions too ;
    They drink of every bitter cup,
    Till, sick, they cast their idols up.

4 My heart, too, after idols sought,
    And roved from the gospel track ;
    And by such rovings I have brought
    A thousand stripes upon my back ;
    Lord, take my foolish heart at last,
    And guide it right, and hold it fast.

899 112th. BERRIDGE.
" Wait ye upon me, saith the Lord," &c.—Zeph. iii. 8.
    O THOU with battering tempest tossed,
    Perplexed and shattered here and there,
    Bewildered on a legal coast,
    And finding no deliverance near,
    On Jesus calling with sad thought,
    But Jesus seems to mind thee not !

2 Soon as thy heart can moaning cry,
    " What must a wretched sinner do ? "
    To Jesus lift thy weary eye,
    For whither else can sinners go ?
    And Jesus will not fail thy hope ;
    But on him wait till he rise up.

3 He will rise up the prey to take ;
    His mighty arm he will make bare ;

He will, for his own mercy's sake,
Bereave thee of thy guilty fear,
And tame the beasts within thy breast ;
But on him wait, till he give rest.

900 112th. BERRIDGE.
" He (Jesus) shall let go my captives."—Isa. xlv. 13.

SAY, wast thou not a captive born,
And art thou not a captive led,
With fetters loaded every morn,
And chained down each night in bed ?
Do not thy lusts beset thee still,
And take thee captive at their will ?

2 Do not rough tempers, proud and base,
Insult and rend thy helpless soul ?
And what can tame the lusts but grace ?
Or what the tempers will control ?
The work for Jesus is prepared,
Who does the work without reward.

3 His blood must purge the conscience clean,
And show a sin-forgiving God ;
His Spirit write the law within,
And guide us on the gospel road ;
And all that seek to him shall know,
That Jesus lets the captives go.

901 112th. BERRIDGE.
" Let my prayer be as incense."—Ps. cxli. 2 ; v. 3.

A GODLINESS which feeds on form,
And lip devotion, barren cheer,
Will satisfy an earthly worm,
Who learns to think and call it prayer ;
Contented with the husky part,
A moving lip and silent heart.

2 O Lord, thy Spirit's aid impart,
And fill me with devotion's fire ;
Create anew my waiting heart,
And heavenly breathings there inspire ;
Bid heart and flesh cry out for thee,
And thou my joyful portion be !

3 Let incense smoking from my breast,
In praise and prayer ascend thy hill ;
And where I rove, or where I rest,
Do thou, O God, surround me still ;
My heavenly intercourse increase,
Till as a river flows my peace.

902 8.8.6.
" If any man thirst, let him come unto me and drink."

LET him who thirsts for heavenly joys,
Come unto Me, the Saviour cries,
    And drink at my spring-head ;
Leave all your boasting self behind,
For from the Saviour you shall find
    A glorious life indeed.

2 I come, O Lord, and thirst for thee ;
Some living water give to me,
    Or I shall faint and die ;

All other means my heart has tried,
All other streams are vain beside
    What flows from Calvary.

3 I long to taste the purple flood,
And feel the virtue of thy blood,
    And gaze and tarry here ;
So shall I sweetly sing and pray,
And serve thee kindly every day,
    Without a guilty fear.

903 8.8.6.
" My house is the house of prayer," &c.—Luke xix. 46.

MY bosom was designed to be
A house of prayer, O Lord, for thee,
    A temple undefiled ;
But vile outrageous thieves broke in,
And turned the house into a den,
    And all its glory spoiled.

2 There anger lies, and lust, and pride,
And envy base its head will hide,
    And malice brooding ill ;
There unbelief the Lord denies,
And falsehood whispers out its lies,
    And avarice gripeth still.

3 Thy help, Almighty Lord, impart,
And drag the tyrants from my heart,
    And chase the thieves away ;
Within my bosom fix thy throne,
And there be loved and served alone,
    And teach me how to pray.

4 [The work is thine to cleanse the place ;
I can but look up for thy grace,
    Nor this without thy aid ;
Then let thy indignation burn,
And all thy foes o'erturn, o'erturn,
    And rear again my head.]

904 8.8.6. BERRIDGE.
" Our sufficiency is of God."—2 Cor. iii. 5 ; Phil. iv. 13.

O LORD, with shame I do confess
My universal emptiness,
    My poverty and pride ;
I cannot keep thee in my sight,
Nor can I think one thought aright,
    Unless thy Spirit guide.

2 I cannot from my idols part,
Nor love the Lord with all my heart,
    Nor can myself deny ;
I cannot pray, and feel thee near,
Nor can I sing with heavenly cheer,
    Unless the Lord be nigh.

3 Since Adam from God's image fell,
On spiritual things we cannot dwell ;
    The heart is turned aside ;

And none can raise to life the dead
But he who raised himself indeed,
And for dead sinners died.

4 Then let this mighty Jesus be
An all-sufficient help for me,
Creating power and will ;
Thy grace sufficed saints of old ;
It made them strong and made them
bold,
And it suffices still. BERRIDGE.

905 8.8.6. Ezek. xxxvi. 26.
" I will take away the stony heart."—

My heart by nature is a stone,
And unconcerned can look upon
Eternal misery ;
Feels no affection for the Lord,
Takes no impression from his word,
But lumpish is and dry.

2 Some tell me I must change my heart,
And undertake the Saviour's part ;
A proud and fruitless strife !
I might as soon the seasons change,
Or make the clouds in order range,
Or raise the dead to life.

3 My shoulders will not bear the load ;
The work is only fit for God,
A work of heavenly grace ;
The Lord, who first created man,
Must now create him new again,
And rear the fallen race.

4 Then unto him I lift my eye ;
My Maker, hear me when I cry,
And give the heart of flesh ;
A heart renewed by faith and love,
That seeks the joys which are above,
And will not feed on trash.

5 [A heart submissive, mild, and meek,
Which hears if Jesus softly speak,
And on his word can feast ;
A heart which prays for great and small,
And dearly loves thy children all,
Yet thinks itself the least.]

906 104th. BERRIDGE.
" I will instruct thee," &c.—Psalm xxxii. 8 ; xxxi. 3.

O WHERE shall I find a guide to direct,
Right skilful and kind, and brave to protect ?
To lovely Mount Zion my heart is now bound,
But many a lion is in the way found.

2 'Tis Jesus can teach the way ye should go,
And out his arm reach to help you on too ;
The doubts that perplex you, the fears that
distress,
The tempers that vex you, his grace can redress.

3 Then may the Lord give me faith in his name,
A faith that will live in water and flame,
A faith that endureth, and feasts on his blood ;
A faith that assureth my sonship with God.

4 [O teach me to love thy Person most sweet,
Nor let my heart rove, but keep at thy feet ;
Be with thee delighted, and clasp thee and twine,
Most firmly united to thy living Vine.

5 And further, I seek the charms of thy mind,
The grace to be meek, and lowly, and kind ;
Forbearing, forgiving, and loving always,
And only be living to publish thy praise.]

907 104th. BERRIDGE.
" Wherewith shall I come? "—Mic. vi. 6—8.

WHEREWITH shall I come before the Most
High,
Who am but a worm, and doomed to die ?

My nature unholy was tainted in birth,
And nursed by folly, brings all evil forth !

2 Whatever I do, some baseness appears ;
Wherever I go, it rings in my ears ;
Pursues me and rages with fulsomest breath,
And tells me its wages are hell after death.

3 No labours of mine, with fasting and tears,
Can purge away sin, or shorten arrears ;
One only sweet fountain of blood that was spilt
Can loosen the mountain of high-crying guilt

908 L.M. KENT.
He that believeth . . hath everlasting life.—Jno. vi. 47.

SAVED is the sinner that believes,
The sacred gospel annals show ;
To him repentance Jesus gives,
And sin's complete remission too.

2 He hears the Spirit's voice within ;
A sacred ray breaks on his eyes ;
He bursts at once the sleep of sin,
And naked now to Jesus flies.

3 Sprinkled with blood his conscience is ;
He feels the sweets of sin forgiven ;
While Jesus' spotless righteousness
Becomes his meetness now for heaven.

4 Jesus, thy Godhead, blood, and name,
O ! 'tis eternal life to know ;
Here let my soul her hold maintain,
When pressed by conscience, wrath, or l[

5 Sin-burdened soul, with tempest tossed,
Thy bark shall every storm outride ;
Grace once received can ne'er be lost,
Nor hell from Christ thy soul divide.

909   S.M.   KENT.
Underneath are the everlasting arms.-Deut. xxxiii. 27.
WHY, drooping saint, dismayed ?
   Does sorrow press thee down ?
   Has God refused to give thee aid,
   Or does he seem to frown ?

2   In darkness or distress,
   His love's the same to thee ;
   Without declension, more or less,
   Immutable and free.

3   Should guilt disturb thy peace,
   Or Satan harass thee,
   Behold the Saviour's righteousness,
   That sets the guilty free.

4   Though he afflicts thy mind,
   'Tis not that he'll destroy ;
   Eternal Wisdom ne'er designed
   To give thee always joy.

5   Beneath thy fainting head
   Thy Father and thy Friend
   His everlasting arms has laid,
   To succour and defend.

910   L.M.   KENT.
Reflecting on past Enjoyment.—Job xxix. 2, 3.
O THAT my soul, as heretofore,
Could with delight and love explore
Those sacred sweets, in Jesus' name,
That once my raptured soul o'ercame !

2 Once I beheld his lovely face,
As full of truth and full of grace ;
Ten thousand thousand suns were dim
In lustre, when compared with him.

3 With his delights my soul was cheered,
With raptures then his voice I heard ;
The word he spake was sweet to me ;
'Twas, " Sinner, I have loved thee."

4 But now those golden hours are fled,
My spirit mourns, with sorrow fed ;
His promise in his word I see,
But fear, alas ! 'tis not for me.

5 O that my Sun, with cheering ray,
Would chase these shades of night away ;
Then shall my soul arise and sing
The healing virtue of his wing.

911   L.M.   KENT.
Those who feared the Lord spake often one to another.
WHEN saint to saint, in days of old,
Their sorrows, sins, and sufferings told,
Jesus, the Friend of sinners, dear,
His saints to bless was present there.

2 As members of his mystic frame,

Together met to bless his name ;
While humbly at his throne we bow,
As " God with us " he's present now.

3 O bless'd devotion ! thus to meet,
And spread our woes at his dear feet ;
Call him our own, in ties of blood,
And hold sweet fellowship with God.

4 His former visits we recount,
On Mizar's hill and Hermon's mount ;
Yet still our souls desire anew
His sweetest, loveliest face to view.

912   104th.   KENT.
He will rest in his love.—Zeph. iii. 17 ; Ps. lxxxix. 33.
SALVATION by grace, how charming the song !
With seraphim join the theme to prolong ;
'Twas planned by Jehovah in council above,
Who to everlasting shall rest in his love.

2 This covenant of grace all blessings secures ;
Believers, rejoice, for all things are yours ;
And God from his purpose shall never remove,
But love thee, and bless thee, and rest in his love.

3 But when, like a sheep that strays from the
     fold,
To Jesus thy Lord thy love shall grow cold,
Think not he'll reject thee, howe'er he reprove ;
For though he correct thee, he'll rest in his love.

4 In Jesus, the Lamb, the Father's delight,
The saints without blame appear in his sight ;
And while he in Jesus their souls shall approve,
So long shall Jehovah abide in his love.

913   8.7.   KENT.
The Gospel Glad Tidings to Sinners.—Heb. vii. 25.
'TIS the gospel's joyful tidings,
   Full salvation sweetly sounds ;
Grace to heal thy foul backslidings,
   Sinner, flows from Jesus' wounds.

2 Are thy sins beyond recounting,
   Like the sand the ocean laves ?
Jesus is of life the fountain ;
   He unto the utmost saves.

3 Hail the Lamb who came to save us ;
   Hail the love that made him die !
'Tis the gift that God has given us ;
   We'll proclaim his honours high.

4 When we join the general chorus
   Of the royal blood-bought throng,
Who to glory went before us,
   Saved from every tribe and tongue,

5 Then we'll make the blissful regions
   Echo to our Saviour's praise ;
While the bright angelic legions
   Listen to the charming lays.

914 C.M. KENT.
Everlasting Love.—Ezek. xlvii. 5; Zech. xiv. 8.
BENEATH the sacred throne of God
  I saw a river rise,
The streams were peace and pardoning blood,
  Descending from the skies.

2 Angelic minds cannot explore
  This deep, unfathomed sea ;
'Tis void of bottom, brim, or shore,
  And lost in Deity.

3 I stood amazed, and wondered when,
  Or why, this ocean rose,
That wafts salvation down to men,
  His traitors and his foes.

4 That sacred flood, from Jesus' veins,
  Was free to take away
A Mary's or Manasseh's stains,
  Or sins more vile than they.

915 L.M. KENT.
" Return unto thy rest, O my soul."—Ps. cxvi. 7.
WHY, O my soul, art thou dismayed ?
Why in these tents of sorrow groan ?
On what have thy fond hopes been stayed,
Still seeking rest, but finding none ?

2 Rest in the promise God has spoke,
In all things ordered well for thee ;
Whose sacred words he'll ne'er revoke,
Nor alter his profound decree.

3 Rest in the oath that he has swore,
Firm as his throne the same shall prove ;
'Twill stand when time shall be no more,
And run coeval with his love.

4 'Tis good to cast an anchor here,
And patient wait, till thou shalt see
Thy hopes for heaven more bright and clear,
Blessed with a surer prophecy.

916 8.7.4. KENT.
" I am the Lord that healeth thee."—Exod. xv. 26.
OFT as sins, my soul, assail thee,
  Turn thy eyes to Jesus' blood ;
Nothing short of this can heal thee,
  Seal thy peace, or do thee good :
    Seek no healing,
  But from Gilead's sovereign balm.
2 Should the tears of deep contrition,
  Like a torrent, drown thy eyes ;
Yet for sin there's no remission
  But in this great Sacrifice ;
    True repentance
Christ to Israel freely gives.

917 8.8.6. KENT.
Hoping in God.—Isa. iii. 10; Ps. xlii. 7-9; Zech. ii. 5.
CEASE, O believer, cease to mourn ;

Return unto thy rest, return ;
  Why should thy sorrows swell ?
Though deep distress thy steps attend,
Thy warfare shall in triumph end ;
  With thee it shall go well.
2 Thy God has said (his word shall stand,
Not like the writing on the sand,
  But firm as his decree)
That, " When thy foes, death, hell, and sin,
On every side shall hem thee in,
  A wall of fire I'll be."
3 Though trouble now thy heart appals,
And deep to deep incessant calls,
  No storm shall injure thee ;
Thy anchor, once in Jesus cast,
Shall hold thy soul, till thou at last
  Him face to face shalt see.

918 8.7.4. KENT.
Spiritual Poverty.—Matt. v. 3; Luke vi. 20; Jas. ii. 5.
BLESSED are the poor in spirit,
  Who their native vileness see,
They are all taught sin's demerit,
  Gladly own salvation free,
    And from Sinai
  To the wounds of Jesus flee.
2 Stripped of all their fancied meetness
  To approach the dread I AM,
They are led to see all fitness
  Centring in the worthy Lamb ;
    And adoring,
  Sing his Godhead, blood, and name.
3 Self-renouncing, grace admiring,
  Made unto salvation wise,
Matchless love their bosoms firing,
  O how sweet their songs arise :
    " None but Jesus ! "
  From his blood their hopes arise.
4 At his throne their sins confessing,
  Now in shame they veil their face,
Weeping, loving, praising, blessing,
  On his head the crown they place ;
    Shouting glory
  To the God of sovereign grace.

919 L.M. KELLY.
" God forbid that I should glory, save in the cross."
WE sing the praise of him who died,
Of him who died upon the cross ;
The sinner's Hope let men deride ;
For this we count the world but dross.
2 The cross, it takes our guilt away ;
It holds the fainting spirit up ;
It cheers with hope the gloomy day,
And sweetens every bitter cup.

3 It makes the coward spirit brave,
   And nerves the feeble arm for fight ;
   It takes its terror from the grave,
   And gilds the bed of death with light.

4 The balm of life, the cure of woe ;
   The measure and the pledge of love ;
   The sinner's refuge here below ;
   The angel's theme in heaven above.

920   8.7.4.   KENT.
Christ's Righteousness.—Isa. xlv. 24 ; 1 Cor. i. 30.

WHEN to worship saints assemble,
   Let the song to Jesus flow.
He forsook his ancient glory,
   Groaned and bled for worms below.
      Ransomed mortals,
   Join to swell the sacred song.

2 Ye who find yourselves polluted,
   Feel your hearts a sink of sin,
Ye shall have by God imputed,
   Righteousness that's white and clean :
      'Tis the garment
   Wove by everlasting love.

3 'Tis Jehovah's own providing ;
   Better, wisdom can't devise ;
From his eye for ever hiding
   Sins of every name and size ;
      He that wears it
   Is by God exalted high.

4 Adam, when the tempter foiled him,
   His bright robes were quickly gone ;
But this righteousness of Jesus
   Once applied, 'tis always on ;
      'Tis their title
   To the mansion love ordained.

921   S.M.   KENT.
" Ye are all one in Christ."—Gal. iii. 28 ; Eph. v. 30.

IN union with the Lamb,
   From condemnation free,
The saints from everlasting were ;
   And shall for ever be.

2   In covenant from of old,
   The sons of God they were ;
The feeblest lamb in Jesus' fold
   Was blessed in Jesus there.

3   Its bonds shall never break,
   Though earth's old columns bow ;
The strong, the tempted, and the weak,
   Are one in Jesus now.

4   When storms or tempests rise,
   Or sins your peace assail,
Your hope in Jesus never dies ;
   'Tis cast within the vail.

5   Here let the weary rest,
   Who love the Saviour's name ;
Though with no sweet enjoyments blessed,
   This covenant stands the same.

922   S.M.   KENT.
The Saints more than Conquerors through Christ.

THE conquest Jesus won
   O'er Satan, sin, and hell,
With all the wonders he has done,
   His saints shall sing and tell.

2   On him shall Zion place
   Her only hope for heaven,
And see, in his dear sacred face,
   Ten thousand sins forgiven.

3   He passed within the vail,
   Did on his bosom bear

   The worthless names that did prevail
   With him to enter there.

4   Worthy the slaughtered Lamb !
   Let ransomed mortals say ;
For who shall sing his lovely name
   In higher notes than they ?

923   C.M.   KENT.
" With my soul have I desired thee in the night."

'TWAS in the night, when troubles came,
   I sought, my God, for thee,
But found no refuge in that name
   That once supported me.

2 I sought thee, but I found thee not,
   For all was dark within ;
Thy tender mercy I forgot
   To me when dead in sin.

3 With cords of his eternal love,
   'Twas thus my soul he drew,
And taught my wretched heart to prove
   His oath and promise true.

4 At length my Sun's refulgent beam
   Through the dark cloud appeared ;
My night of woe was like a dream ;
   My soul was blessed and cheered.

924   L.M.   KENT.
Christ a Refuge from the Storm.—Isa. iv. 6 ; xxxii. 2.

GREAT Rock, for weary sinners made,
When storms of sin distress the soul,
Here let me rest my weary head,
When lightnings blaze and thunders roll.

2 Within the clefts of his dear side,
There all his saints in safety dwell.
And what from Jesus shall divide ?
Not all the rage of earth or hell.

3 Blessed with the pardon of her sin,
My soul beneath thy shade would lie,
And sing the love that took me in,
While others sank in sin to die.

4 O sacred covert from the beams
That on the weary traveller beat,
How welcome are thy shade and streams ;
How bless'd, how sacred, and how sweet !

925   L.M.   KENT.

This Man shall be the peace.—Mic. v. 5 ; Eph. ii. 14.

PEACE by his cross has Jesus made ;
The church's everlasting Head
O'er hell and sin has victory won,
And, with a shout, to glory gone.

2 When o'er thy head the billows roll,
And shades of sin obscure thy soul ;
When thou canst no deliverance see,
Yet still this Man thy Peace shall be.

3 In tribulation's thorny maze,
Or on the mount of sovereign grace,
Or in the fire, or through the sea,
This glorious Man thy Peace shall be.

4 Yea, when thy eye of faith is dim,
Rest thou on Jesus, sink or swim,
And at his footstool bow the knee,
For Israel's God thy Peace shall be.

926   L.M.   KENT.

" Lead me to the rock .. higher than I."—Ps. lxi. 2.

WHEN overwhelmed with doubts and fear,
Great God, do thou my spirit cheer ;
Let not my eyes with tears be fed,
But to the Rock of Ages led.

2 When guilt lies heavy on my soul,
And waves of fierce temptation roll,

I'd to this Rock for shelter flee,
And make my refuge, Lord, in thee.

3 When sick, or faint, or sore dismayed,
Then let my hopes on thee be stayed ;
Thy summit rising to the skies,
Can shield my head when dangers rise.

4 When called the vale of death to tread,
Then to this Rock may I be led.
Nor fear to cross that gloomy sea,
Since thou hast tasted death for me.

927   L.M.   STEELE.

" Thou art my hope in the day of evil."—Jer. xvii. 17.

THOU only Sovereign of my heart,
My Refuge, my Almighty Friend ;
And can my soul from thee depart,
On whom alone my hopes depend ?

2 Whither, ah ! whither should I go,
A wretched wanderer from the Lord ?
Can this dark world of sin and woe
One glimpse of happiness afford ?

3 Eternal life thy words impart ;
On these my fainting spirit lives ;
Here sweeter comforts cheer my heart,
Than all the round that nature gives.

4 Let earth's alluring joys combine,
While thou art near, in vain they call ;
One smile, one blissful smile of thine,
Thou dearest Lord, outweighs them all.

5 Thy name my inmost powers adore,
Thou art my life, my joy, my care ;
Depart from thee ?—'tis death—'tis more
'Tis endless ruin, deep despair !

6 Low at thy feet my soul would lie ;
Here safety dwells and peace divine ;
Still let me live beneath thy eye,
For life, eternal life, is thine.

928   8.8.6.   C.W.

" We have an Advocate with the Father."—1 John ii. 1.

THOU sinner's Advocate with God,
My only trust is in thy blood,
Thou all-atoning Lamb ;
The virtue of thy death impart,
Speak comfort to my drooping heart,
And tell me all thy name.

2 Speak, Lord, and let me find thee near ;
O come and dissipate my fear ;
Declare my sins forgiven ;
Return, thou Prince of Peace ; return,
Thou Comforter of all that mourn,
And guide me safe to heaven.

929   C.M.   HAMMOND.

I was envious at the foolish.—Ps. lxxiii. 3 ; xxxvii. 1.

WHILE others live in mirth and ease,
And feel no want or woe,
Through this dark, howling wilderness
I full of sorrow go.

2 Ah ! wretched soul to reason thus,
And murmur without end !
Did Christ expire upon the cross ?
And is he not thy friend ?

3 Why dost thou envy worldly men,
And think their state so blest ?
How great salvation hast thou seen !
And Jesus is thy rest.

4 What can this lower world afford,
Compared with Jesus' grace ?
Thy happiness is in the Lord,
And thou shalt see his face.

930　　　C.M.　　　KENT.

In these lay a multitude of impotent folk.—Jno. v. 2.

As round the pool, Bethesda named,
　The sick and wounded lay,
And went from hence, though sorely maimed,
　Restored to health away ;

2 So, at the Gospel pool we wait,
　Disordered all by sin ;
In a polluted, dreadful state,
　And lepers all unclean.

3 Lo, here are souls by Satan bound,
　And who shall set them free ?
Speak, Lord, there's mercy in the sound ;
　All power belongs to thee.

4 Descend, descend, thou God of grace,
　Thy saving health display ;
Thy mercy suit to every case ;
　Send none unhealed away.

931　　　8.7.　BAKEWELL & TOPLADY.

"Christ our passover is sacrificed for us."—1 Cor. v. 7.

PASCHAL Lamb, by God appointed,
　Loads of sin on thee were laid ;
By almighty love anointed,
　Thou hast full atonement made.
All thy people are forgiven,
　Through the virtue of thy blood ;
Opened is the gate of heaven ;
　Peace is made 'twixt man and God.

2 Jesus, hail ! enthroned in glory,
　There for ever to abide !
All the heavenly hosts adore thee,
　Seated at thy Father's side.
For thy people thou art pleading ;
　There thou dost their place prepare ;

Ever for them interceding,
　Till in glory they appear.

3 Riches, honour, strength, and blessing,
　Thou art worthy to receive ;
Loudest praises, without ceasing,
　Meet it is for saints to give.
All the bright angelic spirits
　Bring their sweetest, noblest lays ;
Help to sing the Saviour's merits ;
　Help to chant the Saviour's praise.

932　　　8.7.4.　　　KELLY.

The streams make glad the city of God.—Ps. xlvi. 4.

SEE, from Zion's sacred mountain,
　Streams of living water flow ;
God has opened there a fountain,
　That supplies the plains below ;

They are blessed
Who its sovereign virtues know.

2 Through ten thousand channels flowing,
　Streams of mercy find their way ;
Life, and health, and joy bestowing,
　Making all around look gay ;
　　O believer !
　All thy sins are washed away.

3 Gladdened by the flowing treasure,
　All enriching as it goes ;
Lo, the desert smiles with pleasure,
　Buds and blossoms as the rose ;
　　Every sinner
　Sings for joy where'er it flows.

4 Trees of life the banks adorning,
　Yield their fruit to all around,
Those who eat are saved from mourning ;
　Pleasure comes and hopes abound ;
　　Fair their portion !
　Endless life with glory crowned.

933　　　C.M.　　　NEWTON.

The joy of the Lord is your strength.—Neh. viii. 10.

JOY is a fruit that will not grow
　In nature's barren soil ;
All we can boast, till Christ we know,
　Is vanity and toil.

2 But where the Lord has planted grace,
　And made his glories known,
There fruits of heavenly joy and peace
　Are found, and there alone.

3 A bleeding Saviour seen by faith,
　A sense of pardoning love,
A hope that triumphs over death,
　Give joys like those above.

4 To take a glimpse within the veil,
　To know that God is mine ;
Are springs of joy that never fail,
　Unspeakable ! divine !

934　　　C.M.—　　BURKITT, &c.

The Heavenly Jerusalem.—Rev. xxi. 10-27.

JERUSALEM, my happy home !
　Name ever dear to me ;
When shall my labours have an end
　In joy, and peace, and thee ?

2 When shall these eyes thy heaven-built
　And pearly gates behold ; 　　[walls
Thy bulwarks and salvation strong,
　And streets of shining gold ?

3 Why should I shrink at pain or woe,
　Or feel at death dismay ?
I've Canaan's goodly land in view,
　And realms of endless day.

4 Jerusalem, my happy home !
  My soul still pants for thee ;
  Then shall my labours have an end,
  When I thy joys shall see.

935   L.M.   WATTS.
Salvation in Christ alone.—Acts iv. 12; Ps. iii. 8.
LET everlasting glories crown
Thy head, my Saviour, and my Lord ;
Thy hands have brought salvation down,
And writ the blessings in thy word.

2 In vain the trembling conscience seeks
  Some solid ground to rest upon ;
  With long despair the spirit breaks,
  Till made to rest on Christ alone.

3 How well thy blessed truths agree !
  How wise and holy thy commands !
  Thy promises, how firm they be !
  How firm thy hope, thy comfort stands !

936   C.M.   TATE & BRADY.
" O magnify the Lord with me."—Ps. xxxiv. 3, 4.
THROUGH all the changing scenes of life,
  In trouble and in joy,
The praises of my God shall still
  My heart and tongue employ.

2 O magnify the Lord with me,
  With me exalt his name ;
  When in distress on him I called,
  He to my succour came.

937   L.M.
" Holiness becometh thine house, O Lord."—Ps. xciii.
SHALL the believer dare to sin,
Because his sin has been forgiven ?
Shall sovereign grace which makes him clean,
Be thus abused ? Forbid it, Heaven !

2 Hard is that heart which does not melt,
  And blind is that unholy eye,
  Which sees no evil in the guilt,
  For which the Saviour came to die.

3 O blessed Jesus, ne'er may those
  For whom thy precious blood was shed,
  Give cause of triumph to thy foes,
  But shrink from sin with holy dread.

938   8.8.6.   RIPPON'S COL.
Whosoever was not found written in the book of life.
WHEN thou, my righteous Judge, shalt come
To take thy ransomed people home,
  Shall I among them stand ?
Shall such a worthless worm as I,
Who sometimes am afraid to die,
  Be found at thy right hand ?

2 I love to meet among them now,
Before thy gracious feet to bow,
  Though vilest of them all ;
But can I bear the piercing thought :
What if my name should be left out,
  When thou for them shalt call ?

3 Prevent, prevent it by thy grace ;
Be thou, dear Lord, my hiding-place,
  In this the accepted day ;
Thy pardoning voice, O let me hear,
To still my unbelieving fear ;
  Nor let me fall, I pray.

4 Let me among thy saints be found
Whene'er the archangel's trump shall sound,
  To see thy smiling face ;
Then loudest of the crowd I'll sing,
While heaven's resounding mansions ring
  With shouts of sovereign grace.

939   C.M.   TOPLADY.
" The same bringeth forth much fruit."—John xv. 5.
JESUS, immutably the same,
  Thou true and living Vine !
Around thy all-supporting stem,
  My feeble arms I'd twine.

2 I can do nothing without thee ;
  My strength is wholly thine ;
  Withered and barren should I be,
  If severed from the Vine.

3 Quickened by thee, and kept alive,
  I'd flourish and bear fruit ;
  My life I'd from thy sap derive,
  My vigour from thy root.

4 Each moment watered by thy care,
  And fenced with power divine ;
  Fruit to eternal life would bear,
  The feeblest branch of thine.

940   C.M.   TOPLADY.
" The chiefest among ten thousand."—Song v. 10.
COMPARED with Christ, in all beside
  No comeliness I see ;
The one thing needful, dearest Lord,
  Is to be one with thee.

2 The sense of thy expiring love,
  Into my soul convey ;
  Thyself bestow, for thee alone,
  My All in all, I pray.

3 Less than thyself will not suffice
  My comfort to restore ;
  More than thyself I cannot crave,
  And thou canst give no more.

4 Loved of my God, for him again
  With love intense I'd burn ;
  Chosen of thee ere time began,
  I choose thee in return.

5 Whate'er consists not with thy love,
   O teach me to resign ;
   I'm rich to all the intents of bliss,
   If thou, O God, art mine.

941   L.M.   MEDLEY.
" Whom have I in heaven but thee ? "—Ps. lxxiii. 25.
JESUS, my Lord, my Life, my All,
Prostrate before thy throne I fall ;
Fain would my soul look up and see
My hope, my heaven, my all in thee.

2 Here in this world of sin and woe,
I'm filled with tossings to and fro ;
Burdened with sin, and fears oppressed,
With nothing here to give me rest.

3 In vain from creatures help I seek ;
Thou, only thou, the word canst speak
To heal my wounds, and calm my grief,
Or give my mourning heart relief.

4 Without thy peace and presence, Lord,
Not all the world can help afford.
O do not frown my soul away,
But smile my darkness into day.

5 I long to hear thy pardoning voice ;
O speak, and bid my soul rejoice ;
Say, " Peace, be still ; look up and live ;
Life, peace, and heaven are mine to give."

6 Then, filled with grateful, holy love,
My soul in praise would soar above ;
And with delightful joy record
The wondrous goodness of the Lord.

942   L.M.   GOSPEL MAG., 1777.
" I will not leave you comfortless."—John xiv. 18.
O GOD of grace, of love immense,
How free thy favours to dispense !
I to thy mercy-seat repair,
Since thou hast said, " I'll meet thee there."

2 Thou seest my soul by sin opprest ;
O come, and give the weary rest ;
My base backslidings kindly heal,
Apply the balm, thy love reveal.

3 Should I go mourning to the grave,
'Twere just ; yet, Lord, from darkness save.
Does not thy tender word express,
" I will not leave you comfortless " ?

4 Burst thro' the clouds, O Source of Light !
Let joy succeed the weeping night ;
Thy beams shall make my desert blow,
The fruit appear, the spices flow.

5 What thou hast promised I implore,
Supplies from thy exhaustless store.
O righteous Father, just and true,
Give me both grace and glory too.

943   L.M.   W. W. HORNE.
Seeking the Lord's Face.—Ps. xxvii. 8; Isa. xlv. 19.
THE God of grace delights to hear
The plaintive cry, the humble prayer ;
Nor shall the weakest saint complain
That he has sought the Lord in vain.

2 With power to Jacob's seed he speaks ;
His word the heart asunder breaks ;
While grace the rage of sin controls,
And deep repentance melts their souls.

3 " Seek ye my face," Jehovah cries ;
With joy the contrite heart replies,
" Thy face I seek ; with power descend,
From every foe my soul defend ! "

4 A bleeding Christ is all they plead,
And all that guilty sinners need ;
In whose dear name their fervent cries
Before the Lord like incense rise.

944   7s.   R. HILL.
" Tell me where thy flock rests at noon."—Song i. 7.
TELL me, Saviour, from above,
Dearest Object of my love,
Where thy little flocks abide,
Sheltered near thy bleeding side !

2 Say, thou Shepherd all divine,
Where I may my soul recline.
Where for refuge shall I fly,
While the burning sun is high ?

3 Never had I sought thy name,
Never felt the inward flame,
Had not love first touched my heart,
Given the painful, pleasant smart.

4 Turn, and claim me as thy own ;
Be my portion, Lord, alone.
Deign to hear a sinner's call ;
Be my everlasting all !

945   L.M.   HOSKINS.
" Shine forth."—Ps. lxxx. 1-3; 7, 19; Dan. ix. 17.
SAVIOUR of sinners, deign to shine
On this benighted soul of mine ;
O show my wandering feet the way
That leads to realms of endless day.

2 Reveal the path of life and peace,
The road to pure and perfect bliss.
Guide a poor pilgrim safely on ;
Be thou my Shield and constant Sun !

3 'Midst all the dangers that await
My present militant estate ;
Be thou, dear Jesus, ever near,
My soul to keep, my heart to cheer.

4 And when I shall resign my breath,
And walk the gloomy vale of death,
Then may I find the Lord my stay,
And thence to glory wing my way.

946   C.M.   WATTS.
" He hath put away sin," &c.—Heb. ix. and x.

How is our nature marred by sin !
  Nor can it ever find
A way to make the conscience clean,
  Or heal the wounded mind.

2 In vain we seek for peace with God,
  By methods of our own ;
Jesus, there's nothing but thy blood
  Can bring us near the throne.

3 The threatenings of the broken law
  Impress our souls with dread ;
If God his sword of vengeance draw,
  It strikes our spirits dead.

4 But thy illustrious sacrifice
  Has answered these demands ;
And peace and pardon from the skies
  Come down by Jesus' hands.

5 'Tis by thy death we live, O Lord !
  'Tis on thy cross we rest ;
For ever be thy love adored,
  Thy name for ever blest.

947   148th.   BEDDOME.
" Who can tell ? "—2 Sam. xii. 22; Jonah iii. 9.

GREAT God ! to thee I'll make
  My griefs and sorrows known ;
And with a humble hope
  Approach thy awful throne ;
Though by my sins deserving hell,
I'll not despair, for who can tell ?

2 To thee, who by a word
  My drooping soul canst cheer,
And by thy Spirit form
  Thy glorious image there ;
My foes subdue, my fears dispel ;
I'll daily seek, for who can tell ?

3 Endangered or distressed,
  To thee alone I'll fly,
Implore thy powerful help,
  And at thy footstool lie ;
My case bemoan, my wants reveal,
And patient wait, for who can tell ?

4 My heart misgives me oft,
  And conscience storms within ;
But one sweet smile from thee
  At once would make me clean.
If thou be mine, all will be well ;
And why not so ? for who can tell ?

948   S.M.   MATLOCK (?).
He looked for a city, whose maker is God.—Heb. xi. 10.

WHAT is this world to me ?
  This world is not my home ;
A scene of pain, of grief, and woe ;
  When will my Saviour come ?

2 Come, O thou Saviour dear,

And cheer my fainting soul !
Appear, O gracious Lord, appear,
  And make the sinner whole.

3 Give me, O Lord, to prove
  Thy pardoning love so sweet,
That I may ever lay my soul
  At the dear Saviour's feet.

4 Give me thy lowly mind,
  Thy love to me impart,
And grant that I may ever find
  The Saviour in my heart.

949   L.M.   KELLY.
None other name given among men.—Acts iv. 12.

THERE's not a name beneath the skies,
Nor is there one in heaven above,
But that of Jesus, can suffice
The sinner's burden to remove.

2 Sweet name, when once its virtue's known,
How weak all other helps appear !
The sinner trusts to it alone,
And finds the grand specific there.

3 'Twas long before I knew this truth,
And learned to trust the Saviour's name ;
In vanity I spent my youth ;
The thought now fills my heart with shame.

4 But since I've known the life and power
With which his name is richly stored,
The world can keep my heart no more,
Nor can its joys content afford.

5 The things I once esteemed the most
I now account as worthless dross ;
Thy name, dear Saviour, is my boast,
For which the world appears but loss.

950   C.M.   ALLEN & BATTY.
" They led him away to crucify him."—Mat. xxvii. 31.

WHAT object's this which meets my eyes
  Without Jerusalem's gate ;
Which fills my mind with such surprise
  As wonder to create ?

2 Who can it be that groans beneath
  A cross of massy wood ;
Whose soul's o'erwhelmed in pains of death
  And body bathed in blood ?

3 Is this the Man ? can this be he
  The prophets have foretold
Should with transgressors numbered be,
  And for their crimes be sold ?

4 Yes, now I know 'tis he, 'tis he !
  'Tis Jesus, God's dear Son,
Wrapt in humanity, to die
  For crimes that I had done !

5 O blessed sight, O lovely form,
　To sinful souls like me ;
I'd creep beside him as a worm,
　And see him bleed for me.

6 I'd hear his groans, and view each wound,
　Until, with happy John,
I on his breast a place have found
　Sweetly to lean upon.

951　　　　C.M.　　　SWAIN.
Christ, and him crucified.—1 Cor. ii. 2 ; Phil. iii. 10.

HARK ! from the cross a gracious voice
　Salutes my ravished ears ;
" Rejoice, thou ransomed soul, rejoice,
　And dry those falling tears."

2 Amazed, I turn, grown strangely bold,
　This wondrous thing to see ;
And there the dying Lord behold,
　Stretched on the bloody tree !

3 " Sinner," he cries, " behold the head
　This thorny wreath entwines ;
Look on these wounded hands, and read
　Thy name in crimson lines."

4 The power, the sweetness of that voice,
　My stony heart does move ;
Makes me in Christ my Lord rejoice,
　And melts my soul to love.

952　　　L.M.　　　ALLEN & BATTY
Must worship him in spirit and in truth.—Jno. iv. 24.

BELOVED Saviour, faithful Friend,
The joy of all thy blood-bought train,
In mercy to our aid descend,
Or else we worship thee in vain.

2 In vain we meet to sing and pray,
If Christ his influence withhold ;
Our hearts remain as cold as clay,
Till we the Lord by faith behold.

3 Here manifest thyself in peace ;
Thy tender mercies here make known ;
O breathe on us a gale of grace,
And send the cheering blessing down.

4 We humbly for thy coming wait,
Seeking to know thee as thou art ;
We bow as sinners at thy feet,
And bid thee welcome to our heart.

5 Unite our hearts to thee, dear Lamb ;
Vouchsafe to join us all in one,
To love and praise thy gracious name,
Until we meet around thy throne.

953　　　C.M.　　　HOSKINS.
Hope in trouble.—Jonah ii. 4 ; Ps. xxx. 7 ; cxxx. 5.

ALAS ! the Lord my life is gone,
　The Saviour hides his face ;
And I am left to walk alone,
　In this dark wilderness.

2 In vain I read, in vain I pray,
　Or hear salvation's word,
Unless a soul-reviving ray
　Beam from the glorious Lord.

3 Yet would I trust in him that died,
　For Jesus is his name ;
Yet would I in his grace confide,
　For he is still the same.

4 If once his grace renew the heart,
　Jesus will there remain ;
He cannot finally depart,
　But must return again.

5 Then, dearest Lord, teach me to wait
　Thy own appointed time ;
O change my captive, mournful state,
　And witness thou art mine.

954　　　L.M.　　　H. FOWLER.
" Save me, O God."—Ps. iii. 7 ; lxix. 1 ; xxxi. 16.

SAVE me, O God, my spirit cries,
And on thy faithful word relies ;
Save me from sin, my desperate foe,
That fills my soul with every woe.

2 Save me from pride, that angel-form
That swells a poor, weak, sinful worm ;
That moves the tongue, the hands, the eyes,
And often takes me by surprise.

3 Save me from this bewitching world,
That has to death ten thousand hurled ;
Whose charms enchant, and lead astray
From Jesus Christ, the living Way.

4 Save me from Satan's wiles and snares,
From all the malice which he bears
Against thy image, work, and grace,
Against the visits of thy face.

5 Save me from gloomy black despair ;
On thee alone I'd cast my care,
And wait, and pray, and groan, and sigh,
Till thou in mercy drawest nigh.

955　　　112th.　　C.W.　(altered)
" With well doing ye may put to silence.—1 Pet. ii. 15.

WATCHED by the world with jealous eye,
That fain would see our sin and shame,
As servants of the Lord most high,
As zealous for his glorious name,
May we in all his footsteps move
With holy fear and humble love.

2 That wisdom, Lord, on us bestow,
From every evil to depart ;
To stop the mouth of every foe
By upright walk, and lowly heart ;
The proofs of godly fear to give ;
And show the world how Christians live.

956   7s.   NEWTON & UPTON.
" Come unto me, all ye that labour."—Matt. xi. 28.

CHRIST has blessings to impart,
   Grace to save thee from thy fears ;
O the love that fills his heart !
   Sinner, wipe away thy tears.
2 Why art thou afraid to come ?
   Why afraid to tell thy case ?
He will not pronounce thy doom ;
   Smiles are seated on his face.
3 Though his majesty be great,
   Yet his mercy is no less ;
Though he thy transgressions hate,
   Jesus feels for thy distress.
4 Raise thy downcast eyes and see,
   Numbers do his throne surround ;
These were sinners once, like thee,
   But have full salvation found.
5 Yield not, then, to unbelief ;
   Courage, soul, " there yet is room ! "
Though of sinners thou art chief,
   Come, thou burdened sinner, come.

957   L.M.   STEELE.
" I am thy God."—Isa. xli. 10, xliii. 1.

WHY sinks my weak, desponding mind ?
Why heaves my heart the anxious sigh ?
Can sovereign goodness be unkind ?
Am I not safe, since God is nigh ?
2 He holds all nature in his hand ;
That gracious hand on which I live
Does life, and time, and death command,
And has immortal joys to give.
3 'Tis he supports this fainting frame ;
On him alone my hopes recline ;
The wondrous glories of his name,
How wide they spread, how bright they shine !
4 Infinite wisdom ! boundless power !
Unchanging faithfulness and love !
Here let me trust, while I adore,
Nor from my Refuge e'er remove.
5 My God, if thou art mine indeed,
Then I have all my heart can crave ;
A present help in times of need ;
Still kind to hear, and strong to save.
6 Forgive my doubts, O gracious Lord !
And ease the sorrows of my breast ;
Speak to my heart the healing word,
That thou art mine, and I am blest.

958   C.M.   COWPER.
" And Enoch walked with God."—Gen. v. 22, 24.

O FOR a closer walk with God,
   A calm and heavenly frame ;
A light to shine upon the road

That leads me to the Lamb.
2 Where is the blessedness I knew
   When first I saw the Lord ?
Where is the soul-refreshing view
   Of Jesus and his word ?
3 What peaceful hours I then enjoyed,
   How sweet their memory still !
But now I find an aching void
   The world can never fill.
4 Return, O holy Dove ! return,
   Sweet messenger of rest !
I hate the sins that made thee mourn,
   And drove thee from my breast.
5 The dearest idol I have known,
   Whate'er that idol be ;
Help me to tear it from thy throne,
   And worship only thee.
6 So shall my walk be close with God,
   Calm and serene my frame ;
So purer light shall mark the road
   That leads me to the Lamb.

959   C.M.   NEWTON.
" What shall I render unto the Lord ? "—Ps. cxvi. 12.

FOR mercies countless as the sands,
   Which daily I receive
From Jesus my Redeemer's hands,
   My soul, what canst thou give ?
2 Alas ! from such a heart as mine,
   What can I bring him forth ?
My best is stained and dyed with sin ;
   My all is nothing worth.
3 The best returns for one like me,
   So wretched and so poor,
Is from his gifts to draw a plea,
   And ask him still for more.
4 I cannot serve him as I ought ;
   No works have I to boast ;
Yet would I glory in the thought,
   That I shall owe him most.

960   L.M.   NEWTON.
Ask for the old paths . . and walk therein."—Jer. vi. 16.

BY faith in Christ I walk with God,
With heaven my journey's end in view ;
Supported by his staff and rod,
My road is safe and pleasant too.
2 I travel through a desert wide,
Where many round me blindly stray ;
But he vouchsafes to be my guide,
And will not let me miss my way.
3 Though snares and dangers throng my path,
And earth and hell my course withstand,
I triumph over all by faith,
Guarded by his almighty hand.

4 With him sweet converse I maintain ;
  Great as he is, I dare be free ;
  I tell him all my grief and pain,
  And he reveals his love to me.

5 Some cordial from his word he brings,
  Whene'er my feeble spirit faints ;
  At once my soul revives and sings,
  And yields no more to sad complaints.

961   L.M.   NEWTON.
" Lacked ye anything ? "—Luke xxii. 35 ; Deut. ii. 7.
  BE still, my heart ! these anxious cares
  To thee are burdens, thorns, and snares ;
  They cast dishonour on thy Lord,
  And contradict his gracious word.

2 Brought safely by his hand thus far,
  Why dost thou now give place to fear ?
  How canst thou want if he provide,
  Or lose thy way with such a guide ?

3 Did ever trouble yet befal,
  And he refuse to hear thy call ?
  And has he not his promise passed,
  That thou shalt overcome at last ?

4 He who has helped me hitherto,
  Will help me all my journey through ;
  And give me daily cause to raise
  New Ebenezers to his praise.

962   8.8.6.   STEELE (altered).
Shall not walk in darkness, but have the light of life.
  COME, dearest Lord, and melt my heart,
  Thy animating power impart,
    Blest Source of life divine !
  Jesus, thy love alone can give
  The will to rise, the power to live,
    For every grace is thine.

2 If in my soul thy Spirit's ray
  Has ever turned my night to day,
    I bless thee for the same ;
  But O ! when gloomy clouds arise,
  And veil thy glory from my eyes,
    I know not where I am.

3 Without thy life-inspiring ray,
  My soul is filled with sad dismay ;
    Each cheerful grace declines ;
  Yet I must live on thee, dear Lord,
  For still in thy unchanging word,
    A beam of comfort shines.

4 Yes, on thy word alone I'll rest,
  And hang upon thy arm ; thy breast
    Shall be my soft repose.
  With the beloved disciple, I
  Would on thy sacred bosom lie,
    'Midst all my sins and woes.

963   7s.   GOSPEL MAG., 1781.
The Spirit also helpeth our infirmities.—Rom. viii. 26.
  BLESSED Spirit from above,
  Teach, O teach me how to pray ;
  Fill my soul with heavenly love ;
  Lead me the celestial way.

2 When temptations me surround,
  Help me, Lord, on thee to call ;
  When iniquities abound,
  Save, O save me, or I fall.

3 When thou hidest thy lovely face,
  Till the cloud is passed away,
  And I feel the sweets of peace,
  Never let me cease to pray.

4 When I feel my heart like stone,
  When I have no heart to pray,
  At thy feet, O God, I'd groan,
  " Take this stony heart away."

  Holy Spirit, on me shine ;
  Make my evidences clear ;
  Then I'll say that God is mine !
  I shall with the Lord appear !

964   7s.   AMBROSE SERLE.
Let my cry come near before thee.—Ps. cxix. 169.
  IF to thee I breathe my prayer,
  Lord, wilt thou not deign to hear ?
  Shall I seek, but seek in vain ?
  Shall I ask, and not obtain ?

2 Shall the foretaste thou hast wrought,
  Be to disappointment brought,
  (Though thy promise calls it sure),
  Of the life that shall endure ?

3 Lord, to thee I trembling run,
  Void of refuge and undone ;
  And if thou reject my prayer,
  Ruined, lost, I'll perish there !

965   8.7.   GOSPEL MAG., 1781.
" Shall not want any good thing."—Ps. xxxiv. 10.
  TELL us, O our best Beloved,
  Where thou feed'st thy tender flock ;
  Where they rest at noon, discover ;
  Shelter us beneath that rock !
  Let no idol e'er divide us
  From thee, Lord, in whom we live ;
  By thy loving counsel guide us,
  And our souls at last receive.

2 Show us, Lord, thy great salvation ;
  Keep us till the storm shall cease ;
  In the world we've tribulation,
  But in thee a solid peace.
  No good thing shall be denied us ;
  Thou wilt grace and glory give ;
  By thy counsel thou wilt guide us,
  And at last our souls receive.

966   C.M.   NEWTON.

" Happy art thou, O Israel ? "—Deut. xxxiii. 29.

HAPPY are they to whom the Lord
    His gracious name makes known !
And by his Spirit and his word
    Adopts them for his own.

2 He calls them to a mercy-seat,
    And hears their humble prayer,
And when within his house they meet,
    They find his presence near.

3 The force of their united cries
    No power can long withstand ;
For Jesus helps them from the skies,
    By his almighty hand.

4 Then mountains sink at once to plains,
    And light from darkness springs ;
Each seeming loss improves their gains ;
    Each trouble comfort brings.

5 Dear Lord, assist our souls to pay
    The debt of praise we owe ;
That we enjoy a gospel-day,
    And heaven begun below.

967   L.M.   COWPER.

          Jam. v. 13.

Is any among you afflicted, let him pray.—

GOD of my life, to thee I call ;
Afflicted at thy feet I fall ;
When the great water-floods prevail,
Leave not my trembling heart to fail.

2 Friend of the friendless and the faint,
Where should I lodge my deep complaint ?
Where but with thee, whose open door
Invites the helpless and the poor ?

3 Did ever mourner plead with thee,
And thou refuse that mourner's plea ?
Does not the word still fixed remain,
That none shall seek thy face in vain ?

4 That were a grief I could not bear,
Didst thou not hear and answer prayer ;
But a prayer-hearing, answering God
Supports me under every load.

5 Poor though I am, despised, forgot,
Yet God, my God, forgets me not ;
And he is safe, and must succeed,
For whom the Lord vouchsafes to plead.

968   7s.   COWPER.

Lovest thou me ? "—John xxi. 15-17; xiv. 21.

HARK, my soul ! it is the Lord ;
'Tis thy Saviour, hear his word ;
Jesus speaks, and speaks to thee :
" Say, poor sinner, lovest thou me ?

2 " I delivered thee when bound,
And when wounded healed thy wound ;

Sought thee wandering, set thee right,
Turned thy darkness into light.

3 " Can a woman's tender care
Cease towards the child she bare ?
Yes, she may forgetful be,
Yet I will remember thee.

4 " Mine is an unchanging love,
Higher than the heights above ;
Deeper than the depths beneath,
Free and faithful, strong as death.

5 " Thou shalt see my glory soon,
When the work of grace is done ;
Partner of my throne shalt be ;
Say, poor sinner, lovest thou me ? "

6 Lord, it is my chief complaint,
That my love is cold and faint ;
Yet I love thee and adore ;
O for grace to love thee more !

969   L.M.   COWPER.

' He is before all things, and by him all things consist.'

MY song shall bless the Lord of all ;
My praise shall climb to his abode ;
Thee, Saviour, by that name I call,
The great Supreme, the mighty God.

2 Without beginning or decline,
Object of faith, and not of sense ;
Eternal ages saw him shine ;
He shines eternal ages hence.

3 As much when in the manger laid
Almighty Ruler of the sky,
As when the six days' work he made
Filled all the morning stars with joy.

4 Of all the crowns Jehovah wears,
Salvation is his dearest claim ;
That gracious sound well-pleased he hears,
And owns Immanuel for his name.

970   7s.

The Father, the Word, and the Holy Ghost.—1 Jno. v. 7

HOLY Father, God of love !
Throned in majesty above,
Just and true are all thy ways,
Worthy of eternal praise.

2 Fill my heart with thy rich grace ;
Then with joy I'll run my race ;
Christ's fair image on me seal,
And thy love in him reveal.

3 Holy Jesus, Lamb of God,
Send thy healing word abroad ;
Show how strong and kind thou art,
Let me see thy loving heart.

4 Holy Spirit, quickening breath !
Work in us thy precious faith ;
Bless our hearts with gospel peace,
Furnish us with every grace.

5 Breathe upon us from above,
Teach us truth, and give us love ;
All that feel thy quickening flame,
Will adore and bless thy name.

971   8.7.   LYTE *(altered)*.
" Lo, we have left all and followed thee."—Mark x. 28.
JESUS, we our cross have taken,
All to leave and follow thee ;
Naked, poor, despised, forsaken,
Thou, from hence, our All shalt be.
2 Let the world despise and leave us ;
They have left the Saviour too ;
Human hearts and looks deceive us ;
Thou art not, like them, untrue.
3 And while thou shalt smile upon us,
God of wisdom, love, and might,
Foes may hate, and friends disown us,
Show thy face, and all is bright.
4 Man may trouble and distress us,
'Twill but drive us to thy breast ;
Life with trials hard may press us,
Heaven will bring us sweeter rest.

972   8.7.4.   KELLY.
" King of kings and Lord of lords."—1 Tim. vi. 15.
LOOK, ye saints ! the sight is glorious !
See the exalted Saviour now,
From the fight returned victorious ;
Every knee to him shall bow.
Crown him, crown him !
Crowns become the victor's brow !
2 Crown the Saviour ; saints, adore him ;
Rich the trophies Jesus brings !
Saints and angels bow before him,
While the vault of heaven rings ;
Crown him, crown him !
Crown the Saviour King of kings !

3 Hark ! those bursts of acclamation,
Hark ! those loud triumphant chords !
Jesus takes the highest station ;
O what joy the sight affords !
Crown him, crown him !
King of kings, and Lord of lords !

973   7s.   NEWTON
" Not to Sinai, but to Zion."—Heb. xii. 18-24.
NOT to Sinai's dreadful blaze,
But to Zion's throne of grace,
By a way marked out with blood,
Sinners now approach to God.
2 Not to hear the fiery law,
But with humble joy to draw
Water, by that well supplied
Jesus opened when he died.

3 Lord, there are no streams but thine
Can assuage a thirst like mine !
'Tis a thirst thyself didst give ;
Let me, therefore, drink and live !

974   L.M.   KELLY.
" Seek peace."—Ps. xxxiv. 14 ; Rom. xii. 18.
WHILE contests rend the Christian church,
O may I live the friend of peace ;
The sacred mine of Scripture search,
And learn from man, vain man, to cease.
2 O teach me, Lord, thy truth to know,
And separate from all beside ;
This I would guard from every foe,
Nor fear the issue to abide.
3 But keep me, Lord, from party zeal,
That seeks its own and not thy praise ;
This temper I would never feel,
Or when I do, would own it base.
4 Be mine to recommend thy grace,
That sinners may believe and live ;
That they who live may run the race,
And then a crown of life receive.
5 Lord, search my heart ; O search me through !
Detect, destroy what's not thy own ;
Whene'er I speak, whate'er I do,
O may I seek thy praise alone.

975   C.M.   KELLY.
" He shall come, saith the Lord of Hosts."—Mal. iii. 1.
HE comes ; the Saviour full of grace,
By ancient prophets sung ;
The smile of mercy on his face,
And truth upon his tongue.

2 In him the world no beauty sees,
No form nor comeliness ;
Rejected and despised he is,
And plunged in deep distress.

3 But there's a people taught by grace
To know his matchless worth ;
They own him, though accounted base,
And show his praises forth.

4 They own him as the Lord of all,
Their Saviour and their God ;
Before his feet they prostrate fall—
The purchase of his blood.

976   8.7.   BURNHAM.
Christ a Physician.—Matt. ix. 12 ; Mark ii. 17
JESUS is a wise Physician,
Skilful and exceeding kind ;
Through him sinners find remission,
And enjoy sweet peace of mind.
2 Moved with tenderest compassion,
He relieves the wounded heart ;

And the richest consolation
His blest Spirit does impart.

3 This Physician understandeth
All disorders of the soul ;
And no payment he demandeth,
When he makes the wounded whole.

4 Come, ye souls, who now are sighing
Under guilt's distressing chains,
To the Saviour now be flying ;
He will ease you of your pains.

5 What though bad is your condition,
And your wounds you can't endure ?
He, the sinner's wise Physician,
Will effect a perfect cure.

977   L.M.   STEELE.
They that are whole need not a physician.—Lu. v. 31.

DEEP are the wounds which sin has made ;
Where shall the sinner find a cure ?
In vain, alas ! is nature's aid ;
The work exceeds all nature's power.

2 Sin, like a raging fever, reigns
With fatal strength in every part ;
The dire contagion fills the veins,
And spreads its poison to the heart.

3 And can no sovereign balm be found ?
And is no kind physician nigh,
To ease the pain and heal the wound,
Ere life and hope for ever fly ?

4 There is a great Physician near ;
Look up, O fainting soul, and live.
See, in his heavenly smiles appear
Such ease as nature cannot give.

5 See, in the Saviour's precious blood,
Life, health, and bliss abundant flow !

'Tis only this dear sacred flood
Can ease thy pain and heal thy woe.

978   L.M.   MEDLEY.
"Blessed are the poor in spirit."—Mat. v. 3; Lu. vi. 20.

How blessed are they who truly see
Their emptiness and poverty ;
Whose souls are humbled in the dust,
And who in Jesus only trust !

2 Glad they renounce their former pride,
And wholly in his name confide ;
Only in him they make their boast,
Who came to seek and save the lost.

3 They're vile and poor in their own eyes,
But Jesus' love they highly prize ;
They never think they're laid too low
If Jesus on them pity show.

4 To be the meanest they're content,
So Jesus but their souls present
With pardoning grace and heavenly love,
To fit them for the joys above.

5 These are the souls whom Christ will bless
With all the riches of his grace ;
And these are they who soon shall rise
To a bright kingdom in the skies.

979   L.M   MEDLEY.
" Blessed . . which do hunger and thirst."—Mat. v. 6.

JESUS those happy souls does bless,
Who *hunger* for his righteousness ;
Who seek the smilings of his face,
And *thirst* for fresh supplies of grace.

2 They cannot here contented live
On all the dainties earth can give ;
Their souls can feast on nothing less
Than Christ's eternal righteousness.

3 Some sweet foretastes they have below,
But the bright world, to which they go,
Will them a glorious banquet yield ;
There shall their souls be ever filled.

4 May this my blest experience be ;
To *hunger*, Lord, and *thirst* for thee,
And on thy righteousness to live,
Which can both food and comfort give !

5 Then when at death my soul shall rise
To the blest banquet in the skies,
I shall partake the heavenly store,
And feast and sing for evermore.

980   L.M.   STEELE.
" Because I live, ye shall live also."—John xiv. 19.

WHEN sins and fears prevailing rise,
And fainting hope almost expires,
Jesus, to thee I lift my eyes,
To thee I breathe my soul's desires.

2 Art thou not mine, my living Lord ?
And can my hope—my comfort die,
Fixed on thy everlasting word,
That word which built the earth and sky ?

3 If my immortal Saviour lives,
Then my immortal life is sure ;
His word a firm foundation gives ;
Here let me build and rest secure.

4 Here let my faith unshaken dwell ;
Immovable the promise stands ;
Not all the powers of earth or hell
Can e'er dissolve the sacred bands.

5 Here, O my soul, thy trust repose ;
If Jesus is for ever mine,
Not death itself, that last of foes,
Shall break a union so divine.

981   L.M.

If the Lord were pleased to kill us.—Judg. xiii. 23.

WHY should I yield to slavish fears ?
God is the same to endless years ;
Though clouds and darkness hide his face,
He's boundless both in truth and grace.

2 Would e'er the God of truth make known
The worth and glory of his Son ;
His love and righteousness display,
And cast my soul at last away ?

3 Would he reveal my sin and woe,
Teach me my numerous wants to know,
And help me in my darkest frame
To build my hopes on Jesus' name;

4 Would God preserve my soul from hell,
And make his love at times prevail ,-
Would he bestow such mercies past,
And yet reject my soul at last ?

5 Though unbelief may long molest,
And sin and Satan break my rest,
Grace shall at last the victory get,
And make my conquest quite complete.

982   8.7.4.   KELLY.

" It is finished."—John xix. 30; iv. 34; xvii. 4.

" IT is finished ! " Sinners, hear it ;
'Tis the dying Victor's cry ;
" It is finished ! " Angels bear it,
Bear the joyful truth on high :
     " It is finished ! "
Tell it through the earth and sky !

2 Justice, from her awful station,
Bars the sinner's peace no more ;
Justice views with approbation
What the Saviour did and bore ;
     Grace and mercy
Now display their boundless store.

3 Hear the Lord himself declaring
All performed he came to do ;
Sinners, in yourselves despairing,
This is joyful news to you.
     Jesus speaks it,
His are faithful words and true.

4 " It is finished ! " all is over ;
Yes, the cup of wrath is drained ;
Such the truth these words discover ;
Thus the victory was obtained ;
     'Tis a victory
None but Jesus could have gained.

5 Crown the mighty Conqueror, crown him,
Who his people's foes o'ercame !
In the highest heaven enthrone him !
Men and angels, sound his fame !
     Great his glory !
Jesus bears a matchless name.

983   S.M.   C.W.

No man can say that Jesus is the Lord.—1 Cor. xii. 3.

SPIRIT of truth, come down,
Reveal the things of God ;
O make to us salvation known,
And witness with the blood.

2 No man can truly say
That Jesus is the Lord,
Unless thou take the veil away,
And breathe the living word.

3 Then, only then, we feel
Our interest in his blood ;
And cry, with joy unspeakable,
" Thou art my Lord, my God ! "

4 O that we now might know
The all-atoning Lamb !
Spirit of faith, descend and show
The virtue of his name.

5 Inspire the living faith,
Which whosoe'er receives,
The witness in himself he hath,
And joyfully believes.

984   L.M.   C. COLE.

The great trumpet shall be blown.—Isa. xxvii. 13.

HARK ! how the gospel trumpet sounds !
Christ and free grace therein abounds ;
Free grace to such as sinners be ;
And if free grace, why not for me ?

2 The Saviour died, and by his blood
Brought rebel sinners near to God ;
He died to set the captives free ;
And why, my soul, why not for thee ?

3 The blood of Christ, how sweet it sounds,
To cleanse and heal the sinner's wounds !
The streams thereof are rich and free ;
And why, my soul, why not for thee ?

4 Thus Jesus came the poor to bless,
To clothe them with his righteousness ;
The robe is spotless, full, and free ;
And why, my soul, why not for thee ?

5 Eternal life by Christ is given,
And ruined rebels raised to heaven,
Then sing of grace so rich and free,
And say, my soul, why not for thee ?

985   112th.   CENNICK.

" Ho, every one that thirsteth," &c.—Isa. lv. 1.

Ho, ye despairing sinners, hear,
Ye thirsty, sin-sick souls, draw near ;

Here's water, whose all-powerful stream
Shall quench your thirst and wash you clean,
Its healing power has always wrought
Beyond the reach of human thought.

2 Bethesda's pool is not like this,
Nor heals nor cures such leprosies ;
Nor Siloam's streams, nor Jordan's flood
Could to my heart seem half so good ;
'Tis Jesus' blood, that crimson sea,
That washes guilt and filth away.

3 To this dear Fountain I'd repair,
With all the wounds and pains I bear ;
I'd keep my station near its side,
And wash, and drink, and there abide ;
Nor from the sacred streams remove,
Till taken to their source above.

986   C.M.   D. HERBERT.
"And let him that is athirst come."—Rev. xxii. 17.

Ho, poor distressed, thirsty soul,
  The fountain is just by,
Whose waters run both full and free ;
  Come, drink, and never die.

2 O come, poor helpless thirsty soul,
  The call is made to you ;
That God who made you feel your thirst
  Will prove his promise true.

3 O ye who long to feel and see
  Your interest in his blood,
This thing is proved beyond a doubt,
  Because you thirst for God.

4 There's not a sinner out of hell,
  The vilest of the base,
If he is made to trust in Christ,
  Who shall not see his face.

987   C.M.   MEDLEY.
"I will give unto him that is athirst."—Rev. xxi. 6.

O WHAT amazing words of grace
  Are in the gospel found !
Suited to every sinner's case
  Who knows the joyful sound.

2 Come, then, with all your wants and wounds,
  Your every burden bring ;
Here love, eternal love, abounds,
  A deep celestial spring.

3 This spring with living water flows,
  And living joy imparts ;
Come, thirsty souls, your wants disclose,
  And drink with thankful hearts.

4 To sinners poor, like me and you,
  He says he'll freely give,
Come, thirsty souls, and prove it true,
  Drink, and for ever live.

988   7s.   TOPLADY.
"Happy is he that hath the God of Jacob," &c.

HAPPINESS, thou lovely name,
Where's thy seat, O tell me, where ?
Learning, pleasure, wealth, and fame,
All cry out, "It is not here."

2 Not the wisdom of the wise
Can inform me where it lies ;
Not the grandeur of the great
Can the bliss I seek create.

3 Object of my first desire,
Jesus, crucified for me ;
All to happiness aspire,
Only to be found in thee.

4 Thee to praise and thee to know,
Constitute our bliss below ;
Thee to see and thee to love,
Constitute our bliss above.

5 Lord, it is not life to live,
If thy presence thou deny ;
Lord, if thou thy presence give,
'Tis no longer death to die.

6 Source and Giver of repose,
Singly from thy smile it flows ;
Happiness complete is thine ;
Mine it is, if thou art mine.

989   C.M. SPIRITUAL MAG., 1790.
"If the Son shall make you free."—John viii. 36.

YE captive souls, in fetters bound,
  Who feel your misery ;
The way to liberty is found—
  The Son shall make you free.

2 Hear the Redeemer's gracious call :
  "Poor captives, come to me ;
Into my arms for freedom fall ;
  Come, and I'll make you free."

3 Why should you doubt his love or power ?
  To him for refuge flee ;
This is the Lord's appointed hour ;
  He waits to make you free.

4 The souls who are by Jesus freed,
  No more shall bondage see ;
From sin and death they're free indeed ;
  Dear Saviour, make me free.

5 Divorce my soul from every sin,
  Let me thy servant be ;
O make and keep my conscience clean
  To show that I am free.

990   7s.   BURNHAM.
"I cry unto thee daily."—Ps. lxxxvi. 3 ; lv. 17.

JESUS, now thyself reveal ;
Manifest thy love to me ;

Make me, Saviour, make me feel
All my soul's delight in thee.

2 All thy ways I'd well approve,
Under thy dear wings abide ;
Never from thy cross I'd move,
Never leave thy wounded side.

3 Daily I'd repent of sin,
Daily wash in Calvary's blood,
Daily feel thy peace within,
Daily I'd commune with God.

4 Daily I'd thy name adore,
Prize thy word, and love to pray ;
All thy kindness well explore,
Still press on to perfect day.

5 When with evils I'm beset,
Foes advancing all around,
Down I'd fall at thy dear feet,
Wait to see thy grace abound.

991 L.M. TOPLADY.
"Their strength is to sit still."—Isa. xxx. 7, 15.
EMPTIED of earth I fain would be,
The world, myself, and all but thee ;
Only reserved for Christ that died,
Surrendered to the Crucified.

2 Sequestered from the noise and strife,
The lust, the pomp, the pride of life ;
For heaven alone my heart prepare,
And have my conversation there.

3 Constrain my soul thy sway to own ;
Self-will, self-righteousness dethrone ;
Each idol tread beneath thy feet,
And to thyself the conquest get.

4 Detach from sublunary joys
One that would only hear thy voice.

Thy beauty see, thy grace admire,
Nor glow but with celestial fire.

5 Larger communion let me prove
With thee, blest Object of my love ;
But O for this no power have I !
My strength is at thy feet to lie.

992 L.M. KELLY.
"An afflicted and poor people."—Zeph. iii. 12.
"POOR and afflicted," Lord, are thine,
Among the great unfit to shine ;
But, though the world may think it strange,
They would not with the world exchange.

2 "Poor and afflicted," yes, they are ;
Their cup is filled with grief and care ;
But he who saved them by his blood,
Makes every sorrow work for good.

3 "Poor and afflicted ; " yet they sing,
For Jesus is their glorious King ;
"Through sufferings perfect," now he reigns,
And shares in all their griefs and pains.

4 "Poor and afflicted ; " but ere long
They'll join the bright celestial throng
Their sufferings then will reach a close,
And heaven afford them sweet repose.

5 And while they walk the thorny way,
They're often heard to sigh and say,
"Dear Saviour, come ; O quickly come,
And take thy mourning pilgrims home."

993 11s. GRANT.
O thou afflicted, tossed with tempest.—Isa. liv. 11.
O ZION, afflicted with wave upon wave, [save ;
Whom no man can comfort, whom no man can
With darkness surrounded, by terrors dismayed,
In toiling and rowing thy strength is decayed.

2
Loud roaring, the billows now nigh overwhelm ;
But skilful's the Pilot who sits at the helm ;
His wisdom conducts thee, his power thee defends,
In safety and quiet thy warfare he ends.

3
"O fearful, O faithless ! " in mercy he cries ;
"My promise, my truth, are they light in thy eyes ?
Still, still I am with thee ; my promise shall stand ;
Through tempest and tossing, I'll bring thee to
land.

4
"Forget thee I will not, I cannot ; thy name
Engraved on my heart does for ever remain ;
The palms of my hands while I look on I see
The wounds I received when suffering for thee.

5
["I feel at my heart all thy sighs and thy groans,
For thou art most near me, my flesh and my
bones ;
In all thy distresses thy Head feels the pain ;
Yet all are most needful ; not one is in vain.

6
"Then trust me, and fear not ; thy life is secure ;
My wisdom is perfect, supreme is my power ;
In love I correct thee, thy soul to refine,
To make thee at length in my likeness to shine."]

994 S.M. KENT.
"Leaning upon her Beloved."—Song viii. 5.
FROM sin's dark thorny maze,
To Canaan's fertile plains,
A travelling fair one in distress,
On her Beloved leans.

2 Through fire and flood she goes,
A weakling, more than strong ;

Vents in his bosom all her woes,
And leaning moves along.

3 When dangers round her press,
And darkness veils the skies,
She leans upon his righteousness ;
From thence her hopes arise.

4 When guilt, a mighty flood,
Her trembling conscience pains,
Then on his peace-securing blood
This travelling fair one leans.

5 She views the covenant sure ;
Her hopes all centre there ;
And on his bosom leans secure,
Whose temples bled for her.

995   S.M.   KELLY.
" They seek a country," &c.—Heb. xiii. 14; xi. 10.
FROM Egypt lately come,
Where death and darkness reign,
We seek our new, our better home,
Where we our rest shall gain.

2 To Canaan's sacred bound,
We haste with songs of joy ;
Where peace and liberty are found,
And sweets that never cloy.

3 There sin and sorrow cease,
And every conflict's o'er ;
There shall we dwell in endless peace,
And never hunger more.

4 There, in celestial strains,
Enraptured myriads sing !
There love in every bosom reigns,
For Christ himself is King.

5 We soon shall join the throng
And all their pleasure share ;

And sing the everlasting song
With all the ransomed there.

                         MEDLEY.
996   L.M.   Ezek. xlvii. 1-12.
" There is a river," &c.—Ps. xlvi. 4 ;
WHILE the dear saints of God below
Travel this vale of sin and woe,
There is a river through the road,
" Makes glad the city of our God."

2 This river is his heavenly love,
Proceeding from the throne above ;
And all its streams which here are found,
With comfort, joy, and peace abound.

3 Blest river ! great its virtues are ;
Pure river, O how sweet and clear !
Deep river, through the desert way ;
Full river, never to decay !

4 Ye thirsty, poor, and needy souls,

For you this wondrous river rolls.
Though sin and sorrow make you sad,
Yet drink, and let your hearts be glad.

5 Drink, and for ever bless his name,
From whom these streams of mercy came :
Drink, for the fountain's open still ;
Drink, for he says, " Whoever will."

997   C.M.   BURNHAM.
" I go mourning all the day long."—Ps. xxxviii. 6.
LORD, while I wander here below
What ills my soul annoy !
For 'tis of thee I little know,
And ah ! still less enjoy.

2 I often hear the word of life,
And all seems death within ;
Yet feel a strange mysterious strife
Between my soul and sin.

3 I read the truth and think it o'er,
And long to know thy will ;
And wrestle for thy Spirit's power ;
But ah ! how barren still !

4 But shall I from thy throne retreat,
And hopeless, yield to fear ?
No, in the strength of God I'd wait,
Till mercy shall appear.

5 Then still, my soul, fresh cries lift up ;
Stand firm in Zion's ways ;
Till God at length shall crown thy hope,
And fill thee with his praise.

998   104th.   HAMMOND.
" Turn ye to the strong hold, ye prisoners of hope."
YE pris'ners of hope, o'erwhelmed with grief,
To Jesus look up for certain relief ;
There's no condemnation in Jesus the Lord,
But strong consolation his grace does afford.

2 Should justice appear a merciless foe,
Yet be of good cheer, and soon shall you know
That sinners, confessing their wickedness past,
A plentiful blessing of pardon shall taste.

3 Then dry up your tears, ye children of grief,
For Jesus appears to give you relief.
If you are returning to Jesus, your Friend,
Your sighing and mourning in singing shall end.

999   C.M.   NEWTON.
" Will ye also go away ? "—John vi. 68 ; Ps. lxxiii. 25.
WHEN any turn from Zion's way,
(Alas, what numbers do !)
Methinks I hear my Saviour say,
" Wilt thou forsake me too ? "

2 Ah ! Lord, with such a heart as mine,
Unless thou hold me fast,

I feel I must, I shall decline,
  And prove like them at last,

3 Yet thou alone hast power, I know,
  To save a wretch like me ;
  To whom, or whither, could I go,
  If I should turn from thee ?

4 No voice but thine can give me rest,
  And bid my fears depart ;
  No love but thine can make me blest,
  And satisfy my heart.

5 What anguish has that question stirred :
  If I will also go ?
  Yet, Lord, relying on thy word,
  I humbly answer, No.

1000 104th. WINGROVE.
  " There is therefore now no condemnation."
YE tempted and tried, to Jesus draw nigh,
He suffered and died your wants to supply ;
Trust him for salvation ; you need not to grieve ;
" There's no condemnation to them that believe."

2 By day and by night his love is made known ;
It is his delight to succour his own ; [grieve !
He will have compassion ; then why should you
" There's no condemnation to them that believe."

3 Though Satan will seek the sheep to annoy,
The helpless and weak he ne'er shall destroy,
Christ is their salvation, and strength he will
  give ;   [lieve."
" There's no condemnation to them that be-

1001 L.M. NEWTON.
  " The Sabbath of Rest."—Exod. xxxi. 15 ; xxxv. 2.
How welcome to the saints, when pressed
With six days' noise, and care, and toil,
Is the returning day of rest,
Which hides them from the world awhile !

2 Now, from the throng withdrawn away,
They seem to breathe a different air ;
Composed and softened by the day,
All things another aspect wear.

3 How happy if their lot is cast
Where statedly the gospel sounds !
The word is honey to their taste,
Renews their strength and heals their wounds.

4 With joy they hasten to the place
Where they their Saviour oft have met ;
And while they feast upon his grace,
Their burdens and their griefs forget.

5 This favoured lot, my friends, is ours ;
May we the privilege highly prize,
And find these consecrated hours
Sweet earnests of immortal joys.

1002 C.M. MONTGOMERY (*altered*).
Prayer.—Phil. iv. 6 ; Acts vi. 4 ; Dan. ix. 3.
PRAYER is the soul's sincere desire,
  Uttered or unexpressed ;
The motion of a hidden fire,
  That trembles in the breast.

2 Prayer is the burden of a sigh,
  The falling of a tear ;
The upward glancing of an eye,
  When none but God is near.

3 Prayer is the contrite sinner's voice,
  Returning from his ways ;
While angels in their songs rejoice,
  And cry, " Behold, he prays ! "

4 The saints in prayer appear as one,
  In word, and deed, and mind ;

While with the Father and the Son,
  Sweet fellowship they find.

5 Nor prayer is made on earth alone ;
  The Holy Spirit pleads ;
And Jesus, on the eternal throne,
  For sinners intercedes.

6 O thou by whom we come to God,
  The Life, the Truth, the Way !
The path of prayer thyself hast trod ;
  Lord, teach us how to pray.

1003 C.M. WATTS.
Breathing after Holiness.—Ps. cxix. 5, 29-36, 133.
O THAT the Lord would guide my ways
  To keep his statutes still !
O that my God would grant me grace
  To know and do his will.

2 O send thy Spirit down to write
  Thy law upon my heart !
Nor let my tongue indulge deceit,
  Nor act the liar's part.

3 From vanity turn off my eyes ;
  Let no corrupt design,
Nor covetous desires, arise
  Within this soul of mine.

4 Order my footsteps by thy word,
  And make my heart sincere ;
Let sin have no dominion, Lord,
  But keep my conscience clear.

5 Make me to walk in thy commands ;
  'Tis a delightful road ;
Nor let my head, or heart, or hands,
  Offend against my God.

1004 L.M. WATTS.
Original and actual sin confessed.—Ps. li. 1-9; Ro. v. 12

LORD, I am vile, conceived in sin,
And born unholy and unclean ;
Sprung from the man whose guilty fall
Corrupts the race, and taints us all.

2 Soon as we draw our infant breath,
The seeds of sin grow up for death ;
The law demands a perfect heart ;
But we're defiled in every part.

3 Behold, I fall before thy face ;
My only refuge is thy grace ;
Not outward forms can make me clean—
The leprosy lies deep within.

4 Jesus, my Lord ! thy blood alone
Has power sufficient to atone ;
Thy blood can make me white as snow ;
No Jewish types could cleanse me so.

5 While guilt disturbs and breaks my peace,
Nor flesh, nor soul, has rest or ease ;
Lord, let me hear thy pardoning voice,
And make my broken bones rejoice.

1005 C.M. WATTS.
Jesus, the Lamb of God, worshipped.—Rev. v. 11-13.

COME, let us join our cheerful songs
With angels round the throne ;
Ten thousand thousand are their tongues,
But all their joys are one.

2 " Worthy the Lamb that died," they cry,
" To be exalted thus."
" Worthy the Lamb," our lips reply,
" For he was slain for us."

3 Jesus is worthy to receive
Honour and power divine ;
And blessings more than we can give,
Be, Lord, for ever thine.

4 Let all that dwell above the sky,
And air, and earth, and seas,
Conspire to lift thy glories high,
And speak thy endless praise.

5 The whole creation join in one,
To bless the sacred name
Of him that sits upon the throne,
And to adore the Lamb.

1006 L.M. WATTS.
Christ our Wisdom, Righteousness, &c.—1 Cor. i. 30.

BURIED in shadows of the night,
We lie till Christ restores the light ;
Wisdom descends to heal the blind,
And chase the darkness of the mind.

2 Our guilty souls are drowned in tears,
Till his atoning blood appears ;
Then we awake from deep distress,
And sing, " The Lord our righteousness."

3 Our very frame is mixed with sin ;
His Spirit makes our conscience clean ;
Such virtues from his sufferings flow,
At once to cleanse and pardon too.

4 Jesus beholds where Satan reigns,
Binding his slaves in heavy chains ;
He sets the prisoners free, and breaks
The iron bondage from our necks.

5 Poor helpless worms in thee possess
Grace, wisdom, power, and righteousness ;
Thou art our mighty All ; may we
Give our whole selves, O Lord, to thee.

1007 L.M. WATTS.
The Christian Warfare.—1 Tim. i. 18; vi. 12.

STAND up, my soul, shake off thy fears,
And gird the gospel-armour on ;
March to the gates of endless joy,
Where thy great Captain-Saviour's gone.

2 Hell and thy sins resist thy course,
But hell and sin are vanquished foes ;
Thy Jesus nailed them to the cross,
And sang the triumph when he rose.

3 What though thy inward lusts rebel ?
'Tis but a struggling gasp for life ;
The weapons of victorious grace
Shall slay thy sins, and end the strife.

4 Then may my soul march boldly on,
Press forward to the heavenly gate ;
There peace and joy eternal reign,
And glittering robes for conquerors wait.

1008 L.M.
" Quicken us, and we will call upon thy name."

COME, Holy Spirit, calm my mind,
And fit me to approach my God ;
Remove each vain, each worldly thought,
And lead me to thy blest abode.

2 Hast thou imparted to my soul
A living spark of heavenly fire ?
O kindle now the sacred flame !
Teach me to burn with pure desire.

3 Impress upon my wandering heart
The love that Christ for sinners bore ;
And give a new, a contrite heart,
A heart the Saviour to adore.

1009 C.M.
"Heal my soul."—Ps. xli. 4; vi. 2; Jer. xvii. 14.

LORD, I approach thy throne of grace,
    Where mercy does abound,
Desiring mercy for my sin,
    To heal my soul's deep wound.

2 O Lord, I need not to repeat
    What I would humbly crave,
For thou dost know, before I ask,
    The thing that I would have.

3 Mercy, good Lord, mercy I ask ;
    This is the total sum ;
For mercy, Lord, is all my suit ;
    O let thy mercy come.

1010 C.M. STEELE.
"Hear the prayer of thy servant."—Dan. ix. 17.

FATHER, whate'er of earthly bliss
    Thy sovereign will denies,
Accepted at thy throne of grace,
    Let this petition rise :

2 "Give me a calm, a thankful heart,
    From every murmur free ;
The blessings of thy grace impart,
    And make me live to thee.

3 "Let the sweet hope that thou art mine,
    My life and death attend ;
Thy presence through my journey shine,
    And crown my journey's end."

1011 C.M. WATTS.
God's Presence is Light in Darkness.—Luke i. 78, 79

MY God, the spring of all my joys,
    The life of my delights,
The glory of my brightest days,
    And comfort of my nights.

2 In darkest shades if he appear,
    My dawning is begun ;
He is my soul's sweet morning star,
    And he my rising sun.

3 The opening heavens around me shine
    With beams of sacred bliss,
While Jesus shows his heart is mine,
    And whispers *I am his.*

4 My soul would leave this heavy clay,
    At that transporting word,
Run up with joy the shining way,
    To embrace my dearest Lord.

5 Fearless of hell and ghastly death,
    I'd break through every foe ;
The wings of love and arms of faith
    Should bear me conqueror through.

1012 S.M. KELLY.
Himself he cannot save.—Mat. xxvii. 42; Mk. xv. 31.

"HIMSELF he cannot save."
    Insulting foe, 'tis true ;
The words a gracious meaning have,
    Though meant in scorn by you.

2 "Himself he cannot save."
    This is his highest praise.
Himself for others' sake he gave,
    And suffers in their place.

3 It were an easy part
    For him the cross to fly ;
But love to sinners fills his heart,
    And makes him choose to die.

4 'Tis love the cause unfolds,
    The deep mysterious cause,
Why he who all the world upholds,
    Hangs upon yonder cross.

5 Let carnal Jews blaspheme,
    And worldly wisdom mock ;
The Saviour's cross shall be my theme,
    And Christ himself my Rock.

1013 C.M. KELLY.
"Ye shall be my sons and daughters, saith the Lord."

THERE is a family on earth,
    Whose Father fills a throne !
But though a seed of heavenly birth,
    To men they're little known.

2 Whene'er they meet the public eye,
    They feel the public scorn ;
For men their fairest claims deny,
    And count them basely born.

3 But 'tis the King who reigns above,
    That claims them for his own ;
The favoured objects of his love,
    And destined to a throne.

4 But when the King himself was here,
    His claims were set at nought ;
Would *they* another lot prefer ?
    Rejected be the thought !

5 No ; they will tread, while here below,
    The path their Master trod ;
Content all honour to forego,
    But that which comes from God.

1014 8.7.4. KELLY.
"Love as brethren."—1 Pet. iii. 8; Gal. vi. 2.

BRETHREN, let us walk together
    In the bonds of love and peace ;
Can it be a question whether
    Brethren should from conflict cease ?
        'Tis in union
Hope, and joy, and love increase.

2 While we journey homeward, let us
   Help each other in the road ;
Foes on every side beset us ;
   Snares through all the way are strewed ;
     It behoves us
   Each to bear a brother's load.

3 When we think how much our Father
   Has forgiven, and does forgive,
Brethren, we should learn the rather
   Free from wrath and strife to live,
     Far removing
   All that might offend or grieve.

4 Then, let each esteem his brother
   Better than himself to be ;
And let each prefer another,
   Full of love, from envy free ;
     Happy are we,
   When in this we all agree.

1015   S.M.   WATTS.
Divine Compassion.—Ps. ciii. 8-12 ; Isa. xliii. 25.
   My soul, repeat his praise,
   Whose mercies are so great,
   Whose anger is so slow to rise,
   So ready to abate.

2 God will not always chide ;
   And, when his strokes are felt,
His strokes are fewer than our crimes,
   And lighter than our guilt.

3 High as the heavens are raised
   Above the ground we tread,
So far the riches of his grace
   Our highest thoughts exceed.

4 His power subdues our sins,
   And his forgiving love,

Far as the east is from the west,
   Does all our guilt remove.

1016   L.M.   C.W.
"Thy mercy, O Lord, held me up."—Ps. xciv. 18.
   GOD of my life, thy gracious power
   Through varied deaths my soul has led ;
   Oft turned aside the fatal hour,
   Or lifted up my sinking head.

2 Whither, O whither should I fly,
   But to the loving Saviour's breast ?
   Secure within thy arms to lie,
   And safe beneath thy wings to rest.

3 I have no skill the snare to shun,
   But thou, O Christ, my wisdom art :
   I ever into ruin run,
   But thou art greater than my heart.

4 Foolish, and impotent, and blind,

Lead me the way thy saints have known ;
Bring me where I my heaven may find,
The heaven of loving thee alone.

1017   L.M.   NEWTON.
"In my prosperity I said, I shall never be moved."
   THE peace of which I had a taste
   When Jesus first his love revealed,
   I fondly hoped would always last,
   Because my foes were then concealed.

2 But when I felt the tempter's power
   Rouse my corruptions from their sleep,
   I trembled at the stormy hour,
   And saw the horrors of the deep.

3 Now on presumption's billows borne,
   My spirit seemed the Lord to dare,
   Now, quick as thought, a sudden turn
   Plunged me in gulfs of black despair.

4 "Lord, save me, or I sink," I prayed ;
   He heard, and bade the tempest cease ;
   The angry waves his word obeyed,
   And all my fears were hushed to peace.

5 The peace is his, and not my own,
   My heart (no better than before)
   Is still to dreadful changes prone ;
   Then let me never trust it more.

1018   L.M.   TOPLADY.
"He causeth his wind to blow."—Ps. cxlvii. 18.
   AT anchor laid, remote from home,
   Toiling, I cry, "Sweet Spirit, come ;
   Celestial breeze, no longer stay,
   But swell my sails, and speed my way."

2 Fain would I mount, fain would I glow,
   And loose my cable from below ;
   But I can only spread my sail ;
   Thou, thou must breathe the auspicious gale.

1019   L.M.   C.W.
O that I knew where I might find him.—Job xxiii. 3.
   O THAT my load of sin were gone !
   O that I could at last submit
   At Jesus' feet to lay it down,
   To lay my soul at Jesus' feet !

2 When shall my eyes behold the Lamb,
   The God of my salvation see ?
   Weary, O Lord, thou know'st I am ;
   Yet still I cannot come to thee.

3 Rest for my soul I long to find ;
   Saviour, if mine indeed thou art,
   Give me thy meek and lowly mind,
   And stamp thy image on my heart.

4 I would, but thou must give me power,
   My heart from every sin release ;

Bring near, bring near, the joyful hour,
And fill me with thy heavenly peace.

1020 C.M. NEWTON.
But when a stronger than he shall come.—Luke xi. 21.
THE castle of the human heart,
Strong in its native sin,
Is guarded well in every part
By him who dwells within.

2 For Satan there in arms resides,
And calls the place his own ;
With care against assaults provides,
And rules as on a throne.

3 But Jesus, stronger far than he,
In his appointed hour,
Appears to set his people free
From the usurper's power.

4 " This heart I bought with blood," he says,
" And now it shall be mine ; "
His voice the strong one armed dismays ;
He knows he must resign.

5 In spite of unbelief, and pride,
And self, and Satan's art,
The gates of brass fly open wide,
And Jesus wins the heart.

1021 L.M. KELLY.
" By the rivers of Babylon there we sat down," &c.
O ZION, when I think on thee,
I wish for pinions like the dove,
And mourn to think that I should be
So distant from the place I love.

2 A captive here, and far from home,
For Zion's sacred walls I sigh ;
To Zion all the ransomed come,
And see the Saviour eye to eye.

3 While here, I walk on hostile ground ;
The few that I can call my friends
Are, like myself, with fetters bound,
And weariness our steps attends.

4 But yet we shall behold the day,
When Zion's children shall return ;
Our sorrows then shall flee away,
And we shall never, never mourn.

5 The hope that such a day will come
Makes e'en the captive's portion sweet ;
Though now we wander far from home,
In Zion soon we all shall meet.

1022 C.M. WATTS.
" A better country, that is, a heavenly."—Heb. xi. 16.
THERE is a land of pure delight,
Where saints immortal reign ;
Infinite day excludes the night,

And pleasures banish pain.

2 There everlasting spring abides,
And never-withering flowers ;
Death, like a narrow sea, divides
This heavenly land from ours.

3 O could we make our doubts remove,
These gloomy doubts that rise,
And see the Canaan that we love
With unbeclouded eyes ;

4 Could we but climb where Moses stood,
And view the landscape o'er,
Not Jordan's stream, nor death's cold flood,
Should fright us from the shore.

1023 L.M. COWPER.
" I dwell with him that is of a humble spirit."
JESUS, where'er thy people meet,
There they behold thy mercy-seat ;

Where'er they seek thee thou art found,
And every place is hallowed ground.

2 For thou, within no walls confined,
Inhabitest the humble mind ;
Such ever bring thee where they come,
And going, take thee to their home.

3 Dear Shepherd of thy chosen few,
Thy former mercies here renew ;
Here to our waiting hearts proclaim
The sweetness of thy saving name.

4 Here may we prove the power of prayer
To strengthen faith, and sweeten care ;
To teach our faint desires to rise,
And bring all heaven before our eyes.

1024 C.M. C.W
" Create in me a clean heart."—Ps. li. 10; Prov. xx. 9.
O FOR a heart to praise the Lord,
A heart from sin set free,
A heart that's sprinkled with the blood
So freely shed for me.

2 A heart resigned, submissive, meek ;
The great Redeemer's throne ;
Where only Christ is heard to speak,
Where Jesus reigns alone.

3 A humble, lowly, contrite heart,
Believing, true, and clean,
Which neither life nor death can part
From him that dwells within.

4 Thy nature, gracious Lord, impart ;
Come quickly from above ;
Write thy new name upon my heart,
Thy new, best name of Love.

1025   C.M.   NEWTON.

"They shall look on him whom they have pierced."

IN evil long I took delight,
    Unawed by shame or fear,
Till a new object struck my sight,
    And stopped my wild career.

2 I saw One hanging on a tree,
    In agonies and blood,
Who fixed his languid eyes on me,
    As near his cross I stood.

3 Sure never till my latest breath
    Can I forget that look ;
It seemed to charge me with his death,
    Though not a word he spoke.

4 My conscience felt and owned the guilt,
    And plunged me in despair ;
I saw my sins his blood had spilt,
    And helped to nail him there.

5 A second look He gave, which said,
    " I freely all forgive ;
This blood is for thy ransom paid ;
    I die that thou may'st live."

1026   148th.   H. FOWLER.

Where sin abounded, grace did much more abound.

NOT one of Adam's race
    But is by sin undone,
Deep sunk in foul disgrace,
    And righteousness has none ;
And this, when brought through grace to know,
Will sink the sinner very low.

2   He sinks in miry clay,
    And scarce can lift a sigh,
    He tries, but cannot pray,
    Nor lift to heaven his eye ;
His bosom heaves, with guilt oppressed,
But, in himself, can find no rest.

3   In this bewildered state,
    Pursued by guilt and sin,
    He pushes at the gate,
    But cannot enter in ;
Till Jesus opens wide the door,
And saves the helpless and the poor.

4   The prisoner now goes forth ;
    The lame man leaps with joy ;
    He feels the Saviour's worth,
    And lifts his name on high.
On Jesus' head the crown he'll place ;
A sinner saved by sovereign grace.

1027   C.M.   H. FOWLER.

" Their rock is not as our Rock."—Deut. xxxii. 31.

WHAT a polluted world this is,
    A vale of sin and woe !
The sons of earth complain of this,
    But Zion feels it so.

2 The world to creature-objects fly,
    Their maladies to heal ;
But Zion cries to God on high,
    " Do thou thy face reveal.

3 " Saviour divine, reveal thy love ;
    Bright Morning Star, arise,
And lead my thoughts to things above,
    E'en to the upper skies.

4 " This shall create a joy within,
    Beyond what angels know,
And stimulate my powers to sing
    The Saviour's praise below."

1028   L.M.   H. FOWLER.

Joshua's Invitation, in a Gospel sense.—Joshua iii. 9.

COME hither, ye by sin distressed,
And hear the Saviour's faithful word ;
Soon ye shall enter into rest,
And know that he's your conquering Lord.

2 Come hither, ye whose rising fears
Forbid you to exult and sing ;
Whose moments pass in sighs and tears,
Feeling your guilt a dreadful sting.

3 Does Satan tempt you to give up,
And call no more on Jesus' name ?
Cast not away your little hope ;
Come hither, and *behold the Lamb*.

4 Come hither, to the Saviour come,
Vile as thou art in every view ;
In Jesus' house there still is room
For needy sinners, such as you.

5 Power and love in Christ combine,
An able, willing Saviour too ;
Is he a Sun ?   On thee he'll shine.
Is he thy God ?   He'll bring thee through.

1029   S.M.   H. FOWLER.

The troubles of my heart are enlarged.—Ps. xxv. 17.

COME, Saviour, quickly come,
    Let me but feel thee near ;
I'm a poor wanderer far from home,
    Pursued by guilt and fear.

2   The troubles which I meet,
    The evils which I feel,
The miry clay that clogs my feet,
    Entangle, and I reel.

3   Thy hand alone can guide
    My weather-beaten bark ;

And in this stormy sea provide
A safe and solid ark.

4　O shut me safely in ;
Then at the storm I'll smile ;
Nor fear the power of hell and sin,
But triumph all the while.

1030　　C.M.　　H. Fowler.
"I am carnal, sold under sin."—Rom. vii. 14-23.
Lord, what a wretched, wretched heart,
I feel from day to day ;
Vile and unsound in every part ;
Subdue it, Lord, I pray.

2　I groan, and pray, and cry, and strive,
To have it all removed ;
Can it be thus in those who live ?
In those whom God has loved ?

3　Can such besetting evils dwell
In sinners born of God ?
Could black corruption rise and swell
Where Christ applies his blood ?

4　To thee, dear Lord, for light I cry,
On this my darksome path ;
O let thy mercy me supply ;
O Lord, increase my faith.

1031　　H. Fowler.
7s.　　Dan. ix. 7.
"Behold, I am vile."—Job xl. 4 ; Ps. li. 5 ;
What a vile, deceitful heart,
Filled with sin in every part ;
But for free and sovereign grace,
Hell had been my destined place.

2　Called by grace these many years,
Rescued from ten thousand fears ;
Yet a flagrant rebel still,
Tossed about with every ill.

3　Thus I'm burdened, thus I groan,
And my sad condition moan ;
Can a sinner thus beguiled
Be the Lord's adopted child ?

4　Lord, how rich and free thy grace
To appoint a resting-place ;
While within, and all around,
Comforts fail, and sins abound.

1032　　S.M.　　H. Fowler.
"How shall I give thee up, Ephraim ?"—Hosea xi. 8.
"How shall I give thee up ? "
('Tis Jesus speaks the word)
"I am the sinner's only hope ;
I am thy gracious Lord.

2　"Rebellious thou hast been,
And art rebellious still ;
But since in love I took thee in,

My promise I'll fulfil.

3　"I've bound thee up secure,
'Midst all the rage of hell ;
The curse thou never shalt endure,
For I'm unchangeable.

4　"My son, give me thy heart ;
Let me thy sorrows bear ;
'Tis not thy caution, power, or art,
Can save thee from despair."

5　Lord, captivate my soul ;
Subdue the power of sin ;
My vile corruptions, O control ;
Let faith the battle win.

1033　　11s.　　H. Fowler.
"Whither the forerunner has for us entered."
In Jesus combine all the riches of grace,
What glory and grandeur I see in his face ;
Jehovah's eternal and co-equal Son,
Took all our transgressions and made them
his own.

2
Ye children of Zion, now dry up your tears ;
For you the Redeemer in glory appears ;
Now he lives, now he reigns, now he dwells
in the sky,
To answer the needy whenever they cry.

3
Afflicted believer, thy cause he'll maintain ;
Though rough be thy way, he'll revive thee again;
In dark dispensations his kindness he'll prove,
And teach thee to prize his immutable love.

4
What though thy corruptions are many and
strong,
Thy gracious Redeemer will help thee along ;
His promise assures thee, when troubles assail,
Though hell should oppose thee, thy faith
cannot fail.

1034　　L.M.　　H. Fowler.
"The captive exile hasteneth that he may be loosed."
Jesus, my soul's athirst for thee ;
Absent from thee I cannot rest ;
Come now, reveal thyself to me ;
I cannot leave thy throne unblest.

2　My base ingratitude I mourn,
A needy, helpless sinner still ;
Dear Lord, I wait thy sweet return,
Thy gracious promise to fulfil.

3　Ah, whither shall thy prisoner flee ?
Thy captive hastens to be loosed ;
And would repose his trust in thee,
Though oft by sin and sorrow tossed.

4 Jesus is still the sinner's Friend,
Although the billows roll between ;
And since his love is to the end,
Ere long he'll change this gloomy scene.

1035   S.M.   H. FOWLER.
In returning and rest shall ye be saved.-Isa. xxx. 15.
RETURN, my wandering heart,
To thy dear resting-place ;
Nothing in nature, nor in art,
So fair as Jesus' face.

2   A proud and wandering heart,
A bold, rebellious will,
Severely make me daily smart,
And oft my comforts kill.

3   When night's dim shade I feel,
I sigh, I mourn, I groan ;
Do thou, dear Lord, thy face reveal ;
Ah, leave me not alone.

4   Sweet Comforter, descend,
And lead me to the Lamb ;
My absent, present, precious Friend !
Eternally the same.

1036   L.M.   H. FOWLER.
Encouragement for Seekers.—Ps. lxix. 32 ; Isa. xlv. 19.
SEEK ye my face, the Saviour cries ;
My soul, where canst thou find supplies
But in the Lamb, for sinners slain,
Who has not shed his blood in vain ?

2   Does bitter anguish fill thy heart,
And make thee from the promise start ?
Does Satan tempt thee to give up,
No more in Jesus' name to hope ?

3   Art thou afflicted, sore distressed,
Embarrassed and by guilt oppressed ?
Anxious to know thy sins forgiven,
And find an open way to heaven ?

4   Thou shalt obtain the blessing yet ;
Jesus will not thy cries forget ;
Wait on the Lord, take courage still ;
His promise surely he'll fulfil.

1037   7s.   H. FOWLER.
As thy days, so shall thy strength be.-Deut. xxxiii. 25.
DAYS of darkness and distress
Are my portion here below ;
Thorny is the wilderness,
And the Lord will have it so.

2   When enlarged in faith and prayer,
His dear face by faith I see,
On the Lord I cast my care,
Satisfied he cares for me.

3   But when days of darkness come,
And my heart is hard and cold,

Round the wilderness I roam,
Barren, wandering from the fold.

4   Days of fierce temptation too,
Furious as the foaming wave,
Hide the heavens from my view,
Threatening a watery grave.

5   Up I cast my longing eyes,
Tossed like Jonah in the sea ;
Jesus whispers from the skies,
" As thy days, thy strength shall be ! "

1038   8.7.4.   H. FOWLER.
" They that sow in tears shall reap in joy.
SINNERS, in their deep affliction,
Sigh and groan beneath their load ;
Long to read their own election,
And with pleasure say, " My God ! "

Trembling, fearing,
Hoping still in Jesus' blood.

2 Blessed are the souls who tremble
At Jehovah's searching word ;
Contrite hearts cannot dissemble ;
God has slain them with his sword ;
Doubting, fearing,
Still their hope is in the Lord.

3 Mourning saint, whose heart is broken,
Love shall wipe thy weeping eye ;
Ask thy Saviour for this token ;
All thy needs he will supply ;
Fear not, mourner ;
Christ will make you reap in joy.

1039   C.M.   STEELE.
" The grace of our Lord was exceeding abundant."
LORD, we adore thy boundless grace,
The heights and depths unknown,
Of pardon, life, and joy, and peace,
In thy beloved Son.

2 O wondrous gifts of love divine,
Dear Source of every good ;
Jesus, in thee what glories shine !
How rich thy flowing blood !

3 Come, all ye pining, hungry poor,
The Saviour's bounty taste ;
Behold a never-failing store
For every willing guest.

4 Here shall your numerous wants receive
A free, a full supply ;
He has unmeasured bliss to give,
And joys that never die.

1040   8.7.7.   KELLY.

"I said unto thee, Live."—Ezek. xvi. 6; Eph. ii. 4, 5.

WHEN we lay in sin polluted,
 Wretched and undone we were ;
All we saw and heard was suited
 Only to produce despair ;
 Ours appeared a hopeless case ;
 Such it had been, but for grace.

2 As we lay exposed and friendless,
 Needing what no hand could give,
Then the Lord (whose praise be endless)
 Passed by, and bid us live ;
 This was help in time of need ;
 This was grace, 'twas grace indeed.

3 Yes, 'twas grace beyond all measure,
 When he bid such sinners live,
Laid aside his just displeasure,
 And determined to forgive ;
 But he chose our hopeless case,
 With a view to show his grace.

4 And shall we be found forgetful
 Of the Lord, who thus forgave ?
Lord, our hearts are most deceitful,
 'Tis in thee our strength we have ;
 Should'st thou let thy people go,
 They'd forget how much they owe.

5 Keep us, then, O keep us ever !
 While we stand, 'tis in thy strength ;
Leave us not, forsake us never,
 Till we see thy face at length ;
 Hold thy helpless people fast ;
 Save us, Lord, from first to last.

1041   L.M.   KELLY.

"Thus saith the Lord, I remember thee."—Jer. ii. 2.

O WHERE is now that glowing love
That marked our union with the Lord ?
Our hearts were fixed on things above,
Nor could the world one joy afford.

2 So strange did love like his appear,
That love that made him bear the cross,
No other subject pleased our ear ;
The world for this appeared but loss.

3 Where is the zeal that led us then
To make the Saviour's glory known ;
That freed us from the fear of men,
And kept our eye on him alone ?

4 Where are the happy seasons spent
In fellowship with him we loved ?
The sacred joy, the sweet content,
The blessedness that then we proved ?

5 Behold, again we turn to thee ;
 O cast us not away, though vile !
No peace we have, no joy we see,
 O Lord our God, but in thy smile.

1042   L.M.   KELLY.

I am not ashamed of the Gospel of Christ.—Rom. i. 16.

I NEED not blush to own that He,
On whom my hope of heaven is built,
Was crucified on yonder tree,
Since 'tis his blood that cancels guilt.

2 Nor need I blush to call him Lord,
Whom heaven adores with all its hosts ;
Yes, Jesus is by heaven adored,
In him the brightest seraph boasts.

3 What though the world no glory sees
In him my soul admires and loves,

I wonder not—how should he please
The man who of himself approves ?

4 I too could boast of merit once,
And Jesus had no charms for me ;
But all such claims I now renounce ;
No merit but in him I see.

1043   L.M.   KELLY.

"O Lord, rebuke me not in thy wrath."—Ps. xxxviii. 1.

DEAL gently with thy servant, Lord,
And if the rod should needful be,
Thy seasonable aid afford ;
My soul in trouble flies to thee.

2 Thy frown is terrible to bear,
But grace a spring of hope supplies ;
Thy anger more than death I fear,
Thy favour more than life I prize.

3 But much I fear, lest in some hour
Of sore temptation I may fall ;
And, yielding to the tempter's power,
Faithless may prove, and give up all.

4 Lord, save thy worm, for thou alone
Canst keep me in the trying hour ;
Thy help I trust to, not my own,
Thy love, thy wisdom, and thy power.

5 When chastisement shall needful be,
Correct thy worm, but not in wrath ;
A father's hand I fain would see ;
A father's rod no terror hath.

1044   7s.   KENT.

With joy shall ye draw water .. the wells of salvation.

WATER from salvation's wells,
Thirsty sinner, come and draw ;
Grace in Jesus' fulness dwells,
More than men or angels know.

2 'Twas in God, the fount supreme,
　Till the day that Adam fell ;
　Then the first all-healing stream
　Watered Eden's garden well.

3 Far and wide the cleansing flood
　O'er the sin-cursed garden ran ;
　Preaching peace by Jesus' blood,—
　Blissful sound to rebel man.

4 Thousands now around the throne
　Water from this fountain drew ;
　Felt their griefs and sorrows gone ;
　Hymned his praise ; and why not you ?

5 Bring no money, price, or aught,
　No good deeds, nor pleasing frames,
　Mercy never can be bought ;
　Grace is free ; and all's the Lamb's.

1045　　7s.　　KELLY.
"Who will show us any good ? "—Ps. iv. 6.
　"WHO will show us any good ? "
　Thus the hopeless worldling cries ;
　Pleasure, though with zeal pursued,
　Still from his embraces flies.

2 Is there nothing here below
　Can supply the soul with food ?
　Hear the general answer, No !
　"Who will show us any good ? "

3 Must we then all hope resign ?
　Is there nought can yield repose ?
　Saviour, make thy face to shine,
　This is what will heal our woes.

1046　　L.M.　　KELLY.
We hanged our harps upon the willows.—Ps. cxxxvii. 2.
　My harp on yonder willow lies,
　Silent, neglected, and unstrung ;
　My cheerful songs are turned to sighs ;
　Sad is my heart and mute my tongue.

2 Once I could sound the note of praise,
　As loud as others I could sing ;
　But retrospect of former days
　No help in present grief will bring.

3 But why should I give way to grief ?
　I see my remedy at hand ;
　Does not the gospel bring relief
　To such as self-convicted stand ?

4 Yes, 'tis a faithful, cheering word,
　That Jesus came to save the lost ;
　This truth with richest grace is stored,
　And to the vilest yields the most.

1047　　C.M.　　KELLY.
By whom shall Jacob arise ?-Amos vii. 2, 5 ; Ps. xii. 1.

"By whom shall Jacob now arise ? "
　For Jacob's friends are few ;
　And (what should fill us with surprise)
　They seem divided too.

2 "By whom shall Jacob now arise ? "
　For Jacob's foes are strong ;
　I read their triumph in their eyes ;
　They think he'll fail ere long.

3 "By whom shall Jacob now arise ? "
　Can any tell by whom ?
　Say, shall this branch that withered lies,
　Again revive and bloom ?

4 Lord, thou canst tell—the work is thine ;
　The help of man is vain ;
　On Jacob now arise and shine,
　And he shall live again.

1048　　L.M.　　KELLY.
For here have we no continuing city.—Heb. xiii. 14.
　"WE'VE no abiding city here ; "
　This may distress the worldling's mind ;
　But should not cost the saint a tear,
　Who hopes a better rest to find..

2 "We've no abiding city here ; "
　Sad truth, were this to be our home ;
　But let the thought our spirits cheer,
　"We seek a city yet to come."

3 "We've no abiding city here ; "
　Then let us live as pilgrims do ;
　Let not the world our rest appear,
　But let us haste from all below.

4 "We've no abiding city here,"
　We seek a city out of sight,
　Zion its name—the Lord is there ;
　It shines with everlasting light.

5 O sweet abode of peace and love,
　Where pilgrims freed from toil are blest ;
　Had I the pinions of the dove,
　I'd fly to thee, and be at rest.

1049　　L.M.　　KELLY.
So he bringeth them unto their desired haven.
　THE Christian navigates a sea
　Where various forms of death appear ;
　Nor skill, alas ! nor power has he,
　Aright his dangerous course to steer.

2 Why does he venture, then, from shore,
　And dare so many deaths to brave ?
　Because the land affrights him more
　Than all the perils of the wave ;

3 Because he hopes a port to find,
　Where all his toil will be repaid ;

And though unskilful, weak, and blind,
Yet Jesus bids him nothing dread.

4 His destined land he sometimes sees,
And thinks his toils will soon be o'er ;
Expects some favourable breeze
Will waft him quickly to the shore.

5 But sudden clouds obstruct his view,
And he enjoys the sight no more ;
Nor does he now believe it true
That he had ever seen the shore.

6 Though fear his heart should overwhelm,
He'll reach the port for which he's bound ;
For Jesus holds and guides the holm,
And safety is where he is found.

1050   S.M.   C.W. (altered).
"The love of Christ constraineth us."—2 Cor. v. 14.

WHEN shall thy love constrain
This heart thy own to be ?
When shall the wounded spirit gain
A healing rest in thee ?

2 Ah ! what avails my strife,
My wandering to and fro ?
Thou hast the words of endless life ;
Lord, whither shall I go ?

3 My worthless heart to gain,
The God who gave me breath
Was found in fashion as a man,
And died a cursed death !

4 Then may I sin forsake,
The world for thee resign ;
Gracious Redeemer, take, O take,
And seal me ever thine !

1051   C.M.   STEELE.
"Watch and pray."—Matt. xxvi. 41; Mark xiii. 33.

ALAS, what hourly dangers rise !
What snares beset my way !
To heaven O let me lift my eyes,
And hourly watch and pray.

2 How oft my mournful thoughts complain,
And melt in flowing tears !
My weak resistance, ah, how vain !
How strong my foes and fears !

3 O gracious God, in whom I live,
My feeble efforts aid ;
Help me to watch, and pray, and strive,
Though trembling and afraid.

4 Increase my faith, increase my hope,
When foes and fears prevail !
And bear my fainting spirit up,
Or soon my strength will fail.

5 Whene'er temptations fright my heart,
Or lure my feet aside,
O God, thy powerful aid impart,—
My guardian and my guide.

6 O keep me in the heavenly way,
And bid the tempter flee ;
And let me never, never stray,
From happiness and thee.

1052   112th.   TOPLADY.
Gal. vi. 14.
"God forbid that I should glory." &c.—

REDEEMER ! whither should I flee,
Or how escape the wrath to come ?
The weary sinner flies to thee
For shelter from impending doom ;
Smile on me, gracious Lord, and show
Thyself the Friend of sinners now.

2 Beneath the shadow of thy cross
The heavy-laden soul finds rest ;
I would esteem the world but dross,
So I might be of Christ possessed.
I'd seek my every joy in thee,
Be thou both life and light to me.

3 Close to the ignominious tree,
Jesus, my humbled soul would cleave ;
Despised and crucified with thee,
With thee resolved to die and live ;
This prayer and this ambition mine,
Living and dying to be thine.

4 There, fastened to the rugged wood
By holy love's resistless chain,
And life deriving from thy blood,
Never to wander wide again,
There may I bow my suppliant knee,
And own no other Lord but thee.

1053   8.7.   C.W.
"I will love him," &c.—John xiv. 17, 20-23.

LOVE divine, all love excelling,
Joy of heaven, to earth come down !
Fix in us thy humble dwelling ;
All thy faithful mercies crown.
Jesus, thou art all compassion ;
Pure unbounded love thou art ;
Visit us with thy salvation ;
Comfort every sinking heart.

2 Breathe, O breathe thy blessed Spirit
Into every troubled breast !
Let us all in thee inherit ;
Let us find thy promised rest.
Take away the love of sinning ;
Alpha and Omega be ;

End of faith, as its beginning,
Set our hearts at liberty.

3 Carry on thy new creation ;
Pure and holy may we be ;
Let us see our whole salvation
Perfectly secured by thee ;
Changed from glory into glory,
Till in heaven we take our place ;
Till we cast our crowns before thee,
Lost in wonder, love, and praise.

1054 8.7. C.W.
To all them that looked for redemption.—Luke ii. 38.
COME, thou long-expected Jesus !
Born to set thy people free ;
From our fears and sins release us ;
Let us find our rest in thee.
Israel's strength and consolation,
Hope of all the saints thou art ;
Dear desire of every nation,
Joy of every longing heart.

2 Born thy children to deliver,
Born a child and yet a king ;
Born to reign in us for ever,
Now thy gracious kingdom bring.
By thy own eternal Spirit,
Rule in all our hearts alone ;
By thy all-sufficient merit,
Raise us to thy glorious throne.

1055 8.7.4. SWAIN.
We which have believed do enter into rest.—Heb. iv. 3.
COME, ye souls, by sin afflicted,
Bowed with fruitless sorrow down ;
By the broken law convicted,
Through the cross behold the crown !

Look to Jesus ;
Mercy flows through him alone.

2 Sweet as home to pilgrims weary,
Light to newly-opened eyes,
Flowing springs in deserts dreary,
Is the rest the cross supplies ;
All who taste it
Shall to rest immortal rise.

3 Blessed are the eyes that see him ;
Blest the ears that hear his voice ;
Blessed are the souls that trust him,
And in him alone rejoice ;
His commandments
Then become their happy choice.

4 But to sing the " Rest remaining,"
Mortal tongues far short must fall ;
Heavenly tongues are ever aiming,
But they cannot tell it all ;

Faith believes it—Hope expects it—
But it overwhelms them all.

1056 L.M. MEDLEY.
Yet will I look again.—Jonah ii. 4 ; 2 Chron. vi. 38. 39.
SEE a poor sinner, dearest Lord,
Whose soul, encouraged by thy word,
At mercy's footstool would remain,
And there would look, and look again.

2 How oft deceived by self and pride,
Has my poor heart been turned aside ;
And, Jonah like, has fled from thee,
Till thou hast looked again on me !

3 Ah ! bring a wretched wanderer home,
And to thy footstool let me come,
And tell thee all my grief and pain,
And wait and look, and look again.

4 Take courage, then, my trembling soul ;
One look from Christ shall make thee whole ;
Trust thou in him ; 'tis not in vain ;
But wait and look, and look again.

1057 8.7. C.W.
People that walked in darkness have seen a great light.
LIGHT of those whose dreary dwelling
Borders on the shades of death,
Come, and, thy bright beams revealing,
Dissipate the clouds beneath.
The new heaven's and earth's Creator,
In our deepest darkness rise,
Scattering all the night of nature,
Pouring day upon our eyes.

2 Still we wait for thy appearing ;
Life and joy thy beams impart,
Chasing all our fears, and cheering
Every poor benighted heart.
Come, and manifest the favour
Thou hast for the ransomed race ;
Come, thou dear exalted Saviour !
Come, and bring thy gospel grace.

3 Save us in thy great compassion,
O thou mild, pacific Prince !
Give the knowledge of salvation,
Give the pardon of our sins.
By thy all-sufficient merit
Every burdened soul release ;
By the shining of thy Spirit,
Guide us into perfect peace.

1058 7s. C. W. or MADAN (?).
" Whosoever shall not receive the kingdom of God," &c
LORD, if thou thy grace impart,
Poor in spirit, meek in heart,

I shall, as my Master, be
Rooted in humility.

2 Simple, teachable, and mild,
Changed into a little child ;
Pleased with all the Lord provides ;
Weaned from all the world besides.

3 Father, fix my soul on thee ;
Every evil let me flee ;
Nothing want, beneath, above,—
Happy in thy precious love.

1059   S.M.   C.W.

" Lead me in thy truth."—Ps. xxv. 5 : v. 8 ; John xiv. 6.

JESUS, the Truth, the Way,
The sure, unerring Light,
On thee my feeble soul I'd stay,
Which thou canst lead aright.

2 O may thy Spirit, Lord,
Soon as the foe comes in,
His mighty needful help afford,
And stem the tide of sin.

3 May I from every sin,
As from a serpent, fly ;
Abhor to touch the thing unclean,
And rather choose to die.

4 Myself I cannot save ;
Myself I cannot keep ;
But strength in thee I fain would have,
Whose eyelids never sleep.

5 My soul to thee alone
I therefore now commend ;
Since Jesus, having loved his own,
Will love them to the end.

1060   112th.   C.W.

O Israel, return unto the Lord thy God.—Hos. xiv. 1-4.

WEARY of wandering from the Lord,
And now made willing to return,
I hear, and bow me to the rod ;
For now, not without hope, I mourn ;
There is an Advocate above,
A Friend before the Throne of Love.

2 O Jesus ! full of truth and grace,
More full of grace than I of sin ;
Yet once again I seek thy face ;
Open thy arms, and take me in !
All my backslidings freely heal,
And love the faithless sinner still.

3 Thou know'st the way to bring me back,
My fallen spirit to restore ;
O, for thy truth and mercy's sake,
Forgive, and bid me sin no more !

The ruins of my soul repair,
And make my heart a house of prayer.

4 Ah, give me, Lord, the tender heart,
That trembles at the approach of sin ;
A godly fear of sin impart ;
Implant and root it deep within ;
That I may love thy gracious power,
And never dare to offend thee more.

1061   C.M.   C.W.

" There remaineth, therefore, a rest to the people," &c

LORD, I believe a rest remains
To all thy people known ;
A rest where pure enjoyment reigns,
And thou art loved alone.

2 O that I now the rest might know,
Believe and enter in !

Dear Saviour, now the power bestow,
And let me cease from sin.

3 Remove this hardness from my heart,
This unbelief remove ;
To me the rest of faith impart,
The sabbath of thy love.

4 Come, thou dear Saviour, come away !
Into my soul descend ;
No longer from thy creature stay,
My Author and my End.

1062   7s.   KELLY.

King of kings, and Lord of lords.—Rev. xix. 16 ; xvii. 14.

KING of kings, and Lord of lords !
These are great and awful words ;
'Tis to Jesus they belong ;
Let his people raise their song.

2 Rich in glory, thou didst stoop ;
Thou that art the people's hope ;
Thou wast poor, that they might be
Rich in glory, Lord, with thee.

3 When we think of love like this,
Joy and shame our hearts possess ;
Joy, that thou couldst pity thus ;
Shame, for such returns from us.

4 Yet we hope the day to see,
When we shall from earth be free ;
Borne aloft, to heaven be brought,
There to praise thee as we ought.

5 While we still continue here,
Let this hope our spirits cheer.
Till in heaven thy face we see,
Teach us, Lord, to live to thee.

1063   8.7.7.   KELLY.
But ye, brethren, are not in darkness.—1 Thess. v. 4.
NOTHING know we of the season
　　When the world shall pass away ;
But we know, the saints have reason
　　To expect a glorious day ;
　　When the Saviour will return,
　　And his people cease to mourn.

2 O what sacred joys await them !
　　They shall see the Saviour then ;
Those who now oppose and hate them,
　　Never can oppose again.
　　Brethren, let us think of this :
　　All is ours if we are his.

3 Waiting for our Lord's returning,
　　Be it ours his word to keep ;
May our lamps be always burning,
　　May we watch while others sleep.
　　We're no longer of the night ;
　　We are children of the light.

4 Being of the favoured number,
　　Whom the Saviour calls his own,
'Tis not meet that we should slumber ;
　　Nothing should be left undone.
　　This should be his people's aim,
　　Still to glorify his name.

1064   C.M.   WATTS.
" Set your affection on things above."—Col. iii. 2.
How vain are all things here below ;
　　How false, and yet how fair !
Each pleasure has its poison too,
　　And every sweet a snare.

2 The brightest things below the sky
　　Give but a flattering light ;
We should suspect some danger nigh,
　　When we possess delight.

3 Our dearest joys, and dearest friends,
　　The partners of our blood,
How they divide our wavering minds,
　　And leave but half for God !

4 The fondness of a creature's love,
　　How strong it strikes the sense !
Thither the warm affections move,
　　Nor can we call them thence.

5 Dear Saviour, let thy beauties be
　　My soul's eternal food ;
And grace command my heart away
　　From all created good.

1065   C.M.   HAWEIS.
Remember thou me for thy goodness' sake.—Ps. xxv. 7.
O THOU from whom all goodness flows,

I lift my heart to thee ;
In all my sorrows, conflicts, woes,
　　Jesus, remember me.

2 When on my mourning, burdened heart,
　　My sins lie heavily ;
My pardon speak, thy peace impart ;
　　In love remember me.

3 Temptations sore obstruct my way,
　　And ills I cannot flee ;
O give me strength, Lord, as my day ;
　　For good remember me.

4 If on my face for thy dear name,
　　Shame and reproaches be,
All hail reproach, and welcome shame !
　　If thou remember me.

5 The hour is near, consigned to death,
　　I own the just decree ;

Saviour, with my last parting breath,
　　I'll cry, " Remember me."

1066   C.M.   DODDRIDGE.
" Lovest thou me ? "—John xxi. 15-17 ; xiv. 21.
Do not I love thee, dearest Lord ?
　　Behold my heart and see ;
And cast each hated idol down,
　　That dares to rival thee.

2 Do not I love thee from my soul ?
　　Then let me nothing love ;
Dead be my heart to every joy,
　　When Jesus cannot move.

3 Is not thy name melodious still
　　To my attentive ear ?
Do I not in thy word delight
　　The Saviour's voice to hear ?

4 Hast thou a lamb in all thy flock
　　I would disdain to feed ?
Hast thou a foe before whose face
　　I'd fear thy cause to plead ?

1067   S.M.   TOPLADY.   Isa. i. 18.
" Though your sins be as scarlet," &c.—
JESUS, thy light impart,
　　And lead me in thy path ;
I have an unbelieving heart ;
　　But thou canst give me faith.

2 Unrivalled reign within ;
　　My only sovereign be ;
O crucify the man of sin,
　　And form thyself in me.

3 Thy blood's renewing might
　　Can make the foulest clean ;
Can wash the Ethiopian white,
　　And change the leopard's skin.

4   Fulfil thy gracious word,
     And show my guilt forgiven ;
Bid me embrace my dying Lord,
     And mount with thee to heaven.

1068   8.7.   D. TURNER.
"Jesus, have mercy on me."—Mark x. 47.

JESUS, full of all compassion,
     Hear thy humble suppliant's cry ;
Let me know thy great salvation ;
     See, I languish, faint, and die.

2 Guilty, but with heart relenting,
     Overwhelmed with helpless grief,
Prostrate at thy feet repenting,
     Send, O send me quick relief.

3 Whither should a wretch be flying,
     But to him who comfort gives ?
Whither, from the dread of dying,
     But to him who ever lives ?

4 Hear, then, blessed Saviour, hear me !
     My soul cleaveth to the dust ;
Send the Comforter to cheer me,
     Lo ! in thee I put my trust.

5 On the word thy blood has sealed
     Hangs my everlasting all ;
Let thy arm be now revealed ;
     Stay, O stay me, lest I fall !

6 In the world of endless ruin,
     Let it never, Lord, be said,
" Here's a soul that perished suing
     For the boasted Saviour's aid."

1069   C.M.   STEELE.
" Return, ye backsliding children."—Jer. iii. 12, 14, 22.

SEE, Lord, before thy throne of grace
     A wretched wanderer mourn !

Thyself hast bid me seek thy face ;
     Thyself hast said, " Return."

2 And shall my guilty fears prevail
     To drive me from thy feet ?
Thy word of promise cannot fail,
     My tower of safe retreat.

3 Absent from thee, my Guide, my Light,
     Without one cheering ray ;
Through dangers, fears, and gloomy night,
     How desolate my way !

4 O shine on this benighted heart,
     With beams of mercy shine ;
And let thy Spirit's voice impart
     A taste of joys divine !

1070   112th.   R. HILL.
" O Lord, I am oppressed," &c.—Isa. xxxviii. 14.

THOU Friend of friendless sinners, hear,
And magnify thy grace divine ;
Pardon a worm that would draw near,
That would his heart to thee resign ;
A worm, by self and sin oppressed,
That pants to reach thy promised rest.

2 With holy fear, and reverent love,
I long to lie beneath thy throne ;
I long in thee to live and move,
And stay myself on thee alone ;
Teach me to lean upon thy breast,
To find in thee the promised rest.

3 Take me, dear Saviour, as thy own,
And with thy Father plead my cause ;
Be thou my portion, Lord, alone !
O help me to obey thy laws ;
And with thy gracious presence blest,
Give me to find thy promised rest.

4 Bid the tempestuous rage of sin,
With every furious passion die ;
Let the Redeemer dwell within,
And turn my sorrows into joy.
O may my heart, by thee possessed,
Know thee to be my promised rest.

1071   7s.   C.W.
" He shall feed his flock like a shepherd."—Isa. xl. 11

HAPPY soul, that, free from harms,
Rests within his Shepherd's arms !
Who his quiet shall molest ?
Who shall violate his rest ?

2 Jesus does his spirit bear,
Far removes each anxious care ;
He who found the wandering sheep
Loves and still delights to keep.

3 Oh ! that I might so believe ;
Steadfastly to Jesus cleave ;
Only on his love rely,
Smile at the destroyer nigh ;

4 Free from sin and servile fear,
Feel the Saviour always near ;
All his care rejoice to prove,
All the blessings of his love !

5 Shepherd, seek thy wandering sheep ;
Bring me back, and lead, and keep ;
Take on thee my every care ;
Bear me, in thy bosom bear.

6 Let me know thy gentle voice,
More and more in thee rejoice ;
From thy fulness grace receive ;
Ever in thy Spirit live.

1072   C.M.   TOPLADY & C. W.
" Lord, help me."—Matt. xv. 25.

JESUS, Redeemer, Saviour, Lord,
  The weary sinner's Friend ;
Come to my help, pronounce the word,
  Bid my corruptions end.

2 Thou canst o'ercome this heart of mine,
  Thou canst victorious prove ;
For everlasting strength is thine
  And everlasting love.

3 Bound down with twice ten thousand ties,
  Yet let me hear thy call,
My soul in confidence shall rise,
  Shall rise and break through all.

4 Speak and the deaf shall hear thy voice,
  The blind his sight receive ;
The dumb in songs of praise rejoice,
  The heart of stone believe.

5 The Ethiop then shall change his skin ;
  The dead shall feel thy power ;
The loathsome leper shall be clean,
  And I shall sin abhor.

1073   8.7.   TOPLADY (from the German).
" I will put my Spirit within you."—Ezek. xxxvi. 27.

HOLY Ghost, dispel our sadness,
  Pierce the clouds of nature's night ;
Come, thou Source of joy and gladness,
  Breathe thy life, and spread thy light.

2 Come, thou best of all donations,
  God can give, or we implore !
Having thy sweet consolations,
  We on earth can wish no more.

3 Author of the new creation,
  Bid us now thy influence prove ;

Make our souls thy habitation ;
  Shed abroad the Saviour's love.

1074   L.M.   C.W.
" But Christ is All."—Col. iii. 11.

WHEN, gracious Lord, when shall it be
That I shall find my all in thee ?
The fulness of thy promise prove,
The seal of thy eternal love ?

2 Thee, only thee, I fain would find,
And cast the world and sin behind ;
A helpless soul, I come to thee,
With only sin and misery.

3 Lord, I am sick—my sickness cure ;
I want—do thou enrich the poor ;
Under thy mighty hand I stoop—
O lift the abject sinner up !

4 Lord, I am blind—be thou my sight ;

Lord, I am weak—be thou my might ;
A helper of the helpless be,
And let me find my all in thee.

1075   112th.   C. W. (from the German).
" I am crucified with Christ."—Gal. ii. 20 ; v. 24.

THOU hidden love of God, whose height,
Whose depth unfathomed, no man knows,
I see from far thy beauteous light,
And inly sigh for thy repose ;
My heart is pained, nor can it be
At rest, till I find rest in thee.

2 Is there a thing beneath the sun,
That strives with thee my heart to share ?
Ah ! tear it thence, and reign alone,
And govern every motion there.
Then shall my heart from earth be free,
When it has found its all in thee.

3 O crucify this self, that I
No more, but Christ in me, may live ;
Bid all my vile affections die,
Nor let one hateful lust survive.
In all things nothing may I see,
Nothing desire, or seek, but thee.

4 Lord, draw my heart from earth away,
And make it only know thy call ;
Speak to my inmost soul, and say,
" I am thy Saviour, God, thy All ! "
O dwell in me, fill all my soul,
And all my powers by thine control.

1076   L.M.   C.W.
" But in me is thy help."—Hos. xiii. 9 ; Isa. xliii. 11.

JESUS, in whom the Godhead's rays
Beam forth with mildest majesty,
I see thee full of truth and grace,
And come for all I want to thee.

2 Wrathful, impure, and proud I am ;
Nor constancy, nor strength, I have ;
But thou, O Lord, art still the same,
And hast not lost thy power to save.

3 Save me from pride, the plague repel ;
Jesus, thy humble mind impart,
O let the Spirit within me dwell,
And give me lowliness of heart.

4 Enter thyself, and cast out sin ;
More of thy purity bestow ;
Touch me, and make the leper clean ;
Wash me, and I am white as snow.

1077   7s.   C.W.
" I will take away the stony heart."—Ezek. xxxvi. 25.

DEAREST Lord, what must I do ?
Only thou the way canst show ;

Thou canst save me in this hour ;
I have neither will nor power.

2 God if over all thou art,
Greater than the sinful heart ;
Let thy power in me be shown ;
Take away the heart of stone.

3 Take away my darling sin,
Make me willing to be clean ;
Make me willing to receive
What thy goodness waits to give.

4 Teach me, Lord, with all to part ;
Tear all idols from my heart ;
Let thy power on me be shown ;
Take away the heart of stone.

5 Jesus, mighty to renew,
Work in me to will and do ;
Turn my nature's rapid tide ;
Stem the torrent of my pride.

6 Stop the whirlwind of my will ;
Bid corruptions, Lord, be still ;
Now thy love almighty shew,
Cleanse my heart, my mind renew.

1078   L.M.   STEELE.
For he dwelleth with you, and shall be in you.

DEAR Lord, and shall thy Spirit rest
In such a wretched heart as mine ?
Unworthy dwelling ! glorious guest !
Favour astonishing, divine !

2 When sin prevails, and gloomy fear,
And hope almost expires in night,
Lord, can thy Spirit then be here,
Great Spring of comfort, life, and light ?

3 Sure the blest Comforter is nigh ;
'Tis he sustains my fainting heart ;

Else would my hopes for ever die,
And every cheering ray depart.

4 When some kind promise glads my soul,
Do I not find his healing voice,
The tempest of my fears control,
And bid my drooping powers rejoice ?

5 Whene'er to call the Saviour mine,
With ardent wish my heart aspires,
Can it be less than power divine,
Which animates these strong desires ?

6 What less than thy almighty word,
Can raise my heart from earth and dust,
And bid me cleave to thee, my Lord,
My life, my treasure, and my trust ?

1079   C.M.   STEELE.
" Say unto my soul, I am thy salvation."—Ps. xxxv. 3

ETERNAL Source of joys divine,

To thee my soul aspires ;
O could I say, " The Lord is mine,"
'Tis all my soul desires.

2 Thy smile can give me real joy,
Unmingled and refined ;
Substantial bliss, without alloy,
And lasting as the mind.

3 Thy smile can gild the shades of woe,
Bid stormy trouble cease,
Spread the fair dawn of heaven below,
And sweeten pain to peace.

4 My hope, my trust, my life, my Lord,
Assure me of thy love ;
O speak the kind transporting word,
And bid my fears remove.

5 Then shall my thankful powers rejoice,
And triumph in my God,

Till heavenly rapture tune my voice
To spread thy praise abroad.

1080   L.M.   STEELE.
The Heavenly Conqueror.—Rev. iii. 5, 12, 21 ; xii. 11.

To Jesus, our victorious Lord,
The praises of our lives belong ;
For ever be his name adored ;
Sweet theme of every thankful song.

2 Lost in despair, beset with foes,
Undone, and perishing we lay ;
His pity melted o'er our woes,
And saved the trembling, dying prey.

3 He fought, he conquered though he fell,
While with his last expiring breath,
He triumphed o'er the powers of hell,
And by his dying vanquished death.

4 Though still reviving foes arise,
Temptations, sins, and doubts appear,
And pain our hearts, and fill our eyes
With many a groan, and many a tear ;

5 Still may we fight, and still prevail,
In our Almighty Leader's name ;
His strength, whene'er our spirits fail,
Can all our active powers inflame.

1081   L.M.   STEELE.
Longing for Immortality.—2 Cor. v. 4 ; Rom. viii. 23.

SAD prisoners in a house of clay,
With sins, and griefs, and pains oppressed,
We groan the lingering hours away,
And wish and long to be released.

2 Nor is it liberty alone,
Which prompts our restless, ardent sighs ;
For immortality we groan,
For robes and mansions in the skies.

3 Eternal mansions ! bright array !
  O blest exchange ! transporting thought !
  Free from the approaches of decay,
  Or the least shadow of a spot.

4 Bright world of bliss, O could I see
  One shining glimpse, one cheerful ray,
  (Fair dawn of immortality)
  Break through these tottering walls of clay.

5 Jesus, in thy dear name I trust,
  My life, my light, my Saviour, God ;
  When this frail house dissolves in dust,
  O raise me to thy bright abode.

1082   C.M.   SWAIN.
That your love may abound more and more.-Phil. i. 9.
  How sweet, how heavenly is the sight,
    When those that love the Lord,
  In one another's peace delight,
    And so fulfil his word !

2 When each can feel his brother's sigh,
    And with him bear a part ;
  When sorrow flows from eye to eye,
    And joy from heart to heart.

3 When free from envy, scorn, and pride,
    Our wishes all above,
  Each can his brother's failings hide,
    And show a brother's love.

4 When love in one delightful stream
    Through every bosom flows ;
  When union sweet and dear esteem,
    In every action glows !

5 Love is the golden chain that binds
    The happy souls above ;
  And he's an heir of heaven that finds
    His bosom glow with love.

1083   C.M.   STEELE.
Doubtless thou art our Father.—Isa. lxiii. 16 ; lxiv. 8.
  My God, my Father, blissful name !
    O may I call thee mine ?
  May I with sweet assurance claim
    A portion so divine ?

2 This only can my fears control,
    And bid my sorrows fly ;
  What harm can ever reach my soul
    Beneath my Father's eye ?

3 Whate'er thy providence denies
    I calmly would resign,
  For thou art just, and good, and wise ;
    O bend my will to thine.

4 Whate'er thy sacred will ordains,
    O give me strength to bear ;
  And let me know my Father reigns,
    And trust his tender care.

5 If pain and sickness rend this frame,
    And life almost depart,
  Is not thy mercy still the same,
    To cheer my drooping heart ?

6 If cares and sorrows me surround,
    Their power why should I fear ?
  My inward peace they cannot wound,
    If thou, my God, art near.

1084   L.M.   STEELE.
The Inconstant Heart.—Prov. xxviii. 26 ; iii. 5.
  AH, wretched, vile, ungrateful heart,
  That can from Jesus thus depart,
  Thus fond of trifles vainly rove,
  Forgetful of a Saviour's love !

2 In vain I charge my thoughts to stay,
  And chide each vanity away,

  In vain, alas ! resolve to bind
  This rebel heart, this wandering mind.

3 Through all resolves how soon it flies,
  And mocks the weak, the slender ties ;
  There's nought except a power divine
  That can this roving heart confine.

4 Jesus, to thee I would return,
  At thy dear feet repentant mourn ;
  There let me view thy pardoning love,
  And never from thy sight remove.

1085   L.M.   STEELE.
" Commune with your own heart."—Ps. iv. 4 ; xviii. 6.
  HENCE, vain, intruding world, depart ;
  No more allure nor vex my heart ;
  Let every vanity be gone ;
  I would be peaceful and alone.

2 Here let me search my inmost mind,
  And try its real state to find,
  The secret springs of thought explore,
  And call my words and actions o'er.

3 Eternity, tremendous sound !
  To guilty souls a dreadful wound ;
  But O, if Christ and heaven be mine,
  How sweet the accents, how divine !

4 Be this my great, my only care,
  My chief pursuit, my ardent prayer,
  An interest in the Saviour's blood,
  My pardon sealed, and peace with God.

5 Search, Lord, O search my inmost heart,
  And light, and hope, and joy impart ;
  From guilt and error set me free,
  And guide me safe to heaven and thee.

1086   C.M.   STEELE.
" Thy will be done."—Matt. vi. 10; Luke xxii. 42.

PEACE, my complaining, doubting heart,
    Ye busy cares, be still ;
Adore the just, the sovereign Lord,
    Nor murmur at his will.

2 Unerring wisdom guides his hand ;
    Nor dares my guilty fear,
Amid the sharpest pains I feel,
    Pronounce his hand severe.

3 Let me reflect, with humble awe,
    Whene'er my heart complains,
Compared with what my sins deserve,
    How easy are my pains !

4 Yes, Lord, I own thy sovereign hand,
    Thou just, and wise, and kind ;
Be every anxious thought suppressed,
    And all my soul resigned.

5 But O, indulge this only wish,
    This boon I must implore :
Assure my soul that thou art mine,
    My God, I ask no more.

1087   L.M.   STEELE.
Thou shalt make his soul an offering for sin.-Isa. liii. 10

WAS it for sin, for mortal guilt,
    The Saviour gave his vital blood ;
For sin amazing anguish felt,
    The wrath of an offended God ?

2 And shall I harbour in my breast
    (Tremble, my soul, at such a deed)
This dreadful foe, this fatal guest,
    The sin that made the Saviour bleed ?

3 Come, glorious Conqueror, gracious Lord,
    Thy all-prevailing power employ ;

O come, with thy resistless word,
    These hateful enemies destroy.

4 My hope, my all is fixed on thee,
    For thou alone hast power divine ;
O come, and conquer, Lord, for me,
    And all the glory shall be thine.

1088   C.M.   C.W.
" I will not let thee go."—Gen. xxxii. 26; Song iii. 4.

SHEPHERD divine, our wants relieve
    In this our evil day ;
To all thy tempted followers give
    The power to trust and pray.

2 Long as our fiery trials last,
    Long as the cross we bear ;
O let our souls on thee be cast,
    In never-ceasing prayer.

3 Till thou the Father's love impart,
    Till thou thyself bestow,
Be this the cry of every heart,
    " I will not let thee go.

4 " I will not let thee go, unless
    Thou tell thy name to me ;
With all thy great salvation bless,
    And say, ' Christ died for thee.' "

1089   C.M.   KENT.
In-dwelling Sin.—Rom. vii. 14-24 ; Isa. lii. 3.

SOLD under sin, was Paul's complaint ;
    He felt its galling load,
Though he, by calling, was a saint,
    And rightly taught of God.

2 Like him, we daily feel the same,
    And long to be dissolved ;
Oppressed by sins of every name,
    How oft are we involved !

3 But he that feels pollution most,
    Defiled throughout by sin,
Will never of his goodness boast,
    But mourn the plague within.

4 Distressed at heart, he'll tell his God
    He feels it every day ;
And to the fount of Jesus' blood
    For pardon haste away.

5 Sinless perfection we deny,
    The chief of Satan's wiles ;
Do thou, my soul, to Calvary fly,
    As oft as sin defiles.

1090   L.M.   KENT.
" Turn you to the strong hold," &c.—Zech. ix. 12.

PRISONERS of hope, to Jesus turn ;
He's a Strong-hold, ordained for you ;
Gird up your loins, and cease to mourn,
And to the Lamb your way pursue.

2 Though fast in Sinai's fetters bound,
Held in the deepest bondage there,
Yet 'tis the gospel's joyful sound :
" Sinners, to this Strong-hold repair."

3 Turn hither, ye who once were blessed
With life the ways of God to run ;
But now whose hearts are sore distressed,
Because those golden hours are gone.

4 Turn hither, ye who oft have tried,
By works, salvation to obtain ;
See royal robes your shame to hide,
And blood that takes out every stain.

5 His name a tower for strength renowned,
Shall save his people from their sin ;
Free grace shall o'er their sins abound ;
Ye fearing, doubting souls, turn in.

1091 L.M. KENT.
The well of Bethlehem.—2 Sam. xxiii. 15.

How welcome to the soul oppressed,
In sorrow's vale, by raging thirst,
Scorched by the sun's meridian beam,
Is the sweet well of Bethlehem !

2 Prophets of old, and saints the same,
In every age, of every name,
Drank of this soul-reviving stream,
The water sweet of Bethlehem.

3 Water so pure, or half so good,
From nature's fountains never flowed ;
There's curse and death in every stream,
Save in the well of Bethlehem.

4 Wide as the stretch of human woe,
Those death-consuming waters flow ;
Spring up, O well ! be this my theme,
Thou water sweet from Bethlehem.

5 To cheer when faint, when sick to heal,
Its wondrous virtues must prevail ;
My sins to crush, my fears to quell,
Spring up, O stream ! from Bethlehem's well.

6 When nature sinks beneath her load,
Amidst the din of Jordan's flood ;
With this my every fear dispel,
One sip of Bethlehem's sacred well.

1092 C.M. KENT.
Loose him, and let him go.—Jno. xi. 44 ; Isa. xlv. 13.

TILL God the sinner's mind illume,
'Tis dark as night within ;
Like Lazarus in the dreary tomb,
Bound hand and foot by sin.

2 Yet though in massy fetters bound,
To God's free grace a foe,
The Gospel has a joyful sound :
" Loose him, and let him go."

3 Sinners shall hear this joyful sound,
When God designs it so ;
Grace shall beyond their sins abound ;
" Loose him, and let him go."

4 Justice, beholding his attire,
No more appears his foe ;
He says, " I've all that I require ;
Loose him, and let him go."

5 He stands accepted in his name
Whose blood for him did flow ;
The holy law proclaims the same :
" Loose him, and let him go."

1093 C.M. KENT.
" And a man shall be a hiding-place."—Isa. xxxii. 2.

How welcome to the tempest-tossed,

Amidst the storm's career,
While horror spreads from coast to coast,
Is some kind haven near !

2 But far more welcome to the soul
Is that secure abode,
(When terrors o'er the conscience roll)
The Rock prepared of God.

3 Jesus, arrayed in mortal form,
Of whom the prophets tell,
On his dear head, O what a storm
Of awful vengeance fell !

4 To him, my only Hiding-place,
Let me for shelter fly ;
The storm of death draws on apace,
And who can say how nigh ?

5 In that dread moment, O to hide
Beneath his sheltering blood !
'Twill Jordan's icy waves divide,
And land my soul with God.

1094 C.M. KENT.
" And such were some of you."—1 Cor. vi. 11 ; xii. 2.

YE souls redeemed by Jesus' blood,
Salvation's theme pursue ;
Exalt the sovereign grace of God,
For " such were some of you ! "

2 From head to foot defiled by sin,
Deep in rebellion too ;
This awful state mankind are in,
" And such were some of you ! "

3 Whilst they are sinners dead to God,
Ye highly favoured few
Are washed from sin by Jesus' blood ;
For " such were some of you ! "

4 As ye are chosen from the rest,
To grace the praise is due ;
Be sovereign love for ever blest,
For " such were some of you ! "

1095 C.M. WATTS.
" The Word was made flesh."—John i. 14 ; 2 Cor. v. 19.

DEAREST of all the names above,
My Jesus, and my God !
Who can resist thy heavenly love,
Or trifle with thy blood ?

2 'Tis by the merit of thy death
The Father smiles again ;
'Tis by thy interceding breath,
The Spirit dwells with men.

3 Till God in human flesh I see,
My thoughts no comfort find ;
The holy, just, and sacred Three,
Are terrors to my mind.

4 But if Immanuel's face appear,
  My hope, my joy begins ;
  His name forbids my slavish fear ;
  His grace removes my sins.

5 While some on their own works rely,
  And some of wisdom boast,
  I love the Incarnate Mystery,
  And there I fix my trust.

1096   8.7.   BURNHAM.
" I had fainted, unless I had believed."—Ps. xxvii. 13.

  O WHAT dangers, all distressing,
    Snare each mourning pilgrim's feet ;
  Gloomy sorrows still increasing,
    Swell the present changing state.

2 Sometimes things around are cheering ;
    Grace and providence unite ;
  Nought but mercy seems appearing,
    Yielding peace and sweet delight.

3 But new trials soon surround us,
    Griefs and sorrows, sins and cares ;
  Creatures all conspire to wound us,
    And no help from heaven appears.

4 O for faith, and hope, and patience,
    Under every gracious rod ;
  Till at length we sing salvation,
    Wrought by Zion's faithful God !

1097   11s.   KENT.
The Refuge.—Deut. xxxiii. 27 ; Ps. xlvi. 1 ; xlviii. 3.

A REFUGE for sinners the gospel makes known ;
'Tis found in the merits of Jesus alone ;
The weary, the tempted, and burdened by sin,
Were never exempted from entering therein.

2

This refuge for sinners his love did ordain,
In Jesus the Lamb, from eternity slain ;
And if God the Spirit reveal this to you,
Take refuge in Jesus, though hell should pursue.

3

The soul that shall enter in safety shall dwell ;
There's no peradventure of sinking to hell ;
The oath of Jehovah secures him from fear,
Nor shall the avenger of blood enter there.

4

Here's refuge for sinners, whose guilt shall appear
As black as the confines of endless despair ;
Who, stript of all merit whereon to rely,
Are taught by the Spirit to Jesus to fly.

5

Should conscience accuse us, as oft-times it may,
Here's blood that can take its defilement away.

In Jesus the Saviour, the sinner shall view
A city of refuge and righteousness too.

1098   C.M.   WATTS.
Repentance, and faith in the blood of Christ.—Ps. li. 14

  O GOD of mercy, hear my call ;
    My load of guilt remove ;
  Break down this separating wall,
    That bars me from thy love.

2 Give me the presence of thy grace,
    Then my rejoicing tongue
  Shall speak aloud thy righteousness,
    And make thy praise my song.

3 No blood of goats, nor heifers slain
    For sin could e'er atone ;
  The death of Christ shall still remain
    Sufficient and alone.

4 A soul oppressed with sin's desert
    The Lord will ne'er despise ;
  A humble groan, a broken heart,
    Is our best sacrifice.

1099   C.M.   JOB HUPTON.
    Lu. xxii. 62.
" And he wept bitterly."—Mat. xxvi. 75 ;

  JESUS, omnipotent to save
    Exalted Prince of grace !
  Light, life, and love, thou dost bestow
    On men of vilest race.

2 The heart of steel to thee must yield,
    The adamant give way ;
  The stoutest rebel bow and kneel,
    And own thy sovereign sway.

3 Thy dying love, thy mercy felt,
    Makes godly sorrow rise ;
  And tears of penitential grief
    Gush from the sinner's eyes.

4 Pardon through thy dear wounds and
    Thy gracious hand reveals,   blood,
  And thy good Spirit on the heart
    That gracious pardon seals.

5 " I hate my sins, I loathe myself,
    O Lord ! " the sinner cries ;
  " O quell my lust, nor let me fall ! "
    He prays with lifted eyes.

1100   C.M.   Col. iii. 2.   NEWTON.
" Set your affection on things above."—

  LET worldly minds the world pursue,
    It has no charms for me ;
  Once I admired its trifles too,
    But grace has set me free.

2 Its pleasures now no longer please,
    No more content afford ;

Far from my heart be joys like these,
Now I have seen the Lord.

3 As by the light of opening day
The stars are all concealed ;
So earthly pleasures fade away,
When Jesus is revealed.

4 Creatures no more divide my choice ;
I bid them all depart ;
His name, and love, and gracious voice,
Have fixed my roving heart.

5 Now, Lord, I would be thine alone,
And wholly live to thee ;
But may I hope that thou wilt own
A worthless worm like me ?

6 Yes ; though of sinners I'm the worst,
I cannot doubt thy will ;
For if thou hadst not loved me first,
I thee had hated still.

1101   8.7.   W. WILLIAMS.
" There remaineth a rest to the people of God."
JESUS, lead me by thy power
Safe into the promised rest ;
Hide my soul within thy arms ;
Make me lean upon thy breast.

2 Be my guide in every peril,
Watch me hourly, night and day ;
Else my foolish heart will wander
From thy Spirit far away.

3 In thy presence I am happy ;
In thy presence I'm secure ;
In thy presence all afflictions
I can easily endure.

4 In thy presence I can conquer,
I can suffer, I can die ;

Far from thee, I faint and languish ;
O thou Saviour, keep me nigh.

1102   8.7.4.   KELLY.
" It is I ; be not afraid."—John vi. 20 ; Mark vi. 50.
WHY those fears ? behold, 'tis Jesus
Holds the helm, and guides the ship ;
Spread the sails, and catch the breezes,
Sent to waft us through the deep,
To the regions
Where the mourners cease to weep.

2 Though the shore we hope to land on,
Only by report is known,
Yet we freely all abandon,
Led by that report alone ;
And with Jesus
Through the trackless deep move on.

3 Led by him we brave the ocean ;
Each tumultuous storm defy ;
Calm amidst tempestuous motion,
Knowing that the Lord is nigh ;
Waves obey him,
And the storms before him fly.

4 Rendered safe by his protection,
We shall pass the watery waste ;
Trusting to his wise direction,
We shall gain the port at last ;
And with wonder
Think on toils and dangers past.

1103   8.8.6.   TOPLADY.
"A propitiation through faith in his blood."—Ro. iii. 25
O THOU that hear'st the prayer of faith,
Wilt thou not save a soul from death,
That casts itself on thee ?

I have no refuge of my own,
But fly to what the Lord has done,
And suffered once for me.

2 Slain in the guilty sinner's stead,
His spotless righteousness I plead,
And his availing blood ;
His righteousness my robe shall be,
His merit shall atone for me,
And bring me near to God.

3 Then snatch me from eternal death ;
The Spirit of adoption breathe,
And consolation send ;
By him some word of life impart,
And sweetly whisper to my heart,
" Thy Maker is thy Friend."

1104   11s.   S. TURNER or BENNETT.
" Lead me to the rock that is higher than I."—Ps. lxi. 2
CONVINCED as a sinner, to Jesus I come,
Informed by the gospel for such there is room ;
O'erwhelmed with sorrow for sin, will I cry ;
" Lead me to the Rock that is higher than I."
2
O blessed be Jesus, for answering prayer,
And raising my soul from the pit of despair ;
In every new trial, to him will I cry,
" Lead me to the Rock that is higher than I."
3
When sorely afflicted, and ready to faint,
Before my Redeemer I'll spread my complaint ;
'Midst storms and distresses, my soul shall rely
On Jesus, the Rock that is higher than I.

1105   L.M.   MEDLEY.
" But one thing is needful."—Luke x. 42 ; Ps. lxxiii. 25.
JESUS, engrave it on my heart,
That thou the one thing needful art ;

I could from all things parted be,
But never, never, Lord, from thee.

2 Needful art thou to make me live ;
Needful art thou all grace to give ;
Needful to guide me, lest I stray ;
Needful to help me every day.

3 Needful is thy most precious blood ;
Needful is thy correcting rod ;
Needful is thy indulgent care ;
Needful thy all-prevailing prayer.

4 Needful thy presence, dearest Lord,
True peace and comfort to afford ;
Needful thy promise to impart
Fresh life and vigour to my heart.

5 Needful art thou, my soul can say,
Through all life's dark and thorny way ;
In death thou wilt most needful be,
When I yield up my soul to thee.

6 Needful art thou, to raise my dust
In shining glory with the just ;
Needful when I in heaven appear,
To crown and to present me there.

1106   L.M.   E. MOTE.

"It fell not, for it was founded upon a rock."
My hope is built on nothing less
Than Jesus' blood and righteousness ;
I dare not trust the sweetest frame,
But wholly lean on Jesus' name.

2 When darkness veils his lovely face,
I rest on his unchanging grace ;
In every rough and stormy gale,
My anchor holds within the vail.

3 His oath, his covenant, and his blood,
Support me in the whelming flood,
When all around my soul gives way,
He then is all my hope and stay.

4 I trust his righteous character,
His counsel, promise, and his power.
His honour and his name's at stake,
To save me from the burning lake.

5 When I shall launch in worlds unseen,
O may I then be found in him,
Dressed in his righteousness alone,
Faultless to stand before the throne.

1107   L.M.   SWAIN.

"The Spirit itself maketh intercession for us."

WHEN some sweet promise warms our heart,
And cheers us under every care,
It is the Spirit's gracious part
To take that word and fix it there.

2 'Twas he that turned our hearts away
From love of sin and hateful strife ;
His all-creating beams display
The dawn of everlasting life.

3 'Tis he that brings us comfort down,
When we complain and mourn for sin ;
And, while he shows our heavenly crown,
Assures us sin no more shall reign.

4 Our great High Priest, before the throne,
Presents the merits of his blood ;
For our acceptance pleads his own,
And proves our cause completely good.

5 When prayer or praise attempts to rise,
And fain would reach Jehovah's ear,
His all-prevailing sacrifice
Perfumes, and makes it welcome there.

1108   C.M.   NEWTON or COWPER.

"I waited patiently for the Lord."—Ps. xl. 1; xxvii. 13.
BREATHE from the gentle south, O Lord,
And cheer me from the north ;
Blow on the treasures of thy word,
And call the spices forth.

2 Cold as I feel this heart of mine,
Yet since I feel it so,
It yields some hope of life divine
Within, however low.

3 I seem forsaken and alone ;
I hear the lion roar ;
And every door is shut but one,
And that is mercy's door.

4 Here would I wait, and hope, and pray,
Till needed mercy come ;
But lest I faint, or turn away,
Lord, do not tarry long.

1109   L.M.   STEELE.

"Come unto me," &c.—Matt. xi. 28, 29; Isa. lv. 1—3.
COME, weary souls, with sin distressed,
Come and accept the promised rest ;
The gospel's gracious call obey,
And cast your gloomy fears away.

2 Oppressed with guilt (a painful load),
O come and spread your woes abroad,
Divine compassion, mighty love,
Will all the painful load remove.

3 Here mercy's boundless ocean flows,
To cleanse your guilt, and heal your woes ;
Pardon, and life, and endless peace ;
How rich the gift, how free the grace !

4 Dear Saviour, let thy powerful love
Confirm our faith, our fears remove ;

Forgiveness shed through every breast,
And guide us to eternal rest.

1110   C.M.   BEDDOME.
" My times are in thy hand."-Ps. xxxi. 15; Ecc. iii. 1-8.

MY times of sorrow and of joy,
   Great God, are in thy hand ;
My choicest comforts come from thee,
   And go at thy command.

2 If thou shouldst take them all away,
   Yet let me not repine ;
Before they were possessed by me,
   They were entirely thine.

3 Nor let me drop a murmuring word,
   Though the whole world were gone ;
But seek enduring happiness
   In thee, and thee alone.

1111   7s.   W. W. HORNE.
" Unclean, unclean."—Lev. xiii. 45; Job xl. 4.

JESUS, thou alone canst save,
Thou canst raise the dead to life ;
Thy reviving power I crave,
To decide this inward strife.

2 Sin my every power defiles,
Thought, and word, and action too ;
Jesus, in thy mercy smile ;
Cleanse, and make me white as snow.

3 Surely none on earth's so vile,
So polluted as I am ;
Condescend, in love to smile,
O thou sin-atoning Lamb !

4 Fierce, impetuous, o'er my head
Billows of temptation roll ;
Sorrows rise, and joys are fled ;
Darkness veils my shipwrecked soul.

5 'Midst the waves O bear me up ;
In thy strength alone I stand ;
In thy promise is my hope ;
Guide me safe to Zion's land.

1112   L.M.   WATTS.
" Blessed are the poor in spirit."—Matt. v. 3—6.

BLESS'D are the humble souls that see
Their emptiness and poverty ;
Treasures of grace to them are given,
And crowns of joy laid up in heaven.

2 Bless'd are the men of broken heart,
Who mourn for sin with inward smart ;
The blood of Christ divinely flows,
A healing balm for all their woes.

3 Bless'd are the souls that thirst for grace,
Hunger and long for righteousness ;
They shall be well supplied, and fed
With living streams and living bread.

1113   8.8.6.   BERRIDGE.
" The very hairs of your head are all numbered."

How watchful is the loving Lord,
How sweet his providential word,
   To children that believe !
Your very hairs are numbered all ;
Not one by force or chance can fall
   Without your Father's leave.

2 Why should I fear when guarded so,
Or shrink to meet a deadly foe ?
   His mouth is held with bit ;
I need not dread his utmost spite,
Nor can he bark, nor can he bite,
   Unless the Lord permit.

3 No cross or bliss, no loss or gain,
No health or sickness, ease or pain,
   Can give themselves a birth ;

The Lord so rules by his command,
Nor good nor ill can stir a hand,
   Unless he send them forth.

4 Since thou so kind and watchful art,
To guard my head and guard my heart,
   And guard my very hair,
Teach me with child-like mind to sit,
And sing at the dear Saviour's feet,
   Without distrust or fear.

5 So, like a pilgrim let me wait,
Contented well in every state,
   Till all my warfare ends ;
Live in a calm and cheerful mood,
And find that all things work for good,
   Which Jesus kindly sends.

1114   C.M.   NEWTON.
New Year: " Thou makest the outgoings," &c.-Ps. 65, 8.

Now, gracious Lord, thy arm reveal,
   And make thy glory known ;
Hear whilst we plead the Saviour's name,
   And venture near the throne.

2 From all the guilt of former sin
   Let mercy set us free ;
And let the year we now begin,
   Begin and end with thee.

3 Send down thy Spirit from above,
   That saints may love thee more,
And sinners now may learn to love,
   Who never loved before.

4 And when before thee we appear,
   In our eternal home,
May growing numbers worship here,
   And praise thee in our room.

1115   L.M.   NEWTON.
New Year: " My times are in thy hand."—Ps. xxxi. 15.

UPHELD by thy supporting hand,
We pass, O Lord, from year to year ;
And still we meet, at thy command,
To seek thy gracious presence here.

2 Oft feed us, Lord, beneath this vine,
Through the new year, with heavenly bread ;
Oft clothe thy word with power divine,
To break the rocks and raise the dead.

3 Oft by a Saviour's dying love,
To many a wounded heart revealed,
Temptations, fears, and guilt remove,
And be our Sun, and Strength, and Shield.

1116   8.7.   KELLY.
" Stricken, smitten of God, and afflicted."—Isa. liii. 3.

" STRICKEN, smitten, and afflicted,"
See him dying on the tree !
'Tis the Christ by man rejected !
Yes, my soul, 'tis he ! 'tis he !
'Tis the long expected Prophet,
David's son, yet David's Lord ;
Proofs I see sufficient of it ;
'Tis a true and faithful word.

2 Tell me, ye who hear him groaning,
Was there ever grief like his ?
Friends, through fear, his cause disowning,
Foes insulting his distress.
Many hands were raised to wound him,
None would interpose to save,
But the awful stroke that found him,
Was the stroke that justice gave.

3 Ye who think of sin but lightly,
Nor suppose the evil great,
Here may view its nature rightly,
Here its guilt may estimate.
Mark the sacrifice appointed !
See *who* bears the awful load !
'Tis the WORD, the LORD'S ANOINTED,
Son of man, and Son of God.

4 Here we have a firm foundation ;
Here's the refuge of the lost ;
Christ's the Rock of our salvation ;
His the name of which we boast.
Lamb of God for sinners wounded !
Sacrificed to cancel guilt !
None shall ever be confounded
Who on thee their hopes have built.

1117   7s.   KELLY.
The love of Christ .. passeth knowledge.—Eph. iii. 19.

LORD, dissolve my frozen heart

By the beams of love divine ;
This alone can warmth impart,
To dissolve a heart like mine.

2 O that love, how vast it is !
Vast it seems, though known in part ;
Strange indeed, if love like this
Should not melt the frozen heart.

3 Saviour, let thy love be felt,
Let its power be felt by me,
Then my frozen heart shall melt,
Melt in love, O Lord, to thee.

1118   8.7.   ZION'S TRUMPET, 1838.
" Herein is love," &c.—1 John iv, 8-16 ; John xv. 13.

WHAT is love ? My soul would answer,
Nought deserves the endearing name
But the God of love, the Saviour,
Whose dear heart's a constant flame.

2 View him prostrate in the garden,
Wet his locks with dews of night,
Grappling with the powers of darkness,
Sweating blood, amazing sight !

3 Hear his groans, till he, expiring,
Cries triumphant, " It is done ; "
Bearing all the wrathful anger
Which to us was due alone.

4 What is love ? My soul would echo
With the saints in heaven above,
Who, through Jesus, gone to glory,
Sing in concert, " This is love ! "

1119   8.7.   FAWCETT.
" I will guide thee with mine eye."—Ps. xxxii. 8.

JESUS, thou Almighty Saviour,
Prostrate at thy feet I lie ;
Humbly I entreat thy favour,
Condescend to hear my cry.

2 When I was to thee a stranger,
Wandering in forbidden ways,
From the paths of sin and danger
Thou didst call me by thy grace.

3 Let not, then, my foes confound me,
Thou art all my help and hope ;
Let thy arms of love surround me,
Let thy mercy hold me up.

4 Grant me thy Divine direction
In the way that I should go ;
Let thy hand be my protection
From the power of every foe.

5 Gracious Saviour, never leave me,
While my toils and conflicts last ;
To thy kind embrace receive me,
When the storms of life are past.

1120 112th.
The Lord's Supper.—Matt. xv. 26, 27; John vi. 32, 33.

Not worthy, Lord, we must confess,
That we of children's bread should taste,
Yet, trusting in thy righteousness,
We venture to the gospel feast ;
The bread we ask which comes from heaven,
O let some blessed crumbs be given.

2 Lord, set thy cross before our eyes,
With all its wondrous toil and smart ;
And feast us on thy sacrifice,
And show our names upon thy heart ;
Till faith cry out, " I Jesus view,
I trust him now, and feel him too."

1121 L.M. WATTS.
The Lord's Supper.—Luke xxii. 19; Matt. xxvi. 26.

'Twas on that dark and doleful night,
When powers of earth and hell arose
Against the Son of God's delight,
And friends betrayed him to his foes.

2 Before the mournful scene began,
He took the bread and blessed and brake ;
What love through all his actions ran !
What wondrous words of grace he spake !

3 " This is my body broke for sin,
Receive and eat the living food ; "
Then took the cup and blessed the wine—
" 'Tis the new covenant in my blood."

4 " Do this," he cried, " till time shall end,
In memory of your dying Friend !
Meet at my table, and record
The love of your departed Lord."

5 Jesus, thy feast we celebrate,
We show thy death, we sing thy name,

Till thou return, and we shall eat
The marriage-supper of the Lamb.

1122 C.M. COWPER.
Welcome to the Lord's Table.—Matt. xxvi. 26-28.

This is the feast of heavenly wine,
And God invites to sup ;
The juices of the living Vine
Were pressed to fill the cup.

2 O bless the Saviour, ye that eat,
With royal dainties fed ;
Not heaven affords a costlier treat,
For Jesus is the bread.

3 The vile, the lost, he calls to them.
Ye trembling souls appear ;
The righteous, in their own esteem,
Have no acceptance here.

4 Approach, ye poor, nor dare refuse

The banquet spread for you ;
Dear Saviour, this is welcome news
Then I may venture too.

5 If guilt and sin afford a plea,
And may obtain a place,
Surely the Lord will welcome me,
And I shall see his face.

1123 L.M. STEELE.
" Christ died for the ungodly."—Rom. v. 6-8; iv. 25.

Stretched on the cross, the Saviour dies ;
Hark ! his expiring groans arise !
See, from his hands, his feet, his side,
Runs down the sacred crimson tide !

2 But life attends each deathful sound,
And flows from every bleeding wound ;
The vital stream, how free it flows,
To save and cleanse his rebel foes !

3 To suffer in the traitor's place,
To die for man, surprising grace !
Yet pass rebellious angels by—
O why for man, dear Saviour, why ?

4 Can I survey this scene of woe,
Where mingling grief and wonder flow ?
And yet my heart unmoved remain,
Insensible to love or pain ?

5 Come, dearest Lord, thy power impart,
To warm this cold and stupid heart ;
Till all its powers and feelings move
In melting grief and ardent love.

1124 L.M. KELLY.
And call the Sabbath the holy of the Lord, honourable.

I fain would love the day of rest,
Would still esteem this day the best,
But oft, alas ! I've need to say,
" How barren is my soul to-day ! "

2 True, I frequent the house of prayer ;
I go and sit with others there ;
I hear, and sing, and seem to pray,
But oft my mind is called away.

3 I fain would see the Saviour near,
Of him would think, and speak, and hear ;
But vain and sinful thoughts intrude,
And draw my soul from all that's good.

4 Redeemed from earth by Jesus' blood
I fain would give the day to God ;
But, seldom to my purpose true,
'Tis mine to plan, but not to do.

5 Of sinners, Lord, I am the chief ;
O bring thy worthless worm relief !
Revive thy work within my soul,
And all my thoughts and powers control.

1125   L.M.   KELLY.

"Where two or three are met in my name," &c.

How sweet to leave the world awhile,
And seek the presence of the Lord!
Dear Saviour, on thy people smile,
And come according to thy word.

2 From busy scenes we now retreat,
That we may here converse with thee;
Ah, Lord, behold us at thy feet!
Let this the "gate of heaven" be.

3 "Chief of ten thousand," now appear,
That we by faith may see thy face!
O speak, that we thy voice may hear,
And let thy presence fill this place.

4 Then let the worldling boast his joys,
We've meat to eat he knows not of;
We count his treasures worthless toys,
While we possess a Saviour's love.

1126   C.M.   NEWTON.

"It is manna."—Exod. xvi. 15-21; 2 Cor. viii. 15.

THE manna, favoured Israel's meat,
Was gathered day by day;
When all the host was served, the heat
Melted the rest away.

2 In vain to hoard it up they tried,
Against to-morrow came;
It then bred worms and putrefied;
And proved their sin and shame.

3 So truths by which the soul is fed
Must e'er be had afresh;
For notions resting in the head
Will only feed the flesh.

4 Nor can the best experience past
The life of faith maintain;

The brightest hope will faint at last,
Unless supplied again.

5 Dear Lord, while in thy house we're found,
Do thou the manna give;
O let it fall on us around,
That we may eat and live.

1127   L.M.   KENT.

"Awake, O north wind."—Song iv. 16; Isa. lxi. 11.

WHEN Zion's sons, great God! appear
In Zion's courts for praise and prayer,
There, in thy Spirit, deign to be
As one with those who worship thee.

2 Without thy sovereign power, O Lord,
No sweets the gospel can afford;
No drops of heavenly love will fall
To cheer the weary, thirsting soul.

3 Winds from the north and south, awake,
Take of the things of Jesus, take;
Diffuse thy kind celestial dew,
Bring pardon, peace, and healing too.

4 Then shall we count the season dear
To those who speak or those who hear;
And all conspire with sweet accord,
In hymns of joy, to praise the Lord.

1128   C.M.   BERRIDGE.

Prayer.—Ps. xx. 9.

ETERNAL Father, Lord of all,
By heaven and earth adored,
Regard thy guilty creatures' call,
Who would revere thy word.

2 Lord Jesus, Son of God most high,
Of all the rightful heir,
Adored by hosts above the sky,
And by thy people here;

3 Thee, Saviour of the lost, we own,
Incarnate God and Lord,
Refresh us now, and send us down
The blessings of thy word.

4 Thou, Holy Ghost, who dost reveal
The secret things of grace;
And knowest well the Father's will,
And his deep mind can trace;

5 Disclose the heavenly mysteries,
And bring the gospel feast;
Give gracious hearts and opened eyes,
That we may see and taste.

1129   148th.   BARNARD.

"He was moved with compassion."—Matt. ix. 36.

JESUS, we come to meet
With thee, our Lord and King,
To bow before thy feet,
And here thy praises sing:
Compacsion on us have, we pray,
And empty send us not away.

2 May every worldly care
Be banished from our mind;
May we with profit hear;
And peace and comfort find:
Refresh us from thy word, we pray,
And empty send us not away.

3 Our strength will soon decrease,
Unless our souls be fed;
We feel our health and peace
Depend on living bread.
Thy gracious hand now, Lord, display,
And empty send us not away.

4 May all true mourners feel
Their grief exchanged for joy;

Thy love to them reveal,
And all their fears destroy :
That when they leave thy house this day,
They may not empty go away.

5 May all thy children prove
The riches of thy grace ;
Each taste redeeming love,
And see thy smiling face :
So shall we all with pleasure say,
We are not empty sent away.

1130   L.M.   NEWTON *(altered).*
Prayer to God the Spirit.—1 Cor. xii. 6-11 ; i. 5.
O THOU, at whose almighty word
The glorious light from darkness sprung,
Thy quickening influence afford,
And clothe with power the preacher's tongue.

2 'Tis thine to teach him how to speak ;
'Tis thine to give the hearing ear ;
'Tis thine the stubborn heart to break,
And make the careless sinner fear.

3 'Tis also thine, Almighty Lord
To cheer the poor, desponding heart ;
To speak the soul-reviving word,
And bid the mourners' fears depart.

4 Thus, while we in the means are found,
We still on thee alone depend
To make the gospel's joyful sound
Effectual to the promised end.

1131   L.M.   S. TURNER.
" If two of you agree, it shall be done."—Matt. xviii. 19
WE have thy promise, gracious Lord,
Thou wilt be where thy people meet ;
O, then, fulfil thy gracious word,
And make our happiness complete.

2 Thy promise is to two or three,
Who meet together in thy name ;
That for whatever they agree
To ask, they surely shall obtain.

3 We ask thy gracious presence here,
The sweet enjoyment of thy love ;
From worldly thoughts O keep us clear,
And set our hearts on things above.

4 We ask thy Holy Spirit's aid,
Whilst we're engaged in prayer and praise ;
We ask from our great living Head
To be supplied with every grace.

5 We ask for faith a sweet increase,
To find our doubts and fears removed,
To feel the powerful reign of peace,
And every sinful thought subdued.

6 We ask to feel a union sweet,
We ask a blessing on thy word ;

We ask—but all our askings meet
In this—we ask thy presence, Lord !

1132   8.8.6.   KENT.
" I will come unto thee, and I will bless thee."
WHERE two or three together meet,
My love and mercy to repeat,
  And tell what I have done ;
There will I be, says God, to bless,
And every burdened soul redress,
  Who worships at my throne.

2 Make one in this assembly, Lord,
Speak to each heart some healing word,
  To set from bondage free ;
Impart a kind celestial shower,
And grant that we may spend an hour
  In fellowship with thee.

3 Guilt from the troubled heart remove,
Constrain the soul, by love, to love,
  Release from slavish fear ;
Then, though in tents of sin we groan,
We'll sing like those around thy throne,
  Till thou shalt bring us there.

1133   8.7.4.   KELLY.
" The Gospel,—the power of God unto salvation."
MAY the power that brings salvation,
  Now exerted in the word,
By its quickening operation,
  Life impart and joy afford !
    Life to sinners,
  Joy to those who know the Lord.

2 Hark, the voice of love, proclaiming
  Mercy through a Saviour's blood ;
Vain the schemes of human framing,
  This alone is owned of God ;
    'Tis the gospel
  Points to heaven, and shows the road.

1134   8.8.6.   BROWNE *(altered).*
" Lead me in thy truth."—Ps. xxv. 5 ; Isa. xxv. 9.
COME, gracious Spirit, heavenly Dove,
With light and comfort from above,
  Our waiting souls set free ;
Be thou our guardian, thou our guide,
O'er every thought and step preside,
  And draw us after thee.

2 Conduct us safe, conduct us far
From every sin and hurtful snare,
  That we may not thee grieve ;
Apply thy word that rules must give,
And teach us lessons how to live,
  And firmly to believe.

3 Lead us to Christ, our only rest,
 And in his love may we be blest,
  While in his name we meet ;
 Let precious drops of heavenly dew,
 Our courage and our strength renew,
 And make the promise sweet.

1135 8.7.4. KELLY.
"Serve the Lord with fear," &c.—Ps. ii. 11.
IN thy name O Lord, assembling,
 We thy people now draw near,
Teach us to rejoice with trembling,
 Speak, and let thy servants hear :
  Hear with meekness ;
 Hear thy word with godly fear.

2 While our days on earth are lengthened,
 May we give them, Lord, to thee ;
Cheered by hope, and daily strengthened,
 May we run, nor weary be ;
  Till thy glory,
 Without clouds, in heaven we see.

3 There, in worship purer, sweeter,
 All thy people shall adore ;
Tasting of enjoyment greater
 Than they could conceive before ;
  Full enjoyment,
 Full, unmixed, and evermore.

1136 8.7.7. KELLY.
"In blessing I will bless thee."—Gen. xxii. 17.
SAVIOUR ! follow with thy blessing
 Truths delivered in thy name ;
Thus the word, thy power possessing,
 Shall declare from whence it came.
 Mighty let thy gospel be,
 Set the burdened sinner free.

2 Let the word be food to nourish
 Those whom thou hast called thy own ;
Let thy people's graces flourish ;
 May they live to thee alone.
 May we all in Jesus live,
 And to God the glory give.

1137 8.7.4. KELLY.
Save thy people, and bless thine inheritance.—Ps. 28, 9.
GOD of our salvation, hear us ;
 Bless, O bless us, ere we go ;
When we join the world, be near us,
 Lest thy people careless grow ;
  Saviour, keep us,
 Keep us safe from every foe.

2 In the day of thy appearing,
 When the trump of God shall sound,
May we hear it, nothing fearing,

Though all nature sinks around,
  By our Saviour
Raised, and then with glory crowned.

1138 7s. NEWTON.
Dismission.—Heb. xiii. 20, 21 ; Rom. xv. 33.
Now may He who from the dead
Brought the Shepherd of the sheep,
Jesus Christ, our King and Head,
All our souls in safety keep.

2 May he teach us to fulfil
 What is pleasing in his sight ;
 Perfect us in all his will,
 And preserve us day and night.

3 To that dear Redeemer's praise,
 Who the covenant sealed with blood,
 Let our hearts and voices raise
 Loud thanksgivings to our God.

PART VI

OCCASIONAL HYMNS.

1139   C.M.   WATTS (abbreviated).
Man frail, God eternal.—Ps. xc. 1–5.

O GOD, our Help in ages past,
  Our Hope for years to come,
Our Shelter from the stormy blast,
  And our eternal Home.

2 Under the shadow of thy throne
  Thy saints have dwelt secure ;
Sufficient is thine arm alone,
  And our defence is sure.

3 Before the hills in order stood,
  Or earth received her frame—
From everlasting thou art God,
  To endless years the same.

4 [Thy word commands our flesh to dust,
  " Return, ye sons of men " ;
All nations rose from earth at first,
  And turn to earth again.]

5 A thousand ages in thy sight
  Are like an evening gone ;
Short as the watch that ends the night,
  Before the rising sun.

6 Time, like an ever-rolling stream,
  Bears all its sons away ;
They fly, forgotten. as a dream
  Dies at the opening day.

7 O God, our Help in ages past
  Our Hope for years to come,
Be thou our Guard while life shall last,
  And our eternal Home.

1140   L.M   WATTS (abbreviated).
Prayer for Reviving.—Ps. lxxx.

GREAT Shepherd of thine Israel,
Who didst between the cherubs dwell,
And led the tribes, thy chosen sheep,
Safe through the desert and the deep.

2 Thy Church is in the desert now ;
Shine from on high, and guide us through ;
Turn us to thee, thy love restore,
We shall be saved and sigh no more.

3 Hast thou not planted with thy hands
A lovely vine in heathen lands ?
Did not thy power defend it round,
And heavenly dews enrich the ground ?

4 But now her beauty is defaced ;
Why hast thou laid her fences waste ?
Strangers and foes against her join,

And every beast devours the vine.

5 Lord, when this vine in Canaan grew,
Thou wert its strength and glory too :
Attacked in vain by all its foes,
Till the fair branch of promise rose.

6 Fair branch, ordained of old to shoot
From David's stock, from Jacob's root ;
Himself a noble vine, and we
The lesser branches of the tree.

7 'Tis thy own Son, and he shall stand,
Girt with thy strength at thy right hand ;

Thy first-born Son, adorned and blessed
With power and grace above the rest.

8 Oh ! for his sake attend our cry,
Shine on thy churches lest they die ;
Turn us to thee, thy love restore,
We shall be saved and sigh no more.

1141   L.M.   WATTS.
The Church's safety and triumph.—Ps. xlvi.

GOD is the refuge of his saints
When storms of sharp distress invade ;
Ere we can offer our complaints,
Behold him present with his aid.

2 Let mountains from their seats be hurled
Down to the deep and buried there :
Convulsions shake the solid world,
Our faith shall never yield to fear.

3 Loud may the troubled ocean roar,
In sacred peace our souls abide,
While every nation, every shore,
Trembles and dreads the swelling tide.

4 There is a stream whose gentle flow
Supplies the city of our God ;
Life, love, and joy, still gliding through,
And watering our divine abode.

5 That sacred stream, thine holy Word,
That all our raging fear controls ;
Sweet peace thy promises afford,
And give new strength to fainting souls.

6 Sion enjoys her Monarch's love,
Secure against a threatening hour ;
Nor can her firm foundation move,
Built on his truth and armed with power.

1142   L.M.   NEWTON.

Confession and prayer for church and nation.

OH may the power which melts the rock
Be felt by all assembled here !
Or else our service will but mock
The God whom we profess to fear !

2 Lord, while thy judgments shake the land,
Thy people's eyes are fixed on thee ;
We own thy just uplifted hand,
Which thousands cannot, will not, see.

3 How long hast thou bestowed thy care
On this indulged, ungrateful spot !
While other nations, far and near,
Have envied and admired our lot.

4 Here peace and liberty have dwelt,
The glorious gospel brightly shone ;
And oft our enemies have felt
That God has made our cause his own.

5 But ah ! both heaven and earth have heard
Our vile requital of his love ;
We, whom like children he has reared,
Rebels against his goodness prove.

6 His grace despised, his power defied,
And legions of the blackest crimes,
Profaneness, riot, lust, and pride
Are signs that mark the present times.

7 The Lord, displeased, has raised his rod ;
Ah ! where are now the faithful few
Who tremble for the Ark of God,
And know what Israel ought to do ?

8 Lord, hear thy people everywhere,
Who meet to mourn, confess, and pray ;
The nation and thy Churches spare,
And let thy wrath be turned away.

1143   C.M.   STEELE.

Confession and prayer for church and nation.

SEE, gracious God, before thy throne
Thy mourning people bend ;
'Tis on thy sovereign grace alone
Our humble hopes depend.

2 Tremendous judgments from thy hand
Thy dreadful power display ;
Yet mercy spares this guilty land,
And still we live to pray.

3 Great God ! and why is Britain spared ?
Ungrateful as we are ;
O make thy awful warnings heard,
While mercy cries, Forbear !

4 What numerous crimes increasing rise
Through this apostate isle !
What land as favoured of the skies,
And yet what land so vile !

5 How changed, alas, are truths divine,
For error, guilt and shame !
What impious numbers, bold in sin,
Disgrace the Christian name !

6 Regardless of thy smile or frown,
Their pleasures they require ;
And sink with gay indifference down
To everlasting fire.

7 O turn us, turn us, mighty Lord,
By thy resistless grace ;
Then shall our hearts obey thy word,
And humbly seek thy face ;—

8 Then, should insulting foes invade,
We shall not sink in fear ;
Secure of never-failing aid,
If God, our God, is near.

1144   8.7.   NEWTON.

For a revival.

SAVIOUR, visit thy plantation,
Grant us, Lord, a gracious rain !
All will come to desolation,
Unless thou return again :
Keep no longer at a distance,
Shine upon us from on high ;
Lest, for want of thine assistance,
Every plant should droop and die.

2 Surely, once thy garden flourished,
Every part looked gay and green ;
Then thy word our spirits nourished,
Happy seasons we have seen !
But a drought has since succeeded,
And a sad decline we see ;
Lord, thy help is greatly needed ;
Help can only come from thee.

3 Where are those we counted leaders,
Filled with zeal, and love, and truth ?
Old professors, tall as cedars,
Bright examples to our youth !
Some, in whom we once delighted,
We shall meet no more below ;
Some, alas ! we fear are blighted,
Scarce a single leaf they show.

4 Younger plants—the sight how pleasant,
Covered thick with blossoms stood ;
But they cause us grief at present,
Frosts have nipped them in the bud !
Dearest Saviour, hasten hither,
Thou canst make them bloom again ;
Oh, permit them not to wither,
Let not all our hopes be vain !

5 Let our mutual love be fervent,
    Make us prevalent in prayers ;
Let each one esteemed thy servant
    Shun the world's bewitching snares ;
Break the tempter's fatal power,
    Turn the stony heart to flesh ;
And begin, from this good hour,
    To revive thy work afresh.

1145   C.M.

For national reprieve.—Gen. xviii. 32.

WHEN Abram full of sacred awe,
    Before Jehovah stood,
And with a humble, fervent prayer,
    For guilty Sodom sued ;

2 With what success, what wondrous grace,
    Was his petition crowned !
The Lord would spare, if in the place
    Ten righteous men be found.

3 And could a single holy soul
    So rich a boon obtain ?
Great God, and shall thy remnant cry
    And plead with thee in vain ?

4 Britain, all guilty as she is,
    Her several saints can boast ;
And now their fervent prayers ascend—
    And can those prayers be lost ?

5 Are not thy righteous dear to thee
    Now, as in ancient times ?
Or does this guilty land exceed
    Gomorrah in its crimes ?

6 Still there are those who bear thy name,
    Here yet is thine abode ;
Long has thy presence blessed our land ;
    Forsake us not, O God !

1146   C.M.   WATTS.

The promise and sign of Christ's coming.—2 Peter iii.

HELP, Lord, for men of virtue fail ;
    Religion loses ground ;
The sons of violence prevail,
    And treacheries abound.

2 Their oaths and promises they break,
    Yet act the flatterer's part ;
With fair deceitful lips they speak,
    And with a double heart.

3 If we reprove some hateful lie,
    How is their fury stirred !
" Are not our lips our own ? " they cry ;
    " And who shall be our Lord ? "

4 [Scoffers appear on every side,
    Where a vile race of men
Is raised on seats of power and pride,

And bears the sword in vain.]

5 Lord, when iniquities abound,
    And blasphemy grows bold,
When faith is hardly to be found,
    And love is waxing cold—

6 Is not thy chariot hastening on ?
    Hast thou not given the sign ?
May we not trust and live upon
    A promise so divine ?

7 " Yes," saith the Lord, " now will I rise
    And make oppressors flee ;
I shall appear to their surprise,
    And set my servants free."

8 Thy word, like silver seven times tried,
    Through ages shall endure ;
The men that in thy truth confide
    Shall find thy promise sure.

1147   L.M.   WATTS (altered).

The book of nature and the Scriptures.—Ps. xix.

THE heavens declare thy glory, Lord,
In every star thy wisdom shines ;
But when our eyes behold thy word,
We read thy name in fairer lines.

2 The rolling sun, the changing light,
And nights and days thy power confess :
And the blest volume thou hast writ
Reveals thy justice and thy grace.

3 Sun, moon, and stars convey thy praise
Round the whole earth, and never stand ;
So, when thy truth begun its race,
Destined to spread to every land :

4 Nor shall thy living gospel rest,
Till through the world thy truth has run ;
Till Christ has all the nations blessed
That see the light, or feel the sun.

5 Great Sun of righteousness, arise,
Bless the dark world with heavenly light ;
Thy gospel makes the simple wise,
Thy laws are pure, thy judgments right.

6 Thy noblest wonders here we view,
In souls renewed, and sins forgiven ;
Lord, cleanse my sins, my soul renew,
And make thy word my guide to heaven.

1148   C.M.   WATTS.

Imperfection of Nature and perfection of Scripture.

LET all the heathen writers join
    To form one perfect book,
Great God, if once compared with thine,
    How mean their writings look !

2 Not the most perfect rules they gave,
  Could show one sin forgiven,
Nor lead a step beyond the grave ;
  But thine conduct to heaven.

3 I've seen an end to what we call
  Perfection here below ;
How short the powers of nature fall,
  And can no farther go.

4 Yet men would fain be just with God,
  By works their hands have wrought ;
But thy commands, exceeding broad,
  Extend to every thought.

5 In vain we boast perfection here,
  While sin defiles our frame ;
And sinks our virtues down so far,
  They scarce deserve the name.

6 Our faith and love, and every grace,
  Fall far below thy word ;
But perfect truth and righteousness
  Dwell only with the Lord.

1149   8s.   NEWTON.
Vital Knowledge of Christ.—Matt. xxii. 42.
WHAT think you of Christ ? is the test,
  To try both your state and your scheme ;
You cannot be right in the rest,
  Unless you think rightly of him.
As Jesus appears in your view,
  As he is belovéd or not ;
So God is disposéd to you,
  And mercy or wrath are your lot.

2 Some take him a creature to be,
  A man, or an angel at most :
Sure these have not feelings like me,
  Nor know themselves wretched and lost.

So guilty, so helpless am I,
  I durst not confide in his blood,
Nor on his protection rely,
  Unless I were sure he is God.

3 Some call him a Saviour in word,
  But mix their own works with his plan ;
And hope he his help will afford,
  When they have done all that they can :
If doings prove rather too light,
  (A little, they own, they may fail),
They purpose to make up full weight
  By casting his name in the scale.

4 Some style him the Pearl of great price,
  And say he's the Fountain of joys ;
Yet feed upon folly and vice,
  And cleave to the world and its toys :
Like Judas, the Saviour they kiss,

And while they salute him, betray ;
Ah ! what will profession like this
  Avail in his terrible day ?

5 If asked what of Jesus I think,
  Though still my best thoughts are but poor,
I say, he's my meat and my drink,
  My life, and my strength, and my store ;
My Shepherd, my Husband, my Friend,
  My Saviour from sin and from thrall ;
My hope from beginning to end,
  My portion, my Lord, and my All.

1150   8.7.   CROSSE.
Prayer and Praise for national blessings.
LORD of heaven, and earth, and ocean,
  Hear us from thy bright abode,
While our hearts, with deep devotion,
  Own their great and gracious God ;
Now with joy we come before thee,
  Seek thy face, thy mercies own ;
Lord of life, and light, and glory,
  Bless thy church, and guard the throne.

2 Health and every needful blessing
  Are thy bounteous gifts t' bestow ;
Comforts undeserved possessing,
  We before thy footstool bow ;
Young and old do now before thee
  Their united tribute bring ;
Lord of life, and light, and glory,
  Hear the hymn of praise we sing.

3 Thee, with humble adoration,
  Lord, we praise for mercies past ;
Still to this most favoured nation
  May those mercies ever last ;
Britons, then, shall still before thee
  Songs of ceaseless praises sing ;
Lord of life, and light, and glory,
  We are safe beneath thy wing.

1151   C.M.   BOYCE.
Harvest.
GREAT sovereign Lord, what human eye
  Amidst thy works can rove,
And not thy liberal hand espy,
  Nor trace thy bounteous love ?

2 Each star that gilds the heavenly frame,
  On earth each verdant clod,
In language loud to men proclaim
  The great and bounteous God.

3 The lesson each revolving year
  Repeats in various ways ;
Rich thy provisions, Lord, appear :
  The poor shall shout thy praise.

4 Our fruitful fields and pastures tell,
   Of man and beast thy care ;
   The thriving corn thy breezes fill,
   Thy breath perfumes the air.

5 But oh, what human eye can trace,
   Or human heart conceive,
   The greater riches of thy grace
   Impoverished souls receive ?

6 Love everlasting has not spared
   Its best belovéd Son ;
   And in him endless life prepared,
   For souls by sin undone.

1152 C.M.
Seasons.

FOUNTAIN of mercy, God of love,
   How rich thy bounties are ;
   The rolling seasons, as they move,
   Proclaim thy constant care.

2 When in the bosom of the earth
   The sower hid the grain ;
   Thy goodness marked its secret birth,
   And sent the early rain.

3 The spring's sweet influence, Lord, was thine ;
   The plants in beauty grew ;
   Thou gav'st the summer sun to shine,
   The mild refreshing dew.

4 These various mercies from above
   Matured the swelling grain ;
   A kindly harvest crowns thy love,
   And plenty fills the plain.

5 We own and bless thy gracious sway ;
   Thy hand all nature hails ;
   Seed-time, nor harvest, night nor day,
   Summer nor winter fails.

1153 C.M. BURNHAM.
" Heirs together of the grace of life."—1 Peter iii. 7.

GREAT God of order, truth, and grace,
   Fountain of social joys,
   Shine with thy sweet approving smile,
   And crown the nuptial ties.

2 Look on the now united pair,
   And O, the union bless ;
   Here may true friendship ever reign
   In firmest bonds of peace.

3 May each the other kindly help
   To run the shining road ;
   Join with delight in prayer and praise,
   And ever cleave to God.

4 May both be fired with one concern
   For one eternal prize ;

And warmest zeal their souls inflame
   For joys beyond the skies.

5 One be their views, their aim, their end,
   Pure heavenly bliss to prove,
   Meeting at last around the throne,
   To reign in realms of love.

6 There may we all with them unite
   In one harmonious song ;
   And one pure anthem swell the joys
   Of one celestial throng.

1154 C.M. DENHAM.
At the appointment of Deacons.

GREAT Head of influence divine,
   Thy people's choice approve ;
   With favour on our deacons shine,
   And fill us all with love.

2 Instruct them in thy heavenly will,
   For all thy saints to care ;
   Help them their office to fulfil,
   In faith and godly fear.

3 O make them useful, wise, and kind,
   In principle unmoved ;
   Men of one heart, and in one mind,
   In all things well approved.

4 The Church and congregation bless,
   Our gifts and grace increase ;
   May thousands more thy name confess,
   And we all live in peace.

1155 C.M. NEWTON.
Death of a believer.

IN vain the fancy strives to paint
   The moment after death,
   The glories that surround the saints,
   When yielding up their breath.

2 One gentle sigh their fetters breaks ;
   We scarce can say, " They're gone ! "
   Before the willing spirit takes
   Her mansion near the throne.

3 Faith strives, but all its efforts fail,
   To trace her in her flight :
   No eye can pierce within the vail
   Which hides that world of light.

4 Thus much (and this is all) we know,
   They are completely blest ;
   Have done with sin, and care, and woe,
   And with their Saviour rest.

5 On harps of gold they praise his name,
   His face they always view ;
   Then let us followers be of them,
   That we may praise him too.

6 Their faith and patience, love and zeal,
    Should make their memory dear ;
  And, Lord, do thou the prayers fulfil
    They offered for us here !

7 While they have gained, we losers are,
    We miss them day by day ;
  But thou canst every breach repair,
    And wipe our tears away.

8 We pray, as in Elisha's case
    When great Elijah went,
  May double portions of thy grace,
    To us who stay, be sent.

1156   C.M.   IRONS.
Precious Blood.—1 Pet. i. 19.

WHAT sacred Fountain yonder springs
    Up from the throne of God,
  And all new covenant blessings brings ?
    'Tis Jesus' precious blood.

2 What mighty sum paid all my debt,
    When I a bondman stood,
  And has my soul at freedom set ?
    'Tis Jesus' precious blood.

3 What stream is that which sweeps away
    My sins just like a flood,
  Nor lets one guilty blemish stay ?
    'Tis Jesus' precious blood.

4 What voice is that which speaks for me
    In heaven's high court for good,
  And from the curse has set me free ?
    'Tis Jesus' precious blood.

5 What theme, my soul, shall best employ
    Thy harp before thy God,
  And make all heaven to ring with joy ?
    'Tis Jesus' precious blood.

INDEX

OF

FIRST LINE OF EACH VERSE AND FIFTH LINE
OF EIGHT LINE VERSES.

In Christ my treasure 178
In Christ's obedience 471
In covenant from of ... 921
In darkest shades if he 1011
In darkness born I went 748
In darkness or distress 909
In darkness such are 253
In David I see a grea. 549
In each dear place ... 156
In Eden's garden there 153
In endless love, the hol. 525
In every believer two 612
In every changing sce. 531
In every condition, in 329
In every mercy, full ... 61
In every office he sus. 174
In every outward ... 287
In every sore and deep 622
In every state secure 412
In every storm in ... 511
In every time of need 739
In every trying deep 531
In evil long I took 1025
In glory, Lord, may ... 174
In glory, soon, with 411
In guilt's dark ... 837
In heaven, and earth 6
In heaven he lives our 815
In heaven my choicest 482
In him a holiness ... 128
In him a rich ... 574
In him, and him alone 377
In him I hope; in ... 271
In him I stand comple. 604
In him my weary soul 128
In him my treasure's... 171
In him the Father nev. 65
In Him the Gentile 557
In him the world no 975
In him they stand com. 538
In his heart they have 720
In his highest work ... 514
In his own heart the 685
In his remembrance- 832
In his righteousness 759
In holiness the saints 16
In Jesus, and Jesus ... 516
In Jesus combine all 1033
In Jesus' image shining 15
In Jesus, the Lamb ... 912
In Jesus they shall ... 114
In loud complaints he 164
In love to Zion he has 553
In mercy put a stop 646
In Meshech as yet I ... 246
In miseries great ... 663
In mounts of danger... 513
In my Jesus' arms ... 342
In my own breast I ... 740
In myself I have no ... 895
In other ills we find 287
In purest love their ... 375
In rising from the ... 653
In rivers of sorrow ... 162
In season due ... 81
In self I'm polluted ... 595
In six days God ... 358
In spite of unbelief 1020
In such sweet posture 756
In swaddling bands ... 39

In thankful notes your 834
In that dread moment 1093
In the ark the weary 356
In the councils of ... 573
In the day of thy 1137
In the hour of dark ... 43
In the Lord is our ... 491
In the midst of ... 769
In the person of ... 514
In the sad garden on 824
In the watery grave we 649
In the world of end. 1068
In thee all blessings 643
In thee, I every glory 173
In thee shall Israel ... 110
In these he was resolv. 66
In themselves as weak 397
In ties of blood and ... 757
In this alone I can ... 105
In this bewildered sta. 1026
In this dear Christ I 604
In this distress the ... 773
In this I make my gr. 216
In this posture let ... 686

In thy bosom safely ... 349
In thy fair book of ... 4
In thy name, O Lord 1135
In thy presence I am 1101
In thy presence I can 1101
In thy strength may 501
In thy Surety thou 145
In tribulation's ... 925
In union with the ... 921
In vain from creatures 941
In vain I charge my 1084
In vain I read, in ... 953
In vain I seek for ... 884
In vain I withstood 197
In vain men talk of 256
In vain the bright, the 186
In vain the fancy ...1155
In vain the sons of ... 257
In vain the tempter 266
In vain the trembling 935
In vain they seek the 898
In vain to hoard it up 1126
In vain we ask God's 111
In vain we boast ...1148
In vain we tune our ... 25
In vain we search in 57
In vain we meet to 952
In vain we seek for 946
In vast eternity he ... 596
In vineyards planted 22
In worship so divine 38
Increase my faith 1051
Increase our fai. & hope 822
Increase our faith & lov. 608
Indignant Justice stood 134
Indulgent God! how ... 732
Indulgent goodness ... 499
Infidels may laugh ... 77
Infinite in truth and 800
Infinite wisdom ... 957
Infirmities as means 613
Innumerable foes ... 287
Inspire the living ... 983
Instead of this he ... 295
Instruct our minds 434

Instruct them in thy 1154
Into thy heart-breaking 563

Is he a 142
Is he compared ... 142
Is he designed ... 142
Is Jesus my Saviour 577
Is not thy chariot ...1146
Is not thy name 1066
Is the evening-time ... 722
Is then the law of ... 809
Is there a thing 1075
Is there nothing here 1045
Is this, dear Lord, that 289
Is this polluted ... 196
Is this the case ... 621
Is this the Man ... 950
Israel's Strength ...1054
It always is full ... 566
It blows its poisonous 287
It cheers a debtor's ... 756
It gives religion ... 832
It heals the soul of ... 896
It is finished! all is 982
It is finished! O ... 93
It is finished, said ... 306
It is finished, sinners 982
It is the cordial ... 890
It is the Lord ... 261
It is the wine of ... 890
It makes me feel ... 748
It makes the coward... 919
It makes the wounded 135
It rises high and ... 212
It says to the ... 233
It sets time past in ... 226
It softens well the ... 896
It speaks of pardon ... 527
It treads on the world 233
It were an easy part 1012
Its beauties all centre 523
Its blessings though 595
Its bonds shall never 921
Its highest delight ... 595
Its owner is a heavenly 684
Its pleasures now no 1100
I've bound thee up 1032
I've foes and fears of 384
I've scarce a glimmer 384
I've seen an end ...1148

Jehovah God! 668
Jehovah has decreed... 522
Jehovah has said ... 207
Jehovah Jireh 513
Jehovah is my righ. 108
Jehovah is my Sun ... 546
Jehovah, the Saviour 597
Jehovah's awful ... 172
Jerusalem, my happy 934
Jesus all your 147
Jesus, and shall ... 427
Jesus arrayed 1093
Jesus, as water ... 862
Jesus, at thy 294
Jesus before ... 173
Jesus beholds ...1006
Jesus' blood speaks 534
Jesus, cast a look ... 686
Jesus Christ God's ... 857

www.ingramcontent.com/pod-product-compliance
Lightning Source LLC
Chambersburg PA
CBHW031145190526
45286CB00008B/125